W9-AYO-464   01/2012

BLACKLISTED BY HISTORY

PALM BEACH COUNTY
LIBRARY SYSTEM
3650 Summit Boulevard
West Palm Beach, FL 33406-4198

BLACKLISTED BY HISTORY

THE UNTOLD STORY OF

Senator Joe McCarthy

AND HIS FIGHT AGAINST AMERICA'S ENEMIES

M. STANTON EVANS

THREE RIVERS PRESS

NEW YORK

Copyright © 2007 by M. Stanton Evans

All rights reserved.
Published in the United States by Three Rivers Press, an imprint of the
Crown Publishing Group, a division of Random House, Inc., New York.
www.crownpublishing.com

Three Rivers Press and the Tugboat design are registered
trademarks of Random House, Inc.

Originally published in hardcover in the United States by Crown Forum, an
imprint of the Crown Publishing Group, a division of Random House, Inc.,
New York in 2007.

Library of Congress Cataloging-in-Publication Data
Evans, M. Stanton (Medford Stanton), 1934–
   Blacklisted by history: the untold story of Senator Joe McCarthy and
his fight against America's enemies / M. Stanton Evans.—1st ed.
   Includes bibliographical references and index.
   1. McCarthy, Joseph, 1908–1957. 2. Legislators—United States—
Biography. 3. United States. Congress. Senate—Biography. 4. United
States—Politics and government—1945–1953. 5. Communism—
United States—History—20th century. 6. Anti-communist movements—
United States—History—20th century. 7. Internal security—United
States—History—20th century. I. Title.
E748.M143E83   2007
973.921092—dc22   2006037004

ISBN 978-1-4000-8106-6

Printed in the United States of America

10 9 8 7 6 5 4 3

First Paperback Edition

For my mother
JOSEPHINE STANTON EVANS
who knew it all along

and for
TIERNEY McCARTHY
wherever she may be

CONTENTS

PART IV.   MOLE HUNTS

PART V.   HARDBALL

PART VI.   END GAME

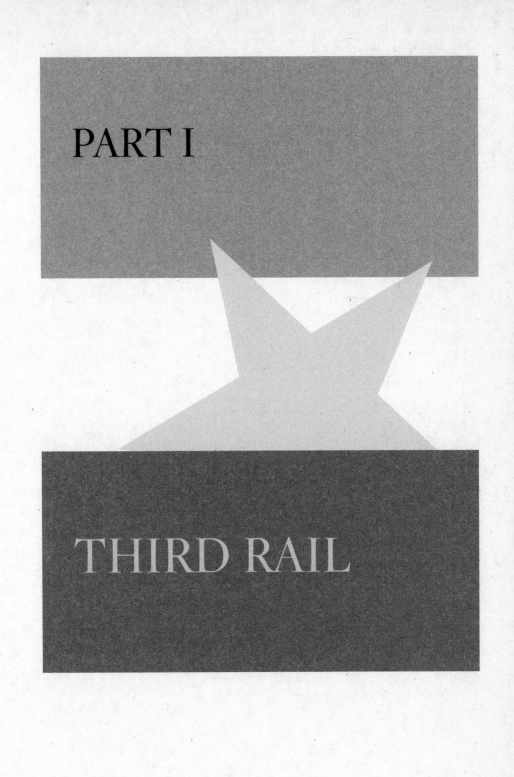

PART I

THIRD RAIL

The Search for Joe McCarthy

I N THE peacetime summer of 1946, the first such summer in half a decade, a State Department official named Samuel Klaus drafted a long confidential memo about the grave security problems that were plaguing the department.

This 106-page report, dated August 3, contained some startling revelations. It discussed, among other things, the number of Soviet agents said to be on the payroll at State, alleged Communist Party members there, and others in the department described as "suspects" or "sympathizers." In the cases of agents and CP members—some thirty-three people altogether—the names (one being Alger Hiss) had been compiled by State's security screeners. As for the suspects and sympathizers, numbering more than ninety staffers, the names weren't available yet as lists were still being assembled.[1]

Information of this type, needless to say, was both ultrasecret and of sensational nature. During the crisis of World War II, when the Soviet Union was our ally against the Nazis, comparatively little attention had been paid to the matter of Communists in the federal workforce. But in the early postwar era, the alliance with Moscow had rapidly unraveled and was being replaced with a series of hostile confrontations that would be dubbed the Cold War. The presence of CP members or fellow travelers in official jobs, formerly viewed with indulgence or ignored, would look shockingly different in 1946 when Sam Klaus composed his memo.

Some four years later, at the height of the loyalty/security furor then raging around the State Department, Sen. Joe McCarthy (R-Wis.) learned about this memo and stirred up a major flap about it. Thanks to the McCarthy pressure, a Senate subcommittee chaired by Sen. Millard Tydings (D-Md.) requested a copy from the department and in due course received one. Thus, one of the most revealing documents ever put together about Red infiltration of the U.S. government was supplied to Congress. But thereafter, so far as the public record shows, the Klaus memo would mysteriously vanish.

In the National Archives of the United States there are at least two places where this report should be on offer. One is the legislative archive of the Tydings panel, which was weighing McCarthy's charges of State Department security breakdown and which unquestionably got a copy. This is reflected in the department's letter of transmittal, which survives and is included in the subcommittee records. So the memo should also be in the files, but isn't.

The other place where this memo ought to be is in the papers of Sam Klaus, held in another section of the Archives. In the index to the Klaus papers, the document is listed, under its proper official heading. However, when the file was examined by this writer it turned out the report again was missing. In this case, at least, we know what happened to it. The file contained a notice where the memo had been, saying it was withdrawn from the Archives in March 1993—not quite half a century after it was written. So this important document is twice over absent from the nation's official records.

Unfortunately for researchers of such matters, this elusive memo is but one of many Cold War papers that have gone AWOL. Some two dozen other documents from the State Department relating to security issues were likewise supplied to Tydings and should be in the Archives also. In these cases handsomely embossed cover sheets, signed by Dean Acheson, Secretary of State in 1950, are still there in the folders. In every case as well, however, the material once enclosed has been stripped from the cover sheet, leaving small wads of paper beneath the staples that held the documents together.

Other historical data that ought to be in the subcommittee records are documents provided to the panel by McCarthy. These included a McCarthy-to-Tydings letter of March 18, 1950, listing the names of eighty loyalty/security suspects at State and elsewhere, some of whose anonymous cases McCarthy had earlier recited to the Senate. Enclosed with the McCarthy list was a letter from the head of the Central Intelligence Agency concerning one of the eighty suspects. In addition, McCarthy that same week gave Tydings a list of two dozen other names as potential subjects of inquiry. All told, a pretty sizable package of information on the most burning issue of that day, and many days thereafter.

As these papers were part of an official proceeding of the Senate—and as we know from other sources they were in fact provided—they should all be in the Tydings archive. Again, however, so far as diligent search reveals, all of them are missing, with no explanation of what happened to them, no hint that they were ever there, and no withdrawal notice. They are simply gone. Since they were documents central to any assessment of McCarthy's charges, their absence is a critical gap in the archival record.* That absence, it bears noting, affects more than our understanding of Joe McCarthy. It affects our knowledge of the issue he was addressing, and thus our comprehension of the Cold War era.

Such problems with McCarthy cases didn't cease with Millard Tydings but would occur also with the records of McCarthy's own committee, when he became himself the chairman of a Senate panel three years later. It's evident that a lot of records here are likewise missing. A notable instance involves the case of Annie Lee Moss, a security suspect in the Army who appeared before McCarthy at an historic committee session. In the hearing record, reference is made to an "Exhibit 18," an FBI report about Mrs. Moss that was obviously important in gauging the merits of the case and what McCarthy had to say about it. But there is no "Exhibit 18" to be found in the archive of the McCarthy panel pertaining to the Moss case.[2]

Nor are such troubles confined to official sources. They extend to private-sector data that should in theory be open to researchers. A significant case in point concerns the famous speech McCarthy delivered in February 1950 at Wheeling, West Virginia, kicking off the whole McCarthy epoch. As is well known, what McCarthy said in this speech became a hotly controverted issue. Much of the dispute revolved around a story in the local morning paper, the *Wheeling Intelligencer,* saying McCarthy claimed to have a "list" of 205 Communists working at the State Department. This quote appears in every book we have about McCarthy and many histories of the Cold War. McCarthy would, however, deny he said it, and whether he actually did so would become, and remain, the cause of vast confusion.[3]

The task of researching the Wheeling speech, and sifting collateral data on it, prompted the thought that, while all discussions of the subject fixate on this one story, there may have been other items in the local paper about such a major event in the life of Wheeling. And if so, these accounts might shed some

---

*In discussion of these cases, there is no suggestion that officials of the National Archives have been remiss in the performance of their duties. In my experience, the archivists are meticulous in safeguarding papers entrusted to their keeping and go to elaborate lengths to prevent any tampering with or removal of such records. In the cases cited, it appears the missing papers were removed from the folders before the archivists ever saw them. (Though, as more recent events suggest, there are people who do try to take things from the Archives, and doubtless some such project could have succeeded in the past if sufficient skill and cunning were devoted to the effort.)

light on what McCarthy did or didn't say there. This hunch, as it turned out, was correct. However, a trip to Wheeling would reveal that these documents, too, were missing.

For one thing, the *Intelligencer* no longer had a morgue of stories from the 1950s. Instead, back issues of the paper were now on microfilm at the Wheeling public library. This seemed fair enough, and as the library was only a couple of blocks away, not an overwhelming problem. However, a visit there produced another disappointment. All issues of the paper, dating to the nineteenth century, were microfilmed and apparently in their appointed places—except the issues that were in question. Conspicuously absent were editions for January and February 1950—the sequence jumping, without explanation, from December 1949 to March 1950. Written inquiry to the librarian produced no reply as to what had happened to these records.

The further thought then occurred that the Library of Congress, which maintains back issues of numerous journals from across the country, might have *Intelligencers* in its holdings. And indeed, the Library does have such a collection—except, again, not these particular issues. According to the notice provided by the clerk who checked the records, the Library had no copies of the *Intelligencer* prior to August 1952. That made three trips to the well, and three times the bucket had come up empty.

This is perhaps enough for now about the subject of disappearing records, which will recur often in these pages. (It should be added that some of the items mentioned did survive in other, less predictable places and were recovered.) However, a couple of connected points need making about primary source material on such issues, and its availability—or lack thereof—to would-be researchers. Again, these problems concern not just the facts on Joe McCarthy but the entire clandestine history of the Cold War.

Among the more voluminous collections of such data are the once-secret records of the FBI. These files are a treasure house of information on Communist penetration of American life and institutions, suspects tracked down by the Bureau, countermeasures taken, and related topics. To its credit, the FBI was watching these matters pretty closely while others allegedly standing guard were dozing, or in the throes of deep denial. The material in the Bureau files is both revealing and extensive.

Thus, to pick some prominent cases, the Bureau knew as early as December 1942 that J. Robert Oppenheimer, the nuclear physicist then becoming a central figure in the atomic energy project, was identified by Communist leaders as a secret party member who had to be inactive because of the wartime work that he was doing. Likewise, in 1945, the FBI obtained credible information that high-ranking government figures Alger Hiss, Lauchlin Currie, and Harry Dexter White were Soviet agents. Also in 1945, the Bureau knew the espionage case of diplomat John Stewart Service and the pro-Red magazine *Amerasia* had been fixed, lied about, and covered up by a cabal of top officials.

Such are but a few of the revelations in the colossal trove of records housed in the J. Edgar Hoover Building, and while they concern some of the more notorious cases that would later come to view are by no means the most astounding. That said, there is still other information in the Bureau files that isn't open to researchers. In case after significant case, entries have been held back or heavily "redacted" (blacked out), sometimes for dozens of pages at a stretch. In nearly every instance, such redactions concern materials fifty years of age and counting. It's hard to imagine any national security interest of the present day that would be threatened by these ancient data.

Considering the stuff that's available in the Bureau records, one has to wonder about the stuff that isn't. *Vide* the memo reprinted overleaf, written in September 1946 by FBI Director Hoover to the Attorney General (at that time Tom Clark) concerning a shadowy Cold War figure named David Wahl. A former federal employee, Wahl had come to notice in one of the most intensive probes ever conducted by Hoover's agents. In this memo, Hoover says Wahl "as early as 1941 . . . was reliably reported to be a 'master spy' for the Soviet government while employed by the United States government in Washington, D.C."[4] After this jolting revelation, however, the next paragraph is blacked out entirely. The obvious question arises: If the Hoover comment that Wahl was "reliably reported" to be a Soviet "master spy" is *left in* the records, what must be in the part that's missing?

These matters are brought up, not to ask the reader's sympathy for the researcher (well, maybe a little), but to suggest the rather parlous state of the historical record concerning some important topics. Without the documents referred to, and without the items blacked out in the records, attempts to chronicle our domestic Cold War, while not entirely futile, are subject to the most serious limits. Lacking these materials, we are left in many cases with secondhand data of doubtful value that are nonetheless recycled from place to place as supposed truths of history.

It's not too much to say, indeed, that the loss of so many primary records has created a kind of black hole of antiknowledge in which strange factoids and curious fables circulate without resistance—spawning a whole other group of research problems. And while this thought again pertains to several aspects of the Cold War, nowhere is it more often true than in discussion of Joe McCarthy. The result has been to ply the public with many apocryphal tales about him and his alleged doings.

Some of these stories are simply fabrications—things McCarthy supposedly said, or did, that can't be confirmed from credible records. In particular, there seems to have been a cottage industry that cranked out purported

REVELATIONS REDACTED

FBI Director Hoover wrote this memorandum concerning an investigative suspect on September 16, 1946. Following an especially startling revelation, an entire paragraph is blacked out in the Bureau's records.

Federal Bureau of Investigation
United States Department of Justice

September 16, 1946

IN REPLY, PLEASE REFER TO
FILE NO. _____

PERSONAL AND CONFIDENTIAL

MEMORANDUM FOR THE ATTORNEY GENERAL

RE: DAVID RALPH WAHL

      In connection with the current investigation concerning known and suspected Soviet espionage agents in the United States, it has been learned that David Ralph Wahl who is presently the Washington representative of the American Jewish Conference with offices at 1706 G Street, N. W., Washington, D. C., and who resides at 3 Lexington Street, Kensington, Maryland, is suspected of being engaged in Soviet espionage activities.

      Wahl is a known contact of numerous subjects being investigated in connection with the Gregory Case about which information has been previously made available to you, and as early as 1941 he was reliably reported to be a "master spy" for the Soviet Government while employed by the United States Government in Washington, D. C.

Respectfully,

J. E. Hoover

John Edgar Hoover
Director

Source: FBI Silvermaster file

statements by McCarthy that have no known valid basis. A leading example is an alleged McCarthy comment that welcomed the support of the Communist Party in the Wisconsin Republican primary of 1946 against Sen. Robert M. La Follette Jr. Nobody has ever been able to verify this quote, despite a considerable effort to do so, and it is almost certainly bogus. Yet it has been recycled many times in treatments of McCarthy.[5]

On top of such inventions, and more common, are episodes from McCarthy's hectic *vita* that did in fact occur but are presented in such a way as to be unrecognizable to anyone somewhat familiar with the record. (Most McCarthy factoids are of this nature, many resulting from the work of the Tydings panel, *fons et origo* of countless errors.) And there are just plain mistakes, some fairly obvious, some more subtle and harder to disentangle. These often stem from jaw-dropping ignorance of the subject matter—not only of McCarthy and his cases, but of other happenings in the Cold War or of American history and institutions. A few such miscues are of serious import, some merely goofy, but all add to the smog bank that veils the story.

We are informed, for instance, by two of the nation's leading dailies—the *Los Angeles Times* and *Washington Post*—that there was once a weird mutant entity of the U.S. government called "Senator Joseph R. McCarthy's House Un-American Activities Committee."* It seems inconceivable, but is obviously so, that there are people writing for major papers who don't know we have a bicameral legislative system, so that a senator wouldn't head a House committee. And while such bloopers are amusing, they can have effects that historically speaking aren't so funny, pinning responsibility on McCarthy for things to which he had no connection (e.g., the House committee's investigation of Reds in Hollywood, often imputed to McCarthy).

One further instance in this vein is worth a bit of notice, as it illustrates not only the ignorance problem but the unwillingness or inability of some who write about such matters to get the simplest facts in order. In this case the offender was the *New York Times,* which in May 2000 published an obituary of a recently deceased New York professor with a domestic Cold War background. This ran on the *Times* obit page under a four-column headline reading, "Oscar Shaftel, Fired After Refusing McCarthy, Dies at 88."[6]

This article said Shaftel, once a teacher at New York's Queens College, had lost his job back in the 1950s when he refused to answer "some questions" about alleged Red connections posed by the "investigations subcommittee of

---

*The *L.A. Times* story using this locution appeared in its Sunday book section on December 29, 2002, the *Washington Post* version in an obituary of a supposed McCarthy victim on July 18, 2004. Running a close third in this know-nothing sweepstakes is the *New York Times,* which used the same remarkable concept in its crossword puzzle. (Clue: "Sen. McCarthy's gp." Answer: "HUAC." 23 down, August 11, 1999.)

the Senate Internal Security subcommittee headed by Senator Joseph R. McCarthy." The obit then went on to offer a lengthy tribute to Shaftel, describe his lonely years of exile, and suggest that, despite this ill treatment, his gallant spirit had remained unbroken.

The errors in this story were stunning, starting with the bedrock fact that Joe McCarthy had nothing to do with the late professor, the committee that brought him to book, or his alleged hardships. Indeed, there was no such thing as "the investigations subcommittee of the Senate Internal Security subcommittee." The security unit, as the name clearly says, was itself a subcommittee (of the Judiciary Committee), its chairman at the time of the Shaftel hearing Sen. William Jenner of Indiana. McCarthy wasn't even a member of this panel, much less the chairman of it.[7]

Almost as odd as the obit itself were the events ensuing when, in my self-appointed role as part-time ombudsman on such matters, I wrote the *Times* about it, giving the facts above related, plus some pertinent data on the case the *Times* account omitted.* Over the course of a month and a half, I sent the *Times* three different missives on the subject without having a letter printed or receiving an answer, made two references to it on C-SPAN talk shows, and enlisted the aid of the late media critic Reed Irvine, who wrote directly to *Times* publisher Arthur Sulzberger trying to get the thing corrected.

This apparently did the trick, as the *Times* at last provided on September 1 (the Friday of the Labor Day weekend) an obscure retraction, tucked into a corrections box between two numbingly soporific items (confusion of Mexican local politicians in a photo, misidentification of birds in Brooklyn). This confessed in bare-bones terms that the *Times* had erred as to the name and chairman of the committee that heard Shaftel. It thus took six weeks, half a dozen efforts, and the labors of two people to get a terse, nit-sized correction in no way comparable in scope or impact to the original mammoth error.

The point of this vignette isn't merely the slapdash and remarkably ignorant reporting of the *New York Times* in its casual slurring of Joe McCarthy, but the extreme difficulty of getting the mistake corrected. The experience has been repeated in other attempts to set the record straight on media treatment of McCarthy and his cases. Responses to these sporadic efforts have always been the same—reluctance to admit or fix the problem, or even to run a letter pointing out the miscue. The prevailing attitude seems to be: We will print any

---

*The *Times* portrayed Shaftel as the long-suffering victim of a witch hunt, hounded from his scholarly post for no good cause and later upheld by court decrees negating the New York laws that brought his ouster. Omitted from this morality play was the fact that Shaftel had been named under oath as a Communist operative at Queens by Dr. William Withers, also a teacher at the college (and formerly head of its economics department). This neglected aspect of the record would seem to have some relevance to a story about an asserted victim dragged before a committee of Congress for no apparent reason.

off-the-wall assertion about McCarthy that comes along, without bothering to check any facts whatever, and if we get called on it won't correct the record.

Why such a mind-set should exist, and what it says about the state of journalistic ethics, are intriguing questions, but less important than the effects of such slovenly reportage on our understanding of the Cold War and Joe McCarthy's involvement in it. Multiply such episodes many-fold, over a considerable span of years, and the cumulative impact in terms of spreading disinformation on McCarthy and his times is obviously enormous.

Finally, less glaring than these journalistic pratfalls, but more harmful, are misstatements that occur in standard biographies of McCarthy and political histories of the era. You might think scholarly looking, footnoted tomes by pipe-smoking academics with years of research to go on are more reliable than ephemeral stories banged out tonight only to be thrown away tomorrow. Such, however, is not the case. These studies, too, are often rife with error. To be sure, the authors know McCarthy wasn't a member of the House or chairman of the Jenner subcommittee, but feature other less easily recognized distortions that are more serious and enduring.

A last anecdote from this unhappy genre may suggest the nature of the academic problem, the more consequential as it involves another record of the federal government pertaining to McCarthy. In 2003, the U.S. Senate released for publication the long-secret transcripts of executive hearings conducted by McCarthy when he headed the Senate Permanent Subcommittee on Investigations in the early 1950s. This was an historical milestone of sorts, as the executive sessions provide detail about a number of controverted cases, in many instances going beyond the public hearings run by McCarthy and his counsel, Roy Cohn.

This major publishing event, however, would be badly marred by the invidious comments and introductory notes of associate Senate historian Donald Ritchie, who edited the hearings for publication. In these notes and press statements of which he was prolific, Ritchie routinely stacked the deck against McCarthy, up to and including glosses that were demonstrably in error. One such episode I discussed with him was the above-noted case of Annie Lee Moss, called before the McCarthy panel in 1954 and portrayed in most histories of the era as a pathetic McCarthy victim. Ritchie's handling of the case, footnoted to three academic studies, reinforced the standard image of Moss as victim and McCarthy as browbeating tyrant.[8]

As will be discussed, this version of the Moss affair is quite false, a fact readily seen if one consults not the usual recycled histories but the voluminous official records on the case. When I got Ritchie on the phone I asked if he by any chance had reviewed these original sources, rather than simply repeating what he had picked up from other academics. When I further indicated that these records showed McCarthy was right about the case and offered to sum up the relevant data, the historian grew irate, said "I am growing very tired of this conversation," and abruptly ended our discussion. The rebuff wasn't all that different from the stonewalling responses of media outlets that have likewise distorted the Moss affair and other of McCarthy's cases.

To pursue other such items from a long syllabus of media/academic error would preempt the contents of this book, which is in large part an effort to redress the many misstatements that have been made in the usual write-ups of McCarthy. Suffice it to say encounters of this kind have made me forever wary of secondhand news that can't be traced to primary records. As an old newspaper adage has it, "If your mother says she loves you, check it out." Unfortunately, many who say and write things about McCarthy simply repeat what they have read somewhere, without the necessary checking. The net effect of such compounded error is an almost complete inversion of the empirical record on McCarthy and his cases.

While trying to unravel such confusions is a main object of this volume, I should stress that I haven't attempted to track down and answer every McCarthy-related error that's out there—which would be the work of a lengthy lifetime—or to quarrel in detail with every author who ever wrote something bad about McCarthy. While disagreements with such authors surface in several places, these passages are somewhat rare, and purely incidental to my purpose: to tell the story of McCarthy and the security problem he was addressing as clearly as I can do it, given my own limitations and the still-inchoate, but developing, condition of the record.

As these comments also suggest, a main emphasis of this study is the importance of finding primary sources on McCarthy, his cases, and the Cold War in general. However, no one person can possibly review all the primary data, which now run to literally millions of pages. Fortunately, there are some excellent scholars and Cold War experts who have done yeoman service in such matters, having devoted endless hours to reviewing, for instance, the *Venona* decrypts (secret messages between Moscow and its U.S. agents), data from the Soviet archives, and details on certain intricate policy matters. Rather than trying to replicate such efforts, I have where appropriate availed myself of these heroic labors—the due bills for which are set forth in the acknowledgments and notes—and sought to combine them with my own researches.

A further aspect of the subject that needs stressing is that, by and large, all of us still know much less than we need to of the total story. In the vast moraine of documents and security data held by the FBI and reposing in the National Archives, there are scores or possibly hundreds of books still waiting to be written—about the rolling coup d'état that transformed the U.S. State Department in the 1940s, the wartime infiltration of the Office of War Information and Office of Strategic Services by Communists and Soviet agents, the conduct of our postwar occupation forces in Germany and Japan, and much else of similar nature. Likewise in need of examination, arguably most of all, is the linkage of such questions to policy outcomes in the early Cold War years affecting the fate of Eastern Europe and much of Asia.

In the present volume, such policy questions are briefly touched on to give some notion of the larger issues at stake in the McCarthy battles of the 1950s. McCarthy was but a single actor in an extended historical drama that stretched out for decades and involved a milling crowd of players who trod the stage before him. Only if that broader context is in some measure understood is there much likelihood of comprehending the McCarthy saga. As the matter currently stands, the real Joe McCarthy has vanished into the mists of fable and recycled error, so that it takes the equivalent of a dragnet search to find him. This book is my attempt to do so.

Hamilton, Virginia
April 2007

CHAPTER 1

An Enemy of the People

THOUGH he's been dead and gone since 1957, Sen. Joseph R. McCarthy (R-Wis.) lives on in American legend with remarkable staying power, unmatched by other notable figures of his day. Not that Presidents Harry Truman and Dwight Eisenhower, two eminent critics of McCarthy in the 1950s, are forgotten. It's just that they don't come up all the time in squabbles of the modern era. Joe McCarthy does, and then some.

Scarcely a week goes by, it seems, without some press reference to McCarthy and his anti-Communist crusading, the "ism" that he spawned, and the harm he supposedly inflicted on the nation. Books and media retrospectives in which he is featured have been many. Any obituary of anybody involved in the security battles of our domestic Cold War is bound to have some mention of McCarthy. He's invoked also when new civil liberties disputes arise—always in grave warnings that, unless we're careful, the dread McCarthy scourge will once more be upon us.

The reasons for all this McCarthyana are well known and don't need much explaining. McCarthy's alleged stock-in-trade was spreading hysteria about an ersatz internal Communist threat and smearing innocent people as subversives, without a shred of fact to go on. In particular, it's said, he launched wild unsupported charges against employees of the U.S. State Department, shattering the lives of hapless victims who never got a chance to answer. Lying and head-line-grabbing accusations were the supposed essence of his method.

This fearsome image of McCarthy has been driven home through years of repetition, with little if any countervailing comment. Whole generations have come of age hearing nothing else about him, assume what they are told is true, and have no cause to doubt it. In this respect as well, the McCarthy case is somewhat distinctive. Other public figures have been savagely treated in their lifetimes but enjoyed a bit of historical comeback later. To look no further than officeholders with varying degrees of political kinship to McCarthy, such reval-uations have occurred with Presidents Richard Nixon and Ronald Reagan, and even with Sen. Barry Goldwater, the conservative champion of the 1960s whose media image in his prime most resembled treatment of McCarthy.

For the junior senator from Wisconsin, however, there has been no re-demption. On the contrary, with the passing of the years and departure from the scene of people who knew anything about him, the negatives are more pro-nounced than ever. He had a pretty bad press when he was alive, but that press is infinitely worse today. Back then he had at least some supporters in book-writing and journalistic circles who set forth a different version of the story. But most of those people are gone as well, or their early work neglected, while defenders of McCarthy in the academic/media world today are so microscopi-cally few as to be practically nonexistent.

So deeply etched is the malign image of McCarthy that the "ism" linked to his name is now a standard feature of the language, defined in all the dictionar-ies as a great evil and routinely used this way by people accusing others of low-down tactics. Nothing could better illustrate the point than that conservatives who think their opponents are making baseless charges are apt to complain about "McCarthyism of the left." This is immortality of a sort, but not the sort anyone aspires to—that of utter and eternal demonization.

That one man should be so vilified for such a lengthy stretch of time would seem strange, except that issues are at stake much larger than the doings of a single politician, however wayward. If McCarthy had killed someone during a spree of drunken driving, or been caught in adultery with a student intern, he would have been denounced and gone into the history books as a scoundrel (or maybe not). But he wouldn't have been rhetorically embalmed, placed on ex-hibit as an "ism," or have his effigy dragged around the public square forever after. All too obviously, such nonstop derogation has occurred, not just to blacken the memory of an individual, but to serve a broader purpose.

McCarthy's literary and journalistic foes, indeed, have made the point ex-plicit. He is treated this way, they tell us, because he crystallized an impulse and a cause that far exceeded his personal failings. He stood for a much wider evil that swept the nation at midcentury—a "Red scare" allegedly fertile of many horrors. In a siege of mass paranoia, it's said, innocent people were hounded out of public life, fired from jobs, and otherwise made to suffer as agents of a fantastic plot that existed only in the fevered brains of know-nothings and vigilantes. As McCarthy was the main avatar of this delusion, continued harping on his crimes is essential to make sure nothing of this dreadful nature will ever again be allowed to happen.

The pervasiveness of this McCarthy image is its most conspicuous feature. Running a close second, however, is the fact that people who talk and write about him in this way, generally speaking, know little of McCarthy, and would be hard-pressed to back their view with plausible specifics, or indeed with anything whatever. The main exceptions to this rule are a relative handful of writers—perhaps a dozen—who do know something of McCarthy and have published harshly critical books about him, often used as sources by journalists and other authors. While there are occasional variations, all these treatments are pretty much the same in substance, and their aggregate impact in conveying the baleful image of McCarthy has been accordingly immense.[1]

In the established version of the story, as told by these writers, McCarthy began his ill-omened anti-Red crusade with a series of mendacious speeches in February 1950, then enlarged on these in Senate hearings conducted by Sen. Millard Tydings (D-Md.) that began the following month. The essence of the McCarthy charges was that the State Department (and other agencies of the U.S. government) had been infiltrated by Soviet agents, members of the Communist Party and their fellow travelers, and that officials supposedly guarding against this danger had first let it happen then covered up the facts about it.

In these early speeches, McCarthy recited what he said were lists of Communists and security suspects—mostly anonymous, some identified by name— as examples of the infiltration problem. These statements triggered fierce disputes before the Tydings panel, in the press, and in public forums throughout the country. McCarthy's charges were denounced as outrageous lies by President Truman, other prominent politicians, the State Department, media pundits, academics, civic leaders, and a vast array of other critics.

At the end of this initial go-round, we're told, McCarthy's charges proved to be completely baseless. The relevant data as conveyed by Tydings and since reprised by countless others showed not only that McCarthy's charges of subversion were false but that he lied about everything else from start to finish. He didn't have any "lists" of Communists or loyalty suspects, had constantly changed his numbers and other aspects of his story, didn't have inside information sources as he claimed, and otherwise deceived the Senate and the country. The whole thing was a "fraud and a hoax," and the American people could rest assured that charges of massive Communist penetration of the State Department were fearmongering nonsense.

In the conventional treatment, this opening McCarthy battle was the template for all that followed. Though discredited in this first encounter, he would simply forge ahead by making other, even wilder charges, smearing other victims, and spreading still more havoc. The rampage would continue unabated until the Army-McCarthy hearings of 1954 and censure proceedings in the Senate a few months later, when he would be condemned in an official action of his colleagues. In these final struggles, McCarthy was at last brought low, destroyed by his own excesses. Such was the mad career of Joe McCarthy, such was his dismal end, and good riddance to him.

Thus in brief compass the universally accepted version of the tale, set forth in all the usual biographies and histories of the era, and recited around the media campfires late at night as standard lore about McCarthy. Few episodes are limned more clearly in the chronicles of the Cold War, or more incessantly repeated. Yet despite its canonical status, as shall be seen, there are numerous problems with this telling of the story. For the moment, the main point to be noted is a further modulation of the ignorance factor, affecting not only members of the general public who admittedly don't know much about McCarthy but also the historians-biographers who have made him the object of their study. As it turns out, despite the many certitudes they express about McCarthy and his cases, these learned gentry in some respects are as innocent of the facts of record as are their trusting readers.

Astonishing as it may seem, very little has been known, by historians or anyone else, about the vast majority of McCarthy's suspects, the security practices of the State Department in 1950, or Communist penetration of the government when he made his charges. This strange epistemological problem stemmed from several causes, the most obvious of which was that most of the McCarthy cases given to the Senate were presented in anonymous fashion and would remain that way for years thereafter. This made it impossible for outside observers to know who the suspects were, or whether they were even in the State Department, much less whether their hypothetical presence there posed any kind of danger.

Aggravating this knowledge gap were secrecy measures that affected virtually every other aspect of the struggle. Some of this was inherent in the superconfidential nature of the subject, but a great deal of it was merely willful. State Department security records were unavailable for public viewing, but also for the most part *terra incognita* to Congress. Efforts by congressional committees to obtain such records ran into countless roadblocks, foremost among them stringent secrecy orders handed down by President Truman. Less accessible yet were records of the FBI, whose investigations were the ultimate source of nearly all such data on State Department or other cases of like nature.

Given all these anonymity/secrecy issues, it's apparent that virtually no one other than the people physically controlling the secret records really knew much about security affairs at State or the facts about McCarthy's cases. How, then, was it possible to make categorical statements about the bogus nature of his charges? And on what basis was it decided that no problem of Communist penetration existed? These were daunting questions, for which a variety of complex responses would be invented. Generally speaking, however, there was one simple, overriding answer that for many in media/academic circles resolved all such knowledge issues: McCarthy's charges of a vast Soviet conspiracy and Communist infiltration were so far out, so alien to the experience of most people, as to defy all credence.

That being so, the denials of the Truman administration and findings of the Tydings panel seemed to carry decisive weight, though nobody could get the specifics on which these were founded. As this not-to-worry version matched what many observers thought to start with, a lack of definite information wasn't seen as a huge problem. The authorities who were supposed to know such things said all was well, few hard facts were available to disprove this, and the shards of data brought forward by McCarthy were dismissed as fictions. Thus the whole drill was premised, not on the availability of proof, but rather on its absence. This seems a strange method of proceeding, but so the matter was expounded at the time, and so it is expounded still.

Luckily, in recent years, the state of our knowledge about such topics has changed in dramatic fashion, and greatly for the better. Things known only to a handful of people circa 1950 are now accessible to journalists and scholars, as many formerly secret records have been made public and certain long-lost documents have surfaced. Most notably, with the fall of the Soviet empire, records from some of the Communist archives have become available to outside researchers. Likewise, information from our own formerly confidential files has become in some measure open to inspection. These new sources supply a wealth of information about what was actually going on fifty or sixty years ago in the dark back alleys of the Cold War.

The most widely noted of these new disclosures are the so-called *Venona* papers, in possession of the U.S. government since World War II but made available to the public only in 1995. These are coded messages, exchanged between the intelligence bosses in the Kremlin and their agents over here, dating to the early 1940s. Having intercepted thousands of these missives, U.S. Army cryptologists succeeded in breaking the code in which they were embedded, and by a painstaking process were able to figure out the meaning of many cables and the matters they pertained to.[2]

In substantial part, the *Venona* messages dealt with efforts of the Soviet global apparatus later known as the KGB and other Red intelligence units to penetrate the U.S. government to engage in spying and other species of subversion. Numerous cables back and forth concern these topics and also provide considerable information about the identities of Communist agents in the

United States then working on behalf of Moscow. This intel was shared by the Army with the FBI in a long-running, super-secret project to track, counter, and ultimately break certain of the Soviet networks.

A second major source of information is a sizable cache of data from the vaults of the former Soviet Union and various of its satellite states, obtained in the early 1990s when the Communists were toppled from power in these countries. These records include extensive data on the activities of the KGB, the Soviet military intelligence service GRU, and correlative doings of the Communist International (Comintern), the worldwide web of Communist parties and controlled front groups that took marching orders from the Kremlin. Such records have been amplified by the memoirs of former intelligence officers in the USSR, Red China, and other Communist nations—plus a handful of revelations from their confreres in the United States and the United Kingdom.[3]

Yet another important source of information—in some ways the most important—is the huge, formerly secret counterintelligence archive of the FBI, which was closely tracking Communist and pro-Communist activities in the United States well before the advent of the Cold War. These records, running to hundreds of thousands of pages, include agent reports, surveillance files, data from wiretaps and informants, and memoranda that synthesize the Bureau's major findings on its cases. These materials have become in part available in recent decades through Freedom of Information requests and legal actions. And while they are often heavily censored, they are a gold mine of information.

There are still other sources to be noted, but these are the main ones. And what they reveal about the clandestine Cold War record is remarkably consistent. Severally and jointly, all of them tell us that the Soviet Union was running a worldwide espionage and influence operation aimed at infiltrating the societies and governments of the West. These efforts were geared to obtaining diplomatic and other official information useful to the Kremlin, securing weapons technology and data, acquiring industrial know-how, and influencing the policies of target nations in favor of the Soviet interest. In the United States specifically, there was indeed an extensive Soviet effort to penetrate our institutions for all these reasons, and this was in many ways successful.

Also confirmed by the new materials is something known from other sources but frequently contested: that the Communist Party USA was a faithful creature of the Soviet Union. Far from being mere indigenous radicals working for peace and social justice, as sometimes argued, the party and its members were subservient tools of Moscow—and those who weren't subservient didn't stay very long as members. The party was funded by the USSR, sent its delegates to Russia to be vetted and receive instructions, and was withal a functioning part of the Kremlin apparatus, enmeshed in spying, policy sabotage and disinformation projects at the behest of Stalin and his agents.

From a composite of all these data, it's evident the Soviet/Communist operation in the United States, as elsewhere, was vast, sophisticated, and effective, nowhere more so than in seeking positions of official influence. The Red networks reached into virtually every important aspect of the U.S. government, up to very high levels, the State Department notably included. All of which was obviously congruent with the warnings of McCarthy and others who sounded the alarm about such matters in the late 1940s and early '50s. There was in fact an immense conspiracy afoot, there were secret Communists burrowing in the woodwork, and these Communists were, in case after case, devoted agents of the Soviet Union.

None of this necessarily means McCarthy was right about specific issues or individuals, which is a separate matter. It would have been possible for him to have had the bigger picture right, more or less, but to have erred as to details (a formula sometimes heard in discussion of these topics). What the disclosures do mean is that the whole question of his cases needs to be reexamined in the light of the new information, and can't be dismissed out of hand with sweeping statements about the absurdity of the larger thesis.

However, there has to date been no revaluation of McCarthy's cases, or effort to reassess his reputation, based on the new disclosures. Despite occasional suggestions that he might have been on to something, the standard treatment of McCarthy and his charges rolls on today as vigorously as ever. Indeed, the usual negative view not only prevails but is reinforced in some excellent studies of *Venona,* the Soviet archival sources, and other now-available records. These comments are usually dicta, without much indication that the authors have made any particular study of McCarthy. To all appearances, these writers have simply rephrased the usual version of the story before proceeding on to the main business of their own researches.

Such reluctance to tackle the McCarthy question in the light of the new information may seem odd, but is understandable in context. "McCarthyism" is the third rail of Cold War historiography—and of our political discourse in general—and any contact with it could prove fatal to writers trying to get their work accepted in academic or mainstream media circles. It's hard enough trying to rewrite the larger history of the East-West struggle and of pro-Communist infiltration on the home front, without the extra burden, God forbid, of reassessing the untouchable likes of Joe McCarthy.*

In attempting such reassessment here, we are fortunate that still other records are now also available for viewing. The most significant of these are several tranches of McCarthy papers that by some miracle have survived the

---

*Which isn't to say that such authors are insincere in their aversion to McCarthy, but rather that they have accepted their assessment of him from the standard histories.

decades—including lists naming his anonymous suspects, backup files pertaining to these, and related data on other of his cases. In addition, there is a large amount of information on the McCarthy suspects strewn throughout the records of the FBI. Other useful databases include the personal files of two of McCarthy's main antagonists in the Senate, Maryland's Millard Tydings and Connecticut's William Benton. The Tydings papers are of special interest, as they include entries that can be cross-checked with McCarthy's records, plus data on security issues that Tydings was surreptitiously receiving from the State Department at the height of the McCarthy furor.[4]*

Any attempted revaluation of McCarthy and his charges is of course very much a matter of specifics, a great number of which—despite lacunae in the records—can be extracted from these sources. And while no summary can possibly do justice to the complex reality of the story, a brief synopsis of what happened on security matters in the federal government before the advent of McCarthy may be helpful in seeing how the infiltration problem came to be and produced the ferocious battles that rocked the country in the 1950s.

By far the most important factor in this sequence was the political astigmatism that prevailed in official circles beginning in the early to mid-1930s and extending—with one notable hiatus—up through the end of World War II. In this roughly ten-year span, Communist entry into the federal government was typically viewed as no big deal, and was thus a relatively easy matter for the comrades to accomplish. Because of the ideological atmospherics of the depression and the war years, few U.S. officials seemed to be concerned about such penetration—though there were some nominal safeguards against it— and in certain instances it was actively encouraged. The Communists and their fellow travelers were prompt to take advantage of these conditions. That's where the problems reflected in *Venona* and other intelligence archives came from.

While many in the federal government were blithely ignorant of such infiltration or considered it of small importance, there were investigative agencies that saw it in a different light. One such was the House Committee on Un-American Activities, which in 1938 began monitoring, in sporadic fashion, Communist or pro-Communist penetration of federal programs and departments. Another was the Federal Bureau of Investigation, which also began tracking the comrades closely at this era. From the early 1940s onward, the FBI picked up on numerous attempts by the Communist Party and Soviet

---

* Valuable also are the archives of State itself, and of such interim units of World War II as the Office of Strategic Services and Office of War Information, both merged into the department at the conclusion of the fighting. Among other significant databases are the executive session transcripts and confidential records of congressional committees that looked into such matters, many also available in the archives. The files of the House Committee on Un-American Activities are the most revealing, but the records of many other panels contain important information also.

agents to infiltrate official agencies and programs, there to engage in theft of secrets, policy sabotage, and pro-Red propaganda.

From these investigations, the Bureau assembled a huge mass of data about the security problem, the places where it was most acute, and a considerable list of suspects on the federal payroll. Beginning in 1942, innumerable FBI reports about these matters were presented to high officials, naming identified Soviet agents, Communist Party members, and fellow travelers in a host of federal agencies. Though the information was extensive, nothing much was done about it at the time or for some while to follow. In many instances, the Bureau reports were challenged or ignored, in others dealt with in hesitant manner. In few cases was there decisive action.

All these responses would be manifest in the U.S. State Department, which inherited via postwar merger hundreds of cases that had developed in the Office of Strategic Services, Office of War Information, and other wartime units where security was especially lax and the penetration most extensive. This merger was of utmost importance in the security troubles that developed later, as the majority of the suspects who turned up at State were alumni of the wartime bureaus. Security officials in the department were uncertain how to deal with this enormous problem, divided in their views about it, and often deadlocked on handling cases. The net outcome was a series of subliminal, halfway measures that got rid of some of the most egregious suspects but left still others on the payroll.

Inevitably, information about all this would make its way to Congress. In the period 1946–48, several flagrant security cases at State and elsewhere became known to members of the House and Senate, who exerted pressures behind the scenes to have some of the more obvious suspects ousted. There then followed a series of congressional investigations, the most famous the Hiss-Chambers case that surfaced in the summer of 1948. At this point, however, congressional efforts to learn more about the problem would be stalled out by secrecy orders from President Truman, denying FBI and other executive data on security problems to members of the Congress. Investigation of State Department and other cases was accordingly stymied, and the whole matter was left hanging behind a veil of *omerta* and denial.

By accident of circumstance and timing, all these combustible elements would come together and reach their flashpoint with the arrival on the scene of the virtually unknown Senator Joe McCarthy in the winter of 1950. As the records clearly show, his lists of cases and much of his information about subversion in the federal government were derived from rosters previously put together by the FBI, State Department security screeners, and some of his congressional colleagues. In most instances, the dossiers had simply been sitting there for two years or more when McCarthy came along and found them. Likewise, the secrecy policy that shrouded the facts about the cases, and would be a huge McCarthy issue, had long been a grievance to the Congress.

McCarthy thus touched off an explosion that had been years in the making. In so doing, he blew the lid off some major security cases, foremost among them the long-buried *Amerasia* scandal, in which hundreds of official documents had been funneled to this pro-Communist publication and the facts about the matter hidden from the public. Linked to this were still other cases tied to events in Asia and the Far East division of the State Department, which harbored many of McCarthy's suspects. As all this followed closely in the wake of the Communist takeover of China in late 1949, McCarthy's charges of pro-Red infiltration occurred at a time when the American people were asking questions about that debacle and the issue of China was front and center.

Still other aspects of McCarthy's timing would give his charges even greater traction. A few weeks before the initial McCarthy speeches on the infiltration problem, Alger Hiss had been found guilty of lying about his connection to former Soviet espionage courier Whittaker Chambers. The Hiss verdict convinced large sectors of the public, if not the intelligentsia, that there had indeed been pro-Soviet infiltration of the State Department, contra many denials and obfuscations. And while anti-McCarthy spokesmen would treat Hiss as a mere unfortunate aberration, the thought occurred to others that if there had been one Soviet agent on the payroll at State, there might well have been more than one, possibly a great many more, just as McCarthy was contending.

Adding to the build-up of concern about security matters was the case of Judith Coplon, an employee of the Justice Department arrested in 1949 for passing secret data to Soviet official Valentin Gubitchev. Early in 1950, also, contemporaneous with the verdict in the Hiss case, nuclear scientist Klaus Fuchs would under tough questioning in England confess that he had been an atom spy for Moscow. And although the case was a British legal matter, it had dire implications for the United States, as Fuchs had spent considerable time at America's secret nuclear project in Los Alamos, New Mexico. It would prove to be but one of many instances in which U.S. and British security woes criss-crossed and interacted.

As the first Senate hearings provoked by McCarthy neared their conclusion in the summer of 1950, there would occur an even more traumatic event that underscored his message. In late June, the armies of Communist North Korea launched an invasion of the non-Communist South, and in a matter of days the United States would be embroiled in a shooting war with the Reds of Asia. Short term, the shock of the invasion eclipsed McCarthy in the headlines and showcased President Truman in a Communist-fighting guise quite different from earlier U.S. policy in the region. Otherwise, the war served to make McCarthy's charges seem more salient. Equally important, what had been merely a Cold War was now armed conflict in the open, and anti-Communist feeling in the country not unnaturally ran high.

While anti-Communism per se was McCarthy's central issue, the secrecy question would be from the beginning a strong subdominant theme, and crucial to the story. Nor was such secrecy confined to withholding data needed to judge McCarthy's charges; it affected nearly every other facet of the struggle, from early New Deal efforts to obscure the problem, to the felonious cover-up of *Amerasia,* to many other topics touched on in the conventional histories. In nearly all such cases, there is a jarring contrast between the accepted version of events and what is actually in the records.

The reasons for all this secrecy were several, but one motive that led all the rest stands out plainly from the data. Officials at the White House, State Department, and elsewhere in the government weren't eager to have the unvarnished facts about the level of Communist penetration on their watch, and their failure to do much about it, set forth clearly before the nation. Joe McCarthy, by some quirk of fate, managed to focus the blazing spotlight of public notice on these issues in a way nobody had ever done before him. He and his charges were thus viewed in certain quarters as a serious menace to be dealt with quickly, and in most decisive fashion. And so in fact they would be.

CHAPTER 2

The Caveman in the Sewer

I N ONE respect at least, the conventional treatment of Joe McCarthy is correct. He was ultimately more important as a symbol or product of the age than for what he did as an individual, however well or ill his personal doings might be rated.

From the standpoint of America's national interests, the most significant thing about the Red-hunting battles of the 1950s wasn't the personal odyssey of somebody named McCarthy but the security situation that existed in the State Department and elsewhere in the government, and the degree of threat that this presented to the nation. These were the things that really mattered then, and that matter still today in sorting out the story. Viewed from this angle, McCarthy was an almost incidental figure who showed up at a particular time when conditions were ripe to push such issues to the forefront. The same might at least in theory have been done by any number of people in Congress, some of whom had been on the job before he got there and knew more about the subject than did he, at least at the beginning. It just happened that the person who actually did it, albeit with copious help from others, was McCarthy.

However, it's also obviously true that there were facets of McCarthy's character, views, and conduct that caused him to play the role he did, in the way he played it, and that influenced the way events unfolded. Whether it was his flamboyant style, rhetorical tactics, or willingness to mix it up with all the reigning powers of his era, there was something about him and his much-lamented methods that got the attention of the public as his predecessors hadn't. Some brief discussion of McCarthy as a personality may thus be helpful by way of background before getting down to cases.

For many people, the standard image of McCarthy as a dreadful human being is defined by the drawings of Herbert Block, better known as Herblock, for decades the editorial-page cartoonist of the *Washington Post.* In the usual Herblock treatment, McCarthy was a swarthy, bearded caveman wielding a gigantic club with which to knock his victims senseless, or an ogreish creature emerging from a sewer manhole bearing a bucket of filth to slosh on his opponents. These oft-reprinted Herblock drawings are doubtless a main source of the impression that McCarthy was some kind of loathsome monster.

There were, however, many verbal renderings of McCarthy that weren't too different from the Herblock version. Among the more notable of these was the word portrait painted by *New Yorker* correspondent Richard Rovere in his book *Senator Joe McCarthy* (1959), depicting its subject as a crazed, barely human, creature. This volume helped establish early on the notion that McCarthy was a brutal villain, guilty of innumerable personal failings as well as official misdeeds. Here are some samples:

> No bolder seditionist ever moved among us—nor any politician with a swifter, surer access to the dark places of the public mind . . . Like Hitler, McCarthy was a screamer, a political thug, a master of the mob, an exploiter of popular fears . . . He was a master of the scabrous and scatological; his talk was laced with obscenity. He was a vulgarian by method as well as probably by instinct . . . He made little pretense to religiosity or to any species of moral rectitude. He sought to manipulate only the most barbaric symbols of America—the slippery elm club, the knee in the groin, and the brass knuckles . . . He was . . . a prince of hate . . . He was morally indecent . . . McCarthy had become liberated from the morality that prevailed in his environment. . . .[1]

And so forth and so on at some length, including charges that McCarthy was a sociopath and nihilist, didn't really believe in the cause he was espousing, and much else of similar nature. Anyone who read this book and believed it to be even a remotely accurate picture of McCarthy could hardly help concluding that he was an amoral, brutal lout with no redeeming features. Nor were Rovere's comments to this effect unusual in the journalism and political comment of the time. Multiply such statements manyfold and there isn't much doubt as to how McCarthy's negative image was established. However, as the record amply shows, there were facets of his life and conduct quite different from this hideous portrait.

Certain data about McCarthy's personal and family background have been many times recited and may be capsuled rather briefly. He was born in Grand

Chute township, outside the city of Appleton in upstate Wisconsin, on November 14, 1908, the son of Timothy and Bridget McCarthy, a second-generation Irish-American couple. Baptized Joseph Raymond, he was the fifth child (out of seven) and third oldest son. The McCarthys were part of the so-called Irish settlement in northeast Wisconsin, flanked by Dutch and German immigrant families who had also moved to the frontier, as it then still was, because of the cheap land and the chance to become property-owning farmers.

The McCarthys were devout Catholics, hardworking, frugal, and self-reliant. Though they weren't destitute, and as working farmers didn't go hungry, there was never much money to go around. The children were expected to do their share of chores, and did. Thus Joe McCarthy from an early age was accustomed to hard work and plenty of it. By most accounts, indeed, he was the hardest working of the lot. But he wanted to be something other than a farmhand, and as a teenager started a business of his own, raising chickens and selling eggs to local grocers. This project did well, but in the winter of 1928 severe weather that injured McCarthy's health and destroyed his flock brought the venture to an end. He then got jobs managing a couple of grocery stores, where his outgoing manner and strong work ethic made him a locally prominent and successful figure.

What most people recalled about McCarthy from this era and his early life in general was his cheerful personality, quite different from the Herblockian image or the fulminations of Rovere. The young McCarthy was gregarious and good natured, well liked by just about everyone who knew him—customers, fellow workers, complete strangers with whom he would strike up a conversation. Combined with his ambition and willingness to work long hours without letup, these qualities seemed to promise greater achievement in the future.

However, the full-time jobs McCarthy held as a teenager kept him from attending high school, and he realized that if he were going to be more than a storekeeper or a farmer he had to get an education. There followed an unusual decision at the age of twenty to enroll at a nearby high school. His experience at the school was something of a community legend. Under an accelerated program then being offered, he completed four years' worth of schooling in nine months, garnering top grades along the way to do so. Again, the keys to his success were willpower and unremitting effort, rising at 5 A.M. and working late at night to do the necessary reading.

From high school McCarthy went on to become a student at Marquette, the Jesuit university in Milwaukee, where he at first pursued a degree in engineering. Halfway through his undergraduate years he switched to prelaw, attended Marquette Law School, and in 1935 received his law degree there. While at Marquette, he held down a number of outside jobs—everything from running a gas station to washing dishes to starting a makeshift moving company. Again he showed a capacity for hard work and impossible hours that amazed his classmates. He exhibited another trait as well that would be significant for his future—an apparently near-photographic memory that allowed him to absorb large masses of material in a hurry and breeze through exams with last-minute cramming.*

Emerging from Marquette Law, McCarthy hung out his shingle in the small town of Waupaca, about thirty miles from Appleton, but in the depression it was hard to make a living at anything and being a small-town lawyer in upstate Wisconsin definitely wasn't the road to riches. Given his friendly nature and willingness to outwork the competition, he hit on the idea of running for public office. His first successful bid was a campaign for circuit judge, though he was still only an inexperienced lawyer and barely thirty. Opposing an incumbent against whom he was thought to have no chance, he succeeded by dint of hard campaigning in pulling off the upset, thus becoming in 1939 the youngest state jurist in Wisconsin.

Nobody including McCarthy himself ever said he was a great legal scholar, but by most accounts he was a pretty good judge. As in everything else he did, he was hardworking and energetic, and soon cleared up an enormous backlog of about 250 pending cases and thereafter kept the docket current. He was also said to have a good intuitive sense of justice. In handling divorce cases, he showed a strong proclivity for defending the rights of women and children. He likewise revealed an inclination to defend consumers and the little guy in general from what he considered overbearing interests, this once more differing from the later image.[2]

With the coming of World War II, McCarthy at the age of thirty-three enlisted in the Marine Corps, getting lots of favorable press notice when he did so. As a state judge, he was exempt from the draft and didn't have to go, but did. He spent most of his service in the South Pacific as an intelligence officer debriefing pilots in combat with the Japanese. It was in this assignment that he got or gave himself the nickname "Tailgunner Joe," acquired from flying a dozen missions or so in which he doubled as photographer/tailgunner. There would be wrangles later about the citations he received for his wartime service and the number of missions he flew, but that he went when he didn't have to and honorably carried out his duties is not disputed.

While serving in the Pacific, McCarthy made no secret of his political ambitions and launched a mostly absentee and unsuccessful primary election bid for the U.S. Senate in 1944 against the Republican incumbent, Alexander Wiley (later McCarthy's Wisconsin colleague in the upper chamber). Though limited

---

*Also at Marquette, McCarthy somehow found time for other ventures, dabbling in campus politics and athletics, getting involved in all-night poker games, and developing something of a reputation as a party reptile. McCarthy was, evidently, a bit of a prankster in college and later in the military service. He was also, it seems, something of a Sergeant Bilko figure, able to round up supplies for sharing with his buddies.

in his ability to campaign, McCarthy as a two-fisted Marine serving in a combat zone came in with a respectable 80,000 votes, prompting him to try again in 1946 when he was back home from the service. This time his opponent in the primary was the supposedly unbeatable Sen. Robert M. La Follette Jr., a name to conjure with in Wisconsin.

The La Follettes were to their state what the Kennedys would later be to Massachusetts, and few people gave McCarthy a chance against this scion of Wisconsin's first political family. La Follette, however, proved to be a reluctant, Washington-based campaigner and otherwise weaker than expected, and McCarthy would emerge from the primary with another stunning upset. He then cruised home to easy victory in the fall, becoming at the age of thirty-eight the youngest U.S. senator in the country.

Such in barest outline was the career of Joe McCarthy before his arrival in the U.S. Senate in January of 1947. Taken at face value, with nothing more to go on, it could be construed as an inspiring Horatio Alger saga, in which a man from humble beginnings ascended to one of the highest offices in the land through toil, pluck, and perseverance. Needless to remark, that isn't how the story is played in most discussions of McCarthy. Instead, as set forth in several standard treatments, the McCarthy *vita* was marked at every step along the way with evil doings, all said to presage the sinister role he was to play in the Red hunts of the 1950s.

In fact, there is virtually no aspect of McCarthy's personal life, dating from his earliest childhood, that hasn't been the subject of *ad hominem* attack. These tales are so many and varied it's hard to keep them all in focus. They include assertions that, as a youngster, he was either a mama's boy or a bully (take your pick); that as a young attorney he was an ambulance-chasing hustler; that he used unethical methods in running for circuit judge and later in his campaign against La Follette; that on the bench he specialized in "quickie divorces" in return for favors; that he was involved in financial shenanigans in the Senate, then cheated on his taxes; that he lied about his war record in the Pacific; that he was a hopeless drunkard; and a good deal else of similar lacerating import.

Given the number and anecdotal nature of these charges, sifting through them is a difficult business. Anecdotal data are hard to verify and depend for their evidential value on whose anecdotes are given credence. A good (or bad) example is the almost universally accepted tale of McCarthy's heavy drinking, attested by countless stories in the standard bios. Yet there were those who observed McCarthy closely—including such harsh McCarthy critics as Jack Anderson and George Reedy—who had a different version: The McCarthy they knew early on was a drink-nurser, concerned to keep his wits about him and thus gain a competitive edge over others who were imbibing. People change, of course, and it may be that if McCarthy succumbed to the bottle, as many witnesses aver, it was in the aftermath of his censure when he was downcast, reviled, and no longer in the limelight. Yet there are those who knew him well at this period also who deny the image of chronic drunkard.[3]

In still other cases, there are negative McCarthy anecdotes that some of his toughest critics tried to nail down but couldn't. The bogus tale of his allegedly welcoming Communist Party support in his campaign against La Follette has been mentioned. Likewise, the "quickie divorce" allegation has recently been debunked in some detail by a particularly stringent McCarthy critic. Yet another item in this vein is the oft-heard charge of cheating on his taxes, a subject that exercised his foes for years and involved a minute ransacking of his finances. Yet when all was said and done, the IRS in 1955 wound up giving McCarthy a $1,056 refund on the grounds that he had *overpaid* his taxes.[4]

Add to all the above the fact that the biographer-critics are by no means agreed as to the scarlet sins committed by McCarthy. While all standard treatments are as one in describing the supposed falseness of his Senate charges, they often vary widely in depictions of his personal evil. In this respect, it's noteworthy that later, more in-depth studies by David Oshinsky and Thomas Reeves dispute many of the lurid tales told by Rovere, Jack Anderson and Ronald May, and other early McCarthy critics, with no evident effort to check the sources. In several instances, Reeves and Oshinsky did such checking and found the previous charges were in error.*

On the other hand, there are McCarthy vignettes that are undoubtedly true in whole or major part: That he was a thrusting young attorney/politician seeking the main chance would be a surprise to no one who knows much about ambitious young attorneys, or politicians; that he used a bit of sharp practice in his race for circuit judge (though mild by the standards of today) seems well documented; that he puffed up his service record and used this for political advantage seems well attested also—though he was hardly the first, or last, to engage in conduct of that nature. To establish the exact degree of truth or falsity of all such charges and arrive at a composite judgment, pro, con, or in between, would be a tremendous labor and result in another book as long as this one.

However, there are obvious grounds on which such an effort would be not only arduous but fruitless. Chief among these is that, in strict logic,

---

*Reeves, whose study of McCarthy's early life and career is a model of exhaustive field research, in particular deflates oft-repeated tales about McCarthy's alleged involvement in financial misdeeds with Pepsi-Cola lobbyist Russell Arundel and the prefab housing company Lustron. In both cases, Reeves concludes, the version supplied by McCarthy's critics at the time, and echoed by Rovere *et al.,* was mistaken. In both cases also, Reeves presents McCarthy as something of a legislative expert on the underlying issues (sugar rationing in the first case, low-cost housing in the other). These findings, and some others of like nature by Oshinsky, are more compelling in that neither writer, to put it mildly, is biased in McCarthy's favor. Reeves and Oshinsky, for example, both debunk the alleged support of McCarthy in 1946 by the Communist Party and the alleged McCarthy quote welcoming such backing from the party. In other respects, unfortunately, these authors were less thorough and fell into errors of their own.

ad hominem attacks have nothing to do with the subject that concerns us—whether McCarthy was right or wrong about his charges of Red infiltration. In theory, he could have been guilty of every personal sin alleged against him and many more, and that still wouldn't tell us what we need to know about the cases. Conversely, he could have been a saint in his personal life but completely wrong about his charges. The proof of the matter, either way, must be found in the documentary record on the cases, to the extent that this can be recovered.

Still, there are aspects of McCarthy's life and career, beyond the mere outline of his schooling and employment, that cast some light on his political conduct and anti-Red crusading. These relate to matters on which there was widespread *agreement* among his friends and critics, rather than a series of dueling anecdotes, and thus concern facets of his nature obvious to all who knew him.

Starting with McCarthy's family background and upbringing, one of the most notable aspects of his persona was his Roman Catholic faith—this directly contrary to the Rovere portrayal of an irreligious and amoral cynic. As attested by friend and foe alike, McCarthy was in fact religious. There are numerous uncontradicted tales on record of his faithfulness in attending Mass, whatever his worldly preoccupations, and while he was no choirboy his Christian faith was an obvious feature of his personal credo and public message. (As a U.S. senator, he was known for his hospitality to Catholic priests and other representatives of the Church who weren't always so recognized by other Catholic members of Congress.)

A second McCarthy trait on which all observers were agreed is that, from college on if not before then, he was a tough customer who wasn't afraid to mix it up with all comers as might be needed. At Marquette, he had been a collegiate boxer, known for his straight-on methods of attack and willingness to take a punch in order to land one. He was powerfully built, strong, and fearless, but in terms of boxing technique, we're told, neither graceful nor proficient. As his critics never fail to note, his headlong boxing methods bore a marked resemblance to his political tactics later, and there is doubtless something to this. (It could likewise be said that his physical courage was in keeping with his wartime decision to join the Marines and go into a combat zone, when he could have stayed out of the service altogether or settled for chairborne duty on the home front.)

A further McCarthy avocation noted in all the studies was his fondness for playing poker. This is frequently cited as an example of his reckless nature, proclivity for bluffing, raising on a losing hand, and so on. Read with any care, however, accounts of McCarthy's poker playing suggest a somewhat different verdict. By the testimony of many who knew him or played against him, he was an extremely good poker player and during his college days and later made considerable money at the table, often covering his living expenses in this fashion. Somebody good enough to make money on a consistent basis playing poker may seem reckless to the kibitzer, and no doubt has a streak of daring in his makeup, but obviously knows what he is doing.

Some other McCarthy traits that couldn't be guessed from the caveman-in-the-sewer image were his keen intelligence and range of knowledge on a wide variety of subjects. His foray into engineering studies would come in handy, for example, in Senate hearings that involved technical/scientific matters, of which there were a fair number. Likewise, his mastery of the public housing issue in his early Senate tenure made him perhaps the foremost expert on that subject in Congress. He also made some study of Russian and astounded listeners at a hearing when he spoke in Russian to a witness who had defected from the Soviet Union.[5]

McCarthy friends and critics would further agree that, as is obvious from his résumé, he was ambitious for success and in a hurry to get it. In this respect, it's evident that his experience taught him there was little he couldn't achieve through willpower and sufficient effort. His skill as a quick study in mastering multiple subjects from high school through law courses at Marquette would have reinforced this notion. It's thus not surprising that when he reached the Senate, rather than being a bashful silent freshman, he plunged into complex issues such as rationing, federal housing programs, and the famous Malmedy episode from World War II*—the main topics to draw his notice early on. He was confident there were few subjects he couldn't handle if he applied himself in diligent fashion.

A final uncontested point about McCarthy was his sympathy for the little guy and common touch in personal dealings. Stories of his befriending elevator operators, clerks, secretaries, and plain everyday people on the sidewalk are legion, recounted by his critics as well as his admirers (when such existed). One of the more amazing but well-supported tales along these lines is that, during a break in his legislative duties, he worked as a common laborer on a North Dakota wheat farm whose proprietor had no idea he was hiring a member of the U.S. Senate.[6]

Such attitudes were reflected in McCarthy's official as well as in his personal conduct—in ways that even his liberal critics, if pushed hard enough, might recognize as valid. In his young political days, he had been at least nominally a New Deal Democrat, and even when he switched to the Republican

---

* "Malmedy" was an atrocity case from World War II in which American soldiers were slaughtered by the Nazis. Later numerous German soldiers were interrogated, put on trial, and convicted in a U.S. military court for complicity in the murders. There were allegations that the defendants had been subject to torture and inhumane treatment to extract confessions. The issue was somewhat similar to the Abu Ghraib episode in the war against Iraq. McCarthy became the main Senate spokesman questioning the methods of interrogation of the German prisoners.

Party was viewed as a "progressive"—all this in keeping with the fluid Wisconsin political scene in the age of the La Follettes. McCarthy's Senate involvements with the issues of low-cost housing and the Malmedy investigation (the latter, contrary to some treatments, a leftward cause célèbre)[7] were in keeping with this background. He was also a strong supporter of antidiscrimination measures, and though often called an "isolationist"—no novelty in Wisconsin—his views and voting record in the Senate were anything but.

Even when McCarthy took his place among more conservative members of the Senate, these early tendencies persisted. Hardly a "progressive" in any accepted meaning of the term, he was first, last, and always a populist in his political leanings. This was indeed the essence of his battle with the State Department and White House, big media outlets, and the establishment in general. Though now portrayed as a public menace and execrated enemy of the people, McCarthy viewed himself, and was viewed by his supporters, as a champion of the average guy against the big elites, self-styled sophisticates, and comfortable interests who usually ran things in the Capital City in whatever way they wanted.

Consistent with such views, McCarthy didn't fit in very well with the Washington social scene or its upscale customs. He remained a steak-and-potatoes guy whose idea of a good time was an all-night pokerfest, a day at the track, or a backwoods hunting party. He had no concern about the clothes he wore, where he dined or when, or material possessions for their own sake. The flip-side of all this was that he was improvident with money and often had to borrow, but would as gladly lend to others, seldom worrying about repayment. He was down home, grassroots, and blue collar all the way, which of course equated to "vulgarian" at *The New Yorker*. Had he been from the South and not Wisconsin, he would have been called a "good ol' boy" and relished the description.

Predictably, McCarthy's aversion to Washington power politics as usual wasn't helpful in the close-knit fraternity of the U.S. Senate and undoubtedly contributed to his later downfall. He was never part of the Senate club that controlled assignments, made the big decisions, and steered the flow of legislation; he showed little deference to its members, and they returned the favor. He went his own way, at his own pace, pursuing subjects that concerned him, and if this put him crossways with the graybeards of the chamber that didn't seem to bother him unduly. He was a maverick from the start and would still be a maverick at the finish.

On the other hand, when McCarthy became the head of his own committee, he was by the testimony of the record and of those who served with him a fair and skillful chairman, correct in dealings with his colleagues and, unless pushed to the very limit, patient with the gavel. This of course is about as different from the standard image as can possibly be imagined. It will accordingly be addressed again, but is briefly mentioned here to round out the picture of McCarthy as a living personality, rather than the deranged and villainous creature of the Herblock drawings and word pictures of Rovere.

In this bundle of McCarthy traits, there are some tentative clues to what he did and why, and the way he did it. Simply noting the highlights, his religious faith, service with the Marines, good ol' boy persona, and status as a self-made man all combined to form a hard-charging political figure who saw Cold War issues in vivid terms of right and wrong, black and white, with little by way of ambiguity (a word seldom used in talking about McCarthy). Nothing could have been further from the temporizing and studied languor that had for so long marked official attitudes on the issue of Communist infiltration and other aspects of the Cold War.

Most histories of the time suggest that McCarthy's vision of the struggle with Moscow was simplistic, paranoid, and Manichaean; based on now-ample records, it might more justly be described as an accurate understanding of the problem. That said, his straight-ahead, take-no-prisoners views and methods did lead him to make mistakes of facts and judgment. In particular, his penchant for multitasking, impromptu statement, and handling quantities of information on the fly caused him to commit errors of detail, a number of which will be noted in these pages. He was a quick starter and free swinger, with some of the ills that this is heir to, though by no means guilty of the many alleged horrors imputed to him.

The impulsive, lone-wolf side of McCarthy's personality would make him a problem in other ways as well—at least for some of his opponents, and occasionally even for his allies. Most notably, and central to the story, he simply couldn't be *controlled.* Considerations of political prudence, to the point of backing off from a cause he considered right, were alien to his nature. He was unwilling to go along to get along, even within his own political party, if he believed fundamental issues were at stake. This made him in Washington terms the worst kind of loose cannon, worrisome to establishmentarian forces in both parties.

Finally, McCarthy also engaged, on some well-known occasions, in harsh political invective against his foes—though scarcely more so, as our Rovere quotes suggest, than the invective used against him. Typically, his toughest political rhetoric was deployed against those who had attacked him, the premier examples being Senators William Benton of Connecticut and Ralph Flanders of Vermont. As Benton was trying to have McCarthy kicked out of the Senate, and Flanders leading the charge for McCarthy's censure, McCarthy in these cases gave as good as he got, though only he would pay a price in the historical record for such exchanges.

Fittingly, given their joint status as villains to forces of the left, one of the best brief descriptions of McCarthy's personality and methods would be offered by FBI Director J. Edgar Hoover. In a 1953 statement to the press, after observing McCarthy in action for better than three years, Hoover put it this way: "McCarthy is a former Marine. He was an amateur boxer. He's Irish. Combine those and you're going to have a vigorous individual, who won't be pushed around . . . Certainly, he is a controversial man. He is earnest and he is honest. He has enemies. Whenever you attack subversives of any kind, . . . you are going to be the victim of the most extremely vicious criticism that can be made."[8]

All this, however, is merely prelude. Again, what matters isn't the kind of person McCarthy was, whether he was quick or slow, drunk or sober, or even what Richard Rovere or J. Edgar Hoover thought about him. What matters in the end is whether he was right or wrong about the cases. And thereby hangs the tale that follows.

CHAPTER 3

He Had in His Hand

UNDOUBTEDLY the most common challenge made in any critique of Joe McCarthy is: Name *one* Communist (or Soviet agent) ever identified by him in his sensational speeches and investigations. That challenge has been posed for fifty years and more—always on the premise that nobody could come up with even one such person. Sometimes, the point is made the other way around, as a flatfooted statement: McCarthy never exposed a single Communist mole, or Soviet spy, despite all his anti-Communist bluster. Such comments appear often in bios of McCarthy and books about the Cold War.

Embedded in these gibes are certain assumptions and ambiguities that need to be cleared up and made explicit. What would it take, for instance, to prove somebody *was* a Communist or Soviet agent? When we note that there are people around these days who still say Alger Hiss was neither, the answer isn't instantly apparent. Hiss, it will be recalled, was convicted in a court of law for having lied about such matters, as were Carl Marzani and William Remington (the latter one of McCarthy's cases before the Senate). And even if such legal verdicts are thought decisive, these are rare exceptions. If conviction in a court of law is to be the standard, we may conclude there were virtually no secret Reds in the U.S. government spotted by Joe McCarthy or anyone else, including FBI Director Hoover and his G-men.

The point about such courtroom verdicts has some other relevance also, as on occasion this too is part of the denunciation of McCarthy: that none of his suspects *went to prison* for their allegedly subversive doings. But of course McCarthy had neither the duty nor the power to put such people in prison (though he certainly thought some of them should have been there), so this is an obvious red herring dragged across the path to confuse the issue. His main goal, oft-stated and sanctioned by the law, was to get his suspects *out of the federal government* and its policy-making system; all the battles in which he was engaged revolved around this central purpose.*

In any event, this way of looking at McCarthy and his cases is a distraction from the critical mass of data we now have about the subject. Most of what we know in life hasn't been filtered through a courtroom, and if we waited until it had been would be incapable of timely action on countless important matters. That Adolf Hitler circa 1940 was a genocidal tyrant who meant to take over Europe wasn't a juridical verdict but one based on real-world evidence in the public record. In like fashion, we know there were Soviet spies and Communist agents in and around the federal government who meant to do us harm, not because a judge and jury said so, but because we have multiple interlocking sources of credible information that reveal this.

A further distinction that needs making concerns the meaning of exposure or identification of Communists or Soviet agents. In no case did McCarthy suggest, nor could he have, that he *personally knew* so-and-so to be a Red, or that he could prove such an accusation through personal sleuthing. Rather, his contention was that there was sworn testimony in the record, or data in security files, indicating somebody was a Communist, had worked for the Soviet embassy, or hung out with Soviet agents (such information usually coming by one route or another from the FBI). When McCarthy said someone was identified as a Communist or henchman of the Kremlin, he meant something of this nature.

All this said, we now consider the rhetorical challenge more directly, on its own less-nuanced merits. Can we in fact name *one* certifiable Communist McCarthy ever came up with in all his speeches and contentious hearings? The answer is that it's indeed hard to cite one such person—just as it's hard to eat one potato chip or salted peanut. Once the process starts, the temptation is to keep going, which would result in a long string of names that would be unintel-

---

* The only instances in which McCarthy tried to send someone to prison were citations for contempt before his committee, which had to be voted by the full committee and thereafter by the entire body of the Senate, then acted upon by the Justice Department and a grand jury. The federal courts in the few cases where all this happened failed for various reasons to convict, which is apparently the basis for this criticism of McCarthy; but these outcomes didn't relate to the substantive merits of the Communist charges. William Remington, on the other hand, was a McCarthy suspect who did go to prison, although his conviction had no direct relation to McCarthy.

ligible without further context, and wouldn't make for lively reading. However, a few examples in this genre, viewed against the backdrop of *Venona,* may help set the stage for things to come. Here, for instance, is a list of ten McCarthy suspects, taken from his Senate speeches and/or hearings in which he figured:

Solomon Adler	Harold Glasser
Cedric Belfrage	David Karr
T. A. Bisson	Mary Jane Keeney
V. Frank Coe	Leonard Mins
Lauchlin Currie	Franz Neumann

This is, to be sure, a heterogeneous group. While all of them came under McCarthy's lens, they did so in different measures and in different settings. Some were in the original bloc of cases he brought before the Senate and Tydings panel (Keeney, Neumann), some were otherwise named in public statements (Bisson, Karr), some later appeared before his subcommittee (Belfrage, Mins), and so on. However, all were McCarthy targets in one fashion or another, and thus per the standard teaching must have been mere innocent victims of his midcentury reign of terror.

Except, when the *Venona* file was published in 1995, all these McCarthy cases were right there in the decrypts, each named significantly in the Soviet cables. From these identifications (and collateral data from the Kremlin archives) it's apparent that, rather than being blameless martyrs, all were indeed Communists, Soviet agents, or assets of the KGB, just as McCarthy had suggested and generally speaking even more so. Thus—apart from people who disbelieve *Venona* (roughly the same people who still believe in Hiss)—we would here seem to have a conclusive answer to the challenge: Can you name *one* Communist or Soviet mole ever unearthed by Joe McCarthy?

These cases are cited here for ready reference simply because they happen to show up in *Venona,* which though of great importance is but one subset of the huge database now available on such matters. If we look to other information sources—reports of the FBI, dossiers from counterintelligence archives, sworn testimony by credible witnesses—it would be possible to identify twenty, thirty, forty, fifty, or more McCarthy targets in like manner. Nonetheless, this particular group provides a good cross section of his cases and the facts he had about them and is thus worth a bit of further notice.

SOLOMON ADLER was an official of the U.S. Treasury Department who served for several years in China during World War II and the early postwar era and came on the McCarthy radar screen on at least two public occasions we know of, suggesting he had been an object of study and discussion in more private sessions. The first such episode was in the Tydings hearings of 1950, triggered by McCarthy's original charges of subversion. Assistant committee counsel Robert Morris, who worked closely with McCarthy in these hearings, was questioning diplomat John Stewart Service, one of McCarthy's foremost targets, about his contacts in Chungking, China, in the 1940s.

It was in this context that Solomon Adler was mentioned, as Morris quizzed Service on his linkage to the Treasury staffer. This line of interrogation, and other questions posed to Service, indicated that McCarthy-Morris at this point had good insight into the bigger picture of events in China, in which Service and Sol Adler both played crucial roles. (There were also indications that the McCarthy forces were privy to wiretap information from the FBI concerning Service, including ties to Adler.)[1]

Adler's name would surface again in 1953, when McCarthy as chairman of the Senate Permanent Subcommittee on Investigations questioned former Treasury employee William Taylor about *his* relationship to Adler—specifically, if Taylor and Adler had by any chance lived together at a house in Chungking. McCarthy in this session also brought up the name of the Chinese national Chi Chao-ting, yet another Adler contact. Again, these questions showed knowledge on McCarthy's part of a larger network in which Sol Adler was a member. Thus Adler was in the sights of Joe McCarthy from a fairly early date and would remain there.[2]

This focus on Sol Adler would be of additional interest when the *Venona* decrypts were published. There we find him duly making his appearance, under the cover name "Sachs," passing information to the comrades about the state of things in China. This fits with other official data that show him to have been part of a Treasury Red combine that included Harry Dexter White, Nathan Gregory Silvermaster, Harold Glasser, V. Frank Coe, and a sizable crew of others. (As indicated by our alphabetical roster, both Coe and Glasser would become McCarthy committee cases also.) Thus, as shall be shown hereafter, Joe McCarthy did not err in targeting Adler, his ties to Service, or his living arrangements while in China.

ADLER was of British birth, and so coincidentally was the second suspect in our lineup—*Cedric Belfrage*. Unlike Adler, who became a U.S. citizen in 1940, Belfrage never did, though he lived and worked in the United States off and on for something like two decades. In the early days of World War II, he was employed by the British Security Coordinator in New York, the famous Canadian spy chief Sir William Stephenson (the man called "Intrepid" by Winston Churchill), who worked in tandem with the ultrasecret American Office of Strategic Services (OSS). In this job, Belfrage had access to U.S. as well as British intelligence data.

At war's end, Belfrage obtained a post with the military government of occupied Germany as a press control officer, supposedly to help advance the cause of "de-Nazification" in the defeated country. In this role he was involved with the licensing of publications, including some of notorious Communist bent (official Allied policy at the time). It was this background that brought him to the notice of McCarthy, looking into U.S. information programs in Europe and possible subversive influence in their operations.

Questioned by McCarthy counsel Roy Cohn as to whether he had been a Communist while carrying out his postwar duties, or if he were a CP member at that very moment, Belfrage declined to answer, seeking shelter in the Fifth Amendment. He refused to answer similar questions concerning fellow journalist James Aronson, his sidekick in this and other ventures. Whereupon the committee called on the Immigration and Naturalization Service to deport Belfrage, and the chairman gave the witness a taste of McCarthyite invective, denouncing "those who come up like you do, especially as an alien, and refuse to answer the questions of the committee—I hope you leave the shores of our country as soon as possible."* After a lot of legal bickering, this in fact occurred, and Belfrage at last left the United States to go back to England.[3]

Belfrage was portrayed at the time as a victim of McCarthyite excesses, punished because he dared dissent from the smothering orthodoxy of the era. Four decades later, however, came the revelations of *Venona*. Here we find numerous mentions of Cedric Belfrage, identified by the cryptologists as the KGB contact "UCN/9," reporting back to Moscow out of William Stephenson's office. *Venona* shows UCN/9 providing data from the OSS about the then-looming struggle for the Balkans—a major focus of Soviet, British, and U.S. intelligence efforts. The decrypts also show UCN/9 trying to sound out British policy toward a second front in Europe to ease Nazi pressure on the Russians, sharing documents with Soviet spy chief Jacob Golos, and otherwise acting as a fount of knowledge for the Kremlin. It would thus appear that Joe McCarthy was not mistaken in seeking the deportation of Cedric Belfrage.

NOR was McCarthy wrong about the case of *T. A. Bisson*. In his early speeches, McCarthy often referred to Bisson and his efforts to advance the Communist cause in China. These comments occurred in connection with McCarthy charges involving the magazine *Amerasia,* the Institute of Pacific Relations (IPR), and Professor Owen Lattimore, a kingpin in the IPR who would become McCarthy's major target. Though Bisson was closely linked to

---

*This is, it must be confessed, a trick quotation. Before this exchange occurred, McCarthy had been called out of the hearing and had turned the gavel over to Sen. Stuart Symington (D-Mo.) as acting chairman. So it was liberal Democrat Symington who spoke these dreadful words to victim Belfrage.

all these cases, it's doubtful many people today know anything about him, except possibly as one of McCarthy's hapless victims. So who was T. A. Bisson? Here is what *Venona* tells us, in a message from Soviet agents in New York back to Moscow Center:

> Marquis [Soviet espionage agent Joseph Bernstein] has established friendly relations with T.A. Bisson (hereafter Arthur) . . . who has recently left BEW [Board of Economic Warfare]; he is now working in the Institute of Pacific Relations (IPR) and in the editorial office of Marquis' periodical [*Amerasia*]. Arthur passed to Marquis . . . copies of four documents: (a) his own report for BEW with his views on working out a plan for shipment of American troops to China; (b) a report by the Chinese embassy in Washington to its government in China . . . (c) a brief report of April 1943 on a general evaluation of the forces on the sides of the Soviet-German front . . . (d) a report by the American consul in Vladivostok. . . .[4]

According to the FBI, the Joseph Bernstein receiving this material was a self-identified Soviet spy who would play an equally sinister role in later cases of subversion. So Bisson not only touted the cause of the Red Chinese, as McCarthy stated, but passed confidential official data to a Soviet intelligence agent. McCarthy thought Bisson was bad news and cited evidence to prove it. But he didn't know for sure how bad, as reflected in these transcripts. That secret would be locked up for fifty years, known only to the Kremlin and the keepers of *Venona*.

BREAKING our alphabetical sequence slightly, we have next the cases of *V. Frank Coe* and *Harold Glasser*, called back to back in the same McCarthy subcommittee hearings in October 1953.* Both were part of the Treasury nexus that included Harry White, Sol Adler, Gregory Silvermaster, and many others. As with Cedric Belfrage, Coe and Glasser were quizzed about Allied policies in the German occupation. This probe sought to develop the espionage angle of a case in which printing plates for occupation currency, issued and redeemable by the United States, were transferred to Soviet control by members of the Treasury network.

In these hearings, ex-Communist Elizabeth Bentley testified that the handover of the currency plates was ordered by her Soviet former bosses and that Red agents in the Treasury followed through and got the job done. Coe and Glasser were questioned about this and other postwar financial issues. Coe was in particular quizzed about a memo he wrote passing along a Soviet request for

---

*These McCarthy subcommittee hearings were in fact conducted by Sen. Karl Mundt (R-S.D.), second-ranking Republican on the panel. (McCarthy himself was at this time conducting the subcommittee's famous investigation of Fort Monmouth.)

more dies to print the occupation money. Asked by Sen. Karl Mundt (R-S.D.), "At the time you wrote that memorandum, were you engaged in espionage activities in behalf of the Soviet government?" Coe replied, "I respectfully, under the protection of the Fifth Amendment, decline to answer the question." When Mundt further asked, "Are you now a member of the Communist Party?" Coe respectfully passed on that one also.

Much the same occurred with Glasser. In cross-examination by McCarthy staffer Thomas LaVenia, the dialogue went as follows: *LaVenia:* "At the time you attended those meetings, were you a member of the Communist Party?" *Glasser:* "I refuse to answer that question on the ground that it may tend to incriminate me." *LaVenia:* "At the time you attended those meetings, were you engaged in espionage?" *Glasser:* "I refuse to answer that question on the ground that it may tend to incriminate me."[5]

Thus Coe and Glasser, both veterans of such encounters in the late 1940s and early '50s, would be added to the pantheon of McCarthy subcommittee martyrs. Eventually, both would also show up in *Venona*—Coe with the cover name "Peak," Glasser with the more appropriate "Ruble." On the *Venona* evidence, Glasser seems to have been an especially valued agent: a pal of Alger Hiss, providing intelligence data to Soviet handlers, talent spotting for the Kremlin. Coe, for his part, would figure in another financial wrangle in the final phases of the war, pertaining to the then anti-Red regime of China and its quest for U.S. funding. In this affair, Coe's efforts would be devoted to blocking aid for an American ally rather than pushing matters forward as he did for Moscow.

EASILY the most important figure on this McCarthy list of ten was *Lauchlin Currie,* an executive assistant to President Roosevelt in the early 1940s whose portfolio included policy toward China. Currie left the government in 1945, and though he was still around when McCarthy came along would flee the country soon thereafter. In trying to retrace the steps by which the U.S. government had been penetrated by Communists and Soviet agents, McCarthy got on the trail of Currie and his multitude of contacts.

Currie was, for instance, closely linked with Owen Lattimore, and with diplomat John Stewart Service, arrested in the *Amerasia* case after sending back a stream of dispatches from China denouncing the anti-Communist leader Chiang Kai-shek. Currie was also extremely thick with John Carter Vincent, the State Department official who played a critical role in shaping U.S. Asia policy in the years before the Red conquest of China.

In addressing the debacle of U.S. China policy, McCarthy charged that "Lauchlin Currie in the White House and John Carter Vincent and subsequently Alger Hiss in the State Department were exercising their influence at the

Washington end of the transmission belt conveying poisonous misinformation from Chungking [to the detriment of Chiang]. The full outlines of Currie's part in the great betrayal have yet to be traced. That it was an important and essential part, I have no doubt."[6]

By "great betrayal" McCarthy meant the strategy of elements in the State and Treasury Departments and White House to torpedo Chiang and advance the fortunes of his Red opponents. This was certainly harsh invective against Currie but totally justified by the record. Like others mentioned, Currie would appear in *Venona* as an agent of influence and spy for Moscow, bearing the cover name "Page." And while he more than did his bit on China, his efforts were by no means confined to Asia.

Venona reveals, for instance, that Currie in 1944 told the KGB President Roosevelt was willing to concede Soviet demands about the Polish-Russian border, which claimed for Stalin the territory he seized in 1939 when he and Hitler jointly invaded Poland and divided it between them. This intel was of utmost value to Moscow, as it showed FDR breaking faith with the Polish government in exile, which opposed the Kremlin land grab. The Soviets thus knew they need not fear a tough U.S. response as they dished the Poles, which they proceeded to do in brutal fashion until they totally conquered Poland.*

LESS important in the larger scheme of things, but significant in his way, was *David Karr*, among the more flamboyant figures in Cold War records. Karr was the subject of one of the bitterest speeches ever delivered by McCarthy—a denunciation of columnist Drew Pearson as a propagandist for pro-Soviet causes. McCarthy's main proof of this was the assertion that Karr, a legman and reporter for Pearson, was a Red agent and that his influence in behalf of Moscow was evident in Pearson's columns savaging anti-Communist spokesmen (McCarthy himself, not so coincidentally, foremost among them).

On December 19, 1950, McCarthy sought to document these charges by reading into the *Congressional Record* a security memo from the Civil Service Commission, including findings that Karr had been a reporter for the *Daily Worker,* a member of the Communist Party, a writer for the Communist-front publication *Fight,* and related data. McCarthy also read into the *Record* testimony by ex-Communist Howard Rushmore, a former editor at the *Worker,* saying he had there given assignments to Karr and that Karr was a party member.

This triggered angry answers from Karr, Pearson, Sen. Clinton Anderson (D-N.M.), and others saying McCarthy had smeared an upstanding newsman. But, as in other cases cited, the evidence of *Venona*—and other Soviet data— indicates McCarthy knew whereof he spoke. Like his fellow suspects, Karr shows

---

*Similar information was provided to the Bentley spy ring by Treasury staffer Harry White.

up in *Venona,* albeit in a different manner. He appears only once, in his own persona and without cover name, providing information to the Soviet agent/TASS correspondent Samuel Krafsur. He also appears in a document gleaned from Russian sources by intelligence expert Herbert Romerstein, as follows:

> In 1978, American Senator Edward Kennedy appealed to the KGB to assist in establishing cooperation between Soviet organizations and the California firm Agritech, headed by former Senator J. Tunney. This firm in turn was connected to the French-American company, Finatech, S.A., which was run by a competent KGB source, the prominent Western financier D. Karr, through whom opinions had been confidentially exchanged for several years between the General Secretary of the Communist Party and Sen. Kennedy. D. Karr provided the KGB with technical information on conditions in the U.S. and other capitalist countries which were regularly reported to the Central Committee.[7]

The description of Karr as a "competent KGB source" underscores the indication in *Venona* that he was an agent of the Soviet interest. So, for that matter, does the reference to Karr as a "prominent Western financier," a status in large part achieved through his linkage to the bizarre Moscow front man Armand Hammer, an even more fantastic Cold War figure whose considerable fortune was based on dealings with the Kremlin.

MARY JANE *Keeney* was among the very first of all McCarthy cases, having been mentioned by him in speeches on the Communist issue in Wheeling, West Virginia, and Reno, Nevada, in February 1950, and on the floor of the Senate a short time later. Though not formally dealt with in testimony to the Tydings subcommittee, she was considered by that panel, the FBI, and the Civil Service Commission to be one of McCarthy's "public cases."

McCarthy didn't talk too often about Mary Jane Keeney (whom he called "Mary Jane Kenney," as did several FBI reports), but what he said was very much on point. In exchanges with Democratic Senate leader Scott Lucas of Illinois, McCarthy put the matter this way: "I gave the name of Mrs. Kenney, who had been listed by the FBI as a courier for the Communist Party, while working for the government. I pointed out that when she was forced out by public pressure and the FBI statement that she ends up where she is today, in one of the educational organizations or in some part of the U.N. organization."[8]

All of which, again, would be backed up by *Venona,* which shows Keeney and her husband Philip to have been Communists and agents of Soviet intelligence. He had worked for a time at OSS, and she at the BEW, and both had occasion to deal with confidential data. She later went to work, like Cedric Belfrage, for the Allied German occupation forces, while Philip would play a similar role in the occupation of Japan.

FBI records show Mary Jane Keeney meeting with Joseph Bernstein, the Soviet agent who received confidential data from T. A. Bisson, and delivering to Bernstein a package he would in turn deliver to a top CP official. The document hand-off was surveilled by Hoover's men and was the obvious basis for the "courier" reference by McCarthy. Bureau files reflect many other meetings between Bernstein and the Keeneys, plus frequent Keeney dealings with a "Colonel Thomas," identified by the FBI as Soviet intelligence agent Sergei Kournakov.

In 1946, on her return from Germany, Mary Jane Keeney did a brief tour of duty at the State Department, but at this time pressures were being mounted by the FBI, security types, and some in Congress to rid the department of such cases. (She was, along with Alger Hiss, one of the "agents" listed in the disappearing Sam Klaus memo of August 1946.) Leaving the department, she moved on to a job at the United Nations, where she was working when McCarthy made his charges. So, despite calling her "Mrs. Kenney" (which he may well have gotten from the FBI), McCarthy described the case with fair precision.

I F LAUCHLIN Currie was the most important of our ten McCarthy cases, the most egregious in many ways was *Leonard Mins*. Called in December of 1953 during a McCarthy probe into pro-Red penetration of defense supply firms, Mins was so flagrant a Communist he had been fired for this reason a decade before from the OSS. Given the reputation of that agency for harboring Reds and Soviet agents, getting removed from it as a subversive was no small distinction.

Mins in the 1930s had written for both the *Daily Worker* and the Communist *New Masses* and had other Red connections. Despite this he had been taken aboard at OSS, where he stayed about a year before being sacked. Indicative of security standards in the war and for some time thereafter, he was then hired by a defense subcontractor dealing with radar-directed weapons for the Navy and stayed at this job for the next three years. In his work on a manual relating to such weapons, he had access to military data.

Among the questions posed to Mins by McCarthy and counsel Roy Cohn were these: "At the time you had access to this material were you a member of the Communist Party?" "Were you at that time on the payroll of the Soviet military intelligence?" "Did you transmit the information which came into your possession while you were working on this manual to Soviet military intelligence?" "At the time [when working for OSS] were you on the payroll of Soviet military intelligence?"[9]

Mins refused to answer all such questions, pleading the protection of the Fifth Amendment—this interlarded with quotes from the historians Suetonius and Tacitus about the decadent days of Rome and evils of informers. Illustrative of McCarthy's patience with such baiting, he permitted all these statements to be offered for the record, plus a diatribe by Mins challenging the jurisdiction of the panel and its effrontery in daring ask him if he were a Soviet agent. Rather than gaveling down this filibuster, McCarthy calmly heard it out, said "motion denied," and proceeded with the hearing.

Subsequently, Mins would appear in *Venona* as an agent of the Soviet military intelligence service GRU, exactly as suggested by the Cohn-McCarthy questions. While with OSS he had reported to the GRU on U.S. efforts to break Soviet codes, Anglo-American war plans, and his own talent-scouting for the Kremlin. Still other Soviet documentation on Mins reveals that he had been a Comintern agent extending back for several decades.

WE CONCLUDE this brief survey with a case that is a bit of an anticlimax, as neither McCarthy nor *Venona* had very much to say about him. This final suspect was *Franz Neumann,* better known as an author and scholar of the so-called Frankfurt school than as a Soviet agent. Nonetheless, he shows up in *Venona* as a source for the KGB (one of many at OSS), and was case No. 59 on the list of suspects McCarthy gave the Tydings panel. Neumann was a refugee from Germany who came to the United States in the middle 1930s. He was taken into the OSS at the outbreak of the war, then transferred into the State Department in October of 1945 along with hundreds of others from that service.

Though Neumann came to the notice of State Department security officials, he apparently kept his head down enough to avoid excessive trouble before McCarthy chanced across him. He was still on the department payroll in 1950, when McCarthy called attention to his case, but seems to have left the department not long thereafter. At all events, Neumann turned out to be a denizen of *Venona* (code name "Ruff") as well as a McCarthy suspect, and so qualifies as yet another answer to the question, Can you name *one* Communist ever identified in the public record by McCarthy?[10]

THOUGH drastically compressed, this is a lot of information all at once about a mixed array of cases. But, considering the glib generalizations tossed around about McCarthy and his victims, the Communists he didn't name, his lack of evidence, and his lying, it's obvious that detailed, specific information is precisely the thing that's needed in such discussion. And, as shall be seen, there are plenty of other security data on McCarthy suspects, derived from sources other than *Venona,* that are as compelling. When these are examined, potential answers to our rhetorical challenge expand in geometric ratio.

Pending that, a few observations are in order about this group of cases.

One is the pattern of verification. In the usual instance, we have someone identified by McCarthy as a Communist, subversive, or security risk, or brought before him to answer charges of this sort made by another witness. Typically, in media/academic handling of such cases, the individual in question would be treated as an innocent victim of McCarthy and/or his "paid informers." Then, when the truth came out at last, it developed that the alleged victim had been a Communist or Soviet agent all along. Seldom if ever does the process work the other way—in which someone initially considered a subversive turns out to be a blameless martyr.

A second significant point about these cases is that, in every instance, the suspects weren't merely ideological Communists—though most of them were surely that; they were also, in pretty obvious fashion, Moscow agents, pledging allegiance to the Soviet Union. This was to some degree inherent in the nature of *Venona,* but would be true in other cases also. The problem with having such people in the U.S. government, in other words, wasn't their political beliefs as such, but the fact that they were fifth columnists working for a hostile foreign power. All were part of a global apparatus, headquartered in the Kremlin, that was far greater in extent than anyone back in the 1950s—up to and including Joe McCarthy—could readily envision.

A third such observation is that these cases were, by and large, deeply rooted. Such as Adler, Coe, Keeney, and Neumann had been on official payrolls for a considerable span of years previous to McCarthy's charges and still were in 1950. How they got there, and what had—or hadn't—been done about them would be essential aspects of the story.

CHAPTER 4

"Stale, Warmed Over Charges"

BEFORE Joe McCarthy, there was Martin Dies. In the latter 1930s and early '40s, Dies would play a role in Congress eerily similar to that filled by McCarthy a decade later. A conservative Democrat from East Texas, son of a former congressman and protégé of Vice President John Nance Garner (a fellow Texan), Dies was the first and longest-serving chairman of what would become the House Committee on Un-American Activities. Formed as a special unit in 1938, and later made a standing committee, the panel would be a storm center of dispute from the beginning, conducting numerous controversial probes into issues of alleged subversion.

Dies was not the first into this minefield, though he would become by an appreciable margin the most famous, at least before the advent of McCarthy. Earlier such investigations had been made by the Overman committee at the era of World War I, Hamilton Fish in 1930, and the Dickstein-McCormack committee in 1934 and '35. But it was Dies who became identified in the public mind with antisubversive, mainly anti-Red, investigations. During his seven years at the helm, the group would be known far and wide simply as the Dies Committee. He pioneered the notion of full-time, ongoing congressional interest in loyalty/security matters.

Virtually everything that would later be said about Joe McCarthy was said first of Martin Dies: that he was conducting "witch hunts," smearing innocent victims, using the Communist issue to advance his own malign agenda, spreading hysteria about a nonexistent menace. As would happen with McCarthy also, it was said that suspects pursued by Dies had been cleared in one fashion or another, that lists of cases he had were phony, that he was undermining the authority of executive agencies and the White House. Spokesmen for left-liberal groups, executive officials, and angry voices in the press assailed him on a nonstop basis. It was the same routine from start to finish.

The similarities between the Dies experience and the later activities of McCarthy stemmed from certain obvious sources. It was the same underlying issue, the same effort to raise an alarm about it, and the same ferocious opposition. In which respect, there was another likeness also—a sharp divide between the people who applauded such investigations and those who bitterly opposed them. Dies was popular with a reflexively anti-Communist public and thus had strong support in Congress, responsive to the voters. But he was disliked intensely by elites, or what were said to be such, in the academy, bureaucracy, and press corps. The same division of opinion, amounting to a cultural chasm, would be apparent in responses to McCarthy.

There were, of course, significant differences between the two Red hunters, which made the path pursued by Dies less rocky at the outset. He was a member of the majority party, chairman of a committee, and backed by conservative southern Democrats who were at that time a powerful element in Congress (this creating frequent tensions between Capitol Hill and the New Deal White House). McCarthy when he began was a junior member of the minority party in the Senate, wouldn't become a committee chairman until three years later, and for most of his relatively brief career was basically a freelance. Yet the similarities between the two security hawks far outweighed such nominal distinctions.

Most to the present point, there were extensive parallels between Dies and McCarthy, not only in terms of general features and broad objectives, but as to many specific topics. Considering that their respective heydays in Congress were roughly ten years apart, it's noteworthy that so many of the groups and individuals who drew their attention turned out to be the selfsame people. This was most often true of various federal employees who became the subjects of investigation, though it extended to others outside of government also.

In turn, it was their common focus on the Reds-in-government issue that made Dies and McCarthy most controversial. It was one thing to be against Communism as a general proposition, or to berate and oppose the open Communist Party (though even this wasn't quite PC back in the 1930s). It was another to zero in on supposedly non-Communist officeholders as secret minions of the party, complicit in the schemes of Moscow. These were the charges that stirred the most vociferous opposition and harsh invective against the accusers. And they were of course the charges that would have been the most outrageous if they had been unfounded.

It so happened, however, that when Dies and his committee came along there had been a recent and fairly extensive penetration of the government by Communists and Soviet agents. This was at the time a novel problem that hadn't previously drawn much notice, and for which there were few security defenses to speak of. To see the changing nature of the issue, we need only scan the report on domestic Communism compiled in 1930 by the Fish committee. For its time a comprehensive wrap-up, this found the CPUSA to be a militant revolutionary group, mostly headed by alien leaders and drawing on a membership base heavily weighted to recent émigrés, many of whom could not speak English. That a Communist Party so led and constituted could penetrate the civilian ranks of the federal government—or make serious efforts to do so—occurred to practically no one.[1]

In the next few years, however, the conditions recorded by the Fish committee, both in the Communist party and in the nation, would be altered in drastic fashion. By the middle 1930s, the party would undergo a complete makeover in public image and at least a partial makeover in composition. In the age of the "popular front," the comrades shelved much of their violent, revolutionary rhetoric; the cause would now be depicted by party boss Earl Browder and his agents as old-fashioned Americanism updated for the modern era. In pursuit of this notion, the party adopted a stance of cooperating with other leftward and conventionally liberal forces for reform and social justice, peace, and other noble objects.

Simultaneously, and no doubt aided by this tactic, there would be an influx into party ranks of native-born Americans, many fresh off the college campus, some from Anglo families dating back for generations. The new arrivals gave the party a different kind of cadre, and cachet, that would be useful to it in numerous projects. Foremost among these was the entry of party members into posts of influence in many walks of life, including academic and media jobs and government work for those inclined in that direction.

Aiding the infiltration process were the pell-mell methods of the First New Deal under President Franklin Roosevelt, who came to power in 1933 in the early stages of the Great Depression. As is well known, Roosevelt and his advisers tried multiple panaceas to deal with unemployment, bank runs, a collapsed stock market, farm problems, and other economic troubles. Subsidies, regulations, and new programs abounded. This hurly-burly meant a lot of federal hiring. It also drew into its vortex all manner of self-styled planners and reformers anxious to get in on the action. And nobody at this time was bothering to vet the new recruits for anti-Red credentials.

As a result of these conditions, a sizable corps of Communists and fellow travelers would wind up on the federal payroll, together with a host of others susceptible to recruitment. The full scope of the penetration is hard to gauge, but there doesn't seem to be much doubt it was extensive. Much of what we know about it is based on the testimony of Whittaker Chambers, a Soviet courier who worked closely with Communist and fellow-traveling federal workers beginning in the early 1930s.

As described by Chambers, a particular concentration point for CP members was the Agricultural Adjustment Administration, a New Deal offshoot of the Department of Agriculture. Here the main Communist leader was one Harold Ware, who contrary to the usual pattern had been in the department for a while before this, and was an enthusiast for Soviet-style collective farming. The group he headed, according to Chambers, included such eventually well-known figures as Alger Hiss, Henry Collins, Nathan Witt, John Abt, Lee Pressman, and Charles Kramer, among a considerable crew of others.

Subsequently, Witt and Kramer would move to the National Labor Relations Board, which became a redoubt of Communist economic/political power later in the decade. Hiss, Collins, and Abt would meanwhile get jobs with congressional committees, and Hiss—the most upwardly mobile of the group—would move to the Department of Justice and then to the State Department. Though State wasn't then the penetration target it would become a few years later, there were already comrades ensconced there in the 1930s. Noel Field, Richard Post, and Julian Wadleigh were among those in the department named by Chambers as members of the apparatus.

A further enclave of CP members and fellow travelers—probably the largest group of all—was in the Treasury Department. Here were employed the influential Harry Dexter White, the Soviet agent Solomon Adler, V. Frank Coe, and several others named by Chambers, all also named by Elizabeth Bentley and in the pages of *Venona*. Added to these were still other party contacts holding federal office: Irving Kaplan of the National Research Project of the Works Progress Administration (WPA), Victor Perlo at the National Recovery Administration (NRA), Hiss's brother Donald in the Department of Labor, and White House assistant Lauchlin Currie. Small wonder Soviet espionage boss J. Peters would brag to Chambers: "Even in Germany, under the Weimar Republic, the party did not have what we have here."*[2]

In explaining how such infiltration happened, Chambers would cite his own experience when, in 1937, he wanted to get a federal job and establish an official identity for the record after leading a mostly underground existence. He said he was referred to Irving Kaplan at the National Research Project and in a matter of days would be on the federal payroll. The research project, per

---

*The scope of the penetration as Chambers saw it is sometimes understated by focusing strictly on the people he named and personally dealt with. In fact, he stressed, the CP agents he managed were all leaders of cell groups, each cell including other members Chambers didn't contact directly. Based on this, he estimated the comrades in his network as perhaps seventy-five in number. He further noted that there were undoubtedly other rings and Communist networks of which he knew nothing, but which based on his general knowledge of CP methods he was certain existed.

Chambers, was a kind of "trapdoor" through which comrades could enter governmental ranks, then move on to other outposts. (And when one got in, he could hire others.)

As to the purpose of such infiltration, Chambers made a couple of further points that in subsequent security debates would be too much neglected. First, that the Communists with whom he worked were, either directly or indirectly, agents of Moscow, albeit with varying levels of commitment, and that the whole operation was managed by Russian or other foreign commissars to whom Chambers as middleman reported. And second, that the object of the infiltration wasn't merely to filch secret papers, though this did occur, but to place people in positions of trust where they could affect the course of policy in favor of the Soviet Union.

Such was the picture of Red penetration circa 1938, as later sketched by Chambers, when the Dies committee was founded. At the outset, like the Fish investigation before it, the committee would survey the scope of Communist activities in American society at large. Only by degrees, as part of a gradual learning process, would it engage the matter of Communists on the federal payroll. In early sessions, the panel looked at Red agitation in the ranks of labor, education, arts and letters, and civic groups of one sort and another. In addition—though this, too, is much neglected—it went after the German-American Bund and other pro-Nazi outfits of the era that were trying to stir up trouble. Otherwise, its foremost project was scrutiny of the innumerable Communist fronts that flourished in the "Red decade."

The Dies disclosures/allegations about Reds in government thus weren't systematic, but occurred in piecemeal fashion as different aspects of the problem surfaced. In one instructive episode, the committee took testimony concerning the Federal Writers Project in New York, another unit of the WPA, set up to give work to unemployed writers. In this project, according to the testimony, more than 100 out of 300 writers had inscribed a book written by Communist party boss Earl Browder, expressing their good wishes to a retiring comrade, the circumstances indicating that the signers were CP members or close-in fellow travelers. If there were 100 such people in a single project, the government-wide problem was arguably in the thousands.[3]

In other instances, Dies would get on the trail of individuals who had pro-Communist or extremely radical records, or had published writings that showed an affinity for Red causes. The committee came up with suspects at the NLRB, Federal Communications Commission (FCC), and, in the early 1940s, Office of Price Administration and the Office of Facts and Figures (progenitor of the Offices of Strategic Services and War Information). Again, these were piecemeal, *ad hoc* disclosures, rather than the findings of a dragnet inquest.

Although the Dies committee had certain ex-Communist witnesses before it to discuss the secret doings of the party—such as ex-Red Ralph de Sola, who helped expose the Writers Project—the more sweeping revelations of Chambers and Bentley were still years in the future. When these formidable witnesses surfaced in the 1940s, they testified, as it were, from the inside out. In the earlier going, Dies didn't have access to their expertise and was working mostly from the outside in.

Accordingly, in trying to gauge the extent of the infiltration problem, Dies and his colleagues would focus on the Communist fronts that flourished in the 1930s, and the membership and sponsor lists of these the committee would assemble. The fronts were the most striking phenomenon of the age, integral to many propaganda successes for the comrades. They would also be, for Dies and his researchers, a potential key to understanding how deeply the Communist Party had penetrated government agencies and programs.

Though portrayed in some historical treatments as an amusing oddity of the age, like marathon dancing or flagpole-sitting, the fronts were no laughing matter. Nor were they of spontaneous nature, or indigenous to the United States. They were serious propaganda operations, devised and guided by Moscow and its agents. A vast number were the handiwork of the German Communist Willi Munzenberg, a famous impresario of deception who spun out groups and publications on demand throughout the 1930s. Relief projects, protest committees, newspapers, manifestoes, art synods, and literary conclaves were all on the Munzenberg agenda.[4]

The point of this activity, as explained by Munzenberg himself, was to promote the Soviet interest through a host of propaganda outlets. "We must," he said, "penetrate every conceivable milieu, get hold of artists and professors, make use of cinemas and theatres, and spread abroad the doctrine that Russia is prepared to sacrifice everything for peace." Or, as his Communist colleague Otto Kuusinen expressed it: "We must create a whole solar system of organizations and smaller committees around the Communist Party . . . smaller organizations working actually under the influence of our party (not under mechanical leadership)."[5]

In simplest terms, a front was a Trojan horse—a metaphor often heard in the rhetorical battles of the time. The idea was to have a group that was under the discipline of the Communist Party but that to the casual viewer seemed something different. In most cases, the front was created *ab initio,* though in others a formerly non-Communist group might be captured and exploited. Two essential aspects of a front were that, while it enlisted as many non-Communists as it could, the control positions were always in reliably Communist hands; and, somewhat easier to spot, the group would invariably parrot and support the propaganda of the Soviet Union.

The proliferation of such groups meshed with other Communist blending tactics of the age. As "progressive" ideas abounded, utopian schemes were preached on street corners, and notions of collectivist planning espoused by many, the comrades seldom had much trouble merging their modified program with the general background noise of the decade. Judged by many public statements, it was hard sometimes to tell who was who. Accordingly, this was the golden era of the fronts, which functioned in virtually every sector of public life—from arts and letters to youth concerns to foreign issues of interest to Moscow such as the Spanish Civil War and the Japanese attack on China.

These are matters of some importance, as they help explain why so many people in the 1930s were drawn to the Red orbit and why a fair number of these would be induced to stay there. In the addled conditions of the time, such notable non-Communist figures as Eleanor Roosevelt and FDR's Interior Secretary, Harold Ickes, could be persuaded to lend their names to pro-Red ventures if these had a plausible cover, since the big-hearted joiners didn't bother to look beyond this. Likewise, less famous people, influenced by such examples, could be brought into the fold and often stick around to be converted. It was precisely in this manner, Elizabeth Bentley would testify, that she was recruited into the Communist Party and thence into the demimonde of Soviet plotting.

For purposes of our survey, the most significant thing about the fronts was their linkage to the Communists-in-government issue. In the 1930s, there was a fair amount of overlap between comrades on the federal payroll and the outside activities of the fronts. This wasn't good tradecraft, was indeed the reverse, especially for CP members in government called on by Chambers, and later by Bentley, to perform secret chores for Moscow. However, in this freewheeling era when nobody was paying much attention to such matters, the comrades often moved back and forth between their day jobs in federal offices and night work or weekend projects cooperating with the agitprop of the fronts.

The resulting degree of interlock between Reds in government service and outside agitation would be noted not only by the Dies committee but also, in the early 1940s, by the Justice Department under Francis Biddle, FDR's Attorney General. This last occurred when the New Deal became for a time atypically concerned about the problem of Red infiltration and supplied a list of fronts to cabinet agencies for guidance in vetting their employees. This was initially a roster of eleven groups, including information that showed their Communist origin and nature, and was most revealing, especially considering the source.[6]

This Biddle list, based on intel from the FBI, spotlighted such organizations as the Washington Book Shop, the Washington Committee for Democratic Action, and an omnibus outfit that spawned numerous other projects called the American League Against War and Fascism, later called for tactical reasons the League for Peace and Democracy (a change in name only). The memo cited chapter and verse on how this group was founded and controlled by the Communist Party and pledged allegiance to the Kremlin.

In its discussion of the League, the Biddle memo cited the confabs called

THE FIRST
"ATTORNEY GENERAL'S LIST"

An excerpt from the list of suspect organizations circulated to top U.S. officials by Attorney General Francis Biddle in early 1942.

STRICTLY CONFIDENTIAL

THE AMERICAN LEAGUE AGAINST WAR AND FASCISM
THE AMERICAN LEAGUE FOR PEACE AND DEMOCRACY

NOTE: The following statement does not purport to be a complete
report on the organization named. It is intended only to
acquaint you, without undue burden of detail, with the
nature of the evidence which has appeared to warrant an
investigation of charges of participation.

It is assumed that each employee's case will be decided
on all the facts presented in the report of the FBI and
elicited, where a hearing is ordered, by the board or
committee before which the employee is given an opportunity to appear.

Please note that the statement is marked "Strictly
Confidential" and is available only for use in administration of the mandate of Public No. 135.

American League Against War and Fascism

The American League Against War and Fascism is the first of three organizations established in the United States in an effort to create public sentiment
on behalf of a foreign policy adapted to the interests of the Soviet Union. Its
successor, the American League for Peace and Democracy, was established in 1937
and it, in turn, gave way in 1940 to the American Peace Mobilization which,
since the German invasion of Russia and the establishment of a pro-war policy by
Communists in the United States, has been known as American Peoples' Mobilization.

A World Congress, devoted to the foundation in each country of a League
Against War and Fascism, was held in Amsterdam in 1932 under the aegis of the
Communist International. It was at this time that Communists throughout the
world were teaching that capitalist forces were about to make war upon the Soviet
Union. The danger that Hitler might soon come into power in Germany accentuated
this belief. The American delegation to the Congress was headed by H. W. L. Dana,
an avowed Communist, who called his group "a workers' delegation". In accordance
with the resolutions of the Congress, organizations having as their stated aim
opposition to war and fascism were founded in the countries in which the Communist
International maintained sections.

The American League Against War and Fascism was formally organized at
the first United States Congress Against War and Fascism held in New York City
September 29 to October 1, 1933. The Manifesto of this Congress called attention
to the "black cloud of imperialist war" hanging over the world and pointed to
the NRA, the CCC and the other policies of the Roosevelt Administration as indications of America's preparedness for war and fascism. Only in the Soviet Union,
the Manifesto continued, has the basic cause of war--monopolistic capitalism--
been removed; the Soviet Union alone among the governments of the world proposes
total disarmament; only by arousing and organizing the masses within each country

(OVER)

by the Communist Party to get the agitation rolling, the presence of known Communists such as Browder himself among the officers and leading speakers, and the flow of funds from Soviet-controlled commercial outfits to underwrite the costs of doing business. And, most of all, the memo noted, there was the League's routine, emphatic, and unwavering praise of Moscow as the world's only champion of peace and justice.*[7]

From the data thus supplied by Biddle, it's apparent that groups such as the League weren't being whimsically singled out as "fronts" but were given this designation for ample reason. The point wasn't lost on Dies, who had much of the material cited in the Biddle memo—a good deal of it originating with the FBI (though the committee had its own information sources also). Dies was early on aware of the Communist nature of the League, would cite it as a Red Trojan horse, and warn of its pro-Soviet nature in reports to Congress.

All this being so, Dies and Co. would be dismayed to learn that the Washington, D.C., chapter of the League consisted almost entirely of federal workers—and these in substantial numbers. Having hammered on the subject for months, and having made the blatantly Communist nature of the group a matter of public record, Dies found that the employees continued their affiliation with it. Whereupon, in October 1939, he would make the names of these employees, 563 in all, a matter of public record also. For this he would be denounced by New Deal officials, countless voices in the press corps, and many historians of the era.

This would be the first of several such employee rosters compiled by Dies that outraged his critics. On other occasions he would take to the floor of Congress and recite some of the more conspicuous cases in the federal workforce, noting their Communist or Communist-front connections. In some instances, he observed, a particular suspect had been let go from one official job only to be transferred to another. In response to this, Dies and others in Congress

---

*The Biddle memo, for instance, stated, "The American League Against War and Fascism was formally organized at the first United States Congress Against War and Fascism in New York City September 29 to October 2, 1933. The Manifesto of this Congress called attention to the 'black cloud of imperialist war hovering over the world.' . . . Only in the Soviet Union, the manifesto continued, "has the basic cause of war—monopolistic capitalism—been removed; the Soviet Union, alone among governments of the world, proposes total disarmament; only by arousing and organizing the masses within each nation for active struggle against the war policies of their own imperialist governments can war be effectively combatted."

To this information the memo added: "Communist affiliation with the American League was reflected in the membership and the leadership which installed Earl Browder [then head of the Communist Party] as vice-president and many Communist leaders on the Executive Board. Resolutions and manifestos of the League were printed in official communist publications and the Federal Bureau of Investigation reports from confidential sources that the League is among those organizations which received financial assistance from the Amtorg Trading Corporation [a Soviet commercial outfit]."

made several efforts to rid the government of such people through use of the appropriations power, withholding the pay of named employees. (This succeeded in a couple of cases but was negated by the courts.)*

All this is worth recalling not only for its intrinsic importance in Cold War history but because it would connect up so closely with the later endeavors of Joe McCarthy. He, too, would develop lists of security suspects on the federal payroll—mostly in the State Department, but in other agencies also. He would make note as well of the fact that such suspects would often be removed from one department only to show up in another. And he would likewise zero in on the matter of Communist-front connections among federal workers and the phenomenal number of these in the records of certain suspects.

Like Dies also, McCarthy was aware that a main object of a front was to lure innocents into unwitting cooperation with the Kremlin, so connection with one such group wasn't necessarily proof of subversive motive. More telling, in McCarthy's view, was membership in or sponsorship of many such organizations. In some instances, this meant involvement with dozens or scores of pro-Red outfits. Also considered indicative of something more than innocent joining was involvement with groups that were notorious Moscow puppets—a view of the matter by no means exclusive to McCarthy.[†]

One such group highlighted by Biddle and the House Committee was the American Peace Mobilization (APM), created by the Communist Party in 1940 at the era of the Hitler-Stalin pact. In the popular front phase of the 1930s, the party had made much of its fierce opposition to Hitler. But now he had joined forces with Stalin, so the propaganda machinery was crudely reversed, with particular stress on opposing U.S. aid to Britain in its then lonely war against the Nazis, allied with Moscow. The APM was the main Communist vehicle for this effort, picketing the White House with placards saying "The Yanks Are Not Coming" and blasting President Roosevelt as a warmonger for his Lend-Lease attempts to help the British.

Then, in June 1941, when Hitler broke his deal with Stalin and invaded Russia, the whole thing suddenly had to be reversed again. Now from a Red standpoint it was imperative to make sure the Yanks *were* coming, to help the Soviet motherland survive the Nazi onslaught. At this juncture, the APM

---

*Among the more famous cases thus pursued by Dies was that of Malcolm Cowley in the Office of Facts and Figures, who had, by the committee's reckoning, been connected with no fewer than seventy-two Red fronts. Close behind in this unusual competition were Dies suspects Goodwin Watson, William Dodd, and Frederick Schuman, all then at the FCC and all with lengthy front records. (Cowley got fired; Watson, Dodd, and Schuman were among the employees whose salaries Congress tried to withhold via an appropriations attainder.)

†Membership in a single designated front group, not to mention several dozen, would be among the indicators supposedly looked at in weighing employee security qualifications under the Truman loyalty program of 1947 and the follow-on Eisenhower program announced in 1953.

stopped its picketing, threw away its peace signs, and morphed into a war-supporting outfit called the American Peoples Mobilization. The group was thus exposed for all to see as a Moscow puppet.

Martin Dies at the time was attentive to the APM and people connected with it. And so later would be McCarthy, one of whose most famous cases was linked to the activities of this notorious front for Stalin. (See Chapter 30.) Still other Moscow fronts, such as the Friends of the Soviet Union, American Friends of the Chinese People, and the American Youth Congress, would figure in charges McCarthy brought before the Senate. Matters of Communist-front affiliation in fact were salient in most of the public cases he presented to the Tydings panel as instances of lax-to-nonexistent security in the State Department of 1950.*

Of course, by the time McCarthy came on the scene, there was a much more extensive database on these matters than when Dies was getting started. Most famously, the Hiss-Chambers confrontation had occurred, Elizabeth Bentley had told her story, and the FBI had assembled a vast storehouse of records on Communist Party machinations. So McCarthy was by no means dependent on inferences from front-group connections to figure out who was who among suspected comrades. Even so, he would continue using data pertaining to the fronts as part of his fact-gathering mosaic, in emulation of Dies before him.

As with the subject of the fronts, there were linkages between Dies and McCarthy concerning many individual suspects. Taking only the McCarthy cases discussed in Chapter 3, it's noteworthy that most of these had been looked at by Dies and/or his successors at the House committee. Of the ten McCarthy cases in that roundup, four—Bisson, Currie, Karr, and Mins—had been subjects of inquiry by Dies. Four others—Adler, Coe, Glasser, and Keeney—would appear before the House committee in its later incarnations. The persistence of these identical cases across so considerable a span of time is an instructive feature of the record.

Perhaps the clearest Dies/McCarthy linkage was the work of famed anti-Red researcher J. B. Matthews. Himself a former Communist fronter and fellow traveler of imposing status, Matthews became disillusioned with the Communists in the mid-1930s and passed over into opposition. Based on his own experience and intensive study of Red tactics, he became the world's foremost authority on the front groups. Appearing as a witness before the Dies panel in August of 1938, he so impressed the committee with his expertise that

---

*Of the nine McCarthy public cases, six involved considerations of this nature. The six were Dorothy Kenyon, Esther Brunauer, Philip Jessup, Owen Lattimore, Frederick Schuman, and Harlow Shapley. See Chapters 16 and 26.

he was hired as its research director, a post he held for the next six years. He would later resurface, in spectacular fashion, as an aide to Joe McCarthy.

Of great value to McCarthy and other Communist hunters was a prodigious volume that was the Matthews magnum opus. This is a huge document, compiled in 1944, called "Appendix IX," so named because it was printed as an adjunct to a series of hearings pertaining to the subject of the fronts. It has to be the largest "Appendix" to anything ever published, far longer than the hearings to which it was connected. It runs to better than 2,000 pages, names some 500 organizations, and lists more than 22,000 people. It contains many minute details about the listed groups, with emphasis on their interlocking nature and ties to the Red apparatus, and would be cited often by McCarthy.[8]

These continuities between the Dies-McCarthy efforts, and the fact that so many of McCarthy's cases had previously been spotlighted by Dies and others, would be well noted by McCarthy's critics and frequently used against him. He was, according to his opponents, dealing in "stale, warmed over charges" already examined and disposed of. This would be one of the foremost allegations made in dismissing the cases he brought before the Senate. The old-hat nature of his information is likewise a feature of every critical book we have about McCarthy and his various lists of suspects.

However, as a moment's reflection may suggest, the casual brush-off of McCarthy's cases on this basis is less than persuasive. It's true that, in the typical instance, McCarthy's charges broke no new ground, quite apart from the efforts of Dies and others in Congress. In fact, just about everything McCarthy had to offer by way of documentation for his charges had been reposing for some time before then in the vaults of the FBI, the Civil Service Commission, and other official security units. McCarthy often noted this himself, saying when he presented a case "this information is nothing new," thus not merely acknowledging the point but making a particular issue of it.

But the fact that the charges were of a certain vintage or derived from previous investigations didn't mean they were false, irrelevant, obsolete, or unimportant. On the contrary, we now know for certain, in case after case they were very much on target, as shown by the witness of *Venona* and other sources cited. A good deal of evidence on such cases was known pre-McCarthy but had been disparaged or pushed aside. His were indeed, "stale, warmed over charges," but they also happened to be charges that were true. And the fact that they were both old and true, while the suspects were in many instances still kicking around on official payrolls, obviously made the security situation worse, not better. How, McCarthy would often wonder, had so many flagrant security cases stayed on in positions of public trust despite the evidence in the record?

CHAPTER 5

Unthinking the Thinkable

THE smooth-talking diplomat in chief, unflappable as ever, was blandly reassuring: Charges of pro-Red chicanery made against a former high official had been carefully looked into, and there was nothing to them. The accused had been unfairly named and had now been cleared by the security screeners. Just another case, it seemed, of wild allegations by reckless people who didn't know the facts of record.

The combative lawmaker who brought the charges wasn't buying. He had further evidence on the matter, he said, the nature of which he couldn't reveal but would give to the appropriate committee. This prompted cries of "smear" and demands that the accuser make his outrageous statements off the floor, without legislative privilege, so that he could be sued for slander.

For Americans of the early 1950s, such unpleasant scenes were all too common, as a three-year verbal slugfest raged between the urbane Dean G. Acheson, Secretary of State in the Truman government, and the Red-baiting, tough-talking Joe McCarthy of Wisconsin. This new dispute had the makings of another go-round—except for one distinctive feature. The episode in question occurred, not in the United States, but in Great Britain. The secretary of state (for foreign affairs, to give him his full title) oozing all the reassurance was the Tory, Harold Macmillan; the legislator who brought the charges, Col. Marcus Lipton, Labor MP for Brixton; and the suspect so triumphantly cleared,

Harold Adrian Russell "Kim" Philby, Red spy par excellence, who would later surface in Moscow as an "intelligence officer" of the Soviet KGB, and extremely proud to say so.[1]

That super mole Kim Philby was cleared by Harold Macmillan and the old-boy network in the United Kingdom speaks volumes about security standards prevailing there in the 1940s and early '50s. As does, indeed, the whole fantastic story of Communist infiltration in which Philby was merely one, albeit a leading, player. The saga of Philby, Donald Maclean, Guy Burgess, Anthony Blunt, James Klugmann, and others of the formidable crowd of Moscow agents who fanned out from the University of Cambridge and wound up in the British government is among the most astounding tales in all the annals of subversion, testimony to the deceptive skills of those who engineered it.[2]

It's testimony as well, however, to the complacency and negligence of the people who let it happen. As the records plainly show, there were plenty of signs along the way that members of the Cambridge clique had Red connections, glaringly obvious in some cases, but these were ignored, discounted, or, in the latter phases of the scandal, shoved under the nearest Whitehall carpet. After all, most of the Philby group had gone to the right schools, belonged to the right clubs, and didn't look or talk the way Bolsheviks were supposed to. It was unthinkable they could be Soviet agents or betray their country. So the evidence of their perfidy was brushed aside until the proof was overwhelming.

The tie-ins of all this to events in the United States were many. Most obviously, the unthinkability factor here was as potent as in England, with effects as deadly for the Western interest. The premier American case was Alger Hiss, also a well-bred, respectable type with all the right credentials, so the evidence against him was downplayed or ignored, just as with the Cambridge comrades. And like Philby, far from being an isolated instance, Hiss was one of a numerous, often upscale, band of brothers. William Remington, Donald Wheeler, Henry Collins, Duncan Lee, Laurence Duggan, Robert Miller, and others involved in Red machinations in the United States had been to the best schools, spoke in cultured accents, and had upper-crust connections. So it followed that they couldn't be Communist agents either.

Underscoring the unthinkability angle in the Hiss affair was that his accuser, ex-Communist Whittaker Chambers, wasn't nearly so presentable an item. Hiss was polished and genteel. Chambers was a pudgy, down-at-the-heels, and generally Bohemian figure. It didn't seem possible on this basis that Chambers was telling the truth and Hiss was lying. Thus, when their epic face-off occurred in 1948 before the House Committee on Un-American Activities, some lawmakers believed the dapper, plausible Hiss and thought frowsy Chambers was the liar. Only when the proof became irresistibly clear did they revise that first impression.

A despondent Chambers had in fact endured the unthinkability syndrome for several years before the final showdown. In this case, our negligence was as shocking as the British, and by some measures even more so. U.S. officials were first given the main elements of the Hiss-Chambers story, not in 1948 when it became a public scandal, but almost a decade before in September 1939. Having left the Communist Party the previous year, and alarmed by the Hitler-Stalin pact, Chambers tried to warn the authorities about Red agents on the federal payroll. Through the good offices of anti-Communist writer/editor Isaac Don Levine, Chambers discussed the problem in detail with Assistant Secretary of State Adolf Berle, a specialist on security matters for the Roosevelt White House.

Chambers would later tell the story again in 1942 and 1945–46 in interviews with the FBI and State Department, and then before the House committee and a grand jury. However, it's obvious from Berle's notes that the essential facts about the matter were available to the White House and the State Department in 1939. Recording several dozen Chambers cases, Berle jotted down the names of Hiss and his brother Donald, Lauchlin Currie, Solomon Adler, V. Frank Coe, and a score of others. Some Chambers identified as Party members, others as fellow travelers, but all as parts of the apparatus.[3]

These notes, backed by those of Don Levine, supplied a pretty good sketch of an extensive pro-Soviet combine inside the U.S. government. So far as anyone can tell, however, the result of these stunning revelations was— nothing. Though a story would be floated that Berle had at the time supplied the information to the FBI, that clearly didn't happen. Nor, so far as the record shows, was anything done about it for years to come. On the contrary, Hiss, Currie, Adler, Coe, and others named by Chambers not only stayed on in their official jobs but played increasingly powerful roles in matters of the highest import. Inertia and self-inflicted blindness were thus as serious here as in Great Britain, and would get a good deal worse before any corrective steps were taken.[4]

Though Hiss was eventually exposed and convicted of lying about his Red affiliations, the same mind-set would shape the reception given other cases, including that of Laurence Duggan, the testimony of Elizabeth Bentley, and, most of all, the charges of McCarthy.[5] Even among those who at last accepted the guilt of Hiss, he was usually viewed as an aberration, not the precursor of a species. That there was a wide-ranging, high-level plot consisting of multiple Alger Hisses, as alleged by McCarthy, was for many in influential places too preposterous for belief. It was either a smear, or paranoia, or a quest for unworthy headlines, or something, but couldn't possibly be the truth. It was, in a word, unthinkable—unthinkable that such a plot existed, or that the people named by McCarthy could be complicit in such betrayal.

As with Chambers and the response to Martin Dies, there was as noted a cultural subtext embedded in the reaction to McCarthy. He was a rough-and-tumble scrapper from the boonies who hadn't been to Yale or Harvard, spoke in blunt phrases, and taunted the smooth sophisticates in the salons of Georgetown and plush corridors of official power. His targets, often as not, were Ivy League respectable types in the mold of Hiss or Duggan. How could one believe such outlandish charges from such a lout, aimed at his social betters? One couldn't, and one didn't.

In which respect, it's worth recalling that Hiss-Chambers, the original McCarthy fracas, and other security battles this side of the Atlantic erupted in the period 1948–50, before the truth about the Philby ring came filtering out from European sources. Guy Burgess and Donald Maclean didn't abscond to Moscow until May of 1951, well over a year after McCarthy's initial speeches. Kim Philby would be cleared of "third man" charges in 1955, only to bolt in 1963. Anthony Blunt wasn't exposed in public as a Soviet agent until the 1970s. Had the truth about the Cambridge spies been general knowledge in 1948 or 1950, it's likely the Chambers allegations, perhaps even the charges of McCarthy, would have been viewed in a different light. If it could happen in Great Britain, it could just possibly happen here. And, in fact, it did.

The parallels between the British and American cases weren't coincidental, but sprang from similar intellectual and moral causes. In both countries, there had been a long decline of faith in Western institutions—beginning with religious faith itself, then spreading to other aspects of a culture that appeared in the depression era of the 1930s to be on its deathbed. To many already afflicted with anomie and dark misgivings, the economic/political crisis of the age looked like the coup de grâce for traditional views and customs. The supposedly ironclad theories of Marx and Lenin and alleged wonders of Soviet planning were thought to have the answers no longer provided by the older culture.

Aiding the transition was the vast flowering of party front groups that has been noted. In these Potemkin village outfits, Communist ideas and projects were presented in appealing masquerade, and many who weren't Communists to begin with, or ever, mingled freely with those who were—Marxism and its subspecies made respectable and fairly trendy by the systemic crisis.

As the 1930s intellectual ferment fed the Communist malaise, it had other adverse effects as well. An alternative answer to the cultural breakdown was the Nazi version of the godless faith, which had just come to power in Adolf Hitler's Germany. As the Brown and Red despotisms fought for supremacy in Europe, each posed as the remedy for the other.* For many in England and the United States, the Communists and the USSR would thus gain added luster as

---

* "Posed" being the operative word, as the two totalitarian systems would in fact cooperate at many levels.

alleged antidotes to Hitler. (A conflict capsuled in the Spanish Civil War of the latter 1930s, as Western leftists flocked to the Loyalist government in Madrid, supported in its fashion by the USSR, in battle against Gen. Francisco Franco, backed by the Italian Fascists and the Nazis.) From this maelstrom came the Philbys and the Hisses, and many others like them, who would be the traitors of our histories.

The British spy cases, however, were linked to events in the United States by more than common causes and similar outcomes. There were innumerable direct connections between the egregious loyalty problems and feckless security measures that prevailed in Whitehall and those that developed in Foggy Bottom and other Washington power centers. Such overlappings reflected, above all else, the global nature of the Soviet project, which was its outstanding organizational feature. The American comrades were part of a worldwide web that included German, French, Chinese, Italian, Japanese, and other agents who took their orders from the Kremlin. The affinities between British and American CP members were aspects of this formidable undertaking. But they were products also of the "special relationship" between the United States and the United Kingdom, with their common political history and language, a linkage that became pronounced in World War II and continued in the Cold War.

Thus, Kim Philby was in the latter 1940s the liaison between the British intelligence unit known as MI6 and intelligence agencies in Washington, and received copious information from his U.S. contacts. Donald Maclean, as second secretary of the British Embassy in D.C., then head of the American desk in London, had access to U.S. intelligence reports and entrée to our atomic energy program. Guy Burgess as attaché for Far East affairs at the British Washington Embassy was privy to official data about our policy in Asia. Among them, the Cambridge spies scooped up a lot of American secrets useful to their Kremlin masters. Britain's unthinkable security problems were our problems also.

Beyond this were intertwinings of British and American personnel, many with specific links to Cambridge (though Oxford also made its contribution). Most visibly, there were Cambridge alums who settled and worked in North America, establishing personal ties that bridged the ocean and would have relevance in the McCarthy era. Among such transplants, one of the more conspicuous—and genteel—was the wealthy American Michael Straight, who spent much of his youth in England and attended Cambridge in the 1930s. Straight would later achieve public notice in the United States as editor of *The New Republic* (cofounded and supported by his family). This small but influential journal was a harsh critic of McCarthy, featuring many articles that deplored his alleged lies and evil doings.[6]

By an odd series of connections, suggestive of the global context, Michael Straight had personal as well as political causes for an aversion to McCarthy.

Straight was linked by marriage to not one but two McCarthy targets—Gustavo Duran and Louis Dolivet—both of foreign birth and both named in U.S. intelligence reports of the time and other data later as Soviet agents. (Duran was married to the sister of Straight's wife, Dolivet to Straight's actress sister.) Duran was one of McCarthy's earliest cases, identified on the Senate floor and before the Tydings panel as a Soviet operative in the Spanish Civil War who had somehow popped up in the U.S. State Department. Dolivet would be named under oath in 1953 McCarthy hearings as a Red propagandist whose books were in our information centers overseas.

Vehement in defense of Duran (less so, in retrospect, of Dolivet), Straight thus had plenty of reasons to deplore McCarthy, which he would do in many formats (including an anti-McCarthy book based on the Army-McCarthy hearings). For Straight, McCarthy personified the evils of crude Red-baiting that saw Communists under every bed. Given all this righteous fervor, it would come as a shock to many to learn that Straight himself had been a Communist under the bed—or perhaps more aptly, given his publishing interests, between the covers. He had been recruited by Communist spy king Anthony Blunt at Cambridge in the 1930s, then sent back to the United States to do the Kremlin's bidding. That the wealthy editor of *The New Republic* had been a CP member and Soviet agent would be yet another unthinkable revelation from the secret annals of the Cold War.*

Whether such linkages mattered—and how—is suggested by an anecdote from Straight himself. He recalled spotting Guy Burgess outside the British Embassy in Washington early in 1951 during the Korean War and realizing Burgess was probably furnishing American military secrets to the Kremlin. Such Burgess spying, Straight reflected, could have cost untold numbers of American lives in the fighting against North Korea and Red China. However, any disclosure of the matter to the FBI would have prompted questions leading back to Blunt and how Straight knew so much about Guy Burgess. So, in the event, Straight did nothing. He preferred to focus his public wrath on the distasteful anti-Communist lowbrow Joe McCarthy. On that particular danger, Straight saw no reason to keep silent.[7]

Michael Straight was not the only member of the Cambridge set to make his way to North America as part of a more general global movement by some well-traveled people. Another was the Canadian E. Herbert Norman, a Cam-

---

*Straight by his own account would break with Moscow—exactly when being less than clear—and under some psychological stress tell his story to the FBI, thereby incidentally exposing Blunt and leading to Blunt's own halfway confession in England. Indicative of the way such things were often handled, while Straight's information was obtained in 1963, it wasn't until 1979 that the facts about the Blunt case were made public. In the meantime, Blunt enjoyed a swank career as director of the Courtauld Art Institute in London and keeper of the Queen's pictures at Windsor Castle—all this plus the honor of a knighthood (revoked in 1979). Likewise, Straight's own partial confession in a memoir—as distinct from his disclosures to the Bureau—didn't occur until 1983.

bridge grad who specialized in Far East affairs and would rise to a high-ranking job in Canada's diplomatic service. In this role, Norman would liaise with U.S. officials and American scholars working on Pacific problems, playing, for instance, a significant part in the postwar occupation of Japan. A Cambridge product even more directly linked to U.S. concerns was Michael Greenberg, a native of Manchester, England, who came to America in 1940 and managed by a feat of bureaucratic magic to wangle a job on the White House staff while still a subject of Great Britain.

Greenberg and Norman would be featured in the McCarthy saga of the 1950s, as both were then named in congressional hearings as agents of the Communist interest.[8] These identifications occurred during an intensive probe of the Institute of Pacific Relations (IPR) conducted by the Senate Internal Security subcommittee, under Sen. Pat McCarran (D-NV), following up on some of McCarthy's unthinkable early charges. The IPR hookup seemed incidental in the case of Norman but decisive in the case of Greenberg. His first important job in the United States was as Professor Owen Lattimore's editorial successor at the Institute; thereafter he would make a smooth transition to the staff of Lattimore's friend and ally Lauchlin Currie at the White House.

As it happened, Michael Straight was also connected in a minor role to the IPR and would meet up with Greenberg and Norman at an IPR conclave in Quebec in 1942. This unusual private group would thus reunite, on the west shore of the Atlantic, three members of the Cambridge circle, far from the storied halls of Trinity and Kings. It was, in a small way, typical of the IPR in action—as its stock-in-trade was networking with like-minded people from many climes to cogitate, and where possible shape, the fate of Asia. Lattimore, Currie, Greenberg, Straight, and Norman were but a few of the peripatetic folk who kept in touch through the IPR and its web of worldwide contacts.[9]

FURTHER indicative of Moscow's global reach through a veritable foreign legion of spies and agents was another unthinkable Communist ring that in some ways outdid the Philby combine. This group too had many U.S. connections, dealt with issues of vital importance to our interests, and would figure prominently in the later McCarthy drama. It was a formidable apparatus, based in Asia, headed by the German-born Communist Richard Sorge, perhaps the most effective secret agent in Soviet history.

Sorge made his mark as a big-time spy for Moscow in Shanghai, China, beginning early in 1930. China was at the time and would remain a hotbed of Red intrigue, where such eminent comrades as Michael Borodin, Gerhart Eisler, Earl Browder, Steve Nelson, Vasili Zarubin, and Eugene Dennis all put in a tour of duty. This parade of talent signified the great importance Moscow attached to the Middle Kingdom—an interest not always matched by American leaders, for whom China was a backwater deserving only passing notice.* In the late 1930s, as Moscow was increasingly concerned about Japan, near neighbor and historic foe of Russia, Sorge was dispatched to Tokyo to help out with that problem also.

Even more than the Cambridge comrades, the Sorge group overlapped with the IPR, understandable as the ring had a Far East focus. Among the leading members of the polyglot Sorge operation were the Chinese Communist Chen Han-seng, the American writer Agnes Smedley, and the German-born naturalized Briton Guenther Stein. In Tokyo the network included the prominent Japanese journalist Hotsumi Ozaki and one Kinkazu Saionji, son of a distinguished family. All would later be named in congressional hearings as Soviet agents tied to Sorge, and all were linked in one fashion or another to the IPR (Saionji as secretary of its Tokyo unit).[10]

Arguably the most direct and intriguing nexus between Sorge and the IPR was the globe-trotting Comintern agent Chen Han-seng. A Communist since 1926, Chen was recruited into the Shanghai combine by Smedley and worked with the ring in both China and Japan. In 1935, fearful of a police crackdown, he decamped to Moscow, then moved on to the United States, where he, too, linked up with Owen Lattimore and the IPR. While at the Institute and the Walter Hines Page School at the Johns Hopkins University (another Lattimore connection), Chen was the main Red Chinese contact with the American comrades. After the fall of China in 1949, he would like others noted in these pages abscond to Beijing and become an official of the Red regime there.[11]

Still other members of the Sorge/IPR extended family had contacts useful to the Moscow cause in Asia. Both Guenther Stein and Agnes Smedley were well familiar with the Chinese Reds based at Yenan in Northwest China and tireless promoters of their interests. Both would likewise become acquainted with U.S. officials posted to China in the 1930s and early '40s. Smedley would be a particular favorite of Gen. Joseph Stilwell, World War II commander of Allied forces in the region, and of his State Department adviser John Paton Davies (who would call Smedley one of the "pure in heart").[12] Stein was a contact of and information source for U.S. diplomat John Service (who also worked for Stilwell), later arrested in the *Amerasia* scandal.

In the spring of 1941, the IPR would develop yet another strategic contact in China as Professor Lattimore moved out of the academic-think-tank shadows directly to the policy forefront. At the prompting of his ally Currie in the White House, Lattimore was named by President Roosevelt as an adviser to Chinese leader Chiang Kai-shek and dispatched to Chungking, wartime capital of Free China. Thus, the IPR contingent now had key personnel at crucial

---

*On the other hand, there were people down the line in the Treasury and State Departments who did concentrate on China, though not in a beneficial manner.

listening posts in both Japan and China, as well as at the center of power back in the United States. Each would have a role to play in the fateful events that led to our involvement in World War II and thereafter in the Cold War.

In Tokyo at this era, the number-one mission of Sorge and his network was to protect the Soviet Union from attack by its historic nemesis, Japan. This task became the more urgent in June of 1941 when Hitler broke his pact with Stalin and invaded Russia, sending the Soviet armies reeling backward. The possibility of a matching onslaught from the East by Germany's Tokyo allies raised in Stalin's hypersuspicious mind the dread specter of a two-front war. Sorge's goal, as he would himself describe it, was to ensure that if Japan, already at war with China, got into the larger global conflict, it wouldn't be through an attack on Russia (or failing this, warn Moscow if such attack was coming).

In this effort, the Soviet master spy was greatly aided by his two IPR-connected Japanese assistants, Ozaki and Saionji. Both had good access to the Tokyo power structure, Ozaki as a respected journalist and adviser to the premier, Prince Konoye, Saionji as a member of the "breakfast group" that counseled the Imperial Cabinet. Each, according to the testimony in the case, used this access to argue that Japan should strike, not north at Russia, but to the south against British, Dutch, or American Pacific outposts to get the resources—especially oil—that the Empire sorely needed.*

As this question was being thrashed out in the Tokyo cabinet, a mirror-image debate was being conducted 7,000 miles away in the United States. Here the issue to be decided was whether to seek a truce with Tokyo, winding down its four-year-old war with China, thus averting a direct clash between Japan and the United States, championing the cause of Chungking. Ambassador Joseph Grew, our envoy to Japan, was working to head off such a conflict and thought there was a chance to do so. However, when it appeared the State Department might be leaning toward a *modus vivendi* with the Empire, members of the IPR brigade sprang nimbly into countervailing action.

Lauchlin Currie, for one, deplored the possibility of such a truce in a memo to FDR, saying any arrangement of this sort would do "irreparable

---

*These advices, whatever their merits from the strategic standpoint of Japan, were fully in keeping with Soviet global interests and Communist propaganda efforts of the era. Stalin and his minions were anxious to keep the Japanese armies pinned down as much as possible through their war with China, hence less available for an attack on Russia. Even better, from Stalin's perspective, if Japan could be embroiled in head-on conflict with the United States. Such involvements could help ensure that the back door to a possible Russo-Japanese war was double-locked and bolted.

As Eugene Lyons would put it in his seminal study *The Red Decade:* "While the invasion of China was under way, Moscow did not relax its efforts to obtain a nonaggression pact with Japan. But no stone was left unturned in the effort to force a Japanese-American conflict . . . The Soviet hope—quite justifiable from the angle of Russia's own *Realpolitik*—was to get Japan and the United States at each other's throats . . ."

damage to the good will we have built up in China." Another U.S. official disturbed by the prospect of a Washington-Tokyo truce was the Treasury's Harry Dexter White. "Persons in our government," White declaimed, "are hoping to betray the cause of the heroic Chinese people." In keeping with this view, according to IPR spokesman Edward Carter, White in November of 1941 alerted him to the *modus vivendi* danger and called an emergency meeting to concert resistance.*[13]

What Carter didn't say and would be discovered later was that White was already working to promote a stiff-necked American policy directly counter to the truce idea, this at the urging of the Soviet KGB. As revealed by Moscow agent Vitaliy Pavlov in his memoirs, he had earlier come to Washington to brief White on the proper stance for the United States to take in discouraging any *rapprochement* with Japan. White, who obviously didn't need much prompting, had followed through, drafting and redrafting a tough memo on the subject for Treasury Secretary Henry Morgenthau, forwarded to the State Department for its guidance.[14]

At this crucial juncture (late November 1941), Professor Lattimore, from his new perch in Chungking, would also get in on the action—firing off a cable to Currie in the White House strongly opposing a diplomatic stand-down with Japan as a betrayal of our friends in China. Chiang Kai-shek, said Lattimore, was dismayed by the possibility of such a truce, so much so that "any *modus vivendi* now arrived at" would be "destructive of the Chinese belief in America."[15] The voices opposing the *modus vivendi* thus formed a considerable chorus on both sides of the Pacific basin.

In the upshot, the Sorge-Ozaki-Saionji advices would triumph in Japan, while those of the Lattimore-Currie-White trifecta would prevail in the United States. There would be no Washington-Tokyo stand-down over China, no Japanese attack on Russia, and no peace in the Pacific. There would instead be Pearl Harbor, as the Japanese at last decided to strike south and reach their *modus vivendi* with Moscow. Whether this would have happened anyway, given the geopolitical tectonics then in motion, there is no way of telling. Enough to note that all these influential people were pushing for a common outcome, and the events that followed were in keeping with their counsels.

All of which was obviously significant in itself but important also in what it portended for the future. For one thing, many key actors in this run-up to Pearl Harbor would make repeat appearances in the later drama of the Cold War, and would there draw the notice of Joe McCarthy. To cite only the more

---

*However, Carter said, by the time he got to Washington for this confab, the *modus vivendi* danger had subsided. "Mr. White assured me," said Carter, "that everything was going to be all right and that there was to be no sellout of China through Japan."

obvious cases, Owen Lattimore, Lauchlin Currie, the IPR, Edward Carter, the Treasury nexus, Agnes Smedley and other alumni of the Sorge ring would all be McCarthy targets in the 1950s. (Ambassador Grew, who got crossways with this crowd on the *modus vivendi* issue, would figure in the later battles also.)

A further linkage between these matters and developments of the McCarthy era was the centrality of the China issue—routinely cited by the IPR brigade as a reason for rejecting any *modus vivendi* with Japan. According to such as Lattimore, Carter, and Currie, it was imperative that we stand fast with our good and faithful ally, Chiang, and do nothing to shake his confidence in our bona fides. A few years later, when Chiang was locked in mortal combat with the Communists at Yenan, the IPR spokesmen who had voiced such great concern about his welfare emerged as his most virulent critics.

Also suggestive of things to come was the synchronous action of so many of these people, acting on a worldwide basis. The positioning, indeed, was nothing short of brilliant. Ozaki and Saionji in Japan, White and Currie in the United States, and Lattimore in Chungking had virtually all the bases covered. The operation was not only global but capable of exerting leverage at crucial vectors and at the highest levels. This, too, would prefigure events that followed in the Cold War, when many of these same players and others like them would frequently act together seeking common objects.

However, by far the most significant thing to follow from all this was the war itself, which drastically transformed power relationships in the world and gave birth to a whole new set of issues in the course of resolving others. Among its many side effects, the war would make the United States and the Soviet Union allies, a condition that gave rise to beliefs and actions spawning many future troubles. In particular, the pro-Soviet atmospherics of the war would accentuate the problem of Communist infiltration that had developed during the Great Depression. What had been a serious problem in the 1930s would now become a truly massive penetration. The story of how all this came about, and its implications for our security interests, is yet another unthinkable chapter from the secret annals of the Cold War.

Equally important, it was in the war years that J. Edgar Hoover and the FBI got their first serious inkling as to the extent of the penetration and began putting together a series of detailed reports that tracked the Red presence in the federal workforce. However, as with the Philby crowd in England and the inert response to Chambers, these FBI memos would in many cases be disparaged or ignored by top officials. A related legacy of the war years was the secrecy in which such intel was mantled, as the facts about the penetration were routinely shielded from Congress and the public. All this occurred in the 1940s, before Joe McCarthy ever came on the security scene, much of it before he was ever elected to the Senate, and it supplied the predicate for just about everything he said and did in the succeeding decade.

Dealing with combustible issues that blew up in the 1950s but had their genesis years before obviously entails the use of flashbacks to explain the elements of the conflict, the stakes involved, and how this or that dispute developed. In later chapters of this essay, a number of switches back and forth between the decades can scarcely be avoided. However, to minimize the distractions and confusions involved in using this device, the following section discusses, in roughly chronological order, some key developments of the war and early postwar years that constitute, so to speak, the immediate prehistory of the McCarthy era.

In this discussion, certain critical events—though greatly compressed—are set forth in fair detail rather than merely being alluded to in passing. This approach has been used, in part, because of the unthinkability factor: Some of the things that happened were so wildly improbable as to defy ready credence, and thus need to be documented rather than simply being asserted. Equally to the point, such details are of the essence in figuring out how the infiltration happened, what was or wasn't done about it, and why it mattered. Once some of these specifics are understood, it becomes possible to understand as well the later unthinkable charges of McCarthy.

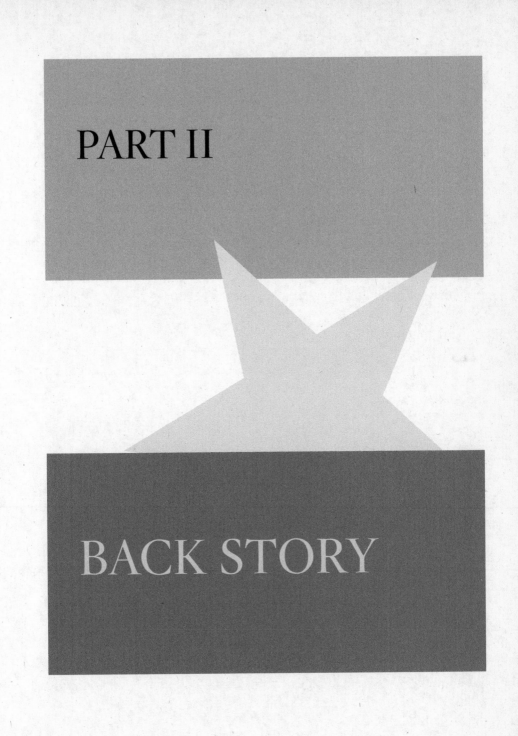

PART II

BACK STORY

CHAPTER 6

The Witching Hour

COMMUNIST penetration of the American government was a long-term process that ebbed and flowed but never ceased entirely. As with other infiltration targets, such as schools, media outlets, civic groups, or labor unions, the purposes were several: to influence policies and programs, make propaganda, disrupt or sabotage things from time to time, and—where chance presented—engage in "intelligence"-gathering operations, otherwise known as spying.

As noted, such infiltration at the official level developed mostly in two phases—one in the depression years, the other during World War II. The net effect of these twin incursions was a sizable Communist presence on the federal payroll, far greater than most histories have suggested. However, in the trough between the rising waves (August 1939–June 1941), the Hitler-Stalin pact exploded, shattering the Communist Party's anti-Nazi image and setting back the penetration effort that prospered in the 1930s. Though these losses would later be recouped, events during the heyday of the pact would have profound effects long after it had ignominiously ended. The seeds of conflict over U.S. security policies for years to come would be sown in the wild zigzags and contradictions of this era.

While it lasted, the spectacle of Brown and Red dictatorships in common harness spurred Congress to decisive action, including stern new laws that treated the two as equal dangers. Foremost among these measures was the Hatch Act, adopted in 1939 and further toughened in 1940, which outlawed the hiring or retention of federal workers who advocated the "overthrow of our constitutional form of government," a rote phrase officially said to mean members of the Communist Party. In May 1941, Congress would adopt a bill of even broader scope, requiring scrutiny of federal workers involved with any "subversive" group whatever. This was Public Law 135, directing that the FBI investigate "the employees of every department, agency and independent establishment of the federal government who are members of subversive organizations or advocate the overthrow of the Federal government," and report back to Congress.[1]

All this was a sharp U-turn, not only from the security nonchalance of the previous decade, but from long-standing Civil Service rules that banned job discrimination based on the "political" views of workers—reflecting a more innocent time when self-styled political parties as agents of a hostile foreign power weren't seen as a serious menace. Concurrent with the strict new guidelines was the unforgiving concept of "reasonable doubt," meaning where such doubt arose security interests would trump the usual safeguards of the system. As the standards were explained in December 1940:

"The United States Civil Service Commission has decided officially that as a matter of policy it will not [favorably] certify to any department or agency the name of any person when it has been established that he is a member of the Communist Party, German Bund, or any other Communist or Nazi organization." And further: "If we find anybody has had any association with the Communists, the German Bund, or any other foreign organization of that kind, that person is disqualified immediately. All doubts are being resolved in favor of the government."[2]

In the enforcement of these hard-nosed rules the relatively open Communist doings of the 1930s would now be used by security agents to advantage. In particular, the membership rolls of front groups that flourished in the Red decade were scanned by the FBI, Justice Department, and House Committee on Un-American Activities as indices of possible trouble. Also, as P.L. 135 raised the question of what was meant by the catchall term "subversive," an official answer was provided: the first "Attorney General's list," quoted in Chapter 4, describing eleven major Communist fronts, circulated early in 1942 by Attorney General Francis Biddle to federal agencies for their guidance.

Had these hawkish notions been adhered to, it's doubtful much further Communist penetration of the federal government could have happened. Such policies, however, would soon be eroded by events and in many instances reversed entirely. When Hitler broke his deal with Stalin and invaded Russia in June of 1941, Moscow was perforce on the side of London and, when we joined the war in December 1941, would be our "noble ally" also. Statements from such as Ambassador Joseph Davies, White House familiar Harry Hopkins, and FDR himself would now echo with praise of Stalin, the Soviet army, and all things whatsoever that were Russian. The Communist Party USA, as Moscow's agent on the scene, basked happily in this springtime for Stalin and reaped a bumper harvest from it.*

Among its many side effects, such pro-Soviet thinking at high levels self-evidently clashed with laws and regulations barring Reds from federal office. The resulting conflict between black-letter law and executive yen to woo the Kremlin would produce a series of angry quarrels between New Deal officials and anti-Red security hawks in Congress—Martin Dies predictably among them.

A main source of friction was P.L. 135 and its order for vetting federal workers. Though circulating his own list of suspect groups in keeping with this mandate, Francis Biddle didn't like it and had used it as a means of needling Dies—suggesting that the House committee itself should do the work of tracking down the data. In the short run this gambit backfired, as Dies responded in the fall of 1941 with another of his lists—a roster of 1,124 federal workers who allegedly were, or had been, members of groups found by the committee, and later by Biddle himself, to be subversive.†

As required by law 135, the FBI would investigate these staffers, producing, in the summer of 1942, a fat report about them running to five volumes (total number of pages not given). This document, however, would never see the light of day, as Biddle and the powers above him were by this time moving in noble-ally mode to scotch the use of fronts as indices for hiring. The Bureau was told to submit its findings in muffled, purely statistical form, the whole running to no more than twenty pages, omitting the names of any groups or individuals. As to the purpose of this edict, one FBI memo explained, Biddle "stated that he was anxious to have the report point out that the Dies information had been worthless."[3]

Thereafter, though Dies tried to revive the issue, the names he submitted—and FBI report about them—would vanish from the public record. More was the pity for the nation, as this much-derided list of suspects, compiled before Pearl Harbor, included numerous big-time Soviet agents who would one day make the headlines—Alger Hiss, Lauchlin Currie, Harry White, and Harold Glasser, to name a notorious handful. Combined with the brush-off of Whittaker Chambers three years before, this deep-sixing of the Dies list gave the comrades the better part of a decade to carry on without much hindrance.

---

* A notable instance of this new policy line was the late-1942 decision of President Roosevelt to let Communist Party boss Earl Browder out of prison, where he had been serving a term for passport violations.

† The three groups used by Dies to track the federal workers—the American League Peace and Democracy, the Washington Book Shop, and the Washington Committee for Democratic Action—were all on the Biddle list of suspect organizations.

As events would show, this episode-of-the-thousand-names was but a single phase in a broader effort to wire around the Hatch Act, P.L. 135, and other measures barring Reds from office. In this pursuit, ingenious distinctions were devised by New Deal wordsmiths, justifying the policy change without bothering to change the statutes, a more difficult and uncertain process. Chief among these subtle concepts was "mere membership" in a subversive group, which, it was argued, could be innocuous in nature. As Biddle would later put it, "activity in the organization, rather than membership, would come closer to reality, and even this can be but one of many facts to be considered in determining fitness for Federal employees."[4]

Applied to front groups, this had some plausible basis, as one object of such "innocents' clubs" was to lure naive peace-seekers or friends of the downtrodden into unwitting concert with the Kremlin. Some scrutiny of that aspect was obviously in order. However, "mere membership" was soon expanded past these prudent limits, embracing not only cited front groups but the Communist Party also. A telltale instance, again from 1942, showed the link between this notion and the pro-Soviet policy now stemming from the White House.

At the outset of the war, a statute administered by the Navy barred Communists as well as Nazis from radio jobs on U.S. merchant vessels, as radio traffic was a vital source of military/strategic data. In May of 1942, however, an order was issued by Navy Secretary Frank Knox rescinding this prohibition. As reflected in official records (doubtless not the total story), the impetus for this reversal came from Knox assistant Adlai Stevenson, later governor of Illinois and candidate for president. Stevenson raised the issue in a memo of April 30, rhetorically asking "whether identification with Communism, even if sufficiently proved, is sufficient grounds to disqualify a man without some further evidence of incompetence or unreliability."[5] Knox sent this to FDR, urging that the ban be lifted, and the President followed suit. The pro-Soviet basis of the change was spelled out in the Navy minutes:

> The Secretary [Knox] . . . said that he had no brief for the activities of the Communist Party, but that the President had stated that, considering the fact that the United States and Russia were allies at this time, and that the Communist Party and the United States effort were now bent toward our winning the war, *the United States was bound not to oppose the activities of the Communist Party,* and specifically, to not disapprove the employment of any radio operator for the sole reason that he was a member of the Communist Party or that he was active in Communist affairs. (Emphasis added.)[6]

In sum, the hiring standards were to be altered and Communists (literally) brought on board, in keeping with the wartime view of Moscow as gallant ally. The far-reaching implications of this mind-set would be borne out by other like reversals. One such occurred the following year when the Civil Service

Commission again revised its guidelines, harking back to the see-no-evil standards of the 1930s. These changes in effect negated both P.L. 135 and the "reasonable doubt" approach of 1940, as civil service investigators were now explicitly told *not* to ask about front groups or other Red connections.*[7]

As customary in such cases, these new rules were set forth in civil liberties language, but the timing of the order and complete *volte-face* in procedure told another story. It's noteworthy that the Washington Book Shop, named specifically in this order as shielded from inquiry, had been included the previous year in the list of suspect outfits passed around by Biddle (and would be included in other such listings later). Thus, in early 1942 federal agencies were expressly warned about the Book Shop in official guidance for their hiring; but by the fall of 1943, investigators were forbidden even to ask if someone were a member.

Thereafter, "mere membership" would show up in other places—always as a rationale for having Communists on the public payroll. A much-controverted case involved the regulations of the Army. Here, too, in keeping with the 1940 standards, existing policy barred Reds as well as Nazis from key positions and from commissions in the service. But in December 1944, a superseding order was issued by the Adjutant General of the Army, saying "no action will be taken . . . that is predicated on membership in or adherence to the doctrine of the Communist Party unless there is a specific finding that the individual involved has a loyalty to the Communist Party which outweighs his loyalty to the United States."[8]

How this comparative weighing of mental states was to be arrived at wasn't explained, nor could any such mind-reading feat well be imagined. Obviously, if *Communist Party membership* didn't raise a loyalty issue, the only way to make such a judgment would be proof of some disloyal action—virtually a criminal courtroom standard for screening military rosters. Absent that, the ruling was carte blanche for known Communists—to say nothing of fronters or mere suspects—to obtain commissions in the Army.†

---

* As a memo drafted by Civil Service official Alfred Klein (November 3, 1943) explained it: "If in the course of the investigation witnesses say that a certain person is a Communist because he is associated with certain persons in a union known or said to be Communist, the investigator should not ask the applicant about his association with these particular individuals. . . . Do not ask any questions whatever involving the applicant's sympathy with Loyalists in Spain . . . no reference should be made to any such organizations as the Abraham Lincoln Brigade or any other of the many Spanish relief groups. . . . Do not ask any question about membership in the Washington Book Shop. . . . Do not ask any questions regarding the type of reading matter read by the applicant. This includes especially the *Daily Worker* and all radical and liberal publications. . . ."

† A glimpse of how this policy came about would be provided a decade later by an Army security officer, Lt. Col. John Lansdale. He testified that, during the war, he was subject to pressure "from military superiors, from the White House and from every other place, because I dared to stop the commissioning of 15 or 20 undoubted Communists. . . . I was being vilified, reviewed, and re-reviewed by boards because of my efforts to get Communists out of the Army and being frustrated by the blind, naïve attitude of Mrs. Roosevelt and those around her in the White House. . . ."

This directive drew the notice, and ire, of Sen. Styles Bridges (R-N.H.), who would later insert a Senate staff report about it in the *Congressional Record.* It also produced some unusual hearings, predictive of events to follow. In February and March of 1945, a House Military Affairs subcommittee chaired by Rep. Ewing Thomason (D-Tex.) reviewed the newly minted Army guidelines. The witnesses were Assistant Secretary of War John J. McCloy, Army intelligence chief Maj. Gen. Clayton Bissell, and Maj. Gen. William Donovan, head of the super-secret OSS. Among them they grudgingly made it plain that the new standards were an open sesame for Communists to enter the Army, get commissions, and gain access to restricted data.[9]

Of the threesome, McCloy was the most knowledgeable on the issue and took the point in explaining it to Congress. Though bearing the title Assistant Secretary, he was relied on heavily by the septuagenarian Secretary Henry Stimson, and was an omnipresent figure on matters relating to defense. This one was no exception, though his explanations of the new ground rules didn't seem too persuasive to the House committee.

Indeed, McCloy's discussion of the new proviso was apparently as baffling to the panel as the matter he was explaining. Much of it was a discourse on "mere membership"—what it meant to be a Communist, whether and how the definition of this had changed, and other philosophic musings.* A moment of clarity occurred when McCloy was asked point blank whether a "person might be a member of the Communist Party and still be commissioned as an officer in the Army of the United States." To which he answered, "Yes, that is so."

General Bissell tried to soften this by saying that, even though the policy was as stated, there weren't to his knowledge any such people in the Army. However, midway in the hearings, Willard Edwards of the *Chicago Tribune* published a list of officers whose records, according to official data, proved these assurances in error. When asked about these individuals, Bissell said they were good soldiers and that their loyalty was unquestioned. Pressed about the Communist charges, he offered only vague demurrers. Pushed harder still, he produced a letter from Stimson denying the relevant security files to Congress. Whereupon discussion foundered.[10]

WHILE all this was going on, still other changes were afoot that affected the issue of Red penetration and the collapse of security safeguards against it. In late 1943 and early '44, reports were received by the FBI and members of the Senate that an effort was under way to abolish counter-intelligence records used in anti-Red investigations. A snapshot of this purge

---

*Based on later information, it appears McCloy himself was responsible for this edict, as an official Army statement describes it as "the McCloy order." It was rescinded in 1946.

was provided by security expert Ben Mandel, who served many years as an investigator and researcher for Congress and more briefly in the State Department.

Mandel told the FBI that, in early 1944, two Budget Bureau officials had "made personal visits to various agencies, such as Civil Service, ONI [Office of Naval Intelligence], Navy Department and G-2 War Department, examining their investigative records." According to Mandel, the duo's "first and principal concern was the subversive files which the various agencies had compiled"— the stated reason for this being that "there was great duplication, and that such investigative activity was unnecessary as the FBI was already making such investigations."[11]

This advice, it seems, was heeded. In June 1944, antisubversive files maintained by the Office of Naval Intelligence in New York and Boston abruptly vanished. According to one ONI staffer testifying to the Senate, these records contained about 100,000 index cards, plus myriad dossiers, reports, and forms that were much consulted. In June 1944, he said, "I remember coming in one day and those files were missing." Similar testimony was given by another staffer shipped out to France in 1943, returning two years later. When he got back, he said, "all the files that were there when I left in 1943 were missing."[12]

As in the change of enlistment standards, developments with security records of the Army would track the experience of the Navy. In May 1944, a directive was issued by the Pentagon to dismantle the G-2 counterintelligence files of the Army and disperse them to the Archives. Questioned about this by Bridges and other members of the Senate, Secretary Stimson and Army Chief of Staff Gen. George C. Marshall professed not to know anything about it. However, Lt. Gen. Joseph McNarney, Marshall's deputy, did know, and indicated the order had come from "higher authority"—which, given the stature of Stimson and Marshall, could only mean the White House.[13]

The removal and/or destruction of G-2 files would be confirmed in other inquests. General Bissell, at a later hearing, gave a less-than-reassuring picture of what had happened to these records. He told investigators, "there are thousands of them that cannot be located, have been destroyed, thousands of them," explaining that "there goes on in any large intelligence organization a sorting out, a re-classification, and a destruction." Bissell's deputy, Col. Ivan Yeaton, enlarged on this description, dovetailing with the timeline on the Navy file removal. Yeaton said that on June 16, 1944, "the whole of G-2 was reorganized right in the middle of the war. . . . The records in every one of the branches were picked up and moved down to the basement."[14]

As suggested by the Mandel interview, the file destruction issue was of compelling interest to the FBI as well as to the Congress. On December 31, 1943, FBI agent George Burton reported to Hoover assistant Mickey Ladd that "certain powerful interests within or near the War Department have undertaken an active program aimed at the dismemberment of the Counter-Intelligence Corps of G-2." Burton had discussed this with Army officials who said "quite frankly that the reason counter-intelligence had been wrecked was that Harry Hopkins and the Secret Service had ordered it to be wrecked."[15]

This seemed sufficiently fantastic, but the explanation given Burton was more so. Officers deploring the asserted wrecking order traced it to the case of Joseph Lash, a former leader of a leftward youth group called the American Student Union and a protégé of the President's wife. When Lash faced conscription in 1942, Mrs. Roosevelt tried to get him a commission in the Navy but was unsuccessful. Instead, Lash was inducted into the Army and kept under G-2 surveillance. Unluckily for all concerned, this led G-2 to conclude that Lash and Mrs. Roosevelt were something more than political buddies, as they were allegedly recorded by a hidden microphone during a hotel-room tryst in Chicago.

According to the G-2 account, when President Roosevelt was advised of this and the recording was played for him, he blew his top and ordered a draconian crackdown. In particular, the FBI was told, Lash and all Army personnel who knew anything about the matter were to be subject to the direst sanctions ("sent to the South Pacific for action against the Japs until they were killed").[16] Since Lash's security file was among those affected by the dismantling order, this bizarre back story appeared to fit the available facts as to why the files would be disposed of.

Years later, Joe Lash would track down the FBI reports on this and deny that such a scandalous thing had happened, and the few historians who refer to it dismiss it as either a smear by FBI Director Hoover or a fantasy concocted by G-2.[17] Whatever the merit of such speculations, it's unlikely this garish tale was the real reason for any dismantling of the records. There were too many other episodes in which Army intelligence files went missing, with no connection to Joe Lash.

An ominous case in point concerned the Katyn Forest massacre of the early war years, when thousands of captive Polish officers were slain in a part of Russia alternately controlled by the Germans and the Russians in fighting once the Hitler-Stalin pact was broken. When the fact of the murders was made public by the Nazis in April 1943, each despotism blamed the other. Since both were perfectly capable of such horrors, either might have done it.

The episode among other ill effects had somber implications for the Cold War future, as Moscow used a request for an independent Red Cross inquiry from the Polish government-in-exile in London as a pretext for breaking off relations, then switched recognition to a Soviet puppet. No such outside inquest would be sanctioned by the Kremlin of that era. However, Col. John Van Vliet, an American officer on the scene as a German POW, examined the bodies and related data and when he got home in 1945 filed a report about the murders. His verdict, borne out by later findings, was that the Soviets were the guilty parties.[18]*

Subsequently, the Van Vliet report was marked "top secret," kept under wraps, then disappeared entirely. A House committee chaired by Rep. Ray Madden (D-Ind.) looked into this grim affair and found that other reports reflecting badly on the Kremlin were likewise disposed of—for instance, dispatches from a Col. Henry Szymanski that criticized the Soviet role in Poland. As the Madden panel reported: "Evidence unearthed by this committee shows that Szymanski's highly critical reports on Soviet Russia were buried in the basement of Army Intelligence (G-2) and subsequently moved to the dead file of that agency."[19]

The Madden committee tried to discover who had done these things and at a minimum who had been handling such papers. Unfortunately for the historical record, the testimony on this point wasn't in public session, and the transcript of the executive hearing itself has vanished from the National Archives. However, the report of the committee summed up the episode as follows:

> More amazing to this committee is testimony of three high-ranking Army officers who were stationed in Army Intelligence (G-2) . . . testifying in executive session, all three agreed there was a pool of "pro-Soviet" civilian employees and some military in Army intelligence . . . who found explanations for almost anything the Soviet Union did. These same witnesses told of tremendous efforts exerted by this group to suppress anti-Soviet reports. The committee likewise learned that top-ranking Army officers who were too critical of the Soviets were by-passed in Army intelligence . . .[20]

THOUGH these are cases from military annals, civilian agencies were not, of course, exempt from similar hazards. The State Department, for evident reasons, would be a target of Soviet attentions, especially during World War II but also for some years before then. As noted by diplomat/historian George F. Kennan, the department in the latter 1930s had a knowledgeable Russian affairs division well versed in Soviet matters, which kept an extensive library and filing system and was famously skeptical on the bona fides of the Kremlin. One day, Kennan relates, an edict would come down as follows:

> The entire shop . . . was to be liquidated, and its functions transferred to the Division of West European Affairs. . . . The beautiful library was to be turned over to the Library of Congress, to be dispersed there by file numbers among its other vast holdings and thus cease to exist as a library. The

---

*This was acknowledged in 1992 by Russia's then-president, Boris Yeltsin.

special files were to be destroyed. . . . I am surprised, in later years, that the McCarthyites and other right wingers of the early Fifties never got hold of the incident and made capital of it; for here, if ever, was a point at which there was indeed the smell of Soviet influence, or strongly pro-Soviet influence, somewhere in the higher reaches of the government.[21]

Other occurrences at State, involving not merely files but people, would give rise to like suspicions. Of particular note were instances in which the policy of the averted gaze toward members of the Communist Party was extended even further—to spies sent here from Moscow, spotted by the FBI, but shielded by some higher power. As with other problems cited, inclinations of this type were evident in the 1930s but increased by several magnitudes during the wartime fling with Stalin.

One such case arose in 1938, involving the Soviet agent Mikhail Gorin, surveilled obtaining confidential data from a civilian staffer of the U.S. Navy. The FBI nabbed both suspects, who were charged with espionage violations and convicted. The naval employee would serve four years in prison, but the Soviet agent would walk free, thanks to State Department intervention. According to the FBI's account, the judge in the case, "on recommendation of the Department of State, and through the authorization of the Attorney General, suspended the execution of Gorin's original sentence and placed him on probation."[22]

Even more troubling to the Bureau was the 1941 case of Soviet superspy Gaik Ovakimian. Having tracked his endeavors in behalf of Moscow, the FBI arrested him for violation of the Foreign Agents Registration Act and thought it had him dead to rights. Again, however, the State Department stepped in to change things. The FBI memo about this says "arrangements were made by the Soviets with the United States State Department for the release of Gaik Ovakimian and his departure for the Soviet Union." The somewhat doubtful reason given for this lenient treatment was that the Soviets would reciprocate by releasing six Americans held by Red officials.*[23]

The release of Ovakimian occurred in July of 1941, a month after Hitler invaded Russia, and may thus have been an early case of foreign policy *realpolitik* thwarting Bureau law enforcement. Thereafter, when the United States was a cobelligerent with the USSR, kid-glove handling of Soviet agents seems

---

*In the event, both ends of this "exchange" (the quote marks are the FBI's) worked strictly to the benefit of Moscow. Of the Americans allegedly detained by Kremlin order, only three would make it to the United States, and two of these were then tracked by the Bureau as contacts of Soviet operatives here—including the wife of Ovakimian's successor as top "resident" in North America, and the wife of a State Department official himself identified as a Soviet asset. (Both wives were likewise identified by the Bureau as Soviet agents.) To judge by the FBI description, the State Department had sent one big apparatchik home to Moscow and got back two small ones for its trouble.

to have been the standard practice. Two instances of no-fault spying for the Kremlin, dating from the middle 1940s, were the cases of Soviet Purchasing Commission official Andrei Schevchenko and a legendary Moscow spy with the un-Russian name of Arthur Adams.

Testimony on these cases was given before the Senate in 1949 by former FBI agent Larry Kerley. Kerley read into the record a condensed and para-phrased version of a secret FBI wrap-up on Soviet activity in the U.S. In the course of this, he referred to Adams and Schevchenko and matter-of-factly told the Senate both had been set free, despite substantial proof of spying, be-cause of State Department orders. "It was simply a matter of policy," he said, "that none of Russia's espionage agents were to be arrested."[24]

A similar version of wartime practice was given by Bureau agent Robert Lamphere—later famous as the main FBI contact with the Army Security Agency in the *Venona* project. Concerning the Schevchenko case, Lamphere would comment: "Justice consulted with the State Department and the deci-sion was made not to arrest Schevchenko but to allow him to leave the country. International repercussions were feared if we arrested and tried a Soviet na-tional during wartime when Russia was our ally. . . ."[25]

In contrast to the benign neglect or positive favor extended to these Krem-lin agents was the stance of some in the U.S. government toward defectors from the Soviet Union. One spectacular case was that of "Jan Valtin" (Richard Krebs), a former Soviet double agent in Nazi Germany who in the 1930s de-fected to the West. Thereafter he wrote an exposé of both the Soviets and the Nazis titled *Out of the Night,* and in 1941 appeared before the Dies committee. The following year, the Immigration and Naturalization Service arrested Valtin-Krebs, locked him up on Ellis Island, and started deportation proceed-ings against him. This action was supposedly based on offenses committed in the 1920s when he was a Soviet henchman (for which he had already been im-prisoned). Thus, while current Soviet agents were allowed to go scot-free, this defecting former agent was to be severely punished.*[26]

Of like nature was the case of Victor Kravchenko, yet another defector from Moscow, who bolted from the Soviet Purchasing Commission's U.S. office in 1944 and made his way to the FBI. Bureau intelligence reports feature a lot of information from Kravchenko, showing he was a valued source in early

---

*The Soviets, for their part, dubbed Valtin-Krebs "one of the most important agents" of the Nazis and wanted him summarily dealt with. People in the United States who knew his background gave no credence to such charges but were well aware that he was a thorn in the side of Moscow. In an appeal to the Attorney General, Max Eastman, George S. Counts, and Eugene Lyons—all former men of the left who had turned against the Kremlin—observed that, since Valtin's arrest, "there has been only silence except in the Communist press, where his detention has been the occasion for frank rejoicing." Luckily for Valtin-Krebs, protests of this nature succeeded in staving off his deportation.

efforts to crack the Kremlin networks. He also would write a best-selling book, *I Chose Freedom*, exposing Soviet espionage and influence operations. Given all of which, an FBI memo from December of 1944 is of chilling import:

> On Friday, December 22, Mr. Ugo Carusi, Executive Assistant to the Attorney General, advised . . . that Mr. [Edward] Stettinius and the State Department were putting the pressure on the Department of Justice to bring about the surrender of Victor Kravchenko to the Russians for return to Russia. Mr. Carusi stated that undoubtedly the pressure was also being put on the State Department by the Soviets. . . . Later that afternoon, Mr. Carusi advised that the Attorney General believed the Bureau should discreetly tip off Kravchenko to the fact that "the heat was on" and that he should flee and carefully hide himself so that he would not be found by government representatives.[27]

On the orders of Director Hoover, the FBI did get this warning to Kravchenko, who thus lived to convey his anti-Soviet message to the public. From which macabre goings-on it's evident that the State Department of the era had some serious internal problems in dealings with our "noble ally." Yet, strange as it may seem, State by and large was among the more conservative, anti-Communist, and security-conscious agencies of the war years. Elsewhere in the federal government, the situation was a good deal worse, with even more sinister implications for the Cold War future.

CHAPTER 7

The Way It Worked

GIVEN the pro-Moscow views and lax security practice of the war, it should hardly be surprising that a formidable crew of Reds, fellow travelers, and Soviet spies wound up on the federal payroll, well in excess of previous levels. It would have been miraculous if they hadn't.

While many agencies were affected, the most seriously compromised were *ad hoc* wartime units thrown together in the early stages of the fighting. These included the Office of War Information (OWI), Office of Strategic Services (OSS), Board of Economic Warfare (BEW), and about a dozen others. Set up on an irregular basis, operating outside normal channels, often changing names and functions, these outfits scrambled to recruit personnel numbering in the thousands with little time, and apparently less desire, for anti-Red security vetting. Even more than the New Deal bureaus, they were custom-built for penetration and would thus figure prominently in security battles that developed later.

By all accounts, the two softest targets were the OWI, headed by broadcaster Elmer Davis and Hopkins crony/playwright Robert Sherwood, and the OSS, where "Wild Bill" Donovan held sway. (Running a close third was the Board of Economic Warfare, whose top officials variously included Vice President Henry Wallace and White House assistant/Soviet asset Lauchlin Currie.) Getting most of the contemporaneous attention was OWI, which being in the information business had a fairly visible profile and drew occasional fire from Congress.

The mission of OWI was supposed to be pro-American and pro-Allied propaganda, consisting of printed materials of all types, plus a multilingual shortwave service beamed at listeners overseas. This required a sizable staff that could deal in foreign-language broadcasts and printed matter, know something of the target nations, translate foreign statements, and so on. It was by its nature a heterogeneous, polyglot operation.

Spurring early criticism of OWI were reports that its productions, especially the foreign broadcasts, were tilted in the Soviet interest. This was a recurring theme in Congress but wasn't limited to such circles. In the summer of 1943, Arthur Krock of the *New York Times* observed that the viewpoints aired in OWI's foreign news and comment "have been closer to the Moscow than the Washington-London line." In another article for the *Times,* Krock suggested that OWI reports on U.S. policy overseas were "seeking to re-shape it according to the personal and ideological views of Communists and fellow travelers in this country."[1]

Similar charges were made by officials of the labor movement, who said OWI played up Red union causes and gave a distorted picture of American workplace issues. Spokesmen for both the AFL and CIO (then rival groups) said the OWI staffer named to handle labor matters had been employed by a Communist-dominated union and was recommended for his job at OWI by two identified Red agents. (This OWI employee was Travis Hedrick, who later worked for the Soviet news agency TASS and took the Fifth Amendment when asked if he had been a member of the Communist Party.)[2]

Joining in the chorus of complaint were representatives of European exile governments, who said OWI broadcasts to and about their homelands were laced with pro-Red propaganda. This was a matter of importance, as there would develop across the map of postwar Europe fierce struggles for political power between Communist and non-Communist forces. Broadcasts to these countries could be used to build up or tear down a given group or leader, according to the whim of those who produced the programs, wrote the scripts, and delivered comment on the airwaves.

Still other wartime developments would bring the agency to the notice of the FBI, security experts such as Ben Mandel (who prepared a report about it for the House Committee on Un-American Activities), and some members of the Congress. Several staffers at OWI would surface in a top-secret Bureau probe of the early 1940s focused on the University of California Radiation Laboratory at Berkeley, seedbed of the atom project.

Featured in this investigation were the American Communist Louise Bransten, her Russian paramour Gregori Kheifetz, and members of a Soviet spy ring based in San Francisco. In the course of this inquiry, the Bureau found that Bransten-Kheifetz had numerous official contacts, including a considerable group at OWI. Some references in FBI accounts dating from 1944–45 are as follows:

> Robin Kinkead, an American citizen residing in San Francisco, was employed by the Office of War Information as a Foreign Propaganda analyst. . . . It is reported that Kinkead has been a contact of Gregori Kheifetz, Soviet vice consul and NKVD agent formerly stationed in San Francisco.
>
> Philip Eugene Lilienthal, a resident of San Francisco, is a native-born citizen who during the war was employed in the Chinese Language Section, Radio Division, Office of War Information, in San Francisco. He is a known contact of Louise Bransten, the reported mistress of Gregori Kheifetz . . .
>
> Joseph Fels Barnes . . . for some time during the war . . . was employed in the Office of War Information as Assistant Director of Overseas Operations in charge of Radio and Publications. . . . Confidential sources have advised that Barnes is a contact of both Louise Bransten and Haakon Chevalier [an identified Communist and member of the San Francisco network].
>
> Charles Albert Page, a State Department employee who has recently been loaned to the motion picture and radio division of the Office of War Information, is a personal friend of Louise Bransten, and an associate of Gerhart Eisler, Otto Katz and Hans Eisler [all identified Comintern agents] . . .[3]

Because of its initial West Coast angle, this probe mainly featured staffers in OWI's Pacific office, where Kinkead and Lilienthal worked, and where others would later draw the notice of the Bureau. One such was a Japanese-American with the euphonious name of Shujii Fujii, who handled Japanese-language matters for OWI, then did a stint for OSS. When asked in a congressional hearing, "Were you a member of the Communist Party when you were working for OWI?" Fujii invoked the Fifth Amendment. He likewise took the Fifth when asked about his party status while on the staff at OSS.[4]

Another instructive case later brought out by Congress was that of journalist William Hinton, sent by OWI to China in 1943 to assist the wartime efforts of Chiang Kai-shek and Allied forces in the region. Hinton also invoked the Fifth when asked by a congressional panel if he were a CP member. After the Red takeover of China, he returned to work with the regime there and was photographed in Chicom gear addressing a Communist Party meeting. As shall be seen, Hinton was one of several U.S. officials involved with affairs of China who wound up on the Beijing payroll.[5]

Among the more prominent staffers in the Pacific sector who would get the attention of security forces was the head of the division, Professor Owen Lattimore of the Johns Hopkins University and the IPR and later a principal target of Joe McCarthy. The FBI would in time develop a huge Lattimore file, running to many thousands of pages, plus thousands of others on the IPR in general. In 1943, the Civil Service Commission zeroed in on two ethnic Chinese who worked for his division, Chew Hong and Chi Kung Chuan. This investigation would itself become in the McCarthy era something of a cause célèbre.

While the Pacific section led the way, the East Coast offices of OWI under Joseph Barnes were fertile of many suspects also. Among these—to pick a few from a lengthy roster—were James Aronson, Julia Older Bazer, and Peter Rhodes. At the conclusion of the war, as seen, Aronson would team up with Cedric Belfrage in the "de-Nazification" of the German press and later take the Fifth when asked about membership in the Communist Party. Julia Bazer, who handled OWI's cable file to Moscow, likewise invoked the Fifth when asked if she were a party member.[6] (Bazer was the sister of Drew Pearson's legman Andrew Older, identified by FBI undercover operative Mary Markward as a Communist agent.)[7] Peter Rhodes worked for both OWI and the Federal Communications Commission (FCC) before moving to the State Department. He would be named by former Soviet courier Elizabeth Bentley as a member of her spy ring.

Drawing attention from the FBI and other security experts were the personnel on various European desks. According to the Mandel report, the chief influence on the German desk was one Paul Hagen (né Karl Frank), a former member of the German Communist Party who became a naturalized American citizen but would develop passport trouble in the 1940s because of alleged security problems.*[8] Hagen was a close friend of the agency's informal guru for Yugoslav affairs, the writer Louis Adamic. An incessant promoter of the Communist Yugoslav leader known as Tito, Adamic had also been linked in a publishing venture with OWI's Alan Cranston. Serving on the Italian desk was one Carlo a Prato, who, according to Eugene Garey, general counsel of a congressional panel that looked into such matters, "was expelled from Switzerland for life as a Soviet agent who received and disbursed funds from Moscow. . . ."[9]

Getting the most public scrutiny in the war were the agency's Polish-language unit and its handling of the Katyn murders. In this instance, OWI chief Elmer Davis had personally gone on the air giving the pro-Soviet version of the story. Thereafter, according to Polish exile groups, OWI refused to broadcast items showing the Kremlin's complicity in the killings. In June 1943, Rep. John Lesinski (D-Mich.) charged that "the story of what happened to thousands of Polish officers who were murdered in the Katyn Forest was completely quashed" by OWI. Ambassador Jan Ciechanowski, who represented the Polish exile government in the United States, likewise asserted that OWI broadcasts on Poland "could only be termed pro-Soviet propaganda." He

---

* Hagen was quite well connected, not only at OWI but elsewhere. A book he wrote featured an introduction by Elmer Davis, and through his friend, Joe Lash, Hagen developed a pen-pal relationship with Mrs. Roosevelt, who tried to help him with his passport troubles (as did Lauchlin Currie).

further charged that "notorious pro-Soviet propagandists and obscure foreign Communists and fellow travelers were entrusted with these broadcasts."*[10]

As many people at the language desks were not American citizens, there was some mystery in the fact that they could so readily enter the United States and go to work for such an important wartime unit. The answer to this puzzle was a private group called Short Wave Research, Inc., the guiding spirits of which included Hagen the German émigré and Edward Carter, a leader of the American Russian Institute and chief officer of the IPR. Short Wave turned out to be another handy trapdoor for entry to federal service, not unlike the National Research Project of the 1930s as described by Whittaker Chambers (as OWI itself would later become a trapdoor to the State Department).

The golden gimmick of Short Wave was that it could recruit and put aliens on its payroll, as OWI at that time could not. Here they would do broadcasting work, translations, script writing, and other chores as Short Wave employees (though on the premises of OWI). The group would then bill OWI for services rendered, taking a 10 percent commission. According to documentation supplied by one Short Wave official, some 60 percent or so of foreign personnel at OWI were recruited in this manner. (Meanwhile, a considerable number of American staffers, according to other inquiries, were inherited from the Federal Writers Project exposed earlier by the Dies Committee.)

As revealed by Short Wave spokesmen, they had another mission as well—helping OWI and the Federal Communications Commission identify malefactors on domestic foreign-language stations who said things that weren't approved of (especially, as further testimony showed, if these were adverse to Moscow). Among OWI staffers working on this censorship project was Alan Cranston, later a U.S. senator from California. As spelled out in congressional hearings, Cranston and others from OWI would confront broadcast officials, backed by the implicit sanction of the FCC with its power over the station license, and suggest that this or that person shouldn't be on the air, or that another should. This was done despite the fact that neither OWI nor FCC had any legal authority over domestic program content.[11]

Testimony on these matters was developed before the House Select Committee on the FCC in 1943–44, and later by the committee on Katyn chaired by Madden. Beyond these inquiries, many aspects of OWI's activities and personnel were brought out in the debates of Congress. Lesinski was especially vocal, but other lawmakers from time to time would join him in spotlighting the

---

* As set forth in FBI reports, three chief players in the United States promoting the Communist cause in Poland were Alexander Hertz; Professor Oscar Lange, a naturalized U.S. citizen of Polish birth who according to the Bureau had links to OWI like those enjoyed by Hagen and Adamic; and Boleslaw "Bill" Gebert, who served on the national committee of the Communist Party USA and received airtime on OWI to express his views on global issues. (When the Communists took over Poland, Hertz, Lange, and Gebert would all go on the payroll of the Red regime there.)

personnel behind the broadcasts. The tenacious Martin Dies discussed a number of OWI employees in his floor presentations. Dies and other congressional critics also delved into the staff setup at the FCC, which not only worked with OWI in targeting domestic foreign-language stations but otherwise exerted its broadcast powers in curious manner.*

Given later partisan battles on these issues, it's worth observing that all congressmen here referred to as critics of OWI were members of the Democratic Party. However, one GOPer who took particular notice of OWI was Rep. Fred Busbey of Illinois, who served on the House Committee on Un-American Activities and often addressed security issues. In November 1943, Busbey supplied a rundown on some twenty-two staffers or broadcasters at OWI who in his view had pro-Communist records and affiliations. Among those he mentioned were Joe Barnes, Robin Kinkead, and the well-known Polish-American Communist Boleslaw Gebert. (Busbey also highlighted the role of Cranston, noting that he was a longtime sidekick of Adamic.) Busbey's remarks on this occasion prefigured the leading role he would play in security battles of the future.[12]

THE problems spotted at OWI were likewise present at OSS, if not a good deal more so. In fact, close students of such matters have long regarded OSS as the most heavily infiltrated of the wartime units, with estimates of the number of Communists there ranging as high as a hundred staffers. This is, however, an estimate only, so the number was conceivably smaller but might also have been a good deal larger. Partially this was the result of Bill Donovan's freewheeling ways, pragmatically using any instrument at hand to accomplish his objectives. As shown in several treatments of the era, OSS under his direction explicitly recruited Communists for certain missions on the premise that they would be good fighters against the Nazis.

Though its posthumous reputation as a den of Communists and Soviet agents would exceed that of OWI, less was known about OSS back in the 1940s. The secret nature of the service allowed its employees to roam about the globe at will, engaging in all sorts of actions concealed from Congress and the public. Some aspects of the problem would, however, come to view when Donovan made his 1945 appearance at the Thomason subcommittee hearings.

At this session, Donovan said there were no Communists on his payroll

---

*As earlier noted, among the FCC staffers discussed at length in Congress were William Dodd, Frederick Schuman, and Goodwin Watson, the last named head of the Foreign Intelligence Broadcast Service for the Commission. All three had lengthy records of Communist-front affiliation. Dodd would later show up in *Venona* as a Soviet intelligence contact.

and that he personally could vouch for the bona fides of his people. In support of this, he cited the cases of two staffers—George Vucinich and David Zablodowsky. Though Donovan considered them true blue, these turned out to be unfortunate choices. Vucinich would show up in *Venona* as a contact of the Soviet GRU. Quizzed later in congressional hearings, he said he hadn't been a Communist while with OSS but refused to say whether he was a party member before or after—claiming the Fifth Amendment on both questions.[13]

As for Zablodowsky, he had been an editor of the publication *Fight,* organ of the American League for Peace and Democracy. Told the League had been named as a Communist front in the list supplied by Biddle, Donovan said he didn't know this. Rather, he said, he had personally interviewed Zablodowsky, who denied he was a Communist, and "Wild Bill" found this persuasive. (Episodes in which supervisors asked employees if they were Reds and accepted denials at face value were fairly common at this era.)

Two other OSS employees vouched for by Donovan were Lts. Milton Wolff and Irving Fajans, both veterans of the Communist-sponsored Abraham Lincoln Brigade that ostensibly fought for the Loyalist cause in Spain. In Donovan's view, Wolff and Fajans were good soldiers and thus certifiably patriotic. But in a later investigation, Wolff refused to say whether he had been a Red while at OSS, served under Soviet officers in Spain, or been involved in the execution of U.S. citizens there (this last asked several times). Fajans also refused to say whether he was a Communist, had been such in Spain, or was trained by foreign commissars in that country.*[14]

Like many others at OSS, Wolff and Vucinich were much involved with affairs of Yugoslavia, which in the early war years were a major focus of U.S. and British clandestine efforts. Guerrilla actions there were encouraged, as Yugoslavia was one of the few spots in Europe where there was serious armed resistance to the Nazi Wehrmacht. It was also a spot where Communist and anti-Communist forces came to an early parting of the ways while the war was still in progress.

When Hitler declared war on Yugoslavia in the spring of 1941, the pact with Stalin was still in force and the sole effective opposition to the German onslaught had been mounted by a breakaway group of Yugoslav army officers. The leading figure of this unit was Serbian Gen. Draja Mihailovich, an anti-Red as well as anti-Nazi leader whose followers were called the Chetniks. Only after Hitler invaded Russia, three months later, did a second, Communist resistance group called the Partisans appear under the leadership of Stalin

---

*In both OWI and OSS, there were competing forces that opposed the pro-Communist factions, so descriptions in this chapter shouldn't be taken as characterizing all employees of these units. It so happened, however, that in many crucial episodes the pro-Communist element held the upper hand.

protégé Josip Broz, who took the nom de guerre of Tito. As would occur with Poland, the rival forces were soon in mortal opposition, and the question for Anglo-American policy was which of the two should be supported.

Beginning in late 1942 and ramping up in '43, broadsides from Moscow and Communist spokesmen in the West would provide an answer, launching a campaign to promote the cause of Tito and denounce Mihailovich as a collaborator and traitor. Though Tito hadn't lifted a finger against the Nazis until they invaded Russia, he was now portrayed as the only legitimate Balkan leader in the battle against Hitler. In the United States this pro-Tito line was promoted by Adamic, Communist writer Howard Fast, and a group called the American Slav Congress, later officially cited as a Communist front. Articles, manifestos, and speeches abounded arguing that Mihailovich was "collaborating with the Nazis" while Tito did all the fighting.*

Though there were people in the U.S. government who resisted this pro-Tito blitz, strong pressures were at work that pushed our policy in this direction. Among these was the predominance of Whitehall interests in the Balkans, where British experience outranked our own by a substantial margin. A contributing factor was the close relationship between Donovan and William Stephenson, the Canadian who ran British intelligence operations in North America. Both were unusual personalities given to unorthodox methods, and they worked together on many projects. (A further parallel was that each unwittingly had as a top assistant a Bentley- and *Venona*-identified Soviet agent—Duncan C. Lee in Donovan's office, and Cedric Belfrage, as noted, at Stephenson's shop in New York City.)[15]

Symbolizing this Anglo-American cooperation was a super-secret Canadian training site called "Camp X," forty miles outside Toronto. One Donovan-Stephenson venture at this location was the recruitment of Canadian-Croatian Communists and veterans of the Spanish Civil War as guerrilla forces for the Yugoslav fighting. The go-between with the Communist vets picked by Donovan was Milton Wolff, whose service with the pro-Moscow cause in Spain was thought to fit him for this duty.

Once guerrilla units were trained for service in the Balkans, they were taken for further briefing to British intelligence headquarters in Cairo, Egypt, then the center of such activities for the region. Here another secret Kremlin agent was at work applying his talents to the Yugoslav question. This was the Cambridge Communist James Klugmann, confrere of Blunt, Philby, Burgess,

---

*As with Poland, the Yugoslav line adopted by the prevailing faction at OWI would draw a strong critique from Congress. Representative Lesinski would charge that the agency was broadcasting unabashedly pro-Tito propaganda, including false reports that Partisan forces had variously invaded Hungary, Austria, Bulgaria, and Romania in their supposedly wide-ranging battle against the Nazis. Helen Lombard of the *Washington Star* likewise reported that scheduled pro-Mihailovich comments had been spiked by OWI officials.

and Maclean. As shown by the researches of David Martin, Nora Beloff, and other recent students of the matter, Klugmann was the guiding presence at Cairo with respect to Yugoslav affairs, shaping estimates of who was doing what in-country, synthesizing field reports, and sending the results to ministries in London.*

Unsurprisingly, with this Cambridge comrade on the job, the message that came through to British leaders was identical to that from Moscow. One bizarre Cairo report said Tito presided over a massive force of 200,000 men who were "pinning down some 14 German divisions in the country." (The true figures for both the Nazis and the Tito forces in Yugoslavia were but a fraction of these numbers.) Another asserted that "the Partisans represent a good and effective force in all parts where only the Quislings [i.e., Nazi collaborators] represent General Mihailovich." A third said Mihailovich units were either "already annihilated or in close cooperation with the Axis [Germans and Italians]."†[16]

Based on a steady stream of such dispatches, London turned decisively toward Tito. In the latter part of 1943, the British Foreign Office concluded "there is no evidence of any effective anti-Axis action initiated by Mihailovich," and that "since he is doing nothing from a military point of view to justify our continued assistance," a cutoff of materials to the anti-Communists was in order. Churchill himself would soon drop Mihailovich entirely and put his chips on Tito.[17]

U.S. intelligence data and clandestine action closely followed the British pattern. A key player in this démarche was Capt. Linn Farish of OSS, an enigmatic and strangely influential early Cold War figure. When Farish parachuted into Yugoslavia in September of 1943 to work with the Partisans and the British, he was quick to absorb the pro-Tito message and repeat it. After being with the Partisans for six weeks, he filed a report back to OSS that was lyrical

---

*Among the methods used in the Klugmann operation, as documented by Martin, were attributing military actions by the Mihailovich forces to the Tito brigades; use of briefing maps that suggested a massive Partisan presence in all sections of Yugoslavia; suppressing news of Nazi statements in which Mihailovich was named as an enemy of the Reich; and construing efforts by Mihailovich to neutralize Italian forces as proof of collaboration, while ignoring identical methods used by Tito.

†On top of these encomia to Tito and denunciations of his anti-Communist foes, the Partisans were depicted as agents of progress, democracy, freedom, equal rights, and literary culture—all this while fighting a heroic guerrilla war against the Nazis. One report to London described these amazing exploits this way:

Partisan policy is . . . constructive rather than destructive . . . witness the rapidity with which throughout the liberated areas, factories, power stations and even railroads are working, while on the cultural side corresponding activity is shown, newspapers are produced, and schools, youth associations are set up, all needless to say, on strictly party lines. In particular a determined effort is being made to combat illiteracy. In all these activities an increasingly active part is being played by women whose emancipation is an important plank in the Partisan platform.

in its praise of Tito, while denouncing Mihailovich and the Chetniks as collaborators with the Nazis and traitors to the Allies.*

Since Farish at this point had no direct knowledge of what Mihailovich was doing, these comments were clearly based on what the Partisans and the British told him. His report also glowed with praise for the Partisans' "free community," in which persons "of any religion or political belief can express an opinion," downplayed the role of the Yugoslav Communist Party in the guerrilla setup, and compared the Tito movement to the American Revolution: "It was in such an environment and under similar conditions that the beginnings of the United States were established."[18]

Though so fawning as to defy belief, these statements were accepted as authentic by policy makers who read them. In fact, this Farish memo, filed on October 29, 1943, would play a crucial role in shaping Allied policy toward the Balkans. By some bureaucratic legerdemain, it was placed directly in the hands of President Roosevelt on the eve of the Teheran conference with Churchill and Stalin that would open one month later. As shown by the records of OSS, Farish's pro-Tito missive was passed quickly from one echelon to the next, with the explicit goal of getting it to FDR in time for the Teheran summit.

This double-time drill succeeded, and the Farish memo was in Roosevelt's hands in time for the Teheran conclave. At the conference on November 29, as reflected in diplomat Charles Bohlen's notes, this U.S. report extolling the Communist Tito and reviling his anti-Red opponent was the first item on the agenda, as the President personally handed it to Stalin (who was no doubt glad to see it). The memo would also receive pride of place in exhibits to the proceedings, where it is again the first item to be dealt with and reproduced in full. (Adding to its apparent authority, Bohlen's notes incorrectly say Farish had been in Yugoslavia for "six months," rather than six weeks.)[19]

Thus did Linn Farish's tribute to Tito and condemnation of Mihailovich make their way to the loftiest reaches of global power. As Churchill was already persuaded, and Stalin needed no persuading, this priming and conditioning of Roosevelt helped seal the doom of anti-Communist forces in the Balkans. When a joint statement was agreed to at Teheran, unstinting aid to Tito was promised and Mihailovich was nowhere mentioned. It would be only a matter of weeks until renunciation of the anti-Communist leader was explicit.

---

* As to who was resisting the Nazis, said Farish, "the Partisans have always fought the Germans and are doing so now. . . . They are a more potent striking force at this time than they have been before. . . . Their present strength is given as 180,000 men." This heroic resistance, he said, was owing to "a handful of men, betrayed and harassed by their own countrymen." As for the treacherous people making things tough for valiant Tito, Farish added: "Whereas the Partisans have fought steadfastly against the Axis occupying forces, other Yugoslav groups have not done so . . . Mihailovich ordered his Chetniks to attack the Partisan forces . . . the Chetnik forces have been fighting with the Germans and Italians against the Partisans."

Some five decades later, when the *Venona* decrypts were published, further information about Linn Farish would come to light. In these records he appears as a contact of the KGB (code name "Attila") meeting with an unidentified Soviet controller ("Khazar") and an official of the Yugoslav Communist apparatus code-named "KOLO." The latter was Sava Kosanovic, who would serve from 1946 to 1950 as Ambassador to the United States from Tito's Red regime in Belgrade. In the *Venona* decrypts, KOLO/Kosanovic appears receiving instructions from KGB boss Pavel Fitin and is discussed as an agent in need of better guidance. Kosanovic also figures in the records of the FBI for 1946, when he was surveilled at a meeting with still another Soviet agent, Nathan Gregory Silvermaster, a leading member of the Elizabeth Bentley spy ring.*

Deprived of U.S. and British aid, Mihailovich was at a hopeless disadvantage, while the cause of Tito, now sponsored jointly by the USSR, the United Kingdom, and the United States in unbeatable combination, would correspondingly flourish. In late 1944, escorted by Russian tanks, Tito entered Belgrade and established a Communist despotism (with plenty of U.S. aid still flowing). Now utterly abandoned, Mihailovich was hunted down by Tito, given a Communist show trial, and put to death. The propaganda campaign of Moscow, Klugmann, Adamic, *et al.*—with a crucial assist from OSS—had brilliantly succeeded. It would be a model for much that was about to happen elsewhere.

---

*These revelations have understandably given rise to the suspicion that Farish was himself a Communist, though other data suggest he was a credulous conduit for pro-Tito propaganda rather than a conscious agent. In June 1944, Farish would write another report of starkly different implication from that filed in October 1943, indicating that the first effort was the result of swallowing Tito and British disinformation, and perhaps some as well from KOLO.

CHAPTER 8

Chungking, 1944

O PINIONS differ as to when the U.S.-Soviet alliance against the Nazis tipped over into the less overt but eventually just as deadly conflict of the Cold War, with its recurring crises overseas and fierce security battles on the home front.

A good case can be made for dating the transition as early as 1943. This was the year of the Nazi retreat from Stalingrad, after which the Soviets knew they were going to withstand the Hitler onslaught and could start planning future onslaughts of their own. Hence the break with the London Poles, acceleration of the anti-Mihailovich *jihad,* and a newly hostile propaganda blitz against the anti-Communist Chiang Kai-shek in China. All this occurred in 1943, causing students of the matter as diverse as Louis Adamic and Joe McCarthy to conclude that World War III had, in effect, been started.[1]

For our purposes, 1944 provides a somewhat clearer demarcation. It takes two to tango, or have a war, and it wasn't until 1944 that people in the West— at least some people—realized such a brand-new war was coming. Also, the line is a bit clearer in 1944 for another reason. This was the year of D-Day, the Allied drive to Paris, and General MacArthur's steady advance across the Pacific on his way back to Manila. Though months of fighting still remained, it was apparent to most observers that the Germans and the Japanese were going to be defeated.

Accordingly, strategists East and West (mostly the former) were laying plans, mustering forces, and jockeying for postwar advantage. And while there would be contests of this type in many places, by far the biggest single prize was China. That this should be the case was, to say no more, ironic. For the United States, China had been the *casus belli,** as our staunch backing for Chiang Kai-shek and refusal to accept Japan's conquests in China were main ingredients in the standoff that exploded at Pearl Harbor.

Now, however, the object of our Asian policy was on its way to being lost before the war was over. Having fought Tokyo to rescue China, we saw the country engulfed instead by civil war, and thereafter by a Communist state as despotic as the Japanese and as hostile to our interests. The outlines of this conflict were also tolerably clear in '44, as the Communist forces of Mao Tse-tung and Chou En-lai had an independent power base at their fastness in Yenan, commanded their own armies, and were visibly preparing for a show-down with Chiang once the Japanese were beaten.[2]

In this unfolding struggle, some of the most important players were people the general public had never heard of. Three particularly worthy of note were functionaries of the U.S. and Nationalist Chinese governments living and working at the makeshift inland capital of Chungking, where Chiang's Kuo-mintang (KMT) regime had moved to evade the Japanese.[†] This trio would have crucial roles to play in the events that sealed the fate of China.

The three officials were, in order of their eventual fame, the American diplomat John Stewart Service, U.S. Treasury attaché Solomon Adler, and the U.S.-educated Chinese economist Chi Chao-ting, who worked for the KMT ministry of finance. This threesome shared a number of interests and aversions, and at least one colossal secret. Though supposedly on the scene in China to help the embattled Chiang Kai-shek, each detested his regime and had an inordinate fondness for his Red opponents. All would do what they could, which was a lot, to injure Chiang and promote the rebels.

Emblematic of this common mission was the somewhat remarkable fact that Service, Chi, and Adler all lived together at a house in Chungking—Service and Adler as roommates on the second floor, Chi on the floor above them. And while we of course have no idea of what generally went on in this unusual household, we do have some specifics. For instance, we definitely know what Service and Adler were doing in their official roles, as this is plainly spelled out in the record: sending back a stream of reports to the American government reviling Chiang, and arguing with increasing fervor that we dump him and embrace the Yenan comrades.[3]

As an employee of the Chungking government, Chi Chao-ting would

---

* As Poland had been the *casus belli* for England.

† Kuomintang = National People's Party.

hardly have set forth such views in an official paper. There is no question, however, that he concurred in private. For something else we know is that Chi was a Soviet agent—a henchman of the Comintern apparatus dispatched to do its work in China. We know the same was true as well of Adler. The documentation that goes to show this is extensive, including the further remarkable fact that both Chi and Adler would abscond to Beijing once the Reds were in control there. Thus, John Stewart Service, one of the most important U.S. officials in China, was living and working at close quarters with two case-hardened Soviet agents—a rare distinction, we can but hope, in diplomatic annals.

Service was the only one of our threesome who would later get much notice. Like several other China hands, including his lifelong friend and fellow diplomat John Davies, he was the son of missionary parents, was born in China, spent much of his life there, and was fluent in the language. A career foreign service officer, he had worked on the U.S. Embassy staff at Chungking with Counselor John Carter Vincent (later head of the China desk and Far East division at State) and would become like Davies a political adviser to Gen. Joseph "Vinegar Joe" Stilwell, wartime commander of U.S. and Chinese forces in the region.

The Stilwell connection was of great significance in the doings of John Service, as "Vinegar Joe" early on conceived a hatred for Chiang Kai-shek, whom he called "the peanut," and other even more insulting nicknames. Stilwell the admirer of Agnes Smedley also idealized the Chinese Reds, and at a later date would voice his desire to shoulder a rifle in the armies of Chu Teh, the Yenan military leader.[4] Stilwell's attitudes gave members of his staff free rein to be as hostile to Chiang as they might wish, and they would exploit the privilege to the fullest.

By the late summer of 1944, Service had landed a coveted spot as a U.S. "observer" at the Communist GHQ in far-off Yenan, a posting for which he had ardently lobbied. Here, as in Chungking but even more so, he would consort with Chou En-lai, the plausible, wily foreign minister of the Reds, and with the usually less accessible Mao. In this assignment Service would also commingle with journalists who made the pilgrimage to Yenan, including Israel Epstein, Guenther Stein, and a fairly sizable crew of others. All in all, given his many contacts and position uniquely on the spot, John Service was a pivotal figure.

Sol Adler never enjoyed the notoriety of Service but was as important. British-born and Oxford-educated, Adler first came to the United States in 1934, made his way to Chicago, and turned up on the faculty of something called the People's Junior College. The dean of this institution, conveniently, was the oft-identified Soviet agent Harold Glasser. (Also, repeating a pattern common in this circle, Adler and Glasser were Chicago housemates.) From Glasser's proletarian college, Adler moved on in 1935 to the National Research Project of the WPA headed by David Weintraub and Irving Kaplan—the same trapdoor through which Whittaker Chambers would gain access to the federal payroll.

From the Weintraub-Kaplan Research Project, it was only a hop and a skip to the Treasury roster, where Adler would move in 1936 to join Harry White and V. Frank Coe, and would eventually reunite with Glasser. Sol Adler was thus a classic study in the ease with which someone having the right (or left) connections could move from one official billet to the next. His smooth upward climb was the more impressive in that, like his countryman Michael Greenberg, he was not yet a U.S. citizen (he wouldn't be naturalized until 1940).[5]

In due course, Sol Adler would turn up in the chronicles of *Venona*. Also, as reflected in the notes of Adolf Berle, he was one of the people Chambers named in his initial revelations as a member of the Treasury Red nexus. Thereafter he would be named as well by Elizabeth Bentley, who informed the Senate: "Solomon Adler . . . was a member of the Silvermaster group. He paid his dues through Mr. Silvermaster to me. Most of the time I was in charge of this group he was in China. But he did send reports to various people, including Harry Dexter White in the Treasury Department, which were relayed to us. . . . He not only was connected with the Silvermaster organization, he had Communist contacts in China. One of these was Chi."[6]

Chi Chao-ting had studied and worked in the United States in the 1930s, taking an advanced degree in economics at Columbia University and obtaining a post as a researcher/writer at the Institute of Pacific Relations. Here he would be yet another confrere of Professor Lattimore, editor of the IPR's quarterly publication. Like Adler, Chi would come to the notice of U.S. security sleuths in the 1940s, but was never given prominent mention. Relatively full disclosure about his activities would have to wait for several decades, when Chi's close friend and fellow IPR member Philip Jaffe would recount the story in a memoir.

As Jaffe told it, Chi was a veteran Comintern agent recruited into the Communist Party in the 1920s, thereafter handling assignments in Europe, the United States, and China—ultimately infiltrating the government of Chiang Kai-shek in behalf of the Red insurgents. Along the way, Chi met and married Jaffe's cousin, Harriet Levine, still another IPR employee (and sometime Lattimore assistant). As Jaffe would recap the story:

> It was through Chi Chao-ting, a cousin of mine by marriage, that I accepted the Communist version of Marxism as a guide to the contemporary world. . . . For a period of more than fifteen years, Chi Chao-ting and I were intimate personal friends and close personal associates. . . . He would ultimately become the economic adviser to H. H. Kung, the Kuomintang finance minister, while simultaneously working clandestinely as an underground operative for Chou En-lai. . . . Upon his death in 1963 in Peking [Beijing] he would be given a hero's funeral.[7]

Quite apart from their common lodgings, our trio—especially Service and Adler—had many interactions. Among the clearest indications of their joint endeavors are the overlapping and interweaving reports Service and Adler sent back to the United States from China (with Chi assisting on occasion as silent partner). While Service was the more prolific, Adler sounded the same political themes, often in the same phraseology, and geared to the same goal of savaging Chiang while talking up the Yenan rebels.

The Service-Adler memos relentlessly hammered a few main themes: The government of Chiang Kai-shek was corrupt, despotic, and ineffective; the Chinese Reds, by contrast, were paragons of virtue, moderate and democratic, beloved of the people; and—most important in the context of the war—only the Communists were carrying on the battle against Japan, while Chiang and his forces at best did nothing and at worst were collaborationists and traitors.

Among the striking features of these memos is how closely they resemble the material being supplied, not long before this, to U.S. and British authorities about the struggle for the Balkans. Point for point, the Service-Adler papers track the comments of Linn Farish, Klugmann-vetted intelligence reports from Cairo, and propaganda broadsides of Adamic—often with the identical images and charges, and sometimes the identical phrasing. It was the same drill throughout, with Chiang the Mihailovich of China, Mao the surrogate for Tito.*

Service's anti-Chiang reports were so voluminous only the merest précis can be offered—though it doesn't take many samples to catch the meaning. In dispatches totaling 1,200 pages, Service couldn't find a good word to say about the anti-Communist Chiang Kai-shek. What poured forth instead was a steady stream of venom, an exercise in which the major challenge appeared to be finding different ways of making the same damaging charges *ad infinitum*. Some of the epithets Service used to describe the KMT leader and his government were as follows:

"Corruption, unprecedented in scale and openness," "the enthronement of reaction," "growing megalomania," "dictatorship," "Gestapo-like organization," "fascist," "undemocratic," "feudal," "reliance on a gangster secret police," "threats and blackmail," "sabotage of the war effort," "the obvious ineffectiveness of the Chinese army," "normally traitorous relations with the enemy," and much more of similar damning nature.[8]

---

* Service himself was fully conscious of this linkage and would stress it in dispatches. In one report, for instance, he commented that "the parallel with Jugoslavia has been drawn before but is becoming more and more apt. It is as impractical to seek Chinese unity with the Kuomintang alone as it was to seek solution of these problems through Mihailovich and King Peter's government in London, ignoring Tito." And, even more explicit: "At present there exists in China a situation closely paralleling that which existed in Yugoslavia prior to Prime Minister Churchill's declaration of support for Marshal Tito."

As there was certainly much to criticize in the ragtag KMT regime, pushed to the limits of financial, physical, and moral endurance by seven years of fighting against Japan and the ravages of wartime inflation, these fierce criticisms might be put down—and often have been—to Service's status as hard-boiled reporter, just conveying "the facts" as he observed them. The just-the-facts rationale, however, is hard to credit when these abrasive comments are compared with his fervent homage to Yenan.

Here, the hard-nosed reporter turned into a swooning groupie. His descriptions of the Communist forces—again echoing the message from the Balkans—read more like propaganda leaflets for the Red regime than the reports of a detached observer. Now the operative words were "progressive," "democratic," "impressive personal qualities," "realism and practicality," "objective and scientific orderliness," "straightforward and frank," "incorruptibility," "a real desire for democracy in China," "aggressive resistance to the Japanese," "complete support of the local population," and on and on in endless variations.[9]

While many aspects of these Service memos might be usefully examined, one in particular is worth a note in passing: the extent to which he presented the Chinese Reds as democratic, nonradical, pro-American, not really Communist, and so on. This point would be important down the line, when there were efforts to exculpate Service and others like him from the charge that they had sugarcoated and helped bring to power the most hideous despotism in global history, measured in terms of total carnage. The charge, as it happens, was entirely true, and well supported by the record.

As with everything else he had to say about events in China, Service would make the same point repeatedly, so there was—and is—no way to miss it. "The Communist political program," he wrote, "is simple democracy. This is much more American than Russian in form and spirit." "They are carrying out democratic policies, which they expect the United States to approve and sympathetically support." "This revolution has been peaceful and democratic. . . . The common people, for the first time, have been given something to fight for." The Communists were following "a policy of self-limitation," marked by their "abandonment of any purely Communist program." "They have a real desire for democracy in China . . . without the need of violent social upheaval and revolution."[*10]

The dispatches of Service's Soviet-agent sidekick Adler were less expansive

---

*The accuracy of this "reporting" may be gauged from the fact that the Chinese Communists Service was describing went on to establish a dictatorship that, gauged by the total number of people killed, would rank foremost in the history of such horrors. Their tactics included mass murder, torture, brainwashing, slave labor, death by famine, and denial of every possible form of personal freedom. There was substantial evidence as to the brutal nature of the Communist forces when Service's words were written.

on these matters, focusing mostly on economic topics—but were similar in tone and content. Frequently, Adler stressed the Mihailovich vs. Tito angle: the alleged ineffectiveness of the KMT in pressing the war against Japan, if not outright collaboration. "The central government," said Adler, "survives in its present form only because of American support and influence and Japanese collusion." Chiang's regime "has lost any interest it ever had in doing anything effective to fight the Japanese," "the war effort is more inert than ever before," "China has done less fighting than any other major ally."[11]

The conclusion Adler drew from all this was the need to "get tough" with Chiang—also a refrain of Service. Adler would explain what he meant by toughness in a message to the Treasury's Harry White in February of 1945. "Our China policy," he wrote, "should be given teeth. It should be made clear to the generalissimo that we will play ball with him only if he plays ball with us." To this end, said Adler, we should support Chiang "*if and only if* he really tried to mobilize China's war effort by introducing coalition government"— meaning coalition with Yenan. (Emphasis in original.) The way to get such a coalition, in Adler's view, was to use the power of the Treasury by withholding financial aid to Chiang, especially a promised loan of $200 million in gold.* This strategy, expounded by one Soviet agent to another, would become within a matter of months official U.S. policy toward China.[12]

The Service-Adler memos were not only congruent in major features, but so drafted as to be mutually reinforcing. In June of 1944, Service would pass along a study of Chiang Kai-shek's ideas on economics done by Adler, calling it "the best analysis" available of the "mixed fascism, feudalism and paternalism which characterize the Generalissimo and the conservative leaders around him who now control China." Service stressed that Adler's role in preparing this report should be "treated as secret" (while indicating that the material had also been worked on secretly by Chi).†[13]

Thereafter, Adler would return the favor. In memos to White, he described the state of things in China—all negative toward Chiang—paraphrasing and quoting Service. These updates included such Service staples as the moderation and democracy of the Yenan Reds, their support by the people, and their valiant efforts to fight Japan, despite lack of help from the worthless Chiang;

---

* "There seems to be no alternative for the Treasury," Adler told White, "but to adopt a negative policy toward China. We should continue to send as little gold as possible to China. For such gold will not be effectively used in combating inflation. . . . We should be tough and tardy in making settlement for U.S. Army expenditures in China. There is no need to have too delicate a conscience in this matter, as the Chinese swindle us right and left at every possible opportunity. . . . We should turn down Chinese requests for goods in civilian lend lease for the ostensible purpose of combating inflation. . . . We should maintain a fairly tight watch on Chinese funds in the United States."

† Service said that sections of the report "have been discussed with a prominent American-trained Chinese economist" who was undoubtedly Chi; in which event, Service was here supplying the U.S. government with the work product of both his Soviet agent housemates.

("The Communists have successfully resisted the Japanese for seven years . . . with no active support from Chungking. . . .") All this came from Service, described by Adler as "the best informed American on internal Chinese politics."[14] Thus, Service quoted Adler as the guru on economic issues, while Adler cited the keen political insights of Service (not pointing out that this drafting of mutual praises in all likelihood occurred over the kitchen table of their flat in Chungking).

Of course, Harry White didn't need Adler—or the Service memos—to tell him Chiang Kai-shek should be reviled and the Reds promoted. The point of these dispatches, like the Klugmann-vetted reports from Cairo and Farish memo at Teheran, was to guide the thinking of policy makers at higher levels. White was diligent in making sure Treasury Secretary Morgenthau saw the Adler memos and selected reports from Service. (Morgenthau's diaries show him exclaiming, "I love these letters from Adler.")[15] Morgenthau would carry the message to the White House, where he had special access to FDR, his long-time neighbor in New York's Hudson Valley. As Lauchlin Currie on the White House staff was receiving similar updates from Service, each series of memos could thus be cited as confirmation of the other.

By Service's own appraisal, his main collaboration with Adler occurred during the visit of Vice President Henry Wallace to Chungking in June of 1944. This proved to be a decisive breakthrough for the strategy of establishing direct U.S. contact with Yenan, which Chiang had bitterly resisted. As Wallace had with him as traveling mentors both Owen Lattimore and John Vincent, he was no doubt well briefed on Chiang's shortcomings and the benefits of liaising with Yenan. (Vincent would later acknowledge that he repeatedly steered the Chiang-Wallace talks in this direction.) Just to make sure, however, Service and Adler got together and drafted a mammoth sixty-eight-page memo on affairs of China to be given to Wallace on his arrival. For official purposes this memo, reprising all the usual notions, was imputed to Service only, with Adler's role, again, sub rosa. We know, however, that the collaboration did occur, as Service himself would later on reveal this.*

ALL this Service-Adler collusion took place within a larger context of interacting forces in the U.S. government aimed at sabotaging Chiang. There were many such forces in and around the State Department, and these would become the subject of a huge debate that erupted in the days of Joe McCarthy.

---

*As Service would describe it: "I was living with Adler then. . . . One night we got to chewing the fat how we ought to do something, write a report, sum up the whole situation. . . . We both sat down, got all worked up, and that night . . . we each wrote out a base summary draft as a starting point. Then he took the two of them and hammered them into one, and I took that and re-wrote it, and we kicked it back and forth. Really it's as much Adler as me. Both of us worked together on it."

Second only to Service himself in pounding home the message was John Davies, who depicted the Yenan regime as "a modern, dynamic popular government," called Chiang's government "politically bankrupt," and declared that "the Communists are in China to stay and China's destiny is not Chiang's but theirs."[16] Still other FSOs would reinforce these notions, playing up the supposed virtues of Yenan and the corruption, inefficiency, and other evils of the KMT. All this was subsequently amplified by press accounts from China that blasted Chiang and praised the rebels.

Less visible at the time, but equally crucial for the fate of China, were manipulations on the Treasury side of things, where concerted efforts were under way to enforce the policy of financial strangulation Adler had set forth to White. Records of this anti-Chiang campaign, including cables, memos and transcripts of meetings, reveal an astounding cast of players—White, Lauchlin Currie, V. Frank Coe, Harold Glasser, and Alger Hiss among them. And, when in the United States, Sol Adler would sit in as well. The operative principle seemed to be that at least two secret Moscow agents had to be in the room— and sometimes more than two—for the meetings to be official. The comrades must have been bumping into each other in the Treasury hallways as they made their way to these important sessions.

Especially notable were scenes in late 1944 and early '45, bracketing the Adler memo to White on cutting off the flow of funds to Chiang. In these conclaves, Morgenthau kept asking his staff about the gold loan promised to KMT finance minister Kung. The Secretary was being badgered by Kung and was asking his advisers why the gold was not delivered. They patiently explained that there were technical issues, shipping problems, glitches; and anyway, the gold would be wasted on the corrupt regime of Chiang. An extremely candid version of the matter would be supplied by White, who admitted in so many words that the loan had been deliberately obstructed.*[17]

After his amazingly frank discussion of the gold loan record, White still undertook to persuade Morgenthau that the Treasury had been right in its obstructionism, "because the money is being badly used." Others from time to time would discuss the issue with Morgenthau in similar fashion, suggesting that the gold be withheld or doled out in driblets. Among those arguing this were Adler, on one of his excursions back to D.C., and V. Frank Coe—who would

---

* "Mr. Secretary," he said, "we have always taken the position we had no legal grounds for withholding the gold; that what we were doing was skating on thin ice and offering excuses and getting by with it as long as we could, and remember because I said we are getting away with it that you better get the President's backing when the [Chinese] begin putting on the heat. It's because, I said, we have no basis for it. We have been successful over two years in keeping them down to twenty seven million and we never understood why the Chinese didn't take it in there [to FDR] and do what they are now doing. The whole thing is we had no basis for it."

later join with Adler in fleeing to Red China. All three of the Morgenthau advisers plying him with this counsel would show up in FBI records, congressional hearings, and *Venona* papers as Soviet agents.*

O N THE merits of what John Service did, as noted, much has been said down through the years to suggest he was merely "reporting" what he saw and couldn't be blamed for having done so. It's noteworthy, however, that what Service allegedly saw wasn't seen by other observers who knew far more about the relevant matters than did he. This was particularly true of his (and Adler's) repeated statements that only the Chinese Communists were fighting the Japanese, while Chiang Kai-shek did nothing.

Gen. Albert Wedemeyer, a true military expert in charge of the war against Japan in China for many months, would flatly contradict these Service-Adler statements. According to Wedemeyer, the Chinese Reds did little fighting against the Japanese and were no help to him in the conduct of the struggle. "No Communist Chinese forces," said Wedemeyer, "fought in any major battles of the Sino-Japanese war. . . ." From intelligence data he was receiving, he said, "I knew that Mao Tse-tung, Chou En-lai and the other Chinese Communist leaders were not interested in fighting the Japanese because their main concern was to occupy the territory which the Nationalist forces evacuated in their retreat."[†18]

In fact, as shown by historians familiar with the Chinese-language Communist sources, the truth of the matter went well beyond this. In his study of the OSS in China during World War II, Naval Academy historian Maochun Yu observes that tales of the Communists' "valiant fighting" (his quote marks) masked a policy of outright collaboration between Yenan and the Japanese invaders. He recounts one episode in which a U.S. reconnaissance team parachuted into northern China only to find the Communists and Japanese camped out a few miles apart and peacefully coexisting; another in which a Japanese puppet ruler was selling arms to the Yenan Reds for use against Chiang's army.

---

*Variations on such techniques abounded. One small but suggestive episode occurred when Kung was in the United States conferring with Morgenthau on financial matters. On hand as Morgenthau aides were White and Adler, while attending as adviser to Kung was Chi Chao-ting. Thus, as in other cases noted, the comrades had both sides of this particular session covered. At one point, Chi and Adler engaged in a technical argument over some piece of business, as though each were speaking up strongly for the interests of his country. In fact, the interests of neither the United States nor Nationalist China were represented in this bit of byplay, as the true masters of Soviet henchmen Chi and Adler were sitting thousands of miles away in Yenan and Moscow.

†So evident was the lack of Communist fighting that even Theodore White, an admirer of the Yenan Reds, was constrained to note the point, commenting that it wasn't the Reds "but the weary soldiers of the Central Government who took the shock, gnawed at the enemy, and died."

The Communists, in a not unusual pattern, were themselves doing what they (and Service) accused the KMT of doing.[19]

Similar findings emerge from other researches in the Chinese-language sources, most notably the definitive biography of Mao Tse-tung by Jung Chang (a former member of the Maoist Red Guards). This massive study, based on mainland Chinese data, makes it crystal clear that Mao had no intention of fighting the Japanese, instead leaving that unpleasant task to the hard-pressed armies of the KMT. This treatment fits the Wedemeyer comment like a glove: Mao's strategy was to let the Japanese destroy or drive out Chiang's forces then have the Communists move in when the Japanese pushed on to grab the territory Chiang relinquished.* On which evidence, the Service memos on this point were not only wrong but a complete inversion of the war-time record.†[20]

However, the clearest and most self-evident indication that Service wasn't "reporting" is simply the nature of his memos. Quite apart from their vengeful tone and spurious content, the most obvious thing about them is that they are works, not of reportage, but of special pleading. Somewhat guarded in the beginning, but increasingly strident later, the Service reports are little more than appeals for abandoning Chiang—again more closely resembling propaganda salvoes than any sort of factual update.

Service sounded this note, for instance, in June of 1944, when he asserted that "for many reasons . . . we might welcome the fall of the Kuomintang, if it could be followed by a progressive government able to unify the country and help us fight Japan . . ."[21] He would return to this thesis later, especially in his Memorandum No. 40, dated October 10, 1944, which was in essence a call for Chiang's overthrow. One of several such memos fired off in October, it was phrased in Adlerian terms of "getting tough" with Chiang, but made it clear that, in Service's view, the best way of getting tough was by toppling Chiang from power entirely. Herewith some samples:

"Our dealings with Chiang Kai-shek apparently continue on the basis of

---

*According to this author: "Mao didn't regard the Sino-Japanese war as a conflict in which all China would fight together against Japan. He did not see himself on the same side as Chiang at all. . . . The war was to him an opportunity to have Chiang destroyed by the Japanese. . . . Mao's basic plan, therefore, was to preserve his forces and expand the sphere of the Chinese Reds. . . . Mao did not want the Red army to fight the invader at all. He ordered Red commanders to wait for Japanese troops to defeat the Nationalists, and then, as the Japanese swept on, to seize territories below the Japanese line. . . . He bombarded his military commanders with telegrams such as 'Focus on creating base areas, not fighting battles.' . . . He said years later that his attitude had been, 'The more land Japan took, the better.'"

†A related point is that much of what Service reported was not what he himself had seen, or even professed to, but rather what he was told by others—especially journalists traveling in the region, who were overwhelmingly hostile to Chiang Kai-shek and favorable toward the Red insurgents. Two journalists whose observations about the alleged facts of Communist popularity with the peasants and staunch resistance to Japan got passed along by Service were Guenther Stein of the *Christian Science Monitor* and Israel Epstein, stringing for the *New York Times.* Both these "journalists," as it happened, would be identified as Soviet agents (Stein as a member of the Sorge spy ring) and thus perhaps not the most impartial sources Service could have consulted.

the unrealistic assumption that he is China and that he is necessary to our cause. . . . Under the present circumstances, the Kuomintang is dependent on American support for survival. But we are in no way dependent on the Kuomintang. We do not need it for military reasons. . . . We need not fear the collapse of the Kuomintang government. . . . We need not support the Kuomintang for international political reasons. . . . We need not support Chiang in the belief that he represents pro-American or democracy groups. . . . We need feel no ties of gratitude to Chiang. . . . There may by a period of some confusion, but the eventual gains from the Kuomintang's collapse will more than make up for this."[22]

Such was the "reporting" John Service provided to U.S. officials as a basis for policy making toward China. As with Linn Farish's take on Mihailovich and Tito and the Klugmann-vetted reports to London, there were people in high places who believed such things and would move to put them into practice. The result was perhaps the most unthinkable aspect of an unthinkable story: a long-running, remorseless U.S. vendetta against Chiang that didn't stop short of projected coup d'état and contemplated murder. (See Chapter 31.)

CHAPTER 9

Reds, Lies, and Audiotape

I N THE fall of 1944, having loosed his October thunderbolts at Chiang, John Service headed back to the United States for what was in essence a two-month furlough. The official purpose of the visit was to consult with his State Department bosses, which he did, but he also did some other things that would be even more critical for his future—and for the secret history of the Cold War.

One revealing aspect of this trip was that it brought Service, for the first time we know of, to the notice of the FBI. According to the Bureau records, he was on his return to have supplied a link between pro-Red forces on the ground in China and their confreres in the United States. As one FBI memo relates: "A highly confidential source, which is completely reliable, has advised that Max and Grace Granich, both of whom have been engaged in Communist and Comintern activities for many years, were advised in the fall of 1944 that Service was returning to Washington from China and that they should contact him because he could furnish fullest details as to the latest developments."[1]

Though omitted from the usual histories, this eye-catching bit of intel—gleaned from a mail intercept by Hoover's agents—would be of keen interest to the Bureau and security sleuths in Congress. Max and Grace Granich were well known to the FBI, appearing in numerous other updates on subversion.

They were also well known in China, where in 1936 and '37 they ran a Moscow-funded news sheet called *The Voice of China*. Their activities in the United States were of like nature, including involvement with the pro-Red journal *China Today,* part of a tangled web of groups and periodicals that agitated the China issue.

Whether the Service-Granich hookup occurred would be a topic pursued off and on by security forces—the results being inconclusive, but indicating Service probably met with Grace, though apparently not with Max.[2] In the meantime, we know for certain he met with others who shared the Granich mission and stance on China, as he would himself reveal this. As he told it in a State Department hearing, two of his main contacts on this trip were Lauchlin Currie and Harry White (a third being Harry Hopkins). This was an intriguing pair of names to mention, as neither Currie nor White was an official of the agency where Service worked. Both were, however, pro-Soviet moles, according to the testimony of Bentley-Chambers and disclosures of *Venona*.

Currie of course had plenty of reason to talk with Service, as China was Currie's portfolio in the White House, there was ongoing contact between them, and Service would perform, as he later put it, as Currie's "designated leaker." The two also had many influential friends in common, most notably Owen Lattimore and John Vincent. The White contact seems more puzzling at first glance, but makes sense when Service's ties to Adler are considered. White was Adler's boss and received regular updates from his minion in the field, re-layed to Morgenthau and others. White also obtained through Adler various reports of Service. There thus would have been no shortage of things for White to check out with the returning FSO.

Yet another intriguing Service link to White occurred in connection with this visit. Shortly after he got back to the United States, Service was asked to give an off-the-record briefing to the Washington branch of the IPR, and did so. In testifying about this talk, Service would somewhat oddly stress that he had official clearance to give it, saying: "I got approval. I talked to Mr. Hopkins, Mr. White, and various other people." Why Service needed approval from White to give this or any other talk was not explained, nor did anyone at the State Department hearing where he said this bother to ask this obvious question.[3]

At all events, Service did talk to the Washington IPR, and would thus plug into the shadowy network of pro-Red China watchers who would now figure decisively in his story. In attendance were the ubiquitous Lattimore, IPR employee Rose Yardumian, State Department official Julian Friedman (an aide to Vincent), and Friedman's friend and federal colleague, Andrew Roth. A former IPR researcher, Roth was at this time a lieutenant in the Far East division of the Office of Naval Intelligence (ONI), liaising with Vincent's

State Department office. He would prove to be a crucial liaison as well in the strange adventures of John Service.*

After his stopover in D.C., Service would head out to his home in California, where he would enjoy a bit of R&R and also pay a visit to the San Francisco office of OWI, yet another significant port of call. As seen, this office had been a subject of FBI inquiry, and according to Bureau records was a redoubt of staffers friendly to the Reds in China. As further reflected in the FBI updates, it was also a favorite stop for Service when in the United States, as he reportedly saw eye-to-eye with the people there who ran its propaganda efforts.

In January, following his California downtime, Service would return to China and take off for Yenan, but his new tour of duty there would be a short one. Back in Chungking, U.S. Ambassador Patrick Hurley had been perusing the anti-Chiang dispatches sent out by Service, especially the vitriolic No. 40, and didn't like what he was reading. He accordingly went on the warpath against Service and kindred FSOs (including John P. Davies) and demanded their recall from China. The result of this was that, by the spring of 1945, Service had been unceremoniously turned around again and sent home to Washington, where he would arrive on April 12, now nursing, if he hadn't before, a serious grudge against Pat Hurley.

O NCE back in D.C., Service would connect up again with the mysterious China-watching network, beginning, so far as the record shows, with Andy Roth. On April 18, Roth suggested to Service that there was a particular person he ought to meet. This turned out to be Philip Jaffe, editor of the pro-Communist journal *Amerasia*, whose memoirs we have quoted, a key member of the pro-Red China combine who according to the FBI reports had specifically asked Roth for an intro to Service.

Philip Jaffe was one of the more unusual characters in the murky byways of subversion. A Russian-born, naturalized U.S. citizen, he was a successful businessman (manufacturer of greeting cards) who seemed to have plenty of money to do the things he wanted. He was also a zealous Marxist and fervent supporter of the comrades at Yenan. (In 1937, he had made a pilgrimage there, along with Lattimore and T. A. Bisson, to meet with Mao and Chou En-lai.) The journal *Amerasia* was one of several propaganda sidelines through which Jaffe sought to advance the Communist cause in China.

---

*Though a bit player in the Service drama, Roth was an intriguing figure, if only for what his career revealed about security standards of the era. In addition to his work at IPR, he had publicly defended the activities of something called the "Free German Committee," a Communist operation based in Moscow. Despite this, he had been commissioned an intelligence officer in the Navy. The former head of ONI explained this, as quoted in a U.S. Senate report, by saying "The fact that an officer was a Communist was not a bar to a commission." As seen, this was a perfectly accurate statement of the wartime practice.

COMRADES

Left to right: Philip Jaffe, Nym Wales (Mrs. Edgar Snow), Owen Lattimore, Red Chinese leader Mao Tse-tung, T. A. Bisson, and Agnes Jaffe in Yenan, China, 1937.

Philip Jaffe Papers, Manuscript, Archives, and Rare Book Library, Emory University

When Roth suggested he meet with Jaffe, Service quickly followed up and the next afternoon saw the editor in his rooms at the Statler Hotel (the present-day Capital Hilton), a few blocks from the State Department offices of that era. This would prove for Service to be a fateful meeting, as it brought him again to the attention of the FBI, in even more incriminating fashion than his first appearance in Bureau records. It would be fateful also for the nation, as it led to one of the most bizarre, and ominous, spy cases in the annals of the Cold War.

For some weeks before this, the FBI had had Jaffe under tight surveillance, including telephone taps, planted microphones, and physical shadowing of his movements. The investigation stemmed from the discovery that elements of a confidential OSS memo had appeared, in some respects verbatim, in the pages of *Amerasia*. This had prompted OSS agents to do a surreptitious entry into Jaffe's New York office, where they found hundreds of U.S. government papers, many bearing "secret," "confidential," or "restricted" markings. In addition, the agents saw an elaborate photographic setup, the more suggestive as *Amerasia* ran no photos.

The OSS gumshoes also noted that, while the papers stemmed from many sources, most seemed to have transited the State Department. The matter was thus referred to State, which called in the FBI to solve the case and nail the culprits. So it was, beginning in mid-March, that the Bureau laid on a massive investigation, soon discovering what seemed to be a booming traffic in official papers being run through *Amerasia*. In the course of this inquest, it turned out that one of Jaffe's main government contacts was Roth. A second was a State Department employee named Emmanuel Larsen. A third frequent Jaffe contact, though unofficial, was journalist Mark Gayn, himself receiving papers from Jaffe. Now, a month into the investigation, the circle was expanded to include the much more imposing figure of John Service.

To judge by the surveillance records, Service seems to have had instant rapport with Jaffe. During their April 19 meeting at the Statler, the two engaged in a rambling talk that covers some twenty-five pages of Bureau transcript. Among other things, Service told Jaffe he had praised an article in *Amerasia* to "the boys at OWI in San Francisco" and said Jaffe was remembered in Yenan from his trip there in 1937. Jaffe replied by saying the recall of Service and others from China "had ruined everything we have been trying to do for years" and complained that he (Jaffe) had "been red-baited."

The conversation then turned to Service's housemates, Chi and Adler. In this context, Jaffe discussed his own links to Chi and praised the sixty-eight-page Service-Adler memo denouncing Chiang Kai-shek prepared for Henry Wallace, calling it "the finest summary written" on the China situation. Jaffe further said the memo had been passed around to general admiration at a recent confab of the IPR. Service voiced neither surprise nor dismay at this, nor did he ask how his confidential memo got into the hands of this private group. He did ask, however, whether his name had been mentioned as an author of the paper, and Jaffe assured him it hadn't.

The talk would then get down to hard specifics of the military scene in China, as Service discussed a commander with a high-sounding title but no troops to speak of, the allegiances of particular warlords, and leaders in the KMT army with varying loyalties to Chiang. All this between two people who, hours before, had presumably been perfect strangers.

The next day, Service upped the ante, bringing to lunch with Jaffe at the Statler a sheaf of papers the editor would take back to New York. This would be one of several such data exchanges, the total number of which would later be disputed. As the nature of the information would be contested also, an entry in the FBI record of this meeting is of interest, as follows: "Service, according to the microphone surveillance, apparently gave Jaffe a document which dealt with matters the [Nationalist] Chinese had furnished to the United States government in confidence. Service stated that the person with whom he was associated in China would 'get his neck pretty badly wrung' if the information got out."

In subsequent conversation, Service would discuss another military issue—the possibility of American forces coming ashore in China, and if so where. This was at the time a topic of importance, as the site of such a landing could have determined whether U.S. troops would link up with the armies of Chiang Kai-shek or with the Communists farther north. Service's comments on this, as recorded by the FBI, were as follows:

> Well, what I said about the military plans is, of course, very secret. . . . That plan was made by Wedemeyer's staff in his absence; they got orders to make some recommendations as to what we should do if we landed in Communist territory . . . they showed me the plans that had been drawn up . . . when we were in Chungking territory, we would have to go on cooperating with them. Those were the orders. But if we landed where the Communists were, without any question they'd be the dominant force.[4]*

All told, Service and Jaffe had at least five such tête-à-têtes in Washington and then on the editor's turf in New York City when Service went there a few weeks later. Also in New York, there would be a series of Service-Jaffe get-togethers with the *Amerasia* crowd—a party at the home of the magazine's co-editor, Kate Mitchell, a Service sleepover at the Gayn apartment, and a group outing to the Long Island digs of T. A. Bisson. There would be also, as in D.C., a Service meeting with staffers of the IPR. All this obviously pleased Jaffe, who according to one FBI memo told an acquaintance on May 15, "Jack Service was in solid."[5] And so, to judge by this incessant round of contacts, he was.

That, however, was only half the story. While these convivial sessions were occurring, agents of the FBI were tracking a lot of other goings-on that riveted their attention. The indefatigable Jaffe, they found, was shuttling back and forth between his Service meetings and yet another set of contacts. These included Communist Party chief Earl Browder, a visiting Red Chinese bigwig from the Maoist stronghold at Yenan, and officials at the Soviet consulate in New York City. An FBI summary on all this informs us:

> In the course of the investigation . . . Jaffe was observed to enter the Soviet consulate in New York on May 31, 1945. He met with Earl Browder, the head of the Communist Party, on four occasions during the investigation. Jaffe also had meetings with Tung Pi-wu, the Chinese Communist representative to the United Nations conference. On April 22, 1945, Browder and his secretary Harold Smith entered Jaffe's residence at 10 a.m. At 10:20 a.m., Tung Pi-wu accompanied by two unidentified Chinese arrived. At 1 p.m. Browder, Smith and Mrs. Jaffe left the premises, returning in half an hour.

---

*Nor was this Service's only comment on the subject. In another exchange, Jaffe came back to the question and Service once more showed his willingness to share military information with his new acquaintance. Jaffe: "Jack, do you think we'll land on the shores of China?" Service: "I don't believe it's been decided. I can tell you in a couple of weeks when Stilwell gets back."

Shortly after 3 p.m., Browder, Smith, Tung Pi-wu and the two Chinese left Jaffe's home.[6]

This nearly five-hour meeting of Jaffe, Browder, and a top Red Chinese official occurred just two days after Jaffe lunched with Service at the Statler, obtaining the documents he would take back to New York. As the Bureau would observe, this marathon session offered ample chance for Jaffe to share with Browder and Tung Pi-wu whatever information was acquired from Service. (A surmise supported by a later Jaffe comment concerning a particular memo: "That's the one Tung Pi-wu didn't want me to publish when he was here.")[7]

Reflecting Jaffe's willingness to provide such materials to members of the Communist global apparatus were still other of his amazing contacts. On May 2, FBI agents surveilled him conferring with Soviet espionage agent Joseph Bernstein, the former *Amerasia* staffer who appears in *Venona* receiving government data from T. A. Bisson. Bernstein knew of Jaffe's ability to come up with official papers and wanted to tap his inside sources. As Jaffe told it, Bernstein made no bones about the fact that he was a spy for Moscow. According to one Bureau wrap-up:

> . . . on May 7, 1945, Jaffe advised Roth that several days previous to their conversation, he had luncheon with an individual subsequently identified as Joseph Milton Bernstein. Jaffe advised Roth that Bernstein had told him he was presently working for a Russian agent and has previously been employed by other Russian espionage agents. Bernstein requested Jaffe to furnish him with Jaffe's sources in the Far Eastern division of the State Department.*[8]

As to Jaffe's periodical, the Bureau made other discoveries that swung things back in the direction of Max and Grace Granich. *Amerasia,* it developed, was a kind of joint descendant of the pro-Communist publications, *Voice of China* and *China Today.* The latter, also edited by Jaffe, was the journal of a subsequently cited Communist front called the American Friends of the Chinese People. Well-known pro-Reds involved in this endeavor—Jaffe, Bisson, Chi, Frederick Field—were likewise on the board of *Amerasia.* All of which suggested to Hoover's agents that they were surveilling something more than an obscure policy-wonk publication with an eccentric taste for secret papers.

---

*This project appealed to Jaffe but also made him nervous. Not that Bernstein was a Soviet spy, but rather that he just possibly wasn't. Suppose Bernstein was a government plant only pretending to work for Moscow? This angle bothered Jaffe, who took pains to check the matter out with Browder and the editor of the Communist *New Masses.* Both advised him he should require Bernstein to say for whom he was working, and by backtracking on this certify his reliability. If Bernstein really were a Soviet spy, he would be "reliable." If not, then not. FBI records show Bernstein in frequent contact with top Soviet agent Gerhart Eisler.

To close the circle, the FBI made four nocturnal visits to the *Amerasia* offices to check out the documents held there. Bureau agents photographed some of these and shared the photos with Justice attorneys to indicate the kind of evidence to be had if arrests were made and papers seized. On this basis, Justice higher-ups decided to proceed with arrests and prosecution. Accordingly, on June 6, FBI agents swooped down on the suspects and took six people into custody: Jaffe, Mark Gayn, and Kate Mitchell in New York; Service, Andy Roth, and Emmanuel Larsen in D.C.

In the course of the arrests, the FBI impounded roughly 1,000 documents from the *Amerasia* office, the apartments of Gayn and Larsen, and the State Department office of Service. On the analysis of the Bureau, about a quarter of these papers concerned military matters in whole or part, and many bore the warning that unauthorized possession was a violation of the Espionage Act. It was, in the view of FBI Director Hoover, "an airtight case," primed and ready for prosecution. (See Chapter 27.)*

And so at first it seemed. In a matter of days, however, the outlook for successful prosecution would be mysteriously altered. At the public level a hue and cry was raised, mostly in the radical press, to the effect that the defendants were being railroaded by evil forces. Simultaneous with this protest, efforts were unfolding behind the scenes to delay the prosecution, and plans to present indictments slacked off and then were halted. As the term of the sitting grand jury was to expire July 2, Justice decided the case should be held over for another. All this was troubling to Hoover, who wrote on June 30: "This is most unfortunate. Case should go to present grand jury, indictments obtained and case set for trial. I don't like all the manipulation which is going on."[9]

These misgivings were well-founded. When a second grand jury was empaneled and Justice made its presentation, the "airtight case" had somehow been punctured, and now collapsed entirely. On August 10, Service, Mitchell, and Gayn were all no-billed—allowed to walk scot-free—while indictments of relatively minor nature were returned against Jaffe, Roth, and Larsen. And when push came to shove, these indictments themselves amounted to little.

For reasons that weren't made clear, the main federal prosecutor chosen to handle these cases was one Robert Hitchcock, called in from upstate New York to be the government's lead attorney. His conduct of the matter seemed, at best, eccentric. At the Jaffe trial, for instance, Jaffe's lawyer said his client indeed had official papers in his possession but "the government does not

---

* Shortly after the arrests, Acting Secretary Joseph Grew would speak likewise for the State Department, saying a "comprehensive security program" was being enforced to stop "the illegal and disloyal conveyance of confidential and other secret information to unauthorized persons." He added that "we heard somebody in the chicken coop and we went to see who was there . . . ample grounds were found to cause the arrests and bring about the charges."

contend that any of the material was used for disloyal purposes." He added that if Jaffe had transgressed, "it seems he has done so from an excess of journalistic zeal." Asked by Judge James Proctor if he agreed, Hitchcock responded: "In substance, yes, your honor. To us, it was largely for the purpose of lending credibility to the publication itself, and perhaps increase its circulation and prestige."

In these brief and amicable proceedings, no word was spoken by Hitchcock about Jaffe's pro-Communist background and connections, the pro-Red nature of his publication, or his meetings with Communist Party chief Earl Browder, Chinese Red leader Tung Pi-wu, officials at the Soviet consulate in New York and the Soviet agent Bernstein. Jaffe was simply depicted, by both defense and prosecution, as a "journalist" who had gone a bit too far with his reporting but hadn't really meant any harm by his aggressive methods.

Thus advised, the judge told Jaffe he accepted "without any doubt the assurance both of your counsel and of the government attorneys that there was no thought or act on your part" injurious to security interests, said Jaffe should be more careful in the future, and fined him $2,500. A few weeks later, a similar drill would occur with Larsen. Thereafter, the charges against Roth were quietly dropped. As far as the federal courts were concerned, the *Amerasia* case was over.[10]

As a political issue, however, it was just beginning. In short order, the handling of the case would come in for pungent criticism from Rep. George Dondero (R-Mich.) and others in Congress, who wondered how such an important case could so quickly and completely crumble. After repeated urgings by Dondero, an investigation of sorts was mounted, chaired by Rep. Sam Hobbs (D-Ala.). This was the first of several inquiries about the case that played out over the next few years; it was also among the most peculiar.

The Hobbs hearings were conducted in executive session, with witnesses not sworn, and a transcript wouldn't be published until four years later, in the midst of the McCarthy furor. The majority members of the panel did, however, file a report that said there was nothing wrong with the way the case was handled and that problems in the prosecution stemmed from errors in seizing evidence in the first place. As Justice official James McGranery told the committee, "None of this evidence was obtained in the manner in which we ordinarily get it. It was very clumsily handled."[11]

In addition to dumping on the methods of securing evidence, which meant dumping on the FBI, Justice spokesmen Hitchcock and James McInerney had downplayed the importance of the purloined papers. In a phrase that would be much repeated, Hitchcock described them as nothing more than "teacup gossip." He also reprised the stance he took at the trial of Jaffe, saying, "We had no evidence of any use to which they were put which was disloyal."[12]

The Hobbs majority bought all this, but the FBI emphatically didn't. When Hoover and his men learned about these statements, they went ballistic, and would set forth in some detail their version of what had happened, their methods of investigation, and the nature of the recovered papers. As the FBI had the documents in its custody, and had studied them with care, it knew they were something other than "teacup gossip."

However, the FBI knew more than this, and its knowledge would fan the flames of outrage even higher. It knew the prosecution had been crudely fixed, and that the very Justice spokesmen who now talked down the case had been complicit in the fixing. The Bureau knew this because it had wiretapped the fixers and had the logs of phone calls in which officials at Justice and elsewhere conspired to throw the case and free John Service.

These wiretaps had been ordered by President Truman for reasons unrelated to *Amerasia*. The new President had certain suspicions concerning veteran New Deal wheelhorse Thomas "Tommy the Cork" Corcoran and had put the Bureau on his trail. In tapping Corcoran, the FBI found him waist-deep in the *Amerasia* quagmire, working with Service's friend and mentor Lauchlin Currie in the White House and higher-ups at Justice to make sure the FSO was not indicted. The taps further showed, per Corcoran's statements, that his longtime partner Benjamin Cohen, soon to be a top official at State, was involved as well, though remaining in the background.*

In these talks, the common premise was that the case would unquestionably be fixed and that Service would walk free and clear from any legal sanctions. Not one of the people being tapped, according to the Bureau records, dissented from this felonious project. There was, however, disagreement among the fixers on how to do it. Corcoran wanted Service to skip the grand jury altogether on the grounds that any such appearance was risky. McInerney, Hitchcock, and Tom Clark, the newly named Attorney General replacing Francis Biddle, thought it better to have Service "cleared" by making an appearance. Corcoran at last consented when assured that there would be no slipup. The following excerpts from the wiretap logs suggest the flavor:[13]

Corcoran to Lauchlin Currie

CORCORAN: What I want to do is get the guy [Service] out. These other fellows want to make a Dreyfus case out of it.

CURRIE: Yeah, the important thing is to get him out.

• • •

---

*On September 15, 1945, a month after the no-billing of Service, Cohen would be named Counselor to the Department. This was the same appointments package that made Dean Acheson Under Secretary of State, replacing Joseph Grew, and named William Benton as an Assistant Secretary. (See Chapter 12.)

CORCORAN: . . . I think our problem is to take care of this kid. Isn't it?

CURRIE: That's right.

• • •

CURRIE: . . . Is this right, Tom? The state undertakes to make its case, the government makes its case why there should be a hearing or a trial, but the defense doesn't answer.

CORCORAN: That's right. He doesn't have to say a damn word.

Corcoran to John Service

CORCORAN: . . . I talked to the Attorney General [Clark] yesterday himself. . . . And again I told him about the understandings we had below about the cutting out of your name before, so there wouldn't be any necessity for your going before the grand jury at all. . . . I did want you to know I'd gone right to the top on this damn thing, and I'm quite sure I'll get it cut out.

Corcoran to James McGranery

CORCORAN: He [Service] was an awfully close friend of Ben's [Cohen] and Ben hoped I'd communicate his concern about this thing to you and Tom Clark. . . . I did communicate this to Tom Clark . . . that Ben's friends over in the State Department told me that McInerney called Service and said, ". . . we know we've got nothing on you, but . . . we think you would like to go yourself before a grand jury on Friday and make a statement yourself that will clear you." And then McInerney said, "I should think the grand jury would clear the whole thing up for you."

• • •

McGRANERY: Well, if what you said in the first instance is correct—that they don't have anything—then why bother with it at all?

CORCORAN: I think they're saying to him, it will be a nice thing for you to do this in order that the grand jury may clear you. I don't think it's smart.

McGRANERY: I'll check it out for you, Tom.

• • •

CORCORAN: Jim, on that thing Ben Cohen told me to watch that I told you about—did you learn anything?

McGRANERY: I didn't get it yet, but I'll watch it for you. . . . I'll take care of it for you. Your man is Service. I got it.

CORCORAN: Yeah. So that we can cut him out. OK?

McGRANERY: All right, Tom.

Corcoran to Tom Clark

CORCORAN: Well, aren't you always afraid of a grand jury and inexperienced people in front of them?

CLARK: Well, I'll tell you, if these boys were antagonistic, I'd say yes. . . . But in this case, from what I understand this morning from these people they don't have any such idea.

CORCORAN: Well, I'm awfully glad of that.

Corcoran to Service

SERVICE: Munter [Service's attorney] talked to Hitchcock yesterday to say I hadn't made up my mind yet and Hitchcock said, "Well, I hope you realize by this time that we want to have Service cleared by a legal body," and Hitchcock is still anxious to have me appear.

CORCORAN: Well, let me put another call in. Only thing is, when I have a flat deal like that you are going to be cleared. . . . I don't like anyone to have to talk before a grand jury.

SERVICE: Well, the statement by Hitchcock yesterday was the most encouraging . . .

CORCORAN: The signals have gone down that you are not to be in this thing. Up at the top the advice is they don't want you to go in there.

• • •

SERVICE: I talked to him [Hitchcock] again and he says he wants to clear me, but it would be very hard for him to do it, and that if I appear before a grand jury and make as good an impression as . . .

• • •

SERVICE: Well, the way Hitchcock talks, there wasn't much chance of clearing myself unless I made an appearance as Exhibit A.

• • •

CORCORAN (*after the decision was reached to go ahead to the grand jury*): Don't worry when you go in. This is double riveted from top to bottom.

Corcoran to McGranery

MCGRANERY: [James] McInerney said that he'd take personal responsibility to see that nothing happened.

Corcoran to Service

CORCORAN: We checked with the A.G. [Tom Clark] and understand that you are all right. Do you feel you are?

SERVICE: Yes.

Nor was Service the only beneficiary of such benign attentions. Indeed, all the *Amerasia* suspects would gain from this solicitude for Service, as it would have been next to impossible to get him off if the facts about Jaffe and all the others had been aired in court. Also, it happened that *Amerasia* co-editor Kate Mitchell had some contacts of her own. Her uncle was an influential attorney in Buffalo, New York, a partner in the same prestigious law firm that, by an odd coincidence, would later become the employer of Robert Hitchcock. Through her uncle, Mitchell obtained a high-powered lawyer in New York City with connections at Truman Justice, which he used to assure her of kindly treatment by the prosecution.*

---

*As recorded in the Bureau transcripts, Mitchell's lawyer told her he had talked with Tom Clark and thereafter with prosecutor Hitchcock. The latter, according to the attorney, said he would meet with

All such assurances would prove to be on target. Service was no-billed by the grand jury in a vote of 20–0, Mitchell by a vote of 18–2, Gayn by a vote of 15–5. Thereafter, the State Department, Service himself, and a legion of his defenders would claim his innocence was now established and that he should never have been arrested in the first place. J. Edgar Hoover and his men, pondering their stash of wiretaps, would reach a very different verdict.

Mitchell in private "the day before we take her to the grand jury so that she would know just what it was going to ask her because I wouldn't like to take her before the grand jury cold. I don't think it would be fair to her."

CHAPTER 10

When Parallels Converged

T HE case of Philip Jaffe's confederate Emmanuel Larsen was settled on November 2, 1945, thus stuffing all but a few scattered remnants of the *Amerasia* scandal into the closet at Truman Justice. That door had, for the moment, closed. Others, however, were about to open.

On November 7, Soviet espionage courier Elizabeth Bentley, having hesitated for some weeks, decided to complete her break with the Communist Party and its Moscow bosses and tell her story to the FBI. It was a compelling saga that jolted even the streetwise, seen-everything agents of the Bureau. And it would move surveillance of pro-Red penetration of American life and institutions to new, hair-raising levels.

In many ways, Bentley was the most important of the ex-Communist witnesses of the era. To say this is no slight to Whittaker Chambers, whose story has been more fully told, most famously in his own moving apologia, *Witness*, and whose confrontation with Alger Hiss would be the stuff of Cold War legend. Yet, measured by what's in official records, the testimony of Bentley had greater impact—far more than one would gather from the usual treatments.

Betty Bentley, as she was known, came from a respectable New England family and was an intelligent, well-educated woman—a graduate of Vassar who did further academic work at Columbia and Italy's University of Florence. Like others of her generation, she was drawn to the Marxist creed for both intellectual and personal reasons. In 1935, she joined the Communist Party, and four years later met Soviet master spy Jacob Golos (real name Jacob Raisin), who would become her mentor, friend, and lover.

Golos, a Russian, was one of the top-ranking Moscow agents in the United States, with far-reaching authority over espionage and other operations. He was, however, in ill health (he would die of heart failure in November 1943) and was already on the radar screens of the Bureau from a previous run-in. For these and other reasons, he used Bentley as a go-between in many dealings. An articulate, native-born American, she could go places and talk to people in a way the obviously foreign Golos couldn't.

Bentley spent some ten years in the party, five as courier and Golos assistant, two more after his death as manager of their many official contacts. In this role, she went back and forth between her Manhattan base and Washington, D.C., where she met regularly with a formidable crowd of Communists and fellow travelers, mostly federal workers moonlighting for the Soviet interest (though sometimes told, as a salve to conscience, that they were merely helping out Earl Browder). On these visits, she collected purloined official data, often in documentary-photographic form, and dues money for the party.

Bentley's knowledge of the Soviet/Communist setup was thus extensive and, at the time she went to the FBI, fairly current. This she proceeded to divulge in a protracted series of debriefings. Before she was done, she would name approximately 150 people as members of or collaborators with the network, many of whom had been in the federal government, or still were, and who had been involved in spying, job placement for fellow Reds, policy sabotage, and pro-Communist propaganda efforts. For the FBI, it was probably the single greatest data haul of the Cold War, rivaled only by *Venona*.

Not that the Bureau simply took Bentley's word about such matters. After recording elements of her story, Hoover's men set out to check the material she provided. In one vivid instance, she told them cell leader Nathan Gregory Silvermaster had a photographic laboratory in his basement, used for copying official papers. The Bureau confirmed the existence of this setup by the disarmingly direct technique of entering the basement, there observing—and photographing—the photographic apparatus.[1]

More typically, the FBI found that much of the Bentley information could be verified from other sources—which members of the group were in close contact with others, where they worked, whom they worked for. Time and again, the Bureau noted, details supplied by Bentley would be confirmed by its backtracking methods. Equally important, there were overlaps between the Bentley cases and disclosures from other investigations, including the seminal Louise Bransten–Gregori Kheifetz inquest of the early 1940s involving the Radiation Lab at Berkeley.

As for *Amerasia,* this was of course fresh in memory for Hoover's agents, and some Bentley revelations concerned players in that drama—Sol Adler, Lauchlin Currie, Frederick Field, and others. The Bureau also went back and looked at its Chambers file and found that, in many cases, suspects named by Bentley were named by Chambers also. Alger Hiss was one such, Currie another, Sol Adler yet another. Also, at this period, other witnesses were emerging who would add to the mosaic. In September of 1945, Igor Gouzenko, a Russian code clerk, had bolted from the Soviet embassy in Canada, and in October Louis Budenz, managing editor of the *Daily Worker,* defected from the Communist Party. Both would provide information congruent with the Bentley-Chambers data.

However, by far the main development in the case was the FBI's decision to lay on a dragnet investigation of Bentley's suspects. At the outset, the Bureau focused on fifty-one of these, of whom it found some two dozen or so then working for the federal government (a number that would later grow), and zoomed in closely on the latter. Others who had recently left the federal payroll—most notably, Currie—were on the watch list also.

From this roundup the FBI assembled a massive file on Bentley's people. Somewhat confusingly called the "Gregory" case (the Bureau's code name for Bentley), this file takes up some 50,000 pages in the declassified FOIA archives and touches on literally thousands of people, scores and possibly hundreds of whom would become potential cases in their own right.* The network, as the Bureau soon discovered, extended out in all directions. There were government staffers in contact with the Bentley people, contacts of those contacts, and so on in ever-widening circles. Also, deeper in the shadows, were identified Russian agents or, in some cases, Red diplomats stationed in D.C. who had dealings with the Bentley suspects.

Piecing all this together, the FBI began to revise its thinking on the nature of the Communist penetration problem. Its West Coast inquiry had spotlighted workers at the Berkeley Lab with links to the Bransten-Kheifetz combine. *Amerasia* had been an eye-opening experience for the Bureau, but the government staffers in that case were few in number. The picture emerging from those probes was one in which sinister outside forces were trying to develop official contacts, and in some cases succeeding, certainly bad enough but seemingly finite and focused.

The Gregory case showed something different—something not only large but already inside the gates, rather than outside looking in. What the Bureau now found itself observing was a vast infiltration, the extent of which was as yet unclear, that affected nearly every significant aspect of the government,

---

*These declassified pages, apparently, amount to only a small fraction—10 percent, perhaps—of the total Bentley records. The "Gregory" designation was confusing because the main suspect in the case, Nathan Gregory Silvermaster, went by this name as well.

including many officials in key positions. (And this didn't include the New York angle, involving still other Bentley cases.)

An early attempt to chart this network was made by Special Agent Fred Youngblood in December of 1945, based on the initial Bentley statements.[2] (See page 127.) Complex as it was, this graphic was a mere beginning, omitting many important players who would come to view as the probe unfolded. As the scope of the problem became apparent, it jarred the FBI out of its usual uninflected Jack Webb prose to what were, for the Bureau, flights of rhetorical fervor. As Chief Special Agent Guy Hottel summed up the matter in a March 1946 memo to Hoover:

> It has become increasingly clear in the investigation of this case that there are a tremendous number of persons employed in the United States government who are Communists and strive daily to advance the cause of Communism and destroy the foundations of this government. . . . Today nearly every department or agency of this government is infiltrated with them in varying degree. To aggravate the situation they appear to have concentrated most heavily in those departments which make policy, particularly in the international field, or carry it into effect. . . . Such organizations as the State and Treasury departments, FEA, OSS, WPB, etc.* Apart from the Russian espionage inherent in this case, there has emerged already the picture of a large, energetic and capable number of Communists, including our suspects, who operate daily in the legislative field, as well as in the executive branch of government . . .[3]

In terms of formal structure, the FBI had found, Soviet espionage and influence operations were usually set up in "parallels"—the term used by the Soviets themselves and adopted by the Bureau. As the word suggests, the clandestine units were supposed to be separate and discreet, not intersecting or overlapping. This was good tradecraft, since it ensured that if one group were blown, it wouldn't lead the authorities to others. Also, having multiple information circuits, the Soviets could compare the data-take from several sources for greater certainty of knowledge.

However, the Bureau also found, the "parallel" image wasn't a very good description of what it was now surveilling. There were indeed separate cells in Bentley's combine, one being the Silvermaster group, another a smaller group headed by a Victor Perlo, plus singleton agents here and there with whom she was working. But the Washington suspects generally speaking weren't very separate, and in some cases weren't discreet. Most of the main figures seemed to know one another, and if they weren't directly linked usually had contacts in common. They also had a penchant for crossing departmental or divisional

---

*FEA = Federal Economic Administration, successor to the Board of Economic Warfare. WPB = War Production Board.

THE FBI CHARTS
THE SOVIET NETWORKS

This December 1945 diagram represents an early FBI effort to trace the many interconnections among American suspects and Soviet agents in the Elizabeth Bentley–"Gregory" investigation.

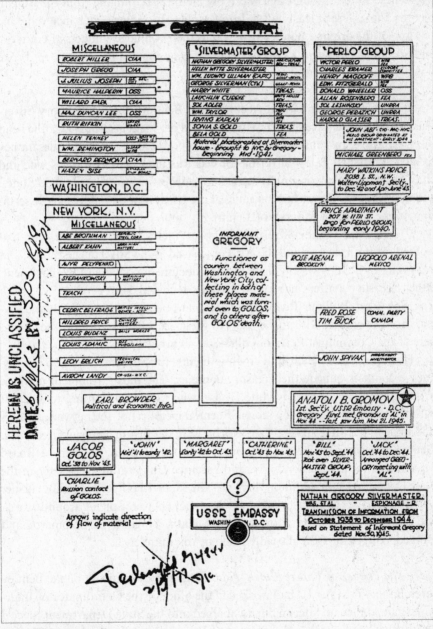

Source: FBI Silvermaster file

lines, talking among themselves, and gathering in social/political conclaves. Far from being true parallels, the lines crisscrossed at many places.

The resulting hologram seen by the Bureau might best be described, not in terms of linear tables, but as a series of overlapping affinity groups or clusters. These were often based on personal friendship or common avocation as much as job description, though that was a big factor also. Judging from the Bureau records, there were at least half a dozen of these groupings, each including one or more of the original Bentley people plus their contacts, contacts of contacts, and so on *ad infinitum*. Looked at in this way, the cast of characters broke down, in part, as follows:[4]

• *The Silvermaster Circle.* According to Bentley, Nathan Gregory Silvermaster, then of the Treasury Department, was her main agent in D.C., the head of an extensive spy consortium that copied official papers and paid dues money to the Communist Party. Silvermaster was Russian-born, as was his wife and chief assistant Helen, originally settled on the West Coast of the United States, and had taken his degree in economics at the University of California (dissertation on the economic theories of Lenin).

Closely linked to the Silvermasters was William Ludwig Ullman, who had worked for the Treasury and the Air Force, lived at the Silvermaster home, and according to Bentley was in charge of the document copying in the basement. Other Treasury staffers named by Bentley included Harry White, V. Frank Coe, Sol Adler, William Taylor, Irving Kaplan, Bela and Sonia Gold, and several more in contact with this circle. All these, said Bentley, were either members of the Communist Party or collaborators in the apparatus.

However, true to their line-crossing habits, the Silvermasters also had extensive contacts outside the Treasury complex. The most prominent of these was Lauchlin Currie in the White House, who ranked, according to Bentley, with Harry White among the most influential members of the network. Others said to be in the Silvermaster-Currie orbit were the Briton Michael Greenberg, George Silverman, a former economist with the Railway Retirement Board who transferred to the Pentagon, and Maurice Halperin of OSS, later in the State Department. In addition, there was the smaller Perlo group, whose leader was then also at the Treasury and whose members were spread around at several outposts (Alger Hiss, Harold Glasser, Harry Magdoff of Commerce, and Donald Wheeler of OSS allegedly being of this number).[5]

• *The Friends of Robert Miller.* Among the most significant of the Bentley cases, Robert T. Miller III had worked in the office of the Coordinator of Inter-American Affairs, an interim bureau merged into the State Department toward the conclusion of the war. A graduate of Princeton, Miller was among the hyperrespectable, unthinkable class of pro-Soviet moles, along the lines of Alger

Hiss or the Cambridge group in England. In the 1930s, he had hied off to Russia and married an American woman, Jenny Levy, who worked at the *Moscow Daily News*. Before entering the government, he published a leftward news sheet on Latin affairs called *Hemisphere* in conjunction with Joseph Gregg, yet another Bentley suspect.

The *Hemisphere* operation would be merged into CIAA, and then again into State. As a result of these transitions, Miller ended up bringing with him to the department several people who had been with him in his previous ventures. The extensive Miller-connected group surveilled by the FBI included Gregg, Philip Raine, Dwight Mallon, E. J. Askwith, Willard Park, Florence Levy, Minter Wood, and Bernard Redmont. Another Miller associate at State—indeed one of his closest allies—was former Budget Bureau official Rowena Rommel.[6] (Various of these Miller contacts—and Miller himself—would show up later in the lists of suspects compiled by Joe McCarthy.)*

• *Alumni of OSS/OWI.* There were numerous transferees from these wartime units still at work in the federal government in the fall of 1945, particularly in the State Department, and Bentley's suspects reflected this migration. The OSS staffers she named as Communists or collaborators with her group included Maurice Halperin, Duncan Lee, Julius Joseph, Helen Tenney (from Short Wave Inc.), and Donald Wheeler. Of these, Halperin and Wheeler moved on to State, while Duncan Lee, a China specialist, would go to work for Thomas Corcoran, now finished with his *Amerasia* labors. Other OSS alumni at the State Department, spotted in the investigation, included Woodrow Borah, Carl Marzani, and David Zablodowsky, a name met with in the testimony of General Donovan before the Thomason subcommittee eight months before this.

While OSS supplied a mother lode of Bentley suspects, OWI contributed also. Some staffers of this agency who had already come to the notice of the FBI have been mentioned in Chapter 7. To the people on that roster, Bentley would add the name of Peter Rhodes, while the FBI investigation would identify still more—Edward Rosskam, Inez Munoz, Alix Reuther, and several others.[7]

• *The Hiss Connection.* Though Chambers was the main witness against Hiss, Bentley would say she knew Hiss to be an agent of the Soviet interest (as would ex-Communists Hede Massing, Nathaniel Weyl, and Budenz). Based on the Chambers-Bentley allegations, the Bureau would zero in not only on Hiss

---

*Of this group Gregg, Park, and Redmont were on the original list of Bentley cases, while the rest were developed through surveillance. Florence Levy was Miller's sister-in-law, and Philip Raine was both a coworker and personal friend of Miller. Rowena Rommel, a much-neglected player, had been instrumental, as she later acknowledged, in bringing Miller himself to State. (Miller would supply another case in which the Bureau was able to give independent confirmation to Bentley, as the FBI had surveilled him in 1941 in personal contact with Golos.)

himself but on his coworkers and allies. As is well known, this became a major investigation in its own right, eventually the most famous of them all, with a totally separate, extensive file in Bureau records.

In the course of this inquiry, the Bureau followed up on a sizable number of Hiss contacts whose names would later appear in security records at State and committees of Congress. This group included Henry Collins, Richard Post, and Julian Wadleigh (all named by Chambers as members of his network). Other more recent Hiss colleagues, not so identified by Chambers but considered by State Department security sleuths to be especially close to Hiss, included Donald Blaisdell, Clarence Nelson, George Rothwell, Paul Appleby, and George Scharzwalder.[8]

• **Amerasia** *and IPR.* While the Bureau was of course intensely conscious of *Amerasia* before it ever talked to Bentley (collaterally but less so of IPR), her testimony would fill in certain blanks and add some further names to the list of suspects in that ongoing investigation. Among those in the *Amerasia*/IPR connection on whom she would provide additional data were Sol Adler, Lauchlin Currie, Frederick Field, Duncan Lee, and Michael Greenberg.

In addition, Bentley would tell the Bureau about the Price sisters, Mildred and Mary, alleged members of the Golos network. Mildred was one of the *Amerasia*/IPR-style activists on China, while Mary had been a staffer for the columnist Walter Lippmann. The Prices, Bentley told the Bureau, were particularly close to Duncan Lee. (Mary also played hostess to meetings of the Perlo group, including OSS employee Donald Wheeler.) Other contacts of Lee, spotted in the investigation, were Robert and Patricia Barnett, both former staffers at IPR (she also formerly of OSS) and both now on the payroll at State.[9]

• *Mary Jane and Philip Keeney.* Though not original Bentley cases, the Keeneys were known to the Bureau from other probes and turned out to have innumerable contacts with her suspects. Indeed, there seemed to be few people in Communist, pro-Communist, and fellow traveling circles they didn't know. Through their multifarious dealings, the Keeneys—especially Mary Jane—came to occupy a special niche in the burgeoning archives of the Bureau. (Both Keeneys show up in *Venona* but were well known to the FBI before it received the decrypts.)

Mary Jane had been at the Board of Economic Warfare, then moved briefly to the State Department, thence to the United Nations. Philip worked at the Library of Congress and OSS, then shipped overseas to help with the occupation of Japan. The Keeneys' range of contacts was prodigious. They knew the Silvermasters, were friends of Max and Grace Granich, were in touch with Philip Jaffe and Joseph Bernstein, hobnobbed with the Owen Lattimores, were friendly with Maurice Halperin of OSS, and had many other such connections. Some of these were unheralded figures who nonetheless show up often in security records: Lois Carlisle, Sylvia Schimmel, and Bowen Smith of the State Department, Alix Reuther of OWI and the War Department, Stanley Graze of OSS and State, David Wahl of BEW, and a formidable list of others.

The Keeneys also had frequent dealings, recorded by the Bureau, with the already noted "Colonel Thomas" (Soviet agent Sergei Kournakov), Samuel Krafsur and Laurence Todd of the Soviet news agency TASS, Czech official Vladimir Houdek, Bulgarian diplomat Boyan Athanassov, and several more of like persuasion. In the manner of Philip Jaffe, Mary Jane moved tirelessly back and forth among officials of the U.S. government, shadowy activists of the left, and identified Soviet or other East bloc agents.[10]

L OOKING at this somewhat bewildering array of people—merely a sample of what's in the records—the Bureau observed a number of items that proved useful in understanding the way things functioned. First, from the interconnections among the suspects, it became apparent that the targets of the various investigations then in progress were at some level all parts of a vast phenomenon, rather than totally distinct endeavors. Whether it was snooping at the Berkeley Lab, purloined papers at *Amerasia,* moles at OWI and OSS, or Soviet agents at Treasury or State, the same names kept popping up from one inquiry to another.

Thus, to take a few examples, Nathan Gregory Silvermaster, who started out on the West Coast, was a close contact of Louise Bransten and of her fellow Communist Steve Nelson. Silvermaster was also acquainted with the Communist writer Bruce Minton, whose real name was Richard Bransten and who was the ex-husband of Louise Bransten.

When they moved East, the Silvermasters connected up with Robert Miller, who was in continuing contact with Maurice Halperin and others from OSS. Halperin and Willard Park were in turn linked with Richard Bransten/Minton. Asking him for contacts in D.C., said Bentley, they were referred to Golos and thus became a part of her apparatus. Park would also be in contact, according to the FBI reports, with Louise Bransten, a cousin of his wife. As Halperin would later aptly comment, "We are all one family when you get down to it."[11]

The Louise Bransten/Kheifetz combine would show up again in one of the most famous of all security probes, that of J. Robert Oppenheimer. Other suspects prominent in this investigation were Haakon Chevalier and George Eltenton, both identified Communist agents tracked by the Bureau. In keeping with the earlier-noted OWI connections of the West Coast group, when Chevalier sought a job at OWI, he got a letter of introduction from Owen

Lattimore to Joe Barnes. George Eltenton's wife meantime was active with the IPR, where both Barnes and Lattimore had worked back in the 1930s.*

The nuclear connections of the D.C. group were many. One of the more famous Silvermaster contacts was Dr. Edward Condon, sometime science adviser to the congressional Joint Committee on Atomic Energy and head of the National Bureau of Standards in the Department of Commerce. Like Oppenheimer, Condon would eventually become the focus of his own FBI investigation and also of a heated conflict between the White House and the Congress.

Yet another case involving Commerce was that of William Remington. Though not part of any of the affinity groups discussed above, Remington was named by Bentley as one of her agents. In a further illustration of how cases commingled, he was a close friend of Bernard Redmont, yet another Bentley suspect, who worked with Robert Miller at State. According to Bentley, it was Remington who brought Redmont into the Communist Party. Such examples could be multiplied indefinitely.

Of course, the mere fact that people's names appeared in this huge compendium of cases didn't mean they were Communists or Soviet agents (though in many instances they quite obviously were), nor did the FBI, backtracking on the Bentley data, so construe things. For that matter, Bentley herself distinguished among her people—some of whom she said were committed CP members or Soviet agents, others timid cooperators on the fringes. Still less was there any certainty about people who showed up as second- or third-tier contacts of the people mentioned.

In some instances, there would later be court tests of such matters, and much later still, confirming evidence from *Venona*. But for the moment the Bureau mainly had Bentley's word about the suspects, which in a court case would be her say-so against theirs. So further evidence was required, and this would be intensely hunted. However, one thing conspicuous early on was that a large number of the people Bentley named, and their interlocking contacts, formed a kind of floating subculture in and around the federal government of distinctive nature.

The point wasn't merely that they knew one another but that they worked together, helped each other get jobs, promotions, and key assignments, cooperated in political projects, and vouched for one another when dicey questions were asked about security matters. Prime movers in this regard, said Bentley, were Harry White and Lauchlin Currie. At Treasury, White ran a virtual job-

---

*A further link between the West Coast group and activity in D.C. would be provided by Gordon Griffiths, a self-admitted Communist who had been on the faculty at UC Berkeley and divulged in a memoir that in the late 1930s to early '40s he had been a member of a CP unit there with both Chevalier and Oppenheimer. During World War II, Griffiths relocated to the nation's capital, where he would figure in one of the significant loyalty/security cases brought by Joe McCarthy in 1950.

placement service, having brought in such as Ludwig Ullman, Frank Coe, and Gregory Silvermaster. When Silvermaster was under fire, Currie would vouch for him as true and loyal. Silvermaster would pass the benefits along, bringing William Taylor to the department; when inquiries were made about Taylor, Harry White would do the honors by vouching for his bona fides.[12]

A second main point about the Bentley people was their great mobility in moving from one job to another. Nor was this merely random. Instead, the transitions were typically quite focused, geared to the main issues of the day, which at this era often meant a diplomatic or other foreign posting. The case of the MacArthur occupation forces in Japan has been noted. In this instance, an unusual group of helpers would be dispatched by the U.S. government to assist the general with his duties. These included John Stewart Service, Owen Lattimore, T. A. Bisson, and Philip Keeney, to cite only the more obvious cases. Also on hand to help out in Japan was the Canadian Herbert Norman, alumnus of both the Cambridge circle and the IPR connection.

A similar crew showed up in Germany to help staff the occupation there. This delegation included Mary Jane Keeney, George S. Wheeler (brother of Donald), Russell Nixon, Ludwig Ullmann, Harold Glasser, V. Frank Coe, James Aronson, Cedric Belfrage, Henry Collins, and Irving Kaplan, all targets of security investigations. Assignments of this sort were run through the office of Assistant Secretary of State John Hilldring. A key member of the Hilldring staff involved in such decisions was Bowen Smith, a good friend of the Keeneys and himself a minor Bureau suspect. Many like assignments would occur at the United Nations Relief and Rehabilitation Administration (UNRRA), in charge of distributing relief supplies and handling displaced persons in the postwar period.*

A further point emerging from the Bureau records concerns the much-emphasized issue of spying. In the case of the Bentley people, the FBI had been told going in that many had plied her with official data, and much of the surveillance was aimed at catching the suspects stealing secrets. This, however, never happened, nor was there much prospect that it would. The main reason usually cited for this is that, shortly after Bentley and Igor Gouzenko bolted, the Soviets ratcheted down their networks, pulled back their Russian controllers, and told their contacts to lie doggo.

But such instructions may not have been the only reason nobody was caught red-handed filching papers or discussing secrets on the phone. Whatever

---

*Also important, as the FBI observed, various of the Bentley people and their contacts were now moving to the new international bodies set up in the last phases of the war and in the early postwar era, where many decisions would be made affecting America's vital interests. Alger Hiss would be the point man in creating and staffing the United Nations, while Harry White would play a comparable role at the International Monetary Fund.

else they were, the Bentley suspects weren't stupid. Despite their casual way in socializing, they were hardly the kind of people to talk about such matters on an open phone line or conduct transactions where they could be watched by Bureau agents. Also, once the heat was on, they knew it, and many a wiretap contains warnings from one suspect to another to be careful about saying anything of substance on the phone. Such concerns became acute in the early months of 1946, when many of the Bentley group were being closely pressed by security agents.

Also, there is a final point that seems even more important in the wider Cold War context. As the postwar diaspora suggested, and as FBI agent Guy Hottel observed to Director Hoover, large numbers of the Bentley people had moved, or were moving, to policy-making jobs that would affect the shape of things to come in the dawning East-West struggle. They were often well placed to guide or implement decisions, not simply kibitz as others did so. And people actually making policy, rather than learning about it secondhand, generally don't have much time—or need—for spying. As Whittaker Chambers had pointed out, it was the policy making that counted.

CHAPTER 11

What Hoover Told Truman

O NCE universally praised and honored, the FBI in recent years has fallen on hard times. The uproar about alleged intelligence failures before the terrorist onslaught of 9/11 is but the latest chapter in a morose, ongoing story that dates back to the 1970s, if not before then.

At that era, we were bombarded with horrific tales of abuses by the Bureau, saying it was trampling private rights and ignoring tenets of the Constitution, creating an American police state. From this agitation there developed laws and guidelines that restricted the powers of the FBI, subjected it to bureaucratic second-guessing, and in general curbed the can-do methods that were once its leading features.

To this skein of woe there have been added, since the 1990s, still other lacerating charges, mostly of the opposite nature: that the FBI was a dismal flop in what was once its foremost mission—combatting the efforts of Communists and Soviet agents to penetrate the U.S. government. Here the Bureau's alleged failings concern, not what it did opposing Red incursions, but what it should have done and didn't. Given the fierce anti-Communism of J. Edgar Hoover and his G-men, this seems the most fantastic charge of all, but is seriously made in certain quarters.

Thus, to take an extreme example, a column by a presumably expert writer in a respected daily makes the remarkable statement that "Soviet intelligence operatives ran through J. Edgar Hoover's FBI like a sieve." This critique suggests the Bureau didn't know "the Communist Party was a support organization for Soviet intelligence," or that its "agent penetrations were numerous at very high levels of the government during and after World War II." The writer adds that, even when tipped off by the Army to the secrets of *Venona,* Hoover and his dim-witted agents failed to get the job done.[1]

A more widely circulated charge relating to *Venona* is that the FBI deliberately withheld its horrific revelations from President Truman. This is a rhetorical twofer, as it both blames the FBI for security lapses in the Cold War and exculpates Truman from charges of inaction, twin objectives in some circles. If only Truman had known about *Venona,* supposedly, he could have taken proper steps against the spies and agents inside the government he headed; but as Hoover withheld the necessary data, Truman was slow to learn the facts and craft the needed measures.*

With all due respect to the learned folk who advance such notions, all of this is moonshine and will be so perceived by anyone who bothers to check the official records. As has been seen, the FBI was neither fooled by nor indifferent to Soviet penetration efforts in the 1940s. Nor was it in doubt that the Communist Party USA was a creature of the Soviet Union, up to its ears in spying, pro-Moscow influence schemes, and other species of subversion. Nor did the Bureau withhold its knowledge of such matters from the Truman White House.

It's fair to say, in fact, that the FBI throughout the war years and early postwar era was the *only* institution of the U.S. government that—as an institution—clearly grasped the Communist problem, devoid of blinkers or delusions. Perhaps the Bureau can be faulted for not picking up on the matter more alertly in the latter New Deal years, but it repeatedly led the way in warning of the Communist danger as of the early 1940s. This was most notably so during the "gallant ally" daze of wartime, when FDR, Harry Hopkins, and their minions were lauding Stalin, letting Earl Browder out of prison, and strewing roses along the path that led the comrades to the federal payroll.

While all this was going on, the FBI was vigilantly on the job against the Soviets and their agents, even as it cracked down on Nazi and Japanese would-be saboteurs in the context of the war. That the Soviets were our military allies didn't obscure for Hoover the fact that they were profoundly hostile to American interests and values. Nor did the Bureau accept the fiction, advanced in 1943, that the Soviet Comintern had been dissolved as an agency of world subversion, or that the "Communist Political Association" announced at this era by Earl Browder was an indigenous American group with no linkage to the Kremlin. The Bureau always knew that this was phony.

---

*This thesis would later be modified to the contention that *Venona* was withheld from Truman, not by the Bureau, but by the Army.

Hoover and his men knew all this, not because of any ideological leanings (though such undoubtedly existed), but because they were paying attention to events—closely watching what the Soviets and American Reds were doing, as opposed to propaganda statements by vice president Henry Wallace or Ambassador Joseph Davies about the peaceable kingdom to come in which the United States and USSR would lie down together in friendship. What the Bureau was observing and recording was the exact reverse of these benighted notions.

To be specific, the FBI as early as 1943 was tracking the efforts of Soviet spies to penetrate the hush-hush American scientific project then getting under way that would produce the A-bomb. This was the seminal Bransten-Kheifetz investigation referred to in Chapter 7. From informants and surveillance, the FBI knew the Soviets and their U.S. helpers were trying to penetrate the atom setup and steal its secrets. Bureau reconnaissance of this conspiracy led to known and suspected agents in other places, producing a series of three closely linked inquiries.

The first of these investigations, called "the Comintern Apparatus" (in FBI shorthand, COMRAP), branched out beyond the atom project to other venues, including Soviet commercial fronts, Red activities among ethnic groups, infiltration of labor unions, propaganda efforts, and a good deal else. COMRAP reports identified hundreds of known or suspected Soviet agents, Communists, and fellow travelers in many walks of life across the nation. All of this, to repeat, was tracked and recorded in the early 1940s.

As COMRAP grew to embrace this range of topics, the Bureau established another file devoted solely to the atom project. This was given the case name "Communist Infiltration of the Radiation Laboratory" (CINRAD) and focused on the interactions of Soviet agents with scientific and technical personnel at the Berkeley Radiation Lab and related outfits. CINRAD unearthed a good deal of specific intel on what the Soviets and their American pawns were doing in their efforts to steal the secrets of the atom. This, too, was in the early 1940s.

Finally, COMRAP/CINRAD led to a group of atom scientists who, based on the accumulating record, appeared to be either Communists themselves or sympathetic to the party. Foremost among these was J. Robert Oppenheimer, a consultant at the Radiation Lab and thereafter the key figure at the super-secret Los Alamos, New Mexico, installation that would produce the A-bomb. As early as December 1942, the FBI had surveillance data indicating Oppenheimer was a Communist who had to be inactive because of the sensitive job he held but was still considered a comrade by CP leaders. Thus, a third file was created, devoted to Oppenheimer and his doings, this too stemming from the early 1940s.

The point of stressing the dates of these investigations, as well as the significant subject matter, is twofold. First, they show the FBI was never thrown off the Communist trail by the propaganda of World War II, which made it as a federal agency unique. Second, the dates show that the FBI was acutely aware of the Communist infiltration problem well before the advent of *Venona*. Needless to remark, *Venona* was of crucial value and contributed in decisive fashion to Bureau knowledge of the Soviet networks. But its decrypts didn't come online to the FBI until April of 1948.*

This trio of interlocking investigations revealed a lot about Soviet/Communist penetration schemes, but more intel was soon to follow. In March of 1945, the *Amerasia* scandal, fix, and cover-up began unfolding before the astonished gaze of Hoover and his agents, and in November of that year the massive Gregory investigation would be unleashed by Bentley. These two further inquiries between them produced about 65,000 pages of now-declassified material that would be blended with thousands of others from COMRAP and CINRAD. The net result was a colossal database the Bureau distilled into a series of revealing memos, long secret from the public.

Though these enormous files and summary memos have been expertly culled from time to time in FOIA actions on specific topics, their vast range, and the information they contain, haven't been a matter of general knowledge. If they had, there could never have been any doubt about the Bureau's awareness of Communist infiltration in the 1940s or suggestions that the FBI withheld security data from top officials. Irrefutable proof about these matters has been there for sixty years, reposing in the Bureau archives.

Because the raw files are so extensive, it's impossible to give any clear notion of their contents, except in merest piecemeal fashion. The reports and summary memos are easier to manage, though even here the scope is daunting, running to several thousand pages of densely packed disclosures. These wrap-ups capsule the findings of the Bureau from one inquiry to the next, show how Hoover and his agents increased their store of knowledge, and indicate how the pieces went together. What follows is a rough précis of some of these reports and memos, in the order of their appearance:

• *The Comintern Apparatus (COMRAP). December 1944.* This is a massive 577-page memorandum, bound in two thick packets, based on the initial probe beginning at the Berkeley Lab. It's a compendium of about 400 names and several score organizations whose activities indicated to the FBI that they were

---

*As to what that knowledge was, it's instructive to compare the FBI's findings at this early time to some of the charges recently made against the Bureau. Compare with the critique above, about the alleged naïveté of the FBI concerning the Communist Party linkage to the Kremlin, certain Bureau comments from 1944: ". . . a number of recent and very striking examples of Comintern operation in the United States emphatically give the lie to pronouncements that the Comintern is dead and to current avowals of loyalty and patriotism by the American Communist Party. Investigations have proved the continued use of Communists in the United States by Soviet agents and have confirmed the operation of an illegal underground apparatus under the direction of Russian Communists and several governmental officers."

part of the Soviet operation. The roster began with the core groups in and around the Lab, then expanded to include such agencies as Amtorg (a Moscow commercial front), the Soviet Purchasing Commission, the activities of Soviet agents Gaik Ovakimian and Arthur Adams, and many others like them.[2]

Among the cast of characters in COMRAP/1944 who would figure in later security wrangles were Oppenheimer, Gregory Silvermaster, Gerhart Eisler, Max Bedacht, Anna Louise Strong, Alfred and Martha Stern, Max and Grace Granich, Victoria Stone, Clarence Hiskey, Haakon Chevalier, Bruce Minton, and a host of others. Also of interest, this report discusses the wartime propaganda and influence operations then going on in U.S. media circles to promote the Communist cause in Yugoslavia and Poland. (Identified as the main pro-Communist gurus in these propaganda efforts were Louis Adamic and Prof. Oscar Lange, a pro-Red expatriate from Poland who would in due course return there.)

• *Philip Jacob Jaffe, was; ETAL: Espionage C, May 11, 1945.* This is an eighty-page report tracking the movements of Philip Jaffe, John Service, Andy Roth, Mark Gayn, and Emmanuel Larsen during a two-week period in April 1945, at the height of the *Amerasia* investigation. The memo is a summary of surveillance records concerning the people named, including the data-take from wiretaps, planted microphones, and physical observations. It is one of a large number of such reports in the *Amerasia* archive, totaling more than 12,000 pages of declassified Bureau records.

Though prepared strictly for the internal uses of the FBI and Department of Justice, and not for wider dissemination, this memo is of great interest for the lay researcher, as it embraces the critical three-day period in mid-April 1945 when Service suddenly appeared on the scene and began his relationship with Jaffe. Included are paraphrases of the first Jaffe-Service talks, the interactions of Jaffe and Roth, the contacts of Jaffe and Larsen, and an overview of Jaffe's dealings with other key figures in the pro–Red China network.[3]

• *Soviet Espionage in the United States, November 27, 1945.* This is a remarkable report of fifty pages, single spaced, that ties together the Bentley data, COMRAP/CINRAD, *Amerasia,* information from defectors (including Victor Kravchenko and Whittaker Chambers), and other Bureau sources. It shows that the FBI, at the threshold of the Cold War, had a detailed, comprehensive understanding of Soviet-Communist operations in the United States. This memo would, for that reason, achieve somewhat legendary status, with parts of it read into the *Congressional Record* by then Rep. Richard Nixon (R-Calif.), cited in testimony before committees, and excerpted in congressional reports and hearings.[4]

Among the individuals who make an appearance in this survey are a number already mentioned: Oppenheimer, Silvermaster, Currie, Bransten-Kheifetz, Harry White, John Service, Sol Adler, Robert Miller, Harold Glasser, and many others. The report also sets forth in brief the case of Alger Hiss, based on the Chambers revelations. Thus, the FBI had a clear bead on Hiss, and passed along key information on him, almost three full years before the matter became a public scandal in the late summer and fall of 1948.

• *"Nathan Gregory Silvermaster," January 3, 1946.* This 484-page report summarizes the Bentley-Gregory case as it stood approximately two months into the investigation. It contains a roster of the Bentley cases, describes efforts of the FBI to check out and follow up her statements, and capsules the results of its surveillance. In all, more than 100 people are mentioned, as are the complex interactions of Silvermaster, White, Maurice Halperin, Joseph Gregg, Victor Perlo, and others. Also revealed are the contacts of various Bentley people with Soviet officials and other Iron Curtain figures. Following is a sample:

> . . . Joseph N. Gregg contacted [Fedor] Garanin [of the Soviet Embassy] while being surveilled by the Bureau. Gregg in turn is known to have been in contact with Peter C. Rhodes of OWI, now transferred to the State Department; Robert T. Miller III, State Department; and Maurice Halperin of the Office of Strategic Services and now with the State Department . . . all of whom were named by Bentley as elements in the espionage unit from which she received . . . information.[5]

• *A memo devoted to Harry Dexter White and his associates in the Treasury Department, February 1, 1946.* (Other versions of this memo also exist.) This twenty-eight-page, single-spaced report was prompted by the fact that White was getting ready to move up to a new post as U.S. executive director of the International Monetary Fund, itself in substantial measure a White creation. Hoover was concerned that in this global job White would "have the power to influence to a great degree deliberations on all international financial arrangements."

This report not only sets forth details on White but traces his many connections with other Treasury staffers: Silvermaster, Ludwig Ullmann, Sol Adler, Harold Glasser, *et al.,* making it clear that an extensive Red apparatus was at work inside the federal government, and had been for some time past. This memo on White—along with other Bureau reports about him—would draw public notice a few years later when a dispute arose between Eisenhower Attorney General Herbert Brownell and former President Truman as to whether relevant data on the case had been provided to the Truman White House.

• *Underground Soviet Espionage Organization (NKVD) in Agencies of the United States Government, February 21, 1946.*[6] Anyone reading the summary of November 27 or the Silvermaster wrap-up could hardly have been in doubt about pro-Red penetration of the federal government, that it reached to very high levels, and that it posed a serious danger. However, just to make sure, the FBI produced this further update, running to 194 pages.

This document highlights more than forty principal suspects who were, or recently had been, in the federal government, and who were members or close contacts of the CINRAD/COMRAP-*Amerasia*-Bentley networks. It thus contains a recap of the usual suspects—Currie, Hiss, Miller, Victor Perlo, Duncan Lee, and some three dozen others. It also contains a notable statement in contrast to the charge that the Bureau was asleep at the wheel concerning the links of the CPUSA to Moscow:

> Soviet espionage has one clear cut advantage over the practice of any other country within the borders of the United States. This advantage centers in the existence of an open and active Communist Party whose members are available for recruitment for any phase of activity desired . . . [such] recruitment is taken in every instance from individuals closely associated with the Communist Party, who in the main are native-born Americans or individuals not native-born but sufficiently familiar with the American way of life to avoid detection.

• *The Comintern Apparatus (COMRAP), March 5, 1946 (summary).* This is a boiled-down (thirty-five-page, single spaced) version of the COMRAP findings, updated and blended with the results of the *Amerasia,* Bentley, and other investigations, in the manner of the November 27, 1945, memo. Its brevity is a helpful feature, making it more manageable than other, more massive documents in the series. This was in fact the purpose of the format, as the summary was intended for the use of top officials unlikely to wade through hundreds of pages of information. (One of those who received this memo was Secretary of State James Byrnes.)[7]

Despite its compact form, this summary is fairly detailed, providing a good overview of the problem as the Bureau then perceived it. Included in its pages are background on Soviet operations and agents in the United States, suspects in OWI and OSS, updates on the Louise Bransten circle, intel on Jaffe and John Service, Bentley's Silvermaster data, and so on. Also included are the Chambers revelations about Alger and Donald Hiss, Henry Collins, Lee Pressman, and Sol Adler. (The Adler-Service roommate connection is brought out in this memo.)

• *Communist Infiltration of Radiation Laboratory (CINRAD), March 5, 1946 (summary).* A companion memo to the COMRAP report of the same date, cast in the same format (thirty-three single-spaced pages) and for the identical purpose: advising top officials of the problem in a condensed and manageable wrap-up that could be read at a single sitting.

This tracks key players in the atom project, explains the wartime division of security tasks between the Bureau and the Army, and shows the extent of the information the FBI had then put together. Among the major figures mentioned are Haakon Chevalier, Joseph Weinberg, Alan Nunn May, Clarence Hiskey, Bernard Peters, and J. Robert Oppenheimer. This report makes yet another reference to the fact that Oppenheimer was said by Communist bigwigs to be a secret party member who had to be inactive in its affairs because of the government work that he was doing.

• *Underground Soviet Espionage Organization (NKVD), October 21, 1946.* A 335-page report that traces the Gregory probe to the time of compilation. Reprising much of the material in the February version, it is more complete, including additional data on individual suspects and showing in greater detail the linkages among them. Noteworthy in this respect is the section on Mary Jane Keeney, discussing her contacts with Joseph Bernstein, David Wahl, Maurice Halperin, and others.

Also set forth in this report is information on such second-tier players as H. Bowen Smith, Duncan Lee, Ruth Rifkin, Cedric Belfrage, Bernard Redmont, Peter Rhodes, and others of like stature. This compilation would have been of special value to security agents, as it is tightly organized, with a full table of contents referring the reader to some fifty-six principal suspects, plus an index relating to hundreds of other people. Though there would be further updates later, this appears to have been the *summa* of the case while the investigation was actively in progress.

THIS survey of Bureau memos is by no means exhaustive. There were other summaries interspersed with these, not to mention that the FBI conducted thousands of investigations of federal workers under provisions of the Hatch Act, P.L. 135, and other statutes. The result of all this investigating and reporting was a huge mass of information concerning the general problem of pro-Red infiltration and innumerable individual suspects employed at federal agencies as of the early to middle 1940s.

Contrary to later aspersions, Hoover and his men weren't compiling this enormous body of data for their own amusement or to have something to hold over people's heads (though there was plenty of such material to work with). The point of all the summaries and updates was to convey the message as clearly and as fully as possible to top officials and trigger some kind of action. These efforts were especially diligent with respect to the Truman White House, which received a Niagara of memos on the major Bentley cases. Also, Hoover made special efforts to get information to Truman via George Allen, a well-known friend of the President who saw him informally and often. Far from withholding anything from Truman, Hoover was ringing alarm bells and supplying intel by every means at his disposal.

Following the Bentley disclosures, for instance, Hoover wasted no time in flagging them to the attention of the White House. Bentley made her first detailed statement to Bureau agents on November 7, 1945. Suggesting the urgency with which Hoover viewed the matter, the next day he had hand-delivered to Truman's aide, Gen. Harry Vaughan, a number of the key details:

> . . . information has been recently developed from a highly confidential source indicating that a number of persons employed by the government of the United States have been furnishing data and information to persons outside the Federal government, who are in turn transmitting this information to espionage agents of the Soviet government . . . The Bureau's information at this time indicates that the following persons were participants in this operation or were utilized by principals in this ring for the purpose in which the Soviet is interested:

> > Dr. Gregory Silvermaster, a long time employee of the Department of Agriculture.
> > Harry Dexter White, Assistant to the Secretary of the Treasury.
> > George Silverman, formerly employed by the Railroad Retirement Board, and now reportedly in the War Department.
> > Laughlin Currie, former Administrative Assistant to the late President Roosevelt.
> > Victor Perlow, formerly with the War Production Board and the Foreign Economic Administration.
> > Major Duncan Lee, Office of Strategic Services.
> > Julius Joseph, Office of Strategic Services.
> > Helen Tenney, Office of Strategic Services.
> > Maurice Halperin, Office of Strategic Services.
> > Charles Kramer, formerly associated with Senator Harley Kilgore.
> > Captain William Ludwig Ullman, United States Army Air Corps.[8]

Thereafter, Hoover would supply the White House with various of the reports detailed above, including the comprehensive summary of November 27, 1945, a condensed version of the same a few weeks later, the Harry White report, the still more comprehensive update of February 21, 1946, the COMRAP and CINRAD summaries of March 5, 1946, and so on in a continuing series. The same memos would be provided to the Attorney General and agencies where the suspects were working. Given this blizzard of Bureau paper, any half-sentient high official of the government had to know, by mid-1946, that a truly massive problem existed.

Reaction to these advices, however, was strangely torpid. After an early flicker of concern, the White House seemed especially inert—indeed, quite hostile to the revelations, and in virtually no case inclined to action. At agencies where the suspects worked, responses weren't a great deal better. In some cases, the reports were simply ignored; in others, they provoked some initial interest, but not much beyond this; in still others, people who received the memos would say they never got them.

Considering the gravity of the problem, Hoover must have felt he was pushing on a string. A recurring subject in the Bureau files is the matter of reports to high officials that somehow got "lost." That reports about such topics would be casually laid aside or "lost" suggests, at best, a thorough indifference to the scope and nature of the trouble. From Hoover's comments it's also apparent he suspected something worse—the passing around of the memos to people who weren't supposed to have them.*

Compounding these Bureau worries was the rankling memory of the *Amerasia* scandal. In that episode, elements in the Justice Department had fixed the case, then tried to blame failure of the prosecution on the FBI.† As other cases now came to public view, such scapegoating would become a familiar tactic. When charges against the Bentley-identified Red agent William Remington surfaced, Commerce Department officials told the press they hadn't been properly briefed about the matter by the Bureau. This despite the innumerable reports on Remington that had been forwarded to Commerce.[9]

Another twist would be provided when the Victor Perlo case began filtering out to the press corps. In this instance, Treasury officials floated a story that

---

*A memo from Quinn Tamm to Hoover in February of 1948 relates that "the report which the Bureau furnished to the Treasury Department in the Gregory case some months ago has been found in a safe in the Treasury Department. You will recall that this is the report which was furnished to Secretary Vinson and was apparently lost by him." In December 1946 it was "stated that the attorney general had mislaid the memorandum on [White-Silvermaster] and wanted to have them before he attended the Cabinet meeting." In an even more troubling report, Hoover himself would recall in 1953: "John Maragon had indicated that he had been in Vaughan's office on many occasions and had seen Mr. Nichols and Mrs. Nesse of the Bureau come in and deliver reports to General Vaughan. He stated furthermore that on occasions General Vaughan had thrown into the wastebasket certain FBI reports after they had been received."

†Echoes of the *Amerasia* case appear in frequent negative Bureau comments about officials at Truman Justice. The FBI files contain numerous Hoover statements concerning James McInerney, who had been prominent in the handling of the case (and would be again when it was revived in 1950). In particular, Hoover considered McInerney to be a leaker, and often said so ("If they would eliminate James McInerney from this case I believe the leaks might stop"). It's also apparent from the files that Hoover had a similar unfriendly view of Justice official Peyton Ford, who would also figure in later conflicts.

they withheld action in the case at the request of the FBI in order to cooperate with its investigation. As the Bureau records make clear, no such request had been made by Hoover, who condemned the Treasury statements as just another attempt to pass the buck. Similar tales would later be told about Alger Hiss, Harry White, and others.

All this would reach a crescendo in the summer of 1948, when some of the loyalty/security cases that had been simmering beneath the surface would be brought out in congressional hearings. Most famously, the House Committee on Un-American Activities conducted its Hiss-Chambers investigation, in which the cases of Silvermaster, Miller, White, Duncan Lee, and others were aired as well. In all these cases, the relevant data had been in the possession of the Bureau—and of responsible higher-ups—for at least two years, and in some instances even longer.

Of course, the press and public knew nothing of this background and were shocked by the revelations of the Hill committees. Rumors and media accounts abounded that the FBI had been dozing, hadn't managed to spot the suspects, hadn't informed top officials of the danger—all this to the great annoyance of Hoover. Accordingly, he ordered the Bureau to prepare an elaborate summary of the reports and memos it had provided on the Bentley suspects. The preparation of such summaries was a common Bureau practice, and many such may be found in the FOIA archives. This was but to be expected of the methodical Hoover, who wanted records on everything the FBI was doing and especially wanted to keep track of the ultrasecret data it was providing on its cases.

What was now prepared, however, was in a class by itself—the mother of all such compilations, showing in detail the huge number of reports that had been supplied about the original Bentley cases, the dates of the reports, and the people who received them. In compiling this prodigious record, the FBI went beyond the written word to make the matter graphic. It drew up a series of elaborate charts—one for each of the primary Bentley suspects in the federal workforce, plus a master chart showing the vast array of warnings that had gone forth from the Bureau. This shows that no fewer than 370 such reports had been supplied, in one fashion or another, to fourteen federal agencies. The bulk of these in turn had gone to the White House and Attorney General. (See page 146.)

From these charts, the proof that the FBI had exerted due diligence and then some in carrying out its investigative and reporting duties was evident at a glance. (Which perhaps explains the fact that this series of charts not only reposes in the general archives of the Bureau but was also in the Official and Confidential records kept by Hoover in his office.) In particular, the massive record of Bureau communications to the White House should put paid to the notion that Hoover would have withheld from Truman the data product from *Venona*.

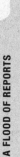

A FLOOD OF REPORTS

This FBI master chart, held in J. Edgar Hoover's personal files, shows the vast array of reports the Bureau sent to high U.S. officials in the early to mid-1940s about major suspects in the Bentley-Gregory investigation.

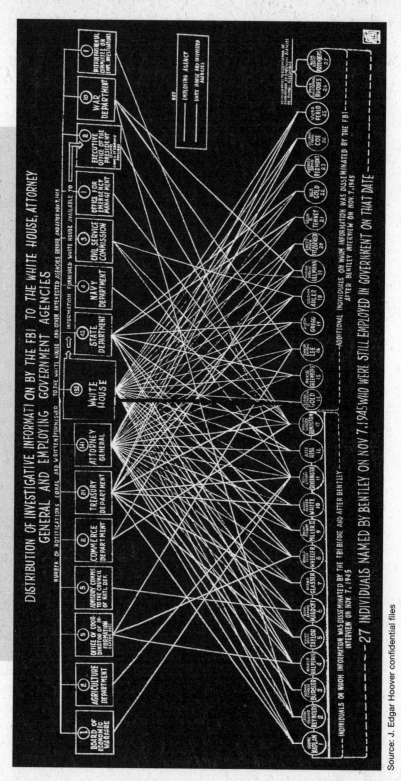

Source: J. Edgar Hoover confidential files

Also apparent from these records is that copious information on the people monitored by the Bureau had been sent to the agencies where the suspects were employed. And while such information would have been of critical importance in every venue of the federal government, in few places were the stakes as high for the security of the nation as at the U.S. State Department—frontline agency in the now rapidly mounting Cold War with Moscow and its global apparatus.

CHAPTER 12

Inside the State Department

A T THE close of World War II, the federal government, like other American institutions, faced problems of conversion to the ways of peace, or
what were thought to be such. Nowhere were the changes more abrupt,
or fraught with meaning for the future, than at the venerable, rococo quarters
of the "old" U.S. Department of State (now the Executive Office Building), due
west of the White House.

Despite the peculiar early security episodes discussed in Chapter 6, the
department of that era still had a reputation as a conservative place, famous
for its straightlaced ways and regard for custom. Beginning in late 1944, however, State would undergo an extreme makeover that drastically transformed
this image. The process took a quantum leap in July of '45, when Edward Stet-
tinius stepped down from a brief caretaker stint as Secretary, to be replaced by
South Carolina's James F. Byrnes, a former senator and Supreme Court justice
and power in the Democratic Party. A few weeks later, the veteran diplomat
Joseph Grew would resign as Under Secretary, to be succeeded by Dean G.
Acheson, a relative newcomer to the department. These top-level changes,
coming in rapid-fire succession, would have profound impact on U.S. policy
overseas and security practice on the home front.

Though Byrnes was an experienced politician with few equals then or later,
he perforce knew little about the inner workings of the State Department and

made no great attempt to change this, managing things through a few trusted aides he brought in to help him. His generally hands-off approach became the more so as he left the country for long spells, attending meetings on global postwar problems. In his absence, whoever was Under Secretary would be Acting Secretary, wielding day-to-day control of the department. Thus the near-simultaneous double switch at the top two positions meant Dean Acheson was now in many respects, if not quite all, the dominant figure at State.

This transition was of critical nature, as Grew and Acheson were then about as far apart on certain pressing issues as could be imagined. Though of similar social and educational background (Groton and Harvard for Grew; Groton, Yale, and Harvard Law for Acheson), they were of different generations and saw things through different lenses. Grew was a respected old-line figure, a forty-year member of the diplomatic corps, and doyen of the Foreign Service. A man of traditional views and courtly mien, he was often at odds with so-called progressives of that day, both in and out of the department.*

Most to the present point, Grew was the official at State who in June of 1945 blew the whistle on the *Amerasia* culprits, saying there had been a noise in the "chicken coop" and that a serious effort was under way to crack down on such offenders. While his role in the affair was otherwise tangential, it ignited a furious outcry by radical elements in the press, denouncing him as a reactionary and calling for his resignation. Two months after this protest erupted, Grew did in fact resign, to be followed rapidly to the exits by some of his closest allies. A mainstay of the older diplomatic culture had been removed from office.

Dean Acheson, a well-connected Washington lawyer and former Treasury official, was of another breed entirely. He had been in the State Department only since 1941—one-tenth as long as Grew—but had already made his mark as a rising figure and point man for the "progressives." This may come as a surprise to modern readers, accustomed to recent books and essays portraying him as a Cold War hawk and ardent foe of Stalin. In 1945, when he assumed the reins of State, Acheson had a very different profile. He was known as an advocate of conciliating Moscow, in sharp contrast to hardliners in the diplomatic corps who wanted to take a tough anti-Red stance in the postwar era. The nature of this backstage struggle would be described by former Assistant Secretary of State Adolf Berle, testifying in the case of Alger Hiss:

---

*Symptomatic of this ongoing conflict, as already seen, was Grew's effort during the run-up to Pearl Harbor to work out a truce between America and Japan, when such as Harry White and Lauchlin Currie were pushing hard for confrontation. Likewise, at the time of the Yalta conference, Grew would oppose some of the more ghastly features of the agreements made there. He would again get crossways with the "progressives" on the matter of a hard vs. soft peace with Japan as the war wound to a conclusion.

As I think many people know, in the fall of 1944 there was a difference of opinion in the State Department. I felt that the Russians were not going to be sympathetic and cooperative. . . . I was pressing for a pretty clean-cut showdown then when our position was strongest. The opposite group in the State Department was largely the men—Mr. Acheson's group, of course, with Mr. Hiss as his principal assistant in the matter. . . . I got trimmed in that fight, and as a result, went to Brazil, and that ended my diplomatic career.*[1]

Though Acheson and his defenders would try to fuzz over or explain away these Berle comments, they would in substance be confirmed by observers from all points on the political compass (J. Edgar Hoover, the Social Democratic *New Leader,* and left-wing journalist I. F. Stone, to name a few). Mainly, however, they were confirmed by Acheson's own acts and statements once he attained a measure of de facto power. In this respect, arguably his most important move was to name John Carter Vincent, a close ally of John Service and the *Amerasia*/IPR contingent, as head of State's Far East division. This was virtually a coup d'état all by itself, as Asia specialists at odds with Vincent were soon out of the department altogether or shunted to the sidelines. Thus, in the wake of the *Amerasia* scandal, elements aligned with Sol Adler's roommate had emerged on top, while opponents of the Service-Vincent faction were all but banished.[†]

These high-level changes, decisive as they were, would be accompanied by other intramural wrangles in which Acheson was a central player. With World War II concluded, the makeshift units thrown together at the outset were dismantled and their staffers shuffled off to other bureaus—the State Department first and foremost. As of October 1945, some 13,000 transferees from OSS, OWI, and other wartime agencies would descend on the department, and while the bulk of these were eventually mustered out, a residue of about 4,000 would remain there. As the interim units had been well salted with identified Communist Party members and fellow travelers, the security woes hatched in the war would thus come home to roost at State.[‡]

---

*This Berle testimony would be brought up when Acheson underwent confirmation hearings as Secretary of State in January of 1949. In response, Acheson made much of the technical quibble that Alger Hiss was not his assistant (a position actually held by Hiss's brother, Donald), and otherwise suggested that he had little or nothing to do with Alger. In fact, as Hiss himself would relate, the two were extremely close. Hiss dealt with Acheson directly on almost a daily basis in 1944 and '45, and would strategize with Acheson in 1946 when Hiss was being forced out of the department.

†Sol Adler himself, meantime, continued on with the Treasury and would play a significant role in the further development of U.S. policy toward China. (See Chapter 31.)

‡A curious aspect of this merger was that it originated in the Bureau of the Budget, not usually thought of as an agency with significant Cold War impact. Truman Budget Director Harold Smith and various of his staffers were not only involved in conflating the wartime outfits into State and other mainline agencies but several such staffers would have roles to play in further security troubles resulting from the merger.

To deal with this enormous problem, an ill-sorted managerial team had lined up for postwar duty under Byrnes. Given primary responsibility for the merger and its tangle of security issues was the new Deputy Assistant Secretary of State for Administration, J. Anthony (Joe) Panuch. A New York lawyer previously with the War Department dealing with intelligence matters, Panuch reported to Donald Russell, a key aide and South Carolina political ally of Byrnes. Panuch thus had a direct line to the top, which he wasn't hesitant in using. Under Panuch in turn was another new appointee, already met with, former Treasury lawyer Samuel Klaus. A somewhat elusive figure, Klaus would wield indefinite but substantial power as counsel to the newly formed Advisory Committee on Personnel Security (ACOPS), in essence the ruling body for security affairs in the department.

Also in the security shop were a group of old-line staffers who had been around a while, had their own ideas on how to do things, and would eventually clash with the new appointees. Members of this seasoned force included Frederick Lyon, director of the Office of Controls (the supervisor of security operations), Robert Bannerman (the main security officer), and Chief Special Agent (CSA) Thomas Fitch, the top in-house investigator. This trio by common repute took a hard-line stance on security cases, as opposed to the more lawyerly, civil libertarian views of Klaus (and to some degree Panuch) and were in frequent contact and close alignment with the FBI. The security setup thus had several interacting parts, which didn't always work together.

Among the first of the problems Joe Panuch set out to handle was the huge group of staffers from OSS—numbering more than 1,000 people—now on the department payroll. As Panuch knew about the troubles that existed in this service, notorious in intelligence circles, the mere fact of having that many of its alumni on board at State was a cause for trepidation. However, Panuch had an even bigger problem with the new arrivals, putting him on collision course with the Acheson forces and touching off an internecine brawl that would split the department down the middle.

At issue in this dispute was an ambitious plan to deploy the staffers from OSS as the new intelligence arm of State, with powers overriding the traditional reporting and analytical functions of the geographic bureaus.* As Acheson would one day make clear, he was an *éminence grise* behind this plan, if not in fact the main one, while Panuch would become its chief backstage opponent. Using his pipeline to Donald Russell and thence to Byrnes, Panuch went to work to scotch the OSS proposal. After peppering Russell with memos highlighting the security dangers involved and the problems with the personnel

---

*Though the struggle was conducted mostly as a bureaucratic turf war—pitting State Department division heads against the OSS contingent—it had serious policy implications. As seen, intelligence data could have decisive influence on policy—for example, whether to back Mihailovich or Tito, or to pull the plug on Chiang Kai-shek in China.

brought in by the merger, Panuch and his departmental allies would win this struggle, but at a sizable cost to be exacted later.[2]

Running parallel with this internal conflict, Panuch and members of his security squad were waging a daily battle to deal with countless individual security cases, mostly though not entirely resulting from the merger. This led to other intramural quarrels, these within the division itself. Ironically, given Panuch's incessant warfare against the OSS intelligence scheme and other like proposals, he and Klaus would be perceived by the old-line staffers as softballs on security issues. Repeated disagreements between these internal factions on how to handle cases would produce a series of deadlocks and halfway measures fertile of many future troubles.

Into the hands of this divided team there now flowed, beginning in the latter weeks of 1945, an urgent stream of FBI reports about alleged security risks, CP members, and Soviet agents said to be in the department, derived from the Bentley/*Amerasia* probes and featuring cases from the merger, though including some indigenous cases also. Based on these data and their own researches, State's security sleuths picked up the trail of numerous suspects. By the spring of 1946, they had the goods on such significant Cold War figures as Alger Hiss, Maurice Halperin, Mary Jane Keeney, Gustavo Duran, Robert Miller, and Carl Marzani—all named in official reports as Communist agents and all now on the rolls at State. And these were only six of many; overall, it would appear, the security team set up case files on several hundred people.

These cases spawned a lot of paperwork, as Robert Bannerman, Klaus, Panuch, and others traded memos on the suspects. Such of these papers as have survived and been discovered are revealing. Among the most important— and longest—is the 106-page memo written by Klaus in the summer of 1946, reviewing the security scene at State, summarizing cases, and urging changes in procedure.* Its most riveting passages concerned security data being provided to the department by the FBI, suggesting a truly massive penetration:

> It is important to note that the department is entirely and practically exclusively dependent on FBI for the type of information which comes from surveillance, wide coverage, and the use of unusual methods of interrogation and investigation. . . . FBI is the sole repository of such information, therefore, as the identity of Communist party members, of sympathizers and fellow travelers, of espionage cases, and of undisclosed foreign agents.
>
> FBI has prepared a chart, now in the possession of Mr. Bannerman, which purports to show the number of "agents," "Communists," "sympathizers," and "suspects" in the State Department as of May 15, 1947.† The tabulation shows:

---

* This is the lost memo referred to in the Prologue.
† Typographical error in original. The true date was May 15, 1946.

Agents 20
Communists 13
Sympathizers 14
Suspects 77

Bannerman states that by July 12 (the date of my interview), the numbers had been reduced to the following:

Agents 11
Communists 10
Sympathizers 11
Suspects . . . . about 74

Since a considerable number of the persons so characterized came with the interim agencies [i.e., the wartime units], continued reductions in force might dispose of more of these.[3]

These comments were startling in themselves, but other findings made them more so. Klaus was right about the chart, but erred as to its authors. In fact, the chart was the department's own creation, drawn up for its internal uses (though utilizing Bureau data). According to the Bureau records, it provided clues, not only as to the number of cases being handled, but also something of their nature. As one FBI account explained it:

> . . . the chart in question was prepared by the State Department and it was noted that it very plainly states that it was prepared in the Reproduction Branch of the State Department and carries the title, "Top Secret, U.S. Department of State, Preliminary Survey of Communist Infiltration, Prepared May 15, 1946". . . . The employees were divided into two groups: (1) Soviet Underground Intelligence Connections. (2) *Amerasia*. There are four charts in all. . . . None of the charts appeared to be a finished product but appeared to be worksheets. The employees are broken down into categories of agents, Communists, sympathizers and suspects. Of the agents (20) and Communists, (13), the State Department has compiled lists (attached). They have not yet been able to compile lists of the sympathizers (14) and suspects (77). They are presently working on this.[4]

In the lists referred to, set forth in this and other Bureau memos, virtually all the names have been blacked out. However, in one version, the identities of two people named as "agents" are given: Alger Hiss and Mary Jane Keeney. Since both were pro-Soviet apparatchiks, as shown by an extensive record, this would seem to be the meaning here of "agents." If 20 moles like Hiss and Keeney had tunneled in at State—plus two dozen others named as Communists or sympathizers, plus 77 further suspects—the problem was obviously immense. Nor was it especially comforting to reflect that, two months after this roster was assembled, there were 11 alleged agents and 10 identified Communists still lingering on the department payroll.

These revelations, however, were not the only eye-catching aspects of

THE KLAUS REPORT

An excerpt from the 106-page memo State Department official Samuel Klaus prepared in the summer of 1946, later read into the *Congressional Record* by Joe McCarthy, showing the number of "agents" and "Communists" then said to be in the department.

-29-

is considerable doubt whether the report was really SECRET derogatory on a security basis.

While this does not apply to Departmental personnel, the fact should be noted as demonstrating a further reliance upon FBI by the Department. Presumably, this check is made by FBI as a matter of accomodation, not of duty. No control us exercised by the Department over the investigation.

(e) It is important to note that the Department is entirely and practically exclusively dependent on FBI for the type of information which comes from surveillance, wide coverage, and the use of unusual methods of interrogation and investigation. CSA appears to have neither the experience nor the facilities to do that type of work and it is apparently not used by any one in that type of work. FBI is the sole repository of such information, therefore, as the identity of Communist Party members, of sympathizers and fellow travelers, of espionage cases, and of undisclosed foreign agents.

(d) FBI has prepared a chart, now in the possession of ████████████, which purports to show a number of "agents", "Communists", "sympathizers", and "suspects" in the State Department as of May 15, 1947. The tabulation shows

```
Agents- - - - - - - - - -20
Communists- - - - - - - -13
Sympathizers- - - - - - -14
Suspects- - - - - - - - -77
```

Bannerman's chart and Klaus's memo. Also of interest, and indicative of the in-house conflict, were the thoughts expressed by Klaus about this mother lode of cases. The FBI, he said, hadn't furnished sufficient proof of its assertions. As to State's own security cops, he added, they took a too-simplistic view of things—were too ready to draw adverse judgments from uncorroborated data. State, he argued, had to do more of its own gumshoeing, in more sophisticated manner, not just rely on rap sheets from the Bureau.

When these comments reached the Lyon-Bannerman forces and the FBI, they drew predictably heated answers. Lyon and Co. thought the FBI investigations of Communist-lining suspects were adequate and solid and, though following up to add details, had no Klaus-like qualms about the information received from Hoover. They also thought Klaus's calls for more elaborate data and lengthier investigations were stalling out the process when prompt and vigorous action was needed. This view appears in several Bureau memos, including one from Hoover assistant Mickey Ladd in October of 1946, based on a talk with Frederick Lyon.

With respect to security matters, said Ladd, "there appears to be the start of a good internal feud" at State. As Lyon told it, he had received instructions to dig up more information on "some 15 or 20 individuals, among whom was Alger Hiss, indicating their implication, if any, in the *Amerasia* case." Lyon's comment on this was that there was already plenty of information on these people, and "that ——— and ——— were attempting to build a paper record to cover up their inactivity in firing Communists in the State Department."*5

Lyon's chat with Ladd reflected something further: active mistrust of Panuch and Klaus, and reluctance to provide them data—suggesting suspicions and concerns beyond mere intramural friction. This lack of feedback would become a chronic theme of Klaus, who blamed the Lyon-Bannerman forces for blocking his own allegedly more sophisticated efforts even as they blamed him for stalling.†

---

*Though the names of the alleged culprits are blacked out in this memo, a subsequent missive from Ladd to Hoover made their identities clear. Concerning an episode of lax security at State, Ladd suggested that it be brought to the attention of Lyon, but added that "since any correspondence directed to Mr. Russell may easily get into the hands of Mr. Panuch or Sam Klaus, it is believed that a letter to Mr. Russell would be highly inadvisable." (In the event, it appears that such a letter was in fact sent to Russell.)

†These crippling conflicts would be noted by congressional staffers who later conducted an in-depth survey of the security office. While their report mainly dealt with other matters, primarily individual cases and the way they were handled, its comments on the internal feuding were explicit. The Lyon-Bannerman group, said the Hill report, had been concerned to eliminate "people of questionable loyalty or regarded as security risks" but had run into frequent roadblocks from Panuch and Klaus, preventing timely and decisive action.

"On numerous occasions," said the report, "Bannerman would recommend that an employee's services be terminated, Lyon would concur in the recommendation, and it would be forwarded to the assistant secretary for administration [Donald Russell]. . . . The common practice was for the file to

Contributing to this paralyzing clash of views were the differing laws and standards earlier noted: On the one hand, the old Civil Service rule that an employee's "political opinions" were nobody's business, compounded by the difficulty of firing someone without protracted legal combat. On the other, the Hatch Act–era standard of "reasonable doubt," saying a government job was a privilege not a right, and that when doubt arose on security grounds the employee could and should be ousted. Further complicating matters was that, in a Civil Service hearing for dismissal, information behind the charges would be disclosed, thus revealing the nature of the data the FBI had gathered. The Bureau was opposed to this, as investigation of the Bentley cases was ongoing.

In an attempt to cut this Gordian knot, Congress in July of 1946 passed, with the assent of Byrnes and Donald Russell, what became known as the "McCarran rider" (drafted by Democratic senator Pat McCarran of Nevada). This gave the Secretary of State the power to discharge, at his discretion, any employee of the department, irrespective of Civil Service rules, if he thought the national interest required it. This theoretically broke the security logjam, but in practice didn't, as State, both then and later, seemed terminally loath to use the power it was given. Dispute about the McCarran rider, when it should be invoked, and why it wasn't, would be central to security wrangles for years thereafter.

What all this discord meant in practice was suggested by the case of Gustavo Duran, who had come to the notice of the Bureau, the security team at State, and several members of the Congress. Duran was of Spanish descent and had served with the anti-Franco forces in Spain in the 1930s. According to former Spanish defense minister Indalecio Prieto (a Socialist and foe of Franco), Duran had been an agent of the Soviet/Communist cause in the Spanish Civil War. By 1946, he had mysteriously turned up as an official in the Latin American division at State and been security-cleared to be there. A memo from Klaus recounts a tense discussion with Mickey Ladd about Duran, and also the case of Carl Marzani, a transferee from OSS. Said Klaus:

> . . . in the course of the conversation, Mr. Ladd took occasion to assert with great emphasis that the State Department should have fired Marzani immediately and asked whether we had got rid of Duran. He said that if these people had been FBI employees they would have been fired at once . . . I . . . told him that, so far as Duran is concerned, we had, after careful consideration of Mr. Ladd's own report, found in Duran's favor and cleared him. We then argued the merits of the Duran case . . . The discussion on

---

be returned with a request for further information. Everyone consulted concerning this seems to be in agreement that Bannerman, Fitch and Lyon were vigorous in their efforts to eliminate suspect individuals from the department and that Samuel Klaus, particularly, and to a lesser degree, Panuch, in a very few instances would concur, and in practically all cases insisted on further inquiry or having the individual classified as no risk."

this point ended with Ladd saying that, if he were a Communist, he would hire me as his lawyer . . .*[6]

HAMPERED by suspicion and legal gridlock, the security squad nonetheless set out to grapple with the mess created by the merger, as well as with a number of homegrown cases that had earlier taken root at State. Reflecting the internal standoff, something like a split decision was arrived at, resulting in more delay and muddle. Officially, "reasonable doubt" prevailed, the more so post–McCarran rider, but this was a strictly formal posture; in fact, even flagrantly obvious cases weren't ousted on their merits. Instead, things were handled in subliminal fashion—"reductions in force" and resignations, rather than outright dismissals. It was all very quiet and proper—aimed at easing people out discreetly, with no legal fuss or public uproar, and in a significant number of cases succeeded.

There were, however, serious drawbacks to these methods. For one, the vast extent of the penetration was kept secret from Congress and the public (and would remain so for years). For another, people who exited in this genteel manner could move on to other federal jobs or, as occurred with many, the United Nations or other global bodies. For yet another, pressuring someone out by these below-the-radar tactics could take months to work (when it did work), meanwhile leaving the suspect in place and risking possible security damage.

All these problems were on display in the most famous of the State Department cases, that of Alger Hiss. State had received several adverse reports on Hiss (including data supplied yet again by Chambers) beginning in the spring of 1945. By early 1946, the case had made its way to the top of the department. According to a Bureau memo of March 13, one State official had "advised in confidence that the Secretary [Byrnes] has on his 'pending' list the name of Alger Hiss, and has stated that Hiss is to be given no further consideration for promotion or assignment to responsible duties in the State Department . . . Secretary Byrnes is of the definite opinion that Alger Hiss should be disposed of, but is concerned over the best manner in which to do it."[7] (The timing of this report suggests Byrnes may well have read the COMRAP summary prepared for him on March 5.) Other State Department memos on Hiss reflect a similar negative judgment.

Thus, by March of 1946 if not before, the highest levels of the department

---

*The available data don't reflect the Lyon-Bannerman view about Gustavo Duran, but based on the congressional-survey comments it's likely they agreed with Ladd. What the larger record makes fairly plain is that Duran was cleared because he had a powerful patron (or patrons) higher up in the department who vouched for his bona fides, thus trumping the objections of security types down at the lower levels. This was a common pattern, not only in the State Department but elsewhere.

were well aware of Hiss but because of uncertainty on how to act took no definite steps to oust him. At that time, given the Civil Service issues, inaction had some faintly plausible basis. However, it's noteworthy that there was no overt move to cashier Hiss even after the McCarran rider was adopted. Instead, as happened in the vast majority of cases, he was quietly pressured to resign, which he finally did, effective in January of 1947. He was thus able to keep his post at State for ten full months beyond the date of Byrnes's comment, and then bow out with seeming honor.*

As would later be discovered, Hiss in this span was anything but idle—using the extra time he was afforded to busy himself with staffing the United Nations, the start-up of which was among his major projects. Congressional investigators would find that, during the spring and summer of '46, Hiss forwarded to the U.N. the résumés of nearly 500 people, many of them his confreres at State, as prospective global staffers. About 50 of these later showed up on the permanent U.N. payroll, while more than 200 others got part-time assignments.†

A real-time hint of what Hiss was doing surfaced in September of 1946, when security agents spotted the apparent leaking of a secret policy memo to journalist Drew Pearson. The document was known to have been in the possession of Hiss's Office of Special Political Affairs (SPA), which triggered an in-depth investigation of that unit. Questioned about the matter by Klaus, Hiss was his usual double-talking self, revealing nothing while raising pedantic smoke-screen issues (whether the memo was being correctly quoted, whether it really matched the Pearson column).

However, the investigators soon uncovered copious information on Hiss, much of it alarming. Among other things, they learned, all kinds of official papers had been funneled to his office, including many on highly sensitive matters (data on the atomic bomb, the course of U.S. policy in China). As for the secret memo, they found it had variously been left sitting around in an open bookcase, taken off the premises by a staffer, and mimeographed in substantial numbers beyond any official need for copies. Such over-ordering, they also found, was standard practice at the SPA. There was thus no telling how many U.S. secrets had passed through Hiss's office to unauthorized outside parties.‡

---

* Like Gustavo Duran, Hiss had a powerful patron—in this case, Dean Acheson.

† The level of Communist penetration among American U.N. employees would eventually become a scandal, explored in the early 1950s by two committees of Congress and a grand jury in New York—the last guided by a precocious Assistant U.S. Attorney named Roy Cohn.

‡ All this was summed up in a scorching letter from Panuch to Hiss deploring "serious security laxness" in the office and intimating tough reprisals. Both in tone and content, this letter would unmistakably have told Hiss the security forces had his number. As to the making of extra copies, Panuch observed, "it appears that over-ordering is a common practice in SPA with respect to classified documents; the security dangers are obvious." Given the timing of this inquiry—September/October

One spin-off of all this was that the security squad began paying more attention, not just to Hiss, but to his subalterns, allies, and coworkers—at State and at the United Nations. A dozen or so names of these show up in department records, most prominently in the memos of Panuch, and many would later appear as well in proceedings of the Congress. Obviously, the investigators didn't assume Hiss was going solo. They acted rather on the premise that he was all too possibly one of many.

And so in fact he was. Simultaneous with the Hiss investigation, the security bloodhounds were on the trail of Robert Miller, named by Bentley as a member of her spy ring. As seen, Miller was a transferee from CIAA who brought other people with him, and was in his way a major figure. The FBI had tracked his connections to the Silvermaster combine, the Maurice Halperin group from OSS, and various outside forces with high subversion quotients. In July of 1946, Bannerman drafted a report on Miller that was basically a digest of the Bureau findings. This reads in part as follows:

> The FBI has established by investigative methods . . . that Mr. Miller is in close and constant association with a group of individuals who are subjects in a current investigation of Soviet espionage activities in agencies of the United States government. It has been determined that Mr. Miller has lunched with, visited the homes of and attended social functions with the subjects of the aforementioned investigation. He further has been in constant association with a number of persons known as Communists, and directly related to Soviet espionage activities in the United States . . .[8]

The Bannerman memo also discussed the problem of bringing formal charges against Miller under Civil Service rules and the trouble this might cause the FBI in surveilling Bentley's people. As the McCarran rider had just been voted, Bannerman suggested Miller might be shown out through that exit. But, again, this didn't happen. Instead, Miller stayed on until mid-December, when he quietly resigned his post, coincident with the long good-bye of Hiss.*

A further protracted and more public case was that of Carl Marzani,

---

1946—it most probably was this investigation that prompted Lyon's talk with Mickey Ladd. If so, this would indicate that Lyon and Co. were not informed as to the nature of the Hiss investigation, thus suggesting still more communication problems. It also suggests that the presence of China-related data in Hiss's SPA was seen as a potential link to *Amerasia*.

*Also of interest was a comment in this Bannerman memo with respect to Maurice Halperin, one of the original Bentley cases, a transferee from OSS and a Miller contact: "He [Halperin] has been requested to resign from the department at the direction of the secretary, as an FBI investigation definitely linked him to a Soviet espionage ring, and revealed that he furnished official information of this government to a Soviet espionage courier." (Halperin had in fact departed on "sick leave" by the time this memo was written.) Thus, the supreme penalty for alleged involvement in a Soviet espionage ring was simply having to resign from the department.

newly arrived from OSS. Marzani was so provable a Communist agent that he would be convicted in a court of law for having denied it to Panuch. Before this happened, however, he also was pressured to resign, which he at first refused to do, and the matter dragged on for months. It was only after this strategy failed that he was finally, and atypically, dismissed via the McCarran rider, this also occurring in December of 1946. The slow pace at which the case developed became a sore point with the FBI and several members of the Congress.*

Nor, in all of this, was the *Amerasia* case forgotten. Though the scandal had been fixed and buried, neither the Bureau nor the security squad at State was dissuaded from following up on its disturbing implications. Service, Jaffe, *et al.* were featured not only in the Bureau's bulging *Amerasia* file but also in the comprehensive memo of November 1945 and COMRAP report of March 1946, all resting on a solid base of wiretaps. Likewise, as seen in the Bannerman charts, the *Amerasia* group at State was thought important enough to merit a section of its own, distinct from all the other cases.

All told, there were something like fifteen people at State who had links to *Amerasia* and/or its think-tank cousin, the Institute of Pacific Relations. Service, Vincent, Hiss, Michael Greenberg, Haldore Hanson, Esther Brunauer, Cora Dubois, and Philip Jessup were examples of such contacts. Another was William T. Stone, a former member of the *Amerasia* board and with Brunauer an incorporator of the American IPR. Stone had worked for Assistant Secretary of State William Benton—as had, intriguingly, Miller, Brunauer, Hanson, and still other security suspects to be considered in their turn hereafter.

On March 22, 1946, Bannerman addressed a memo to Donald Russell concerning Stone, urging that he be removed from the department, once more by way of resignation—and once more showing the weakness of this tactic. Bannerman noted the pro-Communist nature of *Amerasia,* the activities of pro-Soviet editor Philip Jaffe and his flamingly obvious Communist colleague Frederick Field, and Stone's linkage to this duo in the period 1937–41. The memo accordingly concluded:

> . . . it is recommended that action be instituted to terminate the subject's services with the State Department. It is suggested that, to achieve this purpose, an appropriate officer should inform Stone that his continued presence in the department is an embarrassment to the department and that he be

---

*That said, the investigation of Marzani run by Panuch and Klaus was wide-ranging and instructive. As with Hiss and Miller, the State Department records show the extent to which the security team was trying to put the pieces together and trace connections among the players. The Marzani file reflects, for instance, that he was linked with yet another transferee from OSS already met with, David Zablodowsky, who was also pressured to resign (and did). The investigators then found a nexus between Marzani and Robert Miller in the person of Marshall Wolfe—an identified CP member, according to Klaus, who had worked with Marzani in New York, then migrated to D.C., where he hooked up with the Miller combine. While Marzani eventually went to jail, Zablodowsky and Wolfe did rather nicely—both winding up with jobs at the United Nations.

given an opportunity to resign. If Stone should not resign voluntarily action should be instituted under Civil Service Rule XII [i.e., a hearing for dismissal] to terminate his services with the department.[9]

In this case the resignation gambit didn't work, not even slowly. When push came to shove, Stone didn't resign, nor was he fired under Civil Service, or thereafter by the McCarran method. Rather, he stayed on at the department until 1952—a good five years after Bannerman himself departed, and after Stone had been officially cleared by the security team then making such decisions. The episode, and the differing fates of the two parties, were symptomatic of much that would happen in the department in the latter 1940s.

Though halting and uncertain, the subliminal strategy pursued by the Panuch security unit did, after its fashion, get results. Hiss, Miller, Marzani, and others left the building, albeit for the most part sub rosa and at a near-funereal tempo. But, as suggested by the Hiss U.N. maneuvers and secret-memo probe, the costs of this approach were great. Among these was the fact that, while the slow-motion process took effect, the clock was running—not on the suspects, but on the security squad itself. At the beginning of 1947, there would be yet another upheaval in the department, bringing in a new group of players and dismantling the house-divided security team that struggled with the merger.

In the long run, the results of this further changeover were complex. In the short term they were fairly simple, though not for that reason unimportant. When the old security squad departed, it left behind an investigative and enforcement job that, as Panuch himself would comment, was just beginning. The suspects had come on board in a vast incursion, but had been going out by inches. Hiss was finally gone, but there were still in the department many of his allies and lieutenants. Likewise with Robert Miller, several of whose closest friends and contacts remained in their positions. As for the *Amerasia*/IPR contingent, not only did Vincent, Service, Hanson, Stone, *et al.* stay on, they were at this time, thanks to Vincent's elevation, gaining steadily in power. And these affinity groups were representative of others: members of the OSS detachment, retreads from OWI, staunch allies of the Keeneys.

In the meantime, the American people had no idea that any of this had been occurring—had never heard of Alger Hiss or Robert Miller, couldn't have dreamed that twenty alleged Soviet agents had ever been ensconced at State, and were in general blissfully unaware that any security problems at all existed in these early halcyon days of peace. Thanks both to the clandestine nature of the penetration and the subliminal methods used against it, the matter not only dragged out for months but was kept completely secret from the public. All of it, however, would soon become the subject of avid notice by certain members of the Congress.

CHAPTER 13

Acts of Congress

WHEN Martin Dies began compiling his provocative lists of security suspects on the federal payroll, America was at peace, the government was still wrestling with the ills of the Great Depression, and domestic issues were front and center. Accordingly, the places where the suspects worked dealt mainly with such issues. But when Pearl Harbor switched the scene of federal action to the world arena, the trail would lead to the State Department also. Some hints of security trouble there stemmed from the wartime congressional focus on OWI, and then on OSS, as alumni of both units moved en masse to the department.

At war's end, certain members of Congress began to delve into security affairs at State itself. In October of 1945, Rep. George Dondero (R-Mich.) got wind of the *Amerasia* scandal and called for an investigation, resulting in the curious Hobbs inquiry that has been noted. In November, Rep. Paul Shafer, another Michigan GOPer, delivered some scathing comments on staff and policy changes at State, with reference to the transferees from OSS and OWI, the departure of Joe Grew, and the ascendancy of the Acheson forces in the department. A similar critique was made a few weeks later by Rep. Carl Curtis (R-Neb.).[1]

By the early months of 1946, it was apparent that security data from the FBI and the security squad at State were making their way to members of both the House and Senate. In March, Rep. Andrew May (D-Ky.), chairman of the House Military Affairs Committee, demanded the removal from intelligence ranks at State of officials with "Soviet leanings"—a clear reference to the OSS contingent.[2] By April, Sen. Kenneth McKellar (D-Tenn.) was asking the FBI for information on Gustavo Duran and Alger Hiss. Similar interest was expressed by Sen. Kenneth Wherry (R-Neb.) in the matter of Duran.

By mid-summer, concern about security affairs at State was becoming widespread in Congress, as still other lawmakers began to call for information on the penetration problem and press for action. It was at this time that the McCarran rider was adopted, supposedly to ease the way for ousting some of the more flagrant suspects. At this juncture also, yet another Michigan GOPer, Rep. Bartel Jonkman, had a lengthy powwow with Joe Panuch about the Carl Marzani case. In this evidently heated session, Panuch advised his visitor that some forty security suspects had already been eased out of the department, mostly via resignations.

A few days later, Panuch drafted a lengthy memo for Donald Russell reporting on the exchange with Jonkman and passing along some other data indicating that trouble over security issues was building up in Congress. "Sen. [Styles] Bridges [R-N.H.]," said Panuch, "has evidenced a lively interest as to when we are going to begin firings. This is also true of many members of the House. The sentiment clearly seems to be—What is Jimmy Byrnes waiting for?" The following week, Byrnes himself would try to smooth the feathers of another influential solon inquiring about security matters. In a letter to Rep. Adolph Sabath (D-Ill.), Byrnes disclosed that, of 284 State Department employees whose removal had been recommended by security screeners, seventy-nine had been disposed of (this number including the forty previously mentioned by Panuch).*[3]

Thus, members of both parties and both houses were focused on the security shop at State, albeit from different angles, by the latter part of 1946.† The most decisive occurrence on this front, however, had yet to happen: the electoral landslide scored by the congressional GOP in that November's midterm voting. This brought in the first Republican Congress since the early days of the depression, a hiatus in which virtually all the loyalty-security problems at State and other agencies had developed. The GOP had long harbored suspicions of infiltration, had campaigned on an anti-Communist platform, and had every partisan reason to press the issue. So when the 80th Congress came

---

*Though nobody could have predicted it at the time, this Byrnes letter—undoubtedly the handiwork of Panuch and Klaus—would prove to be one of the more significant documents ever drafted in the history of our domestic Cold War.

†Sabath was of the view that State Department security measures of the time were too strict, while Jonkman, Bridges, and others thought they were too lenient.

to town in January of 1947, many individual members and several newly staffed committees were geared up for Red-hunting action, and plenty of it.

B Y ACCIDENT of timing, this Congress took control precisely as further seismic changes were rumbling through State, fracturing a security team that already had its share of troubles. On January 21, a chronically restless Secretary Byrnes had his oft-threatened resignation accepted by the White House and was replaced by Gen. George C. Marshall, just back from a foray to China. As a career military man, Marshall knew even less about the daily workings of the State Department than did Byrnes, and asked the already powerful Acheson to stay on and manage such internal matters for him.* Joe Panuch, at swords' points with the Under Secretary, and now without the shield of Donald Russell, couldn't survive in a department where Acheson was the un-challenged in-house ruler. By close of business on the first day of the Marshall era, Joe Panuch was out of office.[4]

Thereafter, in an exodus that resembled the turnover at the Far East division in late 1945, other members of the security squad would get their walking papers also. Among the first to go was Frederick Lyon. His colleague Robert Bannerman would follow a few months later, and still others of the hard-line faction would soon be ousted. Taking over the security shop were two youngish Acheson protégés who would loom large in disputes to follow: Assistant Secretary of State for Administration John Peurifoy, who assumed the duties of Panuch, and Hamilton Robinson, the new Director of Controls, replacing Lyon.

As the Acheson crew was piped aboard, John Peurifoy faced a forbidding prospect. Not only was he new on the job, he inherited scores of explosive cases left smoldering beneath the decks when Panuch and Lyon walked the plank. To make matters worse, there was the pushy Republican Congress, flexing its investigative powers and focused intently on the doings of his office. Peurifoy thus had to get up to speed while fending off lawmakers who wanted to know about particular suspects, failure to enforce the McCarran rider, security standards being used, and much else involving the security drill at State.

Amid all this turmoil, one factor was unchanging: the semi-official role of Samuel Klaus as record-keeper of the division. Why Klaus was kept on is un-clear, though one plausible reason would seem to be that Hamilton Robinson, the new Director of Controls, voiced legalistic, civil libertarian concerns about security issues identical to those expressed by Klaus the previous August. Also, Klaus was now by default the institutional memory of the office,

---

*Acheson would stay on as Under Secretary through June of 1947, returning as Secretary in January of 1949.

and the Acheson staffers would need briefings on pending cases and replies for questions coming down from Congress. So, in the early days of 1947, Sam Klaus was busy drafting memos, compiling lists of suspects, and framing answers for inquisitive members of the House and Senate.

These Klaus papers, some already noted, provide intriguing glimpses of what had been happening in the security shop in the weeks and months preceding. On February 3, for instance, Klaus memoed one new staffer, summarizing some salient topics. The first item on the list is of interest, considering the direction things would take in the new security age then dawning. "Peake* should be interviewed as soon as convenient for you," said Klaus, "with a view to exhausting the *Amerasia* and Institute of Pacific Relations background. The information obtained should provide a basis for questioning departmental personnel who are associated with either institution. Specific reference should therefore be made to the role played by such persons as William T. Stone, John Carter Vincent and others now in the department. You have a list."[5]

Like the chart in Bannerman's office and earlier effort to get rid of Stone, this indicated that the *Amerasia*/IPR combine at State had been a priority target of the old security squad. Also suggestive, Klaus spotlighted the case of Robert Miller, who had left the payroll in December but many of whose confederates remained there. Klaus stressed the need for inquiry on these cases. "You should," he wrote, "re-examine the case of Florence Levy, sister-in-law of Robert Miller, with a view to making suggestions for additional investigation." And: "The DRA [Latin American] cases should be pursued with special emphasis on the connections of Miller, Marshall Wolfe and Minter Wood."[6]

Three weeks later, Klaus drafted a more detailed update for Hamilton Robinson, stating:

> . . . I have requested Mr. Lyon on several occasions to produce from the files or obtain from the FBI reports allegedly existing which show connections of Mrs. Rowena Rommel and Robert T. Miller III with the notorious Communist Bruce Minton or his family in the Washington area. I have also asked for an investigation of Miller's sister-in-law, who I have found associated with him in a number of enterprises; her name is Florence Levy and she is employed in the department . . . I have also had no report for several months on the status of the investigation into the activities of Minter Wood, another Miller associate.[7]

For reasons to be noted, the idea of looking closely at the kith and kin of Robert Miller probably wasn't something Hamilton Robinson would have relished, but that would surface somewhat later. In the meantime, Klaus was

---

*Undoubtedly Cyrus Peake, a State Department intelligence expert who had been connected to *Amerasia* but resigned from the editorial board because of the journal's pro-Red nature.

drafting still other memos on cases of concern to Congress, arguably his most important duty. Congress not only had the power of legislation, oversight, and funding, all worrisome to State. It could also wield the power of exposure, which might happen with any member who took the trouble to dig in on security issues and speak about them in a public forum.*

Klaus and his colleagues were acutely aware of this and worked hard at keeping the lawmakers appeased, reasonably friendly—or something less than totally hostile—and, above all, quiet.† In another early memo, Klaus suggested a generic way of heading off congressional protest—invoking the prestige of Marshall. Summarizing the views of ACOPS, Klaus reported a consensus that "Secretary Marshall should personally vouch to the members of the House and Senate committees covering Foreign Affairs, State Department appropriations, and Un-American Activities for the adequacy of the present security procedures and of the personnel assigned to handle them."‡8 At this point, Marshall had been Secretary for not quite three weeks, and undoubtedly knew nothing of the combustible issues on which he was to give assurance. This tactic would in due course be used, but couldn't prevent inquiring members from pestering State with their unwelcome questions.

O NE such member was Bartel Jonkman, who had confronted Joe Panuch about the Carl Marzani case, demanding faster action and conceiving an aversion to Panuch that would figure powerfully in his thinking. Now he returned to the fray, determined to pursue the matter further. On February 12, he showed up in Peurifoy's office, where Klaus joined the conversation. Jonkman was irate that Marzani hadn't been fired the previous summer, saying, according to Klaus, "that he felt deceived by Secretary Byrnes, Mr. Russell, and Mr. Panuch" because he thought there was a pledge to do so. (Klaus denied that this was promised.)9

At this meeting, Jonkman, Peurifoy, and Klaus also discussed a further group of suspects, including Miller, then-current and former State employees

---

* It is pretty clear, for instance, that Gustavo Duran, though cleared by State, resigned because of the repeated inquiries from Congress, and the same appears to have been true of Hiss and Carl Marzani. As one Bureau memo relates: "Mr. Russell confidentially informed Mr. Roach [of the FBI] that he was of the opinion that there was nothing wrong with Duran . . . but that if pressure from the Hill continued it may be necessary to accept his resignation to keep Senators McKellar and Wherry quiet."

† Thus, in a memo of February 5, Klaus stressed his earlier theme that the security setup would need revamping, but only "after we have disposed of the few cases which have achieved notoriety—that is, have come to the attention of congressmen."

‡ This memo added: "It is further their [ACOPS'] opinion that short of General Marshall's assurance, it is improbable that anything we can do will fully satisfy every member of the House or Senate who may question the retention of a given person or the loyalty and sincerity of departmental officers."

Jeanne Taylor, Woodrow Borah, Maurice Halperin, and Joseph Gregg. On February 17, Jonkman followed up by requesting more specific data on Borah, Taylor, and seven other pending cases: Just Lunning, Bernard Nortman, Irving Goldman, Helen Yuhas, Minter Wood, Peveril Meigs, and Robert Lehman. In so inquiring, Jonkman showed that he—like several other members—already had certain facts in hand that closely tracked with FBI reports about the Bentley people and their contacts.

The nagging question of dismissals under the McCarran rider was brought up by Jonkman in April when he came back for yet another visit. On this occasion he again raised the issue of Marzani (and fellow OSS alumnus David Zablodowsky), mentioned the case of Haldore Hanson, and inquired again about the forty security suspects eased out in 1946. Klaus drafted a further memo about all this, noteworthy for its clear statement of the methods used in dealing with such cases:

> I told him [Jonkman] that . . . the forty figure was not intended to mean that forty persons were fired for that given reason (being pinks or Reds), but that forty persons who were dismissed on other grounds had derogatory allegations of that character against them and that, in fact, no one was fired for being a Communist. He said that it was his recollection also that Panuch said in that conversation [the previous summer] that no one was actually fired for being a Communist . . . I said that Panuch might have said so because it was the truth.*[10]

The operational, and striking, phrase in this was that, though the likes of Hiss, Marzani, Keeney, Halperin, and Miller had been sheltering in the State Department—when no fewer than twenty alleged Soviet agents had been ensconced there, per Bannerman's charts and Klaus's memo—"no one was fired for being a Communist." The scope and nature of the penetration had thus been finessed and kept out of the employment records, a technique that would be used many times thereafter and lead to still more security problems in the future.

As dogged as Jonkman, and doubtless more troubling to State, was Rep. Karl Stefan of Nebraska. Stefan was a major VIP in the world of Foggy Bottom—the new chairman of the House Appropriations subcommittee that controlled the State Department budget. Making him more formidable still, he

---

*Klaus would explain this more clearly still in yet another of his memos. Justifying the penchant for resignations, he gave the customary reasons—contentious hearings, evidence to be protected. He then added: "In view of that fact, and the cost in time and personnel which investigation entailed, the Department under Secretary Byrnes pursued the policy of requesting and accepting resignations, thus achieving the same end as would be achieved by dismissal." This explanation, written in March of 1947, conspicuously did not address the issue of why such dismissals had been so few after adoption of the McCarran rider, which had occurred nine months before. Equally strange, it failed to note the obvious hazard in such methods—allowing suspects to relocate to other governmental posts and taking an inordinate amount of time to get them out of the department.

seemed to have good information sources and an extensive list of suspects. In March of 1947, he submitted more than three dozen names to the department, describing them as people "whose loyalty to this government has been or is questionable" and asking for a rundown on their cases.

The Klaus response to this, dated March 21, 1947, is one of the more revealing documents on record, as it sets forth in tabular form the then-current status of these cases and the way they were disposed of. The result is a synoptic view of the security scene at State, or a substantial fraction of it, that had developed up through the spring of 1947. It reads as follows:

Persons Still Employed

1. The following have been investigated by the Department and no adverse findings have been made by the Department:

> Haldore E. Hanson[a]
> William Treadwell Stone[a]
> Julian R. Friedman
> T. Achilles Polyzoides
> Elwood N. Thompson
> Dudley Poore
> William P. Maddox
> John Stewart Service[b]
> John Carter Vincent

2. The following are still under investigation by the Department. In the first three cases the employees were previously rated eligible by the Civil Service Commission:

> Theodore J. Geiger (rated eligible by the Civil Service Commission)
> Alexander Lesser (rated eligible by the Civil Service Commission)
> Peveril Meigs (rated eligible by the Civil Service Commission)
> Minter Wood
> John T. Fishburn
> Hugh Borton
> Rowena S. B. Rommel
> David Randolph
> William D. Carter
> Charles A. Thomson

Persons No Longer Employed

1. Carl A. Marzani was discharged on the basis of investigation by the Department under the McCarran Rider.

---

[a]Employment approved by Assistant Secretary Russell in November 1945; it is believed that this was by arrangement with Assistant Secretary Benton.
[b]Cleared by Secretary Byrnes in writing. [Footnotes in original.]

2. H. S. Barton, Jr., was discharged on the basis of investigation by the Department under Rule XII on charges not involving loyalty.

3. In the following cases the Department had completed investigations and no adverse finding had been made at the time of termination:

> Clyde Eagleton (resigned)
> Herbert S. Marks (transferred to Atomic Energy Commission)
> Monroe B. Hall (resigned)
> Abraham Pivowitz (terminated at completion of temporary appointment)

4. In the following cases investigation had not been completed, and no adverse finding was made by the Department.

(a) These persons had previously been rated eligible by the Civil Service Commission:

> Robert T. Miller III (resigned)
> Robin Kinkead (resigned)
> Wayne Vucinich (resigned)
> John N. Hazard (resigned)
> David Zablodowsky (resigned)
> Donald A. Wheeler (resigned)
> Maurice English (resigned)
> Robert Rendueles (resigned)
> Herbert R. Southworth (completion of assignment; involuntary separation)
> Donald H. Cooper (transferred to War Department)

(b) These persons had previously been investigated and approved by OSS:

> Alexander S. Vucinich (resigned)
> William W. Lockwood (resigned)

(c) Others:

> Clifton Read (resigned)
> Alger Hiss (resigned)
> Bess Lomax Hawes (reduction in force)
> Charles A. Page (resigned)[11]

Again, the mere fact that somebody's name appeared in such a lineup didn't mean he or she was thereby labeled a Red or a loyalty risk. Klaus made the point by noting that inquiries on some cases had resulted in "no adverse finding," and that still others had been rated "eligible" by Civil Service. On the other hand, it's also true that someone's having been cleared or rated "eligible" didn't mean much either. (Both Hiss and Miller, for example, were in the "no adverse finding" column, while Klaus had himself been pushing for renewed inquiry on Stone, Vincent, and the Miller network.) Otherwise, what leaps off the page, once more, is the resignation tactic: Of the twenty-three people "no longer employed," fifteen had been permitted to resign, including not only Hiss and Miller but also Charles A. Page, one of the more notorious cases on record.*

Still other congressional troubles, meantime, were developing for the department and its security staffers. One lawmaker who took strong exception to kid-glove, slow-motion methods in dealing with egregious suspects, and to State Department security practice in general, was GOP Rep. Fred Busbey of Illinois, probably the most stringent critic of the department then in Congress. As seen, Busbey had previously gone after OWI, and, in a natural segue, now zeroed in on its successors—the Voice of America and cultural programs that had been folded into State under Assistant Secretary William Benton.[12]

At this time, the department still had a healthy regard for the plenary powers of Congress and was trying to maintain good relations with its members. In an episode that would be unimaginable some months later, Busbey in March of 1947 obtained from Peurifoy a letter which said the congressman "has my complete authority to talk with individuals in the organization concerning their background and the type of work which they are doing."[13] Using this *laisser passer,* Busbey variously traveled to New York to look into VOA broadcast operations, inquired about the art projects sponsored by the cultural division, and visited at least twice with Klaus at State.†

Thereafter, in floor debate on the State Department authorization, Busbey assailed the Benton office, saying "the personnel of the cultural division is in large measure a legacy from Communist-permeated OWI." The congressman read off a list of people in the unit, including Miller, Stone, Hanson, Charles Thomson, Page, and—a new addition to the roll call—Esther Brunauer. Following up on earlier hearings run by Stefan, Busbey also attacked the arts and publication efforts of the division, putting into the *Congressional Record* extensive data about the Communist and Communist-front connections of artists being sponsored by it.

As all of the above suggests, by the spring of 1947 intense concern about security matters at State, and elsewhere, was building rapidly in Congress. Even more to the point, while some lawmakers continued to raise their questions and exert their leverage behind the scenes, such as Busbey, Stefan, John Taber of New York, the powerful and often testy chairman of the House Appropriations Committee, and Rep. Eugene Rees of Kansas, chairman of the Civil Service Committee, were now sounding the alarm in public. (Rees at this period

---

*In addition to submitting his list of suspects, Stefan was at this time also raising inconvenient questions about the various cultural projects promoted by the department. In February he had questioned State official William Benton in private about these matters, and in March would run a series of public hearings on them that were highly embarrassing to the department.

†On the second visit, again indicating the degree to which Congress had developed certain information, Busbey asked Klaus about his secret memo of the preceding summer. Klaus replied that it was, indeed, secret and couldn't be released except by Peurifoy's authorization (which in this case was not forthcoming).

proposed creation of a new freestanding security agency to deal with cases of alleged subversion among federal workers.)[14] Faced with this mounting pressure, the Truman White House sought countermeasures to blunt the issue.

Foremost among these was the Truman loyalty program, in gestation since the 1946 elections but announced precisely at this juncture (March 21, 1947). In a step self-evidently meant to head off the legislative critics, the President unveiled what appeared to be a far-reaching plan to deal with the problems being complained of. A key feature was a proviso that every staffer of the government would be subject to investigation, regardless of position or department. Seemingly more draconian yet, Truman would stipulate that all employees be vetted for "loyalty" to the United States. Despite some ambiguities in the wording, these two aspects together appeared to say the loyalty of every employee of the federal government was prima facie suspect.

To oversee investigation of such matters, Truman directed that complex machinery be set up covering every aspect of the federal workforce. At the apex of the system would be a Loyalty Review Board (LRB) in the Civil Service system, its members presidentially appointed. Under this would be a network of regional boards to hear appeals in disputed cases. Under these in turn would be departmental boards, the basic working units of the program, to hear the cases of accused employees *de novo*. The head of each employing agency would appoint the departmental boards and act as the arbiter of cases, subject to post-audit at higher levels.

In April, shortly after announcement of the loyalty program, the administration began laying plans to present the cases of myriad suspects from the Bentley inquest to a grand jury in New York. This would be a laborious drill, as more than 100 witnesses made appearances before the jury in a marathon procession that went on for months. Such by-now-familiar figures as Gregory Silvermaster, Alger Hiss, Harry White, and William Remington would all be summoned. A full year later, however, there would be no indictments of the Bentley people—the main reason given for this being that the government had only Bentley's word to go on, with no confirming documents or cooperating suspects. It thus appeared that the massive FBI probe of the Gregory case would sputter out in futility after a year and a half of exhaustive effort.*

The loyalty program and grand jury proceedings both signaled that the administration was moving against the internal Communist menace and were obviously meant to send this message. But both had the effect as well of keeping the issue firmly in executive hands, with minimal input from Congress. Both would also take a long time to develop; the grand jury deliberations

---

*Hoover had in fact opposed that effort to seek indictments, reasoning (correctly) on the analogy of the *Amerasia* case that this would predictably result in failure. Toward the end of this phase of the grand jury process, the government would switch signals and instead obtain indictments of a dozen Communist Party leaders, none of whom was a Bentley governmental suspect.

would grind on for eighteen months, while the loyalty plan, though announced in March, wouldn't be fully up and running until the end of 1947. For members of Congress already incensed about delays in ousting suspects, some on the payroll for better than a decade, neither of these drawn-out procedures seemed a valid reason to drop the issue.

Accordingly, the State Department would now play its Marshall card, hoping thus to pacify the critics. In June of 1947, Marshall met with members of the Senate subcommittee on State Department appropriations and was examined on security matters. He duly gave assurances as suggested, received by the senators with little comment. After the session, however, members of the subcommittee handed him a blunt report about security affairs at State that was anything but reassuring. While details about this remarkable report must be deferred, one point is chiefly relevant here: its stress on the Marzani case, the long delay in seeking his dismissal, and the failure of officials at State to invoke the McCarran rider in other cases of like nature.[15]

Whether this particular missive did the job, or whether the cumulative weight of so many critiques proved decisive, the department did now move to enforce the rider, on something like a widespread basis. On June 23, State announced that ten of its employees were being discharged on security grounds, at the discretion of Marshall, using his summary powers of dismissal. Thus, after gathering cobwebs for almost a year, the McCarran rider was unsheathed to fell ten suspects at a stroke. Security hawks in Congress who had been complaining of inaction were, for a while, encouraged.

The ironic outcome of this move, however, was to make the rider more of a nullity than ever. Though the names of the suspended employees were never officially published, they soon became as an anonymous group extremely famous.* A concerted press campaign was mounted, by Bert Andrews of the *New York Herald Tribune* and others, depicting the firings as a gross violation of civil liberties and the ousted staffers as helpless victims. Whether this outcry was cause or pretext, State now flip-flopped again, and rather than entering the employees on its records as security dismissals changed their status to that of having resigned—"without prejudice"—from the payroll. This in effect reverted to the no-fault tactics of the past and basically spelled *finis* for the rider.[16]

While this debacle was unfolding, John Peurifoy made one last attempt to appease the mutinous barons on the Hill. In the late summer and early fall of 1947, in the spirit of his Busbey letter, he granted permission for staffers of the House Appropriations Committee to rummage through State's security files

---

*The names of these employees would eventually be published by the *Washington Times Herald,* suggesting some significant linkages to security inquests that have been mentioned. The ten discharged employees were James Ansara, Harold Bellingham, Woodrow Borah, Hannah Goldman, Irving Goldman, Alexander Lesser, Florence Levy, Bernard Nortman, Leonard Rennie, and Harold Weisberg. (September 21, 1947) Most of these were subjects of or spin-offs from the Gregory investigation.

and make a record of what they found there. This was in essence a follow-up on the requests of Stefan and would produce a much longer list of cases—108, to be exact. The investigators would compile fairly detailed entries on the cases, capsuling data from the files and offering comments about the way things were handled. Named after the chief clerk of the House committee, this roster would in future discussions usually be called "the Lee list." It turned out to be a significant document, as it provided the most comprehensive view of State Department security practice ever supplied to Congress.

It would also be, for all practical purposes, the last such view, as a thick curtain of executive secrecy would soon be drawn across the topic. The provocations for this further *volte-face* occurred in early 1948, shortly after the Lee list was assembled and had started to become a contentious issue. In January and in March, two House committees reviewed the list and questioned State Department officials about its cases. At this time also, the House Committee on Un-American Activities was on the trail of Dr. Edward Condon, an alleged security risk of large dimension who headed the National Bureau of Standards. The committee had its own rap sheet on Condon, but learned there was an FBI report about him at the Department of Commerce, where the Standards Bureau was housed. The committee requested a copy of this report but was turned down flat in a March 4 response from then–Commerce Secretary Averell Harriman, saying such disclosure wouldn't be in "the public interest."

Worse yet, from the perspective of Capitol Hill, was soon to follow. On March 13, a sweeping executive order was issued by President Truman forbidding the provision of any further security data to Congress from any executive unit whatever. The Truman edict said all subpoenas or other requests for such information by Congress should be refused and that "there shall be no relaxation of the provisions of this directive except with my express authority." With this ukase, the era of relatively full disclosure of security information was over. Henceforth, though Hill committees would continue wrestling with security cases—most notably the Hiss-Chambers and William Remington inquests in the summer of 1948—the information they could come up with was strictly what they could develop on their own.[17]

At the outset of this wrangle, the Truman order sparked efforts by outraged members of the House to defend what they considered the rightful powers of that body. The chosen battleground was the case of Condon. A leading spokesman on the issue, prophetic of many things to come, was freshman Rep. Richard Nixon (R-Ca.), a member of the Un-American Activities panel. In March of 1948, Nixon fired off a letter to Averell Harriman and Attorney General Tom Clark demanding that the FBI memo on Condon be disclosed to Congress. Based on what was already known about this memo, said Nixon, it revealed nothing of the Bureau's sources. Accordingly, he said, "the public interest demands that the full text of Mr. Hoover's letter be made public."

This view of the matter was endorsed by the full Un-American Activities panel and the Committee on Interstate and Foreign Commerce, and supported by a lengthy memo from the Legislative Reference Service of the Library of Congress.* All this in turn would be backed by a huge bipartisan majority in the House, which voted by a margin of better than ten to one (300–29) to "direct" that the Condon report be handed over.[18]

Unfortunately for Congress, this brave initial stand against executive secrecy would also be the last one. In amazingly jaunty fashion, President Truman made it clear that he wasn't about to back down from his secrecy order and defied Congress to do anything about it. The lawmakers, he said in paraphrase of Andrew Jackson, had made their ruling, now let them enforce it. This provoked still more congressional outrage and much denunciation of the White House. In a unanimous report about the Hiss case handed down in August of 1948, the House Un-American Activities Committee expressed its frustration this way:

> The committee's investigation of espionage among government workers has been hampered at every turn by the refusal of the executive branch of government to cooperate in any way due to the President's loyalty freeze order [i.e., the secrecy edict] . . . The committee deplores the fact that the executive branch of government will in no way aid the committee in its efforts to protect the national security from those who are doing everything they can to undermine and destroy it.[19]

Equally irate was Sen. Homer Ferguson (R-Mich.), who led the probe of the William Remington case and ran into similar roadblocks. Reviewing this and other secrecy issues, Ferguson warned his Senate colleagues that "some day we shall have to meet the issue head on because the trend to presidential arrogance" in such matters was getting totally out of hand. Congress, he said, "is rapidly being pushed into the intolerable position of having either to legislate through a blind spot or compel the President to answer for his conduct in an impeachment hearing."[20]

Strong words, but words Congress, at this point, was nowhere near ready to back up with action. So the secrecy order would stand, and continue standing long thereafter. In the months and years that followed, the Truman edict would be invoked with metronomic regularity, systematically denying Congress data on any and all loyalty/security suspects in the federal workforce. The lawmakers had thus learned enough about such as Hiss and various of the Bentley cases to know there was a serious problem to be dealt with. But now, as they

---

* The legal eagles at the reference service had prepared a memo on "the Right of Congress to Require Information from the Executive Department," saying it was essential to the legislative/oversight process that Congress have access to data on the performance of executive agents.

saw it, they were estopped from getting the information they needed to gauge the full extent of the danger and take corrective action.

All of which, from the vantage point of Capitol Hill, was rather as if a lid had been clamped down on a boiling kettle. As the laws of physics and politics alike suggest, that was a pretty good formula for an explosion. When it erupted, the shock waves would hit the Truman White House, State Department, and other executive agencies with shattering force, launching yet another security age of starkly different nature.

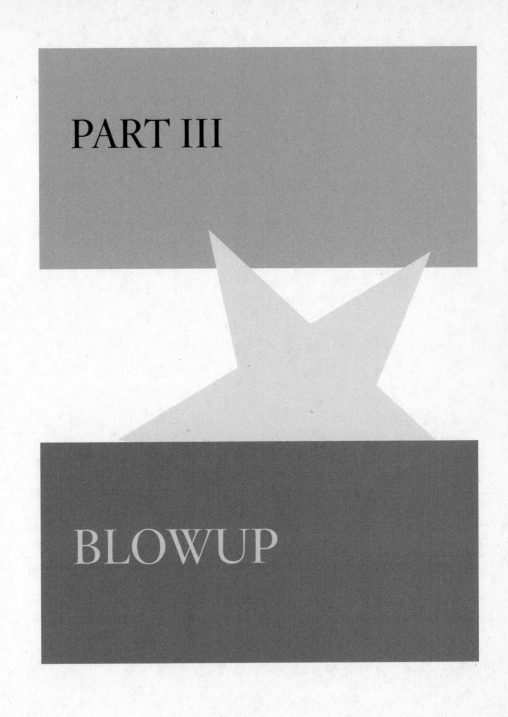

PART III

BLOWUP

CHAPTER 14

Wheeling, 1950

JOE McCarthy stepped into the pages of Cold War history at Wheeling, West Virginia—in many ways a suitable backdrop for his plainspoken message: a hardworking mill and mining town by the Ohio River, perched on the rugged wedge of land that divides Ohio from Pennsylvania. The date was February 9, 1950, a Thursday. The occasion, a Lincoln Day address to the Ohio County (West Virginia) Women's Republican Club, one in a series of political talks McCarthy was to give that month.

Not many people in Wheeling knew much about the speaker, then a young (forty-one) backbencher of the minority party in the U.S. Senate. The Republican ladies were expecting a discussion of farm problems or maybe housing, two specialties of the visiting solon, or perhaps a more generic party-building speech about Abe Lincoln and the GOP. What they heard was something very different—and infinitely more shocking.

However, exactly what they did hear would become, and long remain, a famous item of dispute. In general and without question, McCarthy told his 275 listeners at the Hotel McLure that there was a serious problem of Communist infiltration in the State Department, that this had been improperly dealt with, and that strong measures would be needed to correct it. Other things he had to say would be contested—most notably, and most lasting, just *how many* Communists in the State Department he was alleging. That this numerical aspect should be the focus of debate seems strange, but so the matter would play out.

In the immediate aftermath of the speech, national press attention was modest. The Friday-morning local paper, the *Wheeling Intelligencer,* devoted a front-page story to McCarthy's comments, and the Associated Press sent out a brief account to member papers, about two dozen of whom would use it. All in all, something less than a media firestorm. But by the time McCarthy got to Nevada two days later, the State Department was issuing press releases, McCarthy was expanding on his charges, and the question of what he said at Wheeling was starting to attract some wider notice.

Touching off the battle of the numbers was the *Intelligencer* story, written by a reporter named Frank Desmond. According to this, McCarthy had told his audience in Wheeling: "I have here in my hand a list of 205 that were known to the Secretary of State as being members of the Communist Party and who, nevertheless, are still working and shaping policy in the State Department."[1] The same quote would appear in various AP stories that echoed the *Intelligencer* item and would be recycled many times thereafter. McCarthy, however, would always categorically deny that he had said this.

McCarthy's version of what he said at Wheeling, and other places, was that he did indeed have a "list" of people in the State Department who were "either card-carrying Communists or certainly loyal to the Communist Party," but that the number of these was 57, not 205. He said the larger figure, which he acknowledged using from time to time, wasn't a list but a statistic—derived from the letter Secretary of State James Byrnes had written in 1946 to Rep. Adolph Sabath.* From these differing versions of the speech there grew up an enormous wrangle featured in every book about McCarthy and most political histories of the era.

In one sense, what McCarthy did or didn't say at Wheeling is not a matter of great moment—is, indeed, a derailment from the major issues. The crucial topics to be discussed, after all, were the conduct of the Cold War; whether in this context Soviet spies, Communist agents, or dubious loyalty/security risks had infested the State Department; and if so whether in 1950 they were still burrowing in the woodwork. This could be deduced, not by parsing McCarthy's words and numbers, but by examining the security setup at State and tracking the leads and cases its officials had developed. McCarthy might have said there were 300 Martians in the State Department without affecting this larger issue one way or the other.

However, in another sense, the evidence on McCarthy's talk at Wheeling

---

*Byrnes said there had been 284 State Department employees on whom security screeners made adverse findings, and that 79 of these had been removed from the department as of July 1946. Hence, 205 such employees were then still on the rolls at State.

is important. It was this speech that launched the whole McCarthy era, led to his more detailed address before the Senate, then triggered the Tydings hearings and everything that followed. Moreover, what McCarthy said at Wheeling is significant because his opponents contrived to make it so. To cite only the most obvious examples, the report the Tydings committee produced dwelt on the 205 at length, and Sen. William Benton (D-Conn.) would later use this as his main exhibit in urging the Senate to oust McCarthy. Since then countless articles, books, and media productions have picked up the Tydings-Benton thesis, saying McCarthy falsely claimed to have a "list of 205" at Wheeling, then backed down and changed his story. The subject thus goes to his credibility— and, it's worth noting, that of his critics.

At a distance of more than fifty years, it's of course impossible to reconstruct the facts on Wheeling with any great assurance. All the major players are gone and data that could have answered our questions in definite fashion are, for various reasons, missing. Most obviously, a recording of the speech made by Wheeling radio station WWVA for broadcast that evening was erased, apparently on the following day or perhaps a few days later. Most of the people who heard the speech are doubtless gone as well (though fortunately not all). Nonetheless, we do have a surprising amount of information to draw on in trying to figure out what happened.

The evidence gathered by the State Department, Tydings subcommittee, and Senator Benton to prove McCarthy lied about the Wheeling speech consisted of five items: First, the Desmond article in the *Intelligencer* containing the "205" quotation. Second, a letter from an executive of the paper, Col. Austin Wood, more or less vouching for the Desmond story. Third, a rough draft of the speech McCarthy brought to Wheeling, in which the 205 quote in fact appeared, copies of which had been given to Desmond and representatives of the radio station. Fourth and fifth—and most crucial—depositions from two officials of the station about the broadcast of the lecture.[2]

These affidavits would be central to the indictment of McCarthy, as they served as stand-ins for the lost recording (and were significant for other reasons also). In them, station officials Paul Myers and James Whitaker swore they had checked McCarthy's draft against the talk he had delivered and that he read the text verbatim—in which event, he did indeed lay claim to a "list of 205," since that is what the rough draft stated. Such was, and such is now, the case against McCarthy.

As it happened, all this would be carefully looked at in 1951 by investigators from the U.S. Senate. When Benton brought his charges urging McCarthy's expulsion from that body, they were referred to the Subcommittee on Privileges and Elections (a panel of the Rules Committee), chaired by Sen. Guy Gillette (D-Iowa). As a charge of perjury about the Wheeling numbers was the first item on Benton's list, the Gillette committee sent its staffers up to

West Virginia to dig out the facts about it. The findings they came back with were capsuled in a forty-page memo that is the most comprehensive source of data now available on the subject—and probably was the best source then.[3]

Of particular interest in this memo is the immediate prehistory of the speech, as sketched by the committee staffers. In this account, McCarthy arrived at the Wheeling airport on the afternoon of February 9, where he was met by ex-Congressman Francis Love, former GOP senatorial candidate Tom Sweeney, and reporter Desmond. At this time McCarthy gave a copy of his projected speech to Sweeney for the use of WWVA, and another to Desmond. According to both Love and Sweeney, McCarthy stressed that this was a rough draft he was going to revise before delivery.

The Senator was then driven to the Fort Henry Club in Wheeling, where he said he was going to work on the speech for a couple of hours. At 7:00 P.M. or thereabouts, he was picked up again by Sweeney and driven to the Hotel McLure, where he would deliver his address. Among those in the audience that evening was the editor of the *Intelligencer,* Herman Gieske. As Gieske told the Senate staffers, McCarthy stressed to him as well that the draft supplied to Desmond was not the speech delivered and that any press treatment of the talk should be based on what McCarthy actually said that evening.

In the course of their investigation, the committee staffers interviewed Love, Sweeney, Desmond, Gieske, and others who had been at the meeting. They also talked with station officials Myers and Whitaker about the depositions they had given. From this round robin the investigators learned a number of intriguing things about the draft, the Desmond story, and the Myers-Whitaker affidavits. Their chief findings were as follows:

• According to the investigative memo, reporter Desmond conceded that the "205" quote in his story was taken from the rough draft of the speech, not what McCarthy said at the McLure. As the memo related, Desmond "admits that he did not hear Senator McCarthy make that statement and that, in quoting McCarthy in his news article, he relied on the script which had been delivered to WWVA, a copy of which had also been given to him."[4] The memo later revisited the question in four separate passages:

> "Desmond admitted he 'got the figure' he used in his news article from the script"; ". . . the true source of the figure cited in his news story was the 'rough draft' of the speech which Senator McCarthy had given him"; "Desmond admitted to our investigators that the script was in fact the sole source of the figure '205,' used by him in his news account of the speech"; ". . . the explanation made to subcommittee investigators by Desmond . . . concerning the circumstances surrounding the publication of the news article [and the letter from Austin Wood] show these two items of proffered evidence to be lacking in evidential value on the point at issue."[5]

All of which would seem to make matters pretty clear concerning the draft, the Desmond story, and where the "205" quotation came from.

• As for the depositions of Myers and Whitaker, the Gillette committee inquiry found equally disturbing problems. In particular, it was hard to square their statements that McCarthy read the draft verbatim with the testimony of other people at the dinner. These witnesses were unanimous in saying McCarthy spoke more or less extemporaneously, apparently not following a text at all, rough draft or other. The consensus was that he may have read some sections of the speech but ad-libbed others, waving papers around, pacing behind the podium, and speaking as the spirit moved him.

Meeting chairman William Callahan, for instance, stated: "I have a distinct impression that McCarthy cut, eliminated, passed over, jumped through parts of his speech." Tom Sweeney would agree, recalling: "McCarthy was not reading the speech. It was a combination of both [reading and extemporizing]. He was walking around the platform. He referred to the manuscript from time to time. He did not read the speech." Francis Love concurred: "It seems to me that McCarthy talked extemporaneously but that he had papers in front of him and might have read a paragraph now and then."[6]

Also suggestive on this point, the rough draft of McCarthy's speech included some grossly erroneous population figures that would have shocked everyone present if read verbatim. Most jarringly, the draft said the Soviet Union at that time controlled some "80 billion people" while the population of the free world had shrunk to "500 thousand." Nobody recalled McCarthy saying anything that outlandish, but if the affidavits were true he must have.

Based on this information and close questioning of the men who gave the affidavits, the memo reached a thumbs-down verdict on both depositions. Of one affiant it stated: "On the basis of his own admissions to subcommittee investigators . . . this sweeping certification has been shown to be inaccurate." Of the other: "The accuracy of his affidavit is placed in question by the testimony of five other witnesses who were present during the delivery of the speech [about its impromptu nature] . . . It is difficult to reconcile [the] affidavit with this testimony." Thus, according to the Senate memo, the affidavits on which Tydings-Benton relied went the way of Desmond's story.[7]

• The foregoing, of course, is of a purely negative nature—suggesting that the alleged proofs of what McCarthy said at Wheeling weren't proofs at all, per the investigative findings. Also significant, however, were interviews with several witnesses as to what McCarthy did say, as best they could recall it. Granted the imperfections of memory and inevitable variations of detail, these witnesses were generally agreed in what they remembered. A colloquy with William Callahan reads as follows:

CALLAHAN: . . . McCarthy definitely talked about two different figures. I
have the impression there was a smaller group, which by his information
were known Communists, or known to have Communist connections.
The other group, while he did not have the information to pin it down, he
thought that they could be or probably were in a similar group or connection. What did McCarthy say he said?

[DANIEL] BUCKLEY [one of the investigators]: He said he used the figure 57
concerning Communist suspects and possibly 200 or 205, which figure
he got from the Byrnes letter.

CALLAHAN: The language you just used sounds more familiar . . . it would
be my impression that if McCarthy used 200 or 205 and then the smaller
figure of 57, which he said he used, that would be more in line with what
I believe [occurred].[8]

Like testimony came from former Congressman Love, who had met
McCarthy at the airport and was at the dinner. His recollection was that "there
was certainly another figure mentioned other than the 205 and I think was
stressed more than 205. I am not sure if 205 was mentioned. It seems to me he
talked about another number." Gieske of the *Intelligencer* stated: "I questioned
the '205' which Desmond used in the story and I pressed him closely as to
whether he heard it used. I questioned the authenticity of it. My own recollection is that I did not hear '205' though I was there. My recollection is that Desmond said he was depending on the McCarthy manuscript which was issued
tentatively and subject to change . . ."[9]

Strikingly similar to these comments were the statements of three other
witnesses who heard the speech and who shared their distant memories of it
with the author in March 2000, shortly after the fiftieth anniversary of the
meeting. These were Eva Lou Ingersoll, Douglas McKay, and Ben Honecker,
all young political activists in Wheeling when McCarthy came to visit. Naturally, after so great a lapse of time, total recall of exact details was not to be
expected. Also, on such a notorious topic, the possibility had to be considered
that feedback from other sources might have mingled with firsthand recollection. That said, these interviews jibed with the above, and also, on a most critical matter, with one another.

Most notably, all three of these attendees said McCarthy had spoken impromptu and definitely didn't appear to be reading a text verbatim. Again, the
consensus was that he may have read some of his remarks, ad-libbed others,
seemed to consult his text from time to time but would then make statements
off the cuff. All this reinforced the testimony of witnesses in the Gillette inquiry and thus reconfirmed the central point that the supposedly conclusive
radio affidavits had to have been in error.

As to what McCarthy said exactly, given the lapse of fifty years, the testimony of these latter-day witnesses was understandably mixed, as was that of the Gillette committee subjects. By far the most detailed and vivid account was supplied by Mrs. Ingersoll, who was explicit in saying McCarthy's version of what he said was right, and the Tydings-Benton thesis thus mistaken. The exchange about this went as follows:

> QUESTION: In the summer of 1950, Senator Tydings and other critics of Senator McCarthy contended that here in Wheeling he had said "I have in my hand a list of 205 Communists," or something like that, "in the State Department."
> ANSWER: That was wrong.
> QUESTION: Would you just address what you remember him saying with respect to the 205?
> ANSWER: He spoke of the 205—as I recall, they were being investigated . . . and then he said, "Of the 205, 57 were found to be card-carrying members of the Communist Party." I remember that. And someone told me later that they weren't carrying cards at that time. But I am telling you what he said anyway.
> QUESTION: That's what I want. So, he did not claim to have, in your recollection, a list of 205 Communists?
> ANSWER: No.[10]

The question of course arises as to how Mrs. Ingersoll remembered so distinctly details so hazy in the minds of others. Her answer was that she had definite reason to recall the figures. She said she was so astounded and alarmed by what she heard that she scribbled down the numbers, borrowing a pen from a friend to do so, making notes on a page from her phone bill. Some weeks later she found these in her purse, and remembered them very well thereafter. What she had written down, she said, was first the number "205" and then "57 cc"—the letters standing for "card-carrying Communists." The first was the larger number referred to by McCarthy, the second the list he claimed to have in his possession.*

The two other attendees at the event, McKay and Honecker, while confirming that McCarthy spoke *ex tempore*, were much less certain about the

---

* On this point the questioning went as follows: *Question:* "You had at the time of the meeting made those notes when he was speaking. Is that correct? Then you later pulled the piece of paper out of your purse and said, 'I want to remember this?' . . . " *Answer:* "That is exactly how it happened." *Question:* "Do you remember the note saying . . . that there were 205 of some larger group of suspects? And did those notes say '57 cc' "? *Answer:* "Yes some 57 were found to be [card-carrying Communists]." *Question:* "So that is very vivid in your memory. That is one reason you remember it so well?" *Answer:* "That is right."

Nor, be it noted, did Mrs. Ingersoll wait fifty years to make these assertions. In 1970, she was interviewed by a representative of PBS for a documentary being made about McCarthy. In this interview she gave the same rendition of what McCarthy said at Wheeling.

numbers. Asked about them, McKay said he did recall McCarthy saying he had a "list" of Communists in the State Department and using the figure "205" in this connection. When McKay was asked about the Ingersoll statement, the dialogue went as follows:

> QUESTION: I have just interviewed another person who said the following, and I would ask you to comment about this: That what he said—what she remembered him as saying, and she said she had notes on it—was that there had been a group of 205, and that of these, 57 were card-carrying Communists. You don't recall that?
>
> ANSWER: I don't recall that. He could well have said that, but I do not recall.[11]

Ben Honecker, when asked about the numbers, referred to "200, 205, 55," in that order, but when questioned further didn't recall what numbers were used how. These exchanges went as follows:

> QUESTION: You mentioned the 205, and then you said 55. Do you remember 55 as a number [of suspects] at all?
>
> ANSWER: I have never paid too much attention to the numbers that the politicians use because they can vary from one day to the next.
>
> QUESTION: That is for sure. But you don't specifically remember what he said about that—205, 57?
>
> ANSWER: Nothing.[12]

On net balance—as to specifies and also as to imprecisions—these responses weren't radically different from the replies the Gillette investigators got when they went up to Wheeling (in statements of which these modern witnesses had no knowledge). The chief similarity is the agreement on the impromptu nature of McCarthy's talk; the main difference, the very explicit statement of Mrs. Ingersoll, who seems to have been one of the few people at the event, or perhaps the only person, who made notes of what McCarthy said there.

Beyond such personal reminiscence, there is further evidence bearing on the issue—namely, other press accounts about it. As it developed, the Desmond story was but one of three renditions of the McCarthy talk published in the *Intelligencer,* though the other two receive short shrift, or none, in the conventional histories. One of these was an editorial Herman Gieske wrote the day after the meeting, which not only differed from the Desmond story but closely tracked McCarthy's version.

Gieske's editorial, published Saturday, February 11, stated, *inter alia:* "Senator McCarthy shocked his audience when he charged there are over fifty

THE GIESKE EDITORIAL,
February 11, 1950

This *Wheeling Intelligencer* editorial, written the day after McCarthy's speech at Wheeling, reports the senator as saying there were "over fifty" suspects of Communist affiliation in the State Department, confirming his version of the numbers used at Wheeling.

The Wheeling Intelligencer.

Wheeling, West Virginia

Edward Everett Clucks, Editor — K. C. Ogden, Publisher 1918-1947

Saturday, February 11, 1950 — Telephone Wig. 3600

Published by The Intelligencer Publishing Company

SENATOR JOE McCARTHY'S VISIT TO VALLEY AREA

The visit to our Valley region of Senator Joe McCarthy, of Wisconsin, as the GOP Lincoln Day speaker, was pleasing and stimulating in many particulars, not the least of which was his vehement, forthright arraignment of Communistic infiltration into the U. S. Department of State, now headed by Secretary Dean Acheson. Senator McCarthy, properly, we believe, approached this problem from the standpoint of the American patriot, rather than that of a mere political partisan. This is not surprising, considering that the Senator was a combat flier in the U. S. Marines, with the rank of Captain in World War II.

Senator McCarthy shocked his audience when he charged there are over fifty persons of known Communistic affiliations still sheltered in the U. S. Department of State. When such an allegation is linked with the brazen avowal by Secretary Acheson of his friendship for Alger Hiss, convicted of traitorous revelation of U. S. secrets to a Communist espionage apparatus, the situation becomes one of the most vital concern to every American citizen. Mr. McCarthy was frank and blunt in his avowal of an intense desire to see the supercilious, incompetent Acheson removed from office as a result of a coalition of Republicans and Democrats on a patriotic basis.

"I will work with anyone, Democrat or Republican," said Senator McCarthy, "to attempt to bring about the displacement of Acheson. The truly alarming thing is that these 'enemies from within' actually assist in the formulation of U. S. foreign policy if they do not dominate it."

Senator McCarthy declared that Secretary Acheson cannot be unaware of this Communistic infiltration of which, he said, Alger Hiss was, but one example.

We are in hearty concurrence with Senator McCarthy's approach to this matter. It is not merely a case of partisan politics for the sake of partisan advantage. Mr. Truman, we feel, must be as shocked by Dean Acheson's out-of-character reaction to the Hiss treachery as everyone else in the nation; and although it might be embarrassing to the President to replace still another Secretary of State, it will be more embarrassing as time goes on and the ineptitude, to put it mildly, of Secretary Acheson is more and more conclusively revealed.

If ever there was a time that our country needed a real bi-partisan foreign policy, in which Republicans and Democrats alike would bring to bear their fullest patriotism and highest and keenest intelligence, it is now. Unfortunately, Senator Vandenberg is very ill, suffering pain which according to reports, make it difficult for him to function as of yore. This means, probably, that other Senators will necessarily be drawn into a bi-partisan group

persons of known Communistic affiliations still sheltered in the U.S. Department of State . . . Senator McCarthy declared that Secretary Acheson cannot be unaware of this Communistic infiltration of which, he said, Alger Hiss was but one example." This verification of McCarthy's account of what he said was written, be it noted, within twenty-four hours of the event—not weeks or months thereafter.*[13]

A third rendering of the speech, passed over in the usual histories, also appeared in the *Intelligencer,* and this, too, sharply differed from the Desmond version. The Friday-morning paper, on page 12, printed extensive excerpts from McCarthy's talk that did in general follow the rough draft, but with two major deviations: (a) the erroneous population figures were corrected; and (b)—more significant yet—the passage about the 205 was conspicuously omitted. The obvious implication of the latter is that the statement on the 205 was in fact not uttered by McCarthy.[14]

The neglect of this highly visible feature in the *Intelligencer* by the Tydings panel and historians of the era is extremely puzzling, since it is by far the most extensive media version we have of what McCarthy said that evening. Evidently, the draft was checked over by someone who followed it as McCarthy spoke and who corrected it for errors or changes in the light of what was actually said. The resulting text is obviously a better proxy for the lost recording than the garbled, unpublished, and totally uncorrected draft that Myers-Whitaker said had been declaimed verbatim.

Also, as noted in the Gillette inquiry, there are supplementary sources that recount what McCarthy said in the immediate wake of Wheeling. As he hedge-hopped West by air for other speeches, he made stops at which he met reporters and offered further comment on his charges. Of note was a stopover Friday afternoon in Denver, Colorado, where he talked with a reporter from the *Denver Post.* This encounter is somewhat famous, as it receives a fair amount of play in the usual write-ups. The reason for this is that the *Post* ran a picture of McCarthy peering into his briefcase, with a caption saying: "Sen. Joseph R. McCarthy—Left commie list in other bag." This mocking caption is too much for anti-McCarthy writers to resist, so they have often used it.[15]

However, curiously absent from such accounts is the headline on the story accompanying the photo, in much larger type than the sardonic caption and thus impossible to miss. This reads: "57 Reds Help Shaping U.S. Policy: McCarthy." (See page 189.) Anyone who read the caption on the photo would also have seen this headline, but it is nowhere mentioned in the standard

---

*Some McCarthy critics argue that this editorial may have been written by Gieske on Saturday to help out McCarthy *ex post facto* when a flap developed about the numbers. This speculation is based on a misunderstanding of how newspapers work. An editorial appearing in the Saturday paper would have been written not on that day but on Friday—at which point there was as yet no particular flap about the numbers.

THE *DENVER POST,*
February 11, 1950

Various McCarthy biographies quote the caption on the photo with this story but omit the much larger headline saying that McCarthy used the number "57" in discussing Reds in the State Department—the number he always claimed he used in making his original charges.

57 Red; Help Shaping U.S. Policy: McCarthy

See story on page 1 also.

The state department knows the names of its fifty-seven employes who are card-carrying Communists, Senator Joseph R. McCarthy (Rep.) of Wisconsin insisted Friday afternoon in Denver.

During a half hour stopover at Stapleton air field, he offered to show the list to newsmen, but discovered he had left it in his baggage on the plane. At that time, he said he would give the state department the names "if they ask me for them, but they already know them."

Later, in Salt Lake City, he declined to reveal any names to newsmen, and said he would show the list to Secretary of State Acheson if Acheson would telephone him and "show his sincerity by having a presidential order revoked, at least insofar as the fifty-seven are concerned. (The order prohibits government departments from turning over loyalty records to congressional committees.)

"VARIOUS SOURCES."

"It would be a waste of effort to give Acheson the names, then have him deny they are Communists when we cannot get the records," he declared.

Senator McCarthy asserted that his information came from "various sources, including the un-American activities committee." He explained that the president's loyalty board had listed 289 employes of the state department as "bad risks." Of that number 205 are still working in the department, he said. The fifty-seven card-carrying Commu-

Denver Post Photo.

SEN. JOSEPH R. M'CARTHY.
Left Commie list in other bag.

nists are "not necessarily" all among the "bad risks" designated by the loyalty board, he added.

(In Washington, State Department Press Officer Lincoln White asserted, "We know of no Communist member in the department and if we find any they will be summarily discharged.")

In a Lincoln day address prepared for delivery Saturday night in Reno, Senator McCarthy cited the case of one state department employe who was under investigation by the FBI for "turning over secret information to the Communists" and who has since been promoted to a key position.

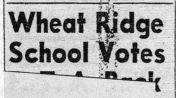

Wheat Ridge School Votes

treatments. So, though our historians have somehow failed to notice, the first independent story we have about McCarthy's comments in the aftermath of Wheeling clearly shows him using the number 57 in referring to his list of suspects—not 205. (Indeed, the same story goes on to give his explanation about 205 as a statistic, not a McCarthy list, much as he would elsewhere explain it.)*

From Denver McCarthy went to Salt Lake City, where he would attend a Republican dinner with Sen. George Malone of Nevada and take part in a radio show, all this still on Friday. This stop produced two further newspaper accounts relating to the numbers—in both of which McCarthy was again quoted as expressly saying he had the names of 57 suspects.† Likewise, when McCarthy and Malone appeared Friday evening with Salt Lake radio personality Dan Valentine, McCarthy said: "Last night I discussed the 'Communists in the State Department.' I stated I had the names of 57 card-carrying members of the Communist Party." Thus, McCarthy's stopover at Salt Lake produced three separate media versions of what he said there, all echoing what he said in Denver.[16]

The story would be much the same on Saturday when McCarthy arrived at Reno, where he was to give an address that evening. On the afternoon of that day, he sent a telegram to Truman using the identical figure appearing in the Denver/Salt Lake stories: "In the Lincoln Day speech at Wheeling Thursday night, I further stated that I have in my possession the names of 57 Communists who are in the State Department at present."[17] That evening, in a speech at the Mapes Hotel, according to the Reno press accounts, he once more made the claim that he had the names of 57 people who were "card-carrying" Communists on the rolls at State.

Finally, the Reno visit provided some further detail pertaining to the rough-draft issue. In the *Nevada State Journal* coverage of the talk appearing on Sunday, February 12, reporter Edward Connors wrote: "Sen. McCarthy who had first typed in a total of 205 . . . scratched out that number and mentioned only '57 card-carrying members . . .'" From this phrasing it would ap-

---

*The same edition of the *Denver Post* that carried this story also had an AP account, datelined Salt Lake City, that recycled the "205" quote from Wheeling. Interestingly, various historians of the era (e.g., Oshinsky, Reeves) conflate this AP dispatch with the "Commie list" caption, making it appear that they occurred in the same story—thus indicating that McCarthy claimed a "list" of 200-plus in Denver. As with the omitted headline stressing "57," this conflation is of a curious nature, since the local Denver story is quite explicit on McCarthy's distinction between the 57 and the 205. (See inset, p. 189.)

†On Saturday, the story in the *Salt Lake Tribune* began: "A charge that at least 57 card-carrying Communists are in the State Department was reiterated in Salt Lake City by Sen. Joseph R. McCarthy (R-Wis.) . . . 'If Secy of State Acheson would call me I could read him the list of 57 names,' Sen. McCarthy said." This story was headlined: "Visiting Solon Cites Reds' Infiltration," with a kicker that read: "Lists 'at Least 57.'" A like story ran in the *Salt Lake Telegram,* which quoted McCarthy as saying: "If Secretary of State Dean Acheson would call me I could read him the list of at least 57 card-carrying Communists who are in his department . . . There may be more. We just have the names of 57."

pear that Connors had a copy of the same rough draft supplied at Wheeling but with the numerical changes penciled in.[18]

It will thus be observed that, in repeated instances immediately following the speech in Wheeling—numbering at least half a dozen—McCarthy invariably claimed to have a "list" of 57 Communists at State, not 205. So far as the available records disclose, there are no exceptions (other than recycled AP accounts) to this consistent usage. Likewise, when he did use the figure 205, he explained that this was a statistical calculation and not a McCarthy "list." McCarthy would make the identical explanation many times thereafter, in many different settings. However, these early instances are of greater evidential value, as they occurred in the immediate aftermath of Wheeling.*

From all of which, the question inevitably arises: Why would McCarthy have claimed on Thursday evening to have a "list of 205" Communists at State, then instantly turn around on Friday and repeatedly say, on so many occasions, something so entirely different? And the self-evident answer has to be that he would not have done so. The plain inference from the data canvassed, mixed with a little common sense, is that what he was saying on Friday must have been what he had said the night before, just as he contended. That verdict is in turn congruent with the findings of the Senate staffers who found no credible evidence he had ever uttered the statement about a "list of 205" in Wheeling to begin with and much evidence to the contrary.

One further point about newspaper treatment of the Wheeling speech is worth brief notice. At the height of the later uproar about the subject, in June of 1950, McCarthy wrote to Herman Gieske asking if he could locate someone who had a recording of the speech as broadcast on WVVA. McCarthy said he was willing to pay up to several hundred dollars for such a recording, but asked the editor not to publicize the fact that McCarthy was the buyer. Gieske complied with this request, running a notice on the front page of the *Intelligencer* on July 6 saying such a recording would be worth considerable money as a "collector's item," not saying McCarthy was the would-be collector.[19] As it turned out, no such recording was discovered. However, McCarthy could not have foreseen this, and by having this item run all but ensured that such a recording would surface if it did exist, and would do so in a public manner. As the Gillette investigators noted, he would hardly have gone to these lengths unless he were confident such a recording would support his version of the numbers.

---

*In anti-McCarthy treatments of all this, as with the Gieske editorial, some of the Friday statements are discussed as though they amounted to "changing his story" in response to a backlash from Wheeling. This ignores the facts (a) that there are no credible data that he ever did tell any other story; (b) that by Friday afternoon, when he got to Denver, there hadn't been much backlash; and (c) that, even if there had been, McCarthy, cooped up in a plane all day, would have had scant occasion to know it.

An instructive gloss on the above is the reaction to the Gillette committee memo by one of McCarthy's severest critics—Senator Benton's aide and confidant, John Howe. As Howe would later write to Benton: "I lost my enthusiasm for the 'perjury' charge when I got a chance that evening, two years ago, to read the report of the committee staff. Now there isn't any doubt that the 205 card-carrying Communists in the State Department appeared in the rough draft. But there is grave doubt that McCarthy actually said it, to the audience or on the air. He ad libbed a great part of the speech, roaming over the stage, and occasionally walking back to glance at his notes. He used at least two figures (doubtless 205 and 57). You'll remember that the next night—where we had the recording [of the Salt Lake broadcast]—he announced that on the previous night he had spoken of 57 card-carrying Communists. The 205 figure, I would then assume, he used in its proper context—based on the letter from Byrnes to Sabath."[20]

Howe then summarized further data from the staff report—Desmond's admission that he had written his story from the draft, the Gieske editorial saying "over fifty," and the business of the depositions. From this overview Howe concluded: "All this has considerably muddied the clarity of the perjury charge, don't you think?" (Benton was less easily persuaded, arguing that the Senate staffers had been biased in McCarthy's favor, but grudgingly acknowledged that the perjury charge was weakened.)

Based on Howe's comments, as well as on its intrinsic merits, the memorandum put together by the Senate staffers was obviously a document of great importance in settling the issue of what McCarthy said at Wheeling. Which makes it of surpassing interest that this fact-laden memo was never printed for public consumption (only nine copies of it were made) and that when the subcommittee issued its final report these findings about the Wheeling numbers were not so much as mentioned. Rather, the whole perjury count against McCarthy—though it was Benton's foremost charge—was simply dropped from the discussion. (This clearly wasn't for reasons of space, as the panel did devote 266 pages of its final report to reproducing McCarthy's financial records. See Chapter 32.)

All too obviously, the data the investigators brought back from Wheeling weren't what the subcommittee's higher-ups were after, so the resulting memo was stuffed in a drawer somewhere and conveniently forgotten.* Subsequently, the memo would all but vanish from chronicles of the era—ignored in most studies of McCarthy, referred to obliquely and not too accurately in a couple, and otherwise consigned to the oblivion of the archives (and hard to locate even there). Likewise, the misgivings expressed by Howe were kept discreetly

---

*A point of considerable relevance later, when McCarthy's failure to cooperate with this committee became one of the two counts on which he would be censured by the Senate. (See Chapter 44.)

private, and may be found today only by rummaging through ancient papers. By such devices do facts of record, for purposes of political history, become officially nonexistent.*

Meanwhile, the contention that McCarthy claimed a "list of 205" Communists at State, then backed off from this and started crawfishing on the numbers, would be enshrined in the report of the Tydings panel as the alleged truth about the speech at Wheeling. From that source it would be repeated, and still is, in countless books, surveys of the Cold War era, and media productions of all types alleging that Joe McCarthy was a liar. The stark contrast between such standard treatments and what is actually in the record would become a model for virtually all discussions of McCarthy now available to readers.

---

*A single—and noble—exception to these comments is the Buckley-Bozell book about McCarthy, which has a quite accurate discussion of the memo, to which the authors were given access. It was this book that prompted Howe to write his note to Benton.

CHAPTER 15

Discourse on Method

C OMPLETING his foray to the West, McCarthy arrived back in Washington on Saturday, February 18, after a brief stopover in Wisconsin, to what seems today a tame reception. The scant coverage he got on his return suggests that, nine days after Wheeling, his charges still hadn't become a press sensation—though that was about to change abruptly.

The Sunday *Washington Post,* for instance, gave no notice at all to his arrival, in contrast to its subsequent nonstop and generally hostile coverage of his doings. The *Washington Times Herald,* sister paper of the *Chicago Tribune* and later McCarthy's main journalistic backer, did somewhat better by him, but only somewhat. It devoted a small item on page five to his return, headlined, "McCarthy to Tell 'Facts on Reds,' " but not saying much besides this.[1]

The *Washington Sunday Star* put McCarthy on page one but devoted only three brief paragraphs to him, below the fold, tagged to a somewhat longer story about Senate Democratic leader Scott Lucas of Illinois. In a statement from Chicago, Lucas had leveled a blast against McCarthy, saying he "simply doesn't have the facts" and demanding "let him name the names." In oblique response to this, the *Star* quoted McCarthy as saying he "intends to present considerable detailed information to the Senate tomorrow" (i.e., Monday) but "refused to say whether he would name the Communists."[2]

This long-distance press exchange between McCarthy and Scott Lucas was predictive of much that happened later. The let-him-name-the-names motif had been a feature of State Department responses to McCarthy for several days before this, so perhaps Lucas was merely echoing what he had seen somewhere about those statements. Or perhaps he already had a game plan of his own. At all events, his comment from Chicago prefigured the main point that he would stress when McCarthy went before the Senate.

On Monday afternoon, apparently between 4 and 5 P.M., McCarthy as advertised rose on the Senate floor to make his charges and present the evidence he had to back them. According to eyewitness accounts, he had stacked before him a large pile of folders from which he would intermittently read material, flourish papers, and offer exhibits for viewing by his colleagues. In a marathon presentation clocked at better than six hours, he recited the cases of some fourscore past, present, and prospective employees of the State Department, all allegedly going to show massive subversion and security breakdown in Foggy Bottom.

Before McCarthy could get into his presentation, however, a number of other things would happen. Almost immediately, he would be challenged by Scott Lucas as to what exactly he said about the 205 at Wheeling and the quote from the Frank Desmond story in the *Intelligencer*. In response, McCarthy would give the explanation of the numbers reviewed in the preceding pages, noting the difference between the 57 names he claimed to have and the statistical 205 derived from Byrnes. He also read in full the text of his speech as he said it had been given in both Wheeling and Reno, the telegram he sent to Truman, and excerpts from the Byrnes letter to Adolph Sabath.

As this was the first occasion on which McCarthy would give his version of what he said at Wheeling-Reno, it's an appropriate spot for a synopsis of these controverted lectures. In these remarks, he said the two speeches were the same and that both had been recorded "so there can be no doubt as to what I said." The recording part was certainly true of Wheeling and apparently true of Reno, but as seen the Wheeling version was erased and nobody ever made that much of an issue of what he said at Reno. (From McCarthy's comments, it doesn't appear he then knew the Wheeling recording had been erased.)[3]

In substance, the speech McCarthy read to the Senate wasn't too different from the text excerpted on page 12 of the *Intelligencer*. It was an impassioned call for all-out American resistance to the designs of Moscow and its agents, depicted as aggressively expanding their empire while the frontiers of freedom were shrinking (hence the population figures). In so stating, McCarthy cast the struggle starkly in religious terms—the confrontation of atheistic communism with the Christian civilization of the West. The United States, he said, had the resources, moral stature, and responsibility to resist this menace but hadn't effectively met the challenge.

The blame for this McCarthy placed squarely on elements in the State

Department, and elsewhere in the federal government, who were either working for the Communist cause or heedlessly permitting others to do so. It was in this context that he mentioned four individuals—John Service, Gustavo Duran, Mary Jane Keeney, and State Department appointee Harlow Shapley—as examples of lax security practice and/or blindness to the Communist danger. (He further mentioned Alger Hiss and Julian Wadleigh, but as both of these had already been dealt with in court proceedings, neither was ever a McCarthy "case.")

In these comments, the centrality of the religious issue was perhaps the most striking feature. It was the Communist denial of God and its "religion of immoralism," McCarthy said, that made the differences between East and West irreconcilable—far more than the many obvious distinctions in political and economic systems. The choice at this fundamental level, in his view, was clear-cut and inescapable, and had to be met without equivocation. "Today," he said, "we are engaged in a final, all-out battle between communistic atheism and Christianity." The message, in both tone and content, was apocalyptic.

Even back in 1950, the strong religious note was a bit unusual for a political stump speech to a secular audience, which in more typical cases might have had a passing reference to such matters but wouldn't have made them a main thesis. Another notable aspect of the talk, which recurred in several places, was its distinctly populist flavor, expressing disdain for the elitists who had become enmeshed in revolutionary causes.

"It has not been," said McCarthy, "the less fortunate or members of minority groups who have been selling out the nation, but rather those who have had all the benefits that the wealthiest nation on earth has to offer—the finest homes, the finest college educations, and the finest jobs the government can give. This is glaringly true in the State Department. There the bright young men who are born with silver spoons in their mouths are the ones who have been the worst."[4]

The glaringest of the glaring, said McCarthy, was Alger Hiss, "who sold out the country which had given him so much" and had been convicted in federal court a few weeks before for having done so, then lying about it under oath. This led in natural sequence to Dean Acheson, who had recently made the famous statement that he wouldn't "turn his back" on Hiss, his erstwhile subordinate in the State Department. In defense of this comment, Acheson had cited the passage in the Book of Matthew ending "I was in prison and you came to me." This reference outraged McCarthy, who denounced "this pompous diplomat in striped pants, with a phony British accent," for blasphemously invoking the words of Christ to justify complaisance toward a traitor.

This was pure essence of Joe McCarthy, combining religious and patriotic themes, populist leanings, and anti-Communist fervor in one package—all of it unloaded on the high official who in his view epitomized what was wrong with American conduct in the Cold War. It was Dean Acheson's fostering care, as McCarthy saw it, that had permitted such as Hiss to flourish. To McCarthy, what Acheson said about Hiss was simply inconceivable—indicative of a mental and moral blindness that threatened the very survival of the nation. (That view would be reciprocated by Acheson and his allies, who thought the inconceivable danger was McCarthy and the "primitives" he represented.)

McCarthy said a number of other things as well—concerning the deals cut by Franklin Roosevelt at the Yalta conference with Joseph Stalin, the 1949 testimony of former FBI agent Larry Kerley about Soviet spying in World War II, and an assertion that the main Cold War evil to be combatted was not espionage, bad as that was, but Communist influence on American conduct overseas. "In discussing the Communists in our government," said McCarthy, "we are not dealing with spies who get 30 pieces of silver to steal the blueprints of a new weapon. We are dealing with a far more sinister type of activity because it permits the enemy to guide and shape our policy."[5]

It was at this point that the paragraph concerning 57 "card-carrying Communists" was inserted, almost in incidental fashion, as illustrative of the policy problem. Again, since this would be so much disputed, it's well to have McCarthy's version of what exactly he had said about the matter, as follows: "I have in my hand 57 cases of individuals who would appear to be either card carrying Communists or certainly loyal to the Communist Party, but who nevertheless are still helping to shape our foreign policy."[6]

Something more than incidental was McCarthy's focus on John Stewart Service. Not only was the Service-*Amerasia* matter mentioned in the Wheeling-Reno text, it became a subject of further comment in its own right. McCarthy rehearsed for the Senate the tale of the *Amerasia* scandal and Service's reports from China touting the cause of the Yenan comrades. He then sharply criticized the way the case had been handled by the Truman administration. The whole affair, he said, showed that something was badly amiss in the State Department and the White House.

Other topics McCarthy mentioned in his prepared remarks, and in impromptu exchanges with his colleagues, were those touched on in earlier comment: resort to the resignation strategy rather than discharging suspects outright, failure to invoke the McCarran rider, the secrecy in which all such topics had been mantled. In which connection, McCarthy made a particular point of the need for Congress to get access to security records rather than merely taking the say-so of the State Department or the White House as to what was in them.

By reading the text of this speech before the Senate, McCarthy plainly wasn't backing down from his previous claim that he knew the identities of 57 people in the State Department "who would appear to be card-carrying Communists or certainly loyal to the Communist Party." In fact, he read the identical number/allegation into the *Congressional Record* in the text of his wire to Truman. In so doing, he bound himself to a hard-line critique of State, the specific number 57 in reference to Communists or their clones at Foggy Bottom, and the contention that he had the names of this many suspects. Unlike the confusion over what was said at Wheeling, all of this was extremely clear and readily documentable from the *Record*.

However, when McCarthy finally got going on his cases, the Senate speech was more varied and nuanced than the text from Wheeling-Reno. This was perhaps to be expected, if only because of the obvious difference between a stump speech to the party faithful and what amounted to a formal proffer of charges in an official setting. There was the further point that the Senate speech discussed a large number of individual cases that varied from one instance to the next and couldn't all be handled in identical fashion. Also, the nature of the evidence itself was mixed, apparently stemming from different kinds of sources.

In this presentation, McCarthy did say, in so many words, that various of the suspects he was describing had been identified by knowledgeable witnesses, FBI reports, and intelligence data as Communist Party members. Other allegations were less direct, though not exactly reassuring: association with known Reds, hiring and promotion of Communists, contacts with suspected Soviet espionage agents, employment by Soviet or pro-Communist groups, and the like. To judge from his presentation, there were certainly a lot of people on his roster—perhaps more than 57—who could plausibly be described as Communists or "certainly loyal to the Communist Party" *if* the McCarthy allegations were correct and current.

All told, McCarthy said, he was going to present information on 81 cases—which, for a variety of reasons, was not precisely the number covered. Reading from what he said were data from "State Department files," or digests thereof, he painted a lurid picture of security meltdown. In reciting the cases, he indicated that he knew the identities of the people he was discussing but supplied no names, listing the suspects by numbers only. Adding to the air of mystery, various contacts of these individuals, alleged espionage agents and such, were also nameless.

While treatment of particular cases must be deferred, a few of McCarthy's comments about some of his suspects are worth a note in passing to get the tenor of the discourse. These statements, in most instances, were somewhat detailed, though brief, and often of sensational nature. They also provided to knowledgeable students of such matters significant clues as to where McCarthy's data had come from. Here, for example, was case No. 1:

"The man involved in case No. 1 is employed in the office of the Assistant Secretary of State. The intelligence unit shadowed him and found him contacting members of an espionage group. A memorandum of December 13, 1946, indicated that he succeeded in having a well-known general intervene with an assistant secretary in behalf of one man who is an active Communist with a long record of Communist Party connections. There is another individual who is very closely tied up with a Soviet espionage agency. There is nothing in the file to indicate that the general referred to knew these two individuals were Communists."[7]

Here was case No. 11: "This individual was an analyst in OSS from July 1943 to August 1945, and was employed in the Division of Map Intelligence in the State Department after August 1945. He is a close pal of a known Communist and has stated it would be a good idea if the Communists were to take over in this country. He is a regular reader of the *Daily Worker.* This individual is not in the State Department at this time, but has a job in the CIA as of today."[8]

Case No. 28: "This individual has been with the State Department as a Foreign Service officer since 1936. He is still holding a high salaried job with the government, and to the best of my knowledge he is now stationed in Frankfurt, Germany. A report of June 1947 indicates that he is a member of the Communist Party, that he attended the Youth International in Russia in 1935. . . . He had been discharged previously from the AFL Federation of Government Employees on the charge of Communistic activity. . . . The file discloses the interesting information that he is a member of the central group, whose task is to spearhead an attack on J. Edgar Hoover and the FBI. . . ."[9]

And case No. 46: "[This] is the case of a man who holds a high position in the State Department. He had been affiliated with the magazine *Amerasia* from May 1937 to November 1941. This magazine consistently followed the Communist Party line. It was under the direction of Philip Jaffe and Frederick Vanderbilt Field [both identified, later self-admitted Communists]. . . . On March 22, 1946 the State Department's own security agency recommended [his dismissal]. . . . The Department took no action on this recommendation."[10]

As to the sources of such information, McCarthy repeatedly said it came from "the State Department's own files" or from the department's "security agency" and was accordingly known to Secretary of State Acheson and his assistants. McCarthy further asserted that, were it not for "some loyal employees" of the State Department, he wouldn't have been able to give such data to the Senate. His references to the State Department's security files were many: "I do not have complete State Department files, information to which we are entitled. . . . I am trying to recite the facts which the State Department's own security agency dug up . . ."[11]

Concerning the security division at State and certain of its "loyal employees" who had tried to enforce more rigorous standards, McCarthy made some suggestive statements about Joe Panuch. These indicated that McCarthy knew something of the internal struggles in the security division—though not, apparently, the full story. They also evinced a high regard for Panuch and his colleagues, in implicit contrast to the Acheson appointees who replaced them. As McCarthy phrased it:

> . . . the information I get—and this is not so much from the files—is that this man Panuch tried to do a job of housecleaning and was given somewhat of a free hand under Jimmy Byrnes in starting to accomplish the job. However, when Byrnes left and Marshall took over—senators will recall Acheson was then Under Secretary—the first official act of General Marshall was to discharge this man Panuch. Obviously, General Marshall did not know anything about the situation. . . . Here is one man who had tried to do the job of housecleaning, and the ax falls.[12]

At several places, McCarthy also expressed the nature of his own role as he conceived it. He wasn't the head of the FBI, or an undercover agent, or a professional security expert. "I do not," he said, "have a counterespionage group of my own." He was not alleging on his own authority that the cases he recited were security risks or Communists, but rather that data to this effect were contained in the records of the State Department. He repeatedly noted that the cases were "nothing new," that many had been kicking around for years but had been ignored or treated with indifference. All of which meant, he said, that it was time for the U.S. Senate to take responsibility for such matters and conduct a thoroughgoing inquest.[13]

Working his way through a mass of data, and subject to countless interruptions and digressions, McCarthy stumbled in several places. Most obviously, he omitted about half a dozen of his cases and, toward the end of his recitation, undoubtedly bleary-eyed, repeated a case already dealt with. Beyond this, as subsequent checking would show, he made a number of other errors: whether a given person was still in the State Department, the date on which something happened, the particular office held by someone at a particular time. Also, as his critics would note, if the security information said someone had been identified as a Communist, he tended to cite the identification as fact—no "allegedly" about it. In prosecutorial mode, he pushed the evidence hard to make an indictment and seldom erred through understatement. Conversely, as such discussion made clear also, he wasn't simply inventing charges out of whole cloth.

All this made for a laborious and lengthy presentation, and it became the more so thanks to a constant barrage of questions and interruptions. A few of these came from McCarthy's Republican colleagues, trying to be helpful and amplifying some of the points that he was raising. Thus, both Homer Ferguson of Michigan and Karl Mundt of South Dakota spoke up to emphasize the resignation strategy that had prevailed at State and elsewhere, and failure to use the McCarran rider. Maine Republican Owen Brewster, an experienced student of such matters, hit hard at the Truman secrecy order and the need for Congress to get the underlying data.[14]

However, these Republican comments and asides were overwhelmed by the sheer volume of Democratic interruptions. Scott Lucas's early challenge on the Wheeling numbers was merely a warm-up for what would follow. Brien McMahon of Connecticut, for one, went after the issue of the State Department files and the summaries McCarthy was reading, intimating that McCarthy was citing only unfavorable items and that the complete files might show something different. This brought a further statement from McCarthy on the need for Congress to get the records. "The Senator understands," McCarthy countered, "that I do not have complete State Department files in these matters. I very greatly wish I did. That is one of the things I hope one of our committees will succeed in getting."

Contributing uniquely to the debate was Sen. Herbert Lehman (D-N.Y.), perhaps the upper chamber's most prominent liberal. At one point, Lehman had a go at the numbers, deducing that McCarthy was talking about "250" names because "I am adding the 57 names to the 205 names which have been mentioned. . . ." McCarthy answered by once more explaining the distinction between the 57 and the 205, the Byrnes letter and related matters. Lehman then asked "whether these names or any substantial number have been submitted to the Secretary of State." To this McCarthy answered that Acheson already had the names and cases in his possession—as all of them came from State itself. Lehman then complained again that "I still do not understand why these names have not been submitted to the Secretary of State."[15]

The numbers and the question of giving the names to State weren't the only things confusing Lehman. An even more curious exchange developed on the question of how, exactly, Communists looked and walked and acted. In discussing two of his suspects (Mary Jane Keeney and Gustavo Duran), McCarthy said that if someone looked, walked, and talked like a Communist, then he probably was a Communist. To this Lehman replied, "If we could spot Communists by the manner in which they walk, our task of fighting Communism would be far simpler than it is." McCarthy explained that he was using the phrase metaphorically and that "I have not . . . seen them physically walk, I am speaking of [their] records . . ." Lehman: "I did not think the senator could describe a Communist by the way Communists look."[16]

As shall be seen, this would not be the last time McCarthy's opponents indulged in questioning of this eccentric nature. However, by far the most persistent—and significant—of the questions aimed at McCarthy concerned, not how the suspects looked and walked, but who exactly they might be and whether he would supply their names, then and there, before the Senate. As presaged in his weekend comments, Scott Lucas went after the question early and returned to it often.

Given the standard treatment of McCarthy and his alleged methods of recklessly smearing people by naming them as Communists or security risks, the series of exchanges on this issue may once more be surprising to modern readers. The facts of the matter, as it happened, were quite the other way around. McCarthy had barely begun his presentation, for example, when Lucas interjected: "I want him to name those Communists. . . . The senator is privileged to name them all in the Senate, and if those people are not Communists the senator will be protected." A few minutes later, Lucas was back with the same demand, referring to "all the Communists he [McCarthy] is going to name. I want to remain here until he names them."[17]

These comments occurred before McCarthy had discussed a single suspect on his roster. When he at last got going on his case No. 1, Lucas was on his feet again, demanding: "Will the senator tell us the name of the man for the record? We are entitled to know who he is. I say this in all seriousness. The Senate and the public are entitled to know who that man is . . ." Thereafter Lucas repeatedly returned to the subject, saying that "whenever the senator names the names," he, Lucas, would assist in the investigation. Still later, Lucas asserted, "The sooner the senator can name these names, the better off we will all be."[18]

McCarthy demurred from all these suggestions, including the notion that he could rely on senatorial privilege to make false identifications without fear of libel.* As instructive as the many demands from Lucas for public naming of the suspects were McCarthy's repeated refusals to do this and the reasons he gave for not complying. Very early in the proceedings, McCarthy stated his position this way:

"The names are available. The senators may have them if they care for them. I think, however, it would be improper to make the names public until the appropriate Senate committee can meet in executive session and get them. I have approximately 81 cases. I do not claim to have any tremendous investigative agency to get the facts, but if I were to give all the names involved, it might leave a wrong impression. If we should label one man a Communist when he is not a Communist I think it would be too bad. However, the names are here. I shall be glad to abide by the decision of the Senate after it hears the cases, but I think the sensible thing to do would be to have an executive session and have a proper committee go over the whole situation."[19]

---

*In this context, McCarthy made a statement he would later regret and which was often used against him: that if the day came when he said something on the floor he wouldn't say elsewhere, he would resign from the Senate. This comment occurred, of course, against the backdrop of his *refusal* to name the names. Once he was required to do so, this high-sounding pledge was impossible to keep, not only because of possible harassment through libel suits, but because news media wouldn't use the names unless they were privileged. McCarthy would conduct an interesting test of this later on when he offered the names of certain suspects to the media off the floor of Congress. No reporter would use them.

McCarthy returned to the subject when McMahon raised the issue of fairness to people on the list of suspects. To this McCarthy replied: "The senator from Illinois [Lucas] demanded, loudly, that I furnish all the names. I told him at that time that so far as I was concerned I thought that would be improper; that I do not have all of the information about these individuals. I have enough to convince me that either they are members of the Communist Party or they are giving great aid and comfort to the Communists. I may be wrong. That is why I said that unless the Senate demanded that I do so, I would not do this . . . It is possible that some of these persons will get a clean bill of health. I know that some of them will not."[20]

Still later, again addressing McMahon, McCarthy stated: "If the senator from Connecticut had been here a little earlier, he would have heard the majority leader demanding that [the identities be made public]. He demanded that I present the names and indict them before the country, without giving them a chance to be heard. I said, 'No, I will not do that unless the Senate demands it. . . . I may be wrong.' That is why I am not naming them"[21]

Nor was even this the end of the matter. Still later in the debate, Sen. Garrett Withers (D-Ky.) also urged McCarthy to name the names, on the unusual theory (voiced earlier by Lucas) that *not* naming them was an unfair practice—allegedly placing all other, innocent staffers of the State Department under a cloud of suspicion. Withers proved to be a full match for Lucas in his persistence, saying: "I should like to ask the senator what reasons he has for not calling names. Does not the senator think it would be a fine thing to let the public know who the guilty are . . . ?" And: "Does not the senator know that I, like all others, am anxious to hear their names?"[22] To all of which McCarthy responded:

"I have stated repeatedly I would go before any Senate committee and divulge the names. I have said further that if it were the feeling of the majority of the Senate that . . . we can do a better job by making the names public on the floor of the Senate, I will be glad to abide by that decision. However, I think that would be a mistake. . . . Let me say that this matter is too important for me to use it as a utensil whereby I can satisfy someone's curiosity. . . . I am convinced of the Communist connections of these persons. . . . Nevertheless, I do not think, as a general proposition, one member of the Senate should arise on the floor of the Senate and should make public the names of 81 persons in that way."[23]

This is a lot about a single matter, but it is a matter of utmost importance in assessing the usual image of McCarthy—and the stance of his opponents. Rather than McCarthy's recklessly naming people in public as Communists or security risks without providing them a chance to answer, it was Senators Lucas and Withers who demanded that precisely such a course be followed, and it was McCarthy who adamantly refused to do so. The record on this is about as clear as such things can get—and is the more suggestive as Scott Lucas wasn't merely one senator among many, but the majority leader of the Senate. Quite obviously, Lucas and Withers were trying to bait McCarthy into committing "McCarthyism" in discussion of his cases, and were indefatigable in their attempts to do so.

THIS background takes on additional relevance in connection with the Senate subcommittee hearings that followed. In his exchanges with Lucas, McCarthy repeatedly said such hearings should be in executive session—this obviously congruent with his refusal to name the names before the Senate. The Lucas reply was equally consistent, matching his demands that McCarthy give the names in public with a curt dismissal of executive hearings.

"As far as I am concerned," said Lucas, "it will not be in executive session. If I have anything to say about it, it will be in the open where every individual in America, every newspaperman, can attend, so that they will know definitely as soon as possible just who is being charged and who is not being charged with being Communists."[24]

As Lucas was the Senate leader, he of course had something to say about it, and did. In obedience to the Lucas-Withers logic that *not* naming the names in public was unfair, arrangements were made to have the hearings in public session. McCarthy had wanted executive sessions, and so did his Republican colleagues on the subcommittee that would weigh his charges, Bourke Hickenlooper of Iowa and Henry Cabot Lodge of Massachusetts. However, they were in the minority and their views did not prevail. As Hickenlooper would tell the Senate (concurred in by Lodge):

> It is a matter of fact that the junior senator from Massachusetts [Lodge] and I . . . at the first executive meeting of the subcommittee, proposed the procedures that the subcommittee meet in executive session, call the senator from Wisconsin before it, and ask him to disclose the names in private, together with whatever information he had in connection with the cases; but the majority of the subcommittee said no, this must be brought out in public . . . the senator from Wisconsin was required, or requested, to come before the committee in public hearings with klieg lights, television and all the rest of such an emotional occasion, there to bring out his cases, name the names, and produce facts.[25]

Accordingly, McCarthy made preparations to appear in public session and brought with him information on various cases, including backup data that would be distributed to the press as well as to the subcommittee. The first of these cases, as it turned out, was Dorothy Kenyon, a onetime New York City judge and former State Department appointee to a U.N. commission on women. Judge Kenyon had an extensive record of affiliation with Communist fronts, which McCarthy was primed to discuss in some detail.

Against the backdrop of the Senate debate, Lucas's statement that there would be no executive sessions, and the recollections of Hickenlooper/Lodge about the way this was settled, the opening exchanges between McCarthy and subcommittee chairman Millard Tydings are instructive. As the hearing commenced, Tydings suddenly announced to McCarthy that it was up to him to decide whether they would be in public or executive session:

> TYDINGS: Senator, at any time that you feel that you want to go into executive session with part of this testimony, if you will indicate that I will call the committee right here together and we will see what the situation is . . .
>
> McCARTHY: Let me make my position clear. I personally do not favor presenting names, no matter how conclusive the evidence is. The committee has called me this morning, and in order to intelligently present the information, I must give the names. . . . Let us take the case of Dor—
>
> TYDINGS: I told you when I invited you to testify that you could testify in any manner that you saw fit. If it is your preference to give these names in executive session we will be glad to have your wishes acceded to. If it is your desire to give them in open session, that is your responsibility.
>
> McCARTHY: Let me say this first case has been handed to the press already. . . . Let us take the case of Dorothy Kenyon.[26]

With that the deed was done. "McCarthyism" had at long last been committed, and McCarthy would henceforth be held responsible for naming the names of his suspects in open session, thus smearing them in public. It was a foretaste of what was to come in the hearings chaired by Millard Tydings and other events of curious nature.

CHAPTER 16

The Tydings Version

IN MOST chronicles of the 1950s and their white-hot security battles, the name and work of Millard Tydings loom exceeding large. This is so for one fairly obvious reason and for one that's less apparent, though critical to our understanding of the era.

The obvious part is that Tydings was a hugely significant player in the drama, occupying center stage for months in a titanic struggle with McCarthy. Not so obvious is that standard treatments of the matter have relied, either directly or indirectly, on information gleaned from Tydings. Indeed, the whole scenario now accepted as historical truth about McCarthy's early cases comes from the report and dicta of Tydings and his subcommittee allies. The accuracy of the Tydings version is thus a matter of some interest.

Like everything else in the McCarthy story, the choice of a committee to weigh his charges and the scope of its investigation were topics of dispute. From a Republican standpoint, the Senate Appropriations Committee was a favored venue, as it included such knowledgeable GOP stalwarts on loyalty/security issues as Homer Ferguson of Michigan and Styles Bridges of New Hampshire. The Democratic leadership, however, preferred the more liberal Foreign Relations Committee, chaired by Tom Connally of Texas—a choice that had some surface merit inasmuch as the State Department was the focus of inquiry.

As the Democrats controlled the Senate, Foreign Relations got the job, to be handled through a special subcommittee. The Republicans did somewhat better on the scope of the investigation, or so it appeared at first. Scott Lucas had wanted to confine the probe strictly to McCarthy's cases, but Ferguson and Sen. Irving Ives (R-N.Y.) objected, urging a much broader survey. The resolution that was adopted, S.R. 231, seemed to promise this, saying the subcommittee was "to conduct a full and complete study and investigation as to whether people who are disloyal to the United States are, or have been, employed by the Department of State."[1]

The fourth-ranking Democrat on the full committee, Tydings became the subcommittee chairman. Serving with him on the majority side were former U.S. Assistant Attorney General Brien McMahon of Connecticut, already met with, and octogenarian Theodore Green of Rhode Island, both reliable New Deal liberals. Hickenlooper of Iowa, a staunch conservative of the Robert Taft wing of the GOP, and Lodge of Massachusetts, a leading party moderate, were the Republican appointees. (To give things a bipartisan aura, the Democrats hoped to bring Lodge over to their views, but in this were doomed to failure.) Washington lawyer Edward Morgan, a veteran of such investigations, would be named chief counsel. Internal security expert Robert Morris was later added to the staff, assisting the Republican members.

On the face of it, the choice of Tydings to lead the probe seemed to be a shrewd one. He was one of the grandees of the Senate, chairing the powerful Armed Services Committee as well as serving on Foreign Relations. First elected in 1926, he was high on the seniority ladder and by all accounts a potent force in backroom dealings. He was known to be tough, a bit imperious, and able. Also, he had an independent image, having opposed the Roosevelt Supreme Court–packing scheme of 1937 and thereafter weathering a purge attempt by FDR in the Democratic primary elections of 1938.

As this last suggests, Tydings was then seen as a conservative Democrat of the southern/border state variety, which meant, first and foremost, an opponent of civil rights. (Maryland at the time was as one with other jurisdictions south of the Mason-Dixon line in having segregated institutions.) But Tydings had another side as well, not so visible to the public. He was closely linked with the foreign policy establishment of the New Deal era and had twice championed Dean Acheson for advancement to high office. Tydings thus provided cover to the right, particularly with southern Democrats, but figured to be a solid ally of the State Department in any showdown with McCarthy. In this he would not disappoint.

THE Tydings panel launched its public sessions on March 8, 1950, in the full glare of the media spotlight, with McCarthy as first witness. The

Senate Caucus Room—scene of many celebrated hearings—was packed wall to wall. Spectators, press, Hill staffers, and executive employees were jammed together, some behind and within a few feet of the committee dais. Klieg lights blazed, flashbulbs popped, and reporters crowded the press tables as they awaited the appearance of the suddenly famous leadoff witness. The McCarthy era in American politics had now begun for certain.

Once things got rolling, the proceedings turned out to be spectacular, unruly, and extremely odd. The executive-session gamesmanship that occurred beforehand was, as it transpired, only one such maneuver among many. For openers, in a replay of what happened on the Senate floor, when McCarthy tried to read a statement he was repeatedly interrupted. (McCarthy himself would calculate that he was interrupted more than 100 times in the course of his presentation. A more impartial source, historian-biographer Lately Thomas, writes that "in his first 250 minutes on the stand [McCarthy] was allowed to read a statement for 17 minutes, and was interrupted 85 times.")[2]

As telling as the number of interruptions was their aggressive nature, obviously meant to rattle McCarthy and knock him off balance. Before he could read a word of his prepared remarks, Senators Tydings and Green launched a salvo of preemptive questions about one of the fourscore cases given to the Senate. This led to an involved exchange in which Tydings and McCarthy cross-talked about different numbers—Tydings referring to case 14, McCarthy for some reason to case 57. Why McCarthy answered as he did remains a puzzle, but motives for the Tydings stress on case 14 are readily unraveled.

Case 14 involved an allegation that an official in the State Department had intervened to have charges against a security suspect dropped. Tydings and Green wanted to know if McCarthy had the name of this meddlesome official and if he would reveal it then and there for all the world to know of. The matter was so urgent, they said, not a further second should be lost in exposing the wrongdoer. To this McCarthy replied that he was prepared to discuss things in a certain order and didn't have information on all cases with him. He would handle that particular case when it came up in proper sequence.

This drew a sharp rebuke from Tydings. "You are," the chairman said, "in the position of being the man who occasioned this hearing, and so far as I am concerned in this committee you are going to get one of the most complete investigations ever given in the history of this republic, so far as my abilities will permit. Now what I am asking you is: Do you or do you not now know the name of this man?"[3]

This raised some eyebrows, as it seemed to say the purpose of the hearings was to investigate McCarthy. It also provoked a strong reaction from the GOP contingent—Hickenlooper and Lodge observing that there were plenty of other cases on McCarthy's roster that looked as serious as this one, and that the sudden clamor to name the wayward official seemed strange considering that the case had been read into the *Congressional Record* two weeks before this. With Lodge, especially, the Tydings-Green preemptive strike turned out to be a grievous error. After McCarthy had been badgered several times without being able to begin his statement, Lodge protested:

> Mr. Chairman, this is the most unusual procedure I have seen in all the years I have been here. Why cannot the senator from Wisconsin get the normal treatment and be allowed to make his statement in his own way, and not be cross-questioned before he has had a chance to present what he has? . . . I think the senator from Wisconsin ought to have the courtesy that every senator and every witness has, of making his own presentation in his own way and not be pulled to pieces before he has had a chance to offer one single consecutive sentence. . . . I do not understand what kind of game is being played here. . . .[4]

Lodge's bafflement was shared by others, but such confusions would be resolved once the facts about the case were known. The official allegedly sinning in case 14 was Joe Panuch, on whom McCarthy had showered praises in his speech before the Senate. (The charge of interference was based on a State Department memo from Robert Bannerman, an intramural critic of Panuch.) Naming Panuch would presumably have embarrassed McCarthy, showing that one of his cases involved someone he had lauded as a hero.

Beyond embarrassment on Panuch, there was a further point to the Green-Tydings questions—to smoke out, and make an issue of, the sources of McCarthy's information. Green, especially prone to candid moments, made this fairly plain, asserting: "The point is, what basis has the senator for his charges on the floor of the Senate?" And again: "I am not asking whether the name is there or not, I want to know how you know it." McMahon came at the matter in even more peremptory fashion: "Will you produce for my inspection," he demanded of McCarthy, "what you have about case No. 14?" When McCarthy demurred from this, McMahon hammered at the issue again: "Will you or will you not produce them [papers relating to case 14] for my inspection right now?"[5]

In fact, it's clear from these exchanges and collateral data that Tydings and Co. knew very well where case 14 and other McCarthy cases—or most of them—had come from. As had by now become apparent to Tydings-Green-McMahon and others, the vast majority of the dossiers McCarthy recited to the Senate were taken from the so-called Lee list, compiled for the House Committee on Appropriations in the fall of 1947 and the subject of House committee hearings in early '48. McCarthy plainly had a copy of this list and based much of his oration on it.

Establishing this, indeed, took no great powers of detection. The similarity between the lists may be seen today by anyone who has both rosters and bothers to compare them. If we can see this now, then obviously Tydings, Green, *et al.* could see it then. (And if they didn't, then certainly the State Department, which knew all about the list, would inform them of it. See Chapter 17.) Armed with such knowledge, one could easily check McCarthy case 14 against the matching Lee list entry and there find the name of Joe Panuch repeatedly mentioned. Hence material ready-made to stage an ambush.

The tactic was suggestive of much to follow. Though professing a stance of judicial impartiality, Tydings indicated by word and deed that he planned to make short work of the upstart from Wisconsin. Going after Panuch and McCarthy's reliance on the Lee list was the equivalent of trying to score an early knockout. It didn't, however, work out in quite the way Tydings intended. In addition to tipping the chairman's hand, offending Lodge, and shocking some observers initially in his corner, his opening gambit proved to be a serious underestimation of McCarthy.

In his prepared comments, when he at last got to make them, McCarthy served up a few surprises of his own—fending off the Tydings onslaught on the Lee list and wrong-footing his opponents in general. Once launched on his charges, McCarthy didn't as expected confine himself to Lee-list suspects but went down another rabbit hole entirely. Over the course of four days on the stand, he would lay out a group of nine public cases, using information drawn from sources other than the Lee list. In the order of his presentation, these cases were as follows:

Judge Kenyon; Ambassador Philip C. Jessup (mentioned briefly in the Kenyon session), a main link between the State Department and the Institute of Pacific Relations; State Department officials Haldore Hanson and Esther Brunauer; Prof. Owen Lattimore of Johns Hopkins University, wheelhorse of the IPR and all-round Asian policy guru; U.N. official and former State Department employee Gustavo Duran, discussed in Chapter 12; State Department UNESCO appointee Harlow Shapley; John Stewart Service, of *Amerasia* fame; and Dr. Frederick Schuman, who had been used by the State Department in 1946 as a lecturer on foreign policy.

Of this group, Duran, Service, and Shapley had been named by McCarthy in his speech before the Senate and elsewhere, but none of them was on the Lee list. In fact, the only one of the nine included in that lineup was Brunauer (who had been McCarthy's case 47 on the Senate floor), and even in this instance McCarthy used non-Lee sources in his stint before the panel. Thus, a showdown on the list was temporarily averted (though Tydings and Co.—and the standard histories—would have much to say about it later).

Generally speaking, McCarthy proved to be a formidable witness, well capable of holding his own against the veteran Tydings. For one thing, he converted the flap about case 14—and many others—into his favorite, long-playing aria: If Tydings really wanted to know about loyalty suspects, the evidence that existed on them and/or officials who failed to do their duty, the subcommittee should subpoena State Department security records, where information of this type abounded. Thus, when Green pressed him about his sources, McCarthy answered: "... I think the senator should be more concerned with finding out whether the information I have given is true or not, than trying to find out my sources of information, if any. He can find out whether the information is true by getting the [State Department] files."[6]

As suggested by this comment, McCarthy took the position that he was providing clues, leads, and names of suspects to be followed up by the subcommittee, in keeping with its Senate mandate. Though their statements varied, the stance of Tydings-Green-McMahon was essentially the reverse: It was up to McCarthy to prove his charges, while they would function as a kind of jury to weigh the evidence presented, rather than an investigative body actively pursuing cases. As Green put it when McCarthy said the panel should check out a cited front group called the League of Women Shoppers, *"That is not the job of the committee."*[7] (Emphasis added.)

When McCarthy finally got to the substance of his charges, he produced far more evidence than expected, and certainly more than was wanted. In the matter of Judge Kenyon, he recited a long list of asserted Communist-front connections on her part, presenting photostats of letterheads, meeting notices, and other documents that showed her affinity with the groups in question. He brought forth similar data on Esther Brunauer, whose alleged front affiliations were fewer in number but of like nature. He further stressed that the case of Brunauer's husband Stephen, an employee of the Navy, was even more significant than hers.

In the case of Haldore Hanson, McCarthy dealt mainly with Hanson's book *Humane Endeavour,* based on the author's activities in China in the 1930s. With Professor Lattimore, the presentation was a mix—citations from his writings, plus considerable background on his linkages to both *Amerasia* and IPR. (In this discussion, McCarthy made it clear he thought the IPR was a security problem requiring serious scrutiny in its own right.)

Measured by sheer quantity of information, McCarthy's most impressive case was that of Gustavo Duran, who had been cleared by the State Department in 1946 over the protests of the FBI, resigned, and then moved on to the United Nations. McCarthy read into the record many documents on Duran drawn from military intelligence, embassy reports, and eyewitness accounts from Spain attesting to Duran's status as a Soviet agent.

In terms of current security practice, McCarthy's main case, once more, was that of Service. Here McCarthy provided background on the *Amerasia* scandal and the mysterious way it had been dealt with, and also supplied an update on what was happening with the case in loyalty/security channels at that moment. As for Professors Schuman and Shapley, both marginal figures,

McCarthy stressed that their significance lay in the phenomenal number and/or nature of Communist fronts that they had joined, which didn't seem to deter the State Department from utilizing their talents.

Taken at face value, McCarthy's testimony on this bloc of cases was a densely packed, well-documented effort, for which Tydings and Co. were manifestly unprepared. Poised to grill McCarthy on the Lee list, they now faced a confident, loquacious witness wielding documents in profusion and making charges based on non-Lee sources. Accordingly, they could do little to challenge him on points of substance and had to settle for counterpunching measures. (In fact, as in his speech before the Senate, McCarthy got certain details wrong, but nobody on the dais knew enough to catch this.)

One Tydings gambit was to drag discussion of Communist front groups down to a *reductio ad absurdum*. When McCarthy mentioned an egregious and officially cited front (the National Council of American Soviet Friendship) and some of the leading comrades in it, Tydings insisted on reading into the record the names of all *other* people connected to the council. As these numbered upward of 100, the process was tedious and time-consuming, and didn't prove anything one way or another unless more was known about the people mentioned. (Responding to this, Hickenlooper sarcastically suggested that when data on a particular suspect were read from the *Register* of federal employees, perhaps Tydings intended to read all the other names in the *Register* also.)[8]

Beyond such improvisations, the majority opted for a sweeping tactic that provided a kind of blanket refutation to all McCarthy charges whatsoever. Green, in yet another flash of candor, would state the method clearly. "The purpose of these hearings," he said, was "to give an opportunity to those who had been charged on the floor of the Senate with disloyalty in the State Department, and who asked to be heard, *to reply to those charges*."[9] (Emphasis added.) This bore no faint resemblance to the wording of S.R. 231 but was indeed the purpose of the hearings, judged by the way that Tydings ran them.

IN THE spirit of Green's comment, the sessions developed a kind of rhythm. McCarthy would make his charges, the person named would come before the panel, deny his allegations, denounce him as a scoundrel, and present a sheaf of endorsements from eminent people saying the accused was a patriot and outstanding public servant. Thereafter the subcommittee, without exception, would adopt these responses as the "facts" about the matter, treating the denials in themselves as conclusive refutation of McCarthy.

Obviously, a right of reply in all such cases was proper and essential, in fairness to the people named and as a first step in any true investigation. But, in the Tydings version, it was virtually the only step that would be taken. Among the clearest illustrations of the method was the case of Philip Jessup, then U.S.

Ambassador at Large and the highest-ranking official on McCarthy's roster. What made the case still more distinctive was that, in contrast to the others, the panel never heard *any* evidence to speak of directly from McCarthy, other than a passing reference to an "unusual affinity . . . for Communist causes"—this said parenthetically in the Kenyon session.[10]

This fleeting mention was enough to trigger an invitation to the globe-trotting envoy to appear before the panel, an opportunity quickly seized. Jessup flew back to the States from Asia and proceeded to give the subcommittee a lengthy rundown of his ancestry and career, famous people who trusted in his judgment, anti-Soviet speeches he made at the U.N., and the *a priori* absurdity of any charges McCarthy might bring against him, though none had as yet been offered. From the standpoint of the Tydings panel, this would be all the evidence needed to reach a verdict on Dr. Jessup.

McCarthy never got a chance to present it, but he had a fairly good rap sheet on Jessup, as he would prove before another Senate panel. Hickenlooper, knowing nothing of the matter, suggested that McCarthy be allowed to cross-examine. This was rejected out of hand by Tydings, who did say, however, in yet another oddball comment: "I think Mr. Jessup might be entitled to interrogate Sen. McCarthy."[11] To this strange remark McCarthy answered that he would be glad to let Jessup ask him any questions he cared to.

Though Tydings himself had just suggested this very process, McCarthy's mild rejoinder provoked another angry outburst. "Just a minute," said Tydings, "we have not asked you as yet, Senator McCarthy."[12] The chairman then proceeded to berate McCarthy for alleged disparities in his numbers (the 205 and 57) and for not having yet produced any proof of card-carrying Communists at State. McCarthy should be questioned on *these* matters, said the chairman, before he could have the privilege of being quizzed by Jessup.

The non sequiturs in this were dazzling, but Hickenlooper correctly deduced from it that McCarthy certainly wasn't going to question Jessup. Hickenlooper then tried to do so himself, using materials borrowed from McCarthy. Predictably, this didn't amount to much, and the hearing soon wound down into a kind of testimonial session in praise of the distinguished witness. "Dr. Jessup," said Green, ". . . let me congratulate you on the way you have so thoroughly cleared whatever charges, so called, have been made against you." McMahon was equally effusive. "Mr. Jessup," he said, "I am proud to have you as a constituent of mine." (Jessup was a resident of Connecticut.)[13] Thus, in its entirety, the Tydings investigation of Philip Jessup.

It might seem things couldn't get more surreal than this, but Tydings and Co. were resourceful in such matters. The appearance of Professor Lattimore was, if anything, even more peculiar. In his star turn before the panel, Lattimore was treated with utmost deference, in sharp contrast to the handling of McCarthy. Throughout, Tydings would refer to the witness as "Dr. Lattimore" (and he would be so denominated in all aspects of the record), though Lattimore held no doctorate or any earned degree whatever from any institution of higher learning.[14] As he began his testimony, Lattimore asked, "May I read uninterrupted?" and Tydings assured him he could.[15] Lattimore then read into the record an enormous statement of about 10,000 words that took an estimated two and a half hours to deliver and consumes some thirty pages of printed transcript.

In the course of this prodigious speech, Lattimore unlike McCarthy encountered zero interruptions, except for pauses to have supporting material entered in the record and occasional prompts and solicitous comments from Tydings (e.g., "Doctor, if at any time you would like to rest for a minute, your statement is long, so do not hesitate to ask for it").[16] Lattimore thus delivered a soliloquy on his life, career, and writings—plus a fierce attack against McCarthy—with no impediment whatever. Only when he concluded were substantive questions permitted, and these, despite some further Hickenlooper efforts, were of a cursory nature.

However, things would get less comfortable for the good doctor a few days later. In a *démarche* Tydings hadn't planned for but McCarthy had, ex-Communist Louis Budenz would appear before the panel—one of several witnesses brought forward by McCarthy/Morris, and by all odds the most important. A former managing editor of the *Daily Worker,* Budenz had broken with the Party about the same time as had Bentley (October 1945) and had appeared in numerous federal court proceedings against it. His information was extensive, as his job had required him to know who was who, promote the party line at any given moment, and ensure that the pages of the *Worker* reflected the proper Moscow view for guidance of the faithful.

When Budenz came before the subcommittee, he obviously stunned the Democratic members who had sat placidly (or perhaps dozed) through the monologue of "Dr. Lattimore" and heard nothing that disturbed them. Budenz matter-of-factly testified that, in the course of his Communist duties, CP top brass had told him Lattimore was an agent of the party and should be so treated in the *Worker.* Budenz recalled four separate episodes of this sort concerning propaganda assignments and related services Lattimore had rendered.[17] This testimony was by far the biggest blockbuster of the hearings, and the most unwelcome.*

For some reason, Budenz didn't receive the kid-glove treatment given Lattimore and Jessup but instead was bombarded with skeptical, insulting questions. Green, who seemed most hostile, asked Budenz if he had ever met

---

*Budenz discussed Lattimore's services to the Communist Party—as related by CP officials—in some detail, stressing that the professor's principal job was to spread propaganda depicting the Chinese Communists as reformers.

Lattimore in person. The colloquy on this would go as follows: *Budenz:* "No, sir, I have not. As a matter of fact, however, I did not see Mr. Alger Hiss, either, but I knew him to be a Communist and so testified before the House Committee on Un-American Activities." *Green: "But you are not reasoning that everyone you have never seen or heard may be a Communist? Is that your argument?"*[18] (Emphasis added.) Budenz allowed that it was not.*

Thereafter, Green lectured Budenz—who had spent several thousand hours working with the FBI—on the urgent need to turn such information over to the Bureau. The senator seemed distraught that Budenz might be sharing data not yet provided to the FBI, and indeed resentful that Budenz was giving any information whatever to the panel. Green further undertook a line of questions suggesting that, since Budenz had been a Communist, and since Communists were known for lying, perhaps this habit of lying was hard to break ("if you believe in some other great cause, the same frame of mind might shift your lying for the cause").[19]

All this was but prologue to the most spectacular witness in the sequence—former Communist Party boss Earl Browder. (Browder had been deposed as party chief in 1945 but retained—as he liked to stress—a good relationship with Moscow.) As Tydings would make quite clear, his main purpose in having Browder on the stand was to rebut Budenz—specifically, to say suspects named by Budenz and/or McCarthy *weren't* members of the Communist Party. The chairman, indeed, was not about to rest until he could wring such statements from this grizzled apparatchik.

Under questioning by Morgan, Browder obligingly denied that he knew Owen Lattimore, T. A. Bisson, Edward Carter, and other people mentioned by McCarthy and/or Budenz to be members of the party. He was fuzzier on Frederick Field and Philip Jaffe; though denying they were engaged in spying, he skated on whether they were party members—with no follow-up or clarification sought by members of the panel. Browder also denied that the Communist Party had tried to place any agents in the State Department or that any Communists had ever worked there.[20]

Browder's ideas of candor may be judged from his assertion that he had "never received any funds from abroad" for the CPUSA or received commands from Moscow. As head of the party, he averred, he had been "an independent executive responsible only to my executive committee." These ludicrous statements drew no riposte from Green about the well-known Communist habit of lying, nor were they subject to follow-up questions, skeptical comments, or rebuke from Tydings.[21]

---

* Hickenlooper would later return to this line of thought in further examination of Budenz, asking if he had ever personally seen Joseph Stalin or V. M. Molotov. Budenz answered that he had not, but knew both of them were Communists.

Hickenlooper then questioned Browder about the meeting at Philip Jaffe's New York home five years before this, attended by Browder and Red Chinese official Tung Pi-wu.* When Hickenlooper asked if either John Carter Vincent or John Stewart Service had been at this meeting, Browder refused to answer. Hickenlooper then read a list of names, nine in all, asking if they were known to Browder as CP members. Two of the people on the list were Dorothy Kenyon and Haldore Hanson. In these cases, as in others, Browder said, "I refuse to answer." This caused great distress to McMahon and Tydings, both of whom implored the witness to reconsider. Appealing to standards of "fairness and truth," Tydings at last got Browder to say neither Kenyon nor Hanson "had any organized connection to the Communist Party."†22

The same ticklish problem would arise again in further discussion of Service and Vincent—this time as to whether *they* were CP members. Once more Browder refused to answer, and again Tydings beseeched him to do so—at least with respect to these two cases. (Browder: "Yes—before it was two other names. Now it is two. Maybe one by one we will get into a list of thousands.")23 This brought a further plea from Tydings, providing another gleam of insight into the object of the hearings. In a courtly appeal to the former CP boss, Tydings said: "I see your point of view, I am not arguing at the moment, *but I do think you are defeating the purpose of this inquiry in a way that you perhaps do not realize,* if you allow this to be obscured, and if you felt that you could answer, in the case of Mr. Vincent and Mr. Service, I would be most grateful."24 (Emphasis added.)

This supplication seems to have touched some better angel in Browder's surly nature, or perhaps turned on a lightbulb in the recesses of his brain, as he at last responded that, "to the best of my knowledge and belief," neither Vincent nor Service had any connection to the Communist Party. The sigh of relief from Tydings is almost audible in the printed record. The chairman said "Thank you, sir," abruptly ended further questions, and soon signaled that the hearing was over. It was a close-run thing, but the purpose of the Tydings inquiry, this day at least, was not defeated.

IN SUCH manner did Millard Tydings investigate McCarthy's cases, concluding with numerous lengthy sessions involving Service and the *Amerasia* scandal. These dragged on into June, with results to be considered. But, before

---

*These questions strongly suggested that information from the FBI's surveillance had made its way to Congress, one of several clues that McCarthy-Morris-Hickenlooper knew more about the *Amerasia* case than they let on in public.

†The locution used here by Browder, who was careful in his choice of words, seemed odd, speaking of an "organized connection." Did this mean there was some *other* kind of connection on the part of Kenyon or Hanson to the Communist Party? Browder's way of putting the matter cried out for clarification, but no effort of this nature was made by an inert committee.

the hearings were ended, the chairman would add a few more distinctive touches suggestive of the Tydings method.

On what turned out to be the last day of formal sessions, June 28, Tydings and Co. were pressing hard to get out a report and write *finis* to the whole endeavor. Green's view was that "we have done all that we need to do in connection with the job that was imposed on us." Tydings likewise opined, "I think our work is pretty well concluded." To this Hickenlooper rejoined, "I don't think it has even started, Mr. Chairman." (He had previously suggested some twenty or thirty potential witnesses—developed by Morris—he thought should be examined.) Lodge for his part proposed a series of questions, eighteen in all, he said had not been answered.*[25]

Morris then raised a case mentioned in a previous session he said deserved some looking into. To this Tydings replied, "Mr. Morris, we can mention cases from now until doomsday." Morris, backed by Lodge, persisted, explaining that the case involved one Theodore Geiger, formerly with the State Department, who had moved on to work for Paul Hoffman of the Economic Cooperation Administration in matters pertaining to foreign aid. "I have gone and gotten witnesses together," said Morris, "who will testify that he [Geiger] was a member of the same Communist Party unit they were."

This cut no ice with Tydings, who told Morris: "Turn it over to the FBI or do something else with it. I would like to get a decision here. We don't want to waste this afternoon."[26] As presaged by this, nothing of substance would be done about the case of Geiger, the questions raised by Lodge, or the twenty or thirty witnesses Hickenlooper wanted to summon. The afternoon would not be wasted on any topics of that nature. Tydings-Green-McMahon then pushed through an opaque arrangement to have Morgan draft a report about the hearings (see Chapter 18), and the Tydings probe was over.

There would, however, be a bizarre footnote to these already unusual hearings, in the form of a federal court decree reflecting on their conduct. This resulted from an unfathomable decision by the subcommittee to bring contempt proceedings against Earl Browder, based on his refusal to answer various of Hickenlooper's questions. As it happened, Browder had never been ordered by Tydings to answer these particular questions, or told he would be cited for contempt if he didn't, or required to state any constitutional basis for refusing.

Given all this, Browder was no doubt amazed to find himself slapped with

---

*These questions were especially pointed and involved such matters as who had promoted and protected Alger Hiss, Berle's assertion about a pro-Soviet clique inside the State Department, soft treatment of Soviet spies Ovakimian and Gorin, the "FBI chart" mentioned in the Klaus report, and other items of like nature. Lodge also wanted to know who had been responsible for obtaining Lattimore and Schuman as speakers at the State Department, the relationship of Lattimore to the Far East desk, and why exactly the dismissal of the ten security suspects in June 1947 had been reversed by the department.

a contempt citation and haled into court to face a possible prison sentence. He mounted an aggressive defense against the charges, assisted by court-appointed attorney Roger Robb, though mainly acting as his own counsel. In these court sessions, among the most fantastic in American judicial history, Browder brought only one witness to the stand to defend him against the Tydings contempt citation. That single witness was Joe McCarthy. Thus, in a scene no Hollywood writer could have scripted, the nation's former Communist boss called in his defense the nation's most famous Communist hunter. It proved to be a wise decision. Asked if Browder had been in contempt of Tydings, McCarthy answered:

> . . . in all my experience as a judge, and a lawyer, I don't know if I have ever seen more perfect cooperation between a witness and the chairman of the committee. When the witness refused to testify it appeared to be with the wholehearted approval of the chair. The chair, in fact, was not interested in eliciting information from the witness which would indicate the presence of Communists in the government. . . . The witness came down and took a very active part in what the chair was trying to do, and that was to conduct a cover up.[27]

These McCarthy statements were addressed directly to Browder, conducting the interrogation. At no point did Browder demur, interrupt, or ask any skeptical questions suggesting McCarthy's comments about a Tydings cover-up were mistaken. Thereafter, Browder's attorney Robb likewise argued that, when "Browder refused to answer those questions, he was doing what the majority of that committee wanted him to do."[28] Having heard McCarthy's testimony and Robb's summation, the court ruled that the defendant in fact hadn't been required to answer Hickenlooper's questions and entered a directed verdict: Earl Browder was acquitted.

CHAPTER 17

Eve of Destruction

BEHIND the scenes at the Tydings hearings, the action was almost as hectic as that unfolding before the cameras. However, much of what went on backstage was starkly different from what was being said in public.

By the terms of S.R. 231, Tydings was to have conducted a "full and complete investigation as to whether personnel who are disloyal to the United States are or have been employed by the Department of State." No such investigation ever happened, or anything remotely like it. Nor did Tydings usually bother saying this was the object of the hearings. Rather, as he often stated, the idea was to have McCarthy come before the panel and present whatever facts he had for its consideration. The burden of proof, and investigation, was squarely on McCarthy.

Demanding that McCarthy put up or shut up was obviously different from the official purpose of the hearings, but even this was fairly distant from what went on in subcommittee sessions and even further from events occurring behind the arras. Tydings came closer to the truth when he told McCarthy, "You are going to get one of the most complete investigations in the history of this republic." To this McCarthy had objected, saying the chairman must have misspoken. The point of the inquest, after all, was to look into the loyalty setup at State, not the doings of McCarthy. Of course, said Tydings, that was what he meant.

As shown by now-available data, Tydings had it right the first time. Both in its regular operations and in more shadowy backstairs dealings, the Tydings panel in fact set out to investigate McCarthy, and did so in systematic fashion. The proofs of this in formerly confidential records are legion. Among the more suggestive is a strategy memo Tydings passed on to counsel Edward Morgan, with cover note, on April 11. This was roughly a month into the hearings, as Tydings in his public, ostensibly objective mode claimed to be suspending judgment on McCarthy's charges.

The memo he sent to Morgan was of a very different tenor—a blueprint for turning the hearings, not merely into an investigation of McCarthy, but into a formal arraignment, trial, and condemnation by the Senate. The Humpty-Dumpty logic of this plan was that, since McCarthy had triggered the hearings to begin with, "the scope of the subcommittee's power to make recommendations is sufficiently broad to include a recommendation that Senator McCarthy be censured." Hence, no problem turning a supposed investigation of loyalty matters in the State Department into an investigation—and indictment—of McCarthy.

Among the complaints against McCarthy prophetically capsuled in this memo was, first and foremost, that he "practiced a fraud and a deceit when he assured the Senate he would read into the *Congressional Record* the text of the speech he delivered at Wheeling. As to its most relevant passage, Senator McCarthy interpolated new language in the Senate reading." (This in reference to the fact that the Wheeling-Reno speech McCarthy read to the Senate didn't mention a "list" of "205 Communists" at State, which Tydings and Co. always insisted had been said at Wheeling.)

The second charge set forth in the memo was that McCarthy also committed "fraud and deceit" concerning the sources of the security data he recited on his fourscore suspects. Linked to this was the further charge that these data weren't either new or current, as "Senator McCarthy's information was in the possession of the Congress in 1947." (Both charges here related to the contention that McCarthy in his Senate speech did nothing but repeat outdated cases from the Lee list, compiled in the fall of 1947.)

To these main counts were added others, all prelude to the inevitable guilty verdict: that McCarthy, "in the sordid pursuit of political advantage, has demeaned the Senate, lowered its prestige and injured its reputation by subjecting matters of world import to partisan attack, wholly divorced from semblance of truth."[1] All in all, something less than judicial calm in weighing evidence from the hearings, which had another ten weeks to run and were supposed to be digging out the facts on possible loyalty risks at State.

Exactly who drafted this philippic isn't indicated on it.* Whatever the

---

* Based on the other evidence in the record, the most likely source of this memo was the State Department. See below.

source, Tydings in his buck slip to Morgan made it plain that the views expressed weren't distasteful and that the charges raised against McCarthy would probably be brought at some date in the future. "This is confidential, for your information," he wrote to Morgan. "Please bring it to my attention at the proper time." The implication was that such a necktie party would be staged, but not at that particular moment. (And, indeed, the main charges in this strategy memo would be repeated, point for point, in the report Tydings gave the Senate three months later.)

Why Tydings may have felt the time was not yet ripe for pressing formal charges against McCarthy is suggested by a worried letter he wrote the following day to Truman. This April 12 missive is of interest for what it says about the chairman's back-channel dealings with the White House, his reading of the political omens, and his real objective in the hearings. It indicates he felt McCarthy and the GOP were scoring heavily on the Communist issue and that the President needed to take dramatic action to stop the bleeding.

To this end, Tydings made two chief proposals. First, that Truman seize the initiative on the subversive question by emphasizing the prosecution of Communist agents on his watch (including, with no apparent sense of irony, Alger Hiss), thus trumping McCarthy's message with the public.* Second, that the President make some adjustment on the matter of State's security files, the withholding of which was being blasted by McCarthy as a cover-up and scandal. With these steps to clear the way, the administration and its allies could go on the offensive against its accusers. In concluding, Tydings made an urgent, and revealing, plea to Truman:

> I strongly recommend for your own welfare, for the welfare of the country and lastly for the welfare of the Democratic party that the present Communist inquiry not be allowed to worsen, but that you take bold, forthright and courageous action which I presume to say will do as much as anything I can think of to give you and your administration and party a tremendous advantage in the coming election.†2

Further suggesting the Tydings mood—and purpose—was a meeting with Democratic members of the Senate in which he voiced concern about the State Department hearings and asked his colleagues for their aid in bringing down

---

* Truman's attitudes toward and statements on the Hiss case are considered in Chapter 24.

† As reflected in the internal papers of the White House, the steps thus recommended would soon be taken. In succeeding weeks, Truman staffers scrambled to position the President as a vigorous, nononsense foe of Communism at home as well as overseas. A key player in this effort was presidential assistant Stephen Spingarn, a specialist in security matters, who plied White House speechwriters with data—for instance, the declining membership of the Communist Party—that allegedly showed Truman's leadership in thwarting the subversive menace. Also, a compromise of sorts would be effected on the matter of the files—all this linked to a concerted blitz against McCarthy in the House and Senate. That Tydings caused all this to happen with his letter may be doubted, but his tactical notions obviously marched with the trend of White House thinking.

McCarthy. The gathering would be recalled by Tydings ally William Benton, who had by 1950 moved from the department to the Senate, where he would be a relentless McCarthy critic. Benton later wrote his assistant John Howe, "I was the first senator by several weeks to go after McCarthy," and explained the comment this way:

> I remember well the meeting in [Secretary of the Senate] Les Biffle's office when Tydings spoke with great distress about the problems of the Tydings' Committee. McMahon was also there. So, too, was Chauvez [*sic*—Sen. Dennis Chavez (D-N.M.)]. I was to make a speech the next day . . . [and] I hastily wrote in the paragraph about McCarthy as a "hit and run propagandist on the Kremlin model" . . . My recollection is that Chauvez followed with another attack on McCarthy and for this Chauvez was bitterly assailed.*[3]

The Tydings pessimism revealed in these vignettes would in due course be tempered by happier thoughts about turning the tables on McCarthy. In this pursuit, the question of the Wheeling numbers would be for Tydings the dominant, virtually all-consuming, issue. Again, the focus on this statistical point seems odd, but the chairman had his reasons. To Tydings, it came to mean not only that McCarthy had been evasive and untruthful but that he had actually committed perjury—since he would deny under oath, in an executive session, claiming a "list" of 205 Reds at State. This perjury angle would become an *idée fixe* with Tydings, as also with Benton.

From the outset of the hearings, a good deal of backstage effort had been devoted by Tydings and his staffers to seeking proof that McCarthy lied about the Wheeling speech. The main item relied on at the beginning was the Frank Desmond story in the *Intelligencer*. Also getting notice in this context was the Edward Connors piece that ran the following Sunday in Reno. This was ambiguous evidence, if that, but for some reason obviously had strong appeal for Tydings. To check these matters out, Tydings-Morgan early on assigned committee staffers to quiz the two reporters.

One Tydings aide, assistant counsel Lyon Tyler, was to have contacted Frank Desmond about the 205 quotation. A Tydings-to-Desmond letter saying Tyler would be coming up to Wheeling gives a pretty good view of the chairman's true investigative interests. Among the questions Tydings posed to Desmond: "From what was the quote . . . referred to taken? Was it handed to you by Sen. McCarthy with the statement that you could print it or words to that effect? Is it an accurate quotation from such paper as Sen. McCarthy gave you?"[4]

---

* Both the Benton and Chavez attacks occurred as mentioned, but Benton, no master of detail as he sometimes admitted, erred as to the sequence. His speech that used this phrasing was delivered on May 9. By this time several well-orchestrated attacks against McCarthy had been made in both the House and Senate.

Evidently the higher-ups at the *Intelligencer* found this too hot for handling in the newsroom, as the answer Tydings received was the letter from newspaper executive Austin Wood, already noted. Wood said he had talked with Desmond and "he tells me there can be no doubt that Senator McCarthy did use the figure '205' in referring to his list of men in the State Department who have been named as members of the Communist Party and members of a spy ring." (The Desmond story and letter from Wood are featured in the Tydings record as exhibits A and B going to show McCarthy lied about the Wheeling numbers.)*[5]

A less helpful sequence played out with Connors, who had reported that McCarthy's written text at Reno contained the passage on the 205 but that this was not in fact delivered. Seemingly intrigued by this, Tydings-Morgan planned to send someone out to Reno to talk to Connors or else bring him to Washington for that purpose. In the event, neither of these things would happen, but the episode did show the Ahab-like zeal of Tydings in tracking down his quarry. As later revealed by Connors, Tydings called him long distance to question him on the 205, its deletion from McCarthy's Reno talk, and related matters. Verifying the magic number was so important that it required the personal sleuthing of the chairman.[6]

None of this, needless to remark, looked like an investigation of loyalty risks in the State Department, in keeping with the Tydings mandate from the Senate. However, it also wasn't, to this point, a very effective investigation of McCarthy. As the Gillette committee analysts would find, neither the Desmond-Wood account from Wheeling nor the Connors Reno story, severally or jointly, was enough to sustain a perjury charge about McCarthy's numbers. These were thin reeds to support so large a burden, and something more robust was needed. By the latter part of April, even as Tydings plumbed the depths of worry about the hearings, his staffers and political allies began to think that they had found it.

On April 12, the day after Tydings sent the strategy memo and cover note to Morgan, the chief counsel would return the favor. He advised the chairman that he had a contact in Wheeling—the attorney for radio station WWVA—who told him the text of the McCarthy speech had been supplied beforehand to the station and that technicians there had monitored its delivery. Specifically, said Morgan, WWVA program director Paul Myers could attest that "McCarthy did not depart from the same in any material respect. It was obvious during the talk that he was reading from the prepared text."[7]

---

*On close inspection, as the Gillette committee investigators would observe, Wood's letter was considerably short of being conclusive. For one thing, it amounted to hearsay, as Desmond himself would have been the obvious person to say whatever it was he had to say about the matter. For another, even in Wood's paraphrase, Desmond had simply said McCarthy used the figure 205 in "referring to" his cases. That wasn't quite the same as claiming a "list" of 205—which was the issue to be settled.

Accepting Morgan at his word, this seems to have been the genesis of the Wheeling affidavits, the allegedly clinching proof of McCarthy's lying, and surrogate for the lost recording. At this stage, however, the story would take an O. Henry twist that equaled in peculiarity anything else that happened in the Tydings saga. As it turned out, not only were Tydings-Morgan stalking McCarthy from town to town to nail him on a perjury count, they were doing so in collusion with the State Department—which they were supposed to be investigating. Indeed, to judge from fairly copious records, it was State that henceforth took the lead in hunting down McCarthy, with Tydings-Morgan simply tagging after.

Exactly how and why the State Department became the chief investigator in an alleged investigation of itself isn't clear, but that it did so is apparent. As Tydings would later explain about the Wheeling affidavits:

> Mr. [Adrian] Fisher, counsel of the State Department, got in touch with the Wheeling, West Virginia radio station over which McCarthy spoke . . . as a result of this conversation, Mr. Rine, the station manager of Radio Station WWVA, sent to Mr. Fisher the manuscript of McCarthy's remarks at Wheeling . . . Following the receipt of this manuscript by Mr. Fisher, a State Department investigator was sent to Wheeling to look into the matter. The result was that the two officials of Radio Station WWVA gave the investigator affidavits to which were attached photostats of the McCarthy manuscript . . .*[8]

That Tydings was not mistaken in this recollection is shown by a letter from Carlisle Humelsine of State to Sen. Harley Kilgore (D-W.Va.), explaining why the department wanted the affidavits and how it came to get them. Noting that State had been accused of misfeasance by McCarthy, Humelsine said it had a strong interest in obtaining whatever information it could about the charges. It had accordingly sent its agents up to Wheeling, where the Whitaker-Myers affidavits had been obtained by "a representative of this department."[9]

In fact, as shown by the Gillette inquiry, State Department involvement with the affidavits was a good deal closer than suggested by these comments. According to the Gillette committee memo, the station officials "explained to our investigators that their original affidavits *were prepared for their signatures by a State Department representative (whose identity they do not know)* and the managing director of station WWVA (Bill Ryan [Rine]) . . ."[10] (Emphasis

---

*Subsequently, Tydings would expand on this reminiscence in an exchange with attorney Edward Bennett Williams, serving as counsel to McCarthy. In this encounter, Tydings acknowledged not only that State Department investigators had obtained the radio affidavits but that he had asked the department to send its representatives to Wheeling for this purpose. (When Williams, with some incredulity, commented, "You used State Department investigators in an investigation of the State Department itself," Tydings responded that the identity of the people obtaining the affidavits was "immaterial.")

added.) Thus, State not only got the affidavits, it helped prepare them in the first place. They were at every step along the way a State Department product.

Much the same was true regarding the other main count in the indictment—that McCarthy in his remarks before the Senate had merely plagiarized the Lee list. The contention that McCarthy had nothing but this list, and that his charges were therefore baseless, would be stressed repeatedly in the Tydings report as proof that he inflicted a "fraud and a hoax" upon the Senate. In these comments the majority members of the panel, or whoever actually did the drafting, would say these Lee list findings were based on "our investigation." But there is in the Tydings record no hint of such investigation beyond the most perfunctory gestures.*

Rather, as with all individual McCarthy suspects, "our investigation" consisted of merely asking the State Department for answers to his charges, then treating the replies as gospel. And of these there was no shortage. Both Peurifoy and Adrian Fisher were prolific in supplying State-friendly memos and purported backup data relating to McCarthy's cases, all received uncritically by Tydings, large chunks of which would surface in the report and appendix to the hearings. (The report alone reprints some seventy pages of State Department press releases—more than a fifth of the total volume.) This visible work product of State's researchers was but a fraction of the material shared with Tydings on a more private basis.

One such back-channel communiqué is a Peurifoy-to-Tydings memo dated May 25, 1950, providing the supposed facts about McCarthy's cases, the names of his anonymous suspects, and keys to coded symbols in the underlying data. Also passed on privately to Tydings were documents produced by Fisher's legal office under the heading "His Own Assertions Classified and Systematized," the acronym for which was HOACS (State Department humor). This was a running tally of McCarthy's statements, with State Department answers, cross-referenced by name and subject matter and updated on a regular schedule. Several hundred pages of this material may be found in Tydings's personal papers.[11]

An equally impressive effort, and even more useful for McCarthy's foes, was a mammoth 168-page "Confidential Memorandum" that summed up the State Department version of his cases and their supposed nexus to the Lee list. This is on its face a veritable hornbook on the subject: a detailed history of how the list was put together, State Department reactions to it at the time, a correlation with McCarthy's cases, and a concordance of parallel quotes from the two rosters.

---

*For example, Tydings staffer Robert Heald talked with Lee researcher Harris Huston, who provided some general comments about the nature of the inquiry. The committee also went through the formality of officially requesting a copy of the list, which it almost certainly already had in its possession, from the House of Representatives.

This weighty though less than totally accurate document reposes in Tydings's personal papers along with the Peurifoy memo of May 25 and various HOACS reports and updates. Unlike these, which clearly indicate the State Department as the source, this one is carefully anonymous—with every page, both top and bottom, labeled "confidential." Its State Department provenance, however, is shown by several features—one of the more obvious being that the above-noted Peurifoy-to-Tydings memo bears the identical top-and-bottom "confidential" markings.*[12]

As significant as the contents of this huge confidential memo was its timing. The document is dated April 14, a few days after the strategy blueprint Tydings sent to Morgan and the chairman's message to the White House urging a concerted plan against its accuser. Equally serendipitous for Tydings, it also coincided with the Morgan memo pointing toward the radio affidavits, which would complete the data package to be used in a well-synchronized offensive against McCarthy. However, these pivotal documents weren't yet secured and would be needed to buttress the Desmond-Wood account of what McCarthy said at Wheeling.

This last piece of the mosaic would be obtained by the State Department during the final week of April. The Whitaker-Myers depositions were prepared/acquired by the department's representative in Wheeling on Tuesday, April 25. The next day, Harley Kilgore, a Tydings ally, would write John Peurifoy at State, asking if he by any possible chance just happened to have hard evidence of what McCarthy said at Wheeling. The day after that, Carlisle Humelsine, in Peurifoy's behalf, supplied the depositions to Kilgore. The whole thing was done in three days flat.[†] Time, apparently, was of the essence.

With the radio affidavits and State's Lee list information now in hand, Tydings met the following evening with Truman and shared with him the data that would "finish the discrediting of McCarthy," as Truman later told his staffers. As also relayed by Truman, according to one aide, the main emphasis of this discussion was on the Lee list cases. Concerning these, the aide reported Truman as saying that "Tydings proposes to have Democrats in the House bring these facts out through a speech on the floor; he believes that, if this plan is followed through, it may go so far as to result in the Senate acting to throw out McCarthy."[13]

---

*Others include the fact that the data imparted were intimately known to State but not to others, that key omissions from an otherwise comprehensive treatment were such as served the interests of the department, and that locutions were used which reflected an internal State Department—not congressional—viewpoint: for example, *"The* [congressional] *investigators . . .* had access to hundreds of files and *their* reasons for selecting these particular cases, and this particular number, *are not known."* (Emphasis added.)

†This instant turnaround of information, from execution of the affidavits to Kilgore's letter to Humelsine's response, suggests that the U.S. postal service, and the wheels of government in general, worked much more rapidly in 1950 than they do today. Or possibly it suggests something else.

Thereafter, on Sunday, April 30, Tydings convened a meeting in his D.C. apartment to put the various pieces together. A rare journalistic version of these backstage doings was supplied contemporaneously by *Newsweek,* which obviously had excellent sources at State and/or the subcommittee. Present at this meeting, said *Newsweek,* were Tydings, Peurifoy, and Morgan, the investigators thus meeting in *ex parte* manner with the agency under investigation. The object of their conclave—related by *Newsweek* in offhand and unattributed quote marks—was the "total and eternal destruction" of McCarthy. As to how this was to be accomplished:

> The time had come, said Senator Tydings, to expose McCarthy. He had discussed it with the President and advised him that the counterattack was to be launched on the floor of the House and Senate. Peurifoy had prepared a memo for Rep. Frank Karsten [D-Mo.], who would reveal on the floor of the House the origin of McCarthy's cases . . . Sens. Harley Kilgore and Matthew Neely* would flash affidavits proving McCarthy had lied to the Senate about his Wheeling speech. The whole strategy was to be kept strictly secret . . .[14]

In the next few days, events would unfold almost exactly as *Newsweek* suggested. On Monday, May 1, the day after the Tydings apartment session, Representative Karsten read into the *Congressional Record* a learned discourse on the Lee list, its history and meaning, all tracking with the "Confidential Memorandum," this obviously being the Peurifoy memo alluded to by *Newsweek.* (See below.) In this Karsten was assisted by Democratic representatives John Rooney of New York and John McCormack of Massachusetts, who likewise displayed a wealth of esoteric knowledge about the Lee list, its supposed obsolescence, and its innocuous nature.[15]

On Tuesday, back at the State Department, John Peurifoy had a press statement at the ready, saying the department had been asked to comment on Karsten's charge the preceding afternoon that McCarthy had inflicted a "fraud and deceit" upon the nation. Peurifoy modestly declined to make this judgment, saying that was for the Senate panel to decide. (Nor did he say who, precisely, had asked for this comment on such exceedingly short notice.) He then proceeded to repeat, yet again, the full-blown State Department version of the Lee list issue, concluding that Joe McCarthy had once more proved to be a flagrant liar.†[16]

The rhetorical chain reaction would conclude the following day in a riotous session of the Senate, as Democratic leader Lucas read into the *Record,*

---

*The other Democratic senator from West Virginia.

†Peurifoy made this comment on the extraneous question, apparently thrown in for ballast, of Owen Lattimore's allegedly having a "desk in the State Department," according to McCarthy. This McCarthy statement, said Peurifoy, contained "not a shred of truth." Concerning which, see Chapter 29.

over strenuous GOP objections, the entirety of the Peurifoy press release on the Lee list cases, describing it as the definitive statement on McCarthy's plagiarism and deceptions. "So far as I'm concerned," said Lucas, "the statement of Mr. Peurifoy . . . which he makes at this time after weeks of investigation, carries a considerable amount of weight on the question of truth and veracity."[17]

Thus was the identical version of the Lee list issue pounded home on three straight days and in three separate forums, by a seemingly diverse but in reality well-coordinated group of critics. And thus also, it may be noted, did Scott Lucas say in so many words that the Lee list "investigation" that struck him as compelling was done by the State Department, not by anyone in Congress. The point would be repeated later in the day, in connection with the Wheeling numbers, when Senators Kilgore and Neely took the floor to make their contributions. Kilgore, flourishing the radio affidavits, read these into the *Record* also, saying they raised the most serious questions about McCarthy's candor. (Nor did Kilgore make any bones about the fact that the affidavits had been supplied to him by State.)

All this was punctuated by another bit of byplay. After reading the Wheeling affidavits, Kilgore turned to Tydings, who fortuitously happened to be present, and asked if the chairman would like to have these depositions for the use of his subcommittee. Tydings responded, "I shall be very glad to have them. I assume they are pertinent."[18] This assumption turned out to be correct, as Tydings would ever after cite these State Department–provided affidavits, not only in the report he gave the Senate, but in many other settings, as conclusive proof that McCarthy lied about the speech at Wheeling.*

Finally, as advertised, Senator Neely pitched in as well, though not quite in the way *Newsweek* suggested. Rather, he harped on the Desmond *Intelligencer* story, coupling this with a flowery tribute to Col. Austin Wood as a great stickler for the facts who would never let something erroneous appear in his newspaper. Then followed a terrific rhetorical onslaught against McCarthy, by obvious implication though not by name, suggesting he was a modern Ananias, the famous liar in the Bible. In which event, said Neely—here closely tracking the *Newsweek* version—McCarthy's "usefulness to the Senate and the country would be totally and eternally destroyed."[19]

All the points thus made on the floor of Congress concerning the Wheeling numbers, the radio affidavits, and the Lee list would thereafter be repeated in the Tydings report, using all of the same arguments and documentation cited

---

* It may well be doubted that Tydings needed Harley Kilgore to obtain these affidavits, or anything else of similar nature, from State. But this exchange established a public record as to why Tydings had the State-originated affidavits in his possession and how exactly he came to get them—with no provable *ex parte* contact between the chairman and the people ostensibly under investigation.

by Karsten, Kilgore, and Co. in their well-orchestrated blitzkreig. Throughout, the coordination of the several players, the timing of their contributions, and the interlocking nature of their statements were impressive. (In which respect, we need only note that Peurifoy, in "responding" to Frank Karsten, was actually responding to himself, as he had per the *Newsweek* account personally supplied the material Karsten was using.) The cumulative impact was all the greater thanks to the notice given these various statements by major media such as the *New York Times,* the *Washington Post,* and many others.

A coda to the above, in further illustration of the pivotal role of the State Department and collegial nature of the project, would be supplied by a White House memo a few days later (May 8), addressed to Truman staffer Donald Dawson, headed: "Continuing the Counter-Offensive Against McCarthy." Attached to this was yet another State Department missive arguing the need for still more saturation bombing of McCarthy. This referred with approval to the rhetorical efforts of Karsten-Rooney-Kilgore-Lucas and urged that "a senator, either Senator Neely, Senator Kilgore, or Senator Lucas . . . should review other violations of senatorial propriety by Senator McCarthy and should indicate that this type of behavior warrants disciplinary action by the Senate either by way of censure or expulsion."[20]

The oddities in all this were striking—perhaps chief among them the argument Karsten, Rooney, Tydings and Co. chose to stress in framing the Lee list part of the indictment: that McCarthy was guilty of gross deceit and should be severely punished for using material from that list without telling the Senate where it came from. Such *unattributed use of sources,* apparently, was a despicable act deserving censure, expulsion from the Senate, and political annihilation of the offender. This was an interesting charge for them to make, as it's clear beyond all cavil that these alleged Lee list experts were themselves reciting—not just in substance but often enough verbatim—material prepared by others, fobbed off as their own researches.*

Indeed, McCarthy's congressional critics, up to and including the Tydings panel, displayed great economy of effort, repeatedly using language, as well as alleged documentation, supplied by their unacknowledged helpers. Consider, in the graphics on the following pages, four passages on the Lee list issue taken from the "Confidential Memorandum" in the left-hand columns, in comparison with matching statements made by McCarthy's foes in Congress, appearing to the right.

---

*On this score, Kilgore and Lucas deserve somewhat higher marks for acknowledging that the material they used derived from State. Of course, in reading a State Department press release, Lucas could not very well have disguised its place of origin.

**Confidential Memorandum,
April 14, 1950**

"On August 8, 1947, the [State] Department announced to all employees that the investigative staff of the House Committee on Appropriations, consisting of Robert E. Lee, Harris Huston, James Nugent and Wilfred Sigerson, was making a study of the department, and that they would be interviewing members of the Department's staff during the next few weeks. Departmental officers were requested to cooperate in making available the information which the investigators would require."

Rep. John Rooney, May 1, 1950

"On the 8th August 1947, the Department announced to all employees that the investigative staff of the House Committee on Appropriations, consisting of Robert E. Lee, Harris Huston, James Nugent and Wilfred Sigerson were making a study of the department and that they would be interviewing members of the Department staff during the next few weeks. Departmental officers were requested to cooperate in making available the information which the investigators would require."

Confidential Memorandum

"It is apparent that the report of the House investigation did not utilize information from the Department of State files which would disprove charges of disloyalty or security risk with respect to each individual. The House investigators' report being not for the primary purpose of challenging the department's conclusion as to disloyalty or security risk did not, in most instances, concern itself with the merits of each case."

Rep. Frank Karsten, May 1, 1950

"It is apparent that the memoranda prepared by the House investigators in 1947 were selective and did not presume to set forth information from the State Department files which would disprove charges of disloyalty with respect to each individual. As a matter of fact, the House investigators' report being not for the primary purpose of challenging the State Department's conclusion as to disloyalty or security risk, did not in most instances concern itself with the merits of each case."

Confidential Memorandum	Tydings Report, July 20, 1950
"It is fair to say, in terms of Senator McCarthy's charges, that the House report was a specialized selection from the State Department's files. Since it is apparent that Senator McCarthy in turn twisted, colored or perverted in many instances the House report, his charges on the Senate floor on February 20, 1950, constituted a double perversion of the Department's file in terms of the situation in 1947."	"In terms, therefore, of the charges made by Senator McCarthy, it is fair and proper to say that the House memoranda were a specialized selection from the files of the State Department . . . [McCarthy] twisted, colored or perverted the House material. . . . In many instances, his speech of February 20, 1950, to the Senate constituted a distortion compounded of the State Department's files in terms of the situation that prevailed, not in 1950, but back in 1947."

Confidential Memorandum	Tydings Report
"There is no factual information on any of the February 20 81 cases which does not exist in its counterpart in the '108 list' . . . where the language of the House investigators was conditional or doubtful, Senator McCarthy's language was positive, unequivocal, and colored . . ."	"There is no factual information relative to any one of the February 20 cases which does not have its identifiable counterpart among the '108 list' . . . In those instances where the language of the House investigators was conditional or doubtful, Senator McCarthy's language is positive, unequivocal, and colored."

It was by such devices and from such sources that the pattern for virtually all subsequent treatments of McCarthy's early cases was established. With no conspicuous exceptions, mainstream bios and histories of the era have taken their cues from Tydings and/or the orations of Karsten and his colleagues, repeating as supposed fact their statements on the Wheeling numbers, the Lee list, and other alleged proofs of McCarthy's lying. Readers of these works have no way of knowing—and the authors themselves don't seem to know—that the whole thing was concocted by the State Department. All of which would seem to be questionable in itself, but becomes the more so when we reflect that the material thus passed on, in case after case, was grossly in error.

From all of which, a number of conclusions are apparent. That Tydings conducted no investigation of the State Department hardly needs much stressing. The true investigative efforts of the subcommittee, such as they were, focused strictly on McCarthy, aimed at discrediting his statements, digging up evidence to be used against him, and otherwise doing whatever might be done to injure him in his set-to with the State Department and the White House. Equally obvious is that, throughout, Tydings was operating in tight collusion with the State Department, as he would in essence admit in later comments. On the central points at issue, Tydings did little more than act as a willing conduit for whatever information—or misinformation—the State Department chose to give him.

Beyond these self-evident gleanings from the backstage history are a couple of other items that bear noting. One is the formidable array of forces that had lined up against McCarthy and were acting in concert to bring about his downfall. To cite only the major players, these included the Truman White House and its agents; the State Department and the apparently limitless resources it was willing to devote to discrediting its obstreperous critic; Tydings himself and other majority members of his panel; prominent members of the Senate, including Lucas, Kilgore, Benton, Chavez, and others; and, in a somewhat unusual cross-pollination between chambers of the Congress, influential figures in the House, including Karsten of Missouri and senior members of that body such as Rooney and McCormack.

A final important point worth noting—in some ways the most important—is the extreme violence of this opposition, which from the beginning took the Catonian view that McCarthy should be not only refuted with answers to his charges but politically annihilated. The attitude throughout was *delenda est McCarthy.* It's noteworthy, indeed, that the idea of censuring McCarthy, expelling him from the Senate, and destroying him as a political figure was voiced so vehemently and so often in this early going in the spring of 1950. Such was, for instance, the note struck in the strategy memo Tydings sent to Morgan, the comments of Truman to his staffers, the secret Tydings apartment confab, and the follow-up memo from State directed to the White House.

Granted that McCarthy had made a lot of people angry, this over-the-top reaction seems quite strange. Assuming he was wrong about his cases, as his critics argued, why not simply show this, thus besting him in the usual manner of our discourse? Why the instantaneous determination to censure him, eject him from the Senate, annihilate him altogether? People in Congress disagree every day, sometimes for years on end, often in the most heated manner, without trying to expel or censure their opponents or destroy them utterly as political figures. Yet such was the fate decreed for Joe McCarthy from the beginning, and such when all was done would be the outcome of his struggle.

CHAPTER 18

A Fraud and a Hoax

S OME two weeks after Chairman Tydings gaveled proceedings to a close, the printed record and report of his subcommittee were ready for transmission to the Senate. True to the spirit of the hearings, both documents would give rise to bitter conflict between the parties and strange occurrences that were puzzling then and remain so decades later.*

Probably the most surreal aspect of the ensuing melee was the matter of the disappearing transcript. Among the first to notice the problem was Henry Cabot Lodge, who received the printed hearings on July 24 and thumbed through them to check up on certain items. When he did he found something missing—his statement at the last full session of the panel, saying many significant topics hadn't been covered and posing a series of questions he said had not been answered. Angrily raising the issue before the Senate, Lodge noted that this entire section of the hearings had vanished.

Addressing Homer Ferguson, who had the floor, Lodge asked: "Is the senator from Michigan aware of the fact that in the printed copy of the hearings on disloyalty there are omitted, beginning at page 1438, about 35 typewritten

---

* A final executive session of the panel was held on July 7. The report of the subcommittee became available on July 17 and the printed hearing record a week later. Senators thus got the report before they could read the transcript.

pages of the transcript of June 28?"* Lodge added that these pages dealt with "some very important matters" and that their disappearance obviously wasn't accidental. The deletion, he said, "could not have been a mistake . . . because after the omission of the large number of pages . . . in the printed copy of the hearings appear the last sentences shown in the typewritten transcript, including the part about adjournment."[1] Somebody had surgically removed thirty-five pages of stenographic record, then tacked on to what was left the concluding phases of the hearing to give the appearance of a completed session.

On even a cursory survey of the omitted pages, it's evident the things discussed were indeed important. They included not only the questions raised by Lodge but Hickenlooper's comments about witnesses not called, the Tydings-Morris exchange about not wasting the afternoon on Theodore Geiger, and other such contentious topics. These items indicated rather clearly that the subcommittee hadn't done a thorough investigation or even made a fair beginning. And now all these items themselves were missing.

The usually mild-mannered Lodge came as close to strong invective as his patrician genes permitted. "I shall not attempt," he said, "to characterize these methods of leaving out of the printed text parts of the testimony and proceedings. . . . I shall not characterize such methods because I think they speak for themselves."† His view of the matter was endorsed by Senators Ferguson, Karl Mundt, and Robert Taft (who likewise noted that the omission couldn't have been accidental). Ferguson was especially vocal, urging that the Tydings panel be reconvened to "undertake an investigation of its own staff, an investigation of who prepared this volume, to determine who is responsible for omitting from the record these vital pages."[2]

That obviously would have been a good idea, but no such determination was made, nor was any clear explanation offered. Tydings apparently was absent from the floor when the protest erupted, leaving it to Brien McMahon to make an awkward effort at amends—saying he thought the printed transcript was complete, but if not the missing pages should be separately printed as an adjunct to the hearings. Lodge was not appeased. "Having had this experience," he said, "I would rather not take a chance. I would prefer to have the portion I have referred to printed in the *Congressional Record.*"‡[3]

---

*Something less than half of that in the printed version. (See below.)

†Later, when Sen. William Knowland (R-Calif.) asked to see the transcript, Lodge said: "I have the one copy, which I have obtained with some difficulty. I shall be glad to let the senator from California have it, but I hope he does not let it out of his sight because I understand that, if he does, he may never see it again."

‡The closest that anything would come to an explanation was a later notation in the Tydings record that, in this session, "members of the subcommittee and staff were canvassing certain procedural matters . . ." This suggested that the portions left out were technical in nature, though almost the entire discussion concerned the substantive inadequacy of the hearings.

In the event, both remedies were adopted. The missing pages were inserted by Ferguson in the *Record* at the conclusion of his remarks and thereafter published also as an addendum to the printed transcript. This resulted in what has to be the most physically peculiar hearing record ever to roll off the government presses: Part I, the original printed transcript, totaling 1,484 pages; Part II, the appendix containing various exhibits, amounting to 1,024 pages; and, bringing up the rear, Part III, the formerly missing section, running to all of 14 printed pages—a forlorn caboose attached to a gigantic freight train. The asymmetry of the three-volume set makes it something of a collector's item and well represents the weirdness of the whole proceeding.

Nor was that all that would develop on the missing pages. It further happened that the deleted portion contained exchanges on the question of issuing a report of the subcommittee, which helped make that document controversial in its own right. Here were recorded not only the complaints of Republican members about things left undone but the replies of Tydings, McMahon, and Green as to why a summary memo on the inquest should nonetheless be drafted.

In trying to overcome GOP objections to doing such a wrap-up, Tydings and Co. had rung the changes on the tentative character of what was being asked for. *Green:* "A draft to date of the work we have accomplished. . . . It doesn't have to be a conclusion . . . just a basis . . ." *McMahon:* Such a draft "doesn't commit us to anything except seeing a memorandum of what we have got. . . . I shouldn't call it a report. I would call it a memorandum of work that has been done." On that tranquilizing note, Tydings suggested that counsel Morgan "prepare a tentative report to be submitted to the members of the committee"—a basis, in Green's phrasing, "for discussion."[4]

Tydings then pushed through a motion to have such a provisional memo drafted. Lodge and Hickenlooper, despite all entreaties, still said no, Green and McMahon voted aye, and Tydings turned to his counsel and said, "Go ahead, Mr. Morgan, and draft your report."* These comments about the nature of what was being voted were among the items that vanished with the missing transcript. This became the more suggestive when it developed that the tentative, no-big-deal memo would in fact be the final report of the subcommittee— seen by neither Lodge nor Hickenlooper before it was printed.

This, too, became an object of dispute when the report was brought before the Senate. Lodge was as angry as he would be about the missing pages. "I never saw the majority report," he said, "until this afternoon. . . . I never had a chance to see what the majority had to say until the thing was in print. . . . [T]here has never been a vote in the subcommittee on this report, because the senator from Iowa has never seen it at all and I saw it just this afternoon at 2 o'clock." Hickenlooper would reinforce and amplify these comments, saying,

---

*In fact, the bulk of it was already drafted, as Tydings would admit when pinned down by Lodge.

"I never saw this proposed report until after it had been printed, and after it had been given to the press . . ."[5]

This seemed bad enough, but other curious revelations were soon to follow. Having been wafted through the subcommittee, the report had been passed on to the full Committee on Foreign Relations, where still other odd mutations had further transformed the harmless memo. As Sen. H. Alexander Smith of New Jersey, a ranking Republican on the full committee, explained, members of the committee had no time to read the report or weigh its merits. Accordingly, said Smith, "It was moved that the Committee on Foreign Relations transmit to the Senate . . . the report of the subcommittee without comment one way or another . . . I doubt that anyone except the chairman of the subcommittee [Tydings] had read the report." So it was decided, Smith concluded, to say the report had been "received" rather than "accepted" by the full committee, "without comment," and thereafter "transmitted to the Senate."[6]

This seemingly technical issue would be discussed at length by other Republican members who knew something of the matter, seconding Smith's recollection of what had happened and his insistence that "the report is not a report of the Foreign Relations Committee" but of the subcommittee only. Senators Brewster, Ferguson, Lodge, and others addressed the point, summed up by Lodge as follows: "I understood that the full committee merely transmitted the report, just the same as the Post Office Department transmits a letter from one person to another. That is clear from the record."[7]

Against that backdrop, when the report came to the floor, Sens. Kenneth Wherry (R-Neb.) and Forrest Donnell (R-Mo.) sought to make it a matter of official record that this indeed wasn't a report of the full committee but only of the subcommittee, which in turn meant, of course, only its three Democratic members. These objections were summarily overridden by Truman's vice president, Alben Barkley, in the chair, and this ruling was sustained in a straight party-line division; the report would thus be attributed in Senate records to the full committee, not simply to the Tydings panel. Meanwhile, Ferguson and Donnell flagged yet another strange development to the attention of their colleagues: The cover sheet of the document, which originally said it was a report of the subcommittee, had already been replaced—again by some hidden hand—with a brand-new cover reading, "Report of the Committee on Foreign Relations."[8]

Thus did a document that started out as an innocuous, tentative memo— "just a basis" for discussion—wind up as an official Senate report with the imprimatur of the full parent Committee on Foreign Relations, with all the authority this was presumably heir to. In the larger scheme of things, these procedural monkeyshines hardly seem significant enough to justify the considerable effort that was obviously devoted to them. However, the stages by which the metamorphosis occurred are worth noting as indicative of the methods being used to steer the matter through the Senate.

More important than this parliamentary shuffle, though obviously connected to it, was what the report had to say in terms of substance. The document was about as one-sided as Edward Morgan, or whoever actually did the drafting, could contrive to make it. The opening sections concerned, not loyalty problems in the State Department, the security setup there, or the merits of specific cases, but the transcendent evil of Joe McCarthy. The essence of it, stated early and repeated often, was that McCarthy had made false allegations, changed his story, and then lied about it to the Senate. McCarthy, not subversives in the Federal workforce or security practice in the State Department, was depicted as the most pressing danger before the nation.

These charges were not only harsh in content but made in the most violent language. The humdrum, provisional memo had somehow evolved into a mass of scathing accusations. "Hoax," "fraud," "deception," "nefarious," "vile," "big lie," "distortion," "half-truth," "untruth," "despicable," "bias," "sinister," and "totalitarian" were among the epithets used—terms seldom seen in any Senate report whatever, much less about a member of that body.[9] Here are a couple of nontentative, unprovisional comments included in its pages:

> Starting with nothing, Senator McCarthy plunged headlong forward, desperately seeking to develop some information, which colored with distortion and fanned by a blaze of bias would forestall a day of reckoning. Certain elements rallied to his support, particularly those who ostensibly fight communism by adopting the vile methods of the Communists themselves. Senator McCarthy and McCarthyism have been exposed for what they are—and the sight is not a pretty one.[10]

And further:

> . . . we are constrained fearlessly and frankly to call the [McCarthy] charges, and the methods employed to give them ostensible validity, what they are: A fraud and a hoax perpetrated on the Senate of the United States and the American people. They represent perhaps the most nefarious campaign of half-truth and untruth in the history of the Republic. For the first time in our history, we have seen the totalitarian technique of the big lie employed on a sustained basis.[11]

In seeking to prove these grim assertions, the report tracked closely with the strategy memo Tydings had sent to Morgan back in April, the 168-page "Confidential Memorandum" that showed up a few days later, and the remarks of Karsten-Kilgore and others who attacked McCarthy on the floor of Congress. As in these prior incarnations, the chief indictment was McCarthy's alleged lying about the Wheeling numbers, the main evidence cited in support of this the Desmond *Intelligencer* story and the radio affidavits. No glimmer of doubt appeared about the authenticity of these items. Based on these supposed proofs, the report treated the "205" quote as fact and made an official finding that McCarthy said it. His use of the number 57, therefore, simply attested to the "ever-shrinking character of the charges" and "constituted misrepresentation of the true facts to the Senate."[12]

After disposing of this all-important topic, the report took up the thesis that McCarthy's 80 anonymous cases were nothing but a recycled version of the Lee list. This, too, followed the game plan of the strategy memo, State Department materials sent to Tydings, and the remarks of Karsten and his congressional teammates. To these were added a clinching argument provided by John Peurifoy of the State Department—that a quartet of committees in the Republican 80th Congress had already looked at these very cases and found nothing to alarm them. And if the cases didn't amount to much in 1948, they obviously amounted to even less in 1950.

Having dealt with these generic questions of State Department security practice, the report next considered the public cases McCarthy had presented to the Tydings panel. As foretold by the conduct of the hearings, the method used throughout was to take the denials of each and every suspect at face value and adopt these as "findings." Whether it was Dorothy Kenyon, Philip Jessup, Esther Brunauer, Owen Lattimore, Haldore Hanson, or John Service, the verdict was the same: The accused was free of subversive taint, was indeed an outstanding scholar or public servant, and McCarthy's charges were baseless slanders.

In fact, Tydings and Co. managed to clear everybody and everything within shouting distance of McCarthy's charges: the State Department; all of the McCarthy suspects, both named and nameless; the IPR (this in connection with the much-lauded Dr. Jessup, a former IPR official); certain periodicals named by McCarthy as subversive; and the Truman Justice Department in the bargain (this in connection with its handling of the *Amerasia* case). Thrown in with all these clearances, the report also succeeded, by indirections, in clearing both Gustavo Duran and Stephen Brunauer, two of the McCarthy public cases, through professing not to judge them as they were supposedly irrelevant to the hearings.

When members of the Senate got hold of this report and had a chance to study it a bit, something close to pandemonium erupted. Lodge and Hickenlooper were already incensed, but were soon joined by others, including conservatives such as Taft and Mundt and moderate GOPers more akin to Lodge, including New York's Irving Ives and New Jersey's Smith. In these exchanges, McCarthy himself was conspicuously silent, though present for various intervening roll calls. He didn't, however, need to say too much, as virtually everything he might have said in answer to the Tydings onslaught was expressed by a small army of his Republican colleagues, from every sector of the party.

Among these, the most knowledgeable critic of the Tydings version was Ferguson, an experienced investigator of security cases. In a lengthy speech,

Ferguson did a complete demolition of the Tydings wrap-up, along the way providing a good deal of background about loyalty-security issues in general. He in particular noted the omission from the report of significant findings by Congress and security investigators in the past. A prime exhibit, he said, was the "chart" (taken from the Klaus memo) reflecting the number of agents, Communists, and so on, in the State Department as of 1946. The document containing these startling data had been obtained by Tydings and was one of the topics raised by Lodge in his series of unanswered questions. The Tydings report made no reference whatever to the substance of this memo.

Summarizing the Klaus disclosures, Ferguson reprised the questions earlier raised by Lodge: "Who are these Communists and agents and sympathizers and suspects? What are their names? Why are they there?" Getting answers to those questions would have been an obvious starting point for any halfway-competent investigation of security affairs at State. The Tydings majority had shown zero interest in such topics, instead focusing mainly on the procedural question of where the "chart" alluded to by Klaus had come from. (See Chapter 23.)

Ferguson cited other omissions also—for instance, that data on Communist penetration of the State Department assembled by the Senate Appropriations subcommittee were nowhere referred to in the report and, he surmised (correctly), nowhere in the Tydings record. Likewise with concerns expressed by Joe Panuch relating to security suspects, the nature of the *Amerasia* papers, and the curious State Department reversal of the 1947 suspensions under the McCarran rider. These important items, Ferguson noted, weren't so much as mentioned in the document now before the Senate.*[13]

Other Republican members would expand on these comments. Senator Ives, a spokesman for the moderate Northeast contingent of the party, recapped the debate about S.R. 231 and what was agreed to in it. He noted that the resolution had been explicitly crafted so as *not* to be limited to McCarthy's cases but rather to look into the matter of State Department loyalty practice in general. Ives suggested that "there may be some who find that if a fraud and a hoax have been perpetrated on the Senate of the United States, and the American people, such perpetration is evident in the apparently deliberate action of the subcommittee in disregarding the will of the Senate."[14]

There were complaints as well about the tone of the report and its abrasive phrasing. The GOP spokesmen noted that, while all McCarthy targets

---

* Beyond this, Ferguson also said, was the problem of outright falsehood. Specifically, he blasted the repeated Tydings statement that "four committees" of the Republican 80th Congress had looked into security affairs at State and exonerated the department. Having served on two such committees in that Congress, Ferguson knew what they had done and denounced this as a fabrication. Why, he asked, did the report repeat, and italicize, "an untruth about four committees of the Republican Congress," contrary to the documented record? (See Chapter 20.)

were given absolution, there were a few alleged villains in the lurid picture sketched by Tydings. Foremost among these was, of course, McCarthy, but there were some lesser culprits also. Remarkably, in what professed to be a report by the subcommittee/committee, two of these malefactors—Lodge and Hickenlooper—were among the subcommittee members.

The report criticized both Republicans by name, referring to their allegedly slack performance in viewing State Department security records. "Amazingly," said the report, "despite Senator McCarthy's insistence that the loyalty files would prove his case . . . Senator Hickenlooper read only 9 of the files and Senator Lodge only 12."[15] Criticism of members of a committee in a report of that very committee was, to say the least, unusual. Of course, Lodge and Hickenlooper could take care of themselves, and did. The situation was quite different with private individuals attacked in the report but given no chance to answer its aspersions.

Among the targets of such attack were journalists Isaac Don Levine and Ralph de Toledano, editors of the anti-Communist journal *Plain Talk,* which specialized in security matters and Cold War issues. In covering the *Amerasia* case, *Plain Talk* had run an article by the mercurial Emmanuel Larsen depicting Philip Jaffe, John Service, and others as part of a cabal to promote the Communist cause in China. This matched with what Larsen told the Hobbs committee in 1946, but he had in considerable measure reversed his field with Tydings, saying the article didn't represent his views and that Levine and/or Toledano had changed its meaning.

Though Hickenlooper urged that the journalists be called to answer these accusations, neither Levine nor Toledano was brought before the panel. Instead, Tydings and Co. not only let the Larsen charges go unanswered but gratuitously reinforced them, saying: "The fact that these persons have been reported to us as professional anti-Communists, whose income and reputation depend on the developing and maintaining of new Communist fears . . . while not deemed necessarily significant, has not been entirely overlooked by the committee." And: *"if true,* this action of Levine and his associates in connection with the *Plain Talk* article is one of the most despicable instances of a deliberate effort to deceive and hoodwink the American people in our history."*[16] (Emphasis added.)

(These comments were noteworthy in themselves but would become the more so when coupled with the Tydings verdict in the case of Owen Lattimore, who like all other McCarthy suspects was cleared in the subcommittee wrap-

---

*The "if true" was a particularly nice touch, a device by which it would be possible to pass along any slur whatever—as in "It has been suggested by some of his critics that Millard Tydings must have been in the pay of the Soviet Union. *If true,* this would have been despicable on the part of Tydings."

up. McCarthy's critique of Lattimore, said the Tydings panel, revealed *"the danger of promiscuous and specious attacks on private citizens and their views."*[17] [Emphasis added.] What was construed as unfair treatment of a McCarthy target who had ample chance to state his case was apparently okay when done to Toledano and Levine, neither of whom was given an opportunity in the hearings to answer the Tydings onslaught.)

A further episode in which the Tydings panel took the unsupported word of Larsen involved Nebraska Republican Kenneth Wherry, minority leader of the Senate. In its sustained criticism of McCarthy, the majority report asserted: "His [McCarthy's] irresponsible statements called for emergency measures [i.e., by his Republican colleagues]. As Senator Wherry told Emmanuel S. Larsen: 'Oh, Mac got himself out on a limb and kind of made a fool of himself and we have to back him up now.' "[18] On reading this, Wherry exploded, categorically denied he had said it, and blasted the Tydings report for repeating as supposed fact a comment by Larsen—whose credibility wasn't the greatest—without even asking Wherry about the matter.

"I was not given an opportunity," said Wherry, "to confront the man who is alleged to have made this statement . . . the statement of this man, whose honor is now being questioned, is being taken at face value, and it is going to be broadcast to the American people."[19] (In this Wherry was more prescient than he imagined, as the statement is often featured, without qualification or mention of his denial, in purported histories of the era.)

Wherry then confronted Edward Morgan, who was on the floor of the Senate as an aide to Tydings, and asked if Morgan had drafted the passage in question. When Morgan accepted responsibility for the language, Wherry became even more enraged and demanded that Morgan be banished from the Senate floor for impugning the honor of a member. This, too, was put to a vote, and also defeated on a party-line division. Subsequently, a still-furious Wherry took a swing at Morgan—a raucous episode that shows up in several books about McCarthy.*

While Wherry was the most irate, other senators weren't far behind. Lodge, already angry, would become still more so when he read the comments on his conduct. "It is this type of petty sniping," he said, "these attempts to hit below the belt, which has made the work of the subcommittee so difficult. If the other statements in the majority's report are no more accurate than these statements about myself, the report will be chiefly valuable as fiction and special pleading.

---

* And tells us something about these books. Thus, David Oshinsky writes about the Wherry-Morgan fisticuffs in the same chapters using, *as authentic,* the alleged Wherry quote about McCarthy being "out on a limb." Oshinsky doesn't inform the reader that the confrontation occurred because Wherry *denied* that he had made this statement.

Indeed this makes the whole document suspect. . . . They must be desperate men indeed to use these personal methods to divert attention from the main issue which is, of course, the total inadequacy of the investigation."[20]

Finally, the GOPers raised some questions as to where the alleged information in the report had come from and who had actually drafted its offending phrases. "Mr. President," said Hickenlooper, "this document is a mysterious and mysteriously prepared document. It is a document whose antecedents, paternity and maternity, might be open to some serious and revealing facets. It is a document whose generation raises questions in the minds of any who has followed this matter rather carefully."[21]

Ferguson voiced the same suspicions, saying: "I am wondering who did write this report. Who is the actual author of the words of the report? . . . Who drew the conclusions in the report? Who helped to write it? Who read it before it was actually put before the Senate?" And further: "I ask again, and I shall continue to ask until I can find out, who wrote this report? Whose words are these strange words in the report? It is a strange document. It is alien and foreign to this body."[22]

In view of matters already noted, these doubts were obviously well founded. Virtually everything in the report pertaining to the McCarthy cases, the Wheeling affidavits, the Lee list suspects, and all the rest had been gift-wrapped and handed to Tydings by the State Department and uncritically accepted by the majority members of the panel. The questions raised by the GOP lawmakers suggest they had some inkling of this, and if not had extremely sensitive antennae for backstage conniving.

This firestorm raged for several days, fed mostly by Republican members. There were some Democratic responses by such as Tom Connally and Sen. Claude Pepper (D-Fla.)—for instance, defending on procedural grounds the decision to attribute the report to the full Committee on Foreign Relations— but the main Democratic innings belonged to Tydings. On July 20, midway in the week-long donnybrook, the chairman took the floor to make a defense of his report, expound its meaning, and offer his own brand of documentation for its contents.

This Tydings presentation, by all accounts, was among the more memorable speeches ever given in the Senate. He recapped the main points of the report—some several times—but did so in histrionic manner, replete with dramatic images, flights of fancy, and physical props of unusual nature. Among these was a series of charts illustrating the Peurifoy thesis that McCarthy's cases had been viewed and dismissed out of hand by four committees of the 80th Congress. Another prop, even more novel in the Senate chamber, was a portable record player—which would prove to be the most remarkable item in the whole performance.

A further striking aspect of this speech was that Tydings, trying to revive his early game plan, repeatedly cited Cabot Lodge as concurring in the report's conclusions. (Lodge would sharply counter that these comments were a misstatement of his position.) Conversely, Tydings launched a slashing attack on Sen. William Jenner of Indiana, who had criticized the Tydings inquest as a "whitewash." Tydings accused the anti-Communist stalwart Jenner of following the Moscow line in his foreign policy voting. "I find," said Tydings, "that Joseph Stalin and the *Daily Worker* and the senator all vote the same way. . . . I looked up the senator's . . . votes, and here they are, one after the other, always, always, always following the same thing that Stalin is saying, that the *Daily Worker* is saying and the junior senator from Indiana is saying."[23]

All this was certainly high drama for the Senate, but the *pièce de résistance* was yet to come—the portable record player Tydings had before him and a phonograph record he flourished as he spoke. These props were part of his denunciation of the speech at Wheeling and the supposed McCarthy claim there to a list of 205 Communists in the State Department. After running through the alleged proofs of McCarthy's lying about the Wheeling numbers— the Desmond story, the affidavits—Tydings said: "Mr. President, I wonder if I could get unanimous consent to play a radio recording of the senator's own voice on one of these occasions. I ask unanimous consent that I may play a record of the senator's own words. I am not asking senators to take my word, but to hear the senator's own voice, who says he has not made such a statement of that character."

When Wherry objected to this as unseemly, Tydings withdrew his request, saying: "I will play this recording off the floor in due time . . . but admission will be by card only." He nonetheless continued holding forth about the phonograph record, saying McCarthy had "told us under oath that was not what he said, but the record stands there to challenge that statement . . . we have a voice here which can speak louder than these other five exhibits I have already shown the Senate [about the Wheeling numbers]." And further:

> One simply cannot beat the sound of a man's voice. . . . All one has to do is read McCarthy's statement in the *Congressional Record* and listen to this recording in order to know that there is not truth in both these statements. . . . What is there other than a fraud and a hoax and a deceit about this whole matter? It ought to make the blood of Americans boil, that they have been told these foul and vile charges—and here is a recording to prove it. And if that is broken, I have duplicates. [Laughter][24]

This show-and-tell by Tydings was by common consent the forensic highlight of the entire proceedings. Subsequently, he would pose for a smiling picture with the record player and recording, obviously pleased with the effect created. (See page 244.) The press would then report that Tydings had a recording of the Wheeling speech proving McCarthy had falsified the numbers, but

TYDINGS'S PROP

Senator Millard Tydings poses with the phonograph record he led the Senate to believe would prove that McCarthy lied about his speech at Wheeling. Tydings never played the record—with good reason, as he had no recording of the Wheeling speech, a fact he later admitted under oath.

AP/World Wide Photos

that Tydings had been prevented from playing the recording for the Senate. Still more cogent proof, it seemed, of Joe McCarthy's outrageous lying.

Except, of course, there was no such recording of McCarthy's speech at Wheeling, the only recording anyone ever knew of having been erased the following day or a few days later by the radio station that made it. From which it followed that Tydings could not have had such a recording, and didn't. The whole thing was an imposture, as the McCarthy forces would prove when they were eventually able to corner Tydings, in a legal setting under oath, allowing no evasion (after demanding, unsuccessfully, that he play the recording as was promised).

The occasion for this definitive proof was a deposition Tydings was called to give in a libel suit between McCarthy and Sen. William Benton of Connecticut. In this face-off McCarthy's attorney, Edward Bennett Williams, closely questioned Tydings about the recording of which he had made such a production. After numerous twists and turns that inched Tydings inexorably toward an answer, Williams finally pinned him down as follows: *Williams:* "Now, we have established this morning, I think pretty conclusively, that you didn't have a recording of the Wheeling speech, Senator Tydings?" *Tydings: "I did not have a radio recording. I had the verbatim copy of his speech, which McCarthy took to West Virginia and which he read."*[25] (Emphasis added.)

So it wasn't McCarthy who falsified the matter, but Tydings, who ostentatiously led his colleagues and the world to think he had a recording of the Wheeling speech when in fact he didn't. What, then, was the record he offered to play before the Senate? The answer, as he acknowledged to Williams, was a recording of the McCarthy radio interview with Dan Valentine in Salt Lake City. But in that broadcast, as seen, McCarthy never laid claim to a list of 205, but instead claimed a list of 57—precisely as he elsewhere contended. So playing that recording would in no wise have proved that McCarthy lied about the Wheeling numbers, but rather the reverse.

Taken all in all, the story of the Tydings hearing/report and their uproarious reception by the Senate was among the wildest episodes in the history of Congress. From the thirty-five omitted pages, to the bait and switch whereby a "tentative" subcommittee memo became the official report of a full committee, to the recording Tydings professed to have but didn't, it was a breathtaking venture in deception. As Tydings himself so aptly phrased it, "What is there other than a fraud and a hoax and a deceit about this whole matter?" What, indeed? Which is as good a segue as any to the elaborate tale, oft told by Tydings and the State Department, of the McCarthy/Lee list cases and their supposed clearance by four committees of the Congress.

CHAPTER 19

Of Names and Numbers

ROBERT E. LEE is of course a famous name in American history: the Union officer from Virginia who opted for his native Southland in the Civil War and became the leader of the Confederate armies.

However, the Robert E. Lee who concerns us here wasn't a Southerner of the nineteenth century but a twentieth-century Irish Catholic from Chicago.* A former FBI special agent (and later a commissioner of the FCC), this Lee had been chief clerk of the House Appropriations Committee in the Republican 80th Congress, some of whose doings have been noted. In the late summer and fall of 1947, he would assign a team of staffers to review security records at the State Department as part of the congressional probe discussed in Chapter 13. He thus became the eponymous father of the much-cited Lee list—108 security cases, identified by numbers only, compiled for the Appropriations panel.

The Lee list, it should be stressed, wasn't simply a list of cases but a document of substance. It included elements that made it a uniquely useful guide to loyalty/security operations at State, the nature of the caseload being handled, and problems that had developed in the security setup. The entries capsuled

---

*The coincidence was strictly that. As the latter-day Lee would entitle his unpublished memoir, *Only the Name Is the Same.* He wasn't a descendant of the general. Ironically, one of the main security suspects in the Bentley inquiry, Duncan C. Lee, was—as he was reputedly fond of noting.

THE LEE LIST

This is the first page of the oft-cited report on 108 security suspects in the State Department, as compiled by staff investigators for the House Appropriations Committee in 1947.

CONFIDENTIAL

1947-48

NO. 1

He was born in New York City in 1918. He was employed as an Economist and Analyst with OSS and the State Department since June 1945. Previous to that he had worked for the Treasury Department and the War Production Board. He is now in Research and Intelligence.

An undated memorandum in the file, which according to T. L. Hoffman, of CSA, was prepared during the week of October 13, 1947, recommended that this subject be terminated as a security risk. The memorandum states that he was an active member and officer of the American Student Union; that he advocated military opposition to Germany in 1937, and opposed conscription in the U.S.A. in 1940. He has been closely associated with several subjects of a Russian Espionage case, and has two brothers who are Communist Party members.

NO. 2

The subject was born in 1903 in Flushing, New York. He was employed on June 1, 1942 with OSS as a geographer. In September 1945 he was transferred to the State Department where he is presently in Research and Intelligence.

The investigative file on this subject has in it information from a Government investigative agency indicating that the subject possesses radical political views, according to neighbors and confidential informants. Three informants reported him a member of several Communist-front organizations and stated he associates openly with Communists. The report in which this information is included is dated July 3, 1942.

A CSA report of April 18, 1946 contains information obtained from another Government agency. The information of that Agency is set out in a report dated April 22, 1942 and indicates that numerous witnesses, including college professors and police officers in California, testified that the subject is a radical and fellow traveler, if not a Communist. He was very friendly and sympathetic towards Harry Bridges and strongly opposed moves to deport him. He was also a friend of Ralph Friedman, Secretary of the Communist Party in Northern California.

A CSA report of November 13, 1946 sets out information obtained by interviewing subject's present and former associates in Washington. Several of his former associates in OSS state he is "left of the New Deal". Another associate stated that subject favors the Chinese Communists over the "Kuomintang" Regime and favors Russia in most respects. The subject reportedly told another associate that he thought Union members should have the right to strike against the Government. A State Department official described him as being extremely Left and said he seemed to be sympathetic to Russia in the Communist experiment. Another Government official said the subject blamed the capitalists for all ills, and further blamed the State Department for all the trouble with Russia during the war and praised Russia and her foreign policy.

Eleven subsequent investigative reports were prepared between November 13, 1946 and September 22, 1947, with most of the witnesses confirming the above-mentioned statements regarding the subject. As of November 1, 1947, the subject's case had been referred to the State Department Loyalty Board but no action had been taken on it.

A-1

Source: Walter Judd papers

data Lee's researchers found of interest and provided links to other cases, suggesting a dense web of contacts extending out in all directions. All things considered, the list probably supplied more useful data on State Department security practice than any other such survey before or after.

To unlock the meaning of all this, however, two sets of keys were needed: the names that went with the numbers, and the identities of sixty-three other people mentioned—each also with a coded symbol—as contacts of the listed cases. The list had attached to it as well a fairly lengthy memo discussing the security drill at State and the officers who ran it. In many ways this candid memo is as informative as the list itself—in some aspects, even more so.*

As has been noted, the Lee list would become a central issue in the security wars of Joe McCarthy. It was central to McCarthy himself, as the vast majority of the cases he initially brought before the Senate were unquestionably taken from its entries. And it was also central to his foes, who used his reliance on the list to discredit him and dismiss his charges as warmed-over data irrelevant to the State Department security scene in 1950.

In his oration to the Senate, McCarthy made several gaffes, but arguably his single biggest miscue was an error of omission—not telling his colleagues he was mining data from this list. The reasons for this aren't entirely clear, as he would elsewhere freely cite the list as an important source of information. Moreover, there were no immediately obvious reasons he shouldn't have quoted from it and ways in which this would have strengthened the point he was making—that such problems had long been known to the State Department yet persisted. Whatever the motive, his failure to cite the list in the beginning allowed his critics to make this a salient issue—deflecting notice from what the security information *said* to the procedural question of where, exactly, *it had come from* (a tactic used in many later conflicts).

Though McCarthy didn't acknowledge the linkage in his speech, that he was borrowing data from the Lee list was apparent to anyone who had a copy of it and could compare it with his cases. This meant, above all others, John Peurifoy and his colleagues at State, who had the records that formed the basis of the list, knew exactly who was on it, and appeared before two House committees that held hearings on it in the winter of 1948. From this store of inside knowledge, State put together what became, and has remained, the canonical treatment of the list and its exploitation by McCarthy—running more or less as follows:

First and foremost, in this telling, when McCarthy went before the Senate he not only had the Lee list, he had *nothing but* the Lee list. Accordingly, he had no inside information sources at State (or anywhere else), as he led his col-

---

*For example, the congressional comments about the nature of the internal feuding in the State Department security shop, quoted in Chapter 12, are taken from this memo.

leagues to believe. Also, since the list was at this point two years old, it was out of date when McCarthy used it, its denizens no longer at the posts they held in 1948. Specifically, it's alleged, McCarthy's famous "57 cases" were merely a subset of the list, lifted from the congressional hearings of 1948, hence obsolete in 1950. Finally, in this account, the list itself was an innocuous business, so tepid and unimportant the House panels holding hearings on it, plus two others in the 80th Congress, viewed it with supreme indifference.[1]

Such is the version of the topic provided in numerous State Department memos, press releases, and backstage communiqués, echoed by the Tydings panel, and repeated in virtually every treatment of McCarthy now in print. In some instances we find variations, including the point hinted at by Tydings, and later made explicit by William Benton and several authors, that since the list consisted only of nameless, numbered cases, McCarthy didn't even know the identities of his suspects.*

Given the wide acceptance of this tale, its accuracy and completeness are obviously questions of importance. However, any attempt to check such matters out runs quickly into roadblocks and blind alleys. Chief among these, as noted, has been the fact that the Lee-McCarthy rosters were both veiled in anonymity, each consisting entirely of numbered, nameless suspects. Researchers dealing with the issue have thus been juggling two sets of unknown people, trying to match one against the other by comparing the contents of the entries.

While this works up to a point, it has some serious drawbacks. In the absence of the names, for instance, it's impossible to nail down by independent means such basic facts as whether any given suspect was even in the State Department when McCarthy brought his charges, which was one of the points to be decided. Equally futile is the hope of weighing cases on their merits, seeing who their (also anonymous) associates were, or tracing them in other records.

Faced with these epistemological problems, writers on the subject have usually been content to take the alleged facts about the cases from the report and dicta of Chairman Tydings. However, critical information needed to gauge the meaning of the lists doesn't appear in the Tydings transcript, appendix, or report, and/or has vanished from the subcommittee archive. What we have instead are the conclusory judgments of Tydings, telling us certain things about the Lee-McCarthy cases, which can be neither disputed nor confirmed without the missing backup data.

Fortunately for the historical record, sets of these materials have survived in other places and can be consulted. It's thus possible to construct a reasonably accurate picture of the Lee list, its linkage to McCarthy's cases, and its significance in general—on all of which the ascertainable facts are markedly

---

*A further modulation, also hinted at by Tydings, is that McCarthy didn't have the names when he went before the Senate but managed to obtain them later.

different from the standard version. Most obviously, and most to the present point, it doesn't happen to be true that, when McCarthy went before the Senate, he had *nothing but* the Lee list. He had other data also, derived from various public (and some not-so-public) sources. That the bulk of his documentation, 80 percent or thereabouts, stemmed from the Lee list is clearly so; that he had "nothing but the Lee list" just as clearly isn't.

Perhaps the most self-evident items in the initial McCarthy speeches not borrowed from the Lee list, though seldom mentioned in this context, were the four cases he talked about in Wheeling-Reno and then reprised before the Senate: John Stewart Service, Mary Jane Keeney, Gustavo Duran, and Harlow Shapley. Where his information came from on this foursome is a matter worth discussing. For the moment, what can be said with complete assurance is that they weren't taken from the Lee list, as none of them is on it.

Of this original group of cases the most significant by far was the Service/ *Amerasia* matter, fixed, lied about, and buried five years before this. Though others tried to dig it up in previous sessions of the Congress, it was McCarthy who almost single-handedly exhumed it. Moreover, it was the Service-*Amerasia* case on which McCarthy demonstrably had inside information sources and would develop others. His constant hammering on the topic would become a cause of chronic angst for his opponents at the White House, State Department, and Truman Justice. (See Chapter 23.)

Beyond these initial non-Lee cases, McCarthy added to his mix of suspects seven staffers at the Voice of America in New York (residuary legatee of the OWI), none of whom was on the Lee list. His comments on these people were sketchy, simply lumping the group together, saying they were instances of "Commies, or persons with Communist connections, recommending each other."[2] However, the fact that he did have this group of non-Lee cases indicates he had, either directly or indirectly, a source at VOA.

In addition, McCarthy in his opening Senate speech brought up the case of William Remington—a very important case indeed in terms of Truman-era security practice. This was another non-Lee case, as Remington worked for Commerce, not for State, and so wasn't in the House committee lineup. Here, too, McCarthy's comments were brief and sketchy, but did indicate he was fleshing out the list with information from other sources. (Remington was case 19 on McCarthy's initial Senate roster.)

Also, in a sort of Adam's rib procedure, McCarthy presented as one of his numbered cases Patricia G. Barnett, an OSS transferee and wife of a Lee list subject who was herself a State Department staffer but not given separate status on the list. She was thus not technically a Lee case, though mentioned in her husband's entry. Finally, when McCarthy gave the subcommittee the list of names that corresponded with his numbers, it included two other non-Lee cases, Philip Jessup and Edward Posniak (neither of whom, however, had been discussed in the speech before the Senate).

All in all, considering the total roster of cases McCarthy cited in his early speeches, a meager sprinkling of new entries—at the outside about fifteen—not completely insignificant, but also no great number of non-Lee suspects. If that was all he had, he really didn't add much to the discussion and would deserve at least some of the scorn that's heaped upon him. However, this leavening of Lee data with further cases was not the only way McCarthy expanded on the list. Far more important in terms of seeing the total security problem at State was his effort to add information *to the list itself,* by updating it as to the whereabouts of the people on it and the handling of their cases.

From the internal evidence of McCarthy's initial talk before the Senate, it's clear that he and his staffers had for some indefinite time before this been backtracking on the Lee list cases—trying to find out what happened to them, whether they were still in the State Department, if they had been transferred to other official posts, and so on. Judging by the information he then had, this effort had to have been under way during his trip to Wheeling-Reno and probably predated it, but was still a work in progress.* In the February 20 speech, his comments on these matters were frequent, including such statements as the following:

". . . this individual still occupies an important position in the State Department." ". . . this individual, who is now one of our foreign ministers . . ." "This man, I know definitely, is in the Office of Information and Education in the State Department." "This individual is with the division of central services." "This man is still in that very important position [at VOA]." ". . . the case of a man who holds a very high position in the State Department." "This individual is in the biographical information division of the State Department." And so on in similar vein for a score of other cases.[3]

In all, McCarthy made such identifications about thirty times in discussing upward of seventy suspects. As Lee's researchers and the FBI had learned before him, it wasn't always easy for an outsider to discover whether someone was in the State Department at any specific moment, given its far-flung global operations, several different employee rosters, and inclination to be less than helpful in supplying information. (See below.) McCarthy in fact erred in certain of

---

*In some versions it's argued that McCarthy had nothing at all when he set out for Wheeling-Reno but somehow came up with the Lee list and other documentation for his speech when he returned to D.C. Considering that he got back to Washington on Saturday and went before the Senate Monday afternoon, the nature of the documentation he had makes this not only unlikely but virtually impossible. There was no way the data reflected in this speech could have been assembled in this forty-eight-hour period, which included much of Saturday and all of a Sunday, when government offices where such information reposed would have been shut down for the weekend.

these comments, mostly with respect to people who had left the department when he thought they were still in it. However, in instances checkable from the records, he was right in perhaps eight cases out of ten, and would correct and update the others.

Indeed, despite occasional miscues, McCarthy's backtracking methods were fairly good, suggesting due diligence had been exerted by him and/or his researchers. To pick an instance previously cited (case 28), he said of one suspect, "He is still holding a high salaried job with the government, and to the best of my knowledge is now stationed at Frankfurt, Germany."[4] This information, as shown by State Department records, was quite correct and wasn't derivative from the Lee list, which didn't say anything concerning Frankfurt. In another case (No. 65), McCarthy said, "This individual is still in the State Department today in the Office of Information and Education."[5] The State Department (hence, inevitably, Tydings) would in effect deny this in its tabulations, but McCarthy's version would be confirmed twice over when checked against official rosters. (See Chapter 25.)

As to former Foggy Bottom staffers who went elsewhere, McCarthy made another valid and important point, already stressed in several places: Thanks to the subliminal tactic of separating suspect employees by resignations, such people were often able to relocate with relative ease at other official postings, including various global bodies created in the postwar era. In particular, McCarthy noted, some of his suspects had turned up at the United Nations. (Thus McCarthy cases Gustavo Duran, Stanley Graze, and Mary Jane Keeney, all formerly at State, got jobs with the U.N. and would be found working there in 1950.)

McCarthy's updates were also suggestive as to the nature and accuracy of his sources. In one instance—his case No. 11—he said, "This individual is not in the State Department at this time, but has a job in the CIA today."[6] This was an interesting thing for McCarthy to have known if he was simply flying blind and bluffing. In another instance, case No. 53, he said the suspect had been named by a "confessed Communist spy" as a member of his spy ring.[7] These statements, as will be shown, were impeccably correct, weren't taken from the Lee list, and thus clearly indicated other sources. And, of course, to track such data in the first place, McCarthy had to know the names that matched the numbers.

All this was in the speech of February 20. McCarthy's appearance before the Tydings panel, beginning on March 8, should have ended speculation as to whether, at least as of that date, he knew the identities of his suspects. To begin with there were his public cases, all named in open sessions of the hearings. These were nine in number, and in tabulations compiled by State, the FBI, and Civil Service, Mary Jane Keeney was added to the mix to make the total of such cases ten. (Why she was considered a McCarthy case, while some others mentioned in his various speeches weren't, is an anomaly in the record, albeit one of many.)

In addition to the public cases, McCarthy would provide to Tydings, in writing, the list of names that went with the dossiers capsuled before the Senate. By registered letter dated March 18, McCarthy gave the panel the names of his eighty suspects, including those skipped over in the *Congressional Record.* (One individual's name was still omitted, because in McCarthy's view he wasn't a suspect but a victim.) This same week (March 14), McCarthy also gave Tydings a list of twenty-five additional people he said were questionable security risks and needed looking into. As three of these overlapped the eighty, McCarthy thus supplied to Tydings *in writing* a total of 102 names as possible subjects for investigation.[8] (See the Appendix for the written lists McCarthy supplied to Tydings.)

There were other overlaps as well, causing some confusion in the numbers. Two of the names on McCarthy's written list of eighty—Esther Brunauer and Philip Jessup—were also among the ten public cases, meaning only eight people from that further roster were new additions to the lineup. Also, in public statements and in the hearings, and in contacts with the FBI, McCarthy and/or Robert Morris in his behalf brought up the names of (at least) fourteen other suspects: Solomon Adler, Joseph Barnes, T. A. Bisson, Stephen Brunauer, Chew Hong, Chi Chao-ting, Chi Kung Chuan, O. Edmund Clubb, Theodore Geiger, Leander Lovell,* Andrew Roth, Charles W. Thayer, David Weintraub, and George S. Wheeler.

As with the *Venona* cases earlier noted, this was a mixed lot, decked out in several guises. These ranged from fairly extensive comment (Bisson, Stephen Brunauer), to references in Morris's cross-examination (Adler), to brief notice in McCarthy speeches (Barnes, Chi Chao-ting), to private contacts with the Bureau (Thayer, Weintraub). However, as the subject is names and whether McCarthy actually had them, all are worth recording. Also, it's evident McCarthy-Morris at this point had in their grasp fragments of the Chi-Adler-Service puzzle and were putting this together.

In sum, McCarthy-Morris brought to the attention of the public, the Senate, and the FBI a total of 124 names of potential security cases past and present, up through the conclusion of the Tydings hearings. (And, considering the incompleteness and/or redaction of the records, this probably isn't the full roster.)† Consequently, it's hard to see how Benton, or any reasonably well-informed observer, could possibly say McCarthy "had no names." Part of the

---

*Leander Lovell was in fact McCarthy's case No. 28. See Chapter 25.

†McCarthy subsequently addressed many more cases than those listed. However, discussion of the point is confined here to the period of the Tydings hearings, as indicative of what McCarthy did or didn't know as of this initial go-round.

Table 1. The Lee List
(alphabetical order, not case numbers)

1. Alexander, Dorothy	37. Kamarck, Andrew	73. Post, Richard
2. Arndt, Ernest	38. Kaufman, Arthur	74. Raine, Philip
3. Barnett, Robert	39. Lansberg, Hans	75. Randolph, David
4. Berman, Harold	40. Lazarus, Theodore	76. Rennie, Leonard
5. Blaisdell, Donald	41. Lemon, Edythe	77. Robinson, Jay
6. Borton, Hugh	42. Lewis, Preston	78. Rommel, Rowena
7. Brunauer, Esther	43. Lifantieff-Lee, P.	79. Rose, Ernest
8. Burlingame, Robert	44. Lindsey, John R.	80. Rosenthal, Albert
9. Cameron, Gertrude	45. Lloyd, David	81. Ross, Lewis
10. Carlisle, Lois	46. Lorwin, Val	82. Ross, Robert
11. Carter, William	47. Lovell, Leander	83. Rothwell, George
12. Demerjian, Alice	48. Lunning, Just	84. Royce, Edith
13. DeMoretz, Shirley	49. McDavid, Raven	85. Rudlin, Walter
14. Dubois, Cora	50. Magnite, Sylvia	86. Salmon, Thomas
15. Elinson, Marcelle	51. Magruder, John	87. Schimmel, Sylvia
16. Eminowitz, Halina	52. Mallon, Dwight	88. Shell, Melvin
17. Ferry, Frances	53. Mann, Gottfried	89. Shevlin, Lorraine
18. Fierst, Herbert	54. Margolies, Daniel	90. Siegal, Herman
19. Fine, Sherwood	55. Margolin, Arnold	91. Smith, Frederick
20. Fishback, Sam	56. Martin, Shirley	92. Smith, Samuel
21. Fishburn, John	57. Martingale, Rose	93. Smothers, Frank
22. Fornos, Joseph	58. Meigs, Peveril	94. Stoianoff, Stoian
23. Fournier, Norman	59. Miller, Robert	95. Stone, William
24. Gordon, Estelle	60. Montague, Ella	96. Taylor, Jeanne
25. Graze, Gerald	61. Moore, Leith	97. Thomson, Charles
26. Graze, Stanley	62. Neal, Fred	98. Thursz, Jonathan
27. Gross, Aaron	63. Ness, Norman	99. Toory, Frank
28. Hankin, Robert	64. Neumann, Franz	100. Tuchscher, Frances
29. Harrison, Marcia	65. Osnatch, Olga	101. Tuckerman, Gustavus
30. Horwin, Leonard	66. Parker, Glen	102. Vincent, John C.
31. Hughes, H. S.	67. Parsons, Ruby	103. Volin, Max
32. Hunt, Victor	68. Perkins, Isham	104. Washburne, Carleton
33. Illyefalvi-Vitez, G.	69. Pesto, Paula	105. Wilcox, Stanley
34. Jackson, Malcolm	70. Peter, Hollis	106. Wilfert, Howard
35. Jankowski, Joseph	71. Polyzoides, T. A.	107. Wood, James
36. Josephson, Joseph	72. Posner, Margery	108. Yuhas, Helen

explanation, no doubt, is the matter of the disappearing data—including the McCarthy letter of March 18, accompanying roster of eighty names, and further list of twenty-two net potential cases. Researchers who look for these items in the official public records aren't apt to find them.

However, we do now have the names, and with them can answer some of the questions glossed over in the standard treatments. (The complete lists of Lee-McCarthy cases are given in Tables 1 and 2, followed by some relevant breakdowns in succeeding tables.) On the substance of the matter, we of course need something more than names and numbers, which in themselves say noth-

Table 2. Names Submitted to Tydings in Writing by McCarthy

(alphabetical order, not case numbers)

1. Arndt, Ernest
2. Askwith, E. J.
3. Barnett, P.
4. Barnett, R.
5. Berman, Harold
6. Blaisdell, Donald
7. Brunauer, Esther
8. Cameron, Gertrude
9. Carlisle, Lois
10. Carter, William
11. Chipchin, Nelson
12. Clucas, Lowell
13. Davies, John Paton
14. Delgado, Mucio
15. Demerjian, Alice
16. Dubois, Cora
17. Erdos, Arpad
18. Ferry, Frances
19. Fierst, Herbert
20. Fishback, Sam
21. Fishburn, John
22. Ford (Fornos), Joseph
23. Gordon, Stella
24. Grad, Andrew
25. Grandahl, T. Conrad
26. Graze, Gerald
27. Graze, Stanley
28. Gross, Aaron
29. Harris, Reed
30. Harrison, Martha
31. Henkin, Louis
32. Horwin, Leonard
33. Hulten, Charles
34. Hunt, Victor
35. Illyefalvi-Vitez, G.
36. Ingram, George
37. Jankowski, John
38. Jessup, Philip
39. Josephson, Joseph
40. Kamarck, Andrew
41. Katusich, Ivan
42. Kaufman, Arthur
43. Lansberg, Hans

44. Lemon, Edythe
45. Less, Esther
46. Lewis, Preston
47. Lifantieff-Lee, P.
48. Lindsey, Richard
49. Lloyd, David
50. Lorwin, Val
51. Ludden, Raymond
52. Magnite, Sylvia
53. Mann, Gottfried
54. Margolies, Daniel
55. Meeker, Leonard
56. Meigs, Peveril
57. Miller, Robert
58. Montague, Ella
59. Neal, Fred
60. Nelson, Clarence
61. Ness, Norman
62. Neumann, Franz
63. Newbegin, Robert
64. Osnatch, Olga
65. Parsons, Ruby
66. Perkins, Isham
67. Peter, Hollis
68. Polyzoides, T. A.
69. Posner, Margery
70. Posniak, Edward
71. Post, Richard
72. Raine, Philip
73. Ramon, Josephine
74. Randolph, Jay
75. Rapaport, A.
76. Remington, William
77. Robinson, Jay
78. Rommel, Rowena
79. Ross, Lewis
80. Ross, Robert
81. Rothwell, George
82. Rowe, James
83. Sanders, William
84. Schimmel, Sylvia
85. Shell, Melvin
86. Siegal, Herman

87. Smith, Frederick
88. Smith, Samuel
89. Stoianoff, Stoian
90. Stone, William
91. Tate, Jack
92. Taylor, Jeanne
93. Thomson, Charles
94. Tuchscher, Frances
95. Tuckerman, Gustavus
96. Vincent, John C.
97. Volin, Max
98. Washburne, Carleton
99. Wilcox, Stanley
100. Wood, James
101. Yuhas, Helen
102. Zablodowsky, David

Additional Names Brought Forward by McCarthy/Morris During Tydings Hearings

103. Adler, Solomon
104. Barnes, Joseph
105. Bisson, T. A.
106. Brunauer, S.
107. Chew Hong
108. Chi Chao Ting
109. Chi Kung Chuan
110. Clubb, O. Edmund
111. Duran, Gustavo
112. Geiger, Theodore
113. Hanson, Haldore
114. Keeney, Mary Jane
115. Kenyon, Dorothy
116. Lattimore, Owen
117. Lovell, Leander
118. Roth, Andrew
119. Schuman, Frederick
120. Service, John S.
121. Shapley, Harlow
122. Thayer, Charles W.
123. Weintraub, David
124. Wheeler, George

**Table 3. Non-Lee-List Names Brought Forward by
McCarthy/Morris During Course of Hearings**

(alphabetical order, not case numbers)

1. Adler	17. Geiger	33. Nelson
2. Askwith	18. Grad	34. Newbegin
3. Barnes	19. Grandahl	35. Posniak
4. Barnett, P.*	20. Hanson	36. Ramon
5. Bisson	21. Harris	37. Rapaport
6. Brunauer, S.†	22. Henkin	38. Remington
7. Chew Hong	23. Hulten	39. Rowe
8. Chi Chao ting	24. Ingram	40. Sanders
9. Chi Kung Chuan	25. Jessup	41. Schuman
10. Chipchin	26. Katusich	42. Service
11. Clubb	27. Keeney	43. Shapley
12. Clucas	28. Kenyon	44. Tate
13. Davies	29. Lattimore	45. Thayer
14. Delgado	30. Less	46. Weintraub
15. Duran	31. Ludden	47. Wheeler
16. Erdos	32. Meeker	48. Zablodowsky

*Wife of Robert Barnett, mentioned in his Lee list entry but not considered a separate case. Not counted in aggregate number of non-Lee cases in text.
†Case provided by McCarthy in connection with Esther Brunauer, wife of Stephen. Latter not considered by Tydings as one of McCarthy's cases since not in the State Department.

ing about the merits of the cases. As with the speech at Wheeling, this purely numerical focus is a bit of a sideshow. But since these matters were stressed so much by Tydings and the State Department, and still are by McCarthy critics, they can hardly be avoided.

One thing that can be readily seen by looking at these several rosters is that when McCarthy went before the Tydings panel—though still leaning on the Lee list—he obviously did have other cases, and in substantial numbers. Of the names he and/or Morris in his behalf brought up through the close of the hearings, no fewer than forty-seven—not quite two-fifths of the total—were not alumni of the Lee list (see Table 3). As is self-evident from these cases, McCarthy thus had additional sources of information beyond the list and his effort to backtrack on its entries.

Another point that can be tested by checking out the lists is the question of obsolescence—the contention that McCarthy's charges were yesterday's news, out of date in 1950. In the State Department–Tydings version, there *had been* security trouble at State, but this had long since been taken care of. Thanks to State's alertness, supposedly, the bad guys had all been rousted well before the advent of McCarthy. As for any listees that remained, these had all been "cleared" somehow by someone (the 80th Congress, the FBI) and thus were not a problem. Several variations on these themes appear in State Department

Table 4. McCarthy/Morris Cases Still in State Department, 1950
(alphabetical order, not case numbers)

1. Askwith*	24. Harrison	47. Raine
2. Barnett, P.	25. Henkin*	48. Rapaport*
3. Barnett, R.	26. Hulten*	49. Rommel
4. Berman	27. Hunt	50. Ross, L.
5. Blaisdell	28. Ingram*	51. Ross, R.
6. Brunauer, E.	29. Jessup*	52. Rothwell
7. Cameron	30. Katusich*	53. Rowe*
8. Carlisle	31. Kaufman	54. Sanders*
9. Chipchin*	32. Less*	55. Schimmel
10. Clubb*	33. Lifantieff-Lee	56. Service*
11. Clucas*	34. Lorwin	57. Shapley*†
12. Davies*	35. Lovell	58. Siegel
13. Delgado*	36. Ludden*	59. Smith, F.
14. Dubois	37. Margolies	60. Stone
15. Erdos*	38. Meeker*	61. Tate*
16. Fierst	39. Montague	62. Thayer*
17. Fishback	40. Nelson*	63. Thomson
18. Fishburn	41. Newbegin*	64. Tuchsher
19. Gordon	42. Neumann	65. Tuckerman
20. Grandahl*	43. Osnatch	66. Vincent
21. Gross	44. Peter	67. Wilcox
22. Hanson*	45. Polyzoides	68. Wood
23. Harris*	46. Posniak*	

*Cases not on Lee list (total 28).
†Held noncompensated employment, hence not counted in aggregate number of State Department staffers elsewhere (Table 5).

memos and the report that Tydings gave the Senate and are repeated often in the standard histories.

But, as the reader may have noted, at no point in this rebuttal is the salient question posed and answered, namely: When McCarthy presented his cases to the Senate and the Tydings panel and in other contemporaneous statements, *how many* of these people were still on the job at State? Since the State Department had all the information at its fingertips, it could have answered this question very plainly. It would have been a simple matter for State itself to take the McCarthy-Morris names, compare them to its employee rosters, and tell the world how many of these people were on its payroll. But State conspicuously didn't do this.

Instead, Peurifoy and Co. compiled for Tydings yet another double-blind, anonymous table, comparing McCarthy's nameless eighty with the corresponding nameless suspects from the Lee list. This was printed in tiny type, without any specific heading, well back in the appendix to the hearings.[9] In this table and related statements it appears that, as of 1950, exactly half of McCarthy's

Table 5.   McCarthy/Morris Suspects in Official Posts Other Than State Department, 1950

1.	Adler	Treasury
2.	Brunauer, S.	Navy
3.	Duran	U.N.
4.	Ferry	CIA
5.	Geiger	ECA
6.	Graze, S.	U.N.
7.	Kamarck	Treasury
8.	Keeney	U.N.
9.	Lloyd	White House
10.	Meigs	Army
11.	Remington	Commerce
12.	Weintraub	U.N.
13.	Zablodowsky	U.N.

Sources: FBI analysis, March 1950; U.N. hearings of Senate Internal Security Subcommittee, 1952–1953; Tydings papers.

McCarthy/Morris Cases on Official Payrolls, 1950

State Department	67
Other	13
Total	80

eighty cases were still at work in the department. This wasn't actually the full muster, but even if it had been was less than totally reassuring. As noted by a few observers mildly sympathetic to McCarthy, forty cases still on the payroll were not exactly nothing. (Elsewhere, State would give the total as forty-one—itself an inaccurate, lowball figure.)

However, this wasn't the major point about the State Department table. As seen, McCarthy/Morris had come up with at least forty-four other names, above and beyond the opening Senate bid of eighty. What happened to these additional cases? The State Department and Senator Tydings, in their statistical comments, dealt with them in summary fashion—by ignoring them entirely. Computations as to McCarthy's number of suspects, the residue of these at State, and overlaps with the Lee list were based solely on the initial eighty (and in some instances not all of these). The other cases for statistical purposes were treated as if they never existed—which *a fortiori* meant not bothering to tell anyone whether the whole contingent, some, or none, were in the State Department workforce.

On the premise that it was McCarthy's job to push matters forward, Tydings would be off the hook for not following up on McCarthy suspects noted only in passing or in other settings—Adler, Bisson, Chi Chao-ting, Joe Barnes—and who weren't explicitly brought up as cases in the hearings.* However, most of the additional names cited by McCarthy-Morris, perhaps three dozen, *were* called to the attention of the panel, only to be ignored by it in rendering its final judgment.

Of this further group of cases, the largest single block was the list of twenty-two net new names provided on March 14. These names weren't an incidental matter but were discussed two different times in the course of the hearings. When McCarthy gave this supplemental list to Tydings, he said these were people who had been of investigative interest to the FBI and that their security files would warrant looking into. Significantly, in view of what later happened, Tydings replied that he and his staff would get right on it, saying: "We will look them up . . . We are glad to have them. We will look into them, examine the files, and make a report."[10]

But Tydings did none of the above—developed no substantive data on the cases and made no report about them. In the upshot, indeed, the subcommittee's majority members refused even to *ask* the State Department officially about these cases. The rationale for this was the put-up-or-shut-up rejoinder: that, since McCarthy himself hadn't presented evidence on these people, the panel would not even deign to view them. That disposed of, the twenty-two names became de facto nonexistent and vanished from the historical record.

While dropping this group of cases down the memory hole was the single most effective measure shrinking the McCarthy caseload, other steps were taken also. We have already seen what happened with Theodore Geiger, dismissed out of hand by Tydings and thus not included in the statistics that would later be tossed around so freely. Also banished from the numerical computations were John Service, Haldore Hanson, Mary Jane Keeney, Gustavo Duran, Charles W. Thayer, O. Edmund Clubb, and all other McCarthy suspects outside the confines of the eighty. (All the people thus named were fully covered by S.R. 231, all were made known to Tydings, and all were non-Lee cases.)[†]

Beyond this, the State Department wasn't above playing statistical games in whittling down the numbers. A prize example was John T. Fishburn, a sometime coworker of Robert Miller, who was both a Lee case and a McCarthy case twice over.[‡] However, when the McCarthy staff prepared the list of 80 names for Tydings, the typist made a clerical error, entering the name as "John T.

---

*And also weren't in the State Department, which may be why McCarthy didn't present them to Tydings. All four, however, were connected closely with some of McCarthy's most important cases— Lattimore/IPR and Service/*Amerasia.*

†With no apparent sense of contradiction, the Tydings report did discuss some of the additional McCarthy cases—Lattimore, Service, Jessup, Hanson—on their alleged merits, but omitted these from its mathematical comments, which simply mirrored those of State.

‡That is, Fishburn's case was presented *in substance* by McCarthy to the Senate, even though McCarthy's typist would later enter the name as Washburn. Thereafter, McCarthy did present Fishburn's

Washburn" (one of two such typing errors in the preparation of the McCarthy names). Anyone comparing the entry with the Lee list could see this was the case of Fishburn, and both the FBI and the State Department, in their internal memos, made this correction.

But for the purposes of its *public* tabulation, the State Department provided a purely deadpan treatment of the typo, tersely noting of the numbered entry keyed to "John T. Washburn": "Never employed in the Department of State."[11] This was indubitably true of the nonexistent Washburn, but not of the real-life Fishburn, who not only *had* been employed at State but was on the payroll when these words were written. Thus was another McCarthy case disposed of and the measure of State's security problem dialed down by yet another calibration. (A virtually identical drill would be conducted in the case of Leander Lovell. See Chapter 25.)

Having threaded through this maze, we return to the original question: How many of McCarthy's cases were still on the State Department roster in 1950? This is an issue of some moment in view of the historical drubbing he has taken for claiming to have had the names of fifty-seven suspects at work in the department when he made his initial speeches. In the Tydings/State Department treatment, this was yet another Lee list fiction—a false and obsolete statistic: There *were* fifty-seven such cases on the rolls *in 1948,* but not in 1950.

If we check out the State Department rosters of the era, we discover McCarthy's use of the number fifty-seven in referring to then-current security cases in State's workforce was indeed mistaken—but erring on the side of understatement. In fact, of the people he and Morris named up through the conclusion of the hearings, no fewer than sixty-seven were still at State in 1950 (see Table 4).* Moreover, at least thirteen of the people he named were at work that year on other official payrolls, often having moved there from State, precisely as McCarthy contended (Table 5).[12] Thus, of the total number of McCarthy/Morris cases, at least eighty were still serving at official posts in 1950.

The point about all this, again, isn't simply who was right or wrong about a particular set of numbers but what the numbers reflected. The State Department–Tydings version was that the security problem was over and done with, and it was in support of this thesis that assiduous efforts were made to obscure and downsize the McCarthy caseload. Hence the lack of specific data, verbal fuzzballs, and submersion of even the misleading total forty as far below the public horizon as ingenuity could sink it. Had the fact been trumpeted to the world that eighty of McCarthy's suspects—double the number acknowl-

---

name to Tydings, as this was one of the 22 additional cases provided on March 14. Fishburn was thus in effect twice cited by McCarthy and twice scrubbed out of the record by State and Tydings. (To confuse matters further, and possibly prompting the typist's error, there was a "Washburne" on both the Lee list and McCarthy's roster.)

*This total excludes Dr. Harlow Shapley, who held a noncompensated appointment.

edged by State and Tydings—were still in official jobs in 1950, the "total and eternal destruction" ensuing might not have been McCarthy's.

Postscript

As to McCarthy's repeated use of the number fifty-seven, all discussions of the topic assume this was derived from House committee hearings in 1948, when John Peurifoy said this many Lee suspects were still on the State Department payroll. From this coincidence of numbers, it's assumed McCarthy was simply reciting a two-year-old statistic as though it were still valid in 1950.

This would have been a pretty dumb thing to do, had McCarthy actually done it. Given the amount of backtracking he and his staffers did about the cases, they unquestionably would have known—and McCarthy often said—that not all of his suspects were still at their former posts. Why, therefore, make innumerable public statements based on the premise that they were? And if McCarthy were stupid enough to do this, how did he then so shrewdly come up with 67 cases still in the State Department workforce?

In trying to resolve such questions, it's useful to remember that the Lee suspects were a subset of a much larger group of State Department cases on whom there had been adverse security judgments of one sort or another. That larger set of cases declined over time as the suspects were disposed of, mostly by the resignation method. Thus, at one point in 1946, there had been 341 such cases; this then dropped to 284 as certain suspects were quietly eased out of the department; this in turn was reduced to the famous 205, and so on.*

Though this constant shifting in the numbers is confusing (the doing of State's often cryptic mathematical methods), it helps to realize that all such figures referred to the same original pool of suspects. It's in addition tolerably clear that McCarthy and his staffers were working, not simply from the Lee list, but from this more extensive group of cases. This in part explains the fact that he came up with suspects who weren't on the Lee list and that the total number of his cases on the payroll in 1950 would be much larger (sixty-seven) than the residue from Lee's selective roster (forty or forty-one, according to State's tabulations).

This discrepancy provided a strong motive for the State Department, Tydings, and the Truman White House to focus *only* on the Lee list cases, ignoring as much as possible the larger group of suspects hovering in the background. This kept the numbers down to more manageable dimensions, a major goal of State Department striving. However, occasionally the department did

---

*Which doesn't necessarily mean the total number of suspects declined in these ratios, as still other cases would be added to State's payroll in the succeeding years, thus pushing the numbers back up to some indeterminate level.

make note of this larger group of people, as in the following fine-print statement to the Tydings panel:

"Investigation by the [State Department] screening committee, including those spotchecked and those reviewed after further investigation, resulted in 341 'disapprovals.' *Of these 341 cases, 58, after receiving full clearance, are still employed by the department [i.e., in 1950].* Of the remaining 283 cases two were discharged under the McCarran rider. The remaining 281 persons were removed through various types of personnel action."[13] (Emphasis added.)

So, by State's own math, *58 of the original group of disapproved cases were still on the payroll in 1950* when McCarthy made his charges. This doesn't necessarily mean these 58 were coterminous with his 57, or included in his ultimate total of 67, though there must have been many overlaps, since everyone was talking about the same group of people. It's also possible that State's total of 58, like McCarthy's 57, was an understatement of the problem.

Evidence of this was provided by journalist Alfred Friendly, writing in *Harper's* (August 1950), setting forth the Lee-list-only thesis and obviously using information (and disinformation) supplied by State. In this oft-quoted essay, Friendly wrote that, "had McCarthy inquired of the State Department," he would have discovered that "of the 284 employees [mentioned in the James Byrnes letter to Sabath] *only about 65 were still on the Department's payroll"* in February 1950. (Emphasis added.) Friendly would have had no way of acquiring such esoteric knowledge about these nameless cases except through his contacts at State (which were undoubtedly quite good). It would thus appear somebody at State came up with a statistic quite close to that appearing in our rosters (Table 4).

This Friendly article also appears to have been the source for various authors holding forth about the supposedly innocuous nature of the Lee list— contending that, based on an examination of its data: "No committee [of the 80th Congress] presented any adverse report or demanded further action. *Republicans rose on the House floor to declare that the State Department's loyalty program was being handled in a satisfactory manner, and that that department, at least, was completely free of subversives."*[14] The truth of these assertions will be considered in the following chapter.

CHAPTER 20

The Four Committees

I N ITSELF, the fact that Joe McCarthy *had the names* of fifty-seven, sixty-seven, eighty, or any other number of suspects on State Department or other official payrolls in 1950 meant little. Naming suspects is one thing; knowing the facts about them is quite another. The true significance of the McCarthy–State Department battle lay, not in lists of names and dueling numbers, but in the substance of the cases. That was the point that really mattered.

It's precisely here, of course, that McCarthy's guilt is said to be the greatest: allegedly smearing innocent people, bringing charges of subversion, security risk, or Communist taint, contrary to the facts of record. So said the State Department and Senator Tydings, and so say all the standard histories. But what exactly was—or is—the basis for these statements? How do we know if McCarthy's charges were true or false? How do the standard histories know it? How did Senator Tydings and the State Department know it then, if in fact they did?

One obvious way of answering such questions would have been a close examination of the State Department loyalty files, but for reasons to be noted such a survey never happened, or at least was handled in such clandestine fashion as to raise grave doubts about the outcome. (See Chapter 21.) Certainly, there was no information available *to the public* showing McCarthy was either right or wrong about his cases. That being so, a substitute answer was invented—an answer that is repeated, *ad infinitum,* in virtually every study we have about the subject.

That answer, like many others in the record, was concocted by John Peurifoy and his researchers at the State Department. As set forth in the "Confidential Memorandum" discussed in Chapter 17 and numerous State Department memos and press releases, the key elements to be weighed concerning McCarthy's anonymous cases were (a) their complete identity with the Lee list on the one hand, and (b) the innocuous, outdated nature of that roster on the other. Between them, supposedly, these factors showed that McCarthy's charges were baseless. Since the Lee cases proved nothing bad about security goings-on at State, it followed that McCarthy's didn't either.

The innocent nature of the Lee list thus became a kind of proxy for the elusive State Department files as proof that McCarthy lied about the substance of his cases. The clinching argument for this view, much repeated by his critics, was that the list had already been examined by no fewer than four committees of the 80th Congress and dismissed as being of no importance. That verdict was the more compelling as the 80th was a Republican Congress, so the committees that screened the list were all headed by Republican members. McCarthy was thus allegedly in the embarrassing spot of making stale, warmed-over charges already laid to rest by members of his own party.*

This State Department thesis was, in the usual manner, adopted wholesale by Tydings. In his version, the Lee list was a ho-hum affair that refuted McCarthy's Senate speech twice over. It hadn't amounted to much to start with—the entries "do not appear in any instance to be concerned with the merits of the cases" (a comment lifted directly from the "Confidential Memorandum"); and by 1950 it was obsolete—the people involved "are not necessarily now in the State Department." McCarthy, hyping these innocent data, had "twisted, colored or perverted" the House material to make something bland seem evil (another pickup, verbatim, from the "Confidential Memorandum").[1]

To prove the harmless nature of the Lee list, Tydings played the trump card dealt by State: Republicans of the 80th Congress had viewed these very cases and reached no McCarthy-like conclusions. On the contrary, said Tydings, "the material was considered by four separate committees of the Republican controlled 80th Congress and was not regarded as justifying a report concerning the matter or the citation of a single State Department employee as disloyal."[2] This version of the topic was repeated at least seven times in his

---

* As John Peurifoy put it in his "response" to Karsten, "all McCarthy has done is to shake 2 years' dust off some old reports . . . *None of these committees suggested that there are any Communists in the State Department* . . . he was simply reciting, somewhat incorrectly, items from this shopworn list of 108 cases." Peurifoy assistant Carlisle Humelsine would reinforce this, saying, "The Senator picked up an old list that was furnished to the 80th Congress. He is riding piggyback on the 80th Congress committee *that made the investigation and cleared the department."* (Emphasis added.)

report and ten times or so in his show-and-tell oration to the Senate. It has been repeated often since.

McCarthy biographer David Oshinsky, for example, informs us at some length that the Lee list was a tepid affair of no great moment. In support of this, he provides a number of innocuous-sounding excerpts, says some Lee list suspects were described by the House investigators as "a bit leftist" or "somewhat left of center," and quotes the file on case 104 as saying "she entertains Negroes and whites, both men and women, in her apartment." From such insipid stuff, in the Oshinsky treatment, did McCarthy fashion horrific charges.[3]

Thomas Reeves provides a similar wrap-up, offering innocuous-sounding snippets from the Lee list, plus some longer quotes that seem even more so. Also, Reeves repeats the clinching argument of Tydings and the State Department—that Republicans of the 80th Congress had viewed these very cases and found nothing to alarm them. In the House Appropriations drill, says Reeves, "no Communists had been discovered, but of the 108 Lee personally questioned the loyalty of 45 or 50. Hearings were held in 1948, and *the State Department defended itself sufficiently to satisfy House Republicans, who declared it free of subversives.*"[4] (Emphasis added.)

As these dismissive treatments of the Lee list are based chiefly on the say-so of Tydings and the State Department, it would appear that those who flog McCarthy for repeating stale, warmed over charges are themselves engaged in the identical practice. The irony rates a note in passing but is a relatively minor issue. Far more significant, of course, is whether these recycled statements on the Lee-McCarthy cases, and hence security affairs at State, are truth or fiction. And if we delve into this a bit, we soon discover that the whole complicated tale of an insipid, harmless roster cleared by Congress is a preposterous fable.

Consider in this respect the Tydings claim that the Lee list entries "do not appear in any instance to be concerned with the merits of the cases," or the tame fragments and soporific quotes supplied by our historians to prove the cases of no importance. Recall also that the list detailed roughly *100 other cases* from which the McCarthy critics might have quoted. If we examine these, we find they are radically different from the ones they deign to give us. Following are some Lee list excerpts that the State Department, Senator Tydings, and our historians forgot to mention:

- Consideration is still being given this applicant, although he is a known Communist Party member, and a recommendation has been made that his brother, who is now employed in the department, be dismissed for security reasons.

- The records in the industrial detail, Chicago police department, list him as a Communist in 1930.

- Both the subject and her husband are known contacts of two suspects in an investigation of Soviet espionage activities in the United States.

- This is a case of failure to closely follow and supervise an important case . . . [an] investigative agency advised that a reliable informant said in November 1944 that a well-known Communist in Newark, N.J., advised him that the subject was a Communist Party member.

- This is a case of appointment to an important position from a security standpoint without prior security clearance . . . [Soviet defector] Victor Kravchenko stated that the applicant had to be a Communist Party member, or a strong sympathizer, in order to hold a position with the Soviet Purchasing Commission as long as he did.

- There are no indications in the file that any investigation has been conducted regarding her background; however, information was received on October 9, 1947, from a former supervisor in the War Department to the effect that she was a Communist.

- In her form 57 she gave as references the names of two employees of the Soviet Embassy . . . A memorandum dated November 17, 1945, from the Office of Controls . . . stated that for the subject to have been an employee of the Soviet Embassy she must have been accepted politically by them.[5]

This is but a brief selection from numerous Lee list entries of similar astounding import. A few cases are comparatively bland and/or concern such non-Communist-related problems as drinking or finances, but these are a small fraction of the total—and, generally speaking, not cases picked up by McCarthy. (For instance, innocuous-sounding No. 104, so helpfully highlighted by Oshinsky, was *not* one of McCarthy's cases.)* The predominant, unrelenting theme is the sheer number of individuals in some way identified as known or suspected Communists, pro-Communists, or fellow travelers; contacts of suspected Communists or targets of espionage inquiries; members of Communist-front groups; people formerly employed by pro-Communist (or Soviet) organizations; and the like.

To be sure, our excerpts don't include such possibly mitigating factors as the denials of the people named, the accuracy and/or motives of their accusers, or other countervailing data—factors that proved of riveting interest to State Department spokesmen. The point is otherwise—namely, what the Lee list was *about,* the matters security agents were addressing, and the items that would have caught the notice of McCarthy. This was emphatically not an innocuous lineup of New Dealers, people who were "a bit leftist," or enlightened friends of racial integration, as our historians would have it.

---

*Nor was it necessarily as innocuous as the quote selected by Oshinsky makes it appear. See note, page 341.

Consider now the Republican 80th Congress to which the Lee list was presented. How plausible is it that the Old Guard, anti-Communist stalwarts of this Congress, looking at such entries, would have summarily "cleared" the State Department, expressed their "satisfaction" with it, or done anything remotely like this? Or, to pick up the State Department–Tydings trump card, that no fewer than *four committees* of this Congress, viewing these sensational data, would have been so content with what they saw that they declined to file reports about it?

If none of this seems likely to have occurred, rest assured it didn't. All these statements are stunning falsehoods—a bold invention of the State Department and Senator Tydings, who apparently banked (with some success) on gulling readers who couldn't or wouldn't go back and check the record. In fact, the Republican legislators who viewed the list, and such related data as they could get their hands on, were appalled by the security drill at State and made innumerable comments that revealed this.

We need go no further to see the point than the committee that compiled the list, whose conduct was in all respects the opposite of that described by Tydings. The relevant hearings of the House Appropriations subcommittee on the State Department, chaired by Rep. Karl Stefan (with full committee chairman John Taber sitting in), were held in January of 1948. At these sessions, members reviewed various entries of the Lee list and questioned State Department officials Peurifoy and Hamilton Robinson about them. These exchanges show quite clearly the charitable/legalistic view of personnel security that prevailed at State (though nominally disavowed from time to time): that suspect employees should receive the benefit of doubt, much as in a court of law.

This stance, for good or ill, was markedly different from that of Taber and Stefan, who argued with considerable force that where any reasonable doubts existed they should be resolved the other way around—which could readily be done under the McCarran rider. Even more to the present point were the comments these lawmakers made about the Lee list cases. Compare with the Tydings treatment, for example, the actual views of Chairman Taber: "I would say this to you, that it *makes me disturbed as to whether we have any representation of the United States in the State Department.* I would feel that if you are going to have anybody employed in the State Department the question of loyalty should be absolutely clear and that we should have people who are representing the United States and whose interest is first the United States."[6] (Emphasis added.)

In similar vein were the remarks of Stefan, who conducted most of the interrogation. No more than Chairman Taber did he suggest that he was satisfied with security goings-on at State, ready to "clear" it and its employees, or viewed the Lee list with indifference. Instead, he said precisely the reverse, as follows: "I am just a man from the prairies of Nebraska, just asking you *why it is that these people are on the payroll* when the people of the United States are trying to get behind the government to fight communism in this country and all over Europe. *And here we find them employed in the State Department."*[7] (Emphasis added.)

Nor, contra Tydings, did House Appropriations neglect to file a report about the matter. A few weeks after this hearing, the full panel submitted a report to Congress that, *inter alia,* discussed the Lee list. This report informs us: "Files on the prospective employees were active, and the individuals at the time of investigation were being considered for employment, even though information of record pointed to their being poor risks. The committee does not feel that the department has been as diligent as it might have been in the selection of its personnel . . . and has not sufficiently exercised the prerogative given it under the so-called McCarran rider . . . It would seem to the committee that any doubt in connection with the employment of personnel in the Department of State should be resolved in favor of the United States . . ."[8]

While this unanimous (hence bipartisan) report was more gently phrased than the views of the committee leaders, in no sense did it amount to clearance of, contentment with, or indifference toward security practice at State. Moreover, Chairman Taber left no doubt whatever as to his continuing intense displeasure when he and Stefan presented their findings to the House in early March. Here are some Taber comments, geared directly to the Lee list, that suggest the measure of his satisfaction:

". . . The hearings which were held upon the State Department appropriations bill demonstrated beyond any question that the first thing for the United States to do is clean up the State Department and get rid of those whose incompetency or disloyalty is a menace to the United States . . . *The investigations of the Appropriations committee indicated a very large number of Communists on the rolls of the State Department . . . they have employed people whose record according to their own files is not such that any loyal American could trust them."*[9] (Emphasis added.)

Finally, to this grim assessment of the Lee list cases Taber added some further thoughts about the State Department officials who appeared before him, specifically Hamilton Robinson, the Director of Controls, who had chief responsibility for such matters. The depth of the chairman's contentment may be judged from these assertions:

A thorough reading of his [Robinson's] testimony before this committee would indicate total incompetence to do the job. . . . There can be no excuse for the failure of the State Department to clean house—to get rid of the incompetents and those about whom there is any question of loyalty. . . . After listening for 1½ hours to the developments of the way the State Department has handled its security operations and to Mr. Robinson's answers . . . I was compelled to say: The testimony that I have heard here makes me wonder whether the United States has any representation in the State Department. I regret to say that nothing has happened to change my opinion.[10]

Thus the House committee that compiled the Lee list, reviewed its contents, and allegedly "cleared" the State Department on this basis; the reader may wish to go back and scan the not-to-worry description of these topics above related and ask who has been misrepresenting what. The contention of the State Department, Senator Tydings, and our historians that the list was viewed as no big deal, that Congress was "satisfied" with security goings-on at State, and that there was no security problem that required addressing, were the exact reverse of what developed from these hearings.

THIS particular inversion of the record is so raw it might seem impossible to top it; however, the liberties taken with the work of a second House committee, also invoked by Tydings, were in some respects still more bizarre than those that shaped the withering comments of Taber and Stefan into bland approval.

This was a House Expenditures subcommittee chaired by Rep. Edgar Chenoweth (R-Colo.) that held hearings on the Lee list cases on March 10 and 12, 1948. In the Tydings version, these hearings likewise showed how pleased Republicans of the 80th Congress were with the security shop at State—though Tydings supplied no evidence to support this. "It is unnecessary," his wrap-up averred, "to relate in this report the results of their investigation and the trend of examination by the subcommittee members which indicated their satisfaction."[11]

It was indeed "unnecessary" to give such details—at least from the standpoint of Tydings. He and his allies at State in fact had plentiful reason not to recall the chill specifics of these hearings. If we consult the astonishing record of these sessions, we find Chairman Chenoweth, Rep. Fred Busbey (R-Ill.), Rep. Walter Judd (R-Minn.) and others grilling Messrs. Peurifoy and Robinson about the Lee list. Again, the difference in perspective is striking. The State Department witnesses hem and haw about the cases, stress the need for compelling evidence, the difficulty of making judgments. The GOPers as frequently insist that dubious loyalty cases be resolved in favor of security interests, no two ways about it.

To this point, the doings of the Chenoweth panel closely tracked the Taber-Stefan sessions. There was, however, a startling and well-nigh incredible difference, brought out by Busbey. It was Busbey who had sparked these hearings to begin with, publicly saying Hamilton Robinson was totally unfit for the post he held and should be ousted (still more of that GOP contentment). The

Illinois solon backed this up by questioning Robinson on the case of Robert Miller. Miller was one of the main suspects on the Lee list—called "the greatest security risk" ever in the department by the House investigators, named by Bentley as a member of her spy ring, and found by the FBI to be in close contact with the Silvermaster combine.

Why, at this juncture, the Busbey focus on Robert Miller? The answer, brought out at the hearing, was that Miller was a friend and kinsman to none other than the gentleman on the stand, the State Department security chief, Hamilton Robinson. As Busbey developed in some detail, Robinson and Miller were not only second cousins but had been extremely chummy. Miller had been best man at Robinson's wedding, they had been friends since the 1930s, their families traded visits and Christmas presents, the relationship had long persisted.

Busbey's point in bringing this up wasn't that Robinson himself was suspect (though the congressman plainly had his doubts), but rather that this State Department security czar should have known Robert Miller for all these years and had not the faintest inkling that his longtime pal was, just possibly, subversive. (This despite the fact that Miller had gone off to Moscow in the 1930s and married Jenny Levy of the *Moscow Daily News,* a Soviet propaganda organ.) As Busbey summed up his position, "I would say that anyone that naïve should not be the Director of the Office of Controls . . ."[12]

Whether or not Busbey was correct in this regard, it does seem a trifle odd that the person chosen by the Marshall-Acheson State Department to handle matters like the Lee list should be a boon companion of "the greatest security risk" it had to offer, in the view of its compilers. Nor was that the total story. It turned out also that Robinson was less than candid about his links to Miller. In fending off Busbey's questions, for instance, he described his connection to this Bentley-identified Soviet agent as a "silly kind of thing" that was long since over.

"Since I have been director of the Office of Controls," said Robinson, "I have had absolutely nothing to do with this man." He added that, after Miller came back from Russia, they had seen very little of each other. "I saw something of him the first year he was back, 1939, 1940, and since I have been in Washington since the fall of 1940, I have seen very little of him. . . . I think I have had lunch with him a couple of times before I took this job and after he left the department. . . ."[13]

From these remarks the casual listener at the time—or reader now—could hardly help concluding that Robinson's connections to Miller were ancient history. The ever-vigilant FBI, however, knew the story was quite different. Thanks to its surveillance, the Bureau knew the Miller-Robinson contacts had continued right up to the very eve of Robinson's elevation to the supersensitive job he now held, which occurred on February 13, 1947. The hairsbreadth nature of the timing is apparent from the surveillance records:

"On February 10, 1947, Bob Miller contacted Hamilton Robinson at the State Department. However, Robinson was not in but subsequently called Miller and advised him the guy he was going to talk to [about] Bob wasn't around the State Department any more. They made arrangements for a luncheon on February 12, 1947, and Miller is to meet Robinson at his office in the State Department." And: "A physical surveillance on February 12, 1947, reflects that Miller entered the office of Hamilton Robinson in room 182 of the State Department building and subsequently left with Robinson at 12:35 P.M. They proceeded by cab to Wearley's Sea Food Restaurant at 418 12th St. N.W. At 2:05 P.M., Miller and Robinson left Wearley's and returned to the State Department, where they departed [*sic*—parted]."[14]

Thus, Robinson's statement that he hadn't had any dealings with Miller *since assuming the office of Director of Controls* may have been technically correct, but in substance couldn't have been more misleading. In fact, Robinson had met with Miller for an obviously extended talk *on the very day before* Robinson assumed his new job—a job he knew he was going to get for at least a week before this. Not exactly ancient history, and not exactly candor from the witness.

Almost as bad as this obfuscation was Robinson's testimony on the ominous background and high-risk security status of Miller. In fact, both he and Peurifoy professed an almost total lack of awareness as to why Miller had left the State Department. This was brought out in committee questioning when Representative Karsten of Missouri asked: "Did you find out why this fellow Miller left the department?" The colloquy then went as follows:

> BUSBEY: You can find out from him [Robinson]; ask him.
> ROBINSON: Not from me, I was not there.
> PEURIFOY: I was not in this position at the time but I understand he resigned.
> BUSBEY: As a matter of fact, Mr. Peurifoy, the man had been under investigation for quite a time before he was permitted to resign, was he not?
> PEURIFOY: I will have to check the record. I did not occupy my position at that time.
> BUSBEY: And that he was just one of the security risks allowed to resign that should have been fired before he was allowed to resign. Now did you know any of his connections with any Communists or any Communist front organizations?
> ROBINSON: Not a one. I did not know any of his friends.[15]

These Robinson-Peurifoy answers were both disingenuous and absurd—not quite the kind of answers one likes to have from security officials being questioned about a suspected espionage agent. At this point, the duo had been in charge of the security shop at State for over a year, with full access to its files, and could not conceivably *not* have known that Miller had been forced out of the department on the basis of intel from the FBI that he was connected to a Soviet spy ring. (As seen in the Bannerman memo on Miller, the whole thing was spelled out in State's own records—information Busbey plainly had in his possession.)

Likewise, Hamilton Robinson had plenty of reason to know, not only the story on Robert Miller, but also that on Miller's friends and contacts. Robinson had been briefed precisely on this point by Sam Klaus in 1947, shortly after the changeover in the security office. Specifically, Klaus had raised with Robinson the cases of Florence Levy (herself distantly related to Robinson by virtue of her kinship to Miller), Rowena Rommel, and Minter Wood. Robinson thus had ample cause to know about the Miller network at State from this point forward, even if he knew nothing about it beforehand. His answer to Busbey was an obvious stonewall.

John Peurifoy's testimony was in some ways even worse. Asked why Miller had left the department, Peurifoy professed not to know much about it, since he hadn't been in his current position at the time. Apart from the inherent implausibility of Peurifoy's not knowing the facts on one of the most notorious cases in the history of the division, there were those FBI surveillance records that once more told a different story. These show that, like his colleague, Peurifoy was stonewalling the committee.

Thus, in early December of 1946, the Bureau monitored a call between Miller and Rowena Rommel, which among other things disclosed that: "Rowena said that she had talked to Jack Peurifoy yesterday . . . [and] that Peurifoy was quite annoyed and startled and asked about Miller." The next day, December 8, the FBI tapped a conversation between Miller and Peurifoy himself, wherein "they discussed Miller's resignation which Miller said was effective Friday, the 13th. From the gist of the conversation it appears that Peurifoy is trying to help Miller in this matter and advised him that he would see his boss and that Miller should come to see him in a few days."[16]

So Peurifoy's supposed ignorance of the Miller case was also feigned, and indicative of all too many responses supplied to Congress about security cases at State, some arguably as bad as Miller. It was for Congress (and the FBI) a disconcerting picture. Quite apart from the wiretap data, enough was brought out in this combustible hearing to show the Robinson-Miller nexus, which was a shocker in itself, and the unwillingness of State Department spokesmen to level with Congress about an identified Moscow agent who had been serving on their payroll. All of which was blandly ignored by Tydings—though his report invoked the very hearing that produced it.

IF THE reader will bear with me, there is, regrettably, even more: yet *another* committee of Congress Tydings cited to prove there was no security mess at State and that Joe McCarthy was a liar. This was the Senate Committee on Appropriations, which in the period 1947–48 questioned Gen. George C. Marshall, then Secretary of State, about security problems in the department. According to Tydings and the State Department, this was the third of the four Republican panels so satisfied with the security shop at State that they declined to file reports about it.

Unluckily for Tydings, Sen. Homer Ferguson had been a member of this very committee (and still was), and had also chaired another panel of the 80th Congress that inquired into security problems of the era—the affair of William Remington, discussed in Chapter 24. With the benefit of this background, Ferguson deftly nailed the Tydings assertion about committees of that Congress as an "untruth" and proceeded to document this before the Senate.

In June of 1947, Ferguson recalled, members of the Senate Appropriations Committee had talked with Marshall about the security drill at State and expressed their grave concerns about it. Members of the panel at this time had also given direct to Marshall a detailed and vigorous report about security conditions then prevailing. Again, far from voicing "satisfaction," this report expressed utmost alarm about the subject, backed with numerous specifics. Ferguson put excerpts from this into the *Record,* and they make electrifying reading now, as they surely must have then:

"It becomes necessary due to the gravity of the situation to call your attention to a condition that has developed and still flourishes in the State Department under the direction of Dean Acheson [then Under Secretary to Marshall]. It is evident that there is a deliberate, calculated program being carried on not only to protect Communist personnel in high places, but to reduce security and intelligence protection to a nullity . . .

"On file in the department is a copy of a preliminary report of the FBI on Soviet espionage activities in the United States, which involves a large number of State Department personnel, some in high official positions. The report has been challenged and ignored by those charged with the responsibility of administering the department with the apparent tacit approval of Mr. Acheson . . . Voluminous files are on hand in the department proving the connections of the State Department employees and officials with this espionage ring."*

As to the Tydings statement that no committee of the 80th Congress had so much as named a single State Department employee as disloyal, Ferguson

---

*This was in all probability the November 27, 1945, summary referred to in Chapter 11, which enjoyed a considerable circulation on the Hill. Given the date of this report, however (June 10, 1947), the FBI memo referred to could have been one of the later wrap-ups—either February 21, 1946, or October 21, 1946.

nailed this as buncombe also. While forbearing to identify them in the *Record,* the Michigan senator noted that nine officials of the department had been specifically named in this report and that under pressure from Congress some of these had been removed. He then resumed reading from the report:

"[These nine] are only a few of the hundreds now employed in varying capacities who are protected and allowed to remain despite the fact that their presence is an obvious hazard to national security. They are blocked by one man in the State Department, a protégé of Acheson, named [blank] . . . who is also the chief instrument in the subverting of the over-all security program. This deplorable condition exists all the way up and down the line. Assistant Secretary of State [Spruille] Braden has also surrounded himself with men like [blank] and [blank], who has a notorious international reputation.* The network also extends into the office of Assistant Secretary [William] Benton."†17

Given the number and vehemence of such statements, the reader may well inquire how Tydings and the State Department could possibly say that *Republicans of the 80th Congress* were content with security affairs at State. The answer to this was artfully simple: First, all the comments quoted, and others like them, were just plain ignored—dropped down the memory hole and forgotten. To fill the resulting gap in data, John Peurifoy managed to find a single statement by a single GOPer—the previously met with Bartel Jonkman—and Tydings would showcase this as the definitive comeback to McCarthy.‡

This Jonkman statement, besides being the view of a lone individual, is peculiar to the point of weirdness—more Lewis Carroll than George Orwell. It indeed says State had shaped up its act, and asserts that preeminent among those deserving credit for this was none other than—Bartel Jonkman. Acting as a "committee of one," the congressman had looked into security matters at State, made complaints, and demanded action—all of which, he indicated, took him about three weeks (with some follow-up visits to confirm things). Thanks to this endeavor, he concluded, there were no longer any security risks on the job at State. *His evidence for this was that John Peurifoy had told him*

---

*This was an obvious reference to Gustavo Duran, who had worked for Braden.

†The report referred to by Ferguson was of further interest as it zeroed in on the case of Hamilton Robinson and his relationship with Miller. Following a discussion of the Marzani case and the year-long delay in doing anything about it, the report asserted: ". . . there followed the substitution of unqualified men for . . . competent, highly respected personnel who theretofore held the intelligence and security assignments in the department. The new chief of controls is a man utterly devoid of background and experience for the job, who is and at the time of this appointment was known to be, a cousin and close associate of a suspected Soviet espionage agent."

‡Representative Jonkman, as we have seen, was indeed actively interested in these issues beginning in the summer of '46, and had exerted pressure on Panuch and Klaus to take measures against Marzani. In the course of this effort, Jonkman became convinced that Panuch was a main source of the security problem, and was thus well inclined toward Peurifoy as the new anti-Panuch in the division. This evidently resulted in Jonkman's willingness to accept Peurifoy statements at face value, which wasn't a wise thing to do.

so—directly. Such is the "report" the State Department and Senator Tydings unearthed to prove Republicans of the 80th Congress were content with the security shop at State.[18]

In sum: Of the "four committees" cited in the Tydings report, three said precisely the opposite of what it represented them as saying. And what they had to say was that the security situation at State was dire, that there were numerous loyalty/security risks (and worse) at large, and that measures to deal with this were shockingly deficient—in essence, the identical theme that would later be sounded by McCarthy. The only "committee" Peurifoy could find to support his position (and the only one actually quoted by Tydings) was Bartel Jonkman's one-man band. Not mincing any words about it, the Tydings-State performance, across the board, was a carefully woven web of lies. Yet it is this version of the matter that we are given in our alleged histories.

CHAPTER 21

File and Forget It

I N THEORY, the State Department loyalty/security files should have cleared up the mysteries about the nature of McCarthy's cases and the merits of his charges. However, because of the way the thing was handled, the files would become a considerable mystery in themselves—the cause of angry conflict at the time and much historical muddle later.

There is nonetheless a good deal to be learned from the curious saga of the files—particularly, as in other cases noted, from the sharp disparity between the show of things out front and the reality behind the arras. The State Department and Tydings panel offered many reassuring comments about these records, what was in them, and what was being done about them, comments often quoted by McCarthy's critics to prove he lied about his cases. Yet, according to the records of the FBI, these statements themselves, time and again, were anything but truthful.

The crucial importance of the security files had been recognized by all concerned from the beginning. The Lee list cases were a précis of certain of these data, and McCarthy, as has been seen, was relying on that list, garnished with his own researches. He took the position that he had gleanings from the records, indicating things were badly amiss with the security drill at State. But, he said, these were simply clues and fragments. The only way to resolve the matter was to produce the security files for examination by the Senate. That would conclusively prove, he said, whether his charges were true or false.

Somewhat inadvertently, McCarthy's view on this was underscored by one of his main opponents, Sen. Brien McMahon of Connecticut. McMahon raised the point that McCarthy might be reading selectively from the security files, omitting information favorable to the suspects. He stressed "the possibility that if we had the whole file before us, as undoubtedly the State Department has, the information the senator from Wisconsin is giving might be contradicted."[1] This was indeed a possibility, and the only way of gauging whether it was more than that would have been to get a look at the files directly.

There were, however, complications. Chief among these was the fact that providing Congress access to security data was something the Truman administration had successfully fought for several years before this. The issue had come up in 1948 in battles over the William Remington case and the matter of Dr. Edward Condon. In both instances, the administration had refused to supply security information to Congress. Likewise, it repented the fact that John Peurifoy had ever let Hill investigators see State Department security records to begin with, leading to the Lee list and congressional probes about it. It was at the confluence of these disputes that Truman issued his secrecy order of March 13, 1948, denying further such information to Congress.

McCarthy was thus going up against an established policy of *omerta*— a blank wall of denial Congress had strenuously protested but was uncertain how to challenge. This wasn't a hopeful augury for his efforts. On the other hand, he had some factors working in his favor. One was that refusal to release the files didn't look very good for Truman—looked, indeed, like he was hiding something. This was a point stressed by Tydings in his advices to the White House. Some concession on the files, he said, was "the only way the Truman administration can kill permanently the rumor and propaganda that 'there must be something bad in those files or Truman would not mind showing them.' "[2]

Also supportive of McCarthy's view was the fact that S.R. 231, under which the Tydings panel functioned, explicitly said the files should be obtained and studied by the subcommittee. The resolution authorized subpoenaing "the complete loyalty and employee files and records of all the employees in the Department of State, . . . against whom charges have been heard."[3] Thus, the demand that the files be provided wasn't merely a personal hobbyhorse of McCarthy but the official posture of the Senate.

All this placed Tydings in a bind, pitting his mandate from the Senate against his allegiance to the White House. His solution to this dilemma was to split the difference—*requesting* that the files be handed over to the committee rather than issuing subpoenas.* And, he soon claimed, this genteel approach was working. On March 10, in the early stages of the hearings, Tydings announced that the State Department had promised the Senate "free and unlimited access" to the files, so there was no need to get stiff-necked about it.[4] A few days later, he would expand on these comments before his colleagues, praising the cooperative attitude of State.

"I have," said Tydings, "asked the State Department to turn over the files to us that have been mentioned. The State Department has indicated a willingness to turn over these files . . . [on the twenty-five additional cases submitted by McCarthy], I have already asked for the records, and I happen to know that the State Department at this very moment is trying to work out a procedure so that we can see the records. I have asked for the files as a gentleman, not a sheriff."[5]

This sounded very well, but it developed that all these assurances were in error—and the error said a lot about the way the files, and the file issue, were being managed. For openers, when Tydings said the State Department would provide "free and unlimited access" to the files, had "indicated willingness" to turn them over, and was "trying to work out" a way to do this, the files weren't even in State's possession. Instead, they were snugly locked up in the White House and had been for at least a week, the better to keep them from the Senate. The State Department couldn't have provided "free and unlimited access" to these records—or any other kind of access—even had that been its purpose.

As occurred throughout the hearings, the FBI was obtaining regular updates on these events, including the commandeering of the files by order of the White House. The motives for this maneuver, per a March 3 Bureau memo, were candidly explained to the FBI by Donald Nicholson of the State Department. "According to Mr. Nicholson," said this report, "the transfer of these files to the White House is for political reasons, and, further, for the reason that the State Department was fearful that the Secretary of State would be served with a subpoena to produce the files, which can now be answered by stating the files were not in the possession of the State Department."[6]

In fact, by having the files brought to the White House, Truman signaled a good deal more than a desire to protect the State Department from subpoena. He also made it plain he and his personal agents were going to micromanage the whole affair from start to finish, thus guarding against any possible slipups. Henceforth, as pressures mounted for release of the security data to defuse the uproar created by McCarthy, there would ensue a vast array of White House restrictions, denials, and preconditions relating to the files that were anything but full disclosure. Many such exceptions and provisos are chronicled in the Bureau archives.

---

*He would later issue such subpoenas, which were ignored by the Truman administration, with no effort thereafter by the Senate to enforce them.

On March 4, for instance, the Bureau's Mickey Ladd reported that Peyton Ford of Justice had said Truman would, at most, show the senators summaries only, not the files themselves. *In extremis,* according to Ford, the President would let Tydings personally view the files and confirm that the summaries were accurate. If it came to that, said Ladd, "the President is going to take the necessary time to sit down and make the senators look at the material in his presence, and . . . he will forbid the taking of any notes whatever." Thereafter, Ladd relayed the further news from his administration contacts that "they are going to insist that the counsel for the committee not be present."[7]

On March 7, the Bureau's Alan Belmont reported that State Department security files on the McCarthy cases "which were transferred to the White House are now being checked over very carefully by former investigators of the old Truman Senate committee." (What they were checking for not stated.) Belmont added that, "now that the 'McCarthy' case files have been transferred to the White House, the State Department is working on 385 loyalty case files (not mentioned by McCarthy) and will also transfer these files to the White House . . ."[8]

So the Truman forces were not only combing through the McCarthy cases sent over from the State Department, looking for something (or several somethings), but were moving to head off subpoenas for other security files that weren't on the McCarthy roster. If this in fact occurred, and there is no reason to suppose it didn't, the White House would have wound up in custody of about 500 loyalty/security dossiers previously held in Foggy Bottom. None of which looked very much like "free and unlimited access" or preparation for full disclosure to the Senate.

Though now physically controlling the files, the White House hadn't solved its PR dilemma. McCarthy kept pounding on the issue, saying that if he were wrong about the security mess at State, the President could readily prove it by releasing the records. Conversely, if the President didn't release them, he must have been concealing something. It was the kind of point McCarthy was very good at making, and he made it often. This was the problem that worried Tydings when he sent Truman his memo of April 12 saying some kind of compromise settlement on the files ought to be arrived at.

This memo seems to have made at least some impression on Truman and his aides, since they followed its prescriptions in several places. Tydings had urged a stepped-up effort to portray the President as a tough Communist fighter while counterattacking against McCarthy. Just such an effort was made, in synch with the onslaught against McCarthy on the floor of the House and Senate. This matched the scenario sketched by Tydings, and so did what happened with the files. The anti-McCarthy blitz in Congress crescendoed on May 3. The very next day, Truman suddenly—and surprisingly—changed direction on the question of the files, or seemed to, saying access would now be granted to the Senate.

This turnabout, in the account of Tydings, was very much his doing. Since the President was against making any *new* disclosures, the chairman told his subcommittee colleagues, he had come at the matter from that angle. He had pointed out to Truman that the files on the Lee list cases had already been looked at by Congress, and since McCarthy's cases were identical with the Lee list, it couldn't do any further harm to let the Senate see these records. Truman bought this distinction, or so Tydings concluded, and the chairman reported back to the subcommittee that the impasse was over.

In summarizing this achievement, however, Tydings made still other comments about the files that proved to be mistaken. "The complete loyalty files of the State Department," he announced, "will be made available to us on the 81 cases mentioned." This statement would be repeated in the report of his committee, to wit: ". . . we have conscientiously reviewed *each and every one of the loyalty files related to the individuals charged by Senator McCarthy.*" And: "[Our inquiry] has included examination of *each of the loyalty files of the so-called 81 individuals accused by Senator McCarthy . . ."* [9] (Emphasis added.)

These assertions, as shall be shown, weren't correct, or even close to being so. But, even if they had been, they represented a drastic limitation on what the Senate investigators would be allowed to look at. By the terms of S.R. 231, the Tydings panel was to have subpoenaed the files of *"all employees of the State Department . . . against whom charges have been heard."* (Emphasis added.) The Truman-Tydings pact said something different. Self-evidently, by its focus solely on the 81 (actually 80) original McCarthy cases, it screened out all *other* cases McCarthy/Morris had brought forward during the conduct of the hearings. As already seen, this would have been a huge exclusion.

Thus, to take the obvious examples, this proviso would have blocked out security records on Owen Lattimore, John Stewart Service, Mary Jane Keeney, Gustavo Duran, Haldore Hanson, O. Edmund Clubb, Theodore Geiger, and other important McCarthy cases who weren't on the list of 80. By the same token, the additional net 22 cases submitted to Tydings on March 14 would have been excluded also. All told, the Truman-Tydings agreement—even had it been adhered to—would have omitted more than a third of all the cases surfaced by McCarthy-Morris.*

While not all these people were in the State Department, the vast majority of them either were or had been—which meant they came within the scope of the Tydings mandate. This drastic shrinkage of the roster of McCarthy cases was thus in clear violation of S.R. 231, but that was only a beginning. There was

---

*This was in all probability the reason Tydings reversed himself so abruptly on the matter of the additional 22 cases, which he originally promised to pursue but then refused to look at. He had made a similar pledge in the case of Gustavo Duran, and that too would be ignored, most likely for identical reasons.

the further point that the Senate would supposedly get only *Lee-list* cases—this on the assumption that all McCarthy suspects were included in that lineup. But not all of McCarthy's original cases overlapped the Lee list. In fact, 10 of the 80 were derived from sources other than that list, and so by the terms of the Tydings-Truman compact would have been withheld from viewing. Added to the 44 cases that weren't on the original list at all, this would have made a total of 54 McCarthy suspects on whom no files would be provided.

All this would seem to have been quite enough by way of limitations, but there was more to follow. The next constraint imposed, according to the FBI reports, was that no files would be provided on cases disposed of prior to the Truman loyalty order of March 1947. This would have blocked out still other records, most conspicuously those of Robert Miller, who left the State Department in December of 1946. Yet, as stressed in the memos of Sam Klaus in early 1947, Miller continued to be an important figure, as various of his close associates remained in the department, and this was still true in 1950. An examination of Miller's file would have been essential in weighing, for instance, the cases of Rowena Rommel and Philip Raine, both close to Miller, both on McCarthy's roster, and both still on the job at State when McCarthy brought his charges.

Though it didn't affect the subcommittee directly, one further sidebar sheds some additional light on the nonstop maneuvering that went on in the handling of these records. While the Tydings panel was seeking access to the files, a parallel survey was supposed to have been conducted by the Civil Service Commission's LRB, headed by Seth Richardson, a well-known Washington lawyer. This was treated at the time, and later, as a significant move by Truman. As the Tydings report would put it, the fact that the LRB was "to review each of the cases which were made available to us for review . . . is salutary, since the public is entitled to the most nonpartisan estimate possible concerning these files."[10]

This too sounded well, but in the event was mere palaver, as the Richardson LRB review amounted to little. For reasons we can only guess at, many significant files were withheld from the Richardson board, just as they would be from the Senate. As Hoover aide Lou Nichols reported on April 10, Peyton Ford at Justice had said ". . . anybody not in the government or [who] is under security or espionage investigation but . . . not covered by the presidential loyalty directive *need not be provided to Mr. Richardson. As specific illustrations Ford mentioned that material on Owen Lattimore, Dr. Harlow Shapley and Gustavo Duran need not be sent to Mr. Richardson."[11] (Emphasis added.)

The specific exclusion of Lattimore, Shapley, and Duran obviously matched with the limits imposed on the Senate panel. There was, however, a further exclusion also. From the Nichols wording, it appears that anybody on the McCarthy list "not in the government" as of that date would be omitted from the files shown the LRB. This would have lopped off another group of cases—Richard Post, Stanley Graze, Jeanne Taylor, and others. These were all McCarthy and Lee list cases but no longer on the federal payroll in 1950.

In view of this restriction, a rather obvious question arises: Would loyalty/security files denied the Richardson board have been given to the Senate? Although the records are unclear, this seems unlikely. In fact, it defies belief that Truman would have shown records to the Tydings panel that were denied to his own appointees. So it's a reasonable inference that anything not provided to Seth Richardson wouldn't have been shown to the likes of Lodge and Hickenlooper (and hence, all too probably, in some manner made known to Morris and McCarthy).

From these considerations, it's evident that, whatever the senators finally looked at when they got to the White House, it couldn't possibly have been "each and every one" of the "so-called 81 individuals accused by Senator McCarthy . . ." This statement, thrice made by Tydings, was demonstrably in error (the Lee list–only proviso itself sufficient to refute it). Still less was there compliance with the mandate of the Senate. In fact, there is no telling what the senators did see—how many files they may have viewed or what was in the folders they were given. The difficulty on this point was made the more severe by the restrictions imposed on the lawmakers themselves when they finally got a chance to see the records.

As presaged in the comments of Peyton Ford, the senators were on a very short leash when they went over to the White House. Two key limits were that they could have no professional staff members (or FBI agents) present, and could take no notes on what they were viewing. As nonspecialists in such matters, they would have had a hard time knowing what certain references might mean (membership in the League for Peace and Democracy or China Aid Council, connections to such as Miller or Mary Jane Keeney), and wouldn't have been able write down information to take back to Morris or other security experts for detailed discussion.

Lodge, for one, considered the situation absurd. On May 12, he visited Hoover seeking guidance. The Director reported that Lodge was "terribly confused about the files in that the files contained no recommendations and in cases where loyalty hearings had not been held by the State Department there was no indication as to why they had not been held. He stated furthermore that in some instances there had been no indication that various leads had been followed out which appeared in the files . . ."*[12]

---

*Lodge would later expand on these comments, saying that "the files which I read were in such an unfinished state as to indicate that examination of each file would have been a waste of time . . ." He added that "in some of the more important cases the report of the FBI full field investigation was missing . . . It should also be noted that the subcommittee was allowed to see the files only under such stringent limitations as to preclude our getting much essential information . . ."

While all this unfolded, McCarthy was raising another media ruckus about the files. It appears from his public statements that he had some inkling of the limits on the number of cases to be examined but not the full extent of the restrictions. He did correctly state, however, that State Department security and personnel records were kept in such a loose-leaf way that it was impossible to tell if something were missing. Beyond this, he said, there was the further point that the files were very sloppily handled and that innumerable people had access to them (at least before they were locked up in the White House). Combined with the lack of a serial or pagination system, the possibilities for weeding or manipulation were many.

(This problem had been flagged to the attention of the Congress in 1947 by the Lee investigators, who noted that security files had been charged out and not returned, that various materials were missing, and that there was no way of checking what had happened to them. "These failures," said their report, "can largely be attributed to the fact that apparently most anyone and everyone in the division has access to the files, removes files and replaces them with very little regulation or control.")[13]

McCarthy, Hickenlooper, and others referred several times to rumors that the files were being rifled, though they had no hard proof that this was occurring. There was, however, proof that it had occurred before. On this point, McCarthy produced depositions from four past and present State Department employees who said they had been involved in a file-stripping operation at the department in 1946. If it had happened once, McCarthy argued, it could happen again. This brought a swift rebuttal from the State Department, Truman Justice, and Tydings saying McCarthy was once more talking through his hat and that no security data were missing from the State Department records.

On June 21, Tydings announced: "I have been advised by FBI agents that all of the material gathered by the FBI touching on the loyalty of the employees in question has been sent to the State Department and are [*sic*] part of the files which our committee examined."[14] This seemed official and conclusive. However, it developed that when Tydings made this statement, the FBI had conducted no analysis of the files, had made no judgment on them, and was nonplussed as to why he said it. When Hoover saw the Tydings comment, he flagged it to the attention of his staff, asking, "Is this correct?" and "Did we make any such check?" The next day, Mickey Ladd responded: "We have made no such file-by-file examination of the State Department files. . . . We have never made any such comment to Senator Tydings."*[15]

---

* Tydings, it appears, had been misled by a passive-voice construction used by Truman Justice. Peyton Ford had written to Tydings on June 16, saying the FBI had furnished the pertinent data and that "the State Department files *have been checked,* and I can assure you that all of the reports and memoranda furnished the State Department are contained in the files." (Emphasis added.) Tydings converted this into his statement that the FBI had done the checking—which it hadn't.

KNOCKOUT

In this letter to McCarthy, FBI Director J. Edgar Hoover categorically denies Senator Tydings's claim that the FBI had investigated State Department security files.

(nited States Department of Ju   re
Federal Bureau of Investigation
Washington 25, D. C.

IN REPLY, PLEASE REFER TO

FILE No.

July 10, 1950

ALL INFORMATION CONTAINED
HEREIN IS UNCLASSIFIED
EXCEPT W----- = SHOWN
OTHERWISE

Honorable Joseph R. McCarthy
United States Senate
Washington, D. C.

My dear Senator:

    I have received your letter dated June 27, 1950 inquiring whether this Bureau has examined the 81 loyalty files which the members of the Tydings Committee have been scrutinizing and whether such an examination by the FBI has disclosed that the files are complete and that nothing has been removed therefrom.

    The Federal Bureau of Investigation has made no such examination and therefore is not in a position to make any statement concerning the completeness or incompleteness of the State Department files.

    For your information, the Federal Bureau of Investigation furnished Mr. Ford, at his request, a record of all loyalty material furnished the State Department in the 81 cases referred to. For your further information, I am enclosing a copy of Mr. Ford's letter to Senator Tydings which I have secured from the Attorney General.

                    Sincerely yours,

                    /s/ J. Edgar Hoover

Enclosure

BY SPECIAL MESSENGER

C
O
P
Y

121-23278- 206

Source: FBI McCarthy file

Thereafter, in an unusual move, Hoover would go public with the FBI denial. On July 10, in response to an inquiry from McCarthy, the Director made a definitive statement on the subject, saying: "The Federal Bureau of Investigation has made no such examination and therefore is not in a position to make any statement concerning the completeness or incompleteness of the State Department files."[16] Tydings was thus caught flat-footed making a claim about the FBI that was categorically denied by Hoover. This was about as close to a total knockout of Tydings, State, and Truman Justice all at once as McCarthy could possibly have hoped for.

Two days later, picking itself up off the canvas, Truman Justice moved to have the FBI conduct the probe Tydings said had already happened. Following this eleventh-hour effort, Attorney General J. Howard McGrath wrote Tydings on July 17, saying such a Bureau inquiry had *now* been made and that, with one exception, "the files contain all of the FBI reports and memoranda furnished to the State Department on these cases." This was two months after Lodge and Co. began examining whatever it was they were given at the White House, and almost a month after Tydings made his erroneous statement on the matter. It was also after the Tydings report had been drafted and made ready for printing. Tydings then shoehorned the McGrath letter into the report at the last minute, thus allegedly proving that McCarthy's file-stripping comments were "utterly without foundation in fact."[17]

For those of a doubting or cynical nature—for instance, Joe McCarthy— this two-month Kabuki dance around the files raised the question of yet another possible shuffle: that the files had had material missing when Lodge and other senators saw them, but that this was put back in when knowledgeable FBI agents came looking for their memos. This speculation draws support from the fact, as spelled out in the Truman guidelines, that *entire files* on the McCarthy cases, not merely portions, would have been withheld from viewing by the Tydings panel. Perhaps the clearest instance is, again, the case of Robert Miller, who was both a Lee list and a McCarthy case but whose file would have been withheld from the Senate according to the Truman provisos. Yet the Miller file was undoubtedly in the folders looked at by the Bureau.

We know this because we have Hoover's memo to McGrath of July 13 summarizing the files that had at last been viewed by the FBI. This says, among other things, that the files on seventy McCarthy cases had been available for inspection. That number, of course, corresponded to the Truman-Tydings stipulation that only Lee list cases could be looked at, this being the total number of overlapping cases. As that total included the file on Miller—a case well known to the Bureau—it follows that this file would have been examined by the FBI, though under the Truman rules it wouldn't have been given to the Senate.

The Hoover memo to McGrath also makes it clear that there were items that should have been in the files but weren't—starting with the 10 McCarthy cases that didn't overlap the Lee list. Hoover told McGrath that, in thirteen other cases, material transmitted from the Bureau wasn't in the files, having been impounded by the President; that in six cases FBI loyalty reports on individuals who had moved on from State "were not in the State Department files" (this evidently reflecting the current-staffer restriction); and that, in five cases, materials from FBI investigations on State Department employees when they were with OSS—which, for reasons noted, could have been important information—"are not in the State Department files."[18]

This breakdown is hard to reconcile with McGrath's assertion that the files inspected by the FBI were complete, with one unspecified exception. All told, the Hoover memo cites more than thirty items that even the Bureau couldn't get a look at. If all this stuff was missing when the FBI agents came calling, the possibility that more was missing when Lodge and Co. were at the White House is plausible indeed. As the administration and its team of analysts/investigators had had at this point better than four months to go through the files at their leisure, some such fiddling seems more than likely.

In the meantime, McCarthy had come up with his depositions from four past and present employees of State saying that, in the late summer and fall of 1946, they had been given the task of expurgating department personnel records. This project had played out over a period of months and hadn't been completed until December of 1946. The depositions included statements such as: "We were instructed *to remove all derogatory material from the personnel files,* and we were instructed to dispose of this material." And: "All of the clerks on this project were to pull out of the files all matters considered derogatory, either morally or politically . . . the [data] I pulled out of the files pertained to either the morals of the person *or in some way reflected on his or her loyalty.*"[19] (Emphasis added.)

In rebuttal to this, State issued another of its myriad press releases saying McCarthy was a liar, and that the project in question was not a "stripping" of the files but simply an effort to "reorganize them into some new, unified system . . ."[20] This amounted to a direct conflict on the facts, in which case the obvious course for an investigative committee of Congress would have been to—investigate. Once more, however, this didn't happen, as the Tydings panel was closing its doors and had its conclusions already written. Though various signers of the depositions were available to testify, they were never called to do so. Nor was any other testimony taken on the issue. Instead, as per the usual drill, Tydings accepted the State Department denials as conclusive and declared the matter settled.

The file stripping/reorganization had occurred in late 1946—which was, as may be recalled, a critical period in the history of the State Department security office. This was the era of Panuch and Klaus, the advent of the resignation strategy, the McCarran rider, and numerous internal battles over the proper way of handling cases. It was also the era, beginning in the fall, in which the realization dawned that brand-new, Republican committees of Congress would soon be empowered to look into security affairs at State. A most interesting time to be conducting a "reorganization" of personnel files of the department.

All that, however, was in 1946—predating the compilation of the Lee list and three-plus years before McCarthy brought his charges. His contention was that, if such a thing occurred before, perhaps still further "reorganization" happened at some later juncture. This was a subject he would continue to pursue and a surmise in which he turned out to be on target. There was indeed more such "reorganization" of the personnel files in the latter 1940s. Details would be provided by Mrs. Helen Balog, supervisor of the State Department Foreign Service file room, in an inquiry conducted by McCarthy in 1953.

In these hearings Mrs. Balog would testify that safeguards pertaining to FSO personnel files were extremely lax, that files were scattered about in a number of places, and that "three or four hundred people" had access to these records. In particular, she said, there was one individual who spent an inordinate amount of time in the file room working on the folders. In view of certain other matters noted, her testimony about this makes dramatic reading:

> QUESTION: Now, Mrs. Balog, was there a time toward the end of 1948 or the beginning of 1949 when you were notified that a certain official of the State Department would be spending some time in the file room?
> ANSWER: Yes, sir.
> QUESTION: . . . Did this official, actually, physically appear down in the file room?
> ANSWER: Yes, sir.
> QUESTION: And did work on the confidential files?
> ANSWER: Yes, sir.
> QUESTION: For how long a period, would you say, did he continue to work on these confidential files in the State Department?
> ANSWER: . . . I am quite sure he was there practically the whole year of 1949.
>
> • • •
>
> QUESTION: Did he ask for the keys so he could spend the night working in the file room on more than one occasion?
> ANSWER: Quite a number.
> QUESTION: Now, would you please tell the chairman and the members of the committee the name of this person in the State Department who worked on these confidential files at night. . . .
> ANSWER: It was John Service.[21]

CHAPTER 22

All Clear in Foggy Bottom

FOR Millard Tydings and the State Department, the magic word was "clearance." Though they couldn't or wouldn't supply details, they told the world McCarthy's charges were humbug since all of his suspects still on the rolls had "clearance." Such accusations had been made before, were carefully looked into, and the employees "cleared"—or, in some versions, "approved." McCarthy's accusations were thus not only warmed over and stale, but false and perjured.

While oft-repeated, this "clearance" mantra was and is beclouded by several types of ambiguity, and considerable falsehood of it own. The main ambiguity involved the question of who, exactly, had issued the clearance that was talked of. Frequently, in making such assertions, State and its defenders used the passive voice—saying suspects *"had been cleared"*—so you couldn't tell what agency or person had done the clearing. This same ambiguity pops up in several histories of the era.

As seen, Tydings and the State Department claimed that four committees of the 80th Congress had done such clearing, but this turned out to be more moonshine. The only such clearance Tydings could come up with was Representative Jonkman's slightly dotty one-man "report," and even this said nothing about any particular targets of McCarthy. All the other committees referred to didn't issue any clearances at all, but instead expressed utmost alarm about security affairs at State. Who, then, supplied such "clearance"?

In State Department memos and press releases there is a kind of answer, or at least something that might appear to be an answer if scanned quickly by unwary readers. These statements often combined the passive-voice construction with yet another verbal fuzzball, dropping a murky reference to the FBI into some backward-running sentence concerning clearance. This much-used technique would lead the casual reader to believe the FBI was among the agencies that did the clearing.

Thus, to cite a prominent instance, John Peurifoy told the Tydings panel that all McCarthy suspects still in the State Department in 1950 "either *had received full FBI field investigations* or had otherwise been processed under the President's loyalty program and the department's security program and *their continued employment approved."*[1] (Emphasis added.) Since this didn't say who did the approving, and since the FBI was front-loaded in the sequence, readers who didn't know much about the matter might suppose (and undoubtedly many did) that the FBI was involved in issuing the approval.

In similar obfuscating vein were the comments of Gen. Conrad Snow, head of the department's loyalty board, extolling the labors of that unit. In the course of this defense, Snow said that since the inception of the Truman loyalty program his board had "had before it over 500 cases of State Department employees *who had been investigated for loyalty by the Federal Bureau of Investigation. . . . and not one case has been found of a present Communist working in the State Department."*[2] (Emphasis added.) Again, the melding of the passive voice with mention of the FBI conveys the notion that the Bureau had something to do, maybe a lot, with the claim Snow was making.

This technique of obliquely dragging in the FBI was so often used by State and its defenders as to suggest a conscious effort at deception. Sometimes the McCarthy critics made the point other way around, arguing that if one said security suspects at the State Department hadn't been correctly dealt with, this was an outrageous criticism *of the FBI.* This line was taken early on by Senators Scott Lucas and Hubert Humphrey (D-Minn.), who contended that if any subversives had been on the State Department payroll, FBI Director Hoover would have long since rooted out the comrades, made such information public, or prosecuted the offenders.

This argument first surfaced in the clash between Lucas and McCarthy when McCarthy made his initial speech before the Senate. To charge that there were any "card-carrying Communists" in the State Department or elsewhere in the federal government, said Lucas, "is to reflect seriously upon the FBI." The FBI, he added, "knows practically every card carrier in the United States and the FBI would not knowingly permit any card carrier to remain in any government department."[3] Hence, McCarthy's allegations of Communists in the federal workforce were clearly bogus.

Humphrey made the identical argument a few weeks later. "Would it not be a dereliction of duty on the part of the Director of the Federal Bureau of Investigation," he asked McCarthy, ". . . if he were not to reveal the identity of a traitor?" Humphrey further challenged McCarthy to say whether "he believed the Director of the Federal Bureau of Investigation has been derelict in the sense that he has not prosecuted what the Senator from Wisconsin calls a top Communist agent?"[4] As Hoover had done neither of these things, the self-evident implication was that McCarthy's charges were phony.

Whatever the variations, all such innuendoes and statements about the FBI were false and had to be known to be so by the State Department, Senator Lucas, Senator Humphrey, or anyone else who had the slightest acquaintance with the subject. In point of fact, the FBI did not, would not, and could not "clear" State Department employees or any others outside the Bureau itself (though it often had pungent off-the-record thoughts to offer about such as Gustavo Duran, Carl Marzani, or John Service). The FBI conducted its investigations, provided the information to State or other employing venue, and the agency took it from there. Any "clearance" that resulted was the responsibility of the employer, not the Bureau.

This was not only generically true with regard to FBI procedures, but was specifically and necessarily true of the State Department and other federal agencies by the terms of Truman's loyalty order. That order expressly named the secretary or other head of an employing department as the arbiter of loyalty questions, rather than lodging this power in some independent unit, as proposed by Rep. Rees of Kansas. In the case of State, this meant Dean Acheson or his designees would decide whether there were any loyalty risks in the department, and thus, not so incidentally, sit in judgment of their own past handling of such cases.*

Nor, just to complete the record, did the Bureau have the power to decide the issue of prosecution, as suggested by Humphrey's challenge to McCarthy. The Bureau could make recommendations on such matters but had neither the power to launch a prosecution nor the authority to conduct one. That was the province of the Attorney General, and we have seen in the *Amerasia* case a singular study of how that power was used by Truman Justice. It's hard to believe Senator Humphrey didn't know the facts about such procedures, and

---

* The sole exceptions to this rule were that, in the case of a decision against an employee, the ruling could be appealed to the central Loyalty Review Board of the Civil Service Commission and that this board could also, at its discretion, pick up cases for post-audit. The first of these provisions, of course, did nothing to reverse a ruling that cleared a suspect, while the second was seldom exercised in adverse fashion toward an employee. At no time, either before or after the Truman program was enacted, was the FBI empowered to "clear" employees or not.

impossible to believe the Tydings panel didn't—as its chief counsel, Edward Morgan, was himself a former Bureau agent.

In short, as with the "four committees," all attempts to invoke the FBI as having been responsible for inaction on, clearance of, or approval for McCarthy's cases were efforts to becloud the subject. The reality was that all the "clearances" being cited were strictly Foggy Bottom issue—clearances the State Department gave its own employees. Thus, the matter to be decided was what clearance by the State Department amounted to and whether in the cases raised by McCarthy it had been correctly granted. McCarthy's point was, exactly, that the department had been clearing people whose records, as best he could determine, indicated they shouldn't be on the payroll. To reply to that critique with the assertion that the employees *had been cleared* was to rephrase the question as the answer. Such circular reasoning was unimpressive to McCarthy, though apparently satisfactory to some historians of the era.

One high official who liked to tout the State Department's clearance record as self-evident proof that its record was a good one was State's loyalty chairman, General Snow. In the fall of 1951, the general mounted a polemical blitzkrieg in defense of State and against McCarthy, repeating and embellishing the broadsides that had been issuing from the department's research warrens since the early days of 1950. In two publicized addresses, Snow in the usual manner accused McCarthy of making baseless charges, stirring up rancor, and misleading the American people as to the department's excellent security record.

The proof of this excellence was the statistic wielded by the general when he said that, since the inception of the loyalty program, not a single Communist "had been found" in the ranks of the department. Nor, in this span, it further developed, had so much as a single loyalty risk been discovered among all of State's thousands of employees.[5] That record supposedly proved that the department was doing a first-rate job in terms of loyalty/security measures.

Others, however, had contemplated this same statistic and drawn a very different conclusion from it. Most notably, a starkly negative judgment on this basis came from the Loyalty Review Board of the Civil Service Commission, President Truman's own creation. In 1951, the clearance-prone Seth Richardson had stepped down as chairman of this outfit, to be replaced by former Sen. Hiram Bingham of Connecticut—a very different breed of chairman. Under Bingham, the board would take a much tougher view of loyalty cases, and in particular a tougher view of what was going on at State. As revealed by records of the board, Bingham and other members were greatly bothered by the State Department loyalty record and said so in explicit fashion.

The person who brought all this to light, as in so many other cases, was the troublesome, interfering Joe McCarthy. Drawing on his supposedly nonexistent sources, McCarthy somehow got hold of the minutes of a meeting of the LRB, the contents of which turned out to be another bombshell. The meeting in question, held on February 14, 1951, involved discussion of loyalty cases at State, including that of Service, and what the board should do about them. From this the talk branched off to other issues, as members expressed concern about the State Department loyalty drill—making it plain that the department's clearance of so many suspects on such a nonstop basis was considered not a good thing but a bad one.[6]

Chairman Bingham capsuled the theme of these exchanges when he said: "I think it fair to say that the State Department, as you know, has the worst record of any department in the actions of its loyalty board . . . [It] has not found anyone—shall I say 'guilty'—under our rules. It is the only [departmental] board that has acted in this way." Bingham further said he had told Dean Acheson that State's loyalty board "was out of step with all other agency boards. In the Post office Department, 10 per cent of all persons examined were found to be worthy of separation from the government. In the Commerce Department, 6½ per cent. The average was about 6 per cent. The State Dept., zero."[7]

Other members of the board chipped in on the matter of State Department clearance and the methods used to grant it. One revealing exchange went as follows: *Question:* "What are you going to do when the attorney who is presenting the charges [in a department hearing] acts as though he were the attorney for the incumbent? I read 100 pages in the record where 3 members of the [department] board were acting as attorneys for the employee." *Answer:* "Oh, you are talking about the State Department. They are taking the attitude that they are there to clear the employee and not to protect the government. We have been arguing with them since the program started."[8]

This led another member to raise the question of whether the Civil Service board was not remiss in letting the situation at State continue. Focusing on the statistical record brandished by Snow, this board member said: "I have been disturbed about the State Department—this remarkable record of never having fired anybody for loyalty, and yet we do nothing about it. . . . I have been troubled about whether or not we owe the duty of having somebody call the attention of the President to the fact that the program simply does not work in that department. . . . It seems to me we assume some responsibility when we sit back for three years and know that the country rests in a false sense of security that we are looking after their interests here when we know darn well that is it completely ineffective in one of the most important departments of the government . . ."[9]

Such comments were the more significant as they came from President Truman's own LRB, not Joe McCarthy or his conservative GOP allies in Congress. Plainly, the views expressed were quite different from the bland assertions of Snow, John Peurifoy, and the Tydings panel—and writers who take such statements at face value—saying the security drill at State was fine and that all its employees should have been cleared because they had been.

Further insight into these matters would be provided by a high-profile series of hearings, beginning in March 1952, in which Snow and Assistant Secretary of State Carlisle Humelsine would be the State Department spokesmen. These were sessions, again, of the Senate Appropriations subcommittee charged with reviewing the performance of the department before granting it more money. Members of the panel included Pat McCarran of Nevada (the subcommittee chairman), the ever-present Ferguson, and—Beelzebub himself—none other than Joe McCarthy.

From a State Department standpoint, this should have been a most welcome showdown, as its officials here had a chance to challenge, face-to-face, the liar who had been spreading falsehoods about their department. Assuming they were themselves telling the truth and knew whereof they spoke, here was a golden opportunity to expose McCarthy, confront him with the solid facts at their disposal, and discredit him in an official public setting. Unfortunately for State, it didn't work out in quite that fashion. In fact, to the intense embarrassment of Foggy Bottom, pretty much the reverse would happen.

These hearings were especially useful as they gave the senators a chance to review, *seriatim,* a sizable number of McCarthy cases and thus elicit certain information not otherwise available in the record. Among these were Esther Brunauer, O. Edmund Clubb, John Paton Davies, Herbert Fierst, Haldore Hanson, Val Lorwin, Peveril Meigs, Edward Posniak, John Stewart Service, and John Carter Vincent. Of course, given the Truman secrecy order, the senators were unable to get substantive data on the cases, but did manage to find out something about the way they had been handled.

Even at this level, obtaining the relevant information was far from easy and the colloquy often went round in circles. Nonetheless, the discussion revealed a lot about the department's procedures, how its clearances were arrived at, and how the statistical record bragged of by Snow had been kept so impeccably free of adverse findings.

Easily the most dramatic moments of the session occurred when McCarthy and Snow went head-to-head concerning the alleged evils and falsehoods of McCarthy. In his orations, Snow had predictably defined the plague of "McCarthyism" as making false and irresponsible charges. McCarthy, backed by Ferguson and McCarran, challenged Snow to support these statements. Ferguson put it this way: ". . . we are going to ask for the proof that these statements by Senator McCarthy were false, and we want your proof. We don't want your conclusion now. . . . Let us have the Hanson file to prove that what he said about Hanson is untrue. Let us have the file on Service. Let us have the file on Davies."

To all these suggestions General Snow demurred, saying he couldn't give information on specific cases and, anyway, he hadn't mentioned these people in his comments. But, said Ferguson, you have made sweeping statements that

McCarthy's charges were false across the board, and these were among his foremost cases. McCarran seconded the motion: "You make a blanket statement and say that what Senator McCarthy says is false from beginning to end . . . you blanketed everything that he said as being false. Now, you will prove to us that they are false."[10]

As might have been expected, this resulted in a complete dead end. The State Department position was, and would remain, that McCarthy was lying about the cases, but its officials couldn't reveal the facts that proved this; so public and Congress would simply have to take their word that he was lying. Getting nowhere with this approach, McCarthy and his colleagues then asked Snow to give specific examples of McCarthy falsehoods—a drill that was also revealing. In response to this, Snow came back with a series of McCarthy statements that were allegedly in error. These items will be somewhat familiar to the reader, as they rehearse points touched on in preceding pages. Some of the exchanges went as follows:

> SNOW: [As an example of McCarthy falsehoods] the accusation is that the State Department had 205, or whatever number he chose to call it, known Communists. . . . He made the same statement over and over again.
>
> McCARTHY: Let me interrupt the witness now. Mr. Snow, are you aware of the fact that the investigators for the Gillette-Monroney Committee went to Wheeling, W.Va., and completely disproved what you have said?
>
> SNOW: I am not aware of that.
>
> McCARTHY: Did you not read that in the paper?
>
> SNOW: No, sir.
>
> McCARTHY: Did you not think that before going out and making that statement, that you should check on matters like that?[11]

A like discussion would ensue on the matter of the State Department security files. In this case, Snow cited McCarthy statements to the effect that the files had been "purged," "raped," "denuded," "tampered with," and "stripped." These statements, said Snow, were self-evidently false; he personally knew the files were intact because he had them in his possession. McCarthy then questioned Snow about the affidavits on this subject submitted to the Tydings panel:

> McCARTHY: Are you aware of the fact that the statements cover a period of time before June 9, 1947 [when Snow took over the State Department loyalty board]? That the raping was before the files were handed over to your board? Are you aware that we have those statements?
>
> SNOW: No sir.
>
> McCARTHY: You never heard of them.
>
> SNOW: Never heard of them; never saw them . . .

McCARTHY: As chairman of the loyalty board, do you not think you have the duty to check these affidavits?

• • •

SNOW: I was so confident that the files had never been rifled that I had no presentiment of any duty to investigate what the basis of your speech was.*[12]

Snow's next example of alleged falsehood was McCarthy's statement that Dean Acheson had ousted the relatively tough-minded security board at State under Joe Panuch. Snow said this was just a procedural changeover, closing down one board and starting up another, and that "Secretary Acheson had nothing to do with either event." Some of the exchanges about this were as follows:

McCARTHY: Let us see if you are telling the truth, or not. One of the men on the original board was Bannerman, is that right?

SNOW: I don't know who was on the original board. It was before my time.

McCARTHY: Do you know whether Panuch was on it?

SNOW: I don't know.

McCARTHY: Do you know who got rid of Bannerman?

SNOW: I don't know anything about that except the board went out of existence before we came in under Secretary Marshall.

McCARTHY: But Bannerman and Panuch were the men having to do with security in the State Department. You know that, do you not?

SNOW: That was before my time.

• • •

McCARTHY: Do you say I lied when I said Acheson had gotten rid of them?

SNOW: Yes.

• • •

McCARTHY: You know that Bannerman and Panuch are no longer there, do you not?

SNOW: I don't know that; no.[13]

Indeed, General Snow seemed to know very little about the topic altogether, prompting the not unreasonable question from McCarthy: ". . . on what theory can you say I was lying when you now tell us you do not know who the men were; you do not know who fired them; you do not even know how they were forced out of the department?" (This riposte was more plausible yet as Acheson did in fact cashier Panuch, albeit in the form of accepting Panuch's

---

*In these exchanges, Snow and McCarthy both veered from the main point—the condition of the files circa 1950. As for Snow's statements on that topic, it seems unlikely he could personally have vouched for the integrity of the files, given their voluminous nature, loose-leaf condition, and accessibility to so many people. Unless Snow had intimate knowledge of every item in these files and photographic recollection, his assurance was an impossibility. Still less could he have vouched for the condition of the files during the five-month period when they were locked up in the White House.

"resignation"—both parties to the encounter making this clear in later comments.) Worse than Snow's apparently bottomless ignorance was the statement of Carlisle Humelsine, who chipped in with the misleading observation that Joe Panuch had not been ousted but "went of his own accord." Panuch himself would say otherwise in testimony before the Senate.[14]

Later, McCarthy addressed the famous issue of the numbers. Questioning the State Department spokesmen, he adverted to the matter of the 205, as revealed in the James Byrnes letter to Adolph Sabath, and wanted to know what had happened with the cases recommended for dismissal in 1946. Humelsine promised to come up with an answer and thereafter supplied the following update:

"The 205 individuals referred to are included in a group of 341 individuals on whom the screening committee of which Bannerman was a member had indicated a preliminary disapproval. Of this entire group, 46 are still employed in the department after having been thoroughly investigated and cleared. . . . Of the remaining 295 cases two were discharged under the McCarran rider. The remaining 293 were removed through various types of personnel action."[15]

As a glance at page 262 will show, this was the identical statement given the Tydings panel two years before, but with a revealing alteration in the figures. In the earlier comment, *58* of the employees were still on the department payroll after having been "investigated" and given "full clearance." In 1952, this number had for some unspoken reason dropped to *46,* while the number "removed" through "various types of personnel action" had risen by the identical margin—from 281 to 293. In other words, a dozen people "cleared" in 1950 had been "removed" by 1952. (What had mainly happened in the interim, of course, was the uproar caused by McCarthy and concomitant pressure on State to tighten its procedures.)

Also of interest in this memo was the vague reference to "various types of personnel action" by which employees were "removed." While no breakdown was given, it's evident from what has gone before that the main such "personnel action" was the resignation method. This resort to resignations was troubling not only to McCarthy and others in Congress, but also to members of the LRB, as revealed in the review board's minutes—the main problem talked of being that employees who thus departed could, and did, get jobs at other federal agencies.*

In questioning Humelsine and Snow, McCarthy brought out several ex-

---

* As one member of the board expressed it: "When they [the State Department] operate as they do— merely showing a resignation by the individual . . . he immediately goes over to another agency and says, 'I have worked for the State Department for five years. Here is my personnel action sheet. I resigned a few weeks ago.' There is nothing in the personnel action sheet to tell the personnel officer that there is an investigation of that person. He gets the job . . . or [the personnel officer] has to go running around . . . to find out if there has been an investigation of this man . . ."

amples of such resignations and the effects of handling cases in this manner. A main exhibit was Peveril Meigs (who had been McCarthy's case No. 3 before the Senate). As McCarthy put it: ". . . I think we ought to know how many of those who resigned got jobs in another department. Take the case of Meigs. He resigned from the State Department while under investigation. He went over to the Army and got a job in the Army. Whether he was handling classified matter or not, I do not know. Their loyalty board held a hearing and ordered him discharged. I am just wondering how many other cases there are somewhat analogous to his."*[16]

Beyond the question of employees moving to other assignments, there was a further aspect of the resignation method developed in these sessions: its contribution to State's unblemished record of never having found a Communist (or loyalty risk) in its employ. The way it worked was fairly ingenious. If an employee resigned while under investigation, the process was instantly halted, the case was pulled out of the system, and the employee was listed in the records as a voluntary separation. No conclusive judgment having been reached, no loyalty risks or Communists would be discovered. This was brought out by McCarthy and McCarran as follows:

> McCARTHY: Mr. Snow, I note the review board objects to your practice of allowing individuals to resign instead of firing them. Do you still take the position that—
>
> McCARRAN: I do not understand that he has anything to do with their resignation.
>
> SNOW: The chairman is correct. I have nothing to do with whether they resign or don't resign . . . and *once they resign, the case leaves the board and we have no further jurisdiction over it.*
>
> McCARTHY: Let me put it this way: Do you know whether you or any other member of your board has ever indicated to an employee that unless he resigns there will be an adverse holding?
>
> SNOW: No. We could not do that. In the first place, that would be physically impossible because *we don't know what conclusions we come to until the hearing is over with.*[17] (Emphasis added.)

At this stage discussion went on to other topics, but the exchange was enough to confirm that resignations short-circuited the process, so that matters were left open-ended and—the point McCarthy was making—no adverse holding would be arrived at. By such methods the department's immaculate record of never having found a loyalty risk in its employ could be kept intact forever.

---

*Meigs was one of the cases listed by Sam Klaus in 1947 as a target of security action, but was then being dealt with cautiously because he was the head of the State Department employees' union. Though McCarthy didn't say so in this exchange, it was his highlighting of the case that brought Meigs to the attention of the Army and almost certainly caused his dismissal. (See Chapter 25.)

An instance of how this worked was the case of William Stone, McCarthy's suspect No. 46 before the Senate. Stone had been recommended for separation by Robert Bannerman as far back as 1946, but had outlasted Bannerman himself in the department and was still on the payroll six years later. After McCarthy had huffed and puffed about the matter, the Stone case was reopened and taken up by the Bingham board for post-audit. While all this was going on, Stone resigned from the department. Humelsine's discussion of the case was revealing:

"His case had been cleared by the department's board and had been sent forward to the Bingham board for post-audit purposes. While it was over there, Stone resigned. . . . [The Central Board thereafter] sent back a form saying that *inasmuch as Mr. Stone had resigned his case would not be post-audited unless he should attempt to come back into the Federal government . . . at the time he resigned he was a cleared employee . . .*"[18] (Emphasis added.) So Stone, too, would remain in the department data banks as "cleared" and State's perfect record would continue.

A further instance in this genre was Edward Posniak. McCarthy had previously read out to the Senate FBI reports indicating Posniak was or had been a Communist Party member. Posniak, too, had been a "cleared employee" in July of 1950 when McCarthy raised the issue. Now, in the hearings with Humelsine and Snow, McCarthy asked what had happened to the case and eventually got the answer: "The department was advised on June 11, 1948, that the FBI had started a loyalty investigation on Edward G. Posniak. He resigned his position with the Department on November 9, 1950."[19] Posniak would be another no-show in State's tabulation of loyalty risks who had ever been on its payroll.

To the resignation method State added yet another, a bit more complex but still useful in keeping the stat sheet free in terms of finding loyalty risks or—more accurately—not finding them. This was to "suspend" employees at midflight in the proceedings, thus placing them in bureaucratic limbo and keeping them there for an extended period. Such suspension didn't amount to an adverse holding but forestalled review of the case by the LRB.

A prime example of this technique was one of McCarthy's more famous cases, that of Esther Brunauer. McCarthy asked Humelsine what had happened to her and was given a series of confusing answers, as Snow and Humelsine couldn't get straight whether the case was before the State Department board or reposing somewhere else in the labyrinthine channels of the system. Despite the obscurity on this, it was agreed that Mrs. Brunauer had been "suspended" *for approximately a year* and that no final determination had been made as to her loyalty/security status.

From this fact the suspicion dawns, and certainly dawned on McCarthy, that the State Department was simply sitting on the case, thus forestalling final resolution. The issue became enmeshed in double-talk when McCarthy tried to press this aspect, asking if the Bingham board could get the case if State indefinitely held it:

> McCARTHY: Is there anything to the suspicion on the part of some that you hold some of these cases indefinitely after a suspension because the Review Board cannot get them until you get through with them? In other words, if you hold the Brunauer case indefinitely, the Review Board can never see it, can they?
>
> HUMELSINE: The Review Board cannot post-audit, but the Review Board could and has the authority at any time, as I understand it, to take the case out of our hands and handle it themselves.
>
> McCARTHY: Has that ever been done?
>
> HUMELSINE: Yes sir, it has been done in two cases.
>
> McCARTHY: In which cases?
>
> HUMELSINE: They took the Service case and one other case, two cases.
>
> FERGUSON: Before you were through with them?
>
> HUMELSINE: No sir; after they had been sent over to them.
>
> FERGUSON: Why do you not answer the Senator's question?
>
> McCARTHY: Why do you not try to answer my question? It is like pulling teeth. I should not have to ask several questions, in order to get the truth.[20]

All this raised a further point of interest to McCarthy and his colleagues: the failure of the State Department to invoke the McCarran rider *in re* Brunauer, Posniak, Hanson, Meigs, Stone, or other cases of like nature. Under this proviso, the elaborate loyalty/security rigamarole could have been avoided altogether. As agreed to by State itself in the days of Byrnes-Russell-Panuch, the rider gave the secretary the power to dismiss any employee whatever if he thought the national interest required it. Not unnaturally, as the rider bore his name, Senator McCarran thought to raise the issue, though Ferguson would address it also.

> McCARRAN: I would like to know what has become of the provision in the law: It happens to be my own language as originally written [quoting the rider].
>
> FERGUSON: That is an absolute discretion and none of this channeling provides for that.
>
> McCARRAN: Not a bit of it.[21]

In response, Humelsine made it clear that, while giving lip service to the rider, the State Department was not only loath to use it but considered it a dead letter.

> HUMELSINE: My understanding is that we were not to use the McCarran rider but to use Public Law 733 [the supporting legislation for the Truman program]. . . . We have used the McCarran rider in a couple of cases. *But nevertheless the President has told us to run our loyalty program under the executive order.* He has told us to run the security program under Public Law 733. (Emphasis added.)
>
> FERGUSON: But you are not using the valuable instrument we gave you. [and later] You are absolutely defying the McCarran rider.[22]

From these comments it appears the Truman loyalty program, allegedly a tough response to the security problem, was de facto a drastic weakening of previous safeguards. In place of the McCarran rider, with its cut-and-dried authority, Truman had substituted an elaborate Rube Goldberg mechanism of multiple boards, ground-up investigations, appeals, ping-ponging cases back and forth between State and Civil Service, indefinite suspensions, delays in delivering relevant files, and other complications that dragged the process out for years.

From the above—and there is a lot more like it in the record—it's apparent that "clearance" of loyalty/security suspects by the State Department meant little. And what little it did mean, quite plainly, was the reverse of what we're told in standard treatments of the subject.

CHAPTER 23

The Man Who Knew Too Much

THERE remains a procedural question to be considered: Did McCarthy have inside information sources about security suspects in the State Department, or elsewhere in the federal government? Or, to adapt a catchphrase from a later era, what did Joe McCarthy know, and when exactly did he know it?

This is on the face of it one of those collateral, off-the-main-theme topics so common to the McCarthy story, like the flap about the Wheeling numbers or, even more on point, fixation with the Lee list as the one and only basis of his charges. As has been noted, efforts to deflect attention from the substance of McCarthy's cases to the question of where they came from were constant features of all his battles, from Tydings to the showdown with the Army.

Yet, more than other sidebars, the subject of McCarthy's sources goes to his bona fides, and that of his opponents—and not just because he intimated that he had such sources while his critics categorically said he didn't. There is the fact that, if McCarthy really were devoid of sources, the quality and currency of the data he wielded would be open to serious question. Conversely, the existence of such contacts would have enhanced the weight and relevance of his charges. Also, there is a tangent bearing on the issue: Though contrasts between public and private statements were par for the course in the McCarthy struggle, nowhere were these more jarring than in discussion of his sources.

That McCarthy had no inside contacts, and was merely bluffing when he claimed to, was part of the original State Department mantra, echoed by Tydings and countless other McCarthy critics. This was of course the flipside of the "nothing but the Lee list" thesis. As seen, some McCarthy foes would push the argument still further—contending that, since the list was simply an anonymous, numbered lineup, he didn't even know the names of the people he was discussing.

Enough has perhaps been said already to suggest these charges are mistaken. In numerous instances cited in Chapter 19, it's obvious that McCarthy and his staffers had been backtracking on and adding to the Lee list entries for some considerable while before he first addressed the Senate. This plainly shows he had the names of his suspects, since without the names he would have been able to check out nothing. It also means, *eo ipso,* that he had to have some source or other beside the Lee list to make additions to its contents.

However, these modest claims about McCarthy's sources badly understate the point at issue. There is plenty of evidence that he had inside contacts in the executive branch and that these were critical to his presentation. There is evidence also that various of these were in the State Department—though exactly how many may have been at State, Civil Service, intelligence agencies, or other places there is no way of knowing. A good deal of relevant material on this may be found in the archives of the FBI, capsuling the views and actions of Truman staffers on the subject.

It is in these long-secret records that the contrast between public and private comment is most vivid. While the official posture of the State Department and Tydings panel was that McCarthy had no inside sources and was lying when he claimed to, the backstage view was very different; Truman officials were convinced that he did have such sources and were desperate to find them. The hunt for pro-McCarthy moles began with his initial Senate speech and would go on for months thereafter.

In this respect as in many others, the leading instance was the case of John Stewart Service. McCarthy frequently mentioned Service and *Amerasia* in his Wheeling-Reno round of talks and reprised the whole affair again in his opening speech before the Senate. In this oration, McCarthy reviewed various salient facts about the case and added: "For some unknown reason, John Service's file has disappeared in the State Department. I have tried to find out where it is, and I have been told it is in the office—quoting the individual over there—of 'the top brass.' "[1]

Here was certainly a claim to inside data that had no connection to the Lee list, indicating that McCarthy had been talking to someone at the State Department about the file on Service. The Tydings panel would in fact quote this very passage as one in a series of McCarthy statements "seemingly designed to suggest that he has confidential sources in the State Department"—the point being that he was faking when he said it. However, these McCarthy comments, and others like them, were very much on target, and the Truman administration knew it.

At the time of McCarthy's Senate speech, the FBI records reveal, the State Department file on Service wasn't at its accustomed place in the department security office but was being prepped elsewhere for delivery to Examiner Cyril Coombs of the Civil Service LRB. Coombs was a stickler for the rules who had been raising questions about the case for months, believing it hadn't been properly handled. For causes that are obscure but may be guessed, there was an immense delay in getting the file over to the LRB, so Coombs didn't receive it until February 24—four days after McCarthy's statement.

All this closely matched McCarthy's version of what had been occurring, a fact well noted by the White House, State Department, and Truman Justice. (As one administration memo put it, "The dates mentioned by Senator McCarthy coincide with other information indicating the Service case was at that time being forwarded to the Loyalty Review Board.")[2] Somebody was apparently feeding inside information to McCarthy, a suspicion that gave the Truman forces many anxious moments.

Things would soon get even more worrisome for the White House, as McCarthy continued to track the Service case with some precision. In statements before the Tydings panel and the Senate, he discussed new loyalty hearings to be held about the case, the whereabouts of the relevant security file, and FBI reports pertaining to it. On March 14, he urged the Tydings panel to find out "if Service was not considered as a bad security risk by the loyalty board of the Civil Service Commission, in a post-audit decision, handed down on March 3 of this year." He added that he understood "a new loyalty board" was to be convened at State to hear the case *de novo.*[3]

This salvo convinced the Truman staffers that McCarthy unquestionably did have inside sources, and they were desperate to find the leak. How desperate would appear later that day, when White House assistant Donald Dawson and Democratic national chairman William Boyle showed up at the FBI in search of plumbers. This visit was suggestive at several levels—including the fact that the chairman of the Democratic National Committee should be involved in such discussion. It further indicated that the Truman forces thought the leak was at the LRB and were ready to make some drastic moves to stop it. The Bureau memo on this informs us:

> Donald Dawson stated the White House had learned that there was a leak in the Loyalty Review Board (Seth Richardson's group) in view of the fact that Senator McCarthy this morning stated that the loyalty case of John Stewart Service . . . was being referred back to the State Department. . . . According to Dawson, McCarthy made this disclosure prior to the time that the board had referred the case . . . and therefore, it was evident to them that the leak

had occurred in the Board. . . . Both Dawson and Boyle wanted to know if the Bureau would investigate the leak. . . . Boyle commented that, "if we can satisfy ourselves as to the identity of the person giving the information to McCarthy we will fire him outright."[4]

Politely but one gathers firmly, the FBI turned down this request, saying it didn't seem to be a criminal matter but an administrative issue for the Civil Service Commission itself to handle. Such at least was the formal answer. More privately, Bureau agents may have reflected on the irony of the Dawson-Boyle approach. John Service had been kept on the State Department payroll for five full years after passing official papers to Philip Jaffe, confidant of Communist bosses and Soviet agents; but anyone caught passing data to Joe McCarthy concerning Service himself would be out on his ear by sundown.

In succeeding weeks, McCarthy continued to be well informed about the Service case and the loyalty program in general. On April 25, 1950, he announced that the Seth Richardson LRB had recently met and agreed that it wouldn't consider the problem of security risks, but would take cognizance only, in McCarthy's words, of "specific acts of disloyalty." He further said that some members of the Richardson board didn't believe membership in the Communist Party was such an act—raising the question of what kind of proof might be availing in these cases (this echoing the "mere membership" business dating back to World War II). Two days later, he would give the names of board members present at this meeting. He then recounted a series of seven FBI reports on Service, the dates on which they were received by the LRB, and the fact that "on March 6, 1950, the Justice Department picked up Service's entire file."[*][5]

Again, the accuracy of these statements may be gauged from the scalded-cat reaction of the Truman forces, who now launched a full-fledged investigation to find the leak and plug it. This was no perfunctory effort, but a high-level probe conducted by Assistant Attorney General Clive Palmer and James Hatcher, chief investigator of the CSC. It involved much sifting of McCarthy's statements for clues, questioning of suspected pro-McCarthy moles—Cyril Coombs foremost among them—and closely studied transcripts of their answers. Ultimately, the investigators filed a report that didn't identify the mole exactly but did contain a number of revealing comments.

This Palmer-Hatcher report, gathering dust for fifty years in the vaults of

---

*McCarthy's statement reads as follows: "During the entire year of 1949, Mr. Service was under investigation by the FBI. Reports were forwarded to the Loyalty Review Board which reflected adversely on his desirability as a State Department employee. On December 28, 1948, the Loyalty Review Board received a copy of such a report, and again on February 18, 1949, March 10, 1949, April 4, 1949, May 11, 1949, September 7, 1949, and September 21, 1949. . . . Service's file was requested by the Loyalty Review Board repeatedly until the year 1949, but wasn't received by it until February 24, 1950."

the FBI, is confirmation that McCarthy's bulletins on the Service case were too close for comfort at the White House, indicating not only that he had inside sources but that these were minutely accurate in their updates. The report observes, for instance, that "Senator McCarthy's statements as revealed in the *Congressional Record* of April 27 indicate that he had received very detailed information concerning what transpired at the April 3 meeting of the loyalty board and also that he had received very complete information pertaining to the receipt of FBI reports."[6]

McCarthy's information in this case supported the view that he had contacts at the LRB, but didn't preclude sources at the State Department also. Questioned by the Truman gumshoes, the unfortunate Coombs insisted that he wasn't the mole and tried to rebut the theory that everything McCarthy knew had to have come from the Review Board. Rather, Coombs argued, the nature of McCarthy's intel suggested it had come from State. One proof of this alleged by Coombs was that McCarthy had several times mentioned a new loyalty board at State to hear the Service case—something Coombs himself was not, he said, aware of.

Whatever his specific sources, McCarthy seemed to have an unusual knack for obtaining security records from someplace. On March 14, the same day he told the Tydings panel about the ping-ponging of the Service file between State and the Review Board, he also regaled the committee with an account of the Gustavo Duran affair. Duran was yet another suspect who wasn't on the Lee list, as he had left the State Department in 1946 and moved on to the U.N. McCarthy's comments made it clear that he knew the case quite well, and he discoursed on it like an expert. Even more to the present point, he introduced into the hearing record a considerable mass of documents on Duran that explored his background in the Spanish Civil War and portrayed him as a Soviet agent.

A week after the Duran presentation, a member of McCarthy's staff would discuss with the FBI security information on Cora Dubois, a former OSS employee and McCarthy suspect who had moved to the State Department in 1945 and was still on the payroll there in 1950. Dubois was McCarthy's case No. 60 on the Senate floor and was also a Lee case. However, the information covered in this exchange obviously wasn't from the Lee list. A March 21 Bureau report on this says that "———— of Senator McCarthy's staff had in his possession a memorandum which contains information regarding [Dubois], a State Department employee. The memorandum quotes information from the report of SA Kelly and SA Clancy of the Bureau in June of 1948."[7]

From the phrasing, it's evident the McCarthy staffer had, not an original FBI report, but a memo quoting or condensing such a report—a not uncommon type of information in State Department and other security records. McCarthy and his researcher J. B. Matthews had a fair number of such memos in backup files about their suspects, and the Dubois memorandum sounds like one of these. In which event, the State Department itself was the most likely source, though the LRB was again a possibility. In any case, the information, dating from June of 1948, clearly wasn't from the Lee list, which was compiled in the fall of 1947 and published in January of 1948.

On March 25, 1950, in executive session, McCarthy flagged to the attention of the Tydings panel the name of Charles W. Thayer, yet another State Department employee who wasn't on the Lee list. While not going into detail, McCarthy indicated that Thayer was an extremely bad security risk who should be ousted. (He would call the case to the attention of the FBI, as well.) This focus on Thayer is of added interest as McCarthy had in his backup files a rather complete dossier on Thayer, which was to all appearances a copy of the investigative record assembled by the loyalty board at State. The most obvious explanation of this material in McCarthy's papers is that someone in the department leaked it to him.[8]

On March 30, McCarthy again took to the Senate floor, setting forth a substantial body of data on several of his cases, including Service, Philip Jessup, and Haldore Hanson. He also at that time read into the *Congressional Record* a paraphrased version of a 1943 confidential letter Owen Lattimore, then with the West Coast branch of OWI, had written to Joe Barnes, his counterpart in the New York office. This Lattimore missive discussed the cases of Chew Hong and Chi Kung Chuan, two ethnic Chinese then working for OWI who were accused of Red connections and were under security investigation by the Civil Service Commission.

These cases would later prove significant not only in the Lattimore dispute but also for the *Amerasia* scandal, in which Chew Hong would figure as a suspect. For now, their main relevance concerns the question of McCarthy's sources. In a subsequent Senate statement, McCarthy would amplify his revelations on the OWI affair by inserting into the *Congressional Record* the full text of the Lattimore letter to Barnes, plus the reports of security screeners who opposed retention of the two Chinese. This was all Civil Service material but would have been supplied to State, since OWI had been absorbed into the department in the latter part of 1945.[9]

In addition to putting such documents in the *Record,* McCarthy on a back-channel basis continued to flag suspects and pass information to the FBI, including the Barnes-Lattimore correspondence, which the Bureau apparently didn't have, and still other data from unknown sources (identities redacted in the records). An April 20 Bureau report reflects that McCarthy provided the FBI a fairly detailed memo on diplomat O. Edmund Clubb (source redacted, but apparently someone familiar with State Department doings in China). At this same period, McCarthy also brought to the attention of the Bureau the names of Leander Lovell and David Weintraub (FBI memos of April 20 and May 1).[10]

Each of these was, in its way, a significant case. Lovell had been McCarthy's suspect No. 28 on the floor of the Senate, but would like John T. Fishburn vanish from the State Department's tabulation of McCarthy cases. Weintraub was of interest to McCarthy as the U.N. official who had been responsible for sending Owen Lattimore on a mysterious mission to Afghanistan. (Weintraub had been identified, somewhat indirectly, in testimony by Whittaker Chambers—confirmed by data from the Soviet archives—as a Communist operative at the National Research Project in the 1930s.)

There would be still other cases of like nature. In early June, McCarthy somehow obtained all or part of the Sam Klaus memo, discussed in Chapter 12, concerning the number of alleged Soviet agents and Communists who had been in the State Department and what Klaus thought was an FBI chart reflecting these statistics. McCarthy read verbatim excerpts from this memo into the *Congressional Record,* including the table that showed the number of asserted agents, Communists, suspects, and so on. As a comparison with the original shows, all these citations were letter perfect.

McCarthy's ability to come up with this report was especially noteworthy as the FBI itself didn't at this point have a copy. As the Bureau learned more about the matter, its comments confirmed the accuracy of McCarthy's statements, the inside nature of his sources, and the likelihood that these were in the State Department. FBI official Mickey Ladd observed, for instance, that State indeed had in its possession a chart that listed individuals under "the exact breakdown given by McCarthy." It was thus apparent, said Ladd, that "the material used by McCarthy originated from the State Department. . . . A copy of this report is undoubtedly in the hands of McCarthy."[11]

Nor were there any alternative sources outside of State known to the Bureau that might have supplied Klaus's memo to McCarthy. As Director Hoover put it, "McCarthy is getting his material out of the State Department because no one else had such a chart in his possession."[12] McCarthy must have had a pretty good pipeline to the State Department to obtain a memo nobody else outside of State, including J. Edgar Hoover, had previously seen or, apparently, even been aware of.

As noted, the Klaus memo and "chart" reflected a phenomenal number of alleged Soviet agents, Communists, and suspects who had tunneled in at State as of the summer of 1946. At that time, the matter had been glossed over by the subliminal way the cases were handled, permitting such as Hiss, Robert Miller, *et al.* to resign in decorous fashion rather than being ousted as security risks, or worse, via the McCarran rider. The whole thing had been swept under the rug, and despite the exposure of Hiss by Congress in the meantime, the full scope of the wartime and postwar infiltration was still a huge and scandalous secret.

McCarthy's having come up with the Klaus report, and its delivery to Tydings after McCarthy made an issue of it, presented the administration with a problem. We may be sure Truman-Acheson forces weren't anxious to have this kind of information spread out on the record, especially not in the context of their death struggle with McCarthy. To handle this dilemma, a somewhat awkward solution was arrived at. While passing on the Klaus report to Tydings, John Peurifoy drafted a convoluted cover letter, tap-dancing around the substance of the memo and dilating on a secondary topic: that the "chart" referred to by Klaus was *not an FBI chart*—which indeed it wasn't—as if this were the major point at issue.[13]

This proved satisfactory to Tydings, who reproduced the Peurifoy letter as the definitive statement on the subject with no more that needed saying about it. (In fact, Tydings liked the letter so much he reproduced it twice—once in the report of the committee and again in the appendix.) Meanwhile, the memo itself and the data it contained would disappear from the hearing record and thereafter from the subcommittee archive. So all that remains in the exhibits is Peurifoy's obfuscating letter, plus a couple of equally obfuscating State Department press releases on the topic.

Thanks to this Peurifoy-Tydings treatment, the "FBI chart" is often cited as an example of McCarthy's lying. (It would form, for instance, one of the ten charges William Benton later brought against McCarthy in urging his ouster from the Senate.) This argument, though oft repeated, was yet another smoke screen. For of course it wasn't McCarthy who said the chart was prepared by the FBI, but the State Department's own official, Klaus. McCarthy made no claim to knowledge of the chart other than what was in Klaus' memo, and his somewhat incredulous statements about FBI involvement with the case were based strictly on its contents. The State Department, not McCarthy, committed the error that was complained of.

So far as the official record shows, these efforts to obscure the substantive meaning of the Klaus report were the main focus of State Department energies in this conflict. Though it seems certain the administration would have wanted to know how McCarthy got the memo, the available data don't reflect this. However, the Truman sleuths would soon be back on the trail of McCarthy's supposedly nonexistent sources. The provocation this time was a McCarthy speech on the floor of the Senate on July 25 concerning Edward Posniak, an employee of the State Department whose name McCarthy had given to Tydings by registered letter of March 18.

In a talk that touched on other facets of the security issue, McCarthy inserted into the *Congressional Record* excerpts from a lengthy Posniak-related document, which he described, and was labeled, as a report from the Civil Service Commission. This consisted of excerpts from nine FBI reports on Posniak, some indicating that he was a very bad security risk indeed. The most shocking of these, said McCarthy, included statements from an FBI undercover agent that he personally knew Posniak to have been a member of the

Communist Party. Yet Posniak, contra the Truman–State Department assurance that all the bad security risks were long ago disposed of, was still at work in the department.

In presenting this material to the Senate, McCarthy struck one of his most effective blows at the elaborate cover-up stitched together by the Truman White House, State Department, and Tydings panel. The FBI data on Posniak were extensive and, for security purposes, highly damning. Yet he had somehow been "cleared" by the State Department's unfathomable loyalty process. (He would a few months later, as noted in Chapter 22, be permitted to resign in discreet, below-the-radar fashion—undoubtedly as a result of the McCarthy pressure—and then pop up at the International Monetary Fund.)[14]

Simultaneously, however, McCarthy had in this case committed one of his own most egregious gaffes, though how and why he did so aren't apparent from the record. While the Posniak data were authentic, the form in which they were packaged wasn't. The alleged "Civil Service Commission" report wielded by McCarthy was not in fact such a report, but rather a document so formatted as to conceal the proximate source of the security data. The FBI files are replete with comments on this, as well as speculation as to where the information may have come from.

If ever there were a case in which McCarthy's critics could have had a field day at his expense, this would seem to be the obvious candidate. Amazingly, however, this wasn't a point much exploited by his foes, who in other cases did far more with less (though Edward Morgan would refer to it while campaigning against McCarthy two years later in Wisconsin).* One possible reason for this default is that the underlying data on the case were so shocking the State Department thought the less said about them the better. Another possible motive, evident from the Bureau updates, is that concern about where the material might have come from was so intense it trumped all other issues.

Some insight into how the matter was viewed inside the administration, and how urgently the Truman forces looked for pro-McCarthy moles, is provided at several places in the Bureau records. In the wake of the Posniak speech, the FBI soon determined that the Civil Service format was ersatz and interviewed officials of the CSC, State Department, and Loyalty Review Board as to possible sources of the information. As one Bureau memo relates:

> Colonel Hatcher pointed out that while the FBI reports referred to in the McCarthy "exhibit" did actually pass through the Office of the Investigative Division, Civil Service Commission, at no time was the [Posniak] material ever contained in the files of the Investigative Division . . . Colonel Hatcher stated his belief that the likely sources of the information in the case were

---

*It's also mentioned in the Anderson-May book as a "forgery," with zero explanation of the contents.

either in the State Department or in the Loyalty Review Board, since these are the only two places where the information reposed.*[15]

Exactly where the "exhibit" came from would remain a mystery. At least two FBI memos indicate that McCarthy staffer Don Surine had said the Posniak file was treated in this fashion to disguise its true proximate source, which led some in the Bureau to think Surine (a former FBI agent) was the person who did it. If so, of course, this still wouldn't have answered the larger question, since it would have raised the further issue of how Surine obtained the reports in question. However, after the death of Sen. Pat McCarran in 1954, the identical document was discovered among his papers, together with other information relating to the case, which may have been the solution to the puzzle.

The Bureau memo on this describes a "photostat [in the McCarran records] of what purports to be a summary of FBI reports in the case of [Posniak] identical with the document distributed on 7-25-50 [by McCarthy] with the exception that Senator McCarthy's copy had identifying information concerning [Posniak] crossed out."[16] The existence of this more complete version of the Posniak file in McCarran's records would suggest that McCarthy may have received the "exhibit" from McCarran, though the reverse was also a theoretical, if less likely, possibility.[†]

The Posniak case subsided, but the search for McCarthy's sources was ongoing. In early 1952, he provoked a further uproar when he discussed yet another suspect who would be enshrined as one of his many martyrs. This was a Truman aide named Philleo Nash, who had moved to the White House from OWI in the 1940s. According to McCarthy, the record showed that Nash had been a close associate of Communist operatives in the United States and Canada. McCarthy added that the LRB file on Nash, like other dossiers earlier noted, had been commandeered by the White House.

Nash denounced McCarthy's charges as a "contemptible lie," and the White House followed suit. Many discussions of the topic echoed these opinions, citing the case of Philleo Nash as yet another example of McCarthy's

---

*As to the accuracy of the McCarthy data, one FBI memo commented that "although the document was proven not to be a [CSC] summary, it did contain considerable excerpts from our loyalty reports." Another stated: "The FBI reports in two of these files, as assembled at LRB, are set up in the same order as McCarthy's 'exhibit' . . . [The McCarthy information] follows exactly the same order of the FBI reports referred to . . . [Also] Senator McCarthy referred to the '173 page transcript' of the hearing afforded [Posniak] by the State Department Loyalty Review Board . . . It would therefore appear that Senator McCarthy had access not only to . . . the FBI reports, but the entire file relating to [Posniak]."

†Supporting the notion that the document may have come to McCarthy by this route was the fact that McCarran, as chairman of the Senate Judiciary Committee, had regular access to FBI reports or summaries thereof, a unique prerogative in the Senate that backbencher McCarthy did not enjoy. If McCarthy received the document from McCarran, a much-respected colleague, he would have had no particular reason to question the form in which it was presented.

smearing innocent people, citing phony data, and all the rest. Again, however, a different scenario is suggested by the confidential record—which in this case includes a backup file on Nash that was in the hands of the McCarthy forces, found in the files of J. B. Matthews. This indicates that McCarthy-Matthews were in possession of a summary of the official loyalty proceedings against Nash, capsuling the charges against him and the concerns of the Bingham LRB, which had urged a rehearing of the matter.[17]

Collateral data on the case appear in the records of the FBI. These show that, in the wake of McCarthy's speech, the Civil Service Commission had hustled over to the Bureau several documents on Nash, including parts of his loyalty file, records relating to his clearance, and a White House request for relevant data on the subject. The purpose of sending these materials to the FBI wasn't to reassess the case of Philleo Nash, but to discover how McCarthy had found out about it. Specifically, the commission wanted to know if the Bureau could link the papers to its new chief suspect in the great McCarthy mole hunt—an LRB employee named Miriam deHaas.

As FBI official Alan Belmont would explain in a memo to Mickey Ladd: "The following material was made available to the Bureau on January 30, 1952, from the Loyalty Review Board files on Philleo Nash, White House aide, so that the Bureau could treat this material for the latent fingerprints and compare the prints with those of Miriam deHaas . . ."[18] The implications of this don't need much explaining. Despite the administration's outraged disclaimers, it wouldn't have been checking fingerprints on records relating to Nash if it thought McCarthy's comments were baseless. All too plainly, it thought the reverse, and wanted to find out who supplied the data to him.*

Miriam deHaas had in fact been on the radar screens of the CSC and Truman Justice for some time before this. She had been a suspect, along with Cyril Coombs, when McCarthy held forth on the Service case in the spring of 1950. Now she was under even more intense suspicion, not only for the Nash disclosures but for transmission to McCarthy of the LRB minutes he had made public. In these minutes, as seen, members of the Bingham Loyalty Board complained about the dismal record of the State Department in rooting out loyalty risks—exchanges highly embarrassing to the department.

This, too, caused a considerable backstage ruckus—not to clear up the security morass at State, of course, but to determine how McCarthy got the minutes. In this case, it turned out Ms. deHaas was indeed the culprit, though not in the way initially thought. Rather, according to the Bureau memos, she had been providing information to the anti-Communist businessman/activist

---

* A still-later FBI memo on Nash confirmed the accuracy of McCarthy's statement: "After McCarthy made this speech, we conducted an inquiry and decided that, based on the information in the speech, McCarthy probably had access to the results of our loyalty investigation of Nash."

Alfred Kohlberg, who in turn had furnished some of it to Senator McCarran and, it seems, also to McCarthy. It doesn't appear from the records of the case, or deHaas's subsequent statements, that McCarthy had any direct contact with deHaas or even knew of her existence. (DeHaas herself would categorically say, while admitting her role in the affair, that she had had zero contact with McCarthy.)[19]

Once more, officials at Truman Justice displayed impressive zeal in tracking down and seeking to punish McCarthy's sources. Not only did they want the de-Haas leakage stopped, they wanted a full-fledged investigation by the FBI, grand jury sessions, and prosecution of the offender. Again, however, the Bureau was slow to get involved, beyond its fingerprint checking, on the grounds that the quarrel between deHaas and the CSC was an internal administrative issue. In November 1952—a further notable contrast with the case of Service— she was abruptly fired, having been given five days' notice.

Still more such cases might be cited, but these suggest the essence of the matter. Throughout, the White House, Department of Justice, and other agencies of the Truman government showed far more interest in tracking down McCarthy's sources than in uncovering alleged Soviet agents or Communist Party members, or in addressing the lax security standards deplored by the LRB. In the view of the Truman administration, the problem with Joe McCarthy was not that he didn't have inside sources of loyalty data but that he all too obviously did. Which was from a national security standpoint beneficial, as information on such cases was sorely needed.

PART IV

MOLE HUNTS

CHAPTER 24

The Trouble with Harry

IT'S IMPOSSIBLE to understand the McCarthy era and its security wars without first understanding something of Harry Truman—which, however, is no easy task. On this subject, and certain others, Truman is a hard man to figure.

In many standard histories and bios, Truman is depicted as a tough cold warrior who bravely faced down Moscow, being teamed in this respect with his foreign policy vicar Acheson at State. Even more to the present point, we're told, Truman cleaned up security problems on the home front, long before the blustering Joe McCarthy came barging in with his outrageous charges. The cleanup was supposedly effected through the Truman loyalty program, announced in March of 1947. Thanks to this draconian effort, it's said, whatever Communists or security risks had got on official payrolls were ousted. Thus, when McCarthy showed up in 1950 he was banging on a door already closed and locked by Truman.

Sad to say, this portrayal of Truman's policy on the home front is almost entirely fiction. That he was a visceral anti-Communist is not in doubt. However, he seemed to know little about the way the Soviets and their U.S. agents functioned, or their presence in the government he headed, and didn't show much interest in learning. This ennui persisted despite the myriad FBI reports supplied to the White House and Truman cabinet about the vast extent and serious nature of the penetration. Accordingly, not only was the security problem not cleaned up by 1950, some of the most flagrant suspects imaginable were flourishing in the federal workforce.

J. Robert Oppenheimer

Foremost among such cases was J. Robert Oppenheimer, the famous nuclear scientist who played a leading role in the atom project of World War II. This was by all odds the most significant security problem in Cold War records, having its genesis in the days of FDR, blossoming into a full-fledged scandal under Truman, then finally coming to public view in the Eisenhower era.

The earliest known mention of Oppenheimer in the FBI reports is a memo from March 28, 1941, which says he had the previous year attended a meeting in the home of Haakon Chevalier, an identified (later self-admitted) Red, along with Communist leaders Isaac Folkoff and William Schneiderman. It was apparently this information, obtained at the era of the Hitler-Stalin pact, that prompted the FBI to put Oppenheimer on its "custodial detention" list of people to be picked up by the Bureau if a national emergency developed. A memo to this effect was issued May 21, 1941, describing his "national tendency" as "Communist."

Further intel on the case did nothing to dissuade the Bureau from this verdict. As part of the COMRAP/CINRAD inquiry, the FBI at this time was keeping a close watch on itinerant Soviet commissar Steve Nelson, then based in California. From surveillance of Nelson and other Communist bigwigs, the FBI recorded numerous references to Oppenheimer, explicitly and repeatedly saying he was a secret member of the party. One such entry in the Bureau archive reads as follows:

> In December, 1942, Julius Robert Oppenheimer was the subject of a discussion between Steve Nelson and Bernadette Doyle, organizational secretary of the Communist Party for Alameda County, California. At this time, Steve Nelson stated that Dr. Hannah Peters had been to visit him and she had stated that Dr. Oppenheimer, because of his employment in a special project, could not be active in the party. . . . Bernadette Doyle answered Nelson by saying that she believes the matter should be taken up with the State Committee regarding the "two Oppys" inasmuch as they were regularly registered and everyone knew that they were Communist Party members.[1]

A similar entry dating from May 1943 recounts a conversation between Bernadette Doyle and one John Murra, "suspected intelligence agent of the USSR." This says "Bernadette Doyle . . . informed John Murra that Mrs. Oppenheimer and her husband were 'comrades' and that the husband was working on a special project in the [Berkeley] Radiation Laboratory . . . Also

"A PARTY MEMBER"

In this excerpt from an FBI report on nuclear scientist J. Robert Oppenheimer, Communist leaders in California are quoted as calling him a secret member of the party as of December 1942.

It is further known that also in October, 1942, Steve Nelson was in contact with Lloyd Lehmann, organizer of the Young Communist League, Alameda County, California. Lehmann advised Steve Nelson that a very important weapon was being developed and that he was in on the research end of this development. Nelson then asked Lehmann if Oppenheimer knew he was a "YCLer" (member of the Young Communist League) and added that Oppenheimer was "too jittery." Nelson went on to state that Oppenheimer at one time was active in the Party but was then inactive and further stated that the reason the Government left Oppenheimer alone was because of his ability in the scientific field. Nelson went on to explain "he worked on the Teachers' Committee, the Spanish Committee, et cetera and he can't cover his past."

In December, 1942, Julius Robert Oppenheimer was the subject of a discussion between Steve Nelson and Bernadette Doyle, Organizational Secretary of the Communist Party for Alameda County, California. At this time, Steve Nelson stated that Dr. Hannah Peters had been to visit him and she had stated that Dr. Oppenheimer, because of his employment on a special project, could not be active in the Party. Accordingly, Bernadette Doyle answered Nelson by saying that she believed the matter should be taken up with the State Committee regarding the "two Oppys" inasmuch as they were regularly registered and everyone knew that they were Communist Party members.

Confidential sources advise that in May, 1943, John V. Murra, a veteran of the Abraham Lincoln Brigade and a suspected intelligence agent of the USSR, was in San Francisco, California, immediately prior to the National Plenum of the Communist Party to be held in New York City June 11 - 13, 1943. John V. Murra contacted Bernadette Doyle, Organizational Secretary of the Communist Party for Alameda County, advising her that he wanted to get in touch with Mrs. Robert Oppenheimer. Bernadette Doyle directed John Murra to call the Joint Anti-Fascist Committee or to call the University of California and to make inquiry there as to how a letter could be addressed to Mrs. Robert Oppenheimer. It is noted that at this time Julius Robert Oppenheimer and his wife were living in New Mexico where Julius Oppenheimer was head of the Los Alamos Laboratory. Bernadette Doyle further informed John Murra that Mrs. Oppenheimer and her husband were "comrades" and that the husband was working on a special project in the Radiation Laboratory of the University of California. Also Bernadette Doyle stated that Oppenheimer was a Party member but that his name should be removed from any mailing lists in John Murra's possession and he should not be mentioned in any way.

According to the same source, Bernadette Doyle in a conversation subsequent to that set out above, indicated to Helen Winter, the wife of Carl Winter, Secretary, Los Angeles County Communist Party, that Kitty Oppenheimer was a member of the Berriman Branch of the Communist Party in Alameda County, California.

- 8 -

Source: FBI Oppenheimer file

Bernadette Doyle stated that Oppenheimer was a Party member but that his name should be removed from any mailing lists in John Murra's possession and he should not be mentioned in any way."*[2]

Despite these and other similar data from the FBI, Oppenheimer was taken on as scientific/administrative head of the nuclear project in the crisis of the war years. This was a huge calculated gamble on the part of Gen. Leslie Groves, military capo of the project, who thought Oppenheimer (under tight surveillance) was a plausible security risk in the conflict with the Nazis. And given the circumstances of the war, with Moscow as our ally, it might be viewed as a risk worth taking that in the end succeeded.

However, with the advent of the Cold War, as Moscow turned from ally to increasingly hostile foe, the global outlook was obviously quite different. By the latter months of 1945, signs of tension with the Soviets were mounting and the FBI was following up Elizabeth Bentley's revelations on the home front. At this time also, Oppenheimer would leave the jurisdiction of the Army and become a subject of direct concern to Hoover and the Bureau. Accordingly, in mid-November 1945, Hoover provided a précis of the case to the White House and to Secretary of State James Byrnes, then overseeing atomic matters for Truman. This three-page memo wrapped up the pertinent data on Oppenheimer, including his involvement with pro-Red causes and individuals. Specifically noted was the information that Communist leaders in California considered him a secret member of the party.[3]

None of this, however, seemed to be of much concern to Truman officials dealing with the famous suspect, who rather than being phased out of America's nuclear setup would now be given still other significant duties involving our atomic secrets. Among the most important of these new jobs was his appointment to the General Advisory Committee on atomic energy (and subsequent election as its chairman), which carried with it a "Q clearance" providing access to confidential data. This was no honorific post, but one of utmost sensitivity, as the GAC would be the source of expertise and guidance for the Atomic Energy Commission in making key decisions.[4]

As this appointment was going forward, Hoover again hustled over to Truman higher-ups the security data on Oppenheimer and the problem he presented—again, however, to no avail. This further report would be dismissed in utterly casual fashion by Truman's staffers, including White House aide Clark

---

*A further FBI entry, based either on an informant report or microphone surveillance, describes a November 1945 Communist Party meeting in Alameda County, as follows: "According to confidential sources, Jack Manley stated at this meeting that he and Steve Nelson were close to Oppenheimer as Oppenheimer was a party member. Manley also stated that Oppenheimer told Steven Nelson several years ago that the Army was working on the atomic bomb . . . Katherine Sanders, a Communist Party functionary also present at this meeting, stated that Oppenheimer was a Communist Party member."

Clifford and Truman's choice to head the AEC, David E. Lilienthal. In these precincts, the fact that Oppenheimer rendered good service in the war, and was otherwise well regarded, trumped the intel from the Bureau. As revealed in AEC hearings on the case, favorable statements from nuclear satraps Vannevar Bush and James B. Conant, who had worked with Oppenheimer in the atom program, meant *"Dr. Oppenheimer's loyalty was prima facie clear despite material contained in the FBI summary."*[5] (Emphasis added.)

And that, believe it or not, was that. There was, Lilienthal added, some discussion with Clark Clifford about a possible "special board" to look into the matter, but "Mr. Clifford did not seem to take this seriously." Nor did Lilienthal himself. He testified that he had forgotten about this proposal entirely and didn't do anything about it. So the question of Oppenheimer's security status apparently just drifted along in bureaucratic limbo until his authorization for a "Q clearance" was formalized in August of 1947.[6]

Further suggestive of then-prevailing security measures is an AEC memo saying that, in fact, Oppenheimer had *already* received such clearance, dating back to February 1947, but for some reason this significant item hadn't been recorded. This memo also states that "Dr. Oppenheimer was previously cleared by the Manhattan District" (the name given the atom project in World War II)—the point being that such prior clearance meant he was now entitled to another.[7] Once more, the fact that a risk taken when the enemy was in Berlin might be a risk of a different nature when the enemy was in Moscow apparently didn't cross the minds of Truman and his people. There are many possible terms for this, but toughness on Cold War security issues obviously isn't among them.

Harry Dexter White

Had Oppenheimer stood alone as an instance of security coma in the Truman years, the case might be put down as a bizarre exception. It was, however, closer to the norm than to unusual conduct for the era. Among other similar episodes was the strange saga of Harry Dexter White and the even stranger handling of the case by Truman.

Though no Oppenheimer in terms of clout or status, White was a significant figure. He wielded enormous influence with Treasury Secretary Morgenthau, had a hand in countless global dealings, and was instrumental in placing his friends and allies in Treasury and other billets. He was also one of the most important Soviet agents named by Whittaker Chambers and Elizabeth Bentley and would later show up in *Venona*. He was accordingly featured in numerous FBI reports about the penetration problem, beginning in late 1945 and continuing for months thereafter.

Notwithstanding all of this, White would in early 1946 be named by Truman as the top U.S. official at the International Monetary Fund, to a large extent White's own creation, stemming from a 1944 global confab held at Bretton Woods, New Hampshire. White was confirmed for this position by the Senate, had his commission signed by Truman, and went on to the IMF when it began operations in the spring of 1946.

All this would become a matter of public knowledge when the appointment blew up into a political scandal in the early 1950s. How, it was asked, could Truman have permitted the advancement of an identified Moscow agent to such a high-ranking post? In trying to provide an answer, Truman came up with three different explanations: that the FBI failed to inform him of the security problem with White; that when he found out about it, he took prompt and effective action; and that he allowed the appointment to go through to cooperate with the FBI in its investigation.

All these responses, besides being mutually inconsistent, were mistaken, as shown by the documented record. Extensive information on the case would be disclosed in 1953 Senate hearings by Eisenhower Attorney General Herbert Brownell and, in a rare appearance of this nature, FBI Director Hoover. Most provably wrong was the contention that the FBI had failed to tell Truman about White, as the Bureau had copious evidence in writing—some already noted—that it supplied a steady stream of reports about the case not only to the Treasury and Truman Justice but directly to the White House.[8]

Thus, taking the matter from the top, White was featured in the Hoover letter of November 8, 1945, delivered by special messenger to Truman aide Harry Vaughan for the President's attention. White was second on the list of suspects named in this letter. He would be named again in the comprehensive Bureau memo of November 27, 1945, delivered to the White House December 4. White would then be the subject of a special memo from the FBI, devoted mainly to his case, dated February 1, 1946, delivered to the White House February 4. There would be other Bureau reports in which White was mentioned, but these are noted because they were all supplied to Truman and his agents before the IMF appointment became official.*[9]

Likewise, the notion that the appointment went forward in cooperation with the Bureau (an argument earlier floated in the case of Victor Perlo) was categorically denied by Hoover. "At no time," said the Director, "was the FBI party to any arrangement to promote Harry Dexter White, and at no time did

---

*The timeline on these reports, plotted against Truman's actions, is instructive. Truman nominated White for the IMF position on January 23, 1946—two and a half months after the first Hoover letter prominently mentioning White and a month and a half after the November comprehensive memo was delivered to the White House. The nomination would not be voted on by the Senate until February 6, at which time Truman also had the February memo geared to White. It's thus clear that Truman and his aides had ample warning that White was an identified Soviet agent before the nomination ever happened, and had a heads-up mainly devoted to White before the matter was voted by the Senate.

the FBI give its approval to such an agreement."[10] In fact, as Hoover further noted, White's move to the IMF impeded the FBI inquiry as the Bureau's investigative powers didn't extend to global bodies.*

A last revealing sidelight to the above: When White had been confirmed and was ready to take up his IMF position, Truman sent a flowery letter to the appointee congratulating him on his fine service to the nation and the new job he was assuming. This Truman missive said he regretted White's departure from the Treasury, but "my regret is lessened . . . in the knowledge that you leave the Treasury only to assume new duties for the government [at IMF] . . . In that position you will be able to carry forward the work you so ably began at Bretton Woods . . . I am confident that in your new position you will add to the distinction of your already distinguished career with the Treasury."[11]

This effusive Truman letter was dated April 30, 1946—almost six full months after he was first warned by the FBI that White was an identified Moscow agent. It was also at a time, according to Truman's later claims, that he was cooperating with the Bureau to crack down on White and others like him.

Alger Hiss

If White and Oppenheimer were proof of indifference to security standards, the case of Alger Hiss was even more so. This was of course the most famous spy scandal of them all. It was also the case that showed the willingness of the Truman administration, not merely to ignore security intel, but to harass the witness who supplied it.

Histories of the Cold War often highlight Truman's statement that the Hiss-Chambers hearings in the summer of 1948 before the House Committee on Un-American Activities were a "red herring." However, things being said and done in private far exceeded in shock value mere criticism of the House proceedings or the term "red herring." (As it happened, the phrase wasn't initially used by Truman but propounded to him in a question by the press, to which he assented.)

As seen, the FBI had provided top officials plentiful information on Hiss, based on the Chambers-Bentley data, beginning in the fall of 1945. It was information of this type that caused Secretary of State James Byrnes to conclude in early 1946 that Hiss should be removed from the department, and that led to

---

*In a further footnote to all the above, Hoover added that if the idea was to contain White and monitor his actions by surrounding him with trustworthy people, the project was aborted early on by the appointment of V. Frank Coe, yet another Bentley suspect, as secretary of the IMF. Indeed, the Coe appointment was in some ways even more telling than that of White. Coe had been named as a suspect in FBI reports to the White House, Treasury, and Truman Justice dated February 23 and 24 and March 4, 1946. Coe wasn't appointed to the IMF until three months later (June '46).

Hiss's slow-motion resignation ten months later. Also, the department security squad under Joe Panuch had been all over Hiss for a considerable time before he was ousted. Multiple FBI reports about the case were meanwhile sent, not only to the State Department, but to the White House and Truman Justice.

Despite this extensive background, when the Hiss-Chambers duel went public in the summer of 1948, the White House and Truman Justice bent their efforts to nailing and discrediting, not Hiss, but Chambers. Elements of the game plan were set forth in an August 16 memo to Clark Clifford from Truman aide George Elsey. Capsuling steps agreed to at a meeting with Attorney General Clark, this included the notation: "Justice should make every effort to ascertain if Whittaker Chambers is guilty of perjury." To this was added the handwritten comment "investigation of Chambers' confinement in mental institution."[12] There were no similar notes suggesting Hiss be measured for a perjury count or that his mental health might be in question. (See page 323.)

Unfortunately for the Chambers-is-crazy thesis (an oft-repeated line of Hiss himself), the FBI found no records of this nature. On August 20, Hoover reported to Clark: "With respect to Whittaker Chambers, there is nothing indicated in the files of the Bureau, or the files of the New York office that Chambers has been institutionalized."[13] Undaunted by this failure, Truman Justice persisted in its efforts to discredit Chambers and, if possible, indict him. Somewhat improbably, this campaign intensified when Chambers came up with documentary proof that Hiss was lying—long-concealed official papers and summaries of secret data Hiss (and White) provided to then–Soviet courier Chambers in the 1930s.

Some of these papers would be produced by Chambers in a deposition taken by Hiss's lawyers in November of 1948, others in microfilm format to the House Committee on Un-American Activities a few weeks later. This sequence would become the stuff of folklore and start Hiss on the road to prison. The Truman forces, however, didn't see it that way. Their unwavering focus was on the crimes of Chambers—the fact that he hadn't previously produced these papers, which indeed meant he hadn't hitherto been completely truthful. This was the angle that appealed to Truman Justice.

Thus a memo to the FBI from Assistant Attorney General Alexander Campbell, reacting to the November deposition, says: "It is desired that an immediate investigation be conducted so that it can be ascertained whether Chambers has committed perjury. In this connection, photostatic copies of these documents should be obtained together with a copy of the deposition given by Chambers."[14]

Other such memos soon made their way to Hoover. One, dated December 2, 1948, reemphasized that Justice wanted "an immediate investigation by the Bureau to determine whether Chambers committed perjury." While telling his agents to proceed as ordered, Hoover noted in the margin: "I can't under-

NAILING CHAMBERS

This memo from Truman aide George Elsey summarizes plans to discredit Whittaker Chambers and, if possible, indict Chambers—not Hiss—for perjury.

DECLASSIFIED
E.O. 11652, Sec. 3(D) and 5(D)
DEPT. OF JUSTICE LTR. 2-26-73
By *ALT* NARS Date *2-6-73*

THE WHITE HOUSE
WASHINGTON

~~SECRET~~

August 16, 1948

Memorandum for Mr. Clifford:

The following represents the consensus of opinion at our meeting this morning with the Attorney General and Mr. Peyton Ford:

(1) The President should not at this time make a statement regarding "spies" along the lines proposed by Mr. Spingarn.

(2) Attention will be given by Justice to the possibility and desirability of referring the question of Soviet espionage in the Federal Government to a bi-partisan commission, such as the Hoover Commission.

(3) Justice should make every effort to ascertain if Whittaker Chambers is guilty of perjury.
(3A) *Investigation of Chambers confinement in mental institution.*

(4) The Attorney General will furnish the White House with a description of the data Miss Bentley claims to have obtained for Soviet agents during the war, and the White House should endeavor to determine how much of this information was freely available to the Soviet Government through routine official liaison between the U.S. and the U.S.S.R. The purpose of this would be to make it clear that Miss Bentley was not successful in transmitting secret material to the Russians that they did not already have.

(5) The White House should ascertain the facts concerning the retention of Mr. Remington in OWMR, his transfer to the Council of Economic Advisers and his subsequent transfer to the Department of Commerce.

G. M. E.

GEORGE M. ELSEY

Source: NSA-CIA *Venona* report

stand why such effort is being made to indict Chambers to the exclusion of Hiss." He would likewise later comment, "I wonder why they don't move against Hiss also."[15] It was—it is—an excellent question.

Luckily for Chambers, he by this time had a vigorous champion in the House committee, spearheaded by chief investigator Robert Stripling and freshman GOP representative Richard Nixon. When these worthies learned of administration plans to railroad Chambers, they raised a vociferous protest, warning of the further uproar that would be caused by any such proceeding. Relative sanity then prevailed and Truman Justice at last switched sides, deciding to drop the Chambers perjury angle and go after Hiss. We can only speculate as to what might have happened had the House committee not been on the job and in possession of probative data Truman Justice couldn't deny or keep sequestered.

Ultimately, Hiss would be convicted of lying about these matters and wind up in a federal prison, so the vindication of Chambers couldn't have been much more conclusive. None of this, however, impressed the alleged security hawk, Harry Truman. As late as 1956, he engaged in the following exchanges in a TV interview reprinted by *U.S. News & World Report. Question:* "Mr. President, is it true that you characterized Richard Nixon's investigation into the Alger Hiss case as a 'red herring'?" *Answer:* "No, but it was. I never characterized it that way but that's exactly what it was." *Question:* "Do you think that he [Hiss] was a Communist spy?" *Answer:* "No, I do not."[16]

O PPENHEIMER, White, and Hiss were three of the most famous spy suspects ever, and none did any credit to security standards at the Truman White House. All of them, however, were handled outside the boundaries of the President's loyalty program. White and Hiss left the government before the program started, and Oppenheimer would be dealt with through other channels. So it's conceivable that, when the loyalty system was adopted, the administration set off on a different path and thereafter took a harder line than that suggested in these cases. Conceivable—but not what happened. In all too many instances, the same mind-set and same results persisted.

One reason for this outcome was the way the Truman program was structured. Despite its allegedly draconian features, the system contained a host of flaws that made it extremely porous. Among these, ironically, was the "loyalty" requirement itself—stipulating that federal employees be vetted only on this basis. This proved to be a protean concept that gave rise to endless troubles. Closely linked with these was the original Truman order (later changed) that such judgments be based on "reasonable grounds" instead of "reasonable doubt," the rule that in theory obtained before this. Together these Truman notions created a twilight zone of fog and hesitation that resulted in the clearance of many suspects. Following are a few examples.

Edward U. Condon

Had Robert Oppenheimer not existed, Dr. Condon might well be rated the scariest security risk in Cold War history. His case exhibited to the fullest the loopholes in the Truman program and the manner in which its supposedly drastic nature became debilitating weakness.

Condon was another nuclear physicist with odd connections, and also with exotic views about security measures and U.S. relations with the Communist bloc of countries. He had served briefly with the wartime atomic setup but lasted for only about six weeks before he and the project managers parted ways. General Groves, who considered Oppenheimer an acceptable risk, did not so consider Condon. Being judged a bigger security problem than Robert Oppenheimer obviously took a bit of doing (though there were some others who shared this dubious distinction).

As to the Soviet Union and East-West relations, Condon not only adopted the prevalent outlook of the war but carried this to utmost limits and persisted with such notions well after the war was over. He had a worrisome habit of hanging out with East bloc officials, including Polish, Czech, and Bulgarian embassy staffers, subsequent to the Communist takeover of these countries. (Chief among these contacts was one Ignace Zlotowski, a Polish embassy figure named by a defecting Red official as an atomic espionage agent.)[17]

Condon's familiars on the home front were of like nature. He and his wife were friends of the Bentley-identified Soviet agent Gregory Silvermaster and of Silvermaster's housemate, Ludwig Ullman. Another such Condon sidekick was John Marsalka—a member of the Silvermaster circle—discharged from the State Department in the 1930s "due to doubts about his loyalty to the United States," to quote congressional findings on the subject.[18] Still another Condon buddy was Edwin Smith, identified as a CP member (taking the Fifth Amendment when asked about this) and an official of the National Council of American Soviet Friendship, an oft-cited front group. (Condon himself was active in the science committee of this outfit.)

This sampling of the Condon *vita* is perhaps sufficient to suggest why Army security types voiced strong objections in 1945 when he wanted to take off on a trip to Russia and had his passport lifted. Yet, despite this well-documented record, the Truman administration that same year appointed him director of the National Bureau of Standards in the Commerce Department, then kept him at this post, over the protests of Congress, for the next six years. The job had major security implications in that the Standards Bureau dealt with all kinds of classified material, including data on nuclear weapons, radar systems, and guided missiles.[19]

A good deal of this background was known to the House Committee on Un-American Activities, which in early 1948 compiled a report on Condon, calling him one of the "weakest links" in the atomic security chain. The committee discovered also that the FBI had filed its own report on Condon, and House members tried to obtain this as part of their inquiry. As seen, the administration flatly refused to provide this report to Congress.

As to the workings of the loyalty program, the Condon case was bleakly revealing. The Commerce Department was apprised of the negative data on Condon in 1946 and became formally cognizant of the problem with delivery of the FBI report about him in the spring of 1947. Thereafter, the department had the case before it for approximately ten months—a period in which Condon enjoyed continuing access to classified data. Finally, in early 1948, the department held a loyalty hearing on the case, which, to the dismay of Congress, resulted in his clearance.

As brought out in House committee hearings, this surreal result was arrived at by dismissing from consideration Condon's linkages to East Bloc officials, Silvermaster and Marsalka, and other similar intel. The reason for ignoring all this information, said the chairman of the Commerce hearing board, was that it concerned "security," whereas the board looked only at the "loyalty" issue. And the board members didn't think they had "reasonable grounds" for finding Condon was disloyal. As the hearing chairman explained, an adverse ruling on this basis was tantamount to a verdict of treason and the board was loath to make this judgment.[20]

So Condon would stay on at the Bureau of Standards, despite the outcries of Congress, until September of 1951. The case clearly illustrated the problems inherent in the elastic, subjective "loyalty" standard decreed by Truman. That aspect, and the secrecy issue, had obvious tie-ins to the later battles of Joe McCarthy. And there was another tie-in also. The head of the Commerce hearing board that cleared Condon, and who gave the reasons for this clearance, was the already met with Adrian Fisher. By the time of McCarthy's set-to with the State Department, Fisher had moved from Commerce to the AEC and thence to Foggy Bottom, where he was active in the effort to discredit McCarthy and provide back-channel data to Senator Tydings in seeking that objective.

Solomon Adler

As has been well noted, the most explosive security scandal of the Truman era was the *Amerasia* case, replete with cover-up, perjury, and grand-jury rigging by a coterie of top officials. Among its many peculiar features, the case provides a suggestive study of the Truman loyalty program in action.

Like countless other security problems, the *Amerasia* scandal had its origins under FDR but would come to public notice under Truman. The case surfaced in the spring of 1945, when Truman had just succeeded to the White House, so his knowledge of it would have been zero at the outset. Also, we're informed that when he first heard about the matter, he ordered a thoroughgoing investigation, which accorded with his hawkish Cold War image.

However, within a few weeks of this brave beginning, everything was thrown into reverse and the case was fixed and buried. All this manipulation happened on Truman's watch and was thus done by people subordinate to him, none of whom so far as we know suffered any official sanctions, and several of whom were in fact promoted. And as the wiretaps that revealed the cover-up were ordained by Truman, it's hard to believe he didn't learn about the fix, especially in its later phases.

Be that as it may, the relevant point for now is the way suspects in the case would fare under the loyalty program of 1947. Chief among these was John Service, the handling of whose case was so singular and important it requires a discussion of its own (see Chapter 27). Suffice it to note that, despite the FBI's extensive data on Service, he was repeatedly cleared by the State Department's see-no-evil loyalty screeners. Also instructive, though getting less attention, was the case of his Chungking roommate, the veteran Soviet agent Adler.

By the time the Truman loyalty program came on line, the FBI had copious intel on Adler. The Bureau knew from microphone surveillance about Service's links to Adler and their activities in China—including some knowledge of their third housemate, Chi Chao-ting. Hoover's men also had good reason to know Adler was a Communist apparatchik, named as such by Chambers and then again by Bentley. The Bureau likewise had cause to know that Adler was one of a sizable group of Soviet agents battening on the Treasury payroll.

Accordingly, in the period 1945–48, the FBI supplied to Justice, Treasury, and the White House a steady stream of reports in which Adler was featured (see page 328). Again, however, these memos didn't make much of a dent with the Truman security screeners. In fact, despite all the Bureau information, Adler, after a department loyalty hearing, would continue with his Treasury duties.[21]

Adler thus, like Service, had several years of official employment remaining following *Amerasia*/Bentley. During this span, he not only stayed on at Treasury but received promotions, pay increases, and key assignments. In 1946, he was a consultant to Gen. George C. Marshall's mission to China; in 1947, he was tasked with providing background data on China to Gen. Albert Wedemeyer, U.S. commander in the region; and from December 1947 until February 1948, he consulted with the State Department on questions of technical/financial aid to Chiang Kai-shek.[22] Given his status as Soviet agent and previous

WARNINGS ON ADLER

As this FBI chart reveals, the Bureau sent high-level government officials a steady stream of reports on Communist apparatchik Solomon Adler.

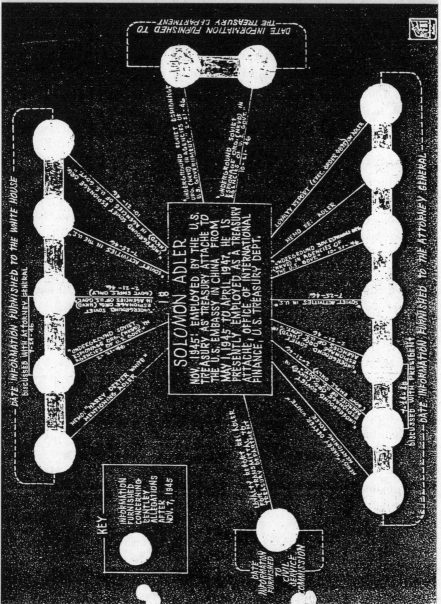

Source: J. Edgar Hoover confidential files

efforts to throttle Chiang, it isn't hard to guess what kind of counsel Adler would have provided in these assignments.

It wasn't until May of 1950, at the peak of the McCarthy uproar, that Adler thought it prudent to leave the Treasury and go back to his native England—not forgetting to put in for back pay and accumulated leave time. Thereafter, he absconded to his real homeland of Communist China, where he lived out his days as an employee of the Red regime he helped midwife to power.

William Remington

The merits of a loyalty system that couldn't flush out the likes of Solomon Adler or Edward Condon don't require much comment. Equally suggestive was the case of William Remington, who for the better part of a decade moved with acrobatic ease from one official billet to another, first under Roosevelt, then under Truman. This occurred despite the fact that Remington, like Adler and so many others, was named in November of 1945 by Bentley as a member of her spy combine.

In the dragnet investigation that followed, the FBI sent out a vast number of reports on Remington to agencies where he worked, the Attorney General, and the White House. In fact, no other target of the probe was the subject of so many reports to top officials. According to Bureau records, the FBI supplied federal agencies no fewer than forty-five memos, written alerts, and oral communications in which the Remington case was mentioned.

The good news was that, on the military side of things, the security data prompted the Office of Naval Intelligence to seek Remington's dismissal as a reserve officer in the Navy. On the civilian side, however, it was Service-Adler redux, as Remington enjoyed an effortless rise to ever more responsible postings. Over the next few years, he was appointed as an economist for the War Conversion and Stabilization Board (1946), served on the staff of the Council of Economic Advisors for the White House (1947), and became chief of the Export Control division at Commerce (1948). The last had serious Cold War implications, as it involved supervision of export-control licenses to the USSR and the Communist bloc in general.

Once more, security intel from the FBI meant little—Commerce officials being totally unaware of the Bureau data or dismissing the case as being of small importance. Among the more amazing revelations was the testimony of Thomas Blaisdell, Remington's chief in several jobs and main sponsor for the export position. Asked by Sen. Homer Ferguson in Senate hearings on the case if he had thought it necessary to check Remington's security status before recommending him for this post, Blaisdell blandly said he hadn't since that wasn't his responsibility.[23]

Other Commerce officials would testify that they knew nothing about FBI reports on Remington, that they assumed he was all right because he worked for the CEA, and that their files showed nothing derogatory on him.[24] These comments were amplified by leaked suggestions from Commerce higher-ups—mirroring the Harry Dexter White case—that the FBI had been remiss in not advising them about the problem. Again, the records of the Bureau showed these buck-passing efforts were in error.

Remington also supplied a further twist in the escalating secrecy battle between Congress and the White House, and his case would shed some light on file-stripping charges of the McCarthy era. Ferguson and his colleagues called for the Commerce security file on Remington, which was in fact delivered. When it arrived, however, it had been picked clean of relevant data. Commerce spokesman Matthew Hale told the lawmakers this weeding had been done in compliance with the Truman secrecy order of March 1948.[25]

The denouement of the case, as far as the loyalty program figured in it, was more astounding yet. In 1949, despite the FBI reports, Remington's separation from the Navy, and a belated disapproval by Commerce, the Seth Richardson LRB cleared him on loyalty charges and returned him to his duties. The rationale for this was that even if Remington had provided data for the Soviets as alleged by Bentley, he did so during World War II, when Moscow was our ally. There was no evidence, said the board, that he was delivering data *in 1949*—thus indicating an adverse finding had to be based on tangible, real-time proof of disloyal conduct in the present.[26]

Like Hiss, Remington would later be convicted in federal court for lying about his Red connections, which meant the Truman loyalty program had been incapable of discharging a flagrant risk found guilty by a jury. Along with Oppenheimer, Condon, Service, and Adler—all holding down significant federal posts in 1950—the Remington case made it clear that the alleged security crackdown under Truman was a myth. And if the Truman screeners could let these sharks slip through the netting, how likely were they to catch the minnows?

CHAPTER 25

A Book of Martyrs

BECAUSE so many of the original McCarthy suspects presented to the Senate were handled on an anonymous basis, judging the merits of the cases has always been a difficult business. So difficult, as has been seen, that most writers on the subject have simply accepted the comments of the Tydings panel and the State Department about the fraudulence of McCarthy's charges, then applied these exculpatory statements back to any particular cases that happened to surface.

Of course, the proper way to do it is the other way around: Get the identities of the suspects, see what's available on them in security records, then draw our own conclusions. However, as the names submitted by McCarthy disappeared from the Tydings subcommittee archive and weren't otherwise part of the official record, nobody outside looking in could know who all the cases were, so backtracking in this manner was precluded. McCarthy would from time to time make some names public, and some would be made known through other channels. But these identifications concerned perhaps only a third of the total caseload, leaving an enormous gap in the historical record.

Now, however, we do have the names of these original McCarthy cases and can check them out from various angles. An earlier chapter considered certain of his suspects, identified in his initial speeches and some other statements, who would later show up in *Venona*. But this too was only a fraction of the total caseload, geared strictly to the *Venona* decrypts. More extensive by far are the records of the FBI, where the names of McCarthy cases abound, while still others would surface in later investigations of the Congress. If we consult these sources, we can find out something about the initial McCarthy suspects, including a fair number of those who vanished from the Tydings record, and what McCarthy knew about them.

E. J. Askwith

Edna Jerry Askwith takes pride of place in this discussion for alphabetical reasons, deriving from her surname. This also put her at the head of the line in McCarthy's supplementary list of potential cases given Tydings on March 14, 1950. This is the list, it may be recalled, that Tydings, the State Department, and most chronicles of the era have treated as nonexistent, thus assuring that Ms. Askwith's name, and case, have been lost to history.

She was one of McCarthy's cases nonetheless, and also one of the FBI's. Professionally, she was a staffer in the State Department office called the Coordinator of Inter-American Affairs, a target-rich division that at various times included Robert Miller, Bernard Redmont, Joseph Gregg, Willard Park, Philip Raine, Dwight Mallon, and John T. Fishburn. (Of these, Miller, Gregg, Park, and Redmont were all original Bentley suspects.) Askwith was also in contact with the Mary Jane Keeney crowd, which included David Wahl, Helen Scott, Alix Reuther, and Samuel Krafsur of the Soviet news agency TASS, among a host of others. As the Miller and Keeney groups both pop up repeatedly in Bureau records, so does Jerry Askwith.

Thus, we find in the Gregory/Bentley file that in 1949 the FBI was conducting a background check on Askwith, in which Dwight Mallon stated that he was her superior at State, gave her a favorable reference, and claimed she wasn't connected to the more dubious characters in the unit. He was aware, he said, "of the fact that persons with whom she was associated in the CIAA were subsequently questioned as to their loyalty but Mallon felt that Miss Askwith's associations with persons such as Bernard Redmont and Robert Miller did not extend beyond a normal office relationship."[1]

The FBI had reason to think otherwise, particularly in the case of Redmont and his wife, Joan, with whom Askwith was in frequent out-of-office contact. It didn't help that Mallon failed to level with the Bureau on this, that he was Askwith's boyfriend, or that both of them had social dealings with the Redmonts. Bureau records show a fairly constant round of contacts among Askwith, the Redmonts, the Raines, the Minter Woods, the Krafsurs, and others in the extended Bentley network.* Also, the Bureau would surveil Askwith attending a party at the home of Alix Reuther along with Mary Jane Keeney and David Wahl.[2]

It would thus appear that Jerry Askwith was a member in good standing of the loose confederation of people who crisscrossed between the Miller and Keeney circles. At least three of the people with whom she was in social contact—Bernard Redmont, Mary Jane Keeney, and David Wahl—were named in Bureau records as Soviet agents (as were her coworkers Gregg and Miller). These linkages were significant from a security angle, as hanging out with even one identified Soviet agent—to say nothing of four or five—was, according to the official regs, a leading sign of trouble.

However, these habitual contacts apparently did nothing to damage Askwith's employment status in Foggy Bottom, as she was still ensconced there in 1950 when McCarthy made his charges. The case suggests the importance of the supplementary list McCarthy gave to Tydings and which thereafter vanished. Disposing of Askwith by this subliminal method meant, among other things, a further whittling down of the McCarthy caseload. She is relevant also in weighing the question of his sources and alleged sole reliance on the Lee list, as she was not a Lee list case (though making an anonymous cameo appearance as "E-18" in the case of Mallon).

Lois Carlisle

A transferee into State from OSS, Lois Carlisle was McCarthy's case No. 58, and unlike Askwith a Lee case also. Among other distinguishing features, she was uniquely close to Mary Jane Keeney, living on the same floor of the Washington, D.C., apartment building where the Keeneys had their lodgings at 215 B St. N.E. (now Constitution Ave.). Based on Bureau records, Carlisle seems to have been among the closest of Mary Jane's innumerable contacts.

Carlisle had a track record that was itself suggestive: OSS, an active member of local #3 of the Communist-dominated United Public Workers Union (the local headed by Peveril Meigs, another McCarthy suspect), and sometime member of the Washington Book Shop, a front group cited by Francis Biddle in 1942—all this plus her tight connection to the Keeneys. Despite all of which,

---

*Thus, on February 14, 1946, a Bureau entry reflected that "at 10:14 A.M. Gerry Askwith contacted Joan Redmont [who] said that she and Bernie would attend her party of 6:45 P.M. tonight." Askwith said that "she, Mallon and others including Alice Raine [wife of Philip] would be in attendance." Thereafter, on March 27, "Helen Scott contacted Joan Redmont saying she had seen Redmont and Jerry Askwith at the Press Club . . . Jerry Askwith subsequently contacted Joan Redmont and asked Joan if she cared if the Krafsurs came on Monday (to a party planned for the Redmonts by Jerry Askwith). . . ." On April 25, Joan Redmont talked with Helen Scott about a dinner with the Minter Woods, mentioning that "Jerry Askwith was also at the Woods."

Carlisle successfully passed at least two loyalty/security checks by the State Department, based on data provided by "several informants interviewed by CSA [who] commented favorably on her loyalty to the United States," per the summary in the Lee list.*[3]

One of those commenting favorably on the loyalty of Carlisle, according to a Bureau memo of February 1947, was none other than—Mary Jane Keeney. This recommendation, however, didn't look too good a few months later. "On July 1, 1947," according to the Lee list, "a government investigative agency [the FBI] advised that it had received information from a highly confidential source of information, whose reliability is unquestioned, that the subject [Carlisle] had been converted to Communism by E-10 [Mary Jane Keeney]." (The unquestioned, highly confidential source was the Keeneys' correspondence, which the Bureau obtained and copied.)[4]

Based on the FBI information about Carlisle's conversion, the case was reopened, but, as the Lee list reflects, there were "no further reports in the files as of October 1, 1947." Given the data on Keeney-Carlisle, Carlisle's background in general, and the statement that she was a convert to Communism by Keeney—all well known to State—it's hard to believe that Lois Carlisle could have survived even the most cursory effort to enforce security standards in the department. Yet she was still on its payroll in 1950 when Joe McCarthy capsuled her case before the Senate and gave her name to Tydings.

Frances Ferry

Among the clearest indications that McCarthy not only knew the identities of his suspects but had been hunting them down with some success before his initial speeches was the case of Frances Ferry (No. 11 on the McCarthy list; No. 8 on the Lee list).

In his opening talk before the Senate, McCarthy summarized some of the derogatory info on Ferry, including allegations that she was a good friend of a person believed to be a Communist† and a regular reader of the *Daily Worker* (intel provided, according to the Lee list, by a former roommate). McCarthy then flatly asserted, "This individual is not in the State Department at this time, but has a job in the CIA as of today."[5] This categorical statement was quite correct and self-evidently wasn't from the Lee list, as Ferry had been at the State Department, not the CIA, when the list was put together.

In addition to noting that Ferry had moved on to the CIA, McCarthy flagged the case directly to the head of that agency, Adm. Roscoe Hillenkoetter. Though we don't have McCarthy's letter, we do have Hillenkoetter's answer,

---

* "CSA" = Chief Special Agent at the State Department security shop.

† McCarthy upgraded this to "known Communist," something he also did in other cases.

dated March 2, 1950, thanking McCarthy for the heads-up on Ferry, saying the CIA took the matter seriously and had conducted an investigation, but concluding Ferry wasn't a loyalty risk despite the derogatory info.[6]

It isn't clear how thorough an investigation of Ferry could have been made by the CIA between McCarthy's speech of February 20 and this response some ten days later. It's obvious, however, that McCarthy must have reached Hillenkoetter almost immediately after the Senate speech for any investigation whatever to have been conducted. It's also obvious that McCarthy knew whereof he spoke as to Ferry's new location, as Hillenkoetter's letter confirms beyond all doubt that she was then on the payroll of the CIA.

It's noteworthy as well that this Hillenkoetter answer was one of the items McCarthy passed on to Tydings by registered letter of March 18, along with the roster of eighty names provided on that occasion, all of which would vanish from the Tydings subcommittee archive. Thus, the documentary information on the case, indicating that McCarthy knew what he did about it and promptly brought it to the notice of the CIA, would go missing from official records.

Herbert Fierst

Among McCarthy's anonymous cases, arguably one of the most consequential was Herbert Fierst. McCarthy himself believed so, as he made Fierst No. 1 on his list of suspects before the Senate and referred to the case as one of the three most significant on his roster.

As recited to the Senate, the allegations concerning Fierst included a charge that he prevailed on an assistant secretary of state to hire two identified Communists and that he had been in contact with members of a Soviet spy ring. "Nonetheless," said McCarthy, "this individual still occupies an important position in the State Department and has access to secret material."[7]

In this instance, we note the usual McCarthy m.o. of taking the Lee material and backtracking on it to see if the individual was still in the State Department, as Fierst indubitably was. As to security specifics, the McCarthy/J. B. Matthews backup files show that the two people Fierst recommended (given only coded symbols in the Lee list) were Henry Collins and Gordon Griffith;* the official who did the hiring was John Hilldring, handling personnel assignments for occupied areas after World War II.

On the Henry Collins aspect, Collins would later confirm the McCarthy information, saying it was Fierst who asked him to come to work at State on postwar occupation matters. According to Whittaker Chambers, Collins was part of the Red network in Washington that Chambers had directed. When asked if he were a member of the Communist Party, Collins took the Fifth Amendment.[8]

---

*So listed in the McCarthy-Matthews file. The surname was actually "Griffiths."

In the case of Gordon Griffiths, he would himself confirm the allegation that he was a CP member, revealing this in a memoir relating to Robert Oppenheimer and their joint membership in a faculty Communist cell at U.C. Berkeley in the latter 1930s. In the postwar era Griffiths, like Collins, did serve with the occupation forces in Europe, though on the staff of the Foreign Economic Administration (FEA) rather than the State Department.[9]

As to the unnamed Soviet agents with whom Fierst was allegedly in contact, per FBI surveillance, one such in the Bureau's judgment was the mysterious David Wahl—"reliably reported" to be a Soviet "master spy," according to Director Hoover. The Bureau files show repeated contacts between Fierst and Wahl, though details about these are among the most heavily blacked-out portions of the record (well over 100 pages concerning Fierst, Wahl, and the two together are redacted).

Interestingly, McCarthy's reference on this point was in the plural—"members"—though the Lee list said only "member." This could have been a slip of the tongue or, more likely from the standpoint of his critics, an attempt to overstate and dramatize the issue. However, the FBI records show that Fierst had been in contact with at least two other people the Bureau spotted as members of the Soviet spy combine: Duncan Lee and Mary Jane Keeney. Thus, McCarthy's use here of the plural form, per the FBI account, was very much on target.

Theodore Geiger

Geiger was the case that Tydings subcommittee assistant counsel Robert Morris thought the panel should take a look at but that Tydings dismissed out of hand because he didn't want to waste the afternoon on topics of that nature. Accordingly, the Geiger case, along with many others, wouldn't receive a public airing and would be ignored by Tydings and the State Department in their tabulations of McCarthy suspects.

Geiger, as Morris knew, had been identified under oath before a New York legislative committee by ex-Communist William Canning as a member of a Communist unit in the latter 1930s. Geiger denied this and, based on this denial, got past the Truman security screeners. Later his new boss, Paul Hoffman of the Economic Cooperation Administration, would issue a ringing endorsement of Geiger. None of this was persuasive to McCarthy, who stayed on the Geiger case and later used it in a critique of Hoffman.

McCarthy's harping on the matter prompted Geiger's attorney, in 1956, to write McCarthy a lengthy letter containing some belated revelations about his client. Contra earlier denials by Geiger, this missive said "there is no question that Mr. Geiger was intellectually committed to Communism in the later 1930s [the period about which Canning testified], but although he wanted to join the

Communist Party and joined an organization thinking it was the party, he never actually became a member." Thereafter, said the lawyer, Geiger became disillusioned by the Hitler-Stalin pact and had broken with the comrades. The attorney then added:

> Mr. Geiger deeply regrets one aspect of his record since his break with Communism in 1940. He regrets that he did not come forward forthrightly at an early date to inform the FBI and other agencies that, although he had not actually been a member of the Communist Party, he was involved in the Communist movement in the late 1930s. Thus when Mr. Hoffman defended him in 1949 and 1950, he did so without the benefit of full disclosure of the pertinent facts by Mr. Geiger. Mr. Geiger rectified this deficiency by telling the entire story fully, cooperatively and candidly to the FBI in 1954. He realized then and realizes now that it would have been in the national interest had he spoken at a much earlier date and that he would thereby have spared himself and others much heartache and embarrassment.[10]

Indeed, it would have been better all around if Theodore Geiger—and a good many others—had told the truth in 1950, instead of spending several years in stonewalling and denial, and if such as Paul Hoffman had been less willing to clear the Geigers of the world absent all the pertinent data. Most of all, in the unfolding of the McCarthy story, it would have been extremely helpful if Millard Tydings had been concerned to learn the truth about the case rather then dismissing it as a waste of time as he rushed to castigate McCarthy.

Victor Hunt

Victor Hunt was McCarthy's case No. 65 before the Senate but wasn't stressed very much as a security problem in his own right. Rather, said McCarthy, Hunt appeared to be under the influence of another, more important suspect, who was McCarthy case No. 81 (Ruby Parsons, formerly with the Voice of America). Hunt would nonetheless provide an interesting test of McCarthy's accuracy and due diligence—and those of the State Department—in supplying data on his cases.

In response to McCarthy's charges, the State Department put out, and Tydings reprinted, materials that showed case No. 65 had resigned from State in April 1949 and thus had been gone for many moons when McCarthy went before the Senate.[11] McCarthy had been quite definite on the point, saying "this individual is also still in the State Department," with no ifs, ands, or buts. So here we seem to have a case in which McCarthy fulfilled the standard image: taking outmoded data and presenting them as current, only to be caught *in flagrante* by the fact-checkers down in Foggy Bottom.

Except that, as it developed, Hunt *was* still at the State Department, if we may credit the department's own employee records (which McCarthy was clearly using). Thus, in the department personnel directory for February 1950, at the precise moment McCarthy made his charges, Victor M. Hunt is plainly listed, along with office location and phone number. Thereafter, in State's *Biographic Register* for 1951, Victor M. Hunt is once more listed, along with a brief *vita*.

How could Victor Hunt have resigned from the State Department in April of 1949 but be listed in State's personnel directory for 1950 and in its *Biographic Register* for 1951? This seems to be quite a puzzle, to which a likely answer is that Hunt may temporarily have transferred out of the department to some other agency and then later come back in, the kind of thing that did occasionally happen in the early postwar era. In that event, by focusing only on the order of his going, it would have been possible to present him as a McCarthy case no longer on the rolls of the department (a tactic that could work as long as the suspect was nameless and couldn't be checked by outside observers against the official employee listings).

As suggested by the history of his superior, Ruby Parsons, who transferred out of State to handle communications for the Army in Europe, this appears to be a plausible scenario in the case of Hunt, though at this late date it's hard to be quite certain. What is certain, in any event, is that the State Department treatment of the matter in its tabulation of the McCarthy cases was in direct conflict with its own employee data. Conversely, McCarthy's wrap-up of the case was well grounded in the official records.

David Demarest Lloyd

Lloyd was McCarthy's case No. 9 on the Senate floor and the case he inadvertently repeated (as case No. 77). Another Lee list alum, Lloyd was the first of the anonymous suspects to be identified in public, as McCarthy had said he was a speechwriter in the White House. Since the number of people thus employed was small, it didn't take long for Lloyd's name to surface, prompting a considerable outcry and much denunciation of McCarthy.

The Lloyd case is instructive in several ways, as it shows McCarthy's backtracking efforts prior to his initial speech and also reveals how erroneous factoids get cranked into the historical record. Both aspects involved noted journalist Jack Anderson, at the time of the McCarthy speech a reporter for Drew Pearson but also on friendly terms with McCarthy (a situation that would later change in drastic fashion).

As Anderson would tell the tale, McCarthy on his return from Wheeling-Reno was looking for information to back his charges. Anderson mentioned the case of Lloyd, said he was working in the White House, and loaned McCarthy Pearson's file on Lloyd—stressing, however, that the data in it were unsubstantiated and had to be checked out. Thereafter, Anderson would write, he was thunderstruck when McCarthy read to the Senate raw unchecked information from the Pearson file as though it were established fact. The episode supposedly convinced Anderson that McCarthy was completely irresponsible and could not be trusted.[12]

This anecdote from Anderson's memoirs has been recycled by other writers as showing that McCarthy would recklessly say things about alleged suspects without bothering to check the information. However, the authors repeating this account, and Anderson himself, should have done some checking of their own before going with the columnist's story. In fact, the data McCarthy gave the Senate on Lloyd were quite plainly taken, not from some Drew Pearson file of murky allegations, but from the entries of the Lee list. There was no substantive statement about Lloyd's affiliations in the McCarthy speech that wasn't derivative from the Lee material—which was official information, not unvetted Pearson gossip[13] (see note below).*

So McCarthy didn't need Jack Anderson or a raw Drew Pearson file to make the case on Lloyd presented to the Senate. What, then, did he get from Anderson that he found of value? The answer is that Anderson knew Lloyd was working at the White House, which information McCarthy in his usual fashion combined with the Lee list revelations. We thus see both McCarthy and his critics in typical action mode—his backtracking on the contents of the list, their passing on secondhand data to his discredit without bothering to consult the record.

Leander B. Lovell

Leander Lovell was another of the strangely disappearing McCarthy cases in the State Department's 1950 tabulation, along with Victor Hunt and John T. Fishburn. In fact, the case was almost a carbon copy of the Fishburn story, arising from similar causes and exploited by State's researchers in like fashion.

In his opening Senate speech, discussing suspect No. 28, McCarthy clearly described the case of Lovell, who was also Lee list case No. 22. Anyone reading the two entries could see they were the same and, from the key provided with the Lee list, identify the case as Lovell. (The FBI, in its analysis, readily made

---

*In fact, the Lee list treatment was a good deal more damaging than McCarthy's, though his second version did include one of his upgrades. *McCarthy on Lloyd:* "Both the individual referred to and his wife—this is in the file of the investigative agency—are members of Communist front organizations. He has a relative who has a financial interest in the *Daily Worker.*" And: "The file indicates he is a very close friend of reported Communists, and that he is closely associated with members of Communist front organizations."

Lee list on Lloyd: "One informant states he is a friend of C-36, of FCC, a reported Communist. He is a member of the National Lawyers Guild and Washington Book Shop. His wife belongs to the 'League of Women Shoppers.' The applicant is a subscriber to 'New Masses' and was closely associated with members of the 'American Peace Mobilization' and 'Washington Committee for Democratic Action' [both cited as Communist fronts by Francis Biddle]. A relative of his has a financial interest in the *Daily Worker.*"

this identification.) In addition, as earlier noted, McCarthy in his backtracking efforts had found out—provisionally but correctly—that Lovell was then stationed in Frankfurt, Germany, information not appearing in the Lee list.

However, McCarthy's office helpers didn't do so well in providing the suspect's name to Tydings. In the Lee list key sequence, Lovell's name immediately followed that of one Hans Lansberg, who wasn't a State Department employee but an applicant. Evidently the McCarthy typist, in matching names and numbers, strayed up a line and typed Lansberg in place of Lovell. Thus, Lansberg's name was supplied to Tydings, though for anyone with a copy of the Lee list the case was obviously that of Lovell.

Exactly as occurred with Fishburn, the State Department pounced on this clerical error to get rid of the case entirely, ostensibly taking the Lansberg designation at face value. Its tabulation says of McCarthy case No. 28, "applicant never employed in the Department of State," which was true of Hans Lansberg but untrue of Leander Lovell, as State's researchers knew better than all others. The department was thus once more able, rather adroitly, to use a McCarthy office typo against him.

Ironically, McCarthy would later flag Lovell's name to the attention of the FBI, trying to confirm the whereabouts of the suspect he had tentatively established. This is reflected in a Hoover memo of April 10, 1950, that quotes a document forwarded by McCarthy asking, "Is Leander Lovell with the State Department in Frankfurt, Germany?" The Hoover memo adds: "Reference is made to him in the Alger Hiss trial. The Taber committee has information on Lovell [e.g., as reflected in the Lee list]."[14]

Lovell thus appeared—like Fishburn—in two different guises in the McCarthy casebook: First in the substantive case presented to the Senate, thereafter in this missive to the FBI. As the Hoover memo suggests, Lovell was known to the Bureau and other security units (the name was one of those Whittaker Chambers gave to Adolf Berle). In February 1950, Lovell was definitely on the State Department payroll, as the department listings show he was then a member of the Foreign Service, and State's *Biographic Register* for this period confirms he was indeed in Frankfurt. So, despite the error by his typist, McCarthy was in substance right about the case of Lovell.

Peveril Meigs

Though no longer in the State Department in 1950, Peveril Meigs was one of McCarthy's stronger cases—vindicating his critique of security practice then prevailing and suggesting his own appreciable impact in getting this corrected.

Meigs, McCarthy case No. 3 (No. 2 on the Lee list), was yet another transferee from OSS. He had an extensive record of radical activities, as capsuled in the Lee list and thereafter to the Senate by McCarthy. Meigs was accordingly on the radarscopes of State Department security types in 1947, but action on the case had been withheld because he was head of the State Department employees' union and the security sleuths were monitoring his contacts.*

When efforts were at last made to get Meigs out of the State Department, the subliminal methods we've reviewed were once more employed. Rather than being fired outright, he was permitted to resign, which he did in 1948. He then moved on to a position with the Army—the kind of thing McCarthy constantly deplored and would specifically stress in the case of Meigs.†

Though he had been prominent on the State Department watch list before he was permitted to resign and make the transfer, Meigs would be cleared for employment under the Truman loyalty program on April 14, 1949.[15] By this action he was "retained" as an economist and educational specialist for the Army. He thus joined the numerous ranks of those with copious derogatory information in the files who stayed on the federal payroll. However, the case would also reveal the sharp reversal in security practice that could occur when McCarthy turned up the heat.

This is reflected in a Bureau memo of March 22, 1950, regarding an inquiry from an Army officer about the case. This says Meigs "has been identified as 'case No. 3' cited by Senator McCarthy . . . It appears [from the Army officer's] closing remarks that the Army is aware of this and may be concerned over the fact that he is apparently still employed by the Army. . . . It appears that the only purpose for [the] call is the probability that the Army is concerned over Senator McCarthy's allegation regarding [Meigs] and is looking for an out."[16]

Thereafter, the Army got Meigs off its hands, this evidently as a result of the McCarthy pressure. The episode is suggestive both as to the workings of the loyalty setup before McCarthy came on the scene and the effect he had when he went public with his charges.

---

*This was, as noted, the local of a national union expelled from the CIO in 1950 on the grounds that it habitually followed the Communist line on labor and all other matters. According to a compilation by the AF of L, which watched such matters closely, other members of this State Department unit included Lois Carlisle, Francis Tuchscher, Sam Fishback, and Marcel Elinson. All these except Elinson were on the McCarthy list of cases. She was the innocuous-sounding case No. 104 selected by historian David Oshinsky for emphasis in discussion of the Lee list, though she wasn't a McCarthy suspect.

†When McCarthy first went before the Senate, it appears he didn't yet know the whereabouts of Meigs, as, in contrast to many other cases, he made no reference to where Meigs was working. However, McCarthy's researchers were on the trail and would discover the suspect was with the Army. (An undated notation in the McCarthy backup file on Meigs records "an individual by this name is listed in the Department of Defense phone directory for February 1950.")

Richard Post

Along with Frances Ferry, the case of Richard Post (McCarthy case No. 53) is among the clearest indications in the record that McCarthy had some good non-Lee sources of security data when he first addressed the Senate.

The case suggests, again, the laxness of State Department standards across the years and McCarthy's ability to come up with information concerning this performance. As it developed, Post was one of the cases on which McCarthy had *not* yet correctly nailed down the whereabouts of the suspect, initially thinking Post was still in the department when he wasn't. This deficiency, however, would be more than compensated by what McCarthy did know (and would be corrected in the roster supplied to Tydings).

In his public résumé of the case, McCarthy gave the Senate the essence of what was in the Lee list—that a "government agency had received information to the effect that he [Post] was a recognized leader in the Communist underground." This was identical to the Lee list information. However, McCarthy then made the still more sensational charge that No. 53 "has been named by a *confessed Communist spy* as part of his spy ring."[17] (Emphasis added). The Lee list had no statement to this effect, its summary of the case containing no mention of a "confessed Communist spy" being the source of the intel on Post or having any connection to the case whatever.

According to the standard treatment, this McCarthy embellishment must mean he was lying, trying to hype the case to make it seem more vivid. However, as shown by now-available records, McCarthy was telling the truth about the case, accurately adding substantive data to the file that weren't taken from the Lee list.

As we now know, the "confessed Communist spy" who named Post as a sometime member of his network was Whittaker Chambers. In fact, Chambers so identified Post on no fewer than five occasions—initially in the statement he gave to Adolf Berle, thereafter in interviews with Raymond Murphy of the State Department in 1945 and '46, then in executive hearings of the House Committee on Un-American Activities in December of 1948 and at last to a U.S. grand jury. Thus, McCarthy's melodramatic addition to the file was not only accurate but known to be so by security agents (including those at the State Department).[18]

Rowena Rommel

While it might not have appeared so at the time, and McCarthy himself didn't say it, Rowena Rommel may have been among the most significant of all his cases, equaling if not surpassing other more famous suspects.

Ms. Rommel had drawn intensive notice from State Department security types at an early date, following the Bentley revelations. A transferee into State from the Bureau of the Budget, she was identified as someone who had a lot to do with reorganization of the department and placing other people in its workforce. The point was stressed, for instance, in early 1946 by security expert Ben Mandel, then working with Raymond Murphy at State, in an interview with Bureau agents.[19]

Thereafter, Rommel would show up on the roster of cases compiled by the Panuch investigators and, according to State Department records kept by Sam Klaus, was recommended for dismissal by security screeners. However, this didn't happen, and she thereafter emerged as one of the suspects on the Lee list. Rep. Fred Busbey then spotlighted her case in a lengthy statement in March 1948, again with emphasis on her role in placing others with dubious security records.[20]

By far the strongest evidence for this critique—in essence admitted by Rommel, according to the Lee list—was that she was the person responsible for bringing Robert Miller to the department. As Miller was a Bentley-identified Soviet agent, this aspect of Rommel's record was in itself sufficient to put security investigators on alert. Add the fact that it was Rommel who discussed Miller's security troubles with him in December of 1946 and tried to intervene with John Peurifoy in his behalf. Finally, it was Rommel's link to Miller that caused Sam Klaus to flag her to the notice of Hamilton Robinson during the changeover at the security office in February of 1947.

So there was quite a paper trail on Rommel, mostly tying her to Miller— "the greatest security risk" the department had harbored, according to the Lee list compilers. As Miller's sponsor at State, confidante while he was there, and champion when he was being ousted, Rommel was obviously thick with this Bentley-identified apparatchik. All of which would have been enough to suggest she was a security risk herself under the most forgiving standards. Yet, like many other cases mentioned, Rommel was still on the State Department payroll in February 1950. She was McCarthy's case No. 51.

Charles W. Thayer

The final case to be considered here is indicative both as to McCarthy's sources and the much-controverted question of his methods. Thayer was yet another transplant from OSS who had become the head of VOA, a frequent target of McCarthy. He wasn't, however, on the list of McCarthy suspects presented to the Senate or the supplementary list supplied to Tydings. (Nor was he a Lee list alum.) His was nonetheless a most revealing McCarthy case.

On at least two occasions in 1950, McCarthy called attention to Thayer, but strictly on a confidential basis. In one instance in March, he mentioned the case in an executive session of the Tydings panel; in another, he flagged it to the notice of the FBI. According to Bureau agent Mickey Ladd, in a memo of March 30, McCarthy "informed me that next week he intends to call on the State Department to fire Charles W. Thayer. In this regard he stated he was not going to call him by name but indicated that in his, McCarthy's opinion, Thayer was one of the worst types of [blacked out]."[21]

These comments are the more noteworthy as McCarthy had in his possession an extensive dossier on Thayer, comprising charges of two different types: allegations that as an officer in OSS in the middle 1940s, Thayer had consorted with and aided pro-Soviet and pro-Tito agents in Yugoslavia, and charges of a more personal nature, concerning alleged homosexual conduct. As earlier noted, this was apparently a State Department loyalty file, and a fairly complete one, running to better than forty pages. That such a file was in the possession of McCarthy says a lot about the kind of information he was then receiving and the inside nature of his sources.[22]

The other point about the Thayer file is that McCarthy, so far as the available records show, never went public with this information, though it was of abundant nature. This says something about his methods and his reluctance to name a suspect using data on personal matters. The Thayer case was of interest also in that he was the brother-in-law of Charles E. Bohlen, a much more imposing State Department figure on whom McCarthy would likewise obtain security data, leading to an historic showdown in the Senate. That famous episode, however, wouldn't happen until three years later.

CHAPTER 26

Some Public Cases

THE McCarthy cases involved in the State Department loyalty hearings ranged from his written lists of 100 or so anonymous suspects, who stayed mostly in the shadows, to big-name targets such as Owen Lattimore, Philip Jessup, and John Service, who got the bulk of the headlines at the time and most of the historical notice later.

Between these extremes of fame were a half-dozen intermediate cases McCarthy read out in open sessions of the Tydings panel and are thus part of the public record, though usually treated in cursory fashion in retrospectives of the era. These cases, as it happens, are of considerable value in gauging the merits of McCarthy's charges, as he provided fairly extensive information on them at the time and more would subsequently be revealed about them.

The cases are of interest also anent the charge that McCarthy was simply recycling data from the Lee list, as virtually none of the documentation he used was derivative from that roster. From a survey of this group of suspects, it's possible to learn something about the evidence McCarthy had, where this in all probability came from, and how accurately he construed it. The cases also reveal a thing or two about State Department security practice of the day and the methods of the Tydings panel in clearing each and every McCarthy suspect.

Dorothy Kenyon

The first name McCarthy brought before the subcommittee, after all the initial sparring, was a surprise to most observers. The case was that of Dorothy Kenyon, a former New York City judge and State Department appointee to a U.N. commission on the status of women. It seemed a curious selection. Judge Kenyon wasn't a well-known or high-ranking official, and her connection to the State Department had recently concluded. She was in all respects a less important case than Jessup, Service, or John Carter Vincent, any one of whom McCarthy might plausibly have led with.

However, some clues as to the choice of Kenyon may be found in the type of information McCarthy was using. His case consisted entirely of a recitation of the numerous Communist-front groups with which the judge had been connected. McCarthy said there were twenty-eight of these, though he didn't actually present this number and a check of the records suggests there were others he could have cited. One obvious feature of this approach is that it was a matter of public information, if one knew where to find it. This would have been for McCarthy a most useful aspect. He couldn't get at the State Department files, but he could, with proper guidance, document the case of Kenyon.

Also, the necessary guidance was now available in the person of J. B. Matthews. Most of the material McCarthy had on Kenyon came from or related to Appendix IX of the House Committee on Un-American Activities, and Matthews was the main compiler of that volume. Matthews would have known a lot about Judge Kenyon and would have had access to or in his possession the documents on which Appendix IX was founded. Putting all of that together not only makes the choice of Kenyon less mysterious but gives us some notion of how McCarthy was at this point proceeding. Having hooked up with Matthews, he would make extensive use of Appendix IX, information on Communist-front affiliations, and the expertise of Matthews in general. And Matthews, as shall be seen, would be a crucial figure in later chapters of the story.

For the moment, the most significant thing about the case was the reaction of Judge Kenyon to the documentation McCarthy presented. To read some sketchy treatments of this affray, one might suppose her appearance was a huge success—that she courageously faced down McCarthy, denounced his charges as spurious and demeaning, and more or less mopped the floor with him in a ringing defense of her views and reputation. An examination of the hearing record, however, does little to support this verdict.

In fact, once Kenyon got through her prepared remarks and was subject to cross-examination by Bourke Hickenlooper, her performance must have left her supporters cringing. An embarrassing episode unfolded as Hickenlooper walked her through a lengthy roster of officially cited Communist fronts and asked about her involvement with them. In this sequence, the clarion tones of her opening statement faded into halfway admissions, hedges, and—most of all—an apparently total loss of memory. Some of her responses—each concerning a separate, officially cited front activity—were as follows:

- "I remember nothing about it. . . . [then, experiencing some recall] I got out very early and washed my hands of it." (Consumers National Federation)
- "I think I made a speech there . . . I had nothing to do with it, according to my records, except to serve for a short period on the Committee for Free Public Education." (American Committee for Democracy and Intellectual Freedom)
- "I haven't the faintest idea. I can't even remember it . . ." (Greater New York Emergency Conference on Inalienable Rights)
- "I haven't any recollection. . . . I don't remember anything about this. . . . I haven't any recollection of it." *Hickenlooper:* "Your name is on the second page." *Kenyon:* "I don't recall having attended the dinner." (Testimonial dinner for the prominent Communist Ferdinand Smith)
- "I have no recollection of anything except the Gerson controversy itself. . . . I have no recollection of it and this seems to me incredible. . . ." (Public group letter defending the naming of well-known Communist Simon Gerson to a staff post with the New York City Council)
- "I have absolutely no recollection of having done anything of the sort. . . ." (Group letter in behalf of the Veterans of the Abraham Lincoln Brigade)
- "I have very little recollection of it myself. . . . I have no recollection of it. . . . So far as I am concerned, I have forgotten everything about it. . . ." (Political Prisoners Bail Fund Committee)
- "I have absolutely no recollection of that whatever, Senator. . . ." (Group letter in behalf of convicted Communist Morris Schappes)
- "I have absolutely no recollection. . . . I have no recollection whatever. . . ." (Films for Democracy)
- "I have absolutely no recollection. . . ." (Citizens Committee to Aid Striking Seamen)
- "I have absolutely no recollection. . . . I have difficulty remembering even this connection with it. . . ." (Conference on Pan American Democracy)
- "I have absolutely no recollection of any such thing. . . ." (Milk Consumers Protective Committee)[1]

From these and similar answers, Ms. Kenyon appeared to be a chronic amnesiac who had trouble remembering much of anything whatever. In which case, it's hard to see how she could have carried out the duties of a judge or those of a State Department appointee to the United Nations. (On the other hand, while experiencing almost total lack of recall about her own involvement with such groups, she did much better in remembering exculpatory data about certain eminent people connected to them.)

Based on the Hickenlooper Q & A, there doesn't seem to be much doubt that Judge Kenyon had been linked with a phenomenally large number of front groups, just as McCarthy contended. The Tydings panel estimated the number at twenty; and while the subcommittee downplayed the significance of these connections, it's well to remember that, from the Biddle era forward, such designations weren't whimsically arrived at. Even more to the point, under the Truman loyalty program, connection with even *one* such group was a factor supposedly weighed in gauging the security status of employees.

Yet, as brought out in the hearings, nobody in the State Department had ever asked Judge Kenyon a single question about these affiliations. This was developed in a further exchange between Hickenlooper and Kenyon:

> QUESTION: Before you took public employment as a representative of this country in the United Nations did any official discuss with you the allegations of your membership in organizations that had been declared subversive?
> ANSWER: Never. They have come and talked to me about other people.[2]

Thus, not only was McCarthy's charge about Kenyon's front connections supported by the hearing record, so was the arguably more important point that the State Department wasn't enforcing the security standards that nominally governed its operations.

Haldore Hanson

Haldore Hanson was the second of the McCarthy public cases and, considering all the factors involved, might easily have been the first.

Hanson was a full-time State Department employee, as Judge Kenyon wasn't. He had previously served on the staff of Assistant Secretary of State William Benton—one of the numerous group of McCarthy suspects once employed in that office. At the time of McCarthy's charges, Hanson headed a division at State that dealt with matters of foreign aid. Most to the present point, he had in the latter 1930s gone on record with some revealing comments about the Communist cause in China, and otherwise had a *vita* that made him an obvious McCarthy target.

McCarthy's Exhibit A was a book Hanson published in 1939 called *Humane Endeavour,** based on his experiences and observations as a journalist in China. The book was full of plaudits for the Red Chinese similar to those

---

*The British spelling was used, as the phrase was lifted from a Gilbert and Sullivan lyric.

expressed a few years later by John Service, a Hanson friend and sometime roommate. In the 1930s, a united front was in effect between the Reds and Chiang Kai-shek against Japan, and in this context Chiang merited some kind words from Hanson, as well as some that weren't so kind. However, Hanson showed no similar ambiguity toward the Red Chinese, on whom he showered lavish kudos. McCarthy quoted some of these comments, and with one exception the quotes were accurate in detail,* leaving no doubt about the author's ardent liking for the Yenan comrades.[3]

The pro-Communist message in the Hanson book came in two different guises: statements in his own behalf as to the nature of the Communist program and its leaders; and the views of others, including the Reds themselves and their admirers, presented as credible evidence on the merits of Mao's revolution. The net effect is a more or less continuous hymn of praise, albeit spread out in different sections and interwoven with other topics not bearing on the issue. Following are some excerpts:

"The Red leaders organized the masses, gave them discipline and something worth fighting for." "Chiang Kai-shek suppressed news of the victory because he feared the popularity of the Communists." "The Red leaders became heroes to thousands of students in China . . . a self sacrificing spirit among these leaders seeped down through the ranks." ". . . the whole [Red] army has a democratic spirit. . . ." "Right wing groups in the China government still want a one party administration. *They are fighting against the democratic revolution as proposed by Mao tse-tung and the Communists.*"[4] (Emphasis added.)

There was more in similar vein, including praise of Mao ("a completely selfless man"), curt dismissal of Communist atheism ("the Chinese leaders are not anti-Christian"), denial of Soviet influence ("the old bogy that Soviet Russia is directing the activities of the Chinese Communists"), and so on. Thrown in as a kind of bonus was a claim that the Soviets themselves had brought reform and progress to Asia: "Russian policy among the Outer Mongolians appealed to the common people by exposing the corruption of the priests and princes; aristocratic privilege was abolished."[†5]

All these effusions were offered by Hanson in his own persona. They were wrapped around the pro-Communist views of others, cited as if they were prosaic, factual statements. Examples in this genre included quotes from Maoist guerrilla leaders, to wit: ". . . we decided to give each village a democratic council and complete political freedom." And: "We wanted to be the first area in China to achieve genuine democracy. . . . The Communist Party, like the liberal group, is placing its faith in the democratic form of government." This

---

*Hanson had described the Chinese Reds as "hard-headed, hard shooting realists" (among other things). McCarthy quoted this as "straight shooting."

†This was also a favorite theme of Professor Lattimore. See Chapter 29.

Red boilerplate was served up by Hanson with no hint of skepticism or need for any possible rebuttal.[6]

In short, McCarthy was not mistaken in saying *Humane Endeavour* was laced with pro-Red propaganda. And there were still other such aspects of the Hanson record that McCarthy correctly noted. One was Hanson's tie-in during the 1930s with the magazine *Democracy,* which McCarthy said was a pro-Communist publication. In seeking to deny this, Hanson cited the involvement with the journal of allegedly distinguished writers and academics of non-Communist outlook. In its usual mode, the Tydings report uncritically accepted this denial and repeated it as a finding.

What this Hanson-Tydings rebuttal omitted was that the chief editors of *Democracy* were the pro-Red author Edgar Snow and his wife Nym Wales, both revealed in Cold War records as agents of the Communist interest (Snow as at best an obedient fellow traveler who took instruction from the Communist Party, Wales as an identified party member). Hanson himself had mentioned Snow and his wife as leaders of this publishing venture in *Humane Endeavour* but forgot to give them credit before the Senate.[7] The Tydings panel, invincibly clueless, made no mention of the couple, apparently knew nothing about them, and made no effort to find out.

All this, however, was but prologue to a major bombshell of the hearings, one of several touched off by Louis Budenz, formerly of the *Daily Worker.* Asked to be specific about people he knew to be concealed members of the Communist Party, Budenz began reciting a considerable list. In order, he named Ella Winter, Joseph Barnes, Victor Yakhontoff, and Guenther Stein. Then came the bombshell: "Haldore Hanson. I knew him only from official reports to be a member of the Communist Party." And further: "I . . . knew this not as a general matter but from official information received. . . . Not gossip around the headquarters; official information. I carried his name with me."[8]

This was one of several such identifications by Budenz that floored the majority members of the panel. They managed, however, to regain their footing in time to clear Hanson in sweeping fashion, finding no indication in his case that there was anything amiss with security goings-on at State. *Humane Endeavour* was just reporting, *Democracy* a respectable journal, and the Budenz testimony "hearsay." These see-no-evil comments don't tell us much about the security drill at State but say a lot as to what it took to raise doubts about that drill with Tydings and his Democratic colleagues.

Esther Brunauer

Mrs. Brunauer was a former official at the American Association of University Women who got into the State Department in 1944, showed up like Hanson

"DR. ESTHER BRUNAUER WILL PRESIDE"

A flyer advertising a 1936 meeting of the American Friends of the Soviet Union and the prominent involvement of Mrs. Brunauer.

"Who Rules

IN

Soviet Russia ?"

A LECTURE BY

MYRA PAGE

Author—Educator—Lecturer

— at —

Typographical Temple,

423 G Street, N. W.

Thursday, June 11th, 1936

8:30 P. M.

DR. ESTHER BRUNAUER, will preside

"A timely and interesting discussion on a much debated subject by a well-known American writer, who has spent 2 years in The Soviet Union. Myra Page is the author of several books. Her most recent one is "Moscow Yankee". She is an instructor at Commonwealth College in Arkansas. Formerly on the staff of the "Moscow Daily News", she is a contributor to the "Nation", "New Republic", and other American periodicals and is on the Editorial staff of the Magazine "Soviet Russia Today".

Admission 35 Cents   Auspices A. F. S. U.

Source: J. B. Matthews papers, Duke University

and several other McCarthy suspects on the staff of Assistant Secretary William Benton, and held various posts in the department dealing with the United Nations.*

She was also a Lee list alum, the only one from that particular roster to become one of McCarthy's public cases. It's noteworthy, however, that McCarthy's presentation of the case to Tydings was derived almost entirely from non-Lee sources. These included data about asserted Communist fronting on her part and loyalty/security information about her husband, Stephen, a scientist working for the Navy.

When Mrs. Brunauer took the stand, she made an impassioned denial of McCarthy's charges and presented a sheaf of testimonials in her behalf from important people. She also tagged McCarthy with at least one alleged error. He said she had served as an assistant to Alger Hiss at the United Nations founding conference in San Francisco. This wasn't so, she countered, as she had worked with the American delegation there while Hiss had been secretary general of the whole shebang. This Brunauer answer, however, was itself a bit of an evasion, obscuring the substantive point at issue.

As it turned out, Mrs. Brunauer had been a State Department staffer at the Dumbarton Oaks conference of 1944, which laid the groundwork for the founding of the United Nations. The executive secretary of the American group at Dumbarton Oaks was Hiss, who thus would have been her superior at this U.N.-related confab. Thereafter, she was a Hiss subordinate in the Office of Special Political Affairs at State. As she had been an aide to Hiss in any event, the statement about the San Francisco conference was hardly an outrageous smear but got ostentatiously counted by Tydings as a McCarthy error.[9]

Other McCarthy allegations about Mrs. Brunauer were well substantiated by the record, though it takes some sleuthing to discern this. One charge was that she had presided at a 1936 meeting of the American Friends of the Soviet Union, an egregious front group, featuring the pro-Soviet speaker Myra Page. In the manner of Judge Kenyon, Mrs. Brunauer claimed to have no recollection of this meeting, but the proof of her involvement was clear (see page 351). It was moreover revealed that she had spoken at yet another gathering of the same front group two years before.

Likewise, there was no denying another McCarthy charge, though Mrs. Brunauer and the Tydings panel did all they could in trying to obscure it: that she had participated in a "call" for a national meeting of the American Youth Congress (AYC)—a group the Communists had famously taken over at its inception, and cited in the Francis Biddle list of 1942. As shown in the McCarthy exhibits, her name appeared on a call for a "Congress of Youth," a conclave of the AYC held in New York City in 1938. According to Mrs. Brunauer, however,

---

* She was in fact, as the backstage records show, a particular favorite and protégé of Benton.

the meeting she sponsored had nothing to do with the subversive AYC. Her denial was, in the usual manner, echoed by the Tydings report, which found "no evidence before the committee that this particular matter was under the domination of the American Youth Congress."[10]

This was, even for Tydings, a bit much. In fact, the evidence linking the Brunauer effort with the AYC was ample. As noted in Appendix IX, the Brunauer-sponsored "call" and accompanying list of cosigners were taken "from the proceedings of the Congress of Youth, *being the fifth national gathering of the American Youth Congress.*" Likewise, a roll call of officers chosen at this meeting tells us, "elected officers listed above *constitute the Cabinet of the American Youth Congress.*"[11] (Emphasis added.) In sum, the conclave Mrs. Brunauer sponsored was a meeting *of* the AYC—information that Tydings and his staffers had in their possession. Her denial was rather like saying the Republican national convention has no connection to the Republican Party.

A related McCarthy charge was that Brunauer had been on the executive board of the American Union for Concerted Peace Efforts (formerly the Committee for Concerted Peace Efforts, the same group with the same leadership—her name appearing under both designations). McCarthy said the group had been identified as subversive by the House Committee on Un-American Activities and that "the leader of the group was Clarence Hathaway, editor of *The Daily Worker.*"[12] Mrs. Brunauer again denied all, saying the Peace Efforts operation was intensely patriotic, there were no Reds or pro-Reds in it, and Clarence Hathaway had no connection to it.

Once more, so far as Tydings was concerned, a denial was a refutation. In discussing the Peace Efforts agitation and clearing Mrs. Brunauer for her involvement with it, his report came down hard on the Clarence Hathaway issue—using the same ingenious phrasing that disposed of inconvenient data about the AYC. "There is no evidence before us," said the report, "to support the allegation that the editor of the *Daily Worker* was involved therewith."[13]

Again, a check of the records shows that the evidence existed—albeit not deemed "before" the Tydings panel—though it also tells us McCarthy made an error of his own in his allusion to it. The basis for his charge was a 1944 report of the House Committee on Un-American Activities that described the Peace Efforts operation as supporting "the same goals as the Communist front American League for Peace and Democracy" and saying Clarence Hathaway was "a leader" in this project (not "the leader," as stated by McCarthy).*[14]

---

*This House committee report was in turn referenced to a story in the *Daily Worker* describing a massive "collective security" petition allegedly signed by 1,000 people and highlighting the names of five "notables" connected with this effort, including such as Henry Stimson, Gov. Elmer Benson of Minnesota—and Clarence Hathaway, editor of the *Daily Worker*. Obviously, the motives of such as Stimson in signing such a petition would have been quite different from those of Clarence Hathaway.

So, sorting out the details, we find that McCarthy upgraded Clarence Hathaway from "a" leader in the Peace Efforts agitation to "the" leader, obviously a different connotation in terms of Communist influence. Over against this we may place the categorical statements of Mrs. Brunauer and the Tydings panel that Clarence Hathaway had no involvement with the enterprise whatever. Thus, neither side in this dispute earned top marks for precision. Readers may judge for themselves which of the two errors was more misleading.

All told, the Communist-front affiliations of Mrs. Brunauer weren't of overwhelming number—nor did McCarthy press the point unduly. Far more significant, he said, was the case of her husband, Stephen, working on classified weapons research for the Navy. Intimating that he knew something of the security record on Stephen, McCarthy raised points he said the Tydings panel should look into: whether Stephen had been subject to security investigation for the past ten years; whether he was a close friend of the absconded Communist Noel Field; and whether Stephen Brunauer himself was not an admitted former member of the Communist Party.*[15]

Tydings gave no credence to any of this, dismissing the case out of hand on the grounds that Stephen wasn't in the State Department. Nonetheless, the panel did manage to give Stephen a "clearance" of sorts, saying of McCarthy's charges: "The record contains a complete denial of these allegations, as well as substantial evidence to support that denial."[16] This was in the inimitable Tydings manner true, as *Brunauer himself* denied the allegations and the subcommittee printed the denial, so "the record" unquestionably did "contain" such a denial. (Likewise, the "substantial evidence" was the material Brunauer presented.) Thus, both Brunauers were in effect cleared by Tydings, based strictly on their own assertions.

To all of this there would be a sequel. In April 1951, a year after the Tydings hearings, both Brunauers were suspended from their official jobs in proceedings under the Hiram Bingham loyalty board. The official summaries of the two cases tracked closely with McCarthy's charges. In the case of Esther, the particulars included allegations that she had been active with the American Friends of the Soviet Union, the Union (Committee) for Concerted Peace Ef-

---

"Collective security" was CP jargon at the time for getting Western nations to help defend the USSR from Hitler—a line instantly reversed with the coming of the Nazi-Soviet pact.

As to the various upstanding and patriotic citizens serving with Mrs. Brunauer on the board of Peace Efforts, there were some she (and Tydings) forgot to mention. One of these was William Hinckley, head of the American Youth Congress; another was Margaret Forsyth, an officer of the American League for Peace and Democracy. As a study of the various boards and panels reveals, there was a considerable overlap between the Peace Efforts agitation and these notorious fronts.

*As would later be brought out by Stephen Brunauer himself, most of the adverse information on his case stemmed from the Office of Naval Intelligence, which he blamed for his ongoing security troubles. McCarthy apparently got his material from the ONI, in which event the most likely conduit was Robert Morris, who had been an officer with that service.

forts, the American Friends of German Freedom (a Paul Hagen operation),* and in the latter 1920s and early '30s had been in close and habitual contact with persons known to be Communist or pro-Communist.

In the case of Stephen, the charges were that he had been linked with Communist or pro-Red groups from 1924 to 1932 and "possibly later," had been an "underground" member of the Communist Party, and kindred allegations. Some of this Stephen admitted, but he said it was ancient history and that he had long since renounced all such sympathies and contacts. These explanations might have been availing had not other items in the record worked against him. Particularly damaging to his case were charges that he tried to obtain a special pass to attend the Bikini atomic tests in 1946, was turned down in these efforts, and then misrepresented the facts about the matter when questioned.[17]

In the end, Stephen was subject to dismissal by the Navy and declined to fight this at a hearing. His case rebounded on that of Esther, who was found not to be disloyal but was adjudged a security risk because of her ties to Stephen. All this occurred, it's worth repeating, under the Truman-Bingham loyalty setup, two years after the cases of both Brunauers had been casually brushed aside by Tydings.

Gustavo Duran

The foregoing episodes tell us something about security practice at the State Department before McCarthy came along and the handling of such matters by Millard Tydings. None, however, was more revealing than the case of Gustavo Duran, one of the most instructive in Cold War records.

In this instance, McCarthy to all appearances assumed the investigative burden Tydings thrust upon him, producing copious documentation on Duran, pointing up the security issues involved, and providing leads for further investigation. The essence of the McCarthy case was the same as that set forth in Chapter 12: that Duran had been named in intelligence reports as a Soviet agent in the Spanish Civil War, despite this had been taken on by State, and thereafter moved with evident ease to the United Nations—where he was employed when McCarthy made his charges.

McCarthy stressed the porous to nonexistent security measures that allowed Duran to enter the State Department and stay there for several years, and raised the further question of how someone with Duran's record had so readily moved to the U.N. On the latter point, Tydings initially concurred, asserting: "Senator McCarthy, I would like to say that your inquiry that we should find out who got him the job in the United Nations . . . will be part of our inquiry. We don't know who he is, whether innocent or guilty, but we will find out anyway."[18]

* See Chapter 7.

In the event, no such inquest would happen. As earlier noted, data on Gustavo Duran were among the records the Truman White House explicitly refused to provide the Tydings panel or the Seth Richardson LRB. As with the twenty-two net additional McCarthy names that were supposed to be followed up by the subcommittee but were dropped entirely, Tydings accepted this constraint as one of his own ground rules, blandly dismissing the Duran case as falling outside the panel's province. This despite the fact that Duran, as a former State Department employee, was clearly within the scope of S.R. 231.*

Among other intriguing features, the Duran affair provided some further clues as to McCarthy's information sources. Virtually all the data McCarthy presented on the case had previously been cited by Reps. Parnell Thomas (R-N.J.) and Alvin O'Konski (R-Wis.), and it seems obvious that McCarthy inherited the files they had assembled. However, as he often did, McCarthy added a special fillip of his own, making the matter still more contentious. The provocation for this was a lengthy cover story in *Time* in October 1951 under the heading: "Demagogue McCarthy: Does He Deserve Well of the Republic?"

As foreshadowed by the phrasing, *Time* concluded that, no, McCarthy certainly didn't deserve well of the republic, and one of the main reasons he didn't was his shameful treatment of Duran. After giving a summary of McCarthy's charges in the case, *Time* offered its own Olympian judgment: "Duran, never a Red, was definitely and clearly anti-Communist."[19] The basis for this flat assertion wasn't clear, and became the less so when McCarthy, in his uncanny fashion, came up with additional data on the case from the files of *Time* itself.

This material confirmed the major points about Duran that McCarthy had made in his indictment and included a 1947 cover memo from James Shepley, then a Washington correspondent for *Time*. Among the topics addressed by Shepley was a defense offered by Duran and his supporters that it was a case of mistaken identity and that some other Gustavo Duran had been the bad guy, now being confused with the good Gustavo. Shepley sardonically debunked this thesis, concluding with the comment that "both Duran and [blank] are considered flatly to be MVD [KGB] secret agents."[20]

McCarthy put all this Shepley material in the *Congressional Record*, prompting protests that he had "stolen" memos belonging to *Time*. (What apparently happened was that someone at *Time* who didn't like what was going

---

* As with Stephen Brunauer, Tydings wasn't content merely to finesse the issue of Duran but handled things so as to tilt the record in the suspect's favor. This was done by inviting Duran to respond to McCarthy's charges as he wished, either in person or in writing. Duran prudently chose the latter, submitting a lengthy statement that ostensibly answered McCarthy's charges and argued that all such assertions were the malicious doing of the Franco regime in Spain. This was reprinted verbatim in the Tydings report, following a skeletal outline of McCarthy's charges, so that the Duran response by volume outstripped the McCarthy version by a ratio of about five to one. Duran was thus able to get his apologia in the record without running the gauntlet of rebuttal or cross-examination.

on there had leaked the Shepley info to him.) When McCarthy then brought the matter to the attention of Henry Luce, *Time*'s founder/publisher answered that the magazine hadn't used the Shepley data because it wasn't conclusively known that Duran was a Soviet agent.[21] (That of course was true, but a far cry from *Time*'s statement that "Duran, never a Red, was definitely and clearly anti-Communist.")

An epilogue to all of this would develop a half-century later when Yale University Press published Soviet archival records pertaining to the Spanish Civil War, under the title *Spain Betrayed,* showing the efforts of the Kremlin to control and exploit the Spanish fighting. The documents included a roll call of Loyalist commanders and their party/ideological affiliations. Listed under the "Communist" designation was Gustavo Duran. Also included were excerpts from the dispatches of the infamous "General Kleber" (Manfred Stern), one of the main Soviet commissars in the Spanish struggle.

These dispatches revealed that, among Kleber's other responsibilities, he was the commanding officer of Duran, and included such statements as the following: "An excellent fellow, intelligent and dedicated to the party, a young party member, Comrade Duran, who served as a translator through the time in Madrid and at the fronts, I made my adjutant and, in fact, my chief of staff." And: ". . . my interpreter and adjutant, Duran, was an absolutely worthy commander and commanded a division." This was high praise indeed from a Soviet proconsul typically sparing in kudos for others.[22]

In these materials, there is no mention of a second Gustavo Duran active in the Spanish fighting who was "definitely and clearly anti-Communist," nor have there to date been any sightings of this doppelgänger in other histories of the conflict. All of which would seem to settle the question of who, in the Duran dispute, "deserved well of the republic."

TWO final suspects in this roster of midlevel McCarthy cases may be handled rather briefly. One was Prof. Frederick Schuman, who, despite a record of Communist-front affiliation exceeding that of Dorothy Kenyon, got invited to address a State Department gathering in 1946 on the then-dawning problems of the Cold War. When McCarthy made an issue of this, the State Department/Tydings answer was that, after all, Professor Schuman had given only one such lecture. That appeared to be true enough, but begged the questions of why he had been invited to give any such lecture at all and who asked him to do so. Some insight on that point would have been helpful in understanding what was then going on at State, but the Tydings panel, in normal mode, saw no reason to pursue it.

The last case in this group, and one of the more ironic, was Prof. Harlow Shapley. His record of Communist-front affiliations rivaled that of Schuman; in addition, he had served as chairman of a notorious Soviet-spawned operation in 1949 called the World Peace Conference. This was so blatant a pro-Moscow venture that none other than Dean Acheson would describe it as a "sounding board" for Communist propaganda.[23] Yet, McCarthy noted, Dr. Shapley had before this twice been appointed by the State Department, when Acheson was Under Secretary, as a U.S. representative liaising with UNESCO, and was still so liaising in 1950. (An instance, it would appear, of the left hand not knowing what the far-left hand was doing.) And these, as noted, were merely some of McCarthy's midlevel suspects. The big McCarthy cases, some very big indeed, were in all respects much more revealing.

Postscript

As to whether loyalty-security problems in the federal government had been cleaned up before McCarthy came on the scene, it's worth pausing to reflect that the vast majority of the suspects discussed in the preceding pages were still serving in official jobs in 1950.

Of the public cases noted in this chapter, Haldore Hanson, Esther and Stephen Brunauer, Gustavo Duran, and Harlow Shapley were all occupying official posts of one sort or another when McCarthy made his charges—though Duran was at the United Nations and Shapley held a noncompensated appointment at State. Among McCarthy's other public cases, to be discussed in more detail hereafter, both John Stewart Service and Philip Jessup were holding down responsible jobs in the department, while Professor Lattimore was off on a mysterious junket for the United Nations.

Among the less celebrated McCarthy cases discussed in Chapter 25, only one—Richard Post—wasn't on an official payroll when McCarthy made his early speeches and went before the Tydings panel. All the others—Askwith, Carlisle, Ferry, Fierst, Geiger, Hunt, Lloyd, Lovell, Meigs, Rommel, and Thayer—were serving in official jobs in 1950. Seven of these were in the State Department, and three had moved from State to other official venues—just as McCarthy contended.

Add to this line-up still other cases discussed in previous chapters: Solomon Adler, O. Edmund Clubb, V. Frank Coe, John Paton Davies, Cora Dubois, Stanley Graze, Mary Jane Keeney, Raymond Ludden, Philleo Nash, Franz Neumann, Edward Posniak, Philip Raine, William Remington, William Stone, John Carter Vincent, David Weintraub, and David Zablodowsky. All these people, too, were found working in official jobs in 1950, mostly at the State Department but also at the White House, Treasury, Commerce, and the global organizations.

This is but a sampling of the total roster of the original McCarthy cases then at official posts, and a considerable number of others would surface in still later inquests. It also doesn't include such notorious suspects as Robert Oppenheimer and Edward Condon—both on the McCarthy radar screen but neither considered one of his cases—also occupying official posts in 1950. From all of which it would appear that loyalty-security problems were by no means over and done with pre-McCarthy. As earlier seen, however, once he applied the blowtorch of public notice to such cases, things had a sudden way of changing.

CHAPTER 27

Tempest in a Teacup

S O FAR AS press and public were aware, the loyalty/security battles of the early 1950s were a partisan shoot-out between the Republican maverick Joe McCarthy and the Democratic administration of the feisty Harry Truman.

That impression was correct up to a point, but didn't go nearly far enough in gauging the scope and nature of the conflict. Nor could it have done so, as some of the heaviest fighting was in secret, the facts about it concealed for decades. Behind the scenes and out of the headlines, a grim twilight struggle was being waged inside the executive branch itself, pitting officials in the Department of Justice against J. Edgar Hoover and a rebellious FBI, keeper of the security data.

At issue in this dispute was what exactly should and shouldn't be said about the McCarthy charges, how much should be disclosed or held back, and how to phrase answers to dicey questions about security problems of the 1940s. Conflicts of this type occurred on several fronts, including the State Department's security records and the cases of specific McCarthy suspects whose files were locked up in the White House. However, by far the biggest single battle involved the *Amerasia* scandal and what to say about it as the Tydings hearings inched their way toward this still-ticking time bomb. In this struggle, the combatants were backed into fairly narrow corners, which made the fighting especially bitter.

From one angle, the position of Truman Justice was the more complex and awkward, which caused its spokesmen to do and say things one has to presume they didn't want to. In the view of the department, the *Amerasia* affair might have been a horror movie titled *The Thing That Wouldn't Die.* Pre-McCarthy, the scandal had been twice buried—first by the fix that let John Service walk, then by the pro forma Hobbs inquiry that found nothing amiss in the way the case was handled. Justice had been involved in both these efforts—the main cover-up at the beginning and the cover-up of the cover-up before the Congress.

Now, thanks to the interfering Joe McCarthy, the whole thing had been exhumed again—a collage of crimes and lies, including theft of official papers, cover-up, perjury, and grand jury rigging—so yet another burial was called for. Wielding the shovel this time was Senator Tydings, who would reprise the Hobbs performance, opining that the case was no big deal and that Truman Justice nobly did its duty by it. Suggestions of a fix, said Tydings, were a "disgusting" smear of prosecutor Robert Hitchcock and an insult to Judge James Proctor.[1]

But of course there had been a fix, though Judge Proctor was completely in the dark about it; Hitchcock, on the other hand, was one of the officials at Justice most deeply implicated in the plot to free John Service. He, James McInerney, and James McGranery had all told the Hobbs committee the case died of its own inertia and shouldn't have happened to begin with. Now they would have to trudge back up Capitol Hill to do the job again in the new hearings prompted by McCarthy.

A federal official fixing any case, one supposes, would be concerned about the implications of such action, but rigging a case of this astounding nature would have made the troubling aspects even more so. Beyond this was the fact that the FBI knew the case was fixed and had the wiretap logs to prove it. And while Justice officials may not have been privy to this early on, they would be advised about it later. All of which added up to a very tight spot for Truman Justice.

Meanwhile, FBI Director Hoover had problems of his own. Though by tradition and Bureau precept nonpolitical and quasi-independent, the FBI was an arm of Justice, taking its orders from the Attorney General and keeping its mouth shut in public on controverted matters. The standing rule was that if anything like *Amerasia* was to be the subject of quotable comment, that would come from the department, not the Bureau. Now, however, the FBI knew the case was rigged and that Justice itself had been complicit. So Hoover's bureaucratic obligations pointed him in one direction, his knowledge of the facts in quite another.

At any given moment, Hoover could have blown the whole thing sky-high, a dread possibility that undoubtedly occurred to officials at Justice—this over against the Bureau's technical subordination, culture of silence, and long history of discretion. Even short of full and purposeful exposure, FBI agents were going to be called before the Tydings panel to be quizzed concerning the scandal and the Bureau's knowledge of it. And Hoover's men weren't about to perjure themselves to protect the higher-ups at Justice.

This situation led to a terrific struggle in which the FBI and Truman Justice repeatedly clashed on what to say to Tydings. The delicate problem facing Justice was how to get enough cooperation from the Bureau to keep the cover-up intact, while alternately trying to appease and muzzle Hoover. It was a daunting task, and with any Senate chairman less in the tank than Millard Tydings couldn't have survived one reasonably active subcommittee session posing some obvious questions.

For one thing, Justice spokesmen would say and do things that enraged the Director, pushing him to the brink of public protest and sometimes beyond it. One high-risk Justice gambit was to put out statements on the alleged views of Hoover and the FBI that were quite different from their real opinions. That such misrepresentations were even attempted, as occurred on several topics, is indicative of the desperation then prevailing in certain quarters.

The main Justice tactic on *Amerasia,* starting with the initial fix, was to downplay the significance of the case, describing it as a trivial matter not worth all the fuss and feathers. The prosecutors, it was said, really didn't have much on the defendants; the evidence had been badly handled; the documents were of no importance. These points were made often by Justice spokesmen and spelled out in a lengthy memo supplied to Tydings explaining why the case had foundered. All this read more like a brief for the defense—which it was—than for the prosecution. And all of it would bring a sharp rejoinder from the Bureau.

While most of this wrangling occurred backstage, one semipublic battle was triggered by journalist Walker Stone of the Scripps-Howard news chain, who reported that Hoover thought the data on *Amerasia* presented a "100 percent airtight case."[2] This was, of course, directly counter to the official line and was picked up and quoted by McCarthy as he hammered away at Service and the *Amerasia* crowd in general. In response, John Peurifoy at the State Department asked Justice for a rebuttal to the McCarthy statements, duly supplied by Assistant Attorney General Peyton Ford, then furnished to the press corps.

Ford sent Peurifoy a letter denying the "airtight" quote, saying "Mr. Hoover did not make the statement which has been attributed to him." James McInerney would follow suit in testimony before the Tydings panel, saying "Mr. Hoover did not make any such statement. . . . He has denied it." John

Peurifoy promptly issued another press release touting Hoover's alleged denial, the not-to-worry view of *Amerasia,* and the chronic lying of McCarthy.[3]

All of this, however, itself was false, and directly counter to Hoover's true opinions. As the FBI records make clear, Hoover obviously did think the case "airtight," most probably said something like this to Walker Stone, and certainly hadn't issued any disavowals of it. On the contrary, he was outraged by the Ford-McInerney comments and took pains to put his thoughts on record to both State and Justice. So, on top of its misrepresentation of Service/ *Amerasia,* Justice was now explicitly misrepresenting Hoover.

Compounding matters, Hoover had protested Ford's letter in draft form, so Justice knew the denial was false even before it was supplied to State. When a draft was sent over for his approval, the Director had told Peyton Ford, "I have carefully reviewed the letter and I cannot approve it." Hoover added that, "with respect to the case itself, I must point out that in the event I had been asked at the time the arrests were made whether I thought we had an airtight case, I would have stated that I thought we had. Further, if I were asked today, I would have to so state."[4]

Apparently unfazed by this, Ford sent the letter anyway, and Peurifoy happily made it public. Hoover was livid. As he wrote Attorney General J. Howard McGrath, "I want you to know that at no time did I ever give any such clearance for the use of my name by either the Department of Justice or Mr. Peyton Ford, and I must certainly protest the use of my name, particularly when that use does not reflect my views."[5] Ford would later tell Hoover the denial had been "inadvertently" mailed to State—some kind of screwup at the office—and that Peurifoy had released it without his knowledge.*

Correlative to the airtight fiasco, Justice, State, and Tydings were doing all they could to downplay the importance of the *Amerasia* papers. In the Hobbs hearings that at last got printed at this juncture, Robert Hitchcock had used the phrase "teacup gossip" to describe the contents of the purloined memos.[†6] Similar trivializing comments would be made by Hitchcock before the Tydings panel, and by James McInerney, now successor to Tom Clark as head of the criminal division at Justice.

McInerney said the idea that the documents had any serious bearing on national defense was "silly" and repeated the "teacup gossip" line to Tydings:

---

*Thereafter, Hoover sent a similar, slightly more restrained, but still acerbic protest to Peurifoy. "Inasmuch as the question appeared to center around whether I made a statement," said Hoover, "I am at a loss to understand why I was not consulted" prior to State's release of the letter. He added that had he been questioned at the time of the *Amerasia* arrests, "I certainly would have been most emphatic in stating that the arrests were thoroughly justified" by the evidence gathered. Peurifoy and State were thus on notice that the Ford rebuttal to McCarthy was bogus.

†The somewhat garbled transcript has him saying "top gossip reports," but "teacup" is undoubtedly what he actually said.

"AIRTIGHT"

To counter McCarthy, the Truman Justice Department denied that FBI Director J. Edgar Hoover considered the *Amerasia*/Service case "airtight," but here Hoover reveals that Justice misrepresented his views about the matter.

copy:ahs

Mr. Peyton For\
The Assistant to the Attorney General   May 4, 1950

Director, FBI

PHILIP JACOB JAFFE, was., ET AL
ESPIONAGE

       With reference to the attached letter to Mr. John E.
Peurifoy, Deputy Under Secretary, Department of State, which you
submitted for my approval, you are advised that I have carefully
reviewed this letter and I cannot approve it. It is suggested
that you may desire to acknowledge Mr. Peurifoy's inquiry by
sending him a copy of my letter to John S. Service dated
April 18, 1950, in reply to his letter of April 12, 1950, wherein
Service asked the same question as that asked by Mr. Peurifoy. A
copy of my letter to John S. Service is attached.

       With respect to the case itself, I must point out that
in the event I had been asked at the time the arrests were made
whether I thought we had an airtight case, I would have stated
that I thought we had. Further, if I were asked today, I would
have to so state.

Attachments

APPROPRIATE AGENCIES
AND FIELD OFFICES
ADVISED BY ROUTING

b7C

100-267360-
NOT RECORDED
53 MAY 9 1950

2 JUN 6 1950

Source: FBI *Amerasia* file

"I would say that with respect to all these documents that they were innocuous, very innocuous documents. If I would estimate that 1 percent of them related to national defense, that would be about right. They had to do with very minor political and economical matters in the Far East. . . . These things impressed me as being a little above the level of teacup gossip in the Far East."*[7]

These comments were infuriating to Hoover and the Bureau, who had the papers in their custody and well knew what was in them. A Hoover memo of May 31 capsules a conversation with Peyton Ford in which the Director recalled that "I said Hitchcock's statement was outrageous." As Hoover further stated: "I told Ford I was outraged that men in the Department like Hitchcock and McInerney had gone up to the [Tydings] committee and made the statements that they did . . . if the documents were actually silly, or 'teacup gossip,' as McInerney put it, then we should not have had the investigation, or arrested people."[8]

The FBI did several analyses of the papers relating not only to this aspect but to others. One such exercise occurred when Republican Bourke Hickenlooper of the Tydings panel issued a statement to the press challenging the "teacup gossip" label. In fact, he said, many papers retrieved from *Amerasia* concerned military and strategic matters that could have affected the war in the Pacific or been of value to the Yenan Reds in the struggle for control of China.

In support of this, Hickenlooper described certain subjects covered in the papers: the location of American naval units in the Pacific as of November 1944; a Navy plan to set up counterintelligence operations in the United States; a document giving the composition of allied forces in Malaysia; a confidential forecast of trends in the Pacific fighting; two 1944 messages from President Roosevelt to Chiang Kai-shek, marked "eyes only," saying General Stilwell should be made commander of all armies in China, including the Communist forces at Yenan.

Hickenlooper also said the papers included a State Department cable, headed "Hull to Chungking," dated June 28, 1944, summarizing the contents of *Amerasia* itself as a source of insight on Far East affairs, including its view that American strategy in Asia should repeat the pattern followed in the Balkans (which, as seen, is more or less what happened). All this sounded rather portentous and not very much like "teacup gossip."

With the dispute thus out in the open, McInerney counterattacked, saying Hickenlooper was in error about the papers. McInerney said he was familiar with the *Amerasia* holdings and no documents such as those described by Hickenlooper were among them.[9] The Iowa senator, said McInerney, was "100 per

---

*In support of this view, McInerney quoted from the Hobbs report saying the documents had little military importance—neglecting to point out that the Hobbs committee based its opinions on what McInerney and other witnesses from Justice told it.

cent wrong" in his assertions. Tydings would, as ever, reinforce the Justice version of the matter.

These exchanges prompted the FBI to go through the papers again to see who was telling the truth about them. In every instance, the Bureau found, documents in the *Amerasia* file matched exactly or very closely with those that Hickenlooper cited. "It would appear," said the Bureau rundown, "that Senator Hickenlooper is correct in his statements as evidenced by the nature of the documents which have been possibly identified and are attached hereto . . . Mr. McInerney is obviously incorrect in his statement that documents containing 'highly secret wartime information' were not among those found in the *Amerasia* case as evidenced by the attached exhibits."[10]

Meanwhile, in another revealing contrast between public spin and backstage candor, Tydings counsel Edward Morgan drafted an angry memo for the subcommittee files, denouncing Hickenlooper's release of info on the papers. This transgression Morgan laid (correctly) at the door of Robert Morris, saying "the fact that these documents and their contents were released to the press presents a very embarrassing problem to the committee and its staff." Morgan's memo, recapping the contents of the disputed papers, makes it clear that the Hickenlooper data were very much on target, though Tydings and McInerney were denying this in broadsides to the press.[11]

In fact, the papers Hickenlooper cited were by no means the only or most important of the *Amerasia* holdings in terms of military content. The extensive FBI compilations disclose one document after another that by title alone could easily be identified as dealing with military, intelligence, and strategic matters. A brief conspectus reveals little by way of "teacup gossip" but a great deal that looks like military data. Following are the headings of some of the reports and official memos taken from the *Amerasia* office:

"Survey of the Efficacy of the Field Units of the ONI [Office of Naval Intelligence] in China"; "Report from Captured Personnel and Materials Branch, Military Intelligence Service, U.S. War Department"; "Typewritten report entitled 'Intelligence Systems,' dated January 9, 1945" (Feb. 10, '45); "Comments on Current Intelligence for the information of OSS Personnel" (Mar. 26, '45); "Military Affairs Report from China" (May 18, '44); "Disclosure of Military Information to the Chinese" (Jan. 8, '44); "Military Attaché Report from China" (May 18, '44).

And further: "A Military Intelligence Division Report classified 'Confidential' bearing the penciled notation 'war plans,' entitled 'Chinese Guerrilla Training School' " . . . "An OWI document dated March 21, 1945, classified 'confidential,' entitled 'Chinese Coast Physical Geography and Coastwise Shipping Routes.' " This bore the penciled notation, "war plans, coastal areas . . . mined areas" . . . "Document classified 'secret' . . . dated March 3, 1944, entitled 'Changes to Order of Battle of Chinese Army as of February 29, 1944' " . . . "A document classified 'secret' prepared by the

Military Intelligence Division dated February 1, 1944, entitled 'Order of Battle of the Chinese Army as of December 31, 1942' . . ."[12]

While downplaying the significance of the *Amerasia* papers, Truman Justice also minimized the gravity of handing them over to the likes of Philip Jaffe, saying it was just a matter of supplying background to a member of the press. Hitchcock had endorsed this line before Judge Proctor and repeated it to Hobbs. At the time of the original fix, according to one Bureau memo, "Hitchcock advised that the main reason for the grand jury not indicting all the defendants was that it felt the practice engaged in by the defendants was a common practice, and that the government agencies involved were the ones who were actually at fault in view of the laxity in caring for official documents."

This line would be repeated by McInerney, saying "the grand jury took the position that these government agencies were very sloppy in their handling of documents, and almost invited this type of violation. Second, that the same thing that was being done by these people was being done by regular newspapers . . ."[13]

Why a grand jury would have believed these things was not made clear. It seems unlikely a federal grand jury, usually guided in such matters by U.S. attorneys, would have independently reached this conclusion, particularly if given the facts about the sensitive nature of the papers. Based on the initial fix, Hitchcock's expressed desire to clear John Service, and the prosecutor's stipulation that it was all just zealous journalism, it's not hard to guess how the jurors might have come to this opinion.

Truman Justice also sought to obscure the Red connections of Jaffe and his contacts with then–Communist Party chief Earl Browder, Soviet agent Bernstein, Chinese Communist Tung Pi-wu, and the Soviet consulate in New York. None of this information had been given to Judge Proctor when Jaffe was in the dock. Now that the case was being revived before the Tydings panel, the department's efforts to gloss over Jaffe's Communist ties would continue and be expanded.

This was one of the points on which Justice and Bureau agents would tangle in hammering out what to say to Tydings. One FBI memo on this relates that "Mr. Ford objected to the conclusions on page 14 pertaining to the Communist connections of Jaffe . . ." (The Bureau draft had stated, "We knew then of the Communist connections of Jaffe, and had every right to assume that the information would have been used, had the practice continued, against the best interests of the United States."*) Such hand-to-hand combat on the phrasing of responses would recur throughout the process.[14]

---

*The Tydings panel would make a particular point of whether the Bureau had actually seen Jaffe handing documents over to Communist espionage agents. The Bureau rejoined by citing the Bernstein connection, the five-hour meeting with Earl Browder and Tung Pi-wu, and the other contacts

These matters were annoying to Hoover but almost minor irritants compared to certain other issues. Foremost among these was that department spokesmen told both Hobbs and Tydings the *Amerasia* case was deplorably weak because it was bungled from the outset. In this view, the case had been tainted by the Bureau's warrantless entries into the premises of *Amerasia* and Larsen's apartment in D.C. (in some versions, also by the earlier entry of OSS). Worst of all, said Justice spokesmen, Larsen had found out about the entry to his lodgings and filed a motion to quash the whole proceeding. It was this Larsen move, supposedly, that caused Justice to fold its hand and get the best deal it could in lame plea bargains with the suspects.

Such arguments were doubly outrageous to the FBI, which not only knew the case was fixed but deeply resented the effort to scapegoat its methods. The Bureau accordingly fought back hard on this one, noting that all the facts about the prior entries had been known to Truman Justice from the outset. Equally to the point, said the FBI, no documents were seized on these occasions. Rather, all evidence used in the indictments had been taken at the time of the arrests—this also known to Justice. As Mickey Ladd put it in a memo to Hoover:

> I informed [prosecutor Tom] Donegan that the Bureau had entered the apartments of the subjects and the office of *Amerasia* prior to the arrests but that no evidence was obtained at that time and that the only documents obtained were those obtained during the course of serving the warrants of arrest; therefore, the documents were obtained legally. The Bureau had no objection to the matter coming out indicating that the Bureau had been in these places prior to the arrests and that this was merely a smoke screen on the part of the department's attorneys.*[15]

This aspect of the backstage struggle is stressed repeatedly in the *Amerasia* records, probably more than any other. The files are replete with disdainful Bureau comments on what Hoover called "the Morgan-McInerney line" scapegoating the FBI for failure of the prosecution. "I have no doubt," said Hoover in one early memo, "Dept. representatives are trying to hang blame on the FBI to cover their own actions." Thereafter, the Bureau would prepare a point-by-point rebuttal of Justice's memo on the case, debunking both the "teacup gossip" line and the bungled-from-the-outset thesis.[16]

Especially galling to the FBI were written questions posed by Tydings, so

---

noted, observing that such sessions gave Jaffe ample opportunity to pass along various of the papers received from Service. The Bureau memo on this then dryly added, "It's not customary for spies to hand over documents in settings where they can be observed doing so."

*To this Lou Nichols would add, concerning one of the Bureau's many confabs with Peyton Ford: "I told him if this reasoning followed certainly the case was already tainted before it was ever given to the Bureau by OSS, that everyone in the government of any responsibility knew of this as well as the Bureau's entry, and if the taint was there, then why didn't somebody think about it before authorizing the arrests, etc. I told him it was rather disgusting."

worded as to suggest the Bureau had derailed the case with its intrusive methods. One question asked by Tydings was "Did you enter these places surreptitiously and by stealth?" Enraged by this, Hoover threatened to expose the fix by way of rebuttal and retaliation. The Tydings language, he told Peyton Ford, "was outrageous, and if this question was going to stand, I was going to insist on putting in the Cohen-Corcoran information" about the rigging of the case, since he didn't "intend to let Senator Tydings smear the record and scapegoat the Bureau in this manner."[17] This undoubtedly sent a chill down some high-level spines at the White House, State, and Justice, and the offending language would be altered.

There was one further aspect of the Justice memo that raised questions about the collapse of the prosecution. The main reason alleged for having to default the case was Larsen's discovery that his apartment had been entered and his motion to quash the evidence on this basis. This didn't occur, however, until late September, some six weeks after the grand jury no-billed Service. The Larsen motion obviously had nothing to do with these proceedings, which as the Bureau knew were simply products of the fix.

I NDEED, though concern to cover up the scandal was generic, the evidence on the deep-sixing of the case shows throughout the intent to exculpate Service. He was the main subject of the manipulations by Thomas Corcoran, Lauchlin Currie, *et al.,* and also the chief object of solicitude by Justice. However, it would have been impossible to bring out all the facts about the Red connections of the Jaffe crowd while simultaneously clearing Service. Thus, all the defendants got a free ride because of his exalted status.

The obsession with whitewashing Service is apparent in every aspect of the record. A prime example arose when Tydings addressed questions to the Bureau and Truman Justice about specific evidence on the FSO. This produced a further dispute between Peyton Ford and Bureau agents concerning Service's talks with Jaffe, in which Service had referred to the "military plans" that were "very secret." Ford wanted to cut this out or change it; the Bureau, hanging tough, insisted it stay in.*[18]

More generally, the official line on Service was that his involvement with *Amerasia* was tangential. He thought Jaffe was a legitimate newsman, was simply providing "background information," and really didn't do much of that. This was of course Service's own explanation of the matter. In his many statements on the subject, Service minimized the number, as well as the nature, of

---

*In a memo to Bureau official Clyde Tolson, Lou Nichols would describe the tussle over this as follows: "[Ford] started to paraphrase the material and referred to Service discussing political matters. We told him this was not true; that Service discussed military plans. He then wrote in military plans. We then told him that Service had specifically termed the military plans as secret. He then wrote this in."

the papers shared with Jaffe. As he told both the State Department loyalty board and the Tydings subcommittee, it was perhaps "eight or ten," and these of no great value.

As with virtually everything else in the *Amerasia* case, these statements were in jarring conflict with the confidential records. On May 25, 1950, the FBI provided James Hatcher, the chief investigator for the Civil Service Commission, a complete rundown on documents traceable to Service that had been found at *Amerasia*.[19] Rather than being "eight or ten," the list included no fewer than fifty papers that, according to the Bureau, had initially come from Service. This huge batch of papers didn't jibe very well with the story of negligible Service-Jaffe contact, few documents provided, or casual "background" chats between the parties.

The solution to this thorny dilemma was to pin the rap on Larsen—a tactic adopted early on by Robert Hitchcock and repeated by McInerney before the Tydings panel. As one FBI memo relates, "Hitchcock stated that he was favorably impressed by Service's statement to him that Service had given no State Department documents to Phil Jaffe. Hitchcock further informed that Jaffe's attorney had told him, off the record, that Larsen had furnished copies of some 1945 Service reports to Jaffe."[20] So Larsen, not Service, was the actual culprit.

This raised some further questions, such as why an experienced prosecutor would be "impressed" by the self-justifying statements of an arrested suspect caught consorting with Red agents. Still more puzzling is why Jaffe's attorney would be so helpful in clearing Service and fingering Larsen. That information on the face of it would have made no difference in Jaffe's own defense. It thus appears the Jaffe forces were as eager to exculpate Service, and make Larsen the fall guy, as was the prosecution.

Hitchcock had made a similar effort to clear Service in testimony before the Hobbs committee. In the exchange with Congressman Frank Fellows of Maine in which the "teacup gossip" line first appeared, Fellows asked, "Was Larsen the man who did all this?" Yes, said Hitchcock, it must have been Larsen, not John Service. "It had to be," Hitchcock explained. "Service was loaned to the Army back in 1943 . . . and did not return to the United States until the 18th day of April 1945, which was approximately 6 weeks prior to the time these arrests were made."*[21]

The meaning of this comment was that, since Service hadn't been in the United States prior to April of 1945, he couldn't have been the source of papers that made their way to *Amerasia* before then, of which there were a sizable number. But as the Bureau knew, this description of Service's whereabouts was grossly in error. In fact, Service had been in the United States from late Octo-

---

*Service in fact got back on April 12.

ber 1944 until January 1945, during which time he met with Andrew Roth, Owen Lattimore, Julian Friedman, the Washington staff of IPR, Harry White, Lauchlin Currie, and others that we know not of. It was on this trip also that he was supposed to get together with Max and Grace Granich, and most probably met with Grace. All these people were part of the extended *Amerasia* network, and Roth was of course directly implicated in the scandal when it broke the following spring.

The logic of the situation was thus the reverse of that suggested by Hitchcock. The prosecutor was saying Service *couldn't* have done it because he wasn't physically in the United States prior to April of 1945; as Service *was* physically in the United States from late October of 1944 until January of 1945, it follows that he very well could have done it. Which doesn't mean he did, merely that he could have. Only a thorough investigation could have brought out the truth about the matter, and a thorough investigation was precisely what the Truman forces were working overtime to stifle.

The rationale for this particular defense of Service was that just because he had written or transmitted a paper found at *Amerasia,* that didn't necessarily mean he supplied it directly. Somebody else with access to diplomatic records might have done so. This same logic was adopted by Service's attorney, Charles Rhetts, in proceedings of the State Department loyalty board, run parallel with the Tydings hearings. Questioning the chronically harried Larsen, Rhetts reviewed a series of Service papers found at *Amerasia,* trying to get Larsen to say he had—or could have—given these to Jaffe.

After a series of questions in which he was repeatedly asked about these papers, Larsen caught the drift and rebelled at being made the patsy. He admitted to having passed along to Jaffe six or eight Service memos relating to Larsen's own research concerns (leading personalities in China), but categorically denied the rest. At one phase of the Q & A, Larsen blurted out to Rhetts, "I realize your point is to gather sufficient evidence to protect Mr. Service" and said he wanted the hearing ended. "I was warned," he said, "to curtail this meeting at any moment when I felt that I was about to fall into a trap that might incriminate me."[22]

Though Larsen wasn't a very appealing figure or reliable witness, one can't help but feel a twinge of sympathy observing so many powerful forces aligning to have him take the fall for Service. Not only was Service's attorney eager to pin the rap on Larsen, so was Truman Justice, so was Tydings, and so, per Hitchcock's statement, was the legal representative of Jaffe. This last alone is sufficient to suggest that, whatever the bumbling and constantly changing stories of Larsen, he wasn't in on the larger scheme and was probably the least sinister figure in the whole unsavory business.

Finally, it's worth noting that the Rhetts-Hitchcock argument on this cut both ways. If Larsen or someone else *might* have passed along Service's reports to Jaffe, it was also possible Service himself *might* have passed along the reports of others. In which case, the total Service-provided haul at *Amerasia* could well have been in excess of fifty papers. But since the fix was in and no proper adjudication attempted, the truth of the matter was not established. Which was, of course, exactly how the Truman forces were content to leave it, then and forever after.

Now, however, the meddling Joe McCarthy had come out of nowhere to revive the case, raising countless troublesome questions and focusing the spotlight of media notice on the long-buried scandal. It was this McCarthy intrusion that provoked the backstage tussle between the Bureau and Truman Justice, which for the administration was bad enough. Worse yet, McCarthy was himself obtaining and making public security intel on the case, contrary to the official line that it was no big deal and Service an innocent briefer of the press corps. This was an unexpected problem that had to be dealt with in decisive fashion if things weren't to get completely out of hand for the Acheson State Department, Truman Justice, and an increasingly worried White House.

CHAPTER 28

Little Red Schoolhouse

HAD McCarthy done nothing more during his uproarious heyday in the Senate, his role in blowing the lid off the *Amerasia* scandal would deserve the plaudits of a grateful nation. This not only because of the intrinsic meaning of the case, but because it was the gateway to still other unthinkable revelations from the darker precincts of the Cold War.

And let there be no mistake that it was McCarthy who led the charge—constantly hammering on the case, digging up security data on Service, and otherwise exerting pressure on the *Amerasia* crowd and those complicit in its doings. Hoover and his agents knew the facts—knew far more than did McCarthy—but had to do their fighting behind the scenes, in a secret war of dueling memos. These inside baseball efforts weren't enough to prevent the Tydings panel and Truman Justice from selling a bogus version of the story. It was McCarthy who would stir up the public wrath and outcry that would be needed if the security woes implicit in the case were to be exposed and proper remedies adopted.

Nor was it simply a matter of Service-Jaffe and the documents that passed between them, or even the laundry list of federal crimes committed by the *Amerasia* fixers. The deeper meaning of the case stemmed from everything that lay behind it, and that would also need to be hauled out for public airing. In going after Service/*Amerasia*, McCarthy was tugging at the visible edges of an enormous network—far larger than he knew—that permeated the federal government and had objects more grandiose than the papers that made their way to Jaffe, important as those papers were.

To grasp the full significance of the *Amerasia* case and the way it was handled pre-McCarthy, we have only to reflect a bit on some of the things that should have happened in 1945 but didn't because the cover-up succeeded. Most obviously, Service and his codefendants weren't correctly brought to book, but that was merely the beginning. Because the fix was in, there was no serious effort to track down the confederates of the *Amerasia* culprits threaded throughout the State Department, Treasury, White House, and other influential places, all diligently working to shape the course of Cold War history in Asia.

Arguably the second-leading suspect in any adequate probe of Service would have been his Soviet agent housemate, Adler, and not far behind would have been Service's other Soviet agent housemate, Chi Chao-ting. From its surveillance of Jaffe, the FBI knew of the Service-Adler tie-in, and from the Bentley probe that shortly followed would obtain her evidence, backed by that of Chambers, that Adler was part of a pro-Soviet combine on the Treasury payroll. Adler nonetheless somehow got past the Truman loyalty screeners, while the facts about his case—along with just about everything else relating to John Service—were buried. Chi Chao-ting, meanwhile, was given only passing notice by security types and would likewise avoid exposure.

Had these two Soviet moles been rooted out in 1945, along with other of Service's allies, the subsequent course of events in Asia might have been quite different. But because the fix was in and the lid was on, this formidable pair of Soviet agents would have further leisure for clandestine action in behalf of Yenan and Moscow. In the case of Adler, this meant another five years as a Treasury staffer, including close involvement in the Marshall mission of 1946, a pivotal episode in the fall of China. In the case of Chi, it meant continuing as a Maoist agent inside the KMT until it fell in 1949, at which point, mission completed, he would abscond to Beijing.

Something else that should have happened in 1945 but didn't was the unmasking of Lauchlin Currie, himself one of the major fixers and a confidant of Service. Based on the Bentley revelations and confirming data from *Venona*, Currie ranked among the most influential Soviet agents ever in the U.S. government, if only by virtue of his portfolio in the White House dealing with affairs of China. And while he would leave that post in 1945, he was still hanging around in the latter 1940s, assured enough of his protected status to bluff his way through House committee hearings in which he self-righteously denounced the Bentley charges. So this Bentley-Chambers-*Venona*–certified Soviet asset was also never brought to justice.*

---

*Currie would eventually flee the country, as would Adler, at the height of the McCarthy furor in 1950.

Three top Soviet agents shielded by a single fix would seem to be enough for any Cold War thriller, but that too was merely a beginning. All these pro-Moscow apparatchiks had contacts in and around the U.S. government, and policy-making circles elsewhere, who needed serious scrutiny in 1945 but also didn't get it. We have noted Adler's links to Harry White, their joint endeavors to sink the gold loan to Chiang, and close liaison in general. Any halfway competent pursuit of Adler would have led back to White, but this pro-Moscow agent would likewise be spared public notice until some three years later. And White, as seen, was *primus inter pares* among a host of pro-Red Treasury staffers, all similarly shielded when White and Adler dodged the spotlight.

Meanwhile, at the State Department and related units dealing with policy toward China were confederates of Service (and Currie) who also merited close inquiry. These made up a considerable list, including John Carter Vincent, John Paton Davies, Haldore Hanson, Raymond Ludden, O. Edmund Clubb, John K. Emmerson, and Julian Friedman, all of State, Owen Lattimore and "the boys" in the Pacific division of OWI, Duncan Lee of OSS, John K. Fairbank of OWI, Benjamin Kizer of UNRRA, T. A. Bisson, and Miriam Farley (the last two soon to be with the occupation forces in Japan), to cite some of the more obvious cases.

This is only a partial roster, but on its face a pretty formidable crew of people on the federal payroll when the *Amerasia* case was buried. The fix thus protected not just a handful of suspects but a whole interlocking network of staffers linked in one way or another to the Service-Adler combine. It was this group that Joe McCarthy in his rough-and-ready fashion set about dragging into public view, case by painful case, in 1950. But a substantial part of the operation could have been exposed in 1945 had steps been taken to follow the tangled threads of *Amerasia* back to their mysterious sources. In the five-year span between the fix and the McCarthy blowup of 1950, the fall of China was accomplished.

And even this, sad to relate, wasn't quite the total story. Supportive of the Service-Adler camarilla, and tightly interwoven with it, was yet another unthinkable operation that also needed scrutiny in 1945 but also managed to evade it. This was the Institute of Pacific Relations, already met with in several places, which included among its leaders, active members, and close collaborators many important players in the China drama. As the IPR was cheek-by-jowl with *Amerasia* in every way that mattered, a cover-up of *Amerasia* was de facto a cover-up of IPR as well, and ensured that this remarkable group would be spared the notice it deserved—until, again, the advent of McCarthy.

Among the most conspicuous features of the IPR was its globe-girdling character, with affiliates in ten countries and contacts in still others, plus many connections in the U.S. government, academy, foundation world, and press corps. This web of contacts was not only extensive but of unusual nature. The constituency of the IPR ranged, quite literally, from hard-core Soviet agents on the one hand to high-ranking State Department officials on the other. At its meetings in the war years and early postwar era, concealed Communist functionaries (and some not so concealed) hailing from Europe, Asia, and North America freely intermingled with movers/shakers in U.S. policy-making circles. It's doubtful there was anything quite like it elsewhere in the annals of the Cold War, or in the history of nations.

A brief sampling of the IPR's array of international contacts has been provided in an earlier chapter. As there noted, the Sorge ring in Asia included such IPR-connected figures as the American writer Agnes Smedley, the German-born Guenther Stein, the Chinese Red agent Chen Han-Seng, and Japanese comrades Ozaki and Saionji. The Cambridge University set, meantime, embraced such IPR familiars as the Briton Michael Greenberg, the Canadian Herbert Norman, and the American Michael Straight. On the official U.S. end of things, the combine included Currie at the White House, Lattimore at OWI, Vincent and Alger Hiss at State—all four serving, at one time or another, as trustees of IPR. The global reach, pro-Red ties, and high-level influence of the group are well suggested by these cases.

Some aspects of this fantastic tale were known to Joe McCarthy in the early going, while others would develop piecemeal later. In his initial speeches to the Senate, McCarthy discussed some of the IPR's remarkable personnel, its links to *Amerasia,* and its entrée to the State Department, contending it had been a baleful influence on our policy toward China. Like everything else he had to say, these charges would be dismissed out of hand by Tydings, the State Department, and most people in the mainstream press who had anything to offer on the subject. Seldom has the unthinkability factor been more pervasive, or effective in its workings.

On the surface, the IPR was a respectable group and always claimed to be such. It had begun in 1925 as a spin-off of the YMCA, part of a larger trend in Christian circles to foster interest in and religious missions to China and other nations of the Far Pacific. Students of the matter agree that, at the beginning, it was a legitimate outfit that did good work in spreading knowledge of events in Asia. Prominent scholars, business leaders, and public officials cooperated with it, served on its boards, and otherwise approved it. The prestige of these eminent people was undoubtedly its major asset.

When McCarthy attacked the IPR before the Senate, the shocked reaction of his foes was geared to this respectable image. Sen. Clinton Anderson (D-N.M.) asked, with obvious incredulity, "Does the senator [McCarthy] mean to convey the impression that the Institute of Pacific Relations, in 1935 and 1936, was under Communist control?" When McCarthy noted the IPR connections of Philip Jessup, the response of the Tydings panel was the same. Jessup's ties to IPR, said Tydings, "do not in any way reflect unfavorably on him when the true character of the organization is revealed . . . men of unquestioned loyalty and integrity have been instrumental in the management of the organization and making financial contributions to it."[1]

This Tydings comment didn't say who all the outstanding people were involved in managing the IPR, but the obvious reference was to the illustrious names appearing on one letterhead or another. Any such allusion, however, was misleading, since most of these distinguished gentry had nothing significant to do with running the organization, as is frequently true with letterhead groups of all persuasions. With few exceptions, these reputable civic leaders, educators, and business moguls knew as much about the doings of the IPR as its real managers chose to tell them—which was *de minimus,* and that only of a flattering nature.

At the real managerial level, things were starkly different from the high-toned image so impressive to Anderson, Tydings, and others who dismissed McCarthy's charges. Here an astonishing cast of characters held forth, controlling the program on a daily basis and pretty much running things as they wanted. Foremost among these inside players was Edward C. Carter, who under various titles and guises was long the dominant figure in the operation. It was Carter who managed the office, raised the money, administered projects, and was involved in all the key decisions. A former YMCA official, he joined the staff of the nascent IPR in 1925 and stayed there in one capacity or another for upward of two decades.

By all accounts, Carter was a natural-born promoter, and used his abilities along these lines to help IPR to grow and, in its fashion, prosper. From a very early date, he would put his imprint on the group in the way that this is commonly done—by hiring the people who actually did the work and ran the program. And the people he hired would tell the tale as clearly as anything could do it. In 1928, to get things rolling, Carter asked a recent Harvard graduate, Frederick V. Field, to serve as his assistant. Not long after, he hired Field's Harvard friend and classmate Joseph Barnes to help out around the office. At about this time as well, Carter brought on another thirtysomething staffer, Owen Lattimore, to edit *Pacific Affairs,* the group's flagship publication.

Carter, Field, Barnes, and Lattimore thus made up the inner core of the IPR as of the early 1930s. They would later be joined by other staffers of similar background and opinions. These included Barnes's wife, Kathleen, Bryn Mawr graduate Harriet Moore, researcher Hilda Austern, and writer/editor Kate Mitchell. Also added to the team, as part of an increasingly multinational setup, was Elsie Fairfax-Cholmeley, who as the name perhaps suggests was English. The global flavor would be enhanced with the addition of Ms. Cholmeley's fellow Briton Michael Greenberg, Chinese nationals Chen Han-Seng and Chi Chao-ting, and the German-born Guenther Stein (as Chungking correspondent). Also added to the roster were the Americans T. A. Bisson,

Harriet Levine, Andrew Roth, Rose Yardumian, and Talitha Gerlach, to name a selected handful.

Unfortunately, the punch line of this recitation has been spoiled, as many of the IPR personnel just cited have previously surfaced at various places in our discussion. As reflected in official records, all of the 17 people thus brought on board by Carter—from Field to Talitha Gerlach—had one unusual attribute in common: Each would be named in sworn testimony, the chronicles of *Venona,* or official reports of Congress as a member of the Communist Party or a collaborator with Soviet intelligence agents.[2]

By any standard, this was a prodigious number of people with a relatively small outfit—or even a relatively large one—to be identified in this manner. Even granted the usual ripostes about witch hunts, kept witnesses, and such, it's hard to imagine how 17 people connected to a single group of modest size could thus be targeted for ulterior reasons by "paid informers." The point would be made by the Senate subcommittee that delved into the character of the organization:

"The IPR . . . was like a specialized flypaper in its attractive power for Communists . . . British Communists like Michael Greenberg, Elsie Fairfax Cholmeley, and Anthony Jenkinson; Chinese Communists like Chi Chao-ting, Chen Han-Seng, Chu Tong, or Y. Y. Hsu; German Communists like Hans Moeller (Asiaticus) or Guenther Stein; Japanese Communists (and espionage agents) like Saionji and Ozaki; United States Communists like James S. Allen, Frederick Field, William Mandel, Lawrence Rosinger, and Alger Hiss."[3]

The inevitable effect of such a lineup was an off-the-charts subversion index, certain to get the attention of people who knew anything about security matters. According to Elizabeth Bentley, indeed, Soviet spy chief Jacob Golos had warned her to steer clear of the IPR because it was so obviously riddled with Reds the FBI was bound to notice. It was, he said, "as red as a rose, and you shouldn't touch it with a 10-foot pole." The comrades of the IPR, Golos told Bentley, were "far too bungling and too much in the open . . ."[4]

Similar testimony would be offered by Louis Budenz, ex–managing editor of the *Daily Worker.* The IPR, he said, was described to him by Communist nabob Alexander Trachtenberg as a "little red schoolhouse," controlled by CP members, to "teach Americans what they need to know about China." Trachtenberg added, per Budenz, that Communist leaders praised the group for its pro-Red propaganda efforts but were troubled by its lack of caution: "They felt the Institute was too much a concentration point for Communists; the control could be maintained without such a galaxy of Communists in it."[5]

From these and collateral data dug up by Senate investigators and the FBI, it appears the august and scholarly IPR had been taken over from within, and by some rather sinister people. The respectable facade, however, remained, and for a considerable time would be impervious to attempts to publicize the capture. An early instance was the effort of businessman Alfred Kohlberg, a dissident member of the group, who staged a protest against its leadership in the middle 1940s. An importer dealing in goods from China, Kohlberg had traveled in the country and knew a fair amount about it. Studying Institute materials, he concluded the IPR was indeed a "little red schoolhouse," and produced an eighty-eight-page documentary memo that sought to show this.

Kohlberg's campaign, however, was unavailing, as the staff of the IPR prepared a vigorous counterblast against him, and the group's executive board endorsed this as adequate answer to his charges. Thereafter, Kohlberg would be branded as a mercenary looking out for his business interests and impugned as head of the "China lobby," an allegedly evil pressure group much execrated by media outlets such as the *Washington Post* and the columns of Drew Pearson. Later, the similarity between the Kohlberg charges and the allegations of McCarthy would be apparent to any who bothered to compare them, and the pro-IPR arguments and unthinkability defenses used in the Kohlberg battle were thrown into the breach against McCarthy.

Though McCarthy was in fact getting IPR material from Kohlberg, this wasn't his only source of information. As seen, McCarthy had a knack for developing data that alarmed his foes, and he displayed that talent in this instance. On March 30, 1950, he told the Senate he had been informed by a former Soviet intelligence officer that Moscow was "having excellent success through the Institute of Pacific Relations," which the Soviets, "through Communists in the United States, had taken over."[6] (This source was Alexander Barmine, whom McCarthy and Morris wanted to bring before the Tydings panel but who wasn't called.) McCarthy also came up with documents, including canceled checks, showing the key role played in the IPR by the millionaire Communist Field, whose deep pockets helped to fund the operation.

Like Kohlberg, McCarthy initially didn't make much headway against the IPR and the massed forces of denial, as the group, like all other McCarthy targets, would be given a clean bill of health by Tydings. This time, however, there would be a morning after. In 1951, the U.S. Senate created the Internal Security subcommittee of the Judiciary Committee—both panels headed by Nevada Democrat Pat McCarran—to investigate subversion of all types and see about the enforcement of relevant statutes. Its first in-depth investigation would be a probe of the IPR—thus picking up the ball where McCarthy had by main strength contrived to push it and Tydings, in his usual manner, dropped it.

The nature and conduct of the McCarran committee were about as distant from those of the Tydings panel as could be imagined. The main resemblance was that McCarran in his way was just as much a Senate lord as Tydings. A longtime leading figure in Nevada politics, McCarran was first elected to the Senate in 1932 and so had two decades of seniority to undergird his legislative powers. As chairman of the Judiciary Committee, he also had leverage over court nominees and high-level appointments at Justice, and was thus a major Senate presence. He was, however, a staunch conservative of a type then still found in the Democratic Party, and often at odds with its reigning New Deal faction.

McCarran's unusual mix of clout and independence would be crucial to his new subcommittee, which was by and large impervious to the executive pressures that had shaped the work of Tydings. The McCarran group was also of bipartisan nature, consisting of conservative Democrats and Republicans who generally saw eye-to-eye on security issues, and all of its reports and findings would be unanimous—this also in sharp contrast to what occurred with Tydings. The panel had another advantage also, not always enjoyed by such committees: It was able to get access to the files of the IPR—running to tens of thousands of pages—and would wield these in effective manner.

Like congressional interest in the IPR as such, the acquisition of these papers owed a lot to Joe McCarthy—whose staffers discovered the location of the files at the New England farm of Edward Carter and shared this information with McCarran, who then obtained them by subpoena. The files included correspondence between IPR officials and their multitude of contacts, internal memos, minutes of meetings, and records of dealings with U.S. officials. Armed with these materials, carefully sorted out and studied, the subcommittee and its staff were able to ask probing questions of IPR spokesmen and their State Department soul mates and elicit some astounding answers.

While McCarran was running his high-profile investigation, a similar but quieter inquest was being conducted by the FBI. This too, at least chronologically, was a follow-up on McCarthy's efforts. The IPR had previously been on the radar screens of the FBI because of the *Amerasia* tie-in, but Bureau interest in the group would ramp up sharply in the wake of McCarthy's charges. The Bureau, too, obtained and studied the files of the IPR, and its inquiries often tracked, and went beyond, the public efforts of McCarran. In the end, both probes would be massive undertakings: some 5,000 pages of public hearings run by McCarran, plus 1,000 pages of exhibits; 24,000 pages of now-declassified records available in the Bureau archives.

These parallel inquests revealed a wide-ranging, intricate operation that assiduously worked to guide official and public thinking, and hence the course of U.S. policy, concerning the world-changing events unfolding in the Far Pacific. The main focus was on China, where Chiang Kai-shek would be locked in mortal combat with the Yenan comrades, but Japan, Korea, India, Indochina, Indonesia, and other Far Eastern nations were on the docket also. The scope of the group's interests and activities, and their sophistication, were impressive.

The IPR exerted its leverage in divers ways, aided by the fact that it specialized in a field where there were few competitors to challenge its expertise and influence. The Far East was *terra incognita* to most Americans, and virtually nobody other than the IPR made it the subject of ongoing, intensive study. The group pumped out innumerable books and pamphlets, published two supposedly authoritative journals, and was successful in getting its materials used by schools, civic groups, and government bodies as allegedly impartial sources on affairs of the Pacific.

A prime example was the Institute's work in World War II, when U.S. officials bought three quarters of a million of its pamphlets for American troops in Asia. In addition, the group provided to the armed forces lecturers, documents, and books pertaining to the region. IPR materials also enjoyed circulation on the home front, where its pamphlets were widely used in schools and its staffers were available as speakers on radio programs, discussion panels, and lecture platforms.

While IPR pamphlets and journals discussed many issues, two themes especially were salient: the upstanding character of the Soviet Union and the merits of the Reds in China. The group's admiring view of Moscow was, for instance, disseminated to American schoolchildren in a pamphlet called "Land of the Soviets." In this work, U.S. youngsters were instructed that "while the Russians are quick to condemn those who display ambition for personal power, they have no praise too high for the person who devotes himself to the common good." And further: "A motive peculiar to the Russian system is the pride of ownership of the Soviet workers. They have a voice in running the factories . . . Each of these has its own village soviet, chosen at a village meeting not unlike our New England town meeting."[7]

A like view of the Communists in China was provided in a 1946 IPR pamphlet concerning the alleged "peasant party" headquartered at Yenan. This publication asserted that, "when we speak of the Chinese Communists, we should remember that they stand for something rather different from what is ordinarily meant by the term 'Communist' . . . They maintain the right of private property and enterprise in the areas under their control . . . They have established a system of popular elections . . . They have long declared that they would support a democratic republic in which not only they themselves but all other Chinese political parties would be represented . . ."[8]

IPR-connected authors were prolific in producing books and essays that echoed these opinions. Israel Epstein, Owen Lattimore, Guenther Stein, Edgar Snow, Lawrence Rosinger, and others churned out volumes that reflected the perspective. Many of these authors wrote for the popular press as well—including such outlets as the *Saturday Evening Post,* the *Atlantic Monthly,* the *New York Times,* and the *New York Herald Tribune.* A specialty of such writers was reviewing one another's books. As the McCarran report concluded:

For some years, the IPR family held a near monopoly on the reviews of books on the Far East published in *The New York Times, The New York Herald Tribune, The Saturday Review of Literature, The New Republic,* and *The Nation* . . . the IPR stalwarts constituted for the American reading public during those years [1945–50] a virtual screening and censorship board with respect to books on the Far East and the Pacific . . . a major preoccupation of the reviewers was the launching of each other's books.[9]

As might be guessed from the above, books and articles by IPR-connected writers took a harshly negative view of Chiang Kai-shek. It was in fact, as noted by McCarthy, an article by Soviet intelligence asset T. A. Bisson in IPR's *Far Eastern Survey* in 1943 that signaled a switch from the previous line of "united front" accommodation with Chiang when he was pinning down a million Japanese who might have threatened Russia, to a stance of all-out opposition. This message would be amplified manyfold when it was picked up by more prominent writers and echoed in more mainstream journals.

IPR did more, however, than write and publish. It was also a main epicenter of the extended network of activists and groups that held rallies, sponsored meetings, and took hard-left positions on China and other Asian issues. The McCarran panel identified a half-dozen outfits closely linked to IPR by common directors, officers, and staffers. These included the Committee for a Democratic Far Eastern Policy, the China Aid Council, the American Friends of the Chinese People and its magazine *China Today,* and the American Russian Institute (all officially cited Communist fronts).

By far the most significant of such overlaps were with *Amerasia*—a link stressed often by McCarthy. In his early speeches and other public statements, he held forth on the personnel who served both with Jaffe's journal and with the IPR—including such as Lattimore, Chi, Field, and Bisson. Everything McCarthy had to say about this was confirmed by the inquiries of the FBI and McCarran. In fact, not only were there overlaps in terms of staffers, editors, and writers, but numerous other linkages also. As one FBI memo reported:

In 1945, Kate Mitchell, associate editor of *Amerasia,* said material furnished by IPR was used in editing *Amerasia.* IPR documents reflected Edward C. Carter favored a merger of *Amerasia* and IPR . . . IPR and *Amerasia* maintained headquarters in the same building and shared a common switchboard from 1937 through 1943. Review of IPR publications and all issues of *Amerasia* reflects approximately 115 individuals who contributed articles to both. . . . In July 1947, when *Amerasia* ceased publication, subscription lists filled by *Far Eastern Survey.*[10]

Thus, though *Amerasia* was more militant and IPR allegedly more scholarly and restrained, the two groups for all intents and purposes were one. The differences in shading were nonetheless important, as IPR's cloak of re-

spectability gave it entrée to policy-making circles where *Amerasia*'s more blatant pro-Red stance might have been offputting. Aiding the process were IPR-
connected U.S. officials Vincent, Hiss, and Currie, their efforts supplemented
by IPR associates and contacts in other federal billets.* In particular, during
the hurly-burly of hiring for World War II, numerous IPR personnel would be
added to official payrolls. The volume of these pickups was so great the FBI
made several compilations, periodically updating the lists and adding other
relevant data. There appeared to be a constantly active revolving door between
the IPR and U.S. agencies dealing with Far Eastern matters.

Before it became the better part of valor to downplay it, IPR was proud of
its presence in the federal workforce and bragged about this to supporters.
Thus, on November 4, 1942, Edward Carter highlighted for one of his contacts
the involvement of IPR in official wartime posts both in the United States and
overseas, plus the doings of IPR personnel in other aspects of the conflict. Excerpts from this letter are of interest in view of later revelations about some of
the people mentioned:

"Lattimore is at the moment back in Chungking as a political adviser to
Chiang Kai-shek, but goes shortly to San Francisco to be Pacific Coast head of
the Office of War Information. . . . Bob Barnett has just returned from a short
visit to Chungking. Michael Greenberg has just joined the Board of Economic
Warfare . . . Jessup is at Columbia training naval officers for reoccupation
service in the Pacific, Chi is acting secretary general of the American British
Chinese currency stabilization board in Chungking. Chen Han-Seng and Elsie
Cholmeley were prisoners in Hong Kong, but they and some of their friends
managed to escape and are now in Free China."[11]

There is more to be said about the IPR and its leaders, but these comments
are perhaps enough to suggest the major points at issue. The Institute was a

---

*Among such contacts, in addition to Hiss, Vincent, and Currie, were Haldore Hanson, Laurence
Duggan, and Michael Greenberg at State; John K. Fairbank, Duncan Lee, Joe Barnes, and Lattimore at OSS/OWI; Benjamin Kizer at UNRRA; Philip Keeney, Herbert Norman, and Bisson with
the postwar occupation forces. All these IPR contacts would be named under oath as members of
the Communist Party or Soviet agents.

The policy leverage of this group was the greater for having still other contacts who weren't
so named but worked closely with the IPR contingent. These included Service, John Paton Davies,
O. Edmund Clubb, John K. Emmerson, and Raymond Ludden, all of the Foreign Service. IPR contacts at State included Robert and Patricia Barnett (both former staffers at the Institute), William
Stone and Esther Brunauer (incorporators of the American IPR), Jay Robinson, Cora Dubois, and
various others. The most important of these was Philip Jessup, who had been a top official at IPR
and would become a leading figure at State.

Among the IPR associates and staffers identified by the FBI as being involved in official wartime services were Barnes, Lattimore, Elizabeth Downing, William Holland, and others at OWI;
Hilda Austern, Hollis Gale, Katrina Greene, and Rose Yardumian with UNRRA; the two Barnetts,
Charles Fahs, Mary Frances Nealy, William Johnstone, Catherine Porter, and several others with the
State Department; Andrew Grad, Miriam Farley, and William Lockwood with the occupation
forces; Irving Friedman with the Treasury, T. A. Bisson with BEW, Jessup and Carter in miscellaneous positions, and on and on.

kind of plexus through which the notions brewed up in *Amerasia* could be filtered, given more respectable mien, and conveyed to IPR familiars in the State Department as policy options for Asia—a great many of which were then adopted. The unanimous conclusions of the McCarran panel supply a good provisional wrap-up:

> The IPR has been considered by the American Communist Party and Soviet officials as an instrument of Communist policy, propaganda, and military intelligence. The IPR disseminated and sought to popularize false information including information originating from Soviet and Communist sources. A small core of officials and staff members who controlled IPR were either Communist or pro-Communist . . . the names of eminent individuals were by design used as a respectable and impressive screen for the activities of the IPR inner core, and as a defense when such activities came under scrutiny . . .
>
> Over a period of years, John Carter Vincent was the principal fulcrum of IPR pressures and influence in the State Department. It was the continuous practice of the IPR to seek to place in government posts both persons associated with IPR and other persons selected by the effective leadership of IPR. The IPR possessed close organic relations with the State Department through interchange of personnel, attendance of State Department officials at IPR conferences, constant exchange of information and social contacts . . . The IPR was a vehicle used by the Communists to orientate American Far eastern policy toward Communist objectives.[12]

Considering the global reach and high-level contacts of the IPR, it's questionable whether the schoolhouse it was running could properly be called "little." But, based on the findings of McCarran and the FBI, there didn't appear to be much doubt about the redness.

CHAPTER 29

"Owen Lattimore, Espionage—R"

THERE were many notable characters linked to IPR, but none more so than its chief ideologue and master wordsmith, Prof. Owen Lattimore of Johns Hopkins University, OWI, *Pacific Affairs, Amerasia,* and several other significant venues. As that résumé suggests, Lattimore was a versatile sort who wore many hats and did so in rapid sequence. He moved back and forth among the academy, government, and press corps, writing books and essays, editing journals, making speeches, and networking with fellow Far East pundits. If there was anything much that needed doing in the way of Asian expertise, Lattimore was the man to do it.

He was also, according to Joe McCarthy, a Soviet agent—one of the most important in the land. Before the Tydings panel, in executive session, McCarthy had branded Lattimore, indeed, the "top Soviet espionage agent" in the country, an allegation that, when leaked to the press, did considerably more damage to McCarthy than to the professor. Subsequently, McCarthy backed off from the espionage angle but still insisted that Lattimore was a leading Moscow agent, and set out to prove it before the Tydings panel and in speeches to the Senate.

Lattimore, McCarthy charged, had been the point man for the Communist line on China, belittling the cause of Chiang Kai-shek and building up the Yenan rebels. This pro-Red outlook, said McCarthy, had suffused the air in

Foggy Bottom and fatally influenced our stance in Asia. "In view of his position of tremendous power in the State Department as the 'architect' of our Far Eastern policy," McCarthy charged, "the more important aspects of his case deal with his aims and what he advocates; whether his aims are American aims or whether they coincide with the aims of Soviet Russia."[1] McCarthy left no doubt he thought the answer was the second.

In the judgment of the Tydings panel, as ever, such charges had no merit. Its report would echo Lattimore himself on his supposed lack of influence (merely "a writer and a scholar," "the least consulted" of all Asia experts), saying "it is ridiculous to suggest that Lattimore was the principal architect of our Far Eastern policy, or, indeed, that he had any effective influence whatever thereon." As to the alleged pro-Moscow nature of his views, said the report, "we do not find that Mr. Lattimore's writings follow the Communist line or any other line, save as his very consistent positions on the Far East may be called the Lattimore line."[2]

So deposing, Tydings gave short shrift to data brought forward by McCarthy. On the question of policy leverage, for instance, McCarthy said Lattimore "had a desk" in the State Department, this indicating obvious access to the halls of power. Lattimore denied it, John Peurifoy of State concurred in the denial, and Tydings treated these statements as facts of record. Likewise, the testimony of Louis Budenz was again shrugged off as "hearsay" and in essence treated as false and perjured. "In no instance," said the panel, "has Mr. Lattimore on the evidence before us been shown to have knowingly associated with Communists." The case revealed, according to Tydings, "the danger of promiscuous and specious attacks on private citizens and their views."[3]

As with other aspects of the IPR dispute, later investigation would paint a contrasting picture of the bespectacled professor. For one thing, even a cursory survey of his career suggests that, in disclaiming any policy clout whatever, Lattimore was much too modest. *Vide* his role as adviser to Chiang Kai-shek, high-level job at OWI in World War II, and stint in 1944 as traveling mentor to Vice President Henry Wallace. Add to these his role in late 1945 and early '46 with an official mission to Japan and drafting its report on measures allegedly needed in that country. Thereafter, in October 1949, he was a major figure at a State Department confab charting the further course of U.S. policy in Asia. And, in 1950, at the time of the Tydings hearings, he was off on a mysterious foreign junket at the behest of U.N. official David Weintraub. All in all, a pretty active official life for a supposedly cloistered, unconsulted scholar.

All that, however, was minor stuff compared to the McCarthy charge that Lattimore's influence, whatever its scope, was deployed in behalf of Moscow. This wasn't an espionage allegation, but in its way was just as bad, and as outrageous to McCarthy critics. It was also, ironically, an aspect of the Lattimore case that could readily be checked by anyone who wanted to make the effort, as his writings often touched on matters involving the USSR, its foreign policy, and its character in general.

Especially helpful in gauging Lattimore's views were two like-titled books published in the early phases of the Cold War, one in 1945 (*Solution in Asia*), the other in 1949 *(The Situation in Asia)*. These books, though devoted to the Far East, were replete with comments on the Soviet Union as an Asian power, its challenge to the U.S. and other Western nations, and related topics—mostly the civil war in China. No one reading these volumes with any care, or knowledge of the issues, could have been in serious doubt about the Lattimore perspective.

By far the most obvious aspect of these books—and many other Lattimore writings—is that he was an indefatigable shill for Moscow, slanting discussion of just about any conceivable subject in favor of the Soviet interest. Other facets of his work were convoluted or opaque, but this part couldn't have been any clearer. A second obvious feature, linked to the first, is that he was an equally strong promoter of the Reds in China, and handled matters relating to them in pretty much identical fashion. The net effect of Lattimore comments on these topics, though approached by indirections, was about as subtle as a chainsaw.

A main Lattimore thesis, much repeated, was that the Soviet Union was a dynamo of political-economic progress that dazzled the people of Asia with its achievements, thus exerting an immense "attraction" that pulled them toward the Moscow orbit. In so arguing, he invariably wrapped the Soviet despotism in familiar buzzwords of the West—"democracy" being most often used, though "freedom" occasionally popped up also. (Nor did he omit respectful bows to Stalin.) Here is one somewhat famous passage, taken from *Solution in Asia:*

> To all of these people (along the Russian frontier from Korea to Manchuria, past Mongolia, Sinkiang and Afghanistan and Iran, all the way to Turkey), the Russians and the Soviet Union have a great power of attraction. In their eyes—rather doubtfully in the eyes of the older generation, more clearly in the eyes of the younger generation—the Soviet Union stands for strategic security, economic prosperity, technological progress, miraculous medicine, free education, equality of opportunity, and democracy, a powerful combination.[4]

It couldn't get more fawning than that, though the Moscow worship was phrased as the humble view of Asians gazing with awestruck wonder across the steppes at the marvels wrought by Stalin. This was a favored Lattimore tactic, used often in his writings, in which the pro-Red message was presented as the innermost thought of large groups of people whose minds he was adept at reading. The virtually identical treatment appears, for instance, in the second of his *Asia* volumes, which tells us that "among Russia's neighbors in Asia, the progress of the Soviet republics of Asia from about 1925 to 1941 inspired awe and wonder."[5]

Lattimore used the same technique in dealing with the Reds of China, where the anonymous masses smitten with the Communist program weren't people in other countries but China's own ubiquitous peasants. They were, he said, much taken with the "democracy," "self-government," and other reforms enacted by the Reds, along with the tangible economic benefits resulting from the Yenan system. The peasants loved all the good things provided by the comrades and thus flocked naturally to their banner. So it wasn't Lattimore who admired the Reds, you see; it was the peasants. Like his friend John Service, Lattimore was just "reporting."

In using the term "democracy" to describe the doings of Moscow and the Red Chinese, Lattimore conceded that these practices weren't *quite* what we in the United States considered democratic—but then dismissed this as being of no importance. "The fact that the Soviet Union also stands for democracy," he wrote, "is not to be overlooked. It stands for democracy because it stands for all the other things," though this wasn't exactly in keeping with our notions. "The fact is," he explained, "that for most of the people in the world today what constitutes democracy in theory is more or less irrelevant. What moves people to act . . . is the difference between what is more democratic and less democratic in practice."[6]

Words like "dictatorship" and "imperialism" do appear in Lattimore's writings—in their usual meanings—but always applied to anti-Communist forces, never to the USSR or Yenan comrades. If places such as Outer Mongolia or the nations of Eastern Europe got dragooned into the Soviet empire, that was merely further proof of Moscow's "power of attraction." "In Asia," Lattimore wrote, "the most important example of the Soviet power of attraction beyond Soviet frontiers is in Outer Mongolia. It is here that we would look for evidence of the kind of attraction that Russia might offer to Korea. Outer Mongolia might be called a satellite of Russia in the good sense; that is to say, the Mongols have gravitated into the Russian orbit of their own accord."[7]

In similar vein, said the professor, peasants in the USSR herded into collective farms found this more appealing than the previous system of private ownership, which had oppressed them. "More and more Soviet peasants in the Ukraine, Siberia, and Soviet Asia," he wrote, "have come to feel that their individual shares in collective farms represent a kind of ownership more valuable to them than the old private ownership under which they were unable to own or even hire machines."[8] Again, the author's mind-reading powers, applied to anonymous, distant masses, were uncanny. (No mention in this discussion, perhaps because of space constraints, of the millions starved to death in Moscow's various man-made famines.)

As these quotes suggest, Lattimore seldom met a Red atrocity he didn't like, or couldn't find an excuse for. Among the more ghastly examples was his comment on the purge trials and acts of murder with which Stalin scourged his party and his country in the latter 1930s. These events shocked many liberals in the West, including the venerable John Dewey, but didn't faze Lattimore in the slightest. On the contrary, he found them not only undismaying but beneficial. Based on his reading about the Stalin purges, he said, it appeared "a great many abuses have been discovered and rectified." He added that "habitual rectification can hardly do anything but give the ordinary citizen more courage to protest, loudly, whenever in the future he finds himself being victimized by 'someone in the party' or 'someone in the government.' That sounds to me like democracy."[9]

Describing this saturnalia of torture and mass murder as "habitual rectification" and the outcome as "democracy" pretty well summed up the Lattimore method. He had similar honeyed words for Stalin's gulag and slave labor camps, most notably in an article for the *National Geographic* after his 1944 trip with Vice President Wallace and John Vincent to the USSR and China. One of the stops along the way was the infamous Magadan-Kolyma gold-mining complex in Siberia, generally considered by students of such matters to have been the deadliest in the Soviet system.

Lattimore, however, found the Kolyma death camp a wonderful place to visit. Among the items that impressed him was the presence at this slave labor complex of "a first class orchestra and light-opera company," plus "a fine ballet group" on tour there. "As one American remarked," he wrote, "high grade entertainment just naturally seems to go with gold, and so does high-powered executive ability." The executive in question was the warden of this huge prison, a General Mishikov, described by survivors of the camp as a particularly odious tyrant. The Lattimore view, as might be guessed, was different. Mishikov, said the professor, "had just been decorated with the order of hero of the Soviet Union for his extraordinary achievement. Both he and his wife have a trained and sensitive interest in art and music and also a deep sense of civic responsibility."

Finally, to top off the whole delightful outing, the Lattimore party found at the Kolyma mines, "instead of the sin, gin and brawling of an old-fashioned gold rush, extensive greenhouses growing tomatoes, cucumbers and melons to make sure the hardy miners get enough vitamins." This rendering of a Siberian slave camp as a sort of art colony *cum* health spa run by cultured esthetes suggests Lattimore was no piker in these matters but ranked with the most abject of Soviet hacks as an apologist for Stalin.*[10]

---

*In *The Great Terror*, Robert Conquest writes: "[I]n Kolyma, the death rate was particularly high . . . the death rate among the miners is estimated in fact at about 30 per cent per annum. . . . In one of the Kolyma penal camps, which had started the year with 3,000 inmates, 1,700 were dead by the end . . ." Of course, without all the cucumbers and tomatoes, the death toll might have been even higher.

Lattimore not only wrote such things himself but counseled others on how to do it. "I think you are pretty cagey," he told Edward Carter, "in turning over so much of the China section of the inquiry to Asiaticus, Han Seng and Chi. They will bring out the absolutely essential radical aspects, but can be depended on to do it with the right touch."[11] The meaning of this was fairly clear, as Asiaticus, Chi, and Chen Han Seng were all veteran Moscow agents, as shown by a voluminous record. (Chen and Chi, already met with, were especially thick with the professor, both at the IPR and elsewhere.)

A further comment addressed to Carter pushed the Lattimore tactic of scoring propaganda points from cover, minimizing direct exposure. "For China," Lattimore wrote, "my hunch is that it will pay to keep behind the official Chinese Communist position, far enough not to be covered by the same label—but enough ahead of the active Chinese liberals to be noticeable . . . For the USSR—back their international policy in general, but without using their slogans and above all without giving them or anyone else an impression of subservience . . ."[12]

The subservience Lattimore didn't want to show in public would be more obvious in private confabs with the Moscow bosses. Among the documents obtained by the FBI and McCarran panel were minutes of meetings in 1936 between Kremlin bigwigs and a delegation from IPR, including Lattimore and Carter. In these sessions, the Soviets complained that *Pacific Affairs* had run an article by the anti-Communist William Henry Chamberlin, and another by the Trotskyite Harold Isaacs—both anathema to Kremlin censors. In response to this tongue-lashing, the IPR spokesmen apologized profusely. "The Isaacs and Chamberlin articles," said Carter, "were great mistakes and would not be repeated in the future." Lattimore's *mea culpa* was that "he had not realized Chamberlin's position, but as soon as he learned of the Soviet opinion about Chamberlin, he canceled an article on the Soviet press which he had asked from Chamberlin."*[13]

Still other such instances from Lattimore's writings might be cited, but these are perhaps enough to suggest the drift of his opinions, his toadying to Moscow, and the rhetorical tactics used to do it. Looking at the total picture, the McCarran committee would conclude that Lattimore was one of a sizable group at IPR who "sought to influence the American public by means of pro-Communist or pro-Soviet content" in their writings, and that "Owen Lattimore, from some time in the 1930s, was a conscious, articulate instrument of

---

*When the Soviets said *Pacific Affairs* should have a "definite aim," Lattimore also picked up on this. He explained that *Pacific Affairs* was an international journal with articles coming in from member countries, and he couldn't dictate to them what to write. He added, however, that if the Soviets themselves would contribute to the publication, their articles could help establish "a general line—a struggle for peace—the other articles would naturally gravitate to that line . . ." He added

the Soviet conspiracy."[14] Data that have come to light in succeeding years do much to confirm this verdict and precious little to refute it.

But was he an espionage agent? McCarthy has taken considerable heat for saying he was, then backing off from this assertion. According to the Tydings panel, this was an absurd suggestion, implausible on its face as well as being a scandalous libel. As in other cases cited, the main evidence invoked by Tydings was intel from the FBI—an extensive Lattimore file assembled by the Bureau, a summary of which was read *in camera* to members of the panel. With the professor on the stand before him, Tydings said this file cleared Lattimore entirely. "[T]here was nothing in that file," said the chairman, "to show that you were a Communist or had ever been a Communist, or that you were in any way connected with any espionage information or charges, so that the FBI file puts you completely, up to this moment, in the clear."[15]

This seemed fairly conclusive, but Tydings would go still further, indicating that FBI Director Hoover concurred in his assessment. Hoover himself, said Tydings, had prepared the summary and was present when it was read, and it was "the universal opinion" of everyone in the room—this phrase in context including Hoover—that the professor was clean as a whistle. So the episode was reported at the time, and so it is recorded in several bios of McCarthy and histories of the era.

However, as has been noted, Tydings had a disconcerting habit of saying things about clearances from the FBI, the contents of security files, and the views of Hoover that turned out on further inquiry to be in error. The Lattimore case was of this nature, only more so. We know this because we have at least part of the file in question, not merely a summary of it as parsed by Tydings. This shows Tydings was again playing fast and loose with facts of record, and especially with the views of Hoover.

On the latter point, indeed, the distortion was so flagrant Peyton Ford of Justice, himself involved in the *Amerasia* "airtight" debacle, felt constrained to comment. According to an April 1950 memo from Lou Nichols of the FBI, Ford "said he couldn't understand what had come over Senator Tydings, as he recalled very distinctly *that the Director had been asked the question as to how he would regard Lattimore's loyalty, and the Director stated if he were on the Loyalty Board he would question it; further the Director had also regarded Lattimore as a security risk and would not have hired him at the Bureau; he [Ford] couldn't understand what Tydings was talking about.*"[16] (Emphasis added.)*

---

that he was "willing to have *PA* reflect such a line," but needed such articles from the Soviets to get the goal accomplished.

*The file further shows Hoover confirming the accuracy of Ford's statement. A version of these private Hoover comments was leaked to Bert Andrews of the *New York Herald Tribune* and published in that paper. The Director, in internal memos complaining about the leak, acknowledged that this report, mirroring the comments of Ford, was a correct rendition of his verdict on the professor.

So once more Tydings had invoked the FBI as a means of discrediting McCarthy and once more the Bureau records show this was a deception. The Tydings statement as to the contents of the file on Lattimore's views and actions was no better. Noteworthy in this regard was the Tydings comment that there was "nothing in that file" to indicate Lattimore was, "or ever had been, a Communist." Considering what's actually in the records, this was an amazing statement, as it's impossible to read the file without encountering a flat refutation of it. Thus section 1, page 1, tells us that, as of May 16, 1941 (during the Hitler-Stalin pact), Lattimore, like Robert Oppenheimer, was on the Bureau's "custodial detention" list, and that his "nationalistic tendency" was described as "Communist."[17] (See page 393.) As this is the very first item in the professor's FBI rap sheet, it's difficult to miss it.

As to why Lattimore was so regarded there is much else in the Bureau archive of kindred nature. The files are replete with data about his links to Communists and Soviet agents, allegations that he stacked the Pacific office of OWI with pro-Red staffers, that he belonged to Communist Party fronts, that his writings were pro-Soviet propaganda. Again, it's hard to imagine any halfway accurate précis of the file that could have omitted all these items. Whether such charges were valid is perhaps—to stretch the point in Lattimore's favor—a debatable question. That such charges appear repeatedly in the Lattimore file quite obviously isn't.

However, the pending issue isn't Communist affiliation *per se,* but the matter of spying, and the supposedly preposterous nature of the charge that Lattimore was an espionage agent. In fact, the FBI file contains numerous allegations that Lattimore was both a Communist (though possibly not holding a party card, as clandestine operatives usually didn't) *and* an espionage agent. And while passages on this are frequently redacted, they leave no doubt the charges were taken seriously by the FBI and were being pursued with vigor.

There is, for instance, the conspicuous fact that most entries in the Bureau's file on the professor are captioned. "Owen Lattimore, Espionage—R." This meant Lattimore was specifically the subject of an espionage investigation, and the "R" in the heading stands for "Russian." As this rubric appears throughout the Bureau's records on the case, it's again hard to see how anyone reviewing the file, or any adequate distillation, could fail to catch it.

There were several charges of this sort, but the one that seems to have triggered the Bureau's active interest occurred in December 1948, when it was running down leads in the Hiss-Chambers case. As part of this inquiry, Hoover's men interviewed Alexander Barmine, the former Soviet intelligence officer who would later draw the notice of McCarthy. In this interview, the file relates, "information [was] received from Barmine in which he stated that General Berzin

HARD TO MISS

This May 1941 FBI custodial detention notice for Owen Lattimore, describing the professor's "nationalistic tendency" as "Communist," appears on page one, section one, of the Bureau's Lattimore file as reflected in the FOIA records.

Baltimore, Maryland
May 16, 1941

M E M O R A N D U M

The following name is submitted for consideration for Custodial Detention in case of a national emergency.

      Name – OWEN LATTIMORE
      Address – 210 Chancery Road
      Nationalistic Tendency – Communist
      Citizenship Status – Unknown

SUMMARY OF FACTS:

      OWEN LATTIMORE is Vice-Chairman of the Maryland Civil Liberties Committee according to correspondence which among other things criticized the FBI and the Dies Committee and on other literature obtained in the Enoch Pratt Library, Maryland Room, Verticle File, under the title, "Maryland Civil Liberties Committee, Baltimore, Maryland".

NOTE:

      The Baltimore Field Division is presently conducting active and vigorous investigation concerning the activities of the above named individual.

COPIES DESTROYED

100- 24628-1

CH-21

MAY

Source: FBI Owen Lattimore file

of the Red Army intelligence at one time identified Lattimore to him as a Russian agent." The general, said Barmine, had wanted him to set up a commercial cover for Soviet espionage in China:

> Informant recalls that Berzin then told him . . . "we have the organization there already" . . . Berzin said the organization was called "the Institute of Pacific Relations" and it was the basis for our network in China . . . At the time Berzin mentioned the fact that the two most promising and brilliant young men that the Soviet military intelligence had in the IPR were Owen Lattimore and Joseph Barnes.[18]

When these Barmine statements made their way to Hoover, he told the Baltimore office of the FBI to get on the case forthwith. "It is . . . noted," said the Director, "that Lattimore was involved in the Philip Jaffe [*Amerasia*] investigation and was a known contact of several subjects in the Gregory case . . . In view of the many allegations concerning the subject . . . it is believed that a thorough and complete investigation should be conducted concerning Lattimore and should be directed at ascertaining whether or not he is or has been in the past engaged in espionage activities . . . The files of the Bureau will be reviewed and you will be furnished with pertinent information concerning his espionage connections."[19]

Subsequent entries refer to still other such allegations, from sources other than Barmine. While so heavily redacted it's hard to assess the statements or glean details, they give some idea of what the additional charges were based on. On June 22, 1949, Hoover sent a memo to the CIA saying "various informants have identified Lattimore as a possible espionage agent," but with further details deleted. However, at the conclusion of the memo, there is reference to a charge that Lattimore, "while acting as an adviser to Chiang Kai-shek, was divulging information to the Russians."[20]

This comment is fleshed out in a Bureau summary of September 1949, which says: "Allegations made by informants unsubstantiated to date linking Owen Lattimore with Soviet espionage. He was suspected of engaging in espionage for a foreign power while in Shanghai, China, in 1927. Sometime prior to 1938 [blacked out] named as working for the Russians in China." On September 16, Hoover sent another memo to the CIA asking help with foreign aspects of the case. After many deletions of specifics, this concluded by asking the CIA "if through your sources additional information regarding the allegations could be ascertained as well as any other information which would indicate Lattimore's connections with the Soviets while in China."[21]

Filling in some blanks is a Truman Justice summary of the case that wound up in the clutches of McCarthy. One of the things this makes clear is that at least some of the charges of Lattimore subversion against the Chiang

Kai-shek regime came from that regime itself. In this memo, an FBI contact identified as "Bureau source T-1" (a high official of a foreign government stationed in the United States) relayed what he said were the views of Chiang. This source "advised the Bureau that in May or June 1948, he had lunched with Generalissimo Chiang Kai shek . . . at which time Chiang said he had no evidence Owen Lattimore was a Communist. However, he (Chiang) had been advised by Tai-li, his director of Chinese military intelligence, that in 1941 while adviser to Chiang Lattimore had been sending coded messages to Yenan from Chungking."[22]

Another intriguing item in this memo brought the matter closer to home. This was a message from the previously noted Soviet agent Chen Han-Seng, a Lattimore contact at both Johns Hopkins University and the IPR and an alumnus of the Sorge spy ring. On January 10, 1948, Chen wrote from Baltimore to Edward Carter, enclosing a six-page memorandum titled "Troops Under Chiang Kai-shek (January 1948)." Chen's cover note to Carter stated: "At the request of Owen L. I have compiled from very confidential sources a list of troops under the Nanking [Chiang Kai-shek] government. The first top copy went to Owen, as it would be useful for his reference. I take the pleasure of forwarding this carbon copy in the hope that it might also be of some interest to you and your office."*[23]

This episode seemed rather puzzling for a mere "writer and scholar," as Lattimore claimed to be, pursuing purely academic interests. Why would such an ivory tower figure ask the veteran Comintern agent Chen Han-Seng for information on troop deployments under Chiang Kai-shek, then locked in a death struggle with the Reds of China? And why, indeed, was this hard-core Moscow agent and member of the Sorge spy ring being sponsored and mentored by Lattimore in the first place?

As the case of Chen suggests, Lattimore spent an inordinate amount of time swimming in a veritable Red sea of officially identified Communist spies and Moscow agents. Among his innumerable contacts of this nature, according to the Bureau and McCarran records, were Chi Chao-ting, Lauchlin Currie, T. A. Bisson, Frederick Field, Michael Greenberg, Mary Jane Keeney, Philip Jaffe, David Wahl, Harriet Moore, Rose Yardumian, Lawrence Rosinger, and Guenther Stein, all earlier noted in these pages. All were also identified under oath to Congress, and in investigations of the Bureau, as Communists, Soviet spies, or agents of influence for the Kremlin.

As the names of Bisson, Chi, Field, and Jaffe further suggest, Lattimore

---

*When confronted by the FBI with the letter from Chen and the enclosed list of Nationalist troops, Lattimore said he had no recollection of ever having seen the letter or the list of troops, nor did he have any recollection of ever having asked Chen for such a roster.

was tight with the *Amerasia* crowd, since all of these had been closely connected, as had he, to that unusual publication. Throw in the names of Andy Roth and Lauchlin Currie and it's obvious Lattimore was linked as well, not just to the journal, but to key figures in the scandal and the cover-up that followed. When we recall that the biggest fish caught in the *Amerasia* net was John Service, yet another Lattimore friend and ally, it's self-evident the professor was tied to this crew by multiple contacts, a fact well noted by the Bureau.

There is one other such *Amerasia* linkage reflected in the Bureau archives, though not recorded in the usual histories. This involved the Chinese national Chew Hong, who worked for Lattimore at OWI in the war years and was then under suspicion by security forces as a Red agent. In an episode uncovered by McCarthy, Lattimore had gone to bat for Chew, overridden the security types at Civil Service, and thus kept Chew on the payroll at OWI (along with Chi Chung Kuan, the father of Chi Chao-ting).

All of that happened in 1943. Two years later came the *Amerasia* case. In this inquiry, the FBI found that many purloined documents had stemmed from OWI, often bearing indications that showed who had had them in his possession. In several cases, these papers had check marks by the name of Chew Hong, suggesting these were his copies. Based on that information, Hoover and his agents considered Chew a prime suspect in the case—and were also taking a look at other Lattimore protégés and allies at OWI. In the *Amerasia* affair, it seemed, all roads led to the professor.*[24]

From these fragments, a number of conclusions are apparent. Most obviously, it's clear that somebody—or several somebodies—alleged that Lattimore had been a Soviet intelligence asset in China in 1927, had been something similar in the 1930s, and then again in 1941–42 when he was advising Chiang. On top of this, according to Barmine, Red Army general Berzin said Lattimore had been a Soviet intelligence agent—an allegation repeated by Barmine in an appearance before McCarran. And it's obvious that Lattimore was linked, in myriad ways, to the *Amerasia* combine.

All this was well known to the Bureau, and all of it was the subject of an active investigation when Joe McCarthy made his charges and Tydings held his hearings. It's thus clear that when Tydings said there was *"nothing in that file . . . to show . . . that you were in any way connected with any espionage information or charges,"* he was once more baldly misstating what's in the records. As the investigation was ongoing, and the redacted fragments are hard to gauge, this doesn't mean the charges were true, or that if they had once been

---

* Added to this is the further fact that the FBI, on the weekend before the *Amerasia* arrests, had surveilled Philip Jaffe, John Service, and Andrew Roth at or in the vicinity of Lattimore's residence in Ruxton, Maryland.

true they remained so in 1950. But, again, the fact that the charges *existed* and were being carefully vetted by the Bureau is an incontestable fact of record.*

As to whether such charges were valid when McCarthy made his later-retracted "espionage" allegation, given the condition of the files, it's hard to judge, but the probabilities are against it (and even if the charges were true it's hard to see how McCarthy could have proved them). Lattimore may well have been coaching or debriefing the *Amerasia* suspects, or receiving intel from Chen, and could have been involved in transmitting such data himself years before from China. However, the likelihood that he was directly engaged in such activity circa 1950 was small, for two reasons. One is that, after he left OWI, he would have had little or no independent access to confidential data worth passing on to Moscow; the other is that he was far too important in his role as propagandist to have been involved in the often petty but always dangerous business of filching papers.

In this connection, the Lattimore ties to Currie are instructive. The two were especially close and worked together on many projects. It was Currie who got Lattimore named adviser to Chiang Kai-shek, then engineered his appointment to travel with Henry Wallace to the USSR and China. As noted, both Currie and Lattimore were tied to the British émigré-Bentley suspect Michael Greenberg, who first worked at the IPR and then smoothly transferred to Currie's operation on the staff of the White House. Currie-Lattimore had also joined forces to get the notorious Communist agent Field an appointment to military intelligence in the war years (an effort that was, fortunately, thwarted).

That Currie himself was engaged in spying we know from the Bentley testimony and the witness of *Venona,* which suggests there was nothing wildly implausible in the notion that his good buddy and alter ego Lattimore might have done the same, had opportunity presented. However, Currie on the White House staff had access to confidential data that Lattimore, generally speaking, didn't. There would have thus been up through mid-1945 (when Currie left the government) a fairly natural division of labor: Currie as Mr. Inside, handling the espionage aspect, Lattimore as Mr. Outside, carrying on the public propaganda.

All this brings us back to that "desk in the State Department" McCarthy said Lattimore had, Lattimore swore he didn't, and the Tydings panel concluded was another McCarthy falsehood. In the files of the IPR, the McCarran

---

* All of which provides a possible clue as to why McCarthy may have made his original espionage statement. At the executive session where he said this, he intimated that he knew something of the contents of the Bureau's Lattimore file—apparently conveyed to him by someone familiar with it (not, he said, J. Edgar Hoover). If McCarthy had such an inside contact, his source would have seen the file in its pristine state, not redacted as we now have it. As McCarthy had by this point got on the trail of Barmine, he could thus have put the various elements together to reach his espionage conclusion.

panel discovered a 1942 Lattimore memo saying: "I am in Washington about four days a week, and when there can always be reached at Lauchlin Currie's office, Room 228, State Department Building, Telephone National 1414, extension 90."[25] Confronted with this, Lattimore said it totally slipped his mind when he was asked if he "had a desk" in the State Department and denied it. Only when the McCarran panel came up with documentary proof did he remember.* But then, as noted, he was a busy man and couldn't be expected to recall such petty details about his crowded wartime schedule.

---

*The distinction was that Currie's office was in the (old) State Department *Building*, not in the State Department offices as such, a point Lattimore belatedly made but could have brought out, perhaps to better effect, had he admitted the connection at the beginning. However, the fact that Currie was the President's top in-house adviser on China, rather than simply one State Department official among many, made the linkage more important, not less.

CHAPTER 30

Dr. Jessup and Mr. Field

I F LATTIMORE was the intellectual guru of the IPR and Edward Carter its organizational spark plug, its most eminent and visible leader holding federal office was Ambassador Philip Jessup.

There were others connected to IPR with past or present government rank as prestigious as that of Jessup, some a good deal more so—Gen. George C. Marshall, former Under Secretary of State Sumner Welles, and other such distinguished figures. In most cases of this kind, however, the tie-in was mainly formal—a matter of lending a name, or sometimes a presence, to help a seemingly worthy outfit. Off-hand associations of that sort didn't mean the people involved knew much about the IPR, its personnel or daily workings.

Jessup was different. Far from being a casual supporter or letterhead decoration, he was actively engaged with the Institute for about a decade and high up in its inner councils. He had served as chairman of the American group, leader of the international body, and head of the IPR research committee, which had oversight of publications. In the period 1939–42, especially, he was in constant contact with Edward Carter, involved in making decisions about meetings, speakers, and research projects, as integral to the functioning of the group as any full-time staffer.

This background became the more important when Jessup went on to become a major figure in the State Department. In March of 1949, he ascended to the post of Ambassador at Large and would be asked by Dean Acheson to play a pivotal public role in the conduct of China policy. Most conspicuously, Jessup would head the committee that crafted the "White Paper," released in August 1949, washing our hands of the anti-Communist Chiang Kai-shek in China, declaring the Communists the winners of the civil war there, and arguing that nothing occurring in that struggle could be laid at the door of State.

The white paper was significant, and would be disputed, not only for what it said but for what it did. At the time it was put together, the fighting was still going on in China, with the Communists controlling about half of the country, mostly in the north, while the forces of Chiang Kai-shek were hanging on in southern China. There were those knowledgeable on the matter, such as Defense Secretary Louis Johnson and Gen. Claire Chennault, who urged that the document not be issued, saying it would strike the final deathblow at the anti-Communist forces, signaling that they were abandoned. The paper was released nonetheless, with exactly the political-psychological effects predicted.

This having been accomplished, Acheson called on Jessup to play a further role in shaping policy toward Asia—to organize and lead a conference of Far East experts to discuss the proper course for the United States to take following the China meltdown. Jessup accepted this assignment, and such a confab was duly held in early October 1949, involving a most unusual mix of speakers and advancing some provocative notions. Thereafter, Jessup would continue as an Acheson confidant on other matters, also mainly geared to China.

Jessup was thus the State Department official who most clearly linked the program of the IPR to policy-making in Foggy Bottom. His only competitor for this honor was John Carter Vincent, who had even more to do with policy but whose connections to IPR, though close, weren't nearly so close as those of Jessup. Making Jessup's role somewhat peculiar was the fact that, despite his IPR involvements, he wasn't an Asia or China expert. His background was in international law, which he taught for many years at Columbia University Law School. As Acheson likewise knew little about Chinese affairs, he and Jessup were on this point oddly twinned, but between them would make a lot of policy on China.

McCarthy had tried to raise the question of Jessup's views and actions before the Tydings panel but got nowhere in the effort. Tydings would hear nothing on the subject from McCarthy, but instead brought the ambassador to the stand to make an impassioned defense of his career, opinions, and credentials, an appearance treated by Sens. Brien McMahon and Theodore Green as a forensic triumph. Histories of the era reflect this view and would lead one to believe McCarthy had nothing to back his stance, simply tried to slander Jessup, and in this was ignominiously defeated. But as with other topics noted, a study of the documentary sources suggests another reading—and in this instance McCarthy was eventually able to get a lot of documents on record.

Of prime importance in the Jessup saga were Senate hearings in September and October 1951 in which his qualifications to be a U.S. delegate to the United Nations were considered, and McCarthy appeared as principal witness in opposition. Here McCarthy would make his case in somewhat orderly manner and debate it with Democratic senators John Sparkman of Alabama, the subcommittee chairman, and the archliberal J. W. Fulbright of Arkansas, inveterately hostile to McCarthy. Likewise, Jessup was on the stand for several hours, cross-examined by Sen. Owen Brewster (R-Maine) and to a lesser extent by Sens. Guy Gillette (D-Iowa) and H. Alexander Smith (R-N.J.), the other members of the panel.

In his critique of Jessup, McCarthy brought forth materials concerning the ambassador's actions and opinions, allegedly proving an "affinity for Communist causes." A vast amount of time was spent on Jessup's links, or lack thereof, to cited Communist front groups. McCarthy said Jessup was connected to five of these, plus a sixth affiliation involving Mrs. Jessup (and Jessup himself somewhat less directly). Details about these matters are perhaps of little intrinsic interest now except to specialists on such issues, but in 1951 they were thought important, and much effort was devoted to parsing them correctly. Their significance for this study is akin to that of the Wheeling numbers, the four committees, or the backstage history of the *Amerasia* scandal, as they go to the question of who was being accurate and honest, who erred as to details, and who was actively trying to obscure the record.

One thing the Sparkman hearings made clear was that McCarthy had his documents in order, and projected them in graphic fashion. His exhibits included the letterheads of Communist fronts, citations of these from official sources, copies of checks the Communist Frederick Field had written to the IPR, and related items. In the case of the asserted fronts, the point was to show the pro-Red character of the group on the one hand and Jessup's connection to it on the other. In all such cases, the McCarthy data were accurate in detail, but in one particular could be faulted, and promptly were, for lack of context.[1]

This was the Committee to Lift the Spanish Embargo, concerning which McCarthy's exhibit showed the nature of the group, its citation as subversive by the Attorney General, and the fact that its literature featured a quote from Jessup and another law professor in support of its position (one of several such quotes in the original document). On examination, and as McCarthy acknowledged, this didn't mean Jessup was a member or sponsor of the group, but rather that it was in sympathy with his views, which was a different matter.

Jessup and his supporters made much of this, and there was logic to their protest. McCarthy countered that the point of the exhibit was that Jessup *opposed* an embargo on the sale of arms to pro-Communist elements in Spain in the 1930s, but *supported* an embargo on arms to England during the Hitler-Stalin pact. This was true, and rather important, but on the merits of the exhibit as such Jessup had his best moments of rebuttal. In the other cases, there was less to be said—though much was attempted—in behalf of Jessup, and this plainly weakened his credibility with the panel. McCarthy's charges relating to these matters, and Jessup's answers, were as follows:

• *The National Emergency Conference for Democratic Rights.* This group had been cited by the House Committee on Un-American Activities and a House Appropriations subcommittee as a Communist front on no fewer than three occasions—in 1943, 1944, and 1947. It was indeed a quite obvious front, including such familiar denizens of the Marxoid left as Franz Boas, Robert Morss Lovett, Lillian Hellman, and numerous others known to students of the genre. (It was also a predecessor to an even more notorious front called the National Federation for Constitutional Liberties—cited in the Francis Biddle list of 1942.)

Philip Jessup was listed as one of the sponsors of the National Emergency Conference, as shown by McCarthy in his photostatic copy of its letterhead. Jessup's response to this was (a) that, à la Dorothy Kenyon, he had "no recollection" of being involved with it and that his name must have been used without his permission; and (b) that anyway, other respectable folk who weren't Communists in the slightest had been involved with it as well. In this category, Fulbright, and later Jessup himself, highlighted the name of Sen. Paul Douglas (D-Ill.), a well-known anti-Communist liberal.[2]

On inspection, these answers didn't appear to be too convincing—the reference to Senator Douglas being especially unhelpful. As emphasized by Senator Brewster, Paul Douglas *had* been a member of the group but in 1940 resigned from it in a testy letter to Franz Boas, precisely because it was so conspicuous a front.[3] Jessup, who said his name was used without his consent and had known about the listing for some time before it was surfaced by McCarthy, had made no similar move to sever the connection. His failure to do so elicited a doubtful comment from Democrat Gillette—a danger sign for Jessup, indicating he was losing ground with moderate members of the panel.*[4]

• *The American Russian Institute.* This was an equally blatant outfit set up in the 1920s by the Soviets and run by their American henchmen to promote the Moscow cause in U.S. discourse. Its leaders, too, were well known in

---

*GILLETTE: But you have taken no action of any kind. You did not consider it of sufficient moment to take any action to determine whether it [Jessup's name] was properly there, or whether it was improperly there, or should be removed?
JESSUP: I have not, sir.

Communist-fronting circles and included such hardy perennials of the breed as Henry Pratt Fairchild, John A. Kingsbury, Joe Barnes, Paul Robeson, and many others of like nature (including Jessup's IPR associate, Edward Carter).

As for Jessup's connections with the ARI, McCarthy produced documentation showing the ambassador had sponsored a formal dinner put on by the group, in company with such as Howard Fast, Corliss Lamont, Albert Rhys Williams, Langston Hughes, Ella Winter, and others from the united-front wars of the 1930s and early '40s. (In fact, as it developed, Jessup had sponsored two such dinners.) This irrefutable evidence produced much twisting and turning by Jessup, assisted a bit in these gyrations by his committee allies.

Jessup's first defense was one of the usual efforts at deconstruction—that, after all, many prominent non-Communists had been connected with the dinners also. He made the further point that he had merely sponsored *the dinners,* not the group itself, though this distinction didn't seem very important to his interlocutors. His main argument, however, was a variation on the mistaken-identity plea made in behalf of Gustavo Duran and some other McCarthy targets—except Jessup argued that, in this case, there was a mistake about the identity of *the organization,* allegedly being confused with another, totally separate outfit.

Keying to a statement in 1948 by Attorney General Clark that included a subversive listing for the American Russian Institute of California—also listed as subversive that year by the California state legislature's Committee on Un-American Activities—Jessup contended this was completely different from the group he dealt with in New York (and made a similar argument about yet a third ARI in Boston). On this basis, Senators Fulbright and Sparkman sprang to his defense, concluding that McCarthy had confused a *good* American Russian Institute in New York with a presumptively *bad* American Russian Institute in California.

All of this, however, was eyewash. In fact, the citation of the American Russian Institute by the House Committee in Appendix IX was of the institute headquartered *in New York*—the very group to which Jessup had lent his name in sponsoring the dinners. Further, the American Russian Institute *of New York* was explicitly cited as a Communist front by Attorney General Clark in a letter to the Loyalty Review Board made public on April 27, 1949.[5] This was two years before Jessup suggested to the Sparkman panel that this particular group had not been so listed.

In addition, on further analysis of the records, it turned out the California citation of the supposedly separate institute out west was lifted, verbatim, from the language of Appendix IX on the allegedly innocent New York unit. So far as the California committee was concerned, that is, the two institutes were essentially one—two branches of a single pro-Red operation. In short, there was no question whatever about the citation of the group to which Jessup had been connected, though, he, Sparkman, and Fulbright did all they could to talk around this.[6]

• *The American Law Students Association.* McCarthy pointed out that this group was listed in Appendix IX as one of several "miscellaneous Communist and Communist-front organizations," and that this listing said its material bore the "union label 209" (the only group in this particular lineup for which this was stated). This was the well-known icon of the Communist Party print shop called Prompt Press.[7] McCarthy further said the American Law Students Association had been connected with a Communist-dominated group already noted, the American Youth Congress—as testified to by the former executive secretary of the AYC, William Hinckley.

This reference occurred in 1939 hearings of the House Committee when Hinckley submitted a list of "the national organizations that have participated in cooperation with the American Youth Congress . . . [including] the American Law Students Association. . . ." Read into the records of the House Committee at that time by J. B. Matthews were the identities of nine student groups said to be affiliated with the United States Student Peace Conference, yet another front operation, these including "American Law Students Association, American Student Union, [and] American Youth Congress . . ."[8]

From these citations it appeared the American Law Students Association had indeed been closely linked with the complex of "youth" outfits revolving around the notorious AYC. By the same token, there was no question that Jessup had been on the faculty advisory board of the Law Students Association at Columbia, as shown by the letterhead of the group. Jessup conceded this but tried to deflect attention to the question of whether the ALSA was somehow organically connected to the AYC (it wasn't) or had been cited on the Attorney General's list (it hadn't). Those secondary arguments need not detain us, however, as the ALSA was clearly listed in Appendix IX, precisely as McCarthy contended.

• *China Aid Council.* This was yet another conspicuous front (discussed in Chapter 28), a spin-off from the American League for Peace and Democracy and itself cited in Appendix IX and other publications of the House Committee. Its character may be judged from the fact that its directors at various times included such now-familiar pro-Moscow apparatchiks as Chi Chao-ting and his kinsman Philip Jaffe, along with Mrs. Edward Carter, wife of the IPR general secretary (who doubled as head of the American Russian Institute), and that its executive director was Mildred Price, named by both Elizabeth Bentley and Louis Budenz as a Communist agent.[9]

As McCarthy discussed at some length before the Sparkman panel, the sponsor in the case of China Aid was Mrs. Philip Jessup, not an unusual arrangement in such matters (e.g., Mrs. Edward Carter). And while acknowledging that Jessup wasn't accountable for the actions of his wife, McCarthy further observed that Jessup had confirmed his own connection with this egregious front when testifying in the trial of Alger Hiss, to wit: "I have never been a member of it. *I have had some association with it . . .* I don't remember specific contacts. *I remember that we had questions of common interest about arranging meetings, publications, things of that kind,* but I have no recollection of detail on it."[10] (Emphasis added.)

These comments referred to Jessup's activity with IPR, which indeed had numerous overlapping interests with the Council and many overlapping personnel, including Jaffe, Chi Chao-ting, and Frederick Field. In fact, as the McCarran panel observed, China Aid and IPR were both strands in the closely interwoven web of groups, including Field's and Jaffe's *Amerasia,* in which the same people would repeatedly surface, promoting the Communist cause in China.

• *Institute of Pacific Relations.* Jessup's IPR connection was by far the most significant such activity on his record. As noted, he wasn't a mere member, dinner sponsor, or letterhead adviser, but a major operative and moving spirit. As for the subversive label, the IPR hadn't been cited by the House Committee on Un-American Activities, but its American Council had been so named by the California panel, and it was this citation that was mentioned by McCarthy.

As Jessup and his supporters could hardly deny his affiliation with IPR, much of their argument concerned the question of whether the California legislative committee had *withdrawn* its citation of the American Council. The answer to this was a bit cloudy but also not of great importance. In 1948, the new IPR executive director, Clayton Lane, was trying to change the image of the group and live down its previous reputation and had protested to the California panel in this connection. The committee wished Lane well in his cleanup endeavor, said perhaps the IPR wasn't technically a front—describing it rather as "Communist-dominated"—and noted that the panel had "in its files a large amount of documentation on the existence of Stalinist activity and the participation by known Communists in the institute's affairs in the past."[11]

This response from the California committee did little to bail out Jessup, as the "Stalinist" past referred to was precisely the time he, Carter, Lattimore, and Field were wielding dominant power at IPR. Of course, even more significant than the matter of citation by the California panel was the *substantive* character of the IPR. As already seen, the McCarran committee would find, after exhaustive investigation, that "the IPR was a vehicle used by the Communists to orientate American Far-Eastern policy toward Communist objectives." That conclusion by a U.S. Senate panel is obviously more on point than the technical issue of citation by a state committee in Sacramento.

To judge by the hearing record, Jessup's verbal gymnastics on all this weren't impressive to moderate Democrat Gillette or moderate GOPer Smith, one or the other of whose votes the ambassador sorely needed. At one juncture, when Jessup claimed to have "disposed of three organizations to which Senator McCarthy referred," Gillette responded, "The statement that the score is 3 to 0 is deceptive." New Jersey's Smith would allude to "these other organizations that you attempted to explain away." Referring to Jessup's having lent his name to the dinners of the American Russian Institute, allegedly without knowing much about it, Gillette asked, "Is that a custom of yours, to authorize the use of your name in connection with organizations that you know nothing about, their purpose, or their policy?"[12]

While Jessup's performance on these issues didn't do much to aid his cause, more substantial problems would develop on another IPR-related topic: his relationship with Frederick Field, longtime wheelhorse of the IPR, flamingly obvious Communist, and zealous Moscow apparatchik. Though Field was a "secret" Communist back then, and would admit it only some years later, it really wasn't much of a secret, as his Communist sympathies were notorious in the late 1930s and early '40s. This was also, as it happened, the period at which Field was working in the closest harmony with Jessup and earning lavish kudos from his colleague for his invaluable services to the IPR and its Far East mission.

A telltale episode, and a critical test for Jessup and others at the IPR, occurred in 1940 when Field announced he was giving up his post at the Institute to become executive head of the American Peace Mobilization. As seen, this was one of the most blatant front groups ever, created during the Hitler-Stalin pact to agitate against American aid to Britain in its death struggle with the Nazis, then allied with Moscow. Among its projects, in which Field would play a leading role, were calling President Roosevelt a warmonger for his efforts to help the British and picketing the White House with posters saying, "The Yanks Are Not Coming." All this ceased instantly on June 22, 1941, after Hitler invaded Russia, at which point Field and the APM ditched their peace signs and came out for U.S. involvement in the war against the Nazis. It couldn't get more obvious than that.

This background was intensely relevant to Jessup, who had not only worked closely with Field at the IPR but wished him a fervent bon voyage when he went off to run his Moscow-sponsored "peace" charade, and stood ready to welcome him back with open arms once that duty was completed. From the perspective of Jessup and the IPR, the only problem with Field's taking the job at APM was that they were losing a top-notch staffer. Their high regard for Field and urgent desire to have him back at the IPR were expressed in this panegyric:

> Throughout his connection with the Institute, he [Field] has been most scrupulous and exacting in maintaining the highest objective standards for his own IPR writing and that of his colleagues. He has combined personal modesty with the capacity to inspire high achievement on the part of others. He has been noted for practical wisdom in counsel and amazing energy in action. The Board of Trustees desire that the officers assure Mr. Field that his job on the American Council staff will be awaiting him when he completes his present work.[13]

What this said, in so many words, was that once the Soviet agent Field finished "his present work" as a public stooge for Moscow, he would be most welcome to return to his old IPR haunts and colleagues. This was Jessup's personal view as well, as he made clear in a concurrent statement. Jessup said he couldn't "acquiesce in Field's complete separation from the direction of the affairs of the American Council," and expressed the hope that "when his new task was completed, it would be possible for him to go back to active leadership in the work of the IPR."[14]

Field's Peace Mobilization stint was followed by the aborted effort of Owen Lattimore and Lauchlin Currie (both closely linked to IPR) to get him a military intelligence job, perhaps not the ideal place, from a U.S. perspective, to have a Soviet agent. Thereafter, Field would take up a career of even more open Red agitation, including writing a regular column for the *Daily Worker* and articles for the Communist *New Masses*. These ventures, combined with his public flip-flopping at the APM, could leave no doubt, even in the minds of the most obtuse, that he was a Communist and Soviet flunky.

Questioned about all this by the Sparkman panel, Jessup said that only when the APM business developed did he have doubts about Field's sincerity and that the light began to dawn that something was amiss with his valued colleague. He was, said Jessup, "no longer able to believe . . . that Field had been sincere in his noninterventionist attitude, an attitude with which I agreed.* That was the first time I suspected Field of being completely insincere and following the Communist Party line." So, though Jessup had been misled before this, the APM gyrations had opened his eyes to the unhappy truth about his sidekick.[15]

However, this new awareness didn't at all affect Jessup's desire to have Field back at the IPR, where the welcome mat was indeed rolled out exactly as had been promised. Field would, for instance, be placed on the IPR nominating

---

* Jessup was a professed isolationist, along the lines of the *Chicago Tribune,* Charles Lindbergh, Herbert Hoover, and Sen. Robert Taft. For some reason, he is just about the only such isolationist from that era who receives friendly treatment in our histories.

committee for 1941 and elected and reelected as a trustee of the Institute until 1947. Jessup and others at IPR also continued to give Field key assignments, as in planning the 1942 conference at Mont Tremblant in Canada. A Jessup letter of November 30, 1942, recommended a list of thirty people as possible members of the IPR secretariat at this conclave. Among those included on this list was Field. Thereafter, Jessup again recommended Field for appointment to the secretariat at the IPR Hot Springs Conference in 1944.

These continued Jessup ties to and reliance on Field were flabbergasting to Senator Brewster, as was brought out vividly in the hearings. Brought out as well was Jessup's matter-of-fact, completely unapologetic outlook about this linkage:

> BREWSTER: The thing that puzzles me, Dr. Jessup, is that here, 2 years after you concluded that Mr. Field was certainly following a line very different from yours . . . when he followed the Communist reversal [on the Hitler-Stalin pact]—you were recommending him as a delegate. Now, how do you explain that?
> JESSUP: I explain it, sir, by the fact that Field was still in the organization and was still a trustee and was still active in the organization.
> BREWSTER: Although you then knew that he was apparently following the Communist line?
> JESSUP: That is correct, sir.

And again:

> BREWSTER: Is it not true that at the time of the switch you knew he was not sincere and was not following the principles you believed and was reverting to the Communist line?
> JESSUP: Yes, sir.
> BREWSTER: And yet for 3 to 5 years thereafter he continued not only intimate relation to the Institute, but here you recommended he be a delegate. That was entirely your own action. You recommended one whom you had every reason to believe had strong Communist inclinations for so responsible an association.
> JESSUP: That is correct, sir.[16]

So whatever one thinks about the charge that Jessup had "an unusual affinity for Communist causes," he definitely had an affinity for the egregious Communist and Moscow agent Field. Nor, in Jessup's recommendations for conference attendees, was Field a very great exception. When the McCarran committee took a closer look at the list of thirty possible conferees Jessup suggested for Mont Tremblant, it found exactly one-third had been named under oath as Communists or Soviet agents. As McCarran counsel Robert Morris explained it:

In reply to [Senator Ferguson's] question about the 10 people who have been identified as part of the Communist organization on that list recommended by Mr. Jessup . . . we have testimony that Benjamin Kizer was a member of the Communist Party; testimony that Lauchlin Currie was associated with an espionage ring . . . John Carter Vincent has been identified as a member; Harry Dexter White as a member of an espionage ring; Owen Lattimore as a member of the Communist organization; Len de Caux as a member of the Communist Party; Alger Hiss as a member of the Communist Party; Joseph Barnes as a member of the Communist Party; Frederick V. Field as a member of the Communist Party; and V. Frank Coe as a member of the Communist Party.[17]

So, to put the larger situation in a nutshell: Jessup's links to Field on the one hand, and to Dean Acheson on the other, meant someone in close and continuing harmony with a notorious Moscow agent had been counseling America's Secretary of State on matters of the highest import. Functionally considered, Jessup was an interface between the nation's diplomat-in-chief and a hard-core operative of the KGB, again probably not the best of security setups. These links became the more significant given Jessup's responsibilities for China, also a specialty of Field as the Communist Party's commissar for affairs of Asia, as testified by both Louis Budenz and Elizabeth Bentley.

That Jessup was a main fulcrum between IPR and the policy-making drill at State was further apparent in the three-day department policy confab of October 1949. This Jessup had well salted with IPR personnel, conspicuously including Owen Lattimore and Lawrence Rosinger, both later identified under oath as agents of the Soviet interest. Some of the most damaging information about this conference was provided by former governor Harold Stassen, at the time of the proceedings president of the University of Pennsylvania.

In the McCarran hearings, which ran contemporaneously with the Sparkman sessions, Stassen testified about this State Department meeting. The governor had attended as a conferee but said he found himself a dissident minority spokesman, opposed by the likes of Lattimore and Rosinger, whom he identified as leaders of the dominant faction. He said the Lattimore-Rosinger group had pushed a comprehensive program, the main elements of which included:

That the United States should recognize the Communist Peoples Republic government under the leadership of Mao tse-tung at an early date . . . That it should be United States policy to turn Formosa over to the Chinese Communist government . . . That the United States should not approve of the blockade of the Communist Chinese coast by the Chinese Nationalists . . . and should send economic aid to the areas of China under Communist control. That no aid should be sent to the non-Communist guerrillas in the South of China, nor to the Chiang Kai-shek forces, and military supplies on route to them should be cut off.[18]

Stassen also said he strongly protested to Chairman Jessup about the trend of this discussion. "I pleaded with him," said Stassen, "not to implement the Lattimore policy . . . He said that the greater logic lay with the Lattimore group." All of this would be vehemently denied by Jessup and the State Department, which claimed it had no plans to do the things Stassen said were thus promoted. (In fact, as shall be shown, it planned to do not only all of this but a good deal more.)

In further interplay between the McCarran and Sparkman hearings, other witnesses would confirm the Stassen comment on Jessup and the question of recognizing Beijing. Gen. Louis Fortier of MacArthur's staff told McCarran he had a discussion with Jessup in early 1950, when the latter was sent by Acheson on a fact-finding trip to Formosa and Japan. In their conversation, said Fortier, Jessup indicated an early intention of the U.S. government to recognize Red China—which the State Department and Jessup would vigorously deny. Senator Smith, in the Sparkman hearings, recalled that he had a similar talk with Jessup, from which he got the identical message.

Concerning all of which Senator Brewster would sum up as follows: "We have now three cases here, the first that of Senator Smith, who had this conversation in which he gained an impression [on the recognition question]; the next that of General Fortier, who had this conversation which he detailed, the third now of Mr. Stassen."[19] So in this case a three-to-nothing count was chalked up by the Senate umpires, not against McCarthy, but to the detriment of Jessup.

In the end, Jessup's performance before the Sparkman panel proved shaky, conflicted, and unpersuasive. Both Gillette and Smith, after much agonizing on the subject, joined Brewster in voting against him, and so the nomination was rejected in committee. The McCarthy case the Tydings panel refused to hear had carried the day with two of the leading moderates in the Senate. It was by far the biggest trophy ever bagged directly by McCarthy. In the meantime, he was on the trail of even bigger game—a hunt in which his aim would be less true, despite the larger target.

CHAPTER 31

A Conspiracy So Immense

MCARTHY'S most controversial speech, deplored by friend and foe alike, was his marathon 70,000-word indictment of Gen. George C. Marshall, presented to the Senate on June 14, 1951, later published in book form, slightly altered and expanded, as *America's Retreat from Victory*.[1]

In going after Marshall, McCarthy was attacking a national icon, and thus bound to get himself in even more hot water than the simmering tub that was his usual daily portion. Pondering the policy blunders of the war and post-war era, he sought an analytical framework for the mournful data. Though apparently no one recalls it, McCarthy occasionally made other geopolitical speeches about the course of Cold War policy and why it was disastrous for our interests. Sometime in early 1951, he came across an explanation that seemed to solve the puzzle: the man responsible for all this woe was George C. Marshall—Truman's Secretary of Defense, former Secretary of State, and Army Chief of Staff during World War II.

It was an open secret in the 1950s, and has been verified since, that this McCarthy speech was drafted by Forrest Davis, a prominent journalist of the era. Davis had prepared the manuscript as a writing of his own (it bears many earmarks of his style), but then gave it to McCarthy—who found in it the *éclaircissement* he was seeking.[2] The thesis of the manuscript/speech/book was that Marshall, at every step along the way in World War II and the early post-war period, made choices that were not only wrong but served the ends of Moscow. The point was documented from the memoirs of key players in the events, a field of study well known to Davis.

The McCarthy-Davis speech reviewed some critical episodes of the war and wartime conclaves, mostly those in which Marshall was on the opposite side from England's Winston Churchill and in agreement with the Russians. Among these was Stalin's demand for an early "second front" in Europe, whereby Anglo-American forces would land on the northern coast of France, as against Churchill's off-touted plan to move up through Italy to the "soft underbelly" of the Balkans. The Churchill scheme would have put U.S. and British forces into Eastern Europe rather than leaving that sector to the Russians. Marshall's views, and the course taken, were closer to Stalin's preference than to Churchill's.*

Next the speech considered the mysterious post–D-Day decision of U.S. officials to pull up short in Europe, letting the Soviets take both Berlin and Prague. This allowed Moscow to stake a de facto claim to half the continent and created countless problems for the West in maintaining access to Berlin. Responsibility for this, and much else that happened in Europe, McCarthy pinned on Marshall. McCarthy-Davis then considered issues hashed out at the Yalta conference in February 1945, with particular focus on whether concessions made there to Stalin were needed to involve him in the Pacific fighting. In some ways this was the most significant aspect of the speech, and of the blunders it was addressing.

FDR's secret Yalta deal with Stalin, McCarthy noted, gave the Soviets control of Manchuria's ports and railway system, while inviting them at virtually no cost to themselves to take possession of this all-important Chinese province. This handover of Manchuria, the speech asserted, was the basis for much that happened later in China, as the Soviets looted the province of Japanese arms and ammunition, then turned much of this plunder over to their Yenan allies.† The speech spotlighted the role of Marshall in this disastrous sequence and the China debacle that followed, most notably his mission there in 1946 on behalf of President Truman.

There were other topics covered, but these were the main ones. In every case, McCarthy argued, Marshall's decisions and weight of counsel helped ad-

---

*Churchill in *The Hinge of Fate* would argue that he really didn't want to invade the Balkans—this stated as a defense against the charge of being anti-Russian. Most students of the matter think he did aim for the Balkans, which in retrospect seems to his credit and not requiring defensive comment.

†As McCarthy phrased it, the goal of U.S. policy at Yalta and after "should have been not how to get the Russians in, but how to keep them out." His discussion of all this closely mirrored that of the *New York Times*'s Hanson Baldwin—frequently referred to in the speech—who noted that intelligence reports showing that the Japanese were already beaten, and that Russia's entry into the war could and should have been avoided, were kept from high-ranking policy makers.

vance the Soviet cause and injured that of Western freedom. From the stand-point of the conventional wisdom, this was all of course outrageous. McCar-thy, however, made the arraignment even more so by adding dicta that went beyond the general's conduct to the question of his motives. In the most fa-mous portions of the speech, McCarthy said:

> How can we account for our present situation unless we believe that men high in this government are concerting to deliver us to disaster? This must be the product of a great conspiracy, a conspiracy on a scale so immense as to dwarf any previous such venture in the history of man. A conspiracy of infamy so black, that when it is finally exposed, its principals shall be forever deserving of the maledictions of all honest men. . . .

And further:

> What can be made of this unbroken series of decisions and actions con-tributing to the strategy of defeat? They cannot be attributed to incompe-tence. If Marshall were merely stupid, the laws of probability would dictate that part of his decisions would serve this country's interest.[3]

McCarthy has taken his lumps for giving this speech from just about everyone who ever made a comment on it. The criticism is deserved, but for reasons slightly different from those suggested in the standard treatments. For one thing, a good deal of what he had to say about the policy blunders was not only true but ur-gently important. The uproar about Marshall's motives tended to obscure this. For another, McCarthy was quite right that an immense conspiracy was afoot—especially with regard to China—though erring as to the role of Marshall.

In discussing all this, it's well to keep in mind that the Marshall speech was distinct from other McCarthy cases. In more typical instances, McCarthy's point was that an Owen Lattimore or Philip Jessup not only held policy views that favored Yenan or Moscow but had pro-Red leanings and connections. There were no charges of this sort concerning Marshall. The case was made strictly on the basis of the policies he favored and their abysmal outcomes.

McCarthy's reasoning here has been condemned not only by his many crit-ics, but by his corporal's guard of backers. Thus William Buckley and Brent Bozell took him to task in their still highly relevant book for the implicit syllo-gism that, because somebody made decisions that produced disasters, the deci-sion maker must have wanted these to happen.[4] Inferring subjective motives from objectively bad effects, said the authors, misreads the fallible nature of the species. That was true enough, up to a point and with some provisos. How-ever, there was another, less subtle problem with the McCarthy enthymeme—in its factual predicates: that Marshall *everywhere* and *always* made wrong decisions or urged mistaken courses, and that in the trend of Cold War policy he was the ruling figure.

Without trying to rehash the long career of Marshall, a few examples may be cited to suggest the factual errors in McCarthy's thesis. One such involved the *modus vivendi* dispute in the run-up to Pearl Harbor. As seen, oft-identified Soviet agents Harry White and Lauchlin Currie were opposed to any such stand-down in Asia, which would have disserved the cause of Moscow. According to all the data we have, Marshall as Army Chief of Staff was on the opposite side of this internal wrangle—for the excellent military reason that the truce being talked of would have given us extra time to improve our weak peacetime defenses before plunging into all-out conflict.[5]

Had Marshall been part of the White-Currie axis, he wouldn't have taken such a view, whatever the military factors. In like manner, his biographers tell us, he battled with Harry Hopkins about the diversion of U.S. ordnance to the Russians and British when this was needed by our forces. (He also reportedly fought Hopkins on the billeting of the pro-Soviet Col. Philip Faymonville to Moscow, another stance that wouldn't have been taken by a Communist-lining Machiavelli.) There is the further point that Marshall's strategic notions for Europe (though not for Asia) were endorsed by Gen. Albert Wedemeyer, a solid anti-Communist who served with Marshall and knew him well.*[6]

None of this, be it said, puts Marshall in the clear for the bad decisions with which he *was* connected—especially those involving China, which were very bad indeed. Here, however, the second axiom kicks in: that Marshall was the Moriarty behind the whole affair, concocting schemes that others followed. On occasion he may have done so, but usually Marshall wasn't making policy but carrying out a line devised by others—following guidance from above, going along with his instructions, being a team player. These were obviously desirable qualities in a soldier; but when the policy thus created was an unrelieved disaster, as occurred in China, Marshall was complicit in the outcome.[7]

The axial period in the China-Marshall story was the fall of 1945, which brought the elevation of John Carter Vincent to the top of State's Far East division and the resignation of Patrick Hurley as U.S. ambassador to China. Though initially naive about the nuances of the China struggle, Hurley knew blatant propaganda when he saw it, was outraged by the anti-Chiang material being cranked out by Service and John Davies, and demanded their recall from China. Like the *Amerasia* scandal that followed, Hurley's charges against the China FSOs were a huge potential stumbling block to the project of sandbag-

---

*Also, on the internal security angle that was McCarthy's own main focus, there are indications that Marshall sought to tighten security measures in the State Department when he was secretary there. It was Marshall, for instance, who in June 1947 ordered the suspension of ten security risks under the McCarran rider and a few weeks later authorized John Peurifoy to permit the House Appropriations Committee probe that produced the Lee list. Though the first of these decisions was reversed, and the second never to be repeated, it's noteworthy that in both cases Marshall's initial moves were geared to better security practice and cooperation with the Congress.

ging Chiang and talking up the rebels. Hurley's comments were thus ignored entirely or ridiculed as the ravings of a blowhard. A proud man used to better treatment, he resigned in late November, to be replaced by Marshall.*

Some three weeks later, Marshall was sent out to China, where he would be greeted by General Wedemeyer, who had succeeded the cantankerous Stilwell as U.S. military commander in the region. According to Wedemeyer, Marshall was fatigued and out of sorts and knew little of the byzantine complexities of the China tangle. Worse still, the old general was gruffly disinclined to hear much of anything Wedemeyer tried to tell him, especially the intractability of the Communist problem and the likelihood that efforts to smooth this over were doomed to failure.

Actually, Marshall did know something of the China conflict—or thought he did. As subsequent inquiry would reveal, he had by this time been well indoctrinated by forces opposing Chiang Kai-shek and congenial to Yenan. We need only note in this respect that he was the friend and patron of Stilwell, whose hatred of Chiang Kai-shek was boundless and who had had many opportunities to transmit this to Marshall. It would have been hard to find a mentor on China as hostile to Chiang or as friendly to the Yenan interest.

Unfortunately, Marshall was now given just such a mentor in the person of John Vincent, a close ally of Service and Soviet agent Lauchlin Currie, pal of Owen Lattimore, and leading member of the IPR group at State. A career FSO, Vincent through the years voiced some unusual views about East-West relations, the Soviet Union, and the struggle for control of Asia. In the latter 1930s, he had been a staunch supporter of Chiang Kai-shek, but in the 1940s turned bitterly against the Chungking leader. Vincent in the war years seethed with hostility to Chiang, expressed this in dispatches, and advanced the notion of using the lever of U.S. aid to force Chungking's compliance with our wishes.[8]

Vincent's efforts in prepping Marshall for his China mission were in keeping with this background. There would be some confusion and contradictory testimony about Marshall's own input into the instructions that framed the purpose of his journey, but not much doubt about the role of Vincent. It was Vincent who in late November of 1945 supplied a background memo that put Marshall in the China picture and then played a leading part in drafting the general's strange "directive": a statement on the objects of the mission in the name of Secretary of State James Byrnes, plus two memos on the subject signed by Truman—the whole package bearing Vincent's imprint and all given to Marshall for his guidance.[9]

Boiled down, the key provisos of these papers were that the goal of the

---

*Thereafter, in what amounted to a preview of the Tydings inquest, Hurley's accusations against Service *et al.* would be deftly smothered in Senate hearings (chaired by Tom Connally of Texas), the self-evident object of which was to discredit Hurley.

mission was to achieve "peace and unity" in China; that to attain this, Chiang must come to terms with other political forces in the country (including—a telltale Vincent phrase—the "so-called Communists"); and that if this weren't done, U.S. aid to Chiang would be suspended. ("A China disunited by civil strife," said one Truman missive, "cannot be considered realistically as a proper place for American assistance.") All this, despite some sinuosities of language, was simply a recap of the formula earlier spelled out by Solomon Adler in advices to Harry White: Use the bludgeon of U.S. aid to force Chiang into a coalition with the Reds, and if Chiang didn't knuckle under such aid should be denied him.*

If this weren't enough to tilt the mission against Chiang, there were forces already on the ground in China to help advance the project. Among Marshall's principal aides was Adler himself, who would brief the general on economic and financial matters, no doubt explaining who was responsible for China's miseries and the merits of withholding aid from Chiang. (According to later findings of the Senate, Marshall so esteemed Adler's advice he countermanded efforts to have the Treasury staffer sent elsewhere.)[10]

How many other Communist moles had tunneled into the Marshall China operation there is no way of telling, but the number seems to have been substantial. As the historian Maochun Yu observes, based on his study of the Beijing sources: "When George Marshall was in China, Communist penetration of American agencies was rampant. . . . Many Chinese typists and interpreters . . . employed by the OSS and the Office of War Information were secret agents working for Yenan. As revealed in recent materials published in China, they stole U.S. documents, organized secret Communist activities, often forged intelligence, and fed American intelligence agencies in China falsified information . . ."[11]

As of December 1945 when Marshall arrived in China—in sharp contrast to what happened later—the Nationalists were winning their struggle with the Yenan rebels. At this period and in the early months of 1946, the Communists hadn't had sufficient time to be equipped and trained adequately by their Soviet sponsors, and were on the run in northern China. Of course, a situation in which Chiang was fighting and winning wasn't "peace and unity," the *idée fixe* of Marshall's mission. So Marshall's most significant early move was to get Chiang to call off his armies—the first in a series of truces the Reds would agree to when they were losing.

---

*Among other anomalies that might be noted, this bizarre formula gave the Communists de facto veto power over U.S. aid to Chiang. All they had to do to force the cutoff was to ensure that "peace and unity" didn't happen—which, to say no more, was their natural inclination—and Chiang, not they, would pay the price. Assuming the Yenan comrades knew of this proviso, which they undoubtedly did given their extreme penetration of the Marshall mission and U.S. offices in China, it would have been impossible to come up with a concept more likely to ensure that "peace and unity" never happened.

In the judgment of such as Joe McCarthy, the McCarran panel, and China experts Anthony Kubek and Freda Utley, this Marshall effort to stay Chiang's winning hand was foremost among a number of crucial measures that turned the tide in favor of Mao. Given the tough anti-Communist outlook of these sources, some such judgment might be expected. However, the identical view would be expressed by the Red Chinese themselves, as set forth in Jung Chang's definitive study of Mao and his tactics. Jung Chang's discussion of all this, titled "Saved by Washington," informs us:

> Marshall was to perform a monumental service for Mao. When Mao had his back to the wall in what could be called his Dunkirk in late spring 1946, Marshall put heavy and decisive pressure on Chiang to stop pursuing the Communists into Northern Manchuria. . . . Marshall's *diktat* was probably the most important decision affecting the outcome of the civil war. The Reds who experienced that period, from Lin Biao to Army retirees, comment in private that this truce was a fatal mistake on Chiang's part.[12]

Despite this and other Marshall truces, nothing could prevent the Reds and the KMT from waging what both knew was a death struggle, even if George Marshall didn't. Accordingly, in July of 1946, as stipulated in his mission statement, Marshall dropped the hammer on Chiang. Continued fighting wasn't "peace and unity," so aid to the KMT would have to be suspended. *Why* peace and unity were absent didn't matter; even if the Communists were the culprits, as Marshall occasionally acknowledged they had been, U.S. sanctions would be imposed strictly on Chiang. (Against the Reds, of course, we had no such leverage, and the Soviets, for some reason, weren't imposing similar sanctions on their Yenan allies.)*

As would later be discovered, the Marshall arms embargo wasn't anything new, but an extension of preexisting secret measures meant to hinder Chiang in his internal battles—the White-Adler sabotage of the gold loan providing the premier example. There had been backstage efforts to deny military aid as well, months before the embargo was adopted. As described by Col. L. B. Moody, an Army ordnance specialist who in the summer of 1945 inspected surplus munitions intended for the KMT, numerous steps were taken by U.S. officials handling these materials to prevent delivery.

These munitions were under the control of the Federal Economic Administration (successor to the Board of Economic Warfare). When the supplies were to be transferred to Chiang, said Moody, the "FEA took every conceivable

---

*This blow against our nominal ally in China was accompanied by another telltale missive, signed by Truman but again the work of Vincent. "There is increasing awareness," this said to Chiang, "that the hopes of the people of China are being thwarted by militarists and a small group of political reactionaries who are obstructing the general good of the nation by failing to appreciate the liberal trend of the times."

action to block or delay shipment of this essential [material], quite likely taking its cue from Embassy officials." Moody noted that, of 153,000 tons of ammunition supposedly meant for Chiang, only about 2 percent got through, "the rest being dumped in the ocean or otherwise disposed of." Captured German rifles supposedly meant for Chiang were likewise interfered with. "One small shipment started," said Moody, "and the project was cancelled on orders from Washington."[13]

Subsequently, under the Marshall arms embargo, not only were the Nationalists prevented from buying weapons and ammunition, they were also barred from receiving munitions already purchased. To make the shutdown as complete as possible, the embargo was coordinated with the British, the most likely alternative suppliers of weapons and ammo to the anti-Communist armies. This policy was kept in place for almost a year—from the summer of 1946 until the late spring of 1947—and would be resumed, again by clandestine methods, in the months that followed.[14]

As with just about everything else pertaining to our policy in China, the arms embargo was mantled in deception. One of the more bizarre developments along these lines occurred in March of 1947, when the White House unveiled the "Truman doctrine" providing military aid to Greece and Turkey, both then under pressure from Communist forces. The President announced the new policy in vaulting terms about resisting Red aggression around the world—all this while the aid cutoff to Chiang continued.

The stark contrast between this doctrine and what was going on in China was brought out in House committee hearings when Dean Acheson as Under Secretary of State went up to Capitol Hill to explain the Truman program. At these hearings, Rep. Walter Judd (R-Minn.) asked the obvious question: Why provide military aid to oppose Red guerrillas in Greece, when we were doing the exact reverse in China? Acheson answered with one of the more disingenuous statements in an Orwellian record. "The Chinese government," he said, "is not in the position at the present time that the Greek government is in. It is not approaching collapse. It is not threatened by defeat by the Communists."[15]

This answer was the more astounding as it would be flatly contradicted in Acheson's own white paper on China—explaining the China-Greece disjunction in terms of Chiang's alleged failings rather than his unthreatened status. It was also the direct opposite of many backstage State Department assertions, then and later, that Chiang was a triage case whose life support should be suspended. Either way, in the Acheson view, Chiang would be denied assistance. If he was winning, he didn't need it. If he was losing, he couldn't use it.

Revealing also were events in early 1948, after the embargo had been lifted and a worried 80th Congress pushed through $125 million in emergency military aid for Chiang. At this point, the foot-dragging that preceded the embargo once more came into play. Gen. Claire Chennault, longtime Air Force commander in China, would testify that the first shipments of this aid, authorized in early April, didn't reach Shanghai until December. Similar testimony was given by Admiral Oscar Badger, who in the summer of 1948 was part of a U.S. military observer group in northern China. Here KMT forces were anxiously awaiting the arms aid they knew was voted, in preparation for decisive battles. Again, however, the assistance was delayed, and wouldn't arrive until late November.*[16]

A third episode offering a gleam of insight into the bottlenecks and slowdowns occurred early in 1949, when Truman, Acheson, and others in high administration councils decided further military aid to Chiang, though approved by Congress, should be halted—on the now-explicit premise that the KMT cause was hopeless. However, when Michigan GOP senator Arthur Vandenberg learned of this and threatened to make a public protest, Truman reversed his field and ordered that the aid go forward. In passing along these new instructions, Acheson told his State Department staffers, *"It is desirable that shipments be delayed where possible to do so without formal action."*[17] (Emphasis added.)

There have been debates down through the years as to whether and to what degree these measures affected the outcome of the civil war in China. The position of the Acheson forces, set forth in the white paper and court histories of the matter, was that neither the formal embargo nor other efforts to withhold aid to Chiang did any harm, that the aid provided was ample, and that he was bound to lose anyway because of his incompetence and corruption. We can hardly settle that question here—except to note that, if sabotage of the gold loan, imposition of the Marshall embargo, and other recurring aid denials didn't seriously injure Chiang, it certainly wasn't for lack of trying.

Nor would there be lack of trying later. In late 1949, with the fall of China and retreat of the KMT forces to the island of Formosa (Taiwan), one might suppose the State Department's anti-Chiang *jihad* would be called off. It was instead redoubled, as the Acheson forces were now determined to pursue Chiang to his island refuge and finish him for good. This effort proceeded along two divergent but complementary lines—one made public at the time, sufficiently astounding in its own right, the other a deep-dyed secret and even more amazing.

The public part of this vendetta was previewed at the State Department policy confab convened by Philip Jessup in October 1949, immediately following the Red takeover on the mainland. The main thrust of discussion at this

---

* And when it got there, the material was only about 10 percent of what had been expected. Equally dismaying to the KMT forces, said Badger, the material was in many respects defective—machine guns without mounts or clips, no loading machines for ammunition belts, no spare parts. "For the KMT forces," Badger testified, "it was the straw that broke the camel's back." (This delivery of defective equipment was yet another aspect in which developments in China matched those that previously unfolded in the Balkans.)

meeting was that the fall of China was by no means the end of the process but merely a beginning; still other Communist advances in the region were expected, and the recommended policy for the United States was to stand back and let these happen. In particular, according to State's Asia gurus, the United States should acquiesce in a Maoist invasion of Formosa—this to be followed by further renunciations elsewhere, most notably in South Korea.[18]

In short order, a good deal of what was recommended at this conclave would become official policy—most immediately with respect to the anticipated attack against Chiang in his island redoubt. By mid-November, Acheson was advising Truman that the new regime in Beijing should be accorded recognition and that "the United States should disengage completely from Chiang Kai-shek" on Formosa. By late December, the State Department was circulating policy guidance to its officials, saying "loss of the island is widely anticipated" and that it was necessary to dispel "the mistaken popular conception of its importance to the United States defense in the Pacific."[19]

Shortly thereafter, on January 5, 1950, Truman made the write-off official, saying no military aid would be provided by the United States to help Chiang protect Formosa. A week after that, Acheson gave the policy its most famous expression in a speech before the National Press Club. In this talk, he explained that the United States was taking the moral high ground by *not* helping Chiang defend the island (because we would never interfere in the internal affairs of another nation), and described our "defense perimeter" in the Pacific in a way that excluded both Formosa and Korea. All in all, a pretty good approximation of major policy themes emerging from the Jessup chin-pull.[20]

While all this was going on, still other anti-Chiang maneuvering was under way, the details of which wouldn't be known for decades. This involved a series of State Department plots aimed at removing Chiang from Formosa ourselves, either by application of American force and pressure or by fomenting a military coup against him. These plans had an ostensible rationale that differed sharply from Acheson's public statements, but the end result in one crucial aspect would have been the same—lights out for Chiang.

In fact, such clandestine plotting against the anti-Communist leader was nothing novel, as there had been similar plans made during World War II. The central figure in these early schemes was Joe Stilwell, in 1944 waging his own nonstop vendetta against Chiang, assisted by such as John Stewart Service—whose poison pen letters home from China increasingly stressed the theme that the generalissimo should be abandoned. At this period, according to Stilwell's deputy Frank Dorn, Vinegar Joe called him in and ordered him to craft a plan for Chiang's exit from the scene by way of outright murder.

"I have been instructed," Dorn quoted Stilwell, "to prepare a plan for the assassination of Chiang Kai-shek. The order did not say to kill him. It said to prepare a plan . . . The Big Boy [Roosevelt] is fed up with Chiang and his tantrums." From Dorn's phrasing, this seemed to mean the order came from FDR, though Dorn speculated it might have come from Harry Hopkins "or one of the senior officers in the Pentagon." Dorn added that, after weighing several options, such a plan was in fact developed, involving the sabotage of a plane carrying Chiang and Mme. Chiang on a projected diplomatic mission.*

Though Dorn was close to Stilwell and presumably knew whereof he spoke, the existence of so fantastic a plot might be considered doubtful had no other evidence on the matter surfaced. However, confirmation that such a Stilwell scheme did exist was provided in 1985 by OSS archivist Eric Saul, based on the records of that unit. This may have been the same assassination plan or a successor, as it involved the OSS, which Dorn didn't mention. According to Saul, Stilwell was convinced that Chiang was simply feathering his own political-financial nest and thus impeding the war effort in China. So Vinegar Joe "set Detachment 101 [of OSS] the task of taking Chiang out of the picture."[21]

In the event, the top-level order to carry out the assassination wasn't given, so Chiang managed to get through the war without being murdered by his U.S. allies. The animus against him nonetheless continued, in the dispatches of Service-Davies-Adler, efforts to deny arms and money to the KMT, and plotting to bring about Chiang's overthrow once he landed on Formosa. There were multiple links between these State Department projects and the earlier schemes of Stilwell, including the fact that two of Vinegar Joe's war-time helpers were on the Acheson team at State in 1949–50: John Paton Davies, formerly Stilwell's political adviser, and Dean Rusk, deputy chief of staff to Dorn.

How long this State Department plotting had been going on isn't clear, but plans seem to have been in a stage of relatively advanced preparation by the early weeks of 1950, which means they must have started fairly soon after the fall of the China mainland. The most explicit early reference to such scheming is a memo by State Department official W. W. Stuart, dated February 20, 1950, which says, "the following discussion of a United States cultivated *coup d'etat* on Formosa is concerned with the procedural aspects of such action" rather than the merits—indicating that the idea had already been mooted and that Stuart was simply considering ways and means.[22] Thereafter, a whole raft of State Department policy papers would be cranked out on the subject, harping on the evils of Chiang, why he shouldn't be allowed to continue on Formosa, and the urgent need to oust him.

After numerous pros and cons on how to get rid of Chiang had been

---

*In the IPR hearings, committee counsel Jay Sourwine would ask John Carter Vincent, "Did you ever hear of a plan to assassinate Generalissimo Chiang Kai-shek?" And "Did you ever see a memorandum or memoranda concerning such a plan in 1945 or 1946?" Vincent said he recollected nothing about such a plan or such a memo, and so the question was left hanging in mysterious fashion until the revelations of Dorn.

kicked around by State Department policy planners, including John P. Davies, George Kennan, and Paul Nitze, Dean Rusk would produce a forty-page *summa* on the subject, capsuling alternative courses of action. This concluded that the best choices for U.S. policy makers were either to compel Chiang to abdicate by American edict or to sponsor a military coup against him. The State Department candidate for leading such a coup was a dissident KMT general named Sun Li-jen.

Rusk made it fairly clear that he favored the second option, which he expressed this way: "The U.S. should inform Sun Li-jen in the strictest confidence through a private emissary that the U.S. government is prepared to furnish him the necessary military aid and advice in the event that he wishes to stage a coup d'état for the purpose of establishing his military control of the island." So, while the stated Acheson policy was that we couldn't get involved in the internal affairs of another nation to help Chiang defend Formosa, we would be willing to get involved enough to overthrow him.*[23]

Of particular interest in all this was the role of Philip Jessup. In early 1950, while various anti-Chiang initiatives were being mooted in Foggy Bottom, Jessup was off on a "fact-finding" tour of Asia, including Formosa and Japan. It was on this journey, according to Gen. Louis Fortier of General MacArthur's Tokyo staff, that Jessup spread the news of further renunciations in Asia through early recognition of the Red regime at Beijing. It was on this journey also that Jessup reported back to Acheson about the apparently weak state of Chiang's defenses on Formosa.

In one report, Jessup said, *inter alia,* that "the Gimo's[†] house is located quite high in the mountains but only about a 20-minute drive from the center of Taipei [capital city of Taiwan-Formosa]. There was one pillbox with one sentry in one of the many curves in the mountain road, and we saw a few soldiers about but there was no great military presence."[24] These Jessup comments, which might in other context be taken as sightseeing observations, assume a somewhat different meaning against the backdrop of State Department plans for toppling Chiang by military action.

In the end, as with the earlier Stilwell efforts, these schemes for a military rising on Formosa would come to naught. The fact that they occurred at all,

---

*Though this wasn't an assassination plot per se, the likelihood that such a scheme would lead to the death of Chiang and those loyal to him was implicit and in keeping with the outcome of such military risings elsewhere. (In which respect the obvious parallel would be the murder of South Vietnam's Ngo Dinh Diem and his brother, after a virtually identical U.S.-supported coup in November 1963 when Rusk was Secretary of State.) According to Frank Dorn, in fact, there was an alternative coup proposal circa 1950 that explicitly envisioned the death of Chiang, though Dorn didn't give the basis for this statement. In any case, the possible demise of Chiang apparently didn't bother Rusk, who considered the chief danger in such a plot was that it might fail and that U.S. involvement might be exposed, which could have been a bit of a PR problem.

†Diminutive for "generalissimo."

COUP

In this May 1950 memo entitled "U.S. Policy Toward Formosa," State Department official Dean Rusk details plans for a U.S.-sponsored coup d'état against America's anti-Communist ally Chiang Kai-shek.

RODUCED AT THE NATIONAL ARCHIVES

DECLASSIFIED
hority *NND 812001*
NARA Date *1/27*

~~TOP SECRET~~

-2-

willing to leave the Island and turn over the civil and military administration to such Chinese and Formosan leaders as the U.S. may designate; that the U.S. will then give military advice and assistance to the commander responsible for the defense of the Island; that the U.S. will expect the provincial administration on Formosa to give high priority to the welfare of the Formosan people; and that the U.S. will order units of its navy to visit Formosa in order to prevent action by or against Formosa for a period during which the problem of Formosa would be made the subject of discussion with other concerned governments.

(2) The U.S. should inform Sun Li-jen in the strictest confidence through a private emissary that the U.S. Government is prepared to furnish him the necessary military aid and advice in the event that he wishes to stage a coup d'etat for the purpose of establishing his military control over the Island. Sun should also be given ample funds (the total might run into several million dollars) to assist him in buying over the other commanders necessary to such an undertaking; he should be given firm assurances of whatever additional funds he might need in this connection during the early stages. Urgent preparations would have to be made to arrange for the shipment from Guam or some other nearby U.S. base of the arms and ammunition necessary to meet Sun's military requirements at the outset of such an undertaking.

There

~~TOP SECRET~~

Source: State Department records, National Archives

however, tells us much about Dean Acheson and his State Department planners and their true place in the history of the Cold War. Quite obviously, there *was* an "immense conspiracy" afoot concerning China, and had been since the middle 1940s. Some of it was made public at the time, some of it was understandably quite secret. All of it, however, is well documented in official records, though ignored in most of the standard histories.[25]*

A CONCLUDING thought concerns the timing of these events—leaving out the secret plots and looking strictly at the policy measures the State Department made public or more or less acknowledged. Mao had proclaimed his "People's Republic of China" on October 1, 1949, and the Jessup policy confab at State mulling further Red advances was convened a few days later. By mid-November, Acheson was advising Truman to recognize Beijing and let Formosa go under. By late December, the State Department was predicting the "imminent fall" of the island and circulating policy guidance explaining why this need not concern us. On January 5, 1950, Truman made the default official, and seven days thereafter, Acheson told the Press Club, and the world, that both Formosa and Korea were beyond the line of our defenses.

From this hurried sequence, it's evident the Service-Vincent-Jessup crowd was controlling U.S. policy in the Pacific, that more capitulations were in prospect, and that things were moving quickly to make these a *fait accompli* before too much dust had settled over the prostrate form of China. While some of this brought squawks from Congress, that apparently didn't bother State's planners unduly, as they briskly forged ahead with their various up-front and backstage schemes for Asia. As of the Acheson Press Club speech, the whole thing was falling rapidly into place and there didn't seem to be any force on the horizon determined or strong enough to stop it. Four weeks later, a virtually unknown Joe McCarthy, expected to make a talk on housing or farm problems, stepped to the podium in Wheeling.

---

*Linking all this back to Marshall and his part in the China debacle: With respect to the early schemes to murder Chiang, it's hard to believe Stilwell would have been involved in such machinations without the knowledge of his longtime friend and mentor—particularly in view of Dorn's suggestive comment that the order for the murder plan possibly came from "senior" levels in the Pentagon. On the other hand, Dorn in his tell-all mode explicitly said that, had Marshall known of such a plot, he would have disapproved it. As Dorn was in effect outing Stilwell, there isn't any *a priori* reason to suppose he would have held back on Marshall.

As to the later episodes of State Department planning against Chiang, all this occurred in late 1949 and early 1950, after Marshall left the department. Acheson had become Secretary of State in January of 1949, and the policy planners involved in these machinations, including such as Dean Rusk and John Paton Davies, were Acheson protégés or selections (as were, in the earlier going, such pivotal players as John Service and John Vincent). The whole show, so far as we can tell, was Acheson's. All of this would tend to support the view that Marshall, whatever his errors and susceptibility to bad counsel, was far from being the master strategist of State Department skulduggery on China.

CHAPTER 32

The Battle with Benton

THE stock image of Joe McCarthy is that of zealous investigator, questioning witnesses, banging the gavel, ferreting out security risks real or imagined (in the conventional version, of course, strictly the latter), and otherwise pursuing suspects in his hunt for concealed subversives. And a good deal of this sort of thing did happen during his brief tenure as a committee chairman. The obverse of the picture, however, is that McCarthy spent as much time being investigated as he did investigating others. Indeed, during his tempestuous ride as America's most famous Communist fighter, investigations of McCarthy proceeded on virtually a nonstop basis.

These anti-McCarthy inquests included: (1) the Tydings probe, which was supposed to investigate the State Department but which as seen was in its backstage doings actually an investigation of McCarthy; (2) an investigation of the 1950 Maryland Senate race in which Tydings was defeated for reelection by Republican John Marshall Butler; (3) an investigation spun off from the Maryland conflict, based on charges brought against McCarthy by Sen. William Benton (D-Conn.); (4) the famous Army-McCarthy hearings in the spring of 1954; and (5) the censure hearings run later that year by Sen. Arthur Watkins (R-Utah), leading to McCarthy's condemnation by the Senate.

These investigations were in substance closely interwoven—especially the

Tydings hearings, the Maryland inquest, the charges brought by Benton, and the Watkins sessions that preceded the vote of censure. Viewed together, these formed a continuing process that never ceased entirely, with each phase leading to the next and common elements persisting. (Ironically, the best-known of these investigations, the Army-McCarthy hearings, were something of a side-bar in terms of content, though undoubtedly contributing to the final outcome in the damage they inflicted on McCarthy.)

Of note in these investigations was the recurrence of the same issues and same cast of characters working up the charges, though subject to certain modifications and substitutions. The most visible single player in the early going was Tydings, who continued to stay on the case long after his own hearings were concluded and also after he had been defeated for reelection. Following close behind was Benton, who had many grievances against McCarthy and a Javert-like obsession with the subject. Other significant players, by happenstance more than design, were senators Guy Gillette (D-Iowa), whose Subcommittee on Privileges and Elections conducted two of the investigations, and Mike Monroney (D-Okla.), a member of this panel, who chaired the Maryland inquiry.

Hovering in the background were unofficial helpers who worked closely with anti-McCarthy forces in the Senate, many staying the course throughout the investigations. These included the columnist Drew Pearson and his assistant Jack Anderson, reporters for the anti-McCarthy *Milwaukee Journal* and *Madison Capital Times* in Wisconsin, Kenneth Birkhead of the Democratic senatorial campaign committee, various associates of Benton, and—particularly in the later phases of the struggle—a liberal lobby group called the National Committee for an Effective Congress. There were others involved as well, but these were the people who worked with unflagging zeal across a span of years to discredit and bring down McCarthy.

Some particulars of the Tydings investigation have been recounted and would have important consequences later. Before these kicked in, however, Tydings himself would pay a price. In November of 1950, he was defeated for reelection, in a bitter contest, by Republican candidate Butler, a relatively unknown conservative Baltimore lawyer with a distinguished-sounding name. This was a fierce campaign marked by debate about the Communists-in-government issue and the conduct of the Tydings hearings, with substantial involvement on the side of Butler by McCarthy aides and allies. The defeat not unnaturally rankled with Tydings, who moved to make an issue of it in a complaint before the Senate, referred to the subcommittee run by Gillette.

From this action grew the Maryland election probe, important mostly as a warm-up but not without significant aspects of its own. This was the inquiry that focused on a tabloid newspaper called "From the Record," published by pro-Butler forces, attacking Tydings for his conduct of the State Department loyalty hearings. The contents of the tabloid tracked closely with material earlier noted—the thirty-five pages of lost transcript, the kid-gloves treatment of "Dr." Lattimore, and the records of other McCarthy suspects cleared by Tydings. Its most noteworthy feature was a composite photograph of Tydings and former Communist Party boss Earl Browder (see inset, page 428). This photograph and other elements of the tabloid are referred to in the usual histories as showing McCarthy and his staffers did something terribly wrong in helping contrive the defeat of Tydings.

Given this standard treatment of the topic, some notice of the Maryland inquest and its more curious sidebars is in order. For one thing, the way the investigation developed was unusual from the outset. Though Tydings could have challenged the legitimacy of the election under relevant rules and statutes, he never actually did this. In fact, even when he brought his charges before the Senate, he specifically said he wasn't trying to overturn the outcome of the voting. The evident purpose of the complaint was thus simply to make an issue against McCarthy—which was in fact what happened.

In its report, the Gillette-Monroney subcommittee found against the Butler campaign on one substantive legal count—that its campaign manager had not properly reported information about financial contributions as required by law (for which offense he was indicted and convicted). Also, the report raised other questions about the compliance of the campaign with Maryland election statutes and the scope of its political spending, allegedly in excess of stipulated limits. There were no intimations, however, that these details about the Butler operation had other than marginal relevance to McCarthy, so there wasn't that much political mileage in them from the standpoint of the Tydings forces.

While not making any legal finding on the matter, the Gillette-Monroney committee did denounce the "From the Record" tabloid, saying it was "scurrilous" and "defamatory," though exactly what was defamatory about it isn't apparent from the report and hearings. As the tabloid consisted almost entirely of allegations that Tydings hadn't properly conducted his investigation of the State Department, this unalloyed description of its contents would seem to have reflected the pro-Tydings version of the issue rather than an impartial verdict.

Somewhat tipping its hand in this respect, the committee also held forth about commentaries on the election by radio personality Fulton Lewis Jr., himself a resident of Maryland, whom Tydings accused of aiding Butler and who was called as a witness in the hearings. However, no parallel interest was shown in the countervailing efforts of columnist/radio commentator Drew Pearson, who took the opposite position on the contest. Likewise, the committee denounced the "From the Record" flyer for its statement that Tydings by

THE COMPOSITE

The famous "composite photo" from the 1950 Maryland Senate election in which John Marshall Butler defeated Millard Tydings. The *Syracuse Post-Standard*, among others, falsely blamed McCarthy for "framing" Tydings with this "fake photograph."

Source: McCarthy Papers I

inaction had impeded delivery of arms to South Korea, but made no similar critique of Tydings's almost identical charges against the GOP, made in the course of his campaigning.*[1]

More telling than these items—and just about the only thing from the Maryland inquest that would be remembered—was the composite photo. This showed Tydings obliquely face-to-face with longtime Communist Party chieftain Browder, making it appear they had been photographed together. Though the caption described the picture as a "composite," it's likely many people looking at the tabloid might not have read the caption carefully or caught the significance of the term "composite."

This photo was the subject of much outrage at the time, and has been since, as no treatment of McCarthy would be complete without a mention of it. And, up to a point, some outrage was in order, as the most likely effect of the composite would have been to lead readers to think it was a single photo when in fact it wasn't. However, as the hearings made clear, neither McCarthy nor his staffers, though supplying other material for the tabloid, had anything to do with the composite. As shown in some detail by the committee sessions,

---

*Tydings's version was, "If we had done what the Republicans wanted in Korea, there would not have been a gun out there." As earlier seen, Tydings had also lashed out at Senator Jenner of Indiana for allegedly voting in lockstep with the aims of Stalin. Charges of this nature apparently weren't "defamation" if made by Tydings, but became so if made against him.

THE TRUTH COMES OUT

The *Post-Standard* issues a retraction acknowledging, inter alia, that McCarthy "was not responsible" for the composite photo of Tydings and Communist Party chief Earl Browder.

THE POST-STANDARD

The Standard......1829   The Post..........1894
The Post-Standard.........1899

Published Every Day in the Year by
THE POST-STANDARD COMPANY
300 East Fayette Street
Syracuse 1, N. Y.

Richard H. Amberg, *Publisher;* **Henry H. Keller**, *Business Manager.*
Robert L. Voorhees, *Editor;* **Albert V. Brewster**, *Managing Editor;* **J. Leonard Gorman**, *City Editor.*

6   Sunday, March 15, 1953

The McCarthy Record

An editorial published in this space Oct. 19, 1951, has been the subject of a suit for libel by Sen. Joseph R. McCarthy of Wisconsin. Since publication of this editorial the statements therein have been subjected to careful study in the light of all the facts now available.

The Post-Standard in the light of all the pertinent facts wishes in fairness to its readers to correct certain statements that were written in good faith and in a sincere belief in their truthfulness but which have nevertheless proved to be untrue and unfair to Sen. McCarthy.

The editorial had criticized Sen. McCarthy because of certain testimony given in a Swiss court by a Charles E. Davis. The Post-Standard relied on this testimony and on that basis felt that Sen. McCarthy had merited severe criticism. The Post-Standard has since gone further into the record and finds that Charles E. Davis has been convicted of forgery and is beyond belief and that Sen. McCarthy had not committed any act deserving of criticism in connection with that matter.

The editorial of Oct. 19, 1951, also imputed to Sen. McCarthy responsibility for a photographic "framing" of Sen. Tydings of Maryland. We are now satisfied that Sen. McCarthy was not responsible for this act and the record shows that responsibility has been clearly fixed on another individual who had no connection with Sen. McCarthy.

The editorial of Oct. 19, 1951, also criticized Sen. McCarthy for a financial transaction with the Lustron Co. The facts in this case are these:

Sen. McCarthy had prepared a book advising veterans how they could finance home purchases and obtain full advantage of all helps and provisions of federal housing laws. He entered into an agreement with the Lustron Co. whereby they undertook to publish and distribute 100,000 copies of this book, to pay him 10 cents a copy for these and 5 cents a copy thereafter. This agreement was entered into after Sen. McCarthy's party, the Republican Party, had been defeated in the 1950 elections and had lost control of Congress and Sen. McCarthy was very unpopular with the Truman Administration. It is not possible therefore that Sen. McCarthy could have been useful to the Lustron Co. with the Truman Administration.

Lustron at that time was about to embark upon a large scale production of homes. There was no public indication that the RFC was about to foreclose. There has never been evidence presented before any committee or elsewhere that Sen. McCarthy in any way attempted to intercede on behalf of Lustron. The Post-Standard is therefore convinced that Sen. McCarthy's part in this transaction was on the same plane as the common practice among legislators of accepting fees for speeches and earning other fees from legitimate services.

The Post-Standard's editorial of Oct. 19, 1951, was in the nature of an omnibus attack on Sen. McCarthy. McCarthy provoked in the mind of the writer by the Charles E. Davis testimony in Switzerland. The nature of this testimony predisposed the writer to think adversely with respect to Sen. McCarthy and to give credence to other allegations that have since been disproved. The Davis testimony on its face appeared to warrant our sharp editorial comments. Inasmuch as Davis on the basis of his record is unworthy of belief we are happy to make these corrections in fairness to Sen. McCarthy, our readers and ourselves.

the tabloid had been put together by Frank Smith, chief editorial writer for the *Washington Times Herald,* and the composite was the handiwork of Smith's colleague Garvin Tankersley, assistant managing editor of the paper.

That McCarthy had no connection to the photo would later be established in a court of law, after the *Syracuse Post-Standard* of New York had run an editorial accusing him of, among other things, having "framed Sen. Tydings . . . with a fake photograph." McCarthy sued the paper for falsely charging him with things he hadn't done, and in an unusual outcome involving a politician and a major daily, won a favorable verdict. The *Post-Standard* thereafter made a small monetary settlement and—even more important for the historical record—issued a retraction, reproduced on page 429, acknowledging that McCarthy wasn't responsible for the picture.*[2] As to further details about the matter, we are once more indebted to the offstage candor of Senator Benton's aide John Howe. Commenting on the composite photo and *Post-Standard* ruling, Howe would write to Benton:

"We showed that McCarthy had helped arrange for the printing of the tabloid; that members of his staff had contributed material to the tabloid and that McCarthy had later defended the tabloid. But in my opinion it would have been impossible for the *Post-Standard* to prove that McCarthy 'was the one who framed Senator Tydings of Maryland with a fake photograph.' All the evidence is that McCarthy himself had nothing to do with the inclusion of any particular story in the tabloid (he was in Wisconsin through its preparation); the then managing editor of the *Times Herald* has testified that he himself had the idea and ordered the work on the 'composite photograph.' And even the Senate subcommittee castigation of McCarthy would not have borne out the phrase, 'was the one who framed,' etc."†[3]

All this was by way of preface to a much more significant investigation of McCarthy by the same subcommittee—this sparked by Senator Benton and following almost immediately in the wake of the election probe. Reading over

---

*The *Post-Standard* attack on McCarthy and subsequent retraction also touched on other topics, including the so-called Lustron deal and the chicanery of one Charles Davis, two further items alleged against McCarthy by Senator Benton and others. As this was one of the few occasions on which a major media outlet set the record straight about such matters, and as both these charges are still used against McCarthy, the full *Post-Standard* editorial is reprinted on page 429.

†McCarthy and his ally William Jenner (a member and future chairman of the parent Rules Committee) added a further comment the Gillette committee failed to make: that the "composite," though misleading as to when and how the pictures were taken, in substance was not misleading, since the import of the composite was to show Browder and Tydings in amiable concourse. In point of fact, such amiable concourse had occurred, as the Maryland senator treated the Marxist capo with utmost civility during his stint before the panel. (This too, as earlier noted, having been established in a courtroom.) So, in the outrage sweepstakes, it was a bit of a judgment call as to which was the more heinous: to print a composite photo suggesting Tydings was on cordial terms with Browder, or for Tydings actually to *be* on cordial terms with Browder. Perhaps the proper answer is that both should be condemned, though only the first gets any notice in the standard treatment.

the Maryland report, and reflecting on the earlier findings of the Tydings panel, Benton became seized of the notion that McCarthy should be ejected from the Senate. This was, it appears, a very quick decision, or possibly one that had been marinating for a while in Benton's mind, or someone else's, before he suddenly acted on it. The Maryland report was handed down by the Gillette-Monroney committee on August 3, 1951; on August 6, Benton rose on the floor of the Senate and offered a resolution—S.R. 187—saying McCarthy should be investigated with a view to ousting him from the chamber.

This resolution, framed as a follow-on to the Maryland inquest, was also referred to the Gillette committee, which thus would continue its preoccupation with McCarthy for months thereafter. On September 28, Benton went before the panel and presented what he described as evidence proving McCarthy guilty of numerous trespasses against the Senate and the nation. In a lengthy indictment, Benton offered alleged documentation for his charges—this mostly derived from the Tydings report of the previous year, garnished with items pulled together by McCarthy critics in the press and Congress.

It was an audacious move, with few precedents in the history of the Senate. However, as a recent addition to that body, Benton was himself in many ways just as much an outsider and maverick as McCarthy, and not much concerned about its traditions and procedures. A former advertising executive, he had made a fair amount of money before entering government service in the 1940s. He had been the partner of Chester Bowles in a successful ad firm and had thereafter gone on to involvement with a host of media ventures ranging from the *Encyclopaedia Britannica* to Muzak, with other projects in between.

This experience apparently made him in the eyes of someone a good candidate for diplomatic duty, as during the early years of World War II he played divers roles with the Coordinator of Inter-American Affairs, some of whose strange staffers have been noted. Then, in the late summer of 1945, he would be brought directly into the State Department as part of the mysterious and crucial appointments package through which Dean Acheson became Under Secretary of State. Benton's title was Assistant Secretary of State for Cultural Affairs, and numerous transferees from OWI and CIAA would be under his direction. Only in 1950 had he ascended to the Senate.*

Benton had thus been in the Senate for about a year and a half when he made his move against McCarthy. Why he did so has been a subject of speculation. The new senator seems to have had conventionally liberal Democratic

---

*It was through a series of coincidences that Benton would arrive in Congress. At the end of 1949 (in an oblique connection to McCarthy), Sen. Raymond Baldwin would resign to accept a Connecticut judgeship, at a time when Benton's former partner Bowles was governor of the state. Bowles appointed Benton to fill the vacant seat, and Benton would then go on in the fall of 1950 to win election on his own—by a margin of about a thousand votes—to fill out the remaining two years of Baldwin's tenure.

notions on most issues, but the obvious motivating factor for his unusual action was his background in the State Department, which had made him at least an indirect McCarthy target in ways that other senators weren't. Indeed, outside the Far East division, it's doubtful any other branch of the State Department contained as many suspects on McCarthy's several lists as did Benton's.

Benton's charges mostly concerned political statements, speeches, and actions by McCarthy that were deemed offensive. The counts were ten in number: (1) that McCarthy lied about the Wheeling speech and numbers when he testified to Tydings; (2) that he engaged in a questionable deal with Lustron, a manufacturer of prefab housing, accepting a fee of $10,000 for a housing booklet put together by McCarthy; (3) that he defamed General Marshall in his speech of June 14, 1951; (4) that he falsely said Senator Tydings "forced" him to give the names of his anonymous suspects in public hearings; (5) that he was guilty of defaming Tydings in the Maryland election tabloid; (6) that he falsely promised to forgo congressional immunity for his charges; (7) that he falsely claimed to have an FBI "chart," as discussed in Chapter 23; (8) that he misrepresented the source of his eighty-one cases given to the Senate (and didn't even know their names); (9) that he ill-treated a committee chairman, Sen. Raymond Baldwin, in the Malmedy investigation; and (10) that his aide Don Surine misrepresented the circumstances under which he left the FBI, and that McCarthy encouraged and suborned the actions of one Charles Davis, who allegedly forged a telegram concerning John Carter Vincent.[4]

Of this list of charges, only one, that involving the Lustron booklet, had anything to do with McCarthy's finances, everything else relating to his political statements and alleged actions, or those of his assistants. As matters developed, however, the financial angle would be the subject of constant embellishment and expansion, grow at an exponential pace, and eventually become the main, indeed virtually the only, point of the investigation. When the final report of the subcommittee was printed, McCarthy's financial doings were in effect the only subject dealt with, and this in most extensive fashion, while all the other charges vanished. Considering the way the inquest started, this seemed a peculiar outcome.

To get to this odd result, a couple of adjustments had been needed in the proceedings of the Subcommittee on Privileges and Elections. One concerned the fact that its main ostensible province, as the name suggests, was the matter of elections. With a few exceptions, and these a bit of a stretch themselves, McCarthy's financial records had no relevance to his election to the Senate, or anybody else's, but these records would be examined in minute detail by subcommittee staffers. McCarthy, in several angry letters to Gillette, vehemently protested this pursuit of his strictly personal doings, but to no avail, as the subcommittee answered that, given its plenary powers, it could pretty much look into anything about McCarthy that it cared to.

A second adjustment required to give the investigation of McCarthy's finances the widest possible ambit involved the wording of Benton's resolution. In his original motion, Benton had asked for an investigation of McCarthy's activities "*since* his election to the Senate," which occurred in the fall of 1946. (Emphasis here and elsewhere in this discussion added.) However, Benton for some reason soon had second thoughts about the matter and asked that the scope of the inquest be broadened. On October 5, a week after his testimony to Gillette, Benton wrote the committee saying he would now also like an investigation of McCarthy's activities "*before* his election to the United States Senate." This widening of the mandate was required, he said, to evaluate McCarthy's general fitness to sit in that august chamber and was needed in "fairness" to McCarthy as well as others.[5]

This suggestion to extend the investigation backward in indefinite fashion was promptly acted on by the committee. On October 15, Chief Counsel John P. Moore notified his staffers that the initial focus on McCarthy's Senate conduct was now to be expanded to include his private actions in the past, and that they were to launch an investigation and make a report "concerning the senator's pre-election conduct also." This would, said Moore, allow senators on the panel to widen or narrow the lens at their discretion—an idea no doubt also prompted by a desire for greater fairness to McCarthy.

From that point on, the investigation became an unlimited fishing expedition into McCarthy's earnings, bank statements, loan records, stock market activity, taxes, and anything else of financial nature the probers could think of, extending back through his whole career since hanging out his lawyer's shingle. Similar data were sought on his father, brothers, brother-in-law, friends, staffers, and supporters, the total inquiry reaching back to 1935—the year McCarthy got out of law school and more than a decade before he was elected to the Senate. The result was a huge batch of personal financial information on McCarthy and just about everyone he ever dealt with—a considerable mass of which would then be spread out on the public record. Following are a few of the items the subcommittee assembled on McCarthy, his family, friends, and staffers:

Appleton State Bank: Bank Examiners re McCarthy loan
Bentley, Alvin and Arvilla P.: income tax return
Bentley, Arvilla P.: Riggs National Bank ledger account
Gomillion, Otis: income tax returns, 1945–1950
Kerr, Jean F.: income tax returns, 1948–1950
Kerr, Jean F. and Elizabeth: Hamilton National Bank/bank account
Kornely, Roman and Olive: Income Tax Returns, 1948–1950

Mack, Walter S. Jr.: Income Tax Returns, 1943–1950
McCarthy, Joseph R.
    Appleton State Bank, Checking Account
    Bank of Commerce and Savings, Washington, D.C.: Account
    Income Tax Return, 1942–1950 (also Tax Return Analysis, 1935–1950)
    Wisconsin State Income Tax Returns, 1948
    Wisconsin State Income Tax Returns, 1949
    Wisconsin State Income Tax Returns, and Analysis, 1935–1951
McCarthy, Stephen T. and Alice: Income Tax Returns, 1945–1950
McCarthy, Timothy C.: Income Tax Returns, 1945–1946
McCarthy, William P. and Julia: Income Tax Returns, 1947–1950[6]

And so forth and so on—the above selections representing only a fraction of the total data assembled. From this trove of information the subcommittee put together a report running to better than 35 pages, backed up by a staggering 266 pages of photographic reproductions of McCarthy's bank records, loan statements, political spending, and stock market dealings, plus financial information relating to his family, friends, supporters, and staffers.

Somewhat strikingly, having had the opportunity to ransack McCarthy's financial records extending back for seventeen years, the committee would make no finding that he had done anything illegal—though its report was heavy on innuendo and loaded questions. What the records mainly showed was that McCarthy typically was strapped for cash, had drastically uneven earnings from one year to the next, borrowed heavily from time to time, once made considerable profit in a stock transaction but more often lost than gained, and engaged in financial dealings with his friends and family. Money was flipped back and forth among funding sources according to whether he fell behind or got somewhat ahead in this ongoing series of transactions.

What all this contributed to the well-being of the republic or dignity of the Senate wasn't immediately apparent, nor is it apparent now.* What it did do, however, was systematically invade McCarthy's privacy, along with that of his family, friends, and staffers, subject him to constant harassment, and allow his political foes to run barefoot through his financial records in search of possible incriminating data.

The other thing accomplished by all this financial sleuthing was to crowd

---

* The closest connection McCarthy's critics could come up with was a charge that, in his unsuccessful Senate race of 1944, various of his relatives contributed money to his campaign that was actually his, derived from a stock market profit. If true, this would have been a circumvention of Wisconsin spending limits and could arguably have justified printing the relevant data (albeit McCarthy in that campaign had not been nominated, much less elected, so the whole subject was out of bounds, per Benton's original resolution). Also, the committee reprinted various financial reports from McCarthy's 1946 campaign for the Senate. What justification there might have been for printing all the other financial information has never been established.

out of the committee's report the other nine counts Benton brought against McCarthy, though these had been investigated at exhaustive length by the panel's staffers. We have already seen the manner in which the investigative memo compiled for this committee on the Wheeling numbers was disposed of. Though this was Benton's foremost supposed proof of McCarthy's lying, constantly harped on by Benton and by Tydings, and backed by the alleged data assembled by the State Department, it dropped completely out of view when the investigators who went up to Wheeling made their report, in essence supporting McCarthy's version of the issue.

A similar fate now befell all other nonfinancial charges in the original Benton lineup: the alleged lying about the Lee list, the FBI chart, the question of being forced to name the names, the Charles Davis business, and so on. These were summarized briefly in the opening passages of the report, then disappeared entirely. The nominal basis for this silent treatment was that the "subcommittee is reluctant to become involved in matters of speeches and statements"—this despite the fact that speeches and statements were involved directly or indirectly in the vast bulk of Benton's charges, and that the subcommittee had spent countless hours of staff time investigating these very topics. What remained, therefore, were 300-plus pages of a committee report devoted almost exclusively to McCarthy's finances.[7]

While all this was going on, as may be imagined, McCarthy himself was not entirely idle. He was hardly the sort to take this kind of thing lying down, and he counterattacked on several fronts. In addition to angry letters to Gillette protesting the thrust of the inquiry, and declining to dignify the ransacking of his finances as a legitimate investigation, McCarthy also trained his sights on Benton. In March 1952, when Benton waived senatorial immunity for having made his multiple charges against McCarthy, McCarthy filed a libel suit for $2 million. Knowing one U.S. senator was unlikely to win such an action against another, McCarthy reasoned, nonetheless, that he would give Benton something to worry about and force him to play goalie for a change instead of simply attacking at his leisure.*

McCarthy also took the offensive in the Senate. On April 10, he filed his own resolution, S.R. 304, containing several allegations against Benton and asking that these be investigated also. This resolution in its turn was referred to the Gillette committee, so that the panel in the summer of 1952 would have two sets of dueling charges before it—Benton's charges against McCarthy and now

---

*In addition, the suit gave McCarthy an opportunity to depose and cross-examine Benton and others on several matters, an exercise that proved illuminating not only on issues that divided McCarthy and Benton but on other topics. It was in this suit that McCarthy attorney Edward Bennett Williams cornered Millard Tydings and forced him to admit that, contrary to his previous representations, he had no recording of the speech at Wheeling. The suit thus turned out to be of historical value, though it never resulted in a legal judgment.

McCarthy's accusing Benton. The disparate handling of the two cases would reveal a lot about the goals and methods of the committee.

The essence of McCarthy's charges against Benton was that the Connecticut senator, while in the State Department, had harbored an inordinate number of identified Soviet agents, Communists, and loyalty/security risks in his division, and had made no discernible effort to get rid of these when informed about them by security officials. McCarthy said he would back these charges by going before the Gillette committee and documenting them case by case. This he did on July 3, 1952, in a five-hour presentation (with Benton standing by to answer). It was a *tour de force* in which McCarthy discussed some cases already noted—William T. Stone, Haldore Hanson, Charles Thomson, Esther Brunauer, Robert T. Miller, and Rowena Rommel. These were all significant security suspects, and all had apparently worked under Benton at one time or another at State.

In the course of this discussion, McCarthy produced a ream of data about the cases—an exercise that, like the Jessup hearings, gave a pretty good glimpse of the documentary sources McCarthy was using. It was here, for instance, that he referred explicitly and repeatedly to the Lee list, but also to reports of the House Committee on Un-American Activities, Appendix IX, hearings of the Senate and House Appropriations Committees, and so on. In addition, he had with him photostats of more esoteric records—for instance, the form by which Charles Thomson had vouched for Gustavo Duran when the latter became a U.S. citizen, and the incorporation papers of the American IPR signed by Esther Brunauer and William Stone.[8]

Likewise, McCarthy traced various interconnections among these former Benton staffers—such as the fact that Rowena Rommel had acknowledged her role in bringing the Bentley-identified Soviet agent Miller to State, or that Haldore Hanson and William Stone both had links to *Amerasia*. For every such assertion, McCarthy had a document at the ready, which he submitted for the hearing record. All told, he presented more than fifty such items out of a total of sixty-two he said he had brought with him.

McCarthy's testimony ran to 213 pages of stenographic transcript, and the exhibits he cited (some running to several pages each) would have pushed the total to better than 300; this was followed by Benton's rebuttal, consuming another 150 pages. There were many twists and turns of testimony, some of a most interesting nature.* The whole thing is fascinating to read, as once more we have McCarthy and a chief antagonist, if not quite face-to-face, then back-to-back, and through the multitude of McCarthy exhibits we can see exactly what proofs he had for his assertions.

---

* Most notably, Benton's claim that he was the man responsible for the McCarran rider—an assertion he tried, without success, to get James Byrnes to verify.

One might suppose this provocative hearing would have spurred some kind of investigation to see what had happened with the cases of Hanson, Miller, Rommel, Thomson, Stone, and others, what Benton's relationship to them had been, whether his ripostes were on target, whether he or McCarthy was correct when testimony conflicted, and the like. So far as the record discloses, however, no such investigation was ever conducted, or contemplated, by the Gillette committee.

One might also have thought that this hearing, featuring so many security cases, the documentation of these by McCarthy, and the angry retorts of Benton, would have been an informative read for students of such matters. Indeed, given its sensational nature and high-profile combatants, it might well have been, as congressional hearings go, something of a best-seller. Such, however, was not to be, as these remarkable hearings were never printed. Instead, like the staff report from Wheeling, they would be quietly buried—consigned to the oblivion of the archives, there to gather dust and cobwebs for upward of five decades.

This failure to print McCarthy's testimony is of interest when we note that the Benton forces feared his appearance before the panel and fervently wished it could be avoided. As the ever-candid John Howe wrote to Benton in April of 1952: "I think you're very right that we don't want McCarthy testifying before the Gillette Subcommittee on his charges against you—with you replying—*because that is the most dramatic setting McCarthy could get.* At the same time, I feel we'll have to demolish these charges, rather than ignore them. And the sooner we do it the sooner we'll be fully on the attack."[9] (Emphasis added.)

In the upshot, McCarthy's testimony couldn't very well be prevented. However, the alternative arrived at, from the standpoint of tailoring the historical record, would turn out even better: have McCarthy testify, producing a one-day press story necessarily meager on details (and this on the Fourth of July, not a great day for newspaper reading), but thereafter simply fail to print the hearing. It thus became, like other items mentioned, a non-event in history. Journalists, historians, and biographers of the future would have no ready access to what McCarthy said, the specifics he presented on the cases, or the documentation he provided by way of backup.[10]

A small but indicative detail—the number of exhibits McCarthy brought with him to the hearing—suggests the nature of this historical problem. He and members of the panel referred several times to "62 exhibits" with which he sought to document his charges. Biographer-critics of McCarthy tell us, however, that this number was phony—that McCarthy had no such number of exhibits. Anti-McCarthy author Robert Griffith says, for instance: "In reality, there were only twenty-four exhibits, hopefully numbered from one to sixty-one." Likewise, David Oshinsky writes: "He presented the committee with twenty-four exhibits, artfully numbered from 1 to 62."[11]

Scanning the hearing record, one wonders what these authors could be thinking. In fact, the stenographic transcript and accompanying photostats clearly show McCarthy presenting some 47 numbered exhibits, plus half a dozen others that were discussed without a particular number being cited. These weren't all given in exact order, as digressions and interruptions caused him to jump around a bit, but a total of well over 50 exhibits is plainly evident from the transcript. So there is no particular reason to doubt McCarthy actually had 62 such exhibits, the obvious inference being that the remaining handful were skipped over in the cut and thrust of a contentious session.

Why, then, do Griffith and Oshinsky say McCarthy had only 24 exhibits? And why say these were "hopefully" or "artfully" numbered? What is that all about? The likely answer appears to be that, in the William Benton papers, there repose a memo by Benton attorney Gerhard Van Arkel and a draft letter by Benton supposedly setting straight misstatements by McCarthy in these hearings. This memo and Benton letter say McCarthy had only 24 exhibits, "deceptively numbered, however, from 1 to 61." This statement, as it happened, was dead wrong and suggests Benton and Van Arkel hadn't checked the transcript on this with any care.* From the near identity of phrasing and of misinformation, it would appear that, directly or indirectly, Griffith-Oshinsky picked up this wildly inaccurate statement from the Benton papers.[12]

The point itself is relatively minor but illustrative of the larger problem. From the casual but caustic asides of our historians, the reader can conclude only that McCarthy was such a pathological liar he would falsify something so petty as the number of exhibits he happened to have with him at a hearing. In fact, the falsification is the other way around, but thanks to the suppression of the hearing record, the information that goes to show this isn't readily accessible to researchers, much less the average reader. From such shoddy materials has the fabric of our standard histories been woven.

To all of which there is an instructive coda. In December 1951, Daniel Buckley, a New York attorney who had been one of the congressional investigators sent up to Wheeling, issued a scathing statement saying, in so many words, the Gillette committee was indeed suppressing the facts about the Benton-McCarthy conflict. Buckley said he had made not one but two trips to Wheeling to interview people who heard the McCarthy speech, and that his findings were supportive of McCarthy's version of the numbers. As Buckley put it:

> The information I developed on the second Wheeling trip did more than merely cast grave doubt and suspicion on Senator Benton's story. The newly unearthed evidence demolished Senator Benton's charges in all material

---

* An inaccurate index to the hearings prepared by the Gillette committee staff shows 25 exhibits—not 24—which seems to be the source of the error. The identical misinformation is contained in the files of the National Committee for an Effective Congress. As Griffith relied heavily on these files in writing *The Politics of Fear*, he may have gotten his erroneous factoid from this source.

respects and thoroughly proved Senator McCarthy's account of the facts to be truthful. Following this experience in Wheeling I was never again assigned to any task of consequence concerning the Benton charges . . .*[13]

But to conclude: The Gillette committee, exercising its plenary powers to do pretty much anything it wanted, suppressed not one but two highly significant documents needed to understand the McCarthy story: the investigative memo from Wheeling relative to the famous numbers, and McCarthy's testimony-*cum*-exhibits that spelled out his accusations of Communist and pro-Communist penetration of Benton's State Department office. In both cases, fortunately, the documents do still exist and can be obtained with a bit of effort, so we can figure out what the standard histories are omitting, or distorting.

There is a great deal of other evidence in the record suggesting the Gillette committee was intent on bringing down McCarthy—including the switch in the scope and purpose of the investigation, the ransacking of his finances, the huge disproportion in the final report between the number of exhibit pages devoted to Benton (13) and the number devoted to McCarthy (266), a similar disproportion in the archival records (21 McCarthy boxes, three pertaining to Benton) and so on. However, the suppressions of the Wheeling report and the McCarthy testimony, in and of themselves, are dispositive of the bias question, both indicating a settled purpose to stack the deck against McCarthy through concealment of official records.

Oh, one more thing: McCarthy's failure to cooperate with, accept invitations to appear in the dock as a defendant for his pre-senatorial personal doings, or otherwise pay proper deference to this committee, was the *only* count subsequently brought against him in the Watkins hearings for which he would be censured by the Senate.

---

*The investigator further disclosed that he had been questioned about the Wheeling matter by Tydings—who as an ex-senator was of course not a member of the committee—and that when Tydings was told "the Benton version of the 57-205 controversy would not hold water" became "highly indignant and irritated." Buckley further noted that Drew Pearson was feeding material to the committee and had access to certain of its confidential records. When he mentioned this to committee member Sen. Margaret Chase Smith (R-Maine), said Buckley, "her answer was, in substance, that we should forget about it."

Omitted from this discussion are various other peculiarities in the doings of the Gillette committee—including the resignation of one other staffer alleging bias, the fact that all but one of the original senators on the panel also resigned before the probe was over, and well-documented machinations behind the scenes by Pearson and others to push the project to completion.

PART V

HARDBALL

CHAPTER 33

The Perils of Power

FOR Joe McCarthy, the early days of 1953 appeared to be the best of times. He had just been sworn in for his second term in the Senate after racking up a comfortable reelection margin in Wisconsin. He was also the new chairman of the Senate Government Operations Committee (formerly the Expenditures Committee) and of its main subcommittee, the Permanent Subcommittee on Investigations (PSI).* In these roles, he would have power to look into a wide range of government functions seeking out malfeasance of all types, power he would waste no time in using.

McCarthy held these posts of influence because, in the 1952 elections, the Republicans had elected majorities in both House and Senate, while capturing the presidency for the first time since 1928, in a national landslide for the popular military leader of World War II, Dwight D. Eisenhower. The congressional margins were slim, especially in the Senate, but enough to install Republican chairmen of committees in both chambers. And among these new chairmen, few were potentially as powerful, or already as famous, as the junior senator from Wisconsin.

Considering that just three years before McCarthy had been an obscure

---

* McCarthy also retained his seat on the all-important Senate Appropriations Committee, which controlled the budgets for executive departments.

backbencher, and then the target of massed opposition from the White House, State Department, and leading members of the Congress—plus indefatigable lobby groups and major sectors of the press corps—he had come a long way in a hurry. In the process, he had the satisfaction of seeing some of his bitterest enemies bite the dust. In 1950, both Millard Tydings and Scott Lucas had been upended, beaten by McCarthy allies John Marshall Butler and Everett Dirksen. In 1952, the roster of the vanquished included his most tenacious foe, William Benton of Connecticut. Also of interest in that election, Senate Democratic leader Ernest McFarland of Arizona was defeated by an unheralded Phoenix city councilman and department store executive named Barry Goldwater, yet another McCarthy ally replacing yet another critic.

Beyond this, in a kind of reverse-English outcome, McCarthy's influence was apparent even in a campaign where he did nothing. This was the much-publicized Massachusetts Senate race between Republican Henry Cabot Lodge, who had served on the Tydings panel, and a young Democratic congressman named John F. Kennedy, scion of a wealthy and politically ambitious family. McCarthy was a hero in heavily Catholic Massachusetts and the GOP had wanted him to campaign for Lodge. But according to several accounts of the affair, Lodge was reluctant to stump in person with McCarthy, which the latter made a precondition for appearing.

If that weren't enough to keep McCarthy out of Massachusetts, there was another factor in the mix. Young Kennedy's father, millionaire tycoon, stock market guru and former ambassador to England Joseph P. Kennedy, was an admirer and backer of McCarthy and didn't want the senator he supported campaigning against his son. In the event, McCarthy steered clear of Massachusetts, young Kennedy survived the Ike landslide, and a political dynasty had taken a giant step toward national power. McCarthy thus cemented his friendship with the Kennedy clan but also made an implacable foe of Lodge. Both outcomes would be significant for McCarthy's future.

Some political analysts would later argue that McCarthy's influence in these elections was overrated, and that the 1952 results in particular owed more to the appeal of Eisenhower than to the polarizing figure of McCarthy. Without bothering to crunch the numbers that make the point, this seems a no-brainer, recalling that McCarthy was subject to a nonstop political/media blitz that Ike as transpartisan national idol never had to weather. Even so, it was hard to overlook the fact that the electoral landscape was littered with the political corpses of those who had gone head-to-head against McCarthy. Liberal Democrats in the Senate could hardly help wondering who among them might be next.

These electoral victories, not to be forgotten, came in the wake of numerous McCarthy triumphs in his loyalty/security battles. There, too, the list of defeated foes was long and would get longer. Philip Jessup, John Stewart Service,

John Carter Vincent, O. Edmund Clubb, Esther Brunauer, William Stone, Edward Posniak, Peveril Meigs, and other such McCarthy targets had been bested in one fashion or another, and there would be still more scalps dangling from his belt before the run was over. And now the main sponsor and protector of such people, Dean Acheson himself, was gone as well—McCarthy's most detested foe swept out of office with the Ike tsunami.

Accordingly, McCarthy was now viewed as a significant force, not just in Wisconsin but across the country. Despite the battering he had taken in his fight with the Truman-Acheson State Department and its many powerful allies, he was seen as one of the most potent political figures in the land. This was recorded with concern, and even a little awe, by commentators in the press corps. William S. White of the *New York Times,* for one, opined that McCarthy's "strange, half-hidden power in the Senate, in the country, and in the world" was "not diminishing as many thought it might after Dwight Eisenhower took office . . . it is still growing."[1]

That verdict would be confirmed, in even more emphatic language, by Jack Anderson, at the time still toiling for Drew Pearson. Pearson/Anderson had done all they could to derail McCarthy, running countless columns trying to debunk his charges, tie him to scandals, and discredit him in general. They had also been in close contact with Benton, the National Committee for an Effective Congress, and staffers of the Gillette committee in their probe of McCarthy's finances. None of it, however, had worked. Looking back on these attempts to do McCarthy in, Anderson ruefully recalled: "By the advent of 1953, we had used up almost our entire bag of tricks against McCarthy, without marked effect. We could comfort ourselves that all the blows we had landed were bound to take their toll in the late rounds, but, Lord, three years had passed since Wheeling, and he was still coming on stronger."[2]

While things thus looked discouraging for his foes and upbeat for McCarthy, there was trouble in the making for the new chairman, and had been for some time before this. By far the biggest cloud on his horizon, and it was a huge one, was that the Republican President, Dwight Eisenhower, disliked him intensely, and the feeling would grow more so as the events of 1953 unfolded. For this dislike, Eisenhower had from his standpoint ample reasons, and there were people in his entourage who did all they could to reinforce them.[3]

In proximate terms, the main cause of Ike's aversion was the George Marshall speech, which had outraged the new President—along with many other people—and figured as a backstage issue in the 1952 election. Eisenhower and Marshall were long-serving military brothers, and an attack on Marshall was tantamount to an attack on Ike as well. Indeed, there was no "tantamount" about it, as Ike himself had come in for criticism in the Marshall speech. Several items discussed in that oration, such as the decision to pull up short in Europe during World War II, allowing the Soviets to take Berlin and Prague, were Eisenhower's doing as much as and by most accounts considerably more than Marshall's.[4]

Underlying these specific issues was a more generic problem, of which bitterness over the Marshall speech was but a symptom, albeit one of galvanizing rancor. Marshall and Ike were both products of the Roosevelt regime, avatars of the peculiar global vision FDR and Harry Hopkins had promoted during World War II. Both generals had been raised to power over the heads of others by the New Deal White House, and perforce were agents of Roosevelt's often-addled wartime notions and inertial carry-through by Truman. You couldn't survey the Roosevelt-Truman record without running across the names of Ike and Marshall.

This put Ike—and the GOP—in a strange position. He had become the successful candidate of a Republican Party pledged to undo the New Deal–Fair Deal program, yet he was in many respects a product and agent of that very program. On domestic issues, where he had never been a player and held relatively conservative views, this wasn't a major consideration. But so far as foreign policy was concerned, he represented, not systemic change from Roosevelt and Truman, but something closer to continuity. Not for him a punishing hard-line critique of what had been done in Eastern Europe, deals cut at Yalta, or the debacle of the Marshall mission to China.

Also, these connections were more than retrospective. Ike was, by inclination and experience, aligned with the Atlanticist wing of the GOP. This was reflected not only in his personal statements, replete with withering comments on party isolationists confided to his aides and diary, but in appointments made and helpers favored.[5] These were on the foreign policy side overwhelmingly from the eastern, internationalist faction of the party, with ties to Wall Street, large corporations, big eastern media outlets, and Ivy League establishment. Such people were generally closer in foreign policy outlook to Dean Acheson than to the GOP in Congress—believers in bipartisan collaboration and consensus with the Democrats rather than sharp-elbowed opposition.

McCarthy, on the other hand, really did believe in repudiating most if not quite all of the Democratic legacy overseas and thought this was one of the main things the new Republican majority in Congress, and new administration in the White House, were elected to accomplish. His idea of the matter, voiced on numerous occasions, was to condemn the postwar Democratic foreign record root and branch, this usually expressed as repudiation of the Roosevelt and "Truman-Acheson" mind-set that led to diplomatic setbacks at Teheran and Yalta, the communization of half of Europe, and the fall of China.

Though frequently derided as an "isolationist," McCarthy was in fact an interventionist—but with provisos. He voted for the Truman doctrine of aid to Greece and Turkey, and (with less enthusiasm) for the Marshall Plan of economic aid to Europe.[6] He believed in standing up to the Soviet/Communist challenge both in Europe and in Asia, as opposed to the Acheson-Marshall policy that blithely sandbagged Chiang Kai-shek (not to mention the backstage plotting) while focusing its main concerns on Europe. Ike, and many of those around him, were closer to the Acheson-Marshall stance than to the more militant, generic anti-Communism espoused by McCarthy and such of his Republican Senate colleagues as Styles Bridges of New Hampshire or California's William Knowland.

Here was an irreconcilable conflict in the making, though there were some who did what they could to reconcile it. One such was Ike's Secretary of State, John Foster Dulles. Though himself an establishmentarian Wall Street lawyer with a history of bipartisan involvement, Dulles was also a bit of a messianic anti-Communist, and so had certain affinities with McCarthy's worldview. He made several attempts early on to bridge the gap between the internal Republican factions, though in the end these proved unavailing, and Dulles himself would in due course become a critic of McCarthy.

Others who sought to bind the disparate elements of the GOP together included the new Vice President, Richard Nixon, raised to that post from a two-year stopover in the Senate. Himself a hero to the anti-Communist right for his part in exposing Alger Hiss, Nixon had the credentials for appealing to McCarthy, while diligently cultivating his role as a faithful second in command to Ike.[7] Nixon's balancing act between such countervailing forces would continue for the next two decades and eventually get him to the White House. (It was only when he reached that long-sought goal that he would fall off the teeter-totter, landing with Henry Kissinger in Red China, thereafter pushing on into the mists of *détente* with Moscow.)

Yet another who sought to hold things together, though he had little time to do it, was the Republican leader of the Senate, Ohio's Robert Taft, who had lost the presidential nomination to Ike the previous summer.* Taft was the highly respected spokesman for Midwest "Old Guard" Republicans in the Senate, unquestionably agreed with McCarthy in his critique of Yalta, the Acheson State Department, the debacle in China, and other foreign issues, and often said so.[8] Yet he was of a very different temper—prudent, measured, and judicious, adjectives seldom applied to Joe McCarthy. Also, out of his unfailing sense of duty, Taft sought to be a good floor leader in the Senate for the new Republican chieftain in the White House.

Over against these would-be peacemakers were members of the Ike entourage, of moderate-to-liberal hue, who did whatever they could to provoke an Ike-McCarthy showdown. These included members of the New York/Tom Dewey wing of the GOP that included former governor Dewey himself, his

---

*Taft died of cancer on July 31, 1953.

sometime campaign manager Herbert Brownell (now Attorney General), former New Hampshire governor Sherman Adams (now White House Chief of Staff), Press Secretary James Hagerty, national security aide Robert Cutler, and two key players seconded to the White House from the Time-Life empire of Henry Luce—counselor C. D. Jackson and speechwriter Emmet Hughes.[9]

Aligned with these advisers were other influential figures not in the immediate retinue but with good access to the President and his palace guardsmen. These included liberal GOP businessman and former U.S. official Paul Hoffman, active in the "Citizens for Eisenhower" brigade in the 1952 elections, trying to corral moderate and liberal votes for Ike; John J. McCloy, who served under both Roosevelt and Truman but was close to Ike and the new power grouping in the White House; and Henry Cabot Lodge, sometime defender of McCarthy in the Tydings hearings but now a determined foe, the new U.S. Ambassador to the United Nations and a trusted Ike lieutenant.[10]

All these Ike counselors had a strong aversion to McCarthy and some had gone so far as to urge an open break even during the course of the election. This had played out in October of 1952, when Ike was scheduled for a joint campaign appearance with McCarthy in Wisconsin. Hughes, Cutler, and other advisers had urged him to include in his remarks on this occasion a ringing defense of Marshall, and thus an in-your-face repudiation of McCarthy. (Eventually, other advice prevailed and Ike didn't do it.) As such a gesture, whatever its supposed merits, could have done nothing but make trouble for the party, the episode suggested that for many in Ike's inner circle detestation of McCarthy was all-consuming.

Now that the election was safely over and Eisenhower in the White House, various of his counselors would continue to urge a shoot-out with McCarthy and constantly sought a chance to stage one. In this they would succeed, though not quite in the early going with the direct effects they hoped for. Ike had an ingrained unwillingness to engage in personal conflict or cause a visible rupture in the political family of which he was now anointed leader. This had nothing to do with any softness toward McCarthy but meant Ike's hostility would be expressed in subliminal ways, behind the scenes and in occasional delphic statements that would in time become more obvious and more frequent.

All these elements would come to the fore as the Ike-McCarthy odd couple set out together, each in his way, to lead the nation in what are now (mistakenly) viewed as the tranquil 1950s. There were other factors also, internal to the McCarthy camp, that would affect events to follow. One such, oblique but still important, was the McCarthy tie-in with the Kennedys.[11] This was one of the strangest alliances in our political history, given the standard image of John Kennedy and his brother Robert on the one hand, and that of Joe McCarthy on the other. Few politicians have had a better historical press than have the

Kennedy brothers, and nobody could possibly have had a worse such press than Joe McCarthy.

Despite these discrepancies in reputation, the affinities between McCarthy and the Kennedys were solid, hence an embarrassment to historians who venerate the Kennedy name but become apoplectic at the mention of McCarthy. As a young congressman, indeed, Jack Kennedy had entered the hard-line anti-Communist lists before the 1950 arrival of McCarthy, denouncing Owen Lattimore, John K. Fairbank, the IPR, and the Acheson policy in China in terms McCarthy himself could not have faulted.[12]

John Kennedy's younger brother Robert was if anything even more attuned to McCarthy's views—inviting the senator to speak at the University of Virginia Law School when Robert was a student there, working for McCarthy after graduation, and asking McCarthy to be the godfather of his firstborn child (the eventual Democratic lieutenant governor of Maryland, Kathleen Kennedy Townsend). So loyal was Bobby to McCarthy that, at a speech by famed CBS broadcaster Edward R. Murrow, who had vehemently attacked McCarthy, the younger Kennedy brother walked out in protest.[13]

The mind boggles at what might have happened if young Robert Kennedy (then twenty-seven) had become, as he and his father devoutly wished, the chief counsel to new committee chairman Joe McCarthy. Kennedy's own political career would doubtless have been different in many ways, and Joe McCarthy's would have been quite different also. And the historians who idolize the first and condemn the second would have an even more awkward task before them in squaring this improbable circle.

However, while Bobby would go to work for McCarthy, his rise to eminence in that office was not to be. Standing in his way was yet another wunderkind, even younger than himself, with a glittering résumé that neither Bobby nor any other candidate for the job could hope to match. His name was Roy M. Cohn, in early 1953 all of twenty-five years old but already a veteran Communist-hunter and in certain circles well regarded. He would accordingly secure the place the Kennedy clan hoped to get for Bobby.

Cohn was the son of a Democratic judge from New York City, closely connected with the still-potent though somewhat rusty Ed Flynn machine, of the Jewish faith, observant though not conspicuously pious. Short of stature and with hooded eyes that made him look perpetually sleepy, Cohn was anything but. He was in fact a prodigy who graduated from Columbia Law School when he was only twenty years old and thus had to wait for half a year before admission to the bar and appointment as an assistant U.S. attorney for the Southern District of New York. The assignment reflected his good connections in Democratic political-legal circles but was arguably justified by his talents.

As Cohn's five years at Justice coincided with a flurry of high-profile legal actions against the Communist Party and those accused of serving its interests, he was soon immersed in cases of this nature. A liberal Democrat by upbringing and affiliation, he now developed considerable anti-Red expertise working on the trials of Communist Party leaders, the case of William Remington, a perjury indictment of Owen Lattimore, and a grand jury investigation of suspected American Communists employed at the United Nations. In the most prominent case of all, and by his own account the most traumatic, he was part of the prosecutorial team that secured the conviction of Julius and Ethel Rosenberg for espionage conspiracy.[14]

All this was more than enough to recommend Cohn, despite his youth, to Joe McCarthy, but there were other factors also. Cohn was close to the influential Hearst columnist/backstage political impresario George Sokolsky and to the Hearst press in general. Sokolsky-Hearst in turn were among the strongest journalistic backers of McCarthy, and it was in part through the recommendation of Sokolsky that McCarthy met with Cohn and offered him the main staff job on the investigations panel.[15]

As events would show, the affinities between McCarthy and Cohn went beyond their anti-Red convictions. Though differing in religious faith, ethnic roots, and social background, they were in many ways political/intellectual soul mates. Both were tough infighters and geared to action more than theory. Both were also quick studies, reputed to have photographic memories, and capable of moving rapidly from one topic to the next at a pace that left their colleagues gasping. Each had a way of cutting through reams of data to get to the core of the issue as he saw it. This meant they were able to do, and did, a vast amount of work in the comparatively brief span in which they were able to run their new committee.

The McCarthy-Cohn combine also had, as might be guessed, the defects of its virtues. The rapid clip at which they acted, their proclivities for multitasking, and the fact that they carried so much information in their heads had an obvious downside, made worse by the fact that neither was renowned as an administrator. Indeed, the McCarthy office and subcommittee were by general reputation haphazard, not to say chaotic, places—stacks of documents and case folders, phones ringing, people coming and going in profusion. All of this was very different from the orderly ways of the FBI or the systematic methods of Robert Kennedy, who made up for lack of surface brilliance with a capacity for driven, focused effort that would become his trademark.

Also on the McCarthy staff was another youthful member who would turn out to be, when all was done, the most significant of them all. This was G. David Schine, heir to a substantial fortune (the Schine hotel and theater chain), graduate of Harvard, and notable young man about town in New York and Boston. Schine, too, was twenty-five at the beginning of 1953 and had the previous year become a friend of Cohn's. When Cohn took over the counsel's job for McCarthy, he brought Schine along as a volunteer consultant. As the affluent Schine was willing to work for nothing, McCarthy had no objection to the arrangement. Thereby were sown the seeds of future troubles.

Of the many internal problems that afflicted the McCarthy staff, the deep-seated enmity between Cohn and Kennedy was by all odds first and foremost. They were both too much driven by ambition and indomitable will to be working partners, and their relationship was at the best of times marked by strain and tension. Both would establish flamboyant track records as over-the-top, type-A personalities, each disdainful of the other. When Bobby in the early 1960s became Attorney General, he would devote much time and energy trying to put Cohn in jail, and Cohn would gladly have returned the favor. These later battles were well presaged by their taut relationship as McCarthy staffers.[16]

Not of course to be omitted from this picture are the senatorial members of the committee, who would have historic roles to play in the rest of the McCarthy drama. *Primus inter pares* was Sen. Karl Mundt (R-S.D.), a veteran Midwest conservative of the Taft wing and former member of the House Committee on Un-American Activities. He had presided over the latter phases of the Hiss-Chambers hearings in 1948 before ascending at the end of the year to the Senate. He was knowledgeable on security issues, a stalwart anti-Communist, and a born ally of McCarthy.

Next up on the GOP side was Everett Dirksen of Illinois, who had defeated Scott Lucas in 1950. Also a former member of the House, Dirksen too had delved into internal security issues before this and knew a fair amount about them. He was a mellifluous, theatrical orator of the old-fashioned type, given to verbal flourishes and courtly phrases. He was nonetheless a shrewd operator behind the scenes who would go on to become Republican leader of the Senate. He too was a McCarthy ally, though one who worked hard to keep lines open to the White House.

The fourth Republican on the PSI was Charles Potter of Michigan. A Purple Heart veteran of World War II, in which he had lost both legs to a land mine, Potter was the most moderate of the GOP contingent, most amenable to approaches from the White House, and thus most easily divided from McCarthy. His susceptibility on this front would be a critical factor in disputes that happened later. Other than their Republican label, common service in the war, and a generic anti-Communism, the affinities between Potter and McCarthy were few.

At the Democratic end of the committee table, the cast of characters was distinguished and would in time become the more so. The ranking Democrat was John McClellan of Arkansas, a long-serving member and future chairman of the panel. Dour, cagey, and conservative, he had been in the Senate since 1943 and was a leader of the Democratic establishment in that chamber, then heavily weighted by seniority toward long-serving Dixie members. These included such as Richard Russell and Walter George of Georgia, Tom Connally of

Texas, and Harry Byrd of Virginia, who had chaired committees under Democratic rule and were still powers to be reckoned with in a closely divided Senate.

Second ranking among subcommittee Democrats was a rising freshman and former member of the House, elected to the Senate in 1952, Henry Jackson of Washington State. "Scoop" Jackson would become a leading defense hawk in the Democratic Party, and in later years a presidential hopeful of moderate, defense-minded elements in the party. He was close to the labor movement, hence liberal on domestic issues, but a hard-liner on security matters. He would become, after a relatively benign beginning, a tough McCarthy critic.

The third committee Democrat was W. Stuart Symington of Missouri. If one had gone to central casting for a presidential character in a movie, Symington would have filled the bill. Tall and of impressive bearing, he not only looked the part but had strong credentials in military matters as a former Secretary of the Air Force under Truman. A successful St. Louis businessman, also elected to the Senate in 1952, Symington was a staunch liberal on domestic issues and would in due course become McCarthy's main antagonist on the panel.

There were of course many more characters in the story, both in the Senate and outside it. These included majority leader Taft and his soon-to-be successor in that role, William Knowland; the conservative GOP godfather of the chamber, Styles Bridges of New Hampshire; the learned Ferguson of Michigan; stalwart McCarthy allies Hickenlooper, William Jenner of Indiana, Herman Welker of Idaho, Goldwater of Arizona, and a numerous cast of others. On the Democratic side, Lyndon Johnson of Texas was already displaying the formidable skills that would soon make him the unrivaled master of the Senate. Liberals such as William Fulbright of Arkansas, Herbert Lehman of New York, and Hubert Humphrey of Minnesota would inevitably be among McCarthy's chief opponents.

In retrospect, it was a fairly illustrious crew that set out in 1953 on the governance of the republic, at the height of its historic clash with Moscow. It included no fewer than four Presidents of the United States, who among them would serve until the 1970s (Eisenhower, John Kennedy, Johnson, Nixon),* two others who would be nominees of their parties (Goldwater, Humphrey), three Vice Presidents (Nixon, Johnson, Humphrey), and a slew of once and future serious contenders for the White House (Taft, Robert Kennedy, Symington, Jackson).† Virtually all the principal leaders of the country for the next generation, and thus for a big chunk of the Cold War, were actors in or products of the Ike-McCarthy era.

---

*Plus a fifth Vice President- and President-to-be just off stage in the U.S. House, Rep. Gerald Ford (R-Mich.).

†It's of note that so many of these came through the Senate, as at this writing no member of that body has been elected President since this group departed.

Outside the ranks of government, there were other consequential figures—mostly in the press corps—who would make their influence felt on a daily basis. On the anti-McCarthy side were ranged some of the most powerful media institutions, journalists, and broadcasters of the epoch. These included the Time-Life empire, the *New York Times,* the *Washington Post,* provincial newspapers such as the *Milwaukee Journal* and *St. Louis Post-Dispatch,* elite broadcaster Murrow of CBS and like-minded radio/TV personalities, columnists Joseph and Stewart Alsop, Drew Pearson, Marquis Childs, and Walter Lippmann—to name only the more famous.

However, back then more than now, there were some heavyweight daily papers on the conservative side of the divide that were zealous backers of McCarthy. Foremost among these were Col. Robert McCormick's *Chicago Tribune* and (until 1954) *Washington Times Herald,* and their top correspondents Willard Edwards and Walter Trohan, the Hearst newspapers including the *New York Journal American,* columnists Sokolsky, Westbrook Pegler, and Walter Winchell, publisher/columnist David Lawrence of *U.S. News & World Report,* and radio commentator Fulton Lewis Jr. Somewhere in the middle, leaning mostly to the right but none too friendly toward McCarthy, were the Scripps-Howard papers, led by the *New York World Telegram and Sun, Washington Daily News,* and correspondent Frederick Woltman.

As those lineups suggest, the media face-off in those days was a good deal more balanced than it would become about a decade later. This meant McCarthy had some important journalistic allies who were able to communicate and amplify his message in a way that wouldn't be possible for a hard-line anti-Red or conservative politician beginning in the 1960s. The existence of such media firepower on the right was a critical factor in McCarthy's ability to get the word out and undoubtedly helped account for some of his early successes with the public.

Also important in the political mix were outside interest groups and lobbies that followed national security issues. In the McCarthy corner were such as the American Legion, conservative business interests and individuals, and a host of patriotic and women's groups who took up the cudgels for rightward causes. On the left end of the spectrum were the Americans for Democratic Action, American Civil Liberties Union, labor leaders of the CIO, some large foundations, academic institutions and liberal church groups, plus the already met with, small but savvy, Committee for an Effective Congress.

Finally, on the McCarthy side of things were researchers, writers, and security experts who provided him with information, advice, and counsel. Among this number were J. B. Matthews, Ben Mandel, and Robert Morris, all specialists on security matters; writers Ralph de Toledano and Freda Utley; journalists/researchers such as Ed Nellor and Howard Rushmore; and a couple of young conservative firebrands just out of Yale—William F. Buckley Jr. and

L. Brent Bozell. All would assist the McCarthy cause, by word or deed, in the struggles that were to follow.

In terms of internal staffing, McCarthy tried to resolve his Cohn-Kennedy dilemma by naming Francis "Frip" Flanagan, a veteran Hill operative who had previously served with the committee, as "general counsel," Cohn as chief counsel, and Robert Kennedy as assistant counsel. It would prove to be a confused and confusing arrangement. Otherwise, both then and later, McCarthy would lean heavily on former agents of the FBI—these including Don Surine, Francis Carr, and James Juliana, among others. The FBI connection was important to both McCarthy and Cohn, with the powerful J. Edgar Hoover, tacitly and sometimes explicitly an ally but also at times a critic, ever watchful in the background.

Of course, in all of this, there was one player whose influence trumped all the rest—the new chief executive in the White House, Dwight D. Eisenhower. It was his administration and his party, by virtue of his nomination and election; his conduct in office and views about the issues that would be decisive, for good or ill, in what would happen from this point forward. His imposing presence, as events soon proved, would transform the political dynamics of the Capital City, the Republican Party, and the nation. However, so far as Congress was concerned, most observers were intently focused on the high-flying Joe McCarthy, wondering what he was going to do and how he would go about it. They would have much to see, and ponder.

CHAPTER 34

Uncertain Voice

B Y FAR the best way of judging the work of Joe McCarthy—and standard treatments of his conduct—is to study the record of Senate hearings at which he presided as committee chairman. Though drastically compressed in time, that record would prove to be substantial and, in many respects, impressive.

McCarthy, Cohn and Co. obviously meant to get a lot accomplished with their new committee and do it fairly quickly. They hit the ground running in early 1953 with a rapid series of investigations, most now forgotten, others that would be much discussed, if none too accurately, in retrospectives of the era. The hectic schedule is suggested by some comparative numbers. In 1952, according to subcommittee case files, the PSI had held only six days of executive hearings, in which eight witnesses were heard, followed by twenty days of public hearings, a leisurely pace for a major panel of Congress. In 1953, under McCarthy-Cohn, all these figures were ratcheted up in dramatic fashion: 95 days of executive hearings, 331 witnesses called, 75 days of public hearings.[1]

Thus, though McCarthy would in effect be chairman of PSI for only about a year and a quarter, his subcommittee did the equivalent of perhaps a decade's work, measured by the previous output, in a concentrated burst of action.* Among the topics covered were tax manipulations and charges of influence peddling, stockpiling practices of the General Services Administration, the condition of State Department employee records, U.S. information services overseas, trade with the Communist bloc of nations, operations of the Government Printing Office, and a series of probes involving security practice in the Army Signal Corps and its several offshoots. This last would be the most extensive and most controverted of all McCarthy inquests, and the most famous.

Thanks to the fifty-year rule governing confidential Senate records, we now have the executive-session transcripts of the McCarthy panel, added to the long-available transcripts of its public hearings, plus some backup files of the committee. Together these comprise thousands of pages of densely packed material covering a host of issues, hundreds of people, and scores of institutions, and giving us a fairly comprehensive view of McCarthy and his staffers going about their daily business. Anyone who reads these hearings and backup records, or any significant portion of them, will be struck by the contrast between the picture they convey and the accepted image of McCarthy.

Among the more conspicuous features of the early subcommittee sessions were McCarthy's frequent comments about the new Republican administration that had just taken office and his relations with his Democratic colleagues. In both cases, the transcripts show, he was generally speaking a model of *politesse*—something nobody could possibly figure out by reading a whole library of books about McCarthy now available to the public.

In his investigations of the State Department files, Voice of America, U.S. Information Service, Army Signal Corps, and other topics, McCarthy repeatedly stressed, as was only common sense, that the problems being looked at were not the doing of the Eisenhower White House, State Department, or Department of Defense. On the contrary, he said, the difficulties complained of resulted from practices of the previous administration and holdovers from the days of Truman. McCarthy metronomically praised the initiatives of the new regime, the improvements Ike and his appointees were making, and the cooperation the committee was getting from these sources.[2]

At the same time, in an unlikely but for a while successful balancing act, McCarthy was, in contrast to later scenes of acrimony, the soul of collegiality with Democratic members—John McClellan first and foremost, but also Stuart Symington and Henry Jackson. These minority members of the panel often took leading roles in the early investigations, were encouraged to do so by McCarthy, and were praised by him in this connection. Exchanges between McCarthy and his Democratic colleagues at this time were not only civil but quite cordial. Conversely, some of the most trenchant questioning of witnesses,

---

*McCarthy's work as committee chairman was to all intents and purposes ended by April of 1954, when he would become embroiled in the Army-McCarthy hearings.

and toughest comments on the problems dealt with, were offered by the Democratic members.

A third conspicuous feature of the hearings was the leeway granted even hostile witnesses, up to and including conduct plainly contumacious. Again contra the usual horror stories, witnesses before the panel were (a) permitted to have counsel present and confer with counsel on an unlimited basis; (b) given time to obtain counsel, and urged to do so if they didn't have such; (c) allowed to say almost anything they wanted, including criticism of McCarthy, challenges to the jurisdiction of the panel, and ideological filibusters of all types—though these always tended in the same direction.

McCarthy was usually patient with such harangues, seldom tried to gavel someone into silence, and would even debate feisty witnesses on extraneous issues as to their legal merits or lack thereof. When a witness wanted to read a defiant manifesto challenging the panel's jurisdiction, rather than instantly ruling this out of order, McCarthy would say, "You may read your statement," placidly sit through the filibuster, announce "The motion is denied," and continue with the hearing. He even viewed with relative equanimity witnesses who took the Fifth Amendment if they plausibly invoked it to protect themselves from possible incrimination.

The main exceptions to these rules involved obstreperous witnesses who invoked the Fifth in far-fetched manner, cloaked refusal to answer in some other guise, or were otherwise stonewalling or evasive. McCarthy wouldn't permit witnesses *both* to engage in such tactics *and* to indulge in long harangues. On the occasions where this combination occurred, he would get his back up, say the committee didn't need any speeches from witnesses who refused to say whether they were Reds or not, and/or dismiss the witness. (An infallible sign of McCarthy's ire was when he addressed the witness as "Mister"—as in, "Mister, we're going to repeat the question until we get an answer.")

Another salient feature of the McCarthy hearings was the rule that no one should be named as a Communist, pro-Communist, or subversive unless the person named was given notice and the opportunity to respond directly—though there were exceptions when another witness would do such naming on an impromptu basis. McCarthy repeatedly admonished people testifying not to use the names of those they were accusing until these conditions could be met with. One result of this procedure was a series of face-to-face encounters in which accusers and accused were brought together in dramatic fashion.*[3]

As these comments are so starkly different from what is typically said

---

*Though the procedure wasn't 100 percent adhered to—for instance, when someone was named in an open hearing by a witness who hadn't been vetted in executive session—McCarthy made a particular point of emphasizing this stricture in public hearings.

A further aspect of the hearings, in contrast to the usual picture, was McCarthy's concern not to intrude on the turf of other panels or duplicate their efforts. This emerged quite clearly, in hearings

about McCarthy's methods, the reader understandably may find them hard to credit. It may thus be useful to note the views about the subject of a Democratic member of the McCarthy panel, as recorded early on by Samuel Shaffer of *Newsweek*. In the spring of 1953, Shaffer provided a lengthy wrap-up for his editors, devoted to McCarthy's doings, including the way he managed his committee. In the course of this, Shaffer quoted an (unnamed) Democratic member of the panel as follows: "I must say I have a more favorable opinion of McCarthy than I used to have before I came on this committee. He is a very able lawyer. He is damn sharp. He is fair and courteous to members of his committee. He doesn't bulldoze the witnesses as much as I expected him to. In fact, he has permitted hostile witnesses to speak at great length."[4]

Though the senator who said this wasn't named, the internal evidence of the memo suggests it was Henry Jackson. The senator was new to the committee, which excludes McClellan, who had already served there with McCarthy. It further appears the senator was a lawyer, which Stuart Symington wasn't. By process of elimination, this left Jackson as the person probably being quoted. As shall be seen, he and McCarthy at this time were working more or less harmoniously together on some significant issues.

A contemporaneous appraisal of McCarthy from a more friendly source, *Chicago Tribune* correspondent Willard Edwards, likewise testified to McCarthy's generally measured conduct, even under provocation. "Many will be astonished by this," said Edwards, "but the fact is that McCarthy is an extraordinarily patient man. He has more self-control than almost any public figure I have encountered in the past two decades. This writer has had . . . almost numberless occasions to marvel at his control under persistent and insulting questions by hostile reporters. . . . An abusive Fifth Amendment witness gets slapped down promptly but ordinarily McCarthy maintains an even temperament . . ."[5]

These generic comments about McCarthy's conduct of the subcommittee would be underscored from time to time by agency heads, including the commander of a military post that was under investigation and even the defense attorney for an accused subversive, remarking on the fairness and courtesy of the proceedings. There were, of course, episodes of an opposite nature also, in which things erupted into violent confrontation, and these instances are the ones that get all the notice in the usual write-ups. Some of these contentious sessions, and why they occurred, will be considered in their turn hereafter.

So much, for the moment, on procedural aspects of the hearings. In terms

---

on the State Department files, when he told his staff not to delve into security aspects as such but to stick to the question of how the files were handled. (For example, "If we find that [the] internal security [subcommittee] is planning to make an all-out investigation of Communist influence, I think we should give them all the cooperation we can, but I do not like to have parallel investigations running at the same time.")

of substance, the early McCarthy investigations often made good headway, mostly concerning issues that engaged his interest when he was a backbencher and freelancer. Among the first of these was the handling of State Department personnel files, which had been a crucial issue in his Homeric battles with the Truman White House. The condition of those files, the hearings showed, was deplorable in the extreme, concerning which the committee would come up with some shocking revelations and also with proposals to fix things.

The star witness in these sessions was Helen Balog, earlier quoted, in charge of some 8,000 files concerning Foreign Service personnel. She testified that, in the State Department file setup, there was no way of telling if something had ever been in the folders, had been extracted, or had otherwise been fooled around with. There was no pagination or serialization system, and no index or control card showing what was in the records. She further said several hundred people had access to the files, that folders were often moved around the building willy-nilly, and that some were kept out of the file room for a year and longer.

In describing this unruly scene, up to and including the matter of John Service's toiling over the files at night, Mrs. Balog testified with utmost candor. She was obviously an intrepid lady. In executive session, however, she expressed concern about possible sanctions from the State Department for having been so outspoken, saying, "I want you people to protect me."[6] John Matson, a departmental witness who seconded Mrs. Balog's description of the files, would testify that he had been demoted to more menial duty after he protested their sloppy handling. (A State Department higher-up would later explain that Matson was a chronic troublemaker.)

The haphazard condition of the files was confirmed by others, including some who had been involved in the practices complained of. The resulting picture was distressing to the committee, as indicated by the comment of one member to a State Department witness: "How do you possibly keep track of derogatory or commendatory letters in that filing system? . . . There is the danger of someone going through it . . . and then there is no way of knowing what is in the file and what went out. . . . Do you not see that you have laid yourself open to all sorts of criticism in the fact that you can't prove or disprove that things are taken out of the file?" Or, as another panel member put it: "If you have a system where anyone can take anything out of the file without it being known that it was taken out, how can you say that it was a good filing system?"[7]

These exasperated comments were a good précis of the situation with the files and the problems this presented, and suggestive of the value of the McCarthy hearings. They were good indicators also of the bipartisan nature of these early inquests, as the statements quoted weren't from McCarthy or his conservative colleagues Mundt and Dirksen, but from Democratic members of the panel—Henry Jackson in the first case, Stuart Symington in the second.

As for relations between McCarthy and the Ike regime, these disclosures about the files, and proposals for improvement, were well received by the new State Department security chief under Dulles, R. W. Scott McLeod, a former FBI agent and onetime staffer for Styles Bridges. McLeod wrote McCarthy, on May 5, 1953, that "the information divulged in the hearings before your committee has been very helpful in indicating areas requiring immediate attention and corrective measures," and said such measures were being taken.[8] In turn, the report of the committee saluted the "commendable attitude" of McLeod in getting the situation righted. It would be the first of many such exchanges, and improvements, resulting from McCarthy's hearings.

Bipartisan cooperation would be apparent also in the next inquiry of the panel, concerning the Voice of America, a much-controverted subagency of the State Department with a high profile in Congress. This was yet another extension of McCarthy's previous interests, as VOA and its personnel had been among his major targets going back to 1950. (A further linkage with issues past was that VOA and related services were inheritors of personnel and programs from the Office of War Information, font of endless security troubles.)

Though the first part of the VOA investigation was purely technical in nature, it produced one of the more horrific and enduring tales about McCarthy's alleged reign of terror. The main issue was the siting of two VOA transmitting stations called "Baker West" and "Baker East," in reference to their planned locations on the Pacific and Atlantic seaboards. Much of the testimony was to the effect that these stations were in the wrong places for global broadcast. Baker West was in the state of Washington, near Seattle, and according to expert opinion this location would subject its signal to interference from magnetic storms. The proper place for such a setup, said several witnesses, would have been to the south, preferably somewhere in California. (Similar but less extensive testimony was given about the location of Baker East.)[9]

There was other information provided in the hearings as to the peculiar nature of the contract for construction of Baker West, a feasibility study done at the Massachusetts Institute of Technology that had initially approved the site, and the qualifications of the VOA official in charge of the operation. The bottom line, however, was that Baker West was being built at the wrong place, would therefore be ineffective, and that the plans for that location should be scrapped.

As with the State Department file probe, there was active participation in these hearings by Democratic panel members. This was most significant in the case of Henry Jackson, who was from Washington State, where Baker West was sited. Despite this, Jackson was critical of the project—a conspicuous refusal on his part to let patronage concerns obscure security interests. That stance would presage his later career as a stalwart in the Democratic Party on defense and security issues. It was also stressed by McCarthy, who praised Jackson for his efforts in the matter, again suggesting the collegiality then prevailing.*[10]

Like the file probe, the investigation of Baker West also had therapeutic value, resulting in suspension of the project. At midpoint in the investigation, however, a personal tragedy struck that would later be alleged as a terrible black mark against McCarthy. On March 5, 1953, a VOA engineer and prospective witness in the Baker West affair apparently committed suicide. The engineer, Raymond Kaplan, on a visit to Cambridge, Massachusetts, fell or walked in front of a truck and was killed. A letter found in his pocket, addressed to his wife and son, was construed as a suicide note and cited as a reproach against McCarthy.

Kaplan's death was, for instance, seized on by the disruptive subcommittee witness William Marx Mandel (who took the Fifth as to whether he was a Communist Party member), declaring that "you, Senator McCarthy, murdered Major Raymond Kaplan by forcing him, by pursuing him to the point where he jumped under a truck."[11] This version of the matter is repeated in several historical treatments of the VOA inquiry as proof of the fear and trembling at the agency caused by McCarthy. All of which, however, would turn out to be another batch of moonshine.

For one thing, it developed, Kaplan was to have been not a defendant but a friendly witness before the panel. As the note to his wife and son revealed, he had become convinced Baker West was in the wrong location and had earlier gone to California to find another spot for the transmitter. His view of the project thus would have supported the point otherwise established in the hearings. His note added, however, that he was afraid of being made a "patsy" (by unspecified parties) for errors committed in the program, that he feared "harassment," and that "I can't take the pressure on my shoulders any more."[12]

As McCarthy at this point had had zero contact with Kaplan and knew little about him except that he was a prospective witness, these comments about not taking the pressure "any more" suggest someone else had been causing Kaplan grief before this. There was evidence also that he had wanted to testify before McCarthy to get his view of the project on record. This was brought out in executive hearings by Dorothy Fried, a coworker knowledgeable about Kaplan's state of mind just before his death, in colloquy with committee probers:

> COHN: As a matter of fact, from what he said to you, he [Kaplan] *was anxious to testify?*

---

*MCCARTHY: I would like to compliment, at this time, if I may, the senator from Washington for the tremendous help he has given us in helping dig out the facts in regard to Baker West. I think he is better informed perhaps than any other senator on the situation out there.

JACKSON: Thank you, Mr. Chairman.

FRIED: Yes.

COHN: Rather than being anything to be afraid of, he would show up very well. Isn't that the impression you got from him?

FRIED: Yes.

McCARTHY: As of this time you cannot think of any reason he would commit suicide, and I gather from your testimony that the people who worked with him find it so unbelievable that some do not think he committed suicide.

FRIED: That is right. The fact that he called up close to five o'clock that evening [of his death], asking us to extend his travel authorization another day . . .

[DON] SURINE (committee investigator): You state that for a few days prior to his last trip to Boston, Mr. Kaplan was quite nervous and upset.

FRIED: Yes, . . . *he said he was very anxious to testify* . . . He seemed a little more nervous to me than he was generally.[13] (Emphasis added.)

From these exchanges it would appear that, whoever was causing Ray Kaplan to be upset and nervous, it wasn't Joe McCarthy. Evidently somebody was trying to scapegoat Kaplan for Baker West and he was eager to put his side of the story before the committee. Tragically, he never got the chance to do so.*

The rest of the VOA investigation mainly concerned, not technical aspects of the setup, but the content of the broadcasts and the Cold War outlook this reflected. The hearings turned up considerable anecdotal evidence of a tendency to soft-pedal the question of Soviet Communism and its aggressive nature, and to disparage anti-Communist spokesmen and causes. There was a distinct suggestion also that people and attitudes from OWI continued to hold sway in these broadcast operations.

While emphasis on these points by McCarthy was no doubt to be expected, some particulars brought out by the hearings, again, may be surprising. One of the more contentious sessions involved McCarthy's effort to find out why VOA higher-ups were canceling the Hebrew-language service beamed to listeners in Israel. Here we find the alleged anti-Semite McCarthy closely quizzing information official Reed Harris as to why this language service, above all others, should be targeted for extinction, and receiving some not-too-persuasive answers.

In particular, McCarthy wanted to know why this decision about the Hebrew-language service had been made precisely at a time when rampant anti-Semitism had openly surfaced in the Soviet bloc—most notably in the "doctors' plot" in Moscow and show trials in Czechoslovakia, both involving

---

* McCarthy gave a very accurate summary of this executive session testimony in a public hearing—which explanation has been ignored by historians in favor of the Mandel version.

Jewish defendants. McCarthy's view of the matter was at one with the head of the VOA Hebrew desk, Dr. Sidney Glazer, and the acting head of the Near East desk, Gerald Dooher, who protested the order to ax the Hebrew-language service. Both argued that Soviet anti-Semitism was a subject that should be hit hard in broadcasts to Israeli listeners.

Reed Harris responded that these were simply turf-protection issues, that the reasons were strictly financial, and that there had been stepped-up attention to the problem of Soviet anti-Semitism in other services of the Voice. The head of the VOA Russian desk, Alexander Barmine, would, however, categorically deny the last, testifying that downplaying the anti-Semitism issue was part of a more general pattern of softening the anti-Soviet message. (This was the same Alexander Barmine who earlier testified that Owen Lattimore had been identified to him as a Moscow agent.)[14]

The committee further brought out the point that the Hindi-language service of VOA, which had been using anti-Communist statements by certain Indian spokesmen, had been told to halt this practice. These instructions had been issued despite the fact, according to the head of the Hindi desk, that the broadcasts were receiving strong responses, reaching the rate of 1,000 letters a month from Hindi listeners. (In an oblique way, this also connected up with some of McCarthy's previous battles, as the Ambassador to India who reportedly wanted a softening of such broadcasts was Chester Bowles, business and political sidekick of William Benton.)

There was testimony to similar effect concerning other foreign-language broadcasts. Dr. John Cocutz, of the East European division of the Voice, said he had been told not to use the word "communism" in broadcasts about our Red opponents in the region, but to use the word "totalitarian" instead. Like testimony was given about Spanish-language broadcasts to Central and South America. Dooher of the Near East desk cited a half-dozen cases in which policy guidance muffled direct criticism of the Communists or the Soviet Union, or cut back on language services that used such comment in their broadcasts.[15]

On the other side of the question, there was evidence of hostility to anti-Communist spokesmen and leaders. Employees of the French-language service testified that, when Whittaker Chambers's *Witness* appeared and a proposal was made to review it on the air, the head of the section had said, "Whittaker Chambers is a psychopath. Don't touch him with a ten-foot pole." In this same unit, as Everett Dirksen personally knew—since he had been asked to participate in the venture—a Lincoln's Birthday broadcast was prepared, mentioning as a supposed highlight that Lincoln had received on the occasion of his reelection a congratulatory letter from Karl Marx. To Dirksen's and McCarthy's simplistic way of thinking, this didn't seem to be effective Cold War propaganda.[16]

In contrast to the alleged softening and blurring of anti-Soviet themes, the Voice had seen its way clear to reporting vigorous press criticism of South Korea's anti-Communist president Synghman Rhee (one of Professor Lattimore's least favorite "little Chiang Kai-sheks") on the eve of a Korean election. This happened while the Korean war was in progress, with South Korea as our ally, and caused Rhee to ban VOA broadcasts from being carried in the country. It provoked the following exchange between McCarthy and VOA policy director Edwin Kretzmann:

> McCARTHY: . . . there is no question but what your broadcasts beamed to South Korea over the VOA's facilities were critical of Synghman Rhee, you say of his methods, just at a time shortly before the elections were held? There is no question about this, is there?
>
> KRETZMANN: That is right, sir.
>
> McCARTHY: And as a result of that, the South Korean government denied facilities of the South Korean radios to the Voice, is that correct?
>
> KRETZMANN: That is correct.
>
> • • •
>
> McCARTHY: Did you carry any favorable comment on these broadcasts about Synghman Rhee?
>
> KRETZMANN: We did not, because we could not find any in either the American press or the European press at the time.[17]

Other discoveries in the VOA investigation suggested a nostalgia for past practices under OWI. One such, recalling the days of Short Wave Research and its backdoor hiring methods, was the outsourcing of script writing and other chores to "purchase order" employees, rather than assigning these jobs to full-time staffers. This technique was used, according to the testimony, to get around security requirements at the Voice: Employees ineligible on security grounds for full-time jobs were often given these assignments. (Though even this, as pointed out by Mundt, was contrary to the law pertaining to the subject.)[18]

The affinity for certain bygone customs extended also to certain people. In numerous cases, the committee learned, much of the broadcasting complained of was the work of holdovers from the days of OWI, a fact that perhaps accounted for the ideological angle of the product. It also developed that a number of VOA officials had backgrounds in left-wing and Marxist politics that they had allegedly repudiated—though evidence of such repudiation was sketchy.

A prime example of such holdovers was Reed Harris, acting head of the information service, who got grilled about the Hebrew-language broadcasts. An alumnus of the Acheson State Department, Harris had come up through OWI and his early doings matched with those of many others from that unit. He had an extensive background of radical left activity, dating from his tenure as a student at Columbia University in the 1930s. Among his other ventures there, he appeared at a rally with then-Communist Nathaniel Weyl and others, protesting the ouster from the Columbia faculty of the Communist Donald Henderson, later a notorious leader of Red causes.

Shortly after leaving Columbia, Harris had written a book, called *King Football,* providing further insight as to his political outlook at that era. The book was, as the title implies, a denunciation of American colleges for over-emphasis on football, but it was other things as well. It contained a rather vigorous trashing of U.S. society in general—attacks on the American Legion, gibes at business institutions, and slams at organized religion—all somewhat tenuously linked to the main thesis. It also contained two separate plugs for the way they did things in the Soviet Union (no football *there*) and cheers for a subsequently cited Communist front called the National Student League.[19]

Questioned on all this by McCarthy, Harris repudiated the book as a youthful indiscretion, saying his views had changed dramatically since he wrote it. There were, however, other items in his record of like nature. He had been, for instance, a member of the League of American Writers, a Francis Biddle–cited front group, was listed as a sponsor of a dinner for yet another cited front, the American Student Union (into which the National Student League had been merged), and appeared on the editorial board of *Directions,* a publication of the Communist-infiltrated Federal Writers Project. In each case, Harris had an explanation: He was in the League of Writers only briefly and got out when he saw the Communist influence there; the use of his name on the editorial board of *Directions* was purely honorary and pro forma; and so on.[20]

Neither McCarthy nor anyone else on the subcommittee argued that Harris had no right to do these things if that had been his inclination, but panel members openly wondered if someone of such background was the proper person to be in charge of Cold War propaganda against the Soviet Union. As Harris vehemently argued that he was now a solid anti-Communist, McCarthy pressed him for something specific attesting to this change of outlook. The same question would be raised by others on the committee, including Karl Mundt and Democratic members of the panel.

"I would like to ask you," said John McClellan, "whether, since you wrote [*King Football*], you have written any articles for publication . . . that refute the philosophy and views you expressed in that book?" Henry Jackson's version was: "I think what Senator Mundt and I are interested in is any contradictory evidence, anything that contradicts that book and your views as there expressed . . . I am trying to get some evidence here which, if you had it, would indicate a contrary position."[21] The Harris answer was that while he had experienced a drastic change of view, he hadn't written anything for publication that revealed this but could offer a vast sheaf of testimonials as to his militantly anti-Communist outlook.

Given Harris's high-ranking job helping run America's Cold War propaganda efforts, the questions raised about all this by the committee members hardly seemed unreasonable. And, from McCarthy's standpoint, there were some other more generic questions that also needed answers. Why, he wondered, did U.S. propaganda officers so often seem to have radical leftist backgrounds, and what was there in the experience of such people that fitted them for the work they were doing? It was a puzzle that would recur in future hearings.

Postscript

While the VOA hearings were unfolding, the McCarthy panel was simultaneously pursuing another inquiry, spawning a brief conflict with the Ike administration that would smolder on for several months and then flare up again the following autumn. This probe, mostly the work of Robert Kennedy, concerned the issue of trade by America's allies with Communist China, at that time still at war with U.S. and U.N. forces in Korea, and the enforcement of official measures to prevent such traffic. Kennedy produced a detailed report about the matter, indicating that efforts to suppress such trade, though mandated by Congress, were in many cases not being enforced, so that critical materials were reaching the enemy in time of warfare.[22]

Though the entire thrust of this Kennedy project was unwelcome in high administration circles, one aspect in particular would become a cause célèbre. According to Kennedy's account of the affair (and also that of *Newsweek*'s Samuel Shaffer), McCarthy staffers had been told by Ike's new foreign aid administrator, Harold Stassen, that the government could do nothing to interdict foreign trade carried by private vessels, many belonging to Greek ship owners. The scope of the law reached the acts of allied governments but not those of private parties.

Whereupon, with Stassen's encouragement (per Kennedy-Shaffer), Kennedy and fellow McCarthy aide George Anastos met with the ship owners and got them to agree not to carry prohibited goods to Communist China. Kennedy and McCarthy would then announce this *coup de main* at a press conference in March of 1953. The episode was testimony both to the effectiveness of Robert Kennedy and the work of the McCarthy panel. But it would also fuel hostility within the administration toward McCarthy and be used against him as an instance of his unlimited hubris, usurping an executive function. Meanwhile, still other such disputes were brewing that would soon explode into the headlines, leading to an even more significant rupture between McCarthy and the White House.

CHAPTER 35

The Burning of the Books

L ANGSTON Hughes was a celebrated black poet and author of the twentieth century who in his younger days was, to say no more, a sympathizer with the Communist Party and the Soviet Union, and whose works expressed this rather freely.

The most famous of many poems that voiced his radical outlook was one called "Goodbye Christ." This said, among other things: "Goodbye Christ, Lord Jehovah, Beat it on away from here, make way for a new guy with no religion at all, A real guy named Marx, Communism, Lenin, Peasant, Stalin, worker, me." In another early work Hughes had written: "Rise workers and fight . . . the curtain is a great red flag rising to the strains of the Internationale." And in another: "Put one more 'S' in the USA to make it Soviet. The USA when we take control will be the USSA."

In the spring of 1953, the McCarthy subcommittee was looking into books carried by U.S. information centers overseas and found a substantial number of works by Langston Hughes—about 200 altogether, including 16 separate titles, on offer in 51 different venues. Though "Goodbye Christ" apparently wasn't in these collections (no exact breakdown was given), the hearings indicated that various works provided were from this phase of his career and reflected the same outlook. The McCarthy panel was of the view that tax-supported information centers overseas, allegedly promoting the cause of the

United States in its war of words with Moscow, shouldn't be featuring material of such nature.

In pursuit of this notion, McCarthy called an expert witness who knew a lot about the works of Langston Hughes and concurred strongly in the negative verdict. One of the exchanges went as follows:

> QUESTION: Now let us take those [Hughes books] that you think followed the Communist line. Do you feel that those books should be on our shelves throughout the world, with the apparent stamp of approval of the U.S. government?
> ANSWER: I was certainly amazed to hear that they were. I was surprised; and I would certainly say "no."

Committee counsel Cohn would further inquire if these works "should be included in a program to fight communism today?" To which the witness answered, "I would [think] not." Quizzed as to whether such books were something "you would want included in our information program," the witness responded, "I would not." Such materials, he said, ought not be on the shelves of tax-supported U.S. libraries overseas.[1]

This threefold assertion that the early works of Hughes shouldn't be in our official information centers came from the world's foremost expert on the writings of Langston Hughes, as the witness being questioned was Langston Hughes himself. He had broken with Communism, he said, and written other things of more patriotic nature. As he put it, "I have more recent books that I would much prefer, if any books of mine are kept on the shelves . . . They contradict the philosophy [of the early works] and they certainly express my pro-democratic beliefs and my faith in democracy."[2]

This vignette is offered to give some perspective on the "book-burning" episode in the saga of Joe McCarthy featured in most histories of the era. According to these treatments, McCarthy, Cohn, *et al.* were setting out to ban or destroy books with which they disagreed, thus stifling freedom of thought and diversity of opinion. The most notorious chapter of the story was an April tour of U.S. reading centers and related posts in Europe by Cohn and committee staffer David Schine. For conducting this survey and asking a lot of nosy questions, the two were derided as intolerant clowns who terrorized innocent State Department employees, outraged Europeans, and richly earned the sobriquet "junketeering gumshoes," bestowed by one irate U.S. official.

As with the companion inquest into the doings of VOA, the voluminous record of the McCarthy panel on U.S. information libraries provides a sharply different reading. The testimony of Langston Hughes was but one example of the extent and nature of the problem with these reading centers and the merits of McCarthy's corrective efforts. As the hearings would suggest, there was a great deal of other material in the centers like the early work of Hughes, but comparatively little, so far as anyone could tell, of a vigorous anti-Communist nature to oppose it.

Had the facilities in question been private, or even public, general-interest libraries, neither McCarthy nor other members of his panel would have been pursuing such an inquest. However, the purpose of the reading centers, per the State Department, was "to utilize . . . books and related materials to advance the idea of America in the struggle against Communism." This was done under Public Law 402, cosponsored by Karl Mundt, which set up the reading centers and other aspects of the information program to promote American interests in the Cold War. As cosponsor of the law, Mundt was presumably knowledgeable of its purpose. He also happened to be an active member of the McCarthy panel delving into the curious way the project had developed.

Given the stated object of the program, it struck McCarthy, Mundt, and others as odd that Communist and pro-Communist writings should be profusely featured in the reading centers. And, based on data from the State Department, the surveys of Cohn and Schine, and other analyses of the setup, profuse would seem to be an apt description. By the committee's best estimates, there were on the shelves approximately 30,000 books by Red and pro-Red writers. Included in this number were veteran Communist bosses and sometime authors Earl Browder and William Z. Foster, who of course made no secret of their Red opinions. Others represented weren't so famous but were well known to students of Communist propaganda and disinformation. As the committee report expressed it:

> A breakdown of some of these authors shows that at least 12 have been in the past either identified under oath as having been involved or implicated in Soviet espionage or had acted in some important or confidential capacity in behalf of Soviet Russia: Cedric Belfrage, Haakon Chevalier, Lauchlin Currie, Israel Epstein, Philip Jaffe, Owen Lattimore, Kate Mitchell, Harriet Lucy Moore, Andrew Roth, Agnes Smedley, Guenther Stein, [and] Victor Yakhontoff. The adverse information on the above individuals was not classified or secret but was available to anyone who could read the public press. Most of them had been the subject of extensive reports published by the Senate Internal Security subcommittee or the House Committee on Un-American Activities.[3]

The report provided still other lists of authors featured in the centers who were known members of the Communist Party or party-liners. These included James S. Allen, Herbert Aptheker, Howard Fast, Doxey Wilkerson, and more of like persuasion. Several authors were called before the panel, quizzed about the volumes in the reading centers, and declined to say if they were members of the Communist Party when they wrote the books in question. The committee also provided information on the books themselves, including numerous quotes in lavish praise of Moscow. Following are some examples:

> "The Soviet Union plays the role of clearing the path, of facilitating world progress, of proving by its own example the superiority of the socialist system" (James S. Allen). "Russia's strength, to put it in a nutshell, lies in her moral and scientific achievements. Russia has introduced moral principle and scientific method into the heart of productive life. That is the prime cause of her matchless strength" (Hewlett Johnson). "The one hopeful light on the horizon [was] the exciting and encouraging conditions in Soviet Russia, where for the first time in history our race problem has been squarely faced and solved" (Eslanda Robeson).[4]

Especially choice were comments on the good life and noble purposes of the USSR by Scott Nearing, a well-known pro-Communist writer, in one of the books in the USIS collection: "The Soviet Union was therefore the symbol of the popular triumph over privilege. Privilege, the world over, recognized the situation and did its best to destroy the Soviets. The overthrow of the Soviet Union would have meant a decisive and overwhelming victory for privilege. While the Union endured, however, it was the logical homeland of the people's struggle."

These effusive tributes to the Kremlin, to repeat, were taken from books in official U.S. reading rooms, allegedly meant to advance American interests in the Cold War. Still other quotations in this vein, from an author whose books were widely offered in the program, included: "The merit of the new [Soviet] constitution and the national policy it institutionalized is seen by the fact that in the midst of a war for survival, the powers of the constitutive republics are not abridged but extended. The war has strengthened this far-sighted policy of the Soviet people." And: "[In the USSR] society undertakes to protect its members from undue hazards of life, requiring work as a means of life, but supplying in return assurance from accident, chance and misfortune."[5]

The author of these pro-Soviet statements, Columbia professor Bernhard Stern, swore he wasn't a Communist at the time of his committee appearance, but took the Fifth when asked if he had been a Party member when he penned his encomia to the Moscow system. Still other such items would be developed by the committee, including the fact that USIS reading centers carried the works of the Rev. Hewlett Johnson (above quoted), known as the "Red Dean" of Canterbury, and the prominent Russian author Ilya Ehrenburg. How books by these two foreign apologists for Moscow would enlighten readers as to the aims of America in the Cold War was hard to fathom. It certainly raised questions in the mind of the skeptical Joe McCarthy.

The standard explanation for having radical books on official shelves was that they showed the diversity of our culture, where even Communists and pro-Communists were allowed their say, and that we had no fear of revealing this to other countries. That subtle message, however, may not have gotten across to patrons of the centers. As McCarthy and others on the panel opined, a more likely inference would have been that, if such books were bought and paid for by American taxpayers and placed in U.S. reading centers, they had a stamp of approval from U.S. officials. Or, if not outright approval, at least represented something our government, or some of its agents, thought people should be reading (which, as suggested by other data, was probably the case).

Considering the Cold War purpose of these centers, the diversity-openness thesis would have been a tenuous rationale for having Communist and pro-Soviet books on offer. But even if that premise were accepted, it still didn't explain the condition of the reading rooms. To raise the obvious point, if "diversity" were the object of the program, then presumably *anti*-Communist books would, at a minimum, have equal billing with Communist and pro-Red volumes. But, so far as anybody could tell, this was not the case.

A prime example, brought out by subcommittee witness Freda Utley, was the selection of USIS books on China and the Far East, the area of her specialization. Having analyzed the catalogues of books available in USIS reading centers in Germany, Miss Utley found the vast preponderance of these works were by such as Owen Lattimore, Guenther Stein, Lawrence Rosinger, and others whose views about these matters have been noted. "I counted some two dozen books," she testified, "which belonged to the Lattimore school on China, and in the China section . . . which I naturally studied in particular as my own subject, I could find practically nothing, almost nothing, that was not favorable to the Chinese Communists."[6]

In the case of Professor Lattimore, the committee found some 161 copies of his books available in 60 USIS reading centers, including not only his several volumes on Far East affairs but also his plangent memoir, *Ordeal by Slander,* dealing with his appearance before the Tydings panel and including a vigorous blast against McCarthy.

It was of course conceivable that, in so vast a system of books and periodicals, some vigorously anti-Communist works existed somewhere to counterbalance the pro-Red material that was cited. Utley and researcher Karl Baarslag would testify that such books did exist in the collections, but that these were few and far between, hard to find, and outnumbered by works of leftward or radical persuasion. Likewise, defenses of the system were more usually geared to arguing that it was okay to carry radical or pro-Communist materials as examples of diversity, free thought, and good old-fashioned plucky dissent in America's great tradition.[7]

From these and other indicators, it was reasonably obvious the reading centers funded by the U.S. government to combat Communism weren't doing this very well, if at all, and were more often nearly doing the reverse. And as the hearings on VOA suggested, the reasons for this weren't too esoteric. In numerous instances the book collections, and the people who chose them, were holdovers from the days of OWI, among the most heavily penetrated and left-ward-tilting federal agencies ever. The contents of the reading centers were pretty much what one might expect given knowledge of that record.

As the McCarthy inquest revealed, old-line personnel who came aboard with OWI during the war had stuck around under the State Department and U.S. occupation forces. Under the Acheson State Department and High Commissioner for Occupied Germany (HICOG) John McCloy, a number of these holdovers had advanced to top positions. Now, however, the rules had changed and the pro-Soviet outlook of the early 1940s and postwar era had been replaced by the harsh new realities of the Cold War. Making things more awkward still, the Truman-Acheson regime was now supplanted by Eisenhower-Dulles. Worst of all, meddlesome committees of Congress, headed by the likes of Joe McCarthy, were taking an interest in the programs and the officials who ran them.

In these conditions, the holdovers did what they could to adjust to the new setup, presenting themselves as "Cold War liberals" battling against the schemes of Moscow, which perhaps in certain cases they were. As with Reed Harris, however, their own previous records and the embedded programs they were running made it hard to sell this. The McCarthy hearings consisted, in considerable measure, of a long string of contradictions and anomalies inherent in an allegedly anti-Soviet program being run by people of completely different background.

Among the clearest examples of such problems was one Theodore Kaghan, in 1953 the acting deputy director of public affairs for HICOG. Kaghan was another alumnus of OWI, and had the kind of résumé one might suspect based on the history of that unit. In 1939, he had signed a nominating petition for a Communist political hopeful, Israel Amter, saying, "I intend to support at the ensuing election" the Communist candidate for office. Kaghan in the 1930s had also been the roommate and coworker of an identified Communist, worked with a Communist-dominated outfit called the New Theater Project, written a play staged by this group, and attended various Communist meetings.[8]

It was further testified, in the Voice of America sessions, that Kaghan had flunked a loyalty-security check when it was proposed that he move from HICOG to VOA (an episode hashed over in the Reed Harris hearings). All in all, not a *vita* on first appraisal well suited to conducting a "psychological warfare" campaign against Moscow, which Kaghan said he was in charge of doing. As with Reed Harris, much of the wrangling between McCarthy/Cohn and Kaghan concerned the question of whether, and to what degree, he had shed the opinions and affiliations of the 1930s and early '40s, and what proof there was that he had done so.

Other highlights (or lowlights) of the Kaghan affair included testimony that pro-Communist manifestations in American information programs weren't limited to USIS reading centers. Kaghan's office had distributed, for instance, at a cost of $50,000, over a thousand copies of an alleged sociological/ historical tract that said of Stalin, "As the accepted leader of world communism he gave the teachings of Marx, Engels and Lenin their present valid form." It further developed that the occupation government had subsidized with U.S. tax dollars a printing plant being used, *inter alia*, for printing Red materials. In yet another instance, a lecturer sponsored by HICOG was traveling about in Germany voicing praises of Soviet leader Georgi Malenkov.[9]

In cases of this type, the holdover mind-set was apparent, as policies in the early postwar era had viewed the Reds in Germany as allegedly "democratic" elements to be encouraged, subsidized, and otherwise supported. According to records from the postwar occupation archives, one of the Americans involved in supplying aid to the Communist Party under this policy had been none other than Theodore Kaghan.[10] The subsidies and other involvements with the Communists, like the condition of the reading centers, suggested the earlier mind-set and embedded features of the program continued in the 1950s.

Confronted by all this information from the McCarthy probe, the Dulles State Department issued an order that books by Communist authors be removed from the reading centers. The full extent to which this was done isn't clear, but a number of such books were indeed removed and in some manner disposed of. This gave rise to the plaint that the books were being "burned," ultimate responsibility for which was placed on McCarthy. In fact, if any books were burned or otherwise destroyed (and apparently some were), McCarthy didn't do it. He frequently stated that people should be able to obtain and read such books if they so desired. His point was simply that pro-Red materials shouldn't be supplied by American taxpayers as part of an alleged Communist-fighting program overseas.

On this, ironically, McCarthy was backed not only by Langston Hughes and the Dulles State Department but also by the new and impeccably liberal HICOG commissioner, James B. Conant, a successor in that post to John McCloy. Under intense questioning on the subject, Conant agreed that tax dollars shouldn't be used to finance Communist or pro-Communist books in U.S. reading rooms. This testimony was particularly telling as it occurred in a direct confrontation with McCarthy—another encounter where we see the caveman face-to-face with an urbane Ivy League opponent. In this exchange, McCarthy by no means came off second best, as he questioned Conant closely about the reading centers. In this colloquy, the former Harvard president at last affirmed that, "I would not be in favor of having books by Communist authors on the shelves. If they are already there, I would be in favor of taking them off."[11]

The same thought was expressed by President Eisenhower, discussing the subject before the press. On this occasion, Ike said that if USIS libraries overseas carried books that advocated Communism, such books should be gotten rid of, "because he saw no reason for the Federal government to be supporting something that advocated its own destruction. That seemed to him the acme of silliness."[12] Again, this was identical to McCarthy's position on the issue. However, Eisenhower's views on the matter, and McCarthy's role in it, were subject to a good deal of backstage influence, which would be used to get him to issue a famous statement of very different implication.

Oddly enough, before all this occurred, there *had* been a mass destruction of books and other printed materials in Germany dictated by the Allied occupation forces of the postwar era. Such publications were destroyed wholesale in 1946, under orders to dispose of Nazi, pro-Nazi, or "militaristic" literature of all types "from the stocks of all publishing concerns, libraries, and public repositories."[13] At that time, and through the intervening years, nobody had protested that, in obeisance to diversity of thought and old-fashioned notions of dissent, pro-Nazi literature should be available in any form whatever, much less presented to the reading public of Europe in libraries run by the U.S. government.

Likewise, no pro-Nazi, pro-Fascist, or related items, as far as the record shows, were discovered in the catalogues or shelves of the information centers in 1953. Neither destruction of pro-Nazi materials in the postwar era, nor the subsequent absence of such materials from the reading centers, provoked a cry of "book burning" or "censorship" from civil liberties spokesmen. Such charges were reserved exclusively for the removal of Communist and pro-Red books from a program allegedly fighting Communism in Europe. As the McCarthy panel summed it up:

> Americans are now asked to believe that it was good to destroy Nazi and Fascist literature, but that it is bad or a crime against culture to remove Communist books from United States Government–sponsored libraries abroad. Book-burning sauce for the Nazi goose was not sauce for the Communist gander. In our opinion, neither the propaganda of the Nazis or the Communists should be encouraged or promoted by the United States Government.[14]

Notwithstanding all the above, the uproar over the USIS investigation and "book-burning" charges would be effectively used against McCarthy and are used against him still. In this campaign, the publicity given the Cohn-Schine tour of Europe was the first of several adverse developments. In fanning such publicity, Theodore Kaghan and others at HICOG played a significant role, as was brought out by the hearings. In so doing, Kaghan was undoubtedly provoked by the fact that his name, and his reported failure to receive a security clearance, had surfaced in the earlier sessions on the VOA, in public testimony by Voice official James F. Thompson.

Kaghan was thus well primed for his encounter with Cohn and Schine, and when the duo embarked on their tour in April, it was Kaghan who dubbed them "junketeering gumshoes" and helped orchestrate resistance to their efforts. One HICOG technique, for which Kaghan disclaimed responsibility but in which his press officer was admittedly complicit, was to assign a full-time escort to shadow Cohn and Schine wherever they went, find out what they were doing, and alert a mostly hostile press corps to their movements.

This monitoring of Cohn and Schine resulted in close press attention all along the way and numerous adversarial questions about the purpose of their visit. When they responded to such questions, they were then attacked for "having press conferences" and shooting off their mouths to foreign newsmen. As Senator Mundt expressed it to Kaghan: "You were contributing to the very thing you criticized. I do not know whether they held press conferences, but I do know that you made it easier for them to hold press conferences by telegraphing in advance where they were going."[15]

Mundt's summary was correct, except that it understated the extent to which U.S. diplomatic personnel had organized the hostile press reception—an effort that involved not only HICOG but other officials of the State Department. Part of the story would be told by Ben Bradlee, at the time press attaché with the U.S. Embassy in Paris, who went on to media fame at *Newsweek* and the *Washington Post*. Bradlee in later years happily recalled the steps he and others had taken to organize press conferences for Cohn and Schine that were meant to be, and were, bear-baiting sessions.

As Bradlee told it, he and other Embassy staffers went out of their way to round up hostile reporters on a Paris Sunday for a merciless thrashing of Cohn and Schine. "We weren't five minutes into it," said Bradlee, "before [Cohn and Schine] realized it was a disaster and they realized they had been set up . . . There wasn't a single question that took them seriously, not a single anything remotely like a friend in the audience . . ." Much pleased with this, Bradlee worked with British correspondents to orchestrate a similarly angry press turnout in London.[16] Such were the services rendered by State Department officials to enhance the image of the U.S. abroad in the early 1950s. And such were the conditions in which Cohn and Schine would be blamed for holding "press conferences" in fact orchestrated by our diplomats in Europe.

The other main adverse development for McCarthy from the book probe was the work of John McCloy. Kaghan and others had been on the staff at HICOG when McCloy was commissioner there, so the revelations of the McCarthy panel inevitably reflected on McCloy. The former high commissioner was not pleased with the investigation and took steps to retaliate against it. Among these were speeches in which he deplored the excesses of congressional inquests, an obvious allusion to the McCarthy hearings. More important, and one of the best-remembered aspects of the story, was his intercession with President Eisenhower to get a public statement that would be construed (correctly) as a slam against McCarthy.

This episode occurred in June of 1953 at Dartmouth College, where Ike was to receive an honorary degree and make some remarks, and McCloy was in attendance. McCloy here took it upon himself to tell Eisenhower that books were being burned by HICOG, this allegedly caused by McCarthy, and that something drastic needed doing. This outraged the President, who included in his remarks the offhand statement: "Don't join the book burners. Don't be afraid to go in your library and read every book as long as any document doesn't offend your ideas of decency. That should be the only censorship. How will we defeat communism unless we know what it is?"[17]

As a reference to the McCarthy hearings, which it was of course assumed to be, this Ike statement left a lot to be desired. The McCarthy probe had nothing to do with libraries in the United States, where Ike's auditors might have read whatever they wished, and Eisenhower himself would go on record as saying Communist books shouldn't be in official reading centers overseas. And if books had been burned by HICOG, this had been done by members of the executive branch under Ike himself, not by McCarthy. As an anti-McCarthy salvo, therefore, the statement was somewhat lacking in coherence. Where attacks on McCarthy were concerned, however, this was never a big problem, and the anti-McCarthy forces were effusive in their praises of Ike's impromptu comment.

While more sinned against than sinning in these proceedings, the McCarthy forces made some PR gaffes that didn't help things. One was in going after Dashiell Hammett, the famous mystery writer, whose books were widely featured in the information program. There were certainly grounds for objecting to Hammett, a hard-core Stalinist active in pro-Red causes who took the Fifth on relevant questions before McCarthy. Among his other ventures, Hammett had been part of a group that went bail for convicted CP leaders, and had gone to prison for refusing to answer questions about that project. He was, in addition, active at this period churning out propaganda pieces promoting Communist and pro-Soviet notions.

McCarthy's position was that, given all the above, the United States shouldn't be featuring Hammett in official information centers overseas, no matter how acclaimed the writer. That view had some abstract merit, but

McCarthy's focus on the author of *The Maltese Falcon* and *The Thin Man* provided a convenient handle to critics of the probe to trivialize the issue and say books with no Cold War implication were being banished. It would have been the better part of wisdom for McCarthy to steer clear of Hammett.[18]

In another dubious move, McCarthy brought the editor of the *New York Post,* James Wechsler, to appear before the panel. Under other circumstances, Wechsler would have been a logical witness in the hearings, as he had a strongly pro-Red background in the 1930s and his books were among those in the reading centers. However, he was also a virulent press critic of McCarthy, so his appearance was inevitably seen as, and no doubt was, a McCarthy effort at retaliation.

In these hearings, Wechsler gave as good as he got, arguing that he was now a tough-minded anti-Communist who had repudiated his pro-Red past, and presenting articles he had written to prove this. McCarthy retorted that Wechsler had a consistent history of attacking the FBI, disparaging ex-Communist witnesses such as Louis Budenz and Elizabeth Bentley, and defending the likes of William Remington (all of which was true). Wechsler was given latitude to respond at whatever length he chose, and fully availed himself of the privilege (a privilege McCarthy never enjoyed in the then-liberal pages of the *Post*).*[19]

However, nothing McCarthy would say or do could cancel the impression that he was simply using the hearing to attack a journalistic critic, and for that reason, as with Hammett, should never have had the editor before the committee. Beyond which, there were other negatives for McCarthy in this particular set of hearings. Among these was the fact that they occasioned a serious breach between McCarthy and Democratic members of the panel, as Stuart Symington and to a lesser extent Henry Jackson took up the cudgels for Wechsler. Like the Ike "book-burner" speech, it was a harbinger of future trouble for McCarthy. He was now stockpiling enemies at both ends of Pennsylvania Avenue.

That said, there is copious evidence that the USIS investigation was far from being the fiasco portrayed in the usual write-ups. The problem in the reading centers and related programs was real, and the investigation McCarthy conducted went a long way to expose this. The point, however, would be buried beneath the avalanche of ridicule stirred up by such as Kaghan, Bradlee, and McCloy, and repeated ever since in discussions of McCarthy.

---

*For readers familiar with the *New York Post* as owned and directed by Rupert Murdoch, it should be pointed out that this newspaper in the 1950s was of the opposite political outlook.

CHAPTER 36

Scott McLeod, Where Are You?

A T THE advent of the new administration, the Republican Party was split along divergent fault lines. Some of these were institutional—as in executive against Congress; some regional—as in the agricultural West/Midwest against the mostly urban North and East; others of a tactical nature—as in how best to get the message over to the public. All of this was standard fare for any administration of either party, and not especially surprising.

In the intramural Republican struggles of the 1950s, however, there was another kind of party schism that went beyond the usual turf wars. This was in essence a battle for the soul of the GOP, the values it espoused, and its role in our political system. Stated in simplest terms, the question was whether the party should present itself as a sharply etched alternative to the Democratic program or as an approximation of it, give or take a few distinctions.

Within the White House and in the Eisenhower Cabinet, there were divisions on many topics relating to this larger issue. Some of Ike's advisers, as might be expected in a Republican administration, were of conservative bent, while others of more pragmatic temper tried to downplay internal conflicts, just trying to advance a common program. But there were still others who pushed hard for liberalization, wanted a more leftward stance on issues, and sought an open break with conservatives in Congress. These attitudes inevitably dictated differing views on what to do about the problem of Joe McCarthy.

A retroactive close-up of this internal struggle would be provided by Ike speechwriter Emmet Hughes, on loan to the White House from the Time-Life empire. In a breezy memoir of the 1950s, Hughes described the players in the new administration, competing forces in the Cabinet, and links between these groups and elements in Congress. He made it plain that he and C. D. Jackson, a fellow Time-Life alum, were the most zealous advocates of a more liberal GOP, though by no means alone in talking up such notions.

Hughes would provide startling insight into his own ideas and motives, and the nature of his influence, in some amazingly candid comments. "I was, and am," he wrote, "of the generation of the New Deal . . . While accidents of age and wartime duty and foreign assignment kept me from voting in any national elections until 1952, I would have voted, without exception, for all Democratic candidates for the presidency . . . In terms of American politics, I most commonly found myself a comrade, in purpose and temper, of the Democrats—and not the more conservative ones. I still do."[1]

Hughes would back these views with specific and often caustic comments on policies and people. He was, for instance, contemptuous of John Foster Dulles ("a surfeit of abstractions and generalizations"), State Department security chief Scott McLeod ("an aggressive superpatriot"), and Ike's conservative Treasury Secretary George Humphrey ("intellectual baggage unencumbered by complexities")—while manifesting his great regard for FDR and the New Deal heritage in general.[2]

Given these liberal and pro-Democratic leanings, the question perforce arises as to what Hughes was doing in a *Republican* White House—much less presuming to sit in judgment of GOP Cabinet members or other leaders of the party. To find the answer to this puzzle, it's useful to recall that, in the 1950s and for a while thereafter, there was indeed an effort under way to new-model the GOP in the image of its opposition. After so many years of Democratic rule, it was argued, the Republican Party could no longer tread the conservative path preferred by the old bulls in Congress.[3]

The vogue of this conception may seem odd today, looking back on the Goldwater-Reagan *risorgimento* that turned the GOP into a staunchly conservative party in both presidential and legislative circles, then carried it on to election wins at state and federal levels. However, such ideas were fairly trendy in the 1950s and early '60s, promoted in major press outlets, and embodied in the presidential hopes of such media-favored liberal GOPers as New York governor Nelson Rockefeller and New York City mayor John V. Lindsay. It was all very New York/East Coast/establishmentarian, and nicely underscored the concept of policy continuity with the Truman-Acheson era. The presence of

Emmet Hughes in GOP regalia, and the views that he advanced, were aspects of this project.

Outside the environs of the White House, there were other influences of like nature. Among the most important of these was the already noted John McCloy, variously head of the Chase Manhattan Bank and Council on Foreign Relations, among many other weighty titles, who had served as assistant secretary of war under FDR and as high commissioner of Germany under Truman. McCloy was close to Dean Acheson, a fellow graduate of Harvard Law, and had played a significant role in policy episodes of the New Deal era.

McCloy was the quintessential establishment figure, with high-level contacts in the GOP as well as in the Democratic party. Eisenhower liked him and reputedly wanted him to be Secretary of State, but had been dissuaded on the grounds that McCloy's New Deal and Acheson ties would be red flags to the still-vigorous old bulls in Congress. McCloy nonetheless remained in close touch with Ike and with such of his top advisers as C. D. Jackson, a New York acquaintance of long standing. McCloy, as his biographer puts it, was "Ike's wise man."[4]

McCloy's wisdom on the foreign policy side was very much of the Acheson school, and his appointments at HICOG were in keeping with this background. Among his staffers there were Theodore Kaghan, Charles W. Thayer, Samuel Reber, Lowell Clucas, and—a true blast from the past—John Paton Davies. All of these had been, or would become, targets of McCarthy. So in addition to disagreements on the issues, McCloy had some very specific reasons not to like McCarthy. The "book-burning" episode was but one example of McCloy's wielding backstairs influence adverse to McCarthy and conservative interests in general.

Suggestive of McCloy's clout was his recommendation that James B. Conant, former president of Harvard, be named as McCloy's own successor at HICOG. Conant was yet another establishment figure who wore several hats—scientist, educator, administrator, politician. He had been a major player in the nuclear program in World War II and was, like McCloy and Acheson, an admirer of J. Robert Oppenheimer, guru of that operation. Conant continued his nuclear interests in the postwar era, and with McCloy and Oppenheimer had helped shape the Acheson-Lilienthal plan for global sharing of the atom. He was also identified with liberal domestic causes, mostly dealing with education.

To Joe McCarthy and other conservatives in Congress, the appointment of the ur-liberal Conant signaled obvious continuity with the Democratic program rather than the Republicans' promised changes. McCarthy accordingly planned a speech, written by the young conservative author William Buckley, in opposition to the nomination. However, these were early days yet and McCarthy was persuaded by Senator Taft to withhold his fire in the interest of party unity. The Conant speech was not delivered.[5]

More troubling than the Conant appointment was the soon-to-follow Ike decision to name Charles E. "Chip" Bohlen as America's new ambassador to Moscow. Few choices could have been more indicative of solidarity with the New Deal outlook. A career diplomat and longtime Russian expert, Bohlen had been a favorite of Harry Hopkins and was linked closely with the Hopkins appeasement policy toward Moscow. Bohlen had served at the wartime conferences in Teheran, Yalta, and Potsdam and was a favored Acheson colleague at State, where he had risen to the role of counselor formerly held by Benjamin Cohen. It was testimony to the power of State's entrenched bureaucracy, as well as to more general leftward pressures on the GOP, that such an appointment could be engineered under the new regime, and suggestive of Eisenhower's views that he would make it.

Short of naming Acheson himself, it would have been hard to come up with a nominee more offensive to conservatives in Congress. Thus, two months into the Ike age, a small mutiny developed as McCarthy and several others voiced displeasure with the nomination. To quell the outbreak, the White House enlisted the reluctant help of Senate Republican leader Taft and his deputy, William Knowland (R-Calif.). Both were staunch conservatives and anti-Communists who had no more use for Bohlen, Yalta, and the Acheson foreign policy than did McCarthy, and had made this plain in many statements.

Both were, however, loyal party stalwarts and grimly agreed to carry the nomination forward in the Senate. To do otherwise, they reasoned, would badly damage the new administration at the very outset. Thus, in one of the richer paradoxes of that day, support for the Hopkins/Acheson holdover Bohlen would become a test of Republican "unity," with two prominent GOP conservatives in the forefront. This would be sufficient to ensure approval of the nomination, whatever Republican senators thought about its merits (which was nil). Enough would grit their teeth and "support the White House," along with Democrats who actually supported Bohlen, to guarantee his confirmation.

The Taft-Knowland logic, however, was unavailing with some in Congress, and McCarthy was inevitably of this number. It's ironic, to say no more, that he is often depicted as a blind partisan who cynically used the anti-Communist issue to bludgeon his Democratic opponents. The truth about McCarthy, and ultimately his main political problem, was that he wasn't nearly partisan enough, at least from the standpoint of the Eisenhower White House. He was far too consistent in his views to support under Ike policies or people he had castigated under Truman.

In Senate floor debate, McCarthy was by no means the leader of the anti-Bohlen forces. Among the first to go after the nominee was the veteran conservative Democrat Pat McCarran. Others taking up the cudgels were Republicans Styles Bridges, Everett Dirksen, Karl Mundt, and Bourke Hickenlooper. McCarthy supported this contingent but spoke less than did some others, reserving most of his floor remarks for a set speech toward the end of the process.

Complicating matters were reports that an FBI loyalty/security check on Bohlen had turned up derogatory data. Rumors and comments to this effect added to the atmosphere of discontent among the anti-Bohlen forces. Also disturbing was a widely bruited tale that Scott McLeod, the new security chief at State, had refused to sign off on the appointment. This story, as it happened, was true, though some unusual methods would be adopted to disguise this.

Based on these allegations, a clamor arose to have the relevant facts brought before the Senate. The wrangle went on for several days, as McCarthy, McCarran, Bridges, and others asked for the security data on Bohlen. In this, for the most part, they were unsuccessful. As to the FBI report, there were as usual strong objections from the Bureau, as well as from the White House, to making such intel public. The dilemma was in part resolved by having senators Taft and John Sparkman (D-Ala.) review a summary of the FBI file and relay their findings to the Senate.

As for Scott McLeod, he had indeed refused to sign off on Bohlen, only to be overruled by Dulles. A much-distressed McLeod considered resigning over the affair, and at one point shared his concerns with FBI Director Hoover. The Hoover memo on their talk, which took place on March 25, 1953, gives this picture:

> Mr. McLeod seemed to be quite depressed . . . as a result of the recent publicity in which his name had played a prominent part incident to the nomination of Mr. Bohlen as Ambassador to Moscow. Mr. McLeod also stated that he had been at the point of resigning several times as a result of the treatment which he had received in this matter but had refrained from doing so up until the time I saw him. Mr. McLeod stated he had made an evaluation of the FBI summary on Bohlen which had been submitted to the Secretary of State, and indicated that he could not conscientiously give Mr. Bohlen a security clearance. He stated he had refrained from appearing before any committee of Congress although he had been sought to appear before several of the committees.[6]

To say Scott McLeod "refrained" from appearing before the Congress was to put it mildly. When the Bohlen security issue surfaced, McCarthy, John McClellan, and others suggested McLeod be called to testify (a suggestion also made privately by Hoover). This, however, the White House was determined to prevent, and McLeod would be strangely unavailable for any such appearance. As McClellan put it, "I felt that Mr. McLeod should be called and that the question as to his differing with the Secretary of State should be cleared up . . . there does seem something a little mysterious—I do not know what it is—about the unavailability of Mr. McLeod."[7]

The matter was indeed mysterious, and also of unusual import. As would later be disclosed, not only had McLeod been ordered not to testify on Bohlen, but steps were taken to ensure that he was physically unavailable to do so. This maneuvering resembled certain practices under Truman—most obviously, the sequestering of the State Department security files in the White House to keep them from the Senate. In this case, however, it wasn't a matter of sequestering files but of sequestering a person.

The Dulles phone logs reveal, for instance, a March 20 talk with Ike Attorney General Herbert Brownell about ways and means of preventing McLeod from being subpoenaed by the Senate, possibly by invoking the Truman secrecy order of 1948. Later that day, in further conversation with Brownell, "the secretary said McLeod was going out of town so that the subpoena could not be served." Logs for the following day reflect that McLeod was then in Concord, New Hampshire, presumably out of the reach of process servers, though how long he would remain there isn't apparent from the record.[8]

While the exact location of McLeod thereafter is uncertain, we are once more indebted to the candor of Emmet Hughes for background data on the disappearance. As Hughes would put it, "For days, someone on the White House staff had to be assigned to make sure that the State Department security chief was kept 'secure' from any public places where a subpoena might be served on him."[9] Thanks to these precautions, McLeod was never called, so the puzzle would remain and deepen. The episode presaged others down the road in which witnesses would be prevented by unusual methods of the Ike regime from testifying to Congress.

Meanwhile, after viewing a summary of the FBI report, Taft and Sparkman would say there was nothing in it reflecting negatively on the loyalty of Bohlen. The seeming contradiction between this Taft-Sparkman "clearance" and Scott McLeod's refusal to provide the same can now to some extent be resolved, as we have the FBI report in question. Though this is as in other cases heavily redacted, it's possible to see how different judgments were arrived at.

The FBI report on Bohlen came in three sections—one involving loyalty issues, another the somewhat different question of security, and one relating to general suitability for the job in Moscow. At the first level, nothing in the record and nobody interviewed said Bohlen was disloyal or pro-Red, that he was a "loyalty risk," or that there were any doubts on this score whatever. So when Taft and Sparkman reviewed the précis, they could correctly say there was no problem of this nature. However, there were noted in the Bureau wrap-up doubts as to whether Bohlen might be a *security* risk, which was an entirely separate matter.

In this category, the question was not subjective loyalty but aspects of personal history indicating flaws of judgment, moral turpitude, or susceptibility to blackmail. Traits that came under these headings included alcoholism, mental or emotional problems, criminal conduct, or sexual peccadilloes. In the case of Bohlen, the factor most often mentioned was the belief that he might be a homosexual. This was closely linked with allegations against his brother-in-law Charles Thayer, who was in fact being discreetly ousted from the Dulles State Department precisely as the Bohlen nomination was going forward.

There was no evidence or testimony of homosexual activity by Bohlen, but there were reports that tied him in with Thayer and others against whom such charges had been made. Bohlen and Thayer were close friends as well as in-laws, moved in the same circles, and had several friends in common who were reputed homosexuals. One such lived in Bohlen's house while the nominee was in Europe, had been arrested on a morals charge, and had been ousted from the State Department for this reason.[10]

Contrary to current notions of gay liberation, a closeted homosexual in the 1950s was considered a grave security risk, especially in a high official posting. Homosexuality was thought so alien to the culture that exposure would be ruinous, which meant a homosexual in public life was seen as a candidate for blackmail. This notion was by no means confined to Joe McCarthy, though he and other security sleuths in Congress and the executive viewed it as axiomatic.*[11]

Ironically, the fight over Bohlen occurred exactly at the time the Eisenhower White House was issuing tough new security regs that stressed the importance of just such matters. Among the criteria to be used in judging an employee's fitness, according to the new Ike decree, were "any criminal, infamous, dishonest, immoral or notoriously disgraceful conduct, habitual use of intoxicants to excess, drug addiction, or *sexual perversion.*" (Emphasis added.) In those non-PC days, the italicized phrase was obvious code for homosexual.[12]

It was apparently this part of the FBI report that made Scott McLeod reluctant to sign off on Bohlen. It was this aspect also that caused Director Hoover to voice a word of caution. As a memo on a March 17 meeting of Hoover with Dulles and Herbert Brownell records: "The Director made it clear that the FBI did not as a usual procedure evaluate any of its reports, but in view of the President's request [for Hoover's opinion], the Director would not be inclined, if he were passing on the question of security, to give Bohlen a complete clearance. The Director pointed out that there was no evidence that Bohlen had engaged in homosexual activities, but it was a known fact that several of his closest friends and intimate associates were known homosexuals."[13]

It further appears much of this was known to McCarthy. The day after the

---

*It was on such grounds, for instance, that the Marshall-Acheson State Department had dismissed some ninety-one people from the ranks in 1947 before McCarthy ever got in the picture.

Hoover-Dulles-Brownell meeting, McCarthy got in touch with Hoover about Bohlen, seeking the Director's guidance. The resulting conversation is suggestive as to what McCarthy knew about the case, his quest for further data, and the tactics he was or wasn't prepared to use in debate before the Senate. Hoover's memo on this informs us:

> Senator Joseph McCarthy called with reference to the Charles Bohlen appointment and the matter of keeping John Davies on. He stated that he was quite concerned regarding the entire picture as there was practically no change and everything was running about the same as it was a year ago. Senator McCarthy wondered whether I would tell him in complete confidence just how bad Bohlen was. I told him, of course, that it was hard to evaluate. . . .
>
> The senator was advised that we had not shown any overt act, but he, Bohlen, had certainly used bad judgment in associating with homosexuals. The senator stated this was a matter he was almost precluded from discussing on the floor; that it was so very easy to accuse someone of such acts but difficult to prove; I agreed, and stated it was a charge often made by persons who wanted to smear someone.[14]

As presaged by these comments, the security angle was now for the most part dropped by McCarthy and other Bohlen critics. Attention switched to the third tranche of the FBI report, involving issues more discussable in public and dovetailing with other facets of Bohlen's record: his suitability for the Kremlin post in terms of general outlook and performance. Numerous sources raised questions on these grounds, far more than any other. Among the most vehement of the critics was former Ambassador to Moscow William Bullitt, himself a onetime confidant of FDR, for whom Bohlen as a junior diplomat had worked in the 1930s. As the FBI report expressed it:

> He [Bullitt] related that Bohlen was in the Embassy from one to two years and that his conduct became "intolerable." He related that Bohlen, during this period, was drinking excessively and that he personally asked for his recall to the Department of State. . . . Bullitt said there is no question concerning the appointee's loyalty to the United States or his moral character . . . [But] he advised that he has the utmost contempt for Bohlen and has told him so to his face. He related that approximately several years ago he called Bohlen a "cheap profiteer on American disaster." He stated that the above related to what he considered a lack of ethics on the part of the appointee. He advised that during the war years the appointee "went along with the theme of Harry Hopkins that the Soviet Union was a peace loving democracy and he has certainly furthered his career by so doing."[15]

Similar comments about Bohlen's views and policy influence were provided by ex-Communist Jay Lovestone and the anti-Communist expert Isaac Don

Levine. Among the more knowledgeable of such critics, having served in the State Department and worked with Bohlen directly, was former Ambassador to Poland Arthur Lane. In 1946, Lane had tried to head off a State Department policy providing a hefty loan to Communist-dominated Poland. Lane linked this and other Moscow-appeasing policies to Bohlen. As the FBI reported:

> Lane stated it never occurred to him that Bohlen, "who had been the personification of our appeasement policy, should be appointed to Moscow." He said Bohlen was personally responsible for the policy which was repudiated in the elections last November. He advised it was Bohlen who suggested to Averell Harriman to go to Moscow in 1945 and make concessions to the Russians . . . Lane stated that in 1946, when he was Ambassador to Poland, Bohlen was the force behind the ninety-million dollar loan to Poland. He stated that it is inconceivable to him that an individual could recommend the economic build-up of a Communist enemy of the United States . . . and advised that he thinks the appointee's assignment is a grave mistake and that "to put an apologist of the Soviet Union, Yalta and the appeasement policy to the Soviet Union in the position of Ambassador to Moscow is wrong."[16]

These comments by two seasoned diplomats refocused the debate back to where it started: whether appointments under the new GOP regime would be continuous with, or divergent from, policies of the preceding era. This was the point most often stressed by McCarthy and other foes of the nomination. In fact, McCarthy in his speech concerning Bohlen said little on security issues, though not omitting them entirely.

In these remarks, McCarthy as usual paid tribute to Ike and Dulles, said they were doing a good job in general and that he supported them wholeheartedly in the positive steps that they were taking.* Having made this obeisance to party unity, McCarthy then moved into his critique of Bohlen. The centerpiece of this was Bohlen's role at Yalta and his defense of the decisions made there. McCarthy reviewed the Yalta provisions concerning Poland, Yugoslavia, and China, and the ensuing communization of these countries. He also reprised some other issues of that time, such as the demand for the unconditional surrender of Japan, efforts to get the Soviets into the Pacific war, and Bohlen's role in these discussions.

Ultimately, however, it came down to Yalta. This was the sticking point for McCarthy, as it was for Dirksen, Bridges, Mundt, and several others. The Republican platform of 1952 had been quite definite on the subject, saying "the Government of the United States, under Republican leadership, will repudiate all commitments contained in secret understandings, such as those at Yalta,

---

*In these passages, he made only a fleeting reference to the FBI report, and singled out Scott McLeod for praise as having recently removed a number of security risks from the State Department (among them Thayer, though his connection to Bohlen wasn't mentioned).

which aid Communist enslavement."[17] It would be hard to get more anti-Yalta than that, yet here was one of the main holdovers from Yalta being appointed to a key position by the new Republican leader in the White House.

This caused much grief for conservatives backing the nomination, who tried to get Bohlen to make some kind of face-saving gesture on Yalta (face-saving for them, if not for Bohlen). Bohlen wouldn't give them the satisfaction, instead rubbing their noses in the capitulation they were making in the name of unity with the White House. A particularly painful exchange occurred between Bohlen and Sen. Homer Ferguson, who pressed the nominee to say the Yalta agreements were in *some* sense mistaken, but failed badly in the effort.

> FERGUSON: You claim now . . . that these agreements were correct govern-
> mental agreements so far as America was concerned, but that the inter-
> pretation put on them by Russia is what caused the . . .
> BOHLEN: I would say, sir, I would go further than that, saying it is not so
> much interpretation as violation . . .
> FERGUSON: Why did we have to surrender the rights of these people and be
> a party to the surrender?
> BOHLEN: I don't consider the agreement at Yalta involved a surrender. It
> involved the opposite.[18]

These comments and resulting news accounts couldn't have been welcome to Taft and Knowland. One headline read: "Bohlen Backs Yalta Pact and the Truman Foreign Policy." The subhead was even worse—a turn of the screw for conservatives backing Bohlen: "Choice as Soviet Envoy Also Defends Acheson at Senate Group Meeting." All of this, of course, merely confirmed McCarthy and other Bohlen critics in their opposition. Everett Dirksen would put it that "I reject Yalta, so I reject Yalta men." McCarthy's version was "in November, 31,000,000 people told us to clean house. That means getting rid of Acheson's lieutenants, including Bohlen."[19]

That Bohlen was completely unapologetic about his role at Yalta and ser-vice with the FDR/Truman/Acheson State Department would be made clear in his memoir published two decades later. In this volume, he continued to defend the Yalta pact and the merits of Acheson's days at State, while gloating over the outcome of his nomination battle.* He likewise made plain his disagreements with Dulles, and even more so with the traditional policy stances of the GOP: " . . . it was clear that my views on relations with the Soviet Union did not coincide with Dulles' and that of the Republican Party."[20] Styles Bridges, or Joe McCarthy, couldn't have said it any better.

---

*This Bohlen chapter is titled "The Defeat of Joseph McCarthy."

THERE is a last detail about the Bohlen struggle requiring mention. This concerned a report from three respected former officials of the State Department—Norman Armour, Hugh Gibson, and Joseph Grew—who had allegedly signed off on the selection and given Bohlen their endorsement. In testifying to the Senate, Dulles said this distinguished trio "unanimously concurred in the view that Mr. Bohlen was uniquely qualified for this particular post." In support of this, the State Department supplied Senator Knowland a copy of the report for use in floor debate on the appointment.

While McCarthy was giving his speech of opposition, he became embroiled in a dispute with Knowland about this report—which turned out to be an omnibus cover memo with a list of names attached—and what it had to say about Bohlen. When Everett Dirksen inquired as to whether the three officials had in fact all given Bohlen their endorsement, McCarthy suggested Dirksen be allowed to see the report, "so there could be no question." This outraged Knowland, who said McCarthy was "challenging my veracity . . . on the floor of the Senate."[21]

This episode is often cited as a deserved rebuke to McCarthy, showing that his slash-and-burn tactics were so extreme even a conservative like Bill Knowland was offended. As may be seen by reading the debate, this is a complete inversion of the record. McCarthy, the transcript shows, wasn't challenging the veracity *of Knowland,* but did think the Senate should know more about the State Department report in question. In so thinking, he was quite correct, as the well-meaning Knowland had been inveigled into carrying water for the department in one of its patented ventures in confusion. The three-wise-man endorsement of Bohlen was indeed open to serious challenge.

The person who nailed this was Dirksen, who happened to be a good friend of Hugh Gibson, one of the alleged endorsers, and had tracked Gibson down to check the matter out directly. Dirksen quoted Gibson as saying that, *"as a matter of fact, he, Mr. Grew and Mr. Armour were not asked to pass on Mr. Bohlen . . . in the instant case, namely the vacancy at Moscow, they were not actually asked, so he made no recommendation whatsoever."*[22] (Emphasis added.) This Dirksen update would be amplified by Gibson himself in an interview with the *Boston Post,* explaining that he had never been asked to sign off on Bohlen.

"Apparently," said Gibson, "there was the grandest lot of shenanigans about words and meanings on the floor of the Senate you ever heard of. As I recall it . . . the day I talked to Mr. Dulles, together with Mr. Grew and Mr. Armour, Dulles told us that certain appointments had already been made— those for London, Paris, Rome, Madrid, and Moscow . . . *Well, now it comes out that we recommended Bohlen. We certainly did not. At least I did not.* We certainly did not consider the names of the persons down for the jobs in the places I mentioned—London, Paris, Rome, Madrid, and Moscow . . ."[23] (Emphasis added.) So, whatever the case with the other signers, Hugh Gibson obviously hadn't endorsed Chip Bohlen.

Thus McCarthy was entirely right in suggesting that the document Knowland was wielding needed a careful look-see, and Knowland was totally out of line in blowing his stack against McCarthy. In studying this exchange, one senses that the honest, earnest Knowland was embarrassed and flustered by the spot he was in, fronting for the always tricky State Department and making a case with a document about which he knew nothing. Throughout all this, McCarthy was quite civil, patient, and complimentary toward Knowland. So McCarthy was not only right in the point he was raising but very much the injured party. Yet the whole thing is portrayed by the usual historians-biographers as yet another outrageous episode in the shameful saga of McCarthy.

None of this, of course, made any difference in the final outcome, as Bohlen would be confirmed by a vote of 74 to 13, to great hosannas from the liberal press. The fledgling Ike administration, however, had learned a valuable lesson about being prudent in its personnel decisions. A telephone log for March 19 reflects a talk between Dulles and White House majordomo Sherman Adams, wherein a cautionary note was sounded about the appointments process, as "Gov. Adams asked how the secretary [Dulles] happened to pick him anyway." Considering the uproar that had occurred, the question was a good one. These second thoughts about selection methods concerned, however, not Ike's new ambassador to Moscow, but the troublesome security officer, McLeod, who had to be sequestered from the Senate.[24] Obviously, the administration would have to be more careful about such appointments in the future.

CHAPTER 37

The Getting of J. B. Matthews

FOR J. B. Matthews, it was déjà vu all over again, only more so. He had been through the whole thing before, with the House Committee on Un-American Activities. Now he would relive the identical nightmare with Joe McCarthy. Except this time it was worse.

His name was Joseph Brown Matthews, but everybody called him J.B. He was circa 1953 the world's foremost expert on the subject of Communist fronts, and had been for years before this. His expertise stemmed from the fact that he had been a fronter himself, indeed something of a legend in that department. As he said in testifying to Congress, "I hope it will not appear immodest, but I was probably more closely associated with the Communist Party's united front maneuvers than any other individual in this country."[1]

All told, Matthews had been directly linked with twenty such maneuvers, and indirectly with many more. Most conspicuously, he had been the first chairman of the Francis Biddle–cited American League Against War and Fascism (aka League for Peace and Democracy). He had been connected, too, with the Friends of the Soviet Union, the Student Congress Against War, the Tom Mooney Committee, and many similar outfits, and well knew the tie-in between such groups and the formal CP operation then headed by Earl Browder.

In 1935, witnessing the takeover tactics of an alleged Communist faction in a bitter strike at Consumers' Research in Washington, New Jersey, and becoming otherwise disenchanted, Matthews by degrees broke with the movement and then turned against it. A record keeper and document hound by instinct and training, he began compiling the most extensive roster of Red front groups ever assembled. He was a natural to testify before (and later work with) the House Committee, just as he would be a natural ally down the road for Joe McCarthy.

In what was in its day a famous episode, Matthews appeared before Dies and Co. in 1938, conducting a tutorial on why the fronts existed, how the CP controlled them, and how unknowing people were inveigled into cooperation. It was on this occasion that he provoked the "Shirley Temple" furor, much trumpeted by foes of the committee both then and later. The incident provides an instructive tale about the debating tactics of certain New Deal stalwarts, as well as a prelude to the travail of Matthews and McCarthy in the 1950s.

In essence, Matthews told the House committee, naive and busy people could be hoodwinked into lending their names to Red causes that looked good on the surface but were something else on close inspection. He cited the fancy Communist newspaper *Ce Soir* in France (a Willi Munzenberg production), which on the approach of its first anniversary solicited and received greetings from some big Hollywood names—Clark Gable, Robert Taylor, James Cagney, "and even Shirley Temple." "No one, I hope," said Matthews, "is going to claim that any one of these persons in particular is a Communist."[2]

This statement is quoted *in extenso* below to make sure the context is clear.* What it obviously said was that the Reds were adept at fooling innocent people into endorsing their endeavors. In the case of the child star Shirley Temple, of course, the endorsement would have come through some adult agent, who perhaps thought sending greetings to the swanky *Ce Soir* might be a shrewd PR move. All in all, a good object lesson in why movie stars and other famous people, or their agents, needed to be careful about the things they lent their names to.

So far, so sensible. But not at all the way the matter would be played by

---

* "The Communist Party relies heavily upon the carelessness or indifference of thousands of prominent citizens in lending their names for propaganda purposes. Here I find you have another good example, and I am not trying to make these persons' names stand out in any odious manner whatsoever. . . . The Communist Party owns outright the newspaper which is regarded by many as the swankiest newspaper published in France at the present time. The name of the newspaper is *Ce Soir*. It is little more than a year old. On the occasion of its first anniversary recently, this Communist paper featured greetings from Clark Gable, Robert Taylor, James Cagney, and even Shirley Temple. The League of Women Shoppers [an officially designated Communist front per the Attorney General's list] boasts of the membership of Miriam Hopkins and Bette Davis. A list of such persons could be expanded almost indefinitely. No one, I hope, is going to claim that any one of these persons in particular is a Communist. . . ."

various liberal politicians and writers of alleged Cold War history. In these precincts, the story became, and would remain, *the House Committee on Un-American Activities had called Shirley Temple a Communist.* The way was led by the voluble Harold Ickes, Roosevelt's Secretary of the Interior, who explained the matter as follows: "They've gone into Hollywood and there discovered a great plot. They found dangerous radicals there, led by little Shirley Temple. Imagine the great committee raiding her nursery and seizing her dolls in evidence."

Not to be outdone in clueless indignation was FDR's Secretary of Labor, Frances Perkins. In denouncing Dies and his committee, Perkins declaimed: "Perhaps it is unfortunate that Shirley Temple was born an American citizen and that we will not have to debate the preposterous revelation of your committee in regard to this innocent and likable child."[3] So, having made the valid point that famous people in Hollywood (and elsewhere), including a noted child star, needed to watch out for Red deceptions, Matthews and Dies were accused of making charges of subversion against Shirley Temple.*

Fast-forward fifteen years, to the summer of 1953. In an effort to smooth out tensions between Kennedy and Cohn and other office problems, Joe McCarthy got the notion of turning to J. B. Matthews as subcommittee staff director. It was a good idea in theory. Matthews had been helping McCarthy all along, starting with the Tydings probe and the data on such as Esther Brunauer and Dorothy Kenyon that McCarthy had read into the record. Matthews, then fifty-nine, was roughly the age of Cohn and Kennedy put together, with a few years to spare, had spent six years as research director for the House Committee, and was universally respected in anti-Communist circles as an expert's expert.

What seemed good in theory turned out to be less good in practice. Some months before this, Matthews had penned an article for *The American Mercury,* a conservative journal of the era, titled "Reds in Our Churches." Given the lead times of such publications, the article would be published in the July 1953 issue, just as McCarthy was appointing Matthews. This proved to be a godsend to McCarthy's foes, a cause of infinite grief for Matthews, and a critical episode in the further tribulations of McCarthy.

Having had his Shirley Temple moment, Matthews perhaps should have known better than to write a magazine piece that—however accurate—would lend itself to similar exploitation. "Reds in Our Churches" began with the arresting statement: "The largest single group supporting the Communist apparatus in the United States today is composed of Protestant clergymen."[4]

---

* Nor are historical references to this episode a great deal better. Thus, in what purports to be a biography of Martin Dies, we read that, among its other failings, "this committee was charged with having accused Shirley Temple of being a Communist," no other explanation offered.

Though apparently few people read any further, this was a comment Matthews would back up, as was his fashion, with a lot of documentation.*

As Matthews was a diligent researcher, the rebuttable presumption would be that, when he made such an assertion, he knew whereof he spoke. And on this subject he knew more than on others. Not only was he a specialist in Communist agitprop, he was also an ordained Methodist minister. He held the bachelor of divinity degree from Drew University and the sacred theology degree from Union Theological Seminary, and had been a missionary-teacher. Among other pursuits before becoming a Red-hunter, he had translated the Methodist hymnal into Malaysian. (He was also a linguist of some note, with a specialty in Oriental languages.)†

Drawing on his extensive knowledge of religious-political matters, Matthews in his *Mercury* essay listed the names of Protestant clergymen who had wittingly or unwittingly lent support to Communist-front groups. The article also highlighted such weird outfits as the People's Institute of Applied Religion, which promoted Marxism to rural churches, and a magazine called *The Protestant,* whose twin specialties were vicious anti-Catholic invective and thinly veiled Red propaganda.‡5 While offering a mass of data on such topics, he stated in his wrap-up: "It hardly needs to be said that the vast majority of Protestant clergymen are loyal to the free institutions of this country, as well as loyal to their solemn trust as ministers of the Gospel. In a sense, the overwhelming majority is embarrassed by the participation of a minority in the activities of the most sinister conspiracy in the history of the world."6

In sum, a heavily empirical piece, dealing with a serious problem. It could and should have provoked questions, not only about the sources of the Matthews data for those who might have wondered about them, but about the thing he was describing, why it existed, and what the people engaged in such

---

*In purely mathematical terms, the basis for this comment was an earlier Matthews estimate that, over the previous seventeen years, some 3,500 professors in U.S. educational institutions had lent their names to or otherwise supported Communist causes—"many of them as dues paying members, many others as fellow travelers, some as all-out espionage agents, and some as unwilling dupes of subversion." In that same span, said Matthews, the number of Protestant clergymen involved with such activities was twice as large—totaling more than 7,000.

†Beyond this, Matthews had made a study of such curious groups as the Methodist Federation for Social Action, the work of such leftward-tilting preachers as Harry Ward and Jack McMichael, and others topics of like nature. Based on his seminary training, he was familiar with the doctrine of the "social gospel," the way some theologians tried to cross-breed this with Marxism, and confusions promoted on this basis concerning "peace" or "social justice." (To see these linkages in our own day, we need only consider the strange political antics of the National and World Councils of Churches, or the "liberation theology" movement in some Latin nations.)

‡Matthews quoted from *The Protestant* an editorial titled "God's Red Army": "It is not because Russia has saved us that we thank God for the Red Army. . . . It is simply because of what Russia is and because of the quality of the Red Army itself, the spiritual quality of its soldiers, the way its soldiers feel toward its people, the way its soldiers feel toward their enemies. This is why, listening to our innermost voice, we hear ourselves thanking God for the Red Army."

activity had to say about it. However, virtually no such discussion would happen. Instead, as with the Shirley Temple furor, the response would be a deafening mix of demagoguery and misinformation.

Ironically, the Matthews points about Red attempts to manipulate the clergy had earlier been made by him in his memoir, *Odyssey of a Fellow Traveler* (1939), and in testimony before the House committee.[7] But most McCarthy-Matthews critics apparently hadn't read these earlier efforts, so the *Mercury* article struck them as a thunderbolt—and a most welcome opportunity. In short order, a huge outcry would be fomented to the effect that Matthews had attacked *all Protestant ministers,* was smearing *an entire group of people,* and was an *anti-Protestant* bigot. Such comments would be offered from press and pulpit and echo from many official places, including the U.S. Senate and—ultimately—the White House.

As the reader may have guessed, this outcry was in no way spontaneous, and would never have occurred at all if Matthews hadn't been named to his new position with McCarthy, who was, of course, a Roman Catholic. In and of itself, an article in *The American Mercury,* whatever people might have thought about it, wouldn't have sparked a national uproar. But if it could be linked to McCarthy—*the Roman Catholic McCarthy*—that was a different matter. Accordingly, an extensive effort was now made by McCarthy's foes to manufacture a wave of protest about the *Mercury* piece and exploit the "anti-Protestant" religious issue against him.

In this respect, there were some other continuities between the salad days of the HCUA and the McCarthy epoch. In the early 1940s, numerous left-wing groups had been mobilized to attack and if possible defeat more conservative members of Congress. One such outfit was called the Coordinating Committee for Democratic Action, the executive director of which was a leftward activist named Maurice Rosenblatt. The thesis of this group, attuned to the exigencies of the war years, was the need to expose and root out "pro-fascist" elements in American life—a worthy object, no doubt, but one that got defined in malleable terms capable of much expansion.*

The elasticity of the "pro-fascist" charge was noted by Martin Dies, who drew attention to the work of the Coordinating Committee in a floor speech in early 1943. Dies read into the *Congressional Record* excerpts from a Coordinat-

---

*According to Rosenblatt and his admirers, the Coordinating Committee began as a kind of guerrilla theater operation devoted to neighborhood wartime projects in New York (with an affiliate in Boston). Among these were broadsides attacking, and street confrontations with, the allegedly anti-Semitic followers of Father Coughlin, a Catholic radio priest of the 1930s. In due course, the Committee would go national with its efforts, a process aided by its merger with yet another outfit called Friends of Democracy, headed by the mystery writer Rex Stout. In various Coordinating Committee/Friends of Democracy publications, the political targets ranged from anti-Semites like Gerald L. K. Smith on the one hand to more mainstream figures such as Cabot Lodge and Joseph Kennedy on the other.

ing Committee pamphlet titled "Your Congressman and Pearl Harbor," which sought to tag certain members of Congress as pro-fascist. This broadside alleged that some of the solons "felt a kinship for the attackers," that "various senators and representatives cooperated intimately with fascist groups," and that in monitoring "all pro-fascist groups" the Coordinators had noted efforts to use "the floor of Congress as a forum for working against democracy."[8]

Dies further said Maurice Rosenblatt had been running some of his fascist-spotting activities out of the government office of one Gardner Jackson, a New Deal appointee. (In support of this, Dies cited long-distance phone records of Rosenblatt calls made and received through Jackson's office.)[9] Gardner Jackson, as it happened, was one of the better-known activists in Red-front doings of the 1930s and early '40s—including the Washington Committee for Democratic Action and the National Federation for Constitutional Liberties (both on the Francis Biddle list) and the Washington Tom Mooney Committee, a spin-off of the Peace and Democracy operation.

Fast-forward once more to the 1950s, and the emergence on the political scene of a lobbying group called the National Committee for an Effective Congress. A main thesis of this committee was that Joe McCarthy was another Hitler who urgently needed to be stopped before he spread the pall of fascism any further. The executive director of the NCEC turned out to be the selfsame Maurice Rosenblatt, and serving on its board of advisers, along with a numerous cast of others, was the selfsame Gardner Jackson. Still more déjà vu for J. B. Matthews, and still more incipient trouble for McCarthy.

While the NCEC had other functions, mostly backing liberal candidates for office, its top priority in the early 1950s, bar none, was its campaign to bring down McCarthy. To this end it ran something called the (McCarthy) Clearing House, nerve center of a wide-ranging anti-McCarthy mechanism connected to divers liberal journalists, labor officials, leftward lobbies, and politicians. (In a further parallel with the earlier Rosenblatt group, the NCEC conducted some of its operations out of government quarters—an office of Sen. Earl Clements [D-Ky.], then head of the Democratic senatorial campaign committee.)

The NCEC was linked in one way or another with just about every major opponent of McCarthy, including William Benton, Millard Tydings, Drew Pearson, authors Jack Anderson and Ronald May, staffers of the *Milwaukee Journal,* and many others. Members of this loose backstage alliance included Senate Democratic staffer Kenneth Birkhead, liberal activist Robert Nathan, Benton aide John Howe, and Benton attorney Gerhard Van Arkel. (As that roster suggests, it was very much a Benton-connected setup, and Benton himself was active in raising money for it.) Also important, the NCEC had entrée to the new GOP administration, mainly through liberal businessman Paul Hoffman, an Ike supporter and confrere of Rosenblatt's committee.

By 1953, the NCEC had succeeded in securing funds from such wealthy donors as Chicago millionaire Marshall Field, and had hired a researcher, working out of the Clements office, to press its agenda on a full-time basis. It got a letterhead printed up indicating that an "effective" Congress meant an extremely liberal one, which featured on its advisory board, along with Gardner Jackson, a number of McCarthy foes and targets—including such noteworthy figures from earlier Cold War battles as Paul Appleby, Michael Straight, and Telford Taylor.

When McCarthy first named Matthews staff director, the NCEC sprang into action, assembling a dossier on the appointee that, to judge from the group's description, was none too flattering to Matthews, and sought to get this to members of the Senate. When the *Mercury* piece appeared, Rosenblatt and Co., sensing a golden chance to stir up a really massive protest, redoubled their efforts to lobby against McCarthy with his colleagues. The NCEC also launched a concerted drive to reach newsmen, liberal activists, and clerical contacts to fan the flames of indignation against Matthews as an anti-Protestant bigot.[10]

The NCEC would later claim credit for having stirred up the Matthews furor, and at least some of that credit, if such it be, was deserved. The group had extensive press contacts and undoubtedly helped provoke a lot of the hostile media comment about Matthews-McCarthy. Still more significant, perhaps, were its efforts to put pressure on Michigan senator Charles Potter, a Republican member of the McCarthy subcommittee, through contacts with high-ranking Protestant clergy in Detroit. The committee also made particular efforts to get its materials into the hands of John McClellan, the ranking Democrat on the McCarthy panel.

In the event, the media outcry and political firestorm resulted in Matthews's resignation—and much else besides. The Democrats on the PSI demanded that Matthews be ousted and upbraided McCarthy for having hired him in the first place. More critical yet, under the orchestrated pressure from back home, Charles Potter joined the anti-Matthews chorus, and by combining with the three Democratic members made a majority against McCarthy on his own subcommittee. There was thus no alternative for McCarthy now but to unload Matthews.

As the NCEC exulted, the consequences of all this were many. Committee official George Agree would later say its foremost success in all of 1953 had been "the getting of J. B. Matthews, in which the Clearing House provided the initial spark, the biographical dossier that fired up Senator McClellan, the contacts with clergy around the country whose pulpit and press reaction helped particularly with Senators McClellan and Potter." As to the larger meaning of the struggle, the NCEC would put it: "Opportunities like the Matthews episode have arisen before and will arise again. The difference this time seems to have been the presence on the Hill of people armed with detailed information about Matthews, who were seeking an opening and ready to take advantage of it."[11]

That lesson would be remembered, and used in other contests. However, the

NCEC was perhaps taking a few more bows than it deserved to, as other and even more powerful forces were also in the field, likewise seeking to exploit the religious issue against McCarthy. Here we are once more indebted to some inside players for explaining how they pushed the onslaught to the highest levels—getting the President himself to attack McCarthy in a carefully crafted statement on the Matthews affair that would cause the greatest possible damage.

Part of the story would be told by journalist Joseph Alsop, the rest by Emmet Hughes and other White House staffers. As usually happened, Ike's advisers were of two minds on how to handle the Matthews flap, but top aide Sherman Adams decided it was just the ticket for doing in McCarthy. In his newspaper column, Alsop recounted not only what had happened in the White House, but also the larger implications of the tactic. "President Eisenhower," said Alsop, "has at last opened hostilities against Sen. Joseph R. McCarthy . . . [via] Ike's decisive statement denouncing the slander of the Protestant clergy by McCarthy's pet investigator, J. B. Matthews."

"The real interest of this statement," Alsop added, "lies in a vital background fact. The White House actively sought the opportunity, indeed, created the opportunity, to strike this hard blow at the Wisconsin senator. . . . The President's chief of staff, former Gov. Sherman Adams of New Hampshire, was the man who decided that Matthews offered the long-awaited 'really good issue' on which the President could take his stand against McCarthy. . . . Rather cleverly, the White House then took steps to stimulate a telegram denouncing Matthews. . . . This was to give the President a reason to speak . . . the intention to strike at McCarthy was abundantly clear."[12]

Emmet Hughes would fill in some blanks, recounting White House confabs in which it was decided to solicit a protest relating to Matthews from the National Conference of Christians and Jews, a liberal-leaning church group. Hughes further disclosed that Ike's "response" was written before the solicited "protest" ever made it to the White House. This streamlined method, however, was not without its glitches. Disconcertingly, while Hughes and other staffers were anxiously awaiting the NCCJ protest with the answer already drafted, the message of clerical outrage didn't arrive as scheduled.* In the meantime, word reached the White House that McCarthy had decided to jettison Matthews, and concern was rampant that this would remove the pretext for Ike's readymade rejoinder. A priceless chance to trash McCarthy would be wasted.

Accordingly, at the request of Hughes, Vice President Nixon and Deputy Attorney General William Rogers detained McCarthy on Capitol Hill in an extended gabfest as he was on his way to announce the Matthews resignation. This gave Hughes and others just the time required to get the NCCJ "protest"

---

*It had made its way to the desk of Ike aide Bernard Shanley, who wasn't in on the plot, and was holding the letter for discussion.

to the President, obtain his approval for the "response," and release it to the press. (A further minor foulup was that mimeograph stencils for the Ike message and press release had already been prepared, but because of editing changes had to be done over.)[13]

So the thing at last went forward, and the next day's papers featured the clerical "protest" and Eisenhower's "response," both as mendacious as they were synthetic. Each was a classic of the genre, blandly misstating the nature of the issue, as per the Shirley Temple furor. The NCCJ "protest" referred to an alleged "sweeping attack on the Protestant clergy" made by unnamed parties, and said that "destroying trust in *the leaders of Protestantism, Catholicism or Judaism by wholesale condemnation*" was to be lamented. Ike's answer, drafted by Hughes, likewise asserted, "I want you to know at once that I fully share the convictions that you state. . . . *Generalized and irresponsible attacks that sweepingly condemn the whole of any group of citizens* are alien to America."[14] (Emphasis added.)

Of course, Matthews hadn't engaged in "wholesale condemnation" of the "leaders" of any faith, nor had he "sweepingly" condemned the "whole of any group of citizens." He had indeed done the reverse, pointing out that the Protestant clergy he criticized were a minority, and that the vast majority of such churchmen were loyal to both faith and country. None of that, however, made any difference. The important thing was to blitz McCarthy, and the blitzing had been accomplished.

The implications of all this would be greatly amplified by press coverage of the Ike/clergy statements and the sudden Matthews exit. Of particular note was the Murray Marder story the next morning in the *Washington Post,* played in what used to be called in the newspaper business "Second Coming" fashion—gigantic, eight-column headlines spread across the top of page one. The treatment was comparable to that given the attack against Pearl Harbor, the Normandy invasion, or the dropping of the A-bomb. Nor did the *Post* neglect to print in full, as done with the most important documents of state, the complete texts of the totally ersatz Ike/clergy correspondence.[15]

These events were instructive at many levels, most obviously as to the conventional notion that McCarthy was guilty of unprovoked attacks against the executive branch under Ike and thus responsible for conflict within the party. In the Matthews affair we see the exact reverse, as forces within the White House assiduously worked to discredit McCarthy on a matter that had no relevance to the executive branch whatever. The issue at stake was strictly the internal staffing of a Senate committee, which was no business of the White House. It nonetheless provided Hughes, Adams, *et al.*, a chance, in Alsop's phrasing, "to strike this hard blow" against the hated maverick.

At a deeper level, the most significant aspect of the case was the effort of McCarthy's foes to stir up the furies of religious conflict—specifically, to inflame Protestant sensibilities against the Catholic McCarthy. This was no trivial matter, as there were many sections of the country where anti-Catholic feeling ran strong (a condition that would get more notice a few years later during the presidential campaign of John F. Kennedy). This purpose was implicit throughout the Matthews ruckus, but would be made crystal clear by Drew Pearson, whose office worked closely with the NCEC in this and other anti-McCarthy battles.

In his comments on the Matthews affair, Pearson held forth on the theme that McCarthy's choice of Matthews had outraged Protestants—not failing to emphasize, wherever possible, that McCarthy was a Roman Catholic. The columnist also linked Matthews with the Roman Catholic Father Charles Coughlin, and noted that Matthews-McCarthy had been supported in the pages of *Our Sunday Visitor,* the nation's largest publication for lay Catholics. So deposing, Pearson concluded that "given Matthews' background," McCarthy should have known that "Protestants would be outraged" by the choice of Matthews. Pearson thus managed to stamp "Catholic" all over the Matthews-McCarthy combine, while tut-tutting about the "tragic" religious conflict thus created.[16]

From this treatment, readers of Pearson's column could have concluded only that Matthews, like McCarthy, was a Roman Catholic, and that the two of them were engaged in a wholesale attack against the nation's Protestant churches. That Matthews was not a Catholic but a Protestant, and a former Methodist minister in the bargain, was nowhere mentioned in these effusions. Thus were religious hatreds deliberately fanned for political reasons by forces allegedly speaking out for tolerance in our discourse.

Bad as all this was for McCarthy, still other ill effects would follow. Based on this incident, McClellan and the Democratic members of the subcommittee demanded greater say-so in the hiring of staff, and when this turned into a conflict with McCarthy and Republican members, began a boycott of the panel that went on for the remainder of the year. (Robert Kennedy would at this time leave the panel also, to return later as counsel to the Democratic senators.) This was a level of rancor far beyond the usual divisions in the Senate. It also meant some of the most significant investigations of the committee would be conducted without any Democratic members present.*

Taken all in all, the Matthews uproar and its effects must be accounted among the stranger episodes in our political history. Everything about it was fake: the misrepresentation of what Matthews said, and the manufactured

---

*Reviewing the record on this episode, of pivotal importance in the relations of McCarthy to the White House, the comments of Sherman Adams are of interest, as he was by the report of both Alsop and Hughes the triggerman in the scheme to go after Matthews. In his own account of the affair, Adams would make his grim hostility to McCarthy plain, but otherwise provide a study in obfuscation. Nobody relying on his treatment would know the cooked-up nature of the "protest," the ersatz nature of the Ike response, or the role of Adams himself in causing this to happen. The whole thing is presented by Adams at face value as a spontaneous venture in righteous outrage.

outcry; the staged "protest" to the White House, its canned response, and the falsehoods embedded in both statements. Add to all of this the hyped press accounts and envenomed columns of Drew Pearson. That this campaign of poisonous disinformation succeeded—and is even now presented as historical truth in write-ups of the era—is an astonishing fact of record, the more so as its impact on the work of the McCarthy panel was both disruptive and long-lasting. (What had been done to J. B. Matthews was deplorable also, but obviously of zero concern to orchestrators of the protest.)

Meanwhile, the folks at the NCEC, vetted by a major battle with McCarthy, had tasted blood, liked the flavor, and were anxious for another serving. In which connection, they would subsequently be in close contact with an eccentric Republican member of the Senate, Ralph Flanders of Vermont, whose vagaries would lead him to become point man for still other attacks against McCarthy. Likewise, back at the White House, Hughes, Sherman Adams, and others had at last precipitated an open break between Ike and McCarthy, far transcending the earlier squabble about Chip Bohlen. Some members of the administration were now in a fighting mood, anxious to have it out with McCarthy and alert to other occasions like the Matthews fracas. And of these, as the McCarthy panel proceeded with its labors, there would be no shortage.

THOUGH it didn't receive much attention in the wake of the Matthews battle, the McCarthy committee at this period, despite the pressures converging on it, continued with some productive investigations. One such, relevant to the charge that McCarthy "never exposed a single Communist," involved the Government Printing Office, which handled all sorts of printed matter for the federal government, proceedings of the Congress and countless documents for the executive branch, military data and reports on many classified subjects.

The GPO investigation focused mainly on Edward Rothschild, an identified member of the Communist Party who worked in the assembly room where confidential documents were put together. Rothschild would be named under oath as a CP member by a fellow worker at the office, and his wife would likewise be named by an undercover agent for the FBI. Both Rothschilds responded to these identifications by pleading the Fifth Amendment.

A number of tangible outcomes would result from this investigation. Among the most important were committee findings about loyalty/security standards at GPO, which went far to explain how the likes of Edward Rothschild continued to hold a job there. As established by the hearings, the loyalty board at GPO had operated in such a way as to guarantee that virtually no one on its payroll could be found a loyalty risk, whatever the evidence against him.

Two of the tenets under which this board had functioned were (a) a loyalty proceeding would hear only witnesses *favorable* to the employee, and (b) "mere membership" in the Communist Party wasn't considered a disqualifying factor. The reader will perhaps recognize the second as a concept favored in the security fog of World War II—which in this case persisted for eight full years into the era of the Cold War. Also, the penalty at GPO for removing documents from the premises, as Rothschild was accused of doing, was a brief period of suspension. Under standards of this sort, adverse FBI reports about Rothschild did nothing to affect his employment status. He thus continued to have access to classified material that passed through the printing office—including nuclear secrets of the Navy.[17]

In the wake of these hearings—still being described as irresponsible, hit-and-run, and ineffective by the press corps decades later[18]—wholesale changes were made in procedures at the GPO. Rothschild was discharged the day after he took the Fifth Amendment before McCarthy, thus concluding a run of fourteen years of almost unlimited access to documents in the print shop. Also, fifteen other GPO employees accused of pro-Red activity were moved to less sensitive jobs while their cases were under review.

Even more significant than the ouster or transfer of employees, the entire loyalty board of the GPO was fired and new security standards were adopted, concomitant with tougher government-wide guidelines announced by the Attorney General. A month after the hearings, the new head of the GPO, Public Printer Raymond Blattenberger, wrote McCarthy thanking him for the committee's disclosure of security problems there, and recounting the steps being taken to ensure that these would not continue.*

As to McCarthy's conduct of the hearings, Blattenberger's further comments are worth noting. The printer concluded his letter by saying: "The inquiry by your subcommittee focused my immediate attention on the matters described above, and I wish to express my appreciation for the courtesy and the cooperation extended to me by the subcommittee and its staff." If that weren't astonishing enough, McCarthy received a similar accolade from Rothschild's attorney, Charles Ford, who had exercised in behalf of his client the various privileges afforded by the panel. "I think the committee session . . . ," said Ford, "is most admirable and most American. I think they are to be admired for it."[19]

These comments echoed those that had followed the investigation of the State Department's filing system. Even more to the point, perhaps, they presaged events that would unfold as the PSI began the most contentious and historic investigation of McCarthy's tenure.

---

*As to the changes in regulations and the removal of the old loyalty board, Blattenberger said: "The new security regulations issued by the Attorney General, in my opinion, are far superior to the old loyalty proceedings which formerly existed. The actions which have been taken remove from key security positions all of the top officials who were concerned with the former loyalty program. Since the new security regulations present a completely different approach, I believe that our security practice can be administered best by persons who were not trained to think in terms of the old loyalty procedure."

CHAPTER 38

The Moles of Monmouth

I N THE spring of 1953, Joe McCarthy got a cryptic phone call from an
intelligence officer in the Army who said he had some important security
data to share with the new committee chairman. McCarthy would meet
with the mysterious caller, who did have such information, including a confidential memo about a hush-hush Army research setup vital to the nation's
defenses. This would be the start of the longest-running, most complex, and
most controverted of all McCarthy inquests. It would also be the start of endless trouble for McCarthy.

Though the memo in question was never published, a good deal would
eventually be learned about it—and even more would be said about it—in
some flamboyant Senate hearings. The memo was a two-and-a-quarter-page
précis of an FBI report, dated January 1951, culled from an original Bureau
document running to fifteen pages. The subject was the security drill at an
Army Signal Corps research post called Fort Monmouth, based at Eatontown,
New Jersey, on the Jersey Shore, about an hour's drive from New York City. As
later described before the Senate, the memo listed thirty-four workers at Monmouth who had been subjects of FBI investigation, though specifics on the
cases were deleted from the bobtailed version.* To judge by the comments of

*Inserted in place of these original entries were the terms "derogatory" or "no derogatory" [data].

those who read it, most notably including Joe McCarthy, the memo indicated serious security trouble at Monmouth and related units.

This was but one of many leads about the Army Signal Corps that would reach McCarthy in the spring of 1953 and later. Based on such tips, the committee launched what would become a protracted series of investigations that branched off to several aspects of the Signal Corps, other military bases, and firms that supplied materials, technical expertise, and other services to the Army. These interlocking probes would run from the late summer of 1953 through the spring of '54, when they would be brought to a sudden halt by stunning Army charges of malfeasance against McCarthy and his counsel Roy Cohn, and their equally stunning answers.

As the above suggests, while Fort Monmouth would become the major focus of the McCarthy inquest, the panel looked at a number of other things as well. Some of these were arguably as important as Monmouth itself, though they weren't the subject of public hearings, didn't garner any headlines, and are omitted from the usual histories. Taken together, they indicated that security problems in the Signal Corps were many, ongoing, and of most serious nature. One particular instance is worth special mention, as it overlapped in several ways with what later happened at Fort Monmouth.

In this case, the McCarthy probers pulled together data relating to alleged infiltration and security infractions at the Pentagon-based Signal Corps Intelligence Agency (SCIA), nerve center and receiving point for military telecommunications, hence an obvious target for penetration. Charges of lax security at this unit had been brought in the latter part of 1951 by ten Signal Corps officials, alleging that staffers of pro-Red sympathy and background had infiltrated its operations. The complainants further said that important classified papers had vanished from the files and never been recovered.[1]

The officials pressing these allegations included Col. O. J. Allen, executive officer of the SCIA, civilian research chief Edwin Webb, scientific division chief Robert Stilmar, and seven others of some stature in the program. Following their initial charges, certain apparently flagrant suspects were removed from their positions. But thereafter, according to the complaining officials, the probe had been stalled out and a proper cleanup never happened. The ten then took the unprecedented step of petitioning Congress for an outside investigation. This resulted in a brief flicker of congressional interest and public notice in the early weeks of 1952, but thereafter little or nothing would ever be heard about the topic.[2]

McCarthy staffers would gather considerable evidence on all this, including information on alleged penetration of the intelligence unit and the nature

---

(This presumably was done by the Army, as the standard practice of the FBI was to supply information on such cases but leave evaluation to the receiving agency.)

of the in-house struggle over what to do about it. One thing they discovered was that the flap at SCIA had rebounded strongly against the ten accusers. The group had been told by top officials to back off, stop pressing their complaints, and otherwise keep quiet about the subject. Singled out for special admonition was Colonel Allen, who received a letter of reprimand from Chief Signal Officer Gen. George C. Back, accusing Allen of stirring up trouble by supporting "the disruptive group" that brought the lax security charges and being "disloyal" to his superiors.[3]

While this internecine conflict was unfolding, and then mysteriously vanishing from public view, a parallel and ultimately more famous battle was under way up the road at the Monmouth complex in New Jersey. Here, too, the committee would discover, there had been allegations of serious security trouble, suspicious characters on the scene, and inadequate safeguards for the nation's secrets. As with the SCIA, there had also been fierce disagreements between opposing forces in the Army as to what to say and do about security problems that were complained of. There would be consequences as well for those who pressed such issues in too vigorous fashion.

THE installation called Fort Monmouth was in fact a sprawling network of labs spread out among several New Jersey towns and other Northeast locations, doing research on confidential military projects. Radar, missile defenses, antiaircraft systems, and other devices involving advanced electronics were all on the agenda. There were four main research labs, the one most often mentioned in the McCarthy hearings called Evans Signal. In addition, there were half a dozen or so commercial scientific outfits—including the Federal Telecommunications Laboratory (FTL), RCA, General Electric, and other defense suppliers—who subcontracted technical projects for the Army. It was a far-flung, high-tech affair, all supposedly quite secret.

Investigations by the McCarthy panel were often geared to past endeavors of McCarthy and his staffers, and the Monmouth probe was no exception. In this case, the experience was Cohn's. During his five-plus years at Justice, he had been involved in prosecuting several high-profile antisubversive cases. The most famous of these was the trial of Julius and Ethel Rosenberg, accused of conspiracy to commit atomic espionage, found guilty, and sentenced to death. Against that somber backdrop, Cohn would predictably take notice when word reached him of security ills at Monmouth. The installation had been a scene of action in the 1940s for Julius Rosenberg, then a Signal Corps inspector, and to a lesser extent for his convicted coconspirator, Morton Sobell, and two other accused members of the spy ring, Joel Barr and Al Sarant.

The McCarthy investigation would eventually gather extensive evidence on the Rosenberg-Sobell aspect of the case, plus many other specific data about security problems at the complex. However, by far the most comprehensive overview of the security scene at Monmouth would be provided—after some initial hesitation—by Captain Benjamin Sheehan, a G-2 counterintelligence specialist from First Army headquarters in New York.*

Contrary to accepted versions of the story, the Sheehan information wasn't old-hat material but stuff of fairly recent vintage. As suggested by the two-and-a-quarter-page memo passed to McCarthy, security affairs at Monmouth had been of pressing interest to the Army itself in the early days of 1951. According to the Sheehan data, this interest had thereafter escalated sharply, leading to a whole series of internal Army investigations. These included probes of personnel and security practice at Monmouth proper, plus a special sub-investigation at the Federal Telecommunications Lab, the Signal Corps subcontractor of most concern to Army gumshoes.

In November of 1951, according to Sheehan, G-2 at the Pentagon had become sufficiently concerned about the security situation at Monmouth to order a preliminary investigation by officials at the complex. The results of this initial survey brought Sheehan himself into the picture as head of a five-man counterintelligence squad sent down from G-2 of the First Army. The Sheehan probe commenced in February of 1952—about the time the SCIA investigation was shutting down and roughly a year before McCarthy got his alert about security goings-on at Monmouth.

In the course of its investigation, the First Army squad discovered what Sheehan described as "an extremely critical situation" at Monmouth and was on the trail of "a parallel situation at the FTL." The G-2 inquest, per Sheehan, revealed a "serious security problem at Fort Monmouth arising from the presence of an immensely large number of employees of questionable loyalty working there . . ." Making matters worse, the G-2 investigators discovered a worrisome history of laxness in handling confidential papers—the two problems together presenting a security challenge of huge dimensions.

"Shortly after we began the investigation," said Sheehan, "it became apparent that highly classified documents pertaining to our nation's latest defensive and offensive secrets were being treated as personal property by many of the technical personnel employed there, and that they were having these documents indiscriminately reproduced and that they were taking them home with them." Sheehan and Co. accordingly recommended that immediate steps be taken "to neutralize the effectiveness of suspect individuals" and that stringent measures be adopted to crack down on the handling of official papers.[4]

---

*Sheehan's role in the McCarthy probe was somewhat ironic, as when he was first called before the panel in executive session he refused to provide any information, citing the usual secrecy orders. Later he had a change of heart, mostly prompted per his description by the serious nature of the security problem at the complex and the inadequacy of measures relating to it. His information accordingly wouldn't be provided until 1954, by which time McCarthy was bogged down in other issues.

Again contra some later versions of the matter, Sheehan and others in the Army explicitly viewed the Monmouth probe as an espionage investigation. Thus, a First Army G-2 disposition form of June 2, 1952, contained the stipulation: "Examine into indications of an espionage ring at Fort Monmouth, and between FTL and Monmouth employees," while an August 1952 report by the Sheehan team bore the subheading "Indications of Espionage." Subsequently, said Sheehan, when the Monmouth data were relayed to Pentagon higher-ups, "the Army accepted our report as one of espionage, and completely concurred." One top G-2 official, he added, "agreed that the situation had a very definite appearance of espionage" and said "our latest Signal Corps developments were appearing in the hands of the North Korean Communists."[5]

This series of internal probes culminated in the latter months of 1952, when Sheehan and Co. would formally present their findings to their superiors in the Army. But thereafter, as with the SCIA investigation, the Monmouth probe would grind to an abrupt and puzzling halt. "We had finally gotten the word to the Pentagon," said Sheehan, "and there our investigation to all intents and purposes died." He added that he was told to lay off the inquiry and was subject to reprimand when he continued to push it—this, too, resembling the probe at the SCIA and the fate of Colonel Allen.[6]

There matters rested in early 1953 when McCarthy got his heads-up on Monmouth and tasked his committee with following up on leads pertaining to the Signal Corps and its components. According to the Army records, McCarthy had shown interest in Monmouth by the first of April, but the VOA and USIS investigations then in progress meant the Signal Corps inquiry wouldn't get rolling until the summer. Executive hearings of peripheral nature would begin in August, followed by more substantial efforts in September, October, and November, with public hearings starting in December. It would prove to be a long haul and a formidable undertaking: some 200 potential witness interviews, 126 people heard in executive sessions, 39 of these in public hearings.

On the main points at issue, the McCarthy probe would confirm and amplify the findings of Captain Sheehan: Monmouth had long been an information sieve and security debacle in the making, and in many respects continued to be such when the McCarthy investigation started. Among other revelations, the probers found the complex and related installations were chockablock with security suspects, some of the most flagrant nature. The probers also found, as had Sheehan, a long history of laxness in handling official papers.

The McCarthy investigators discovered a number of other things as well. One was that the Communist Party had established a special unit in the vicinity of the research setup, called the Shore Club, which included former Monmouth employees among its members and which, according to extensive testimony, had as its object ferreting information out of Monmouth. Another was that numerous security suspects were indeed ensconced among Monmouth's suppliers, most notably the Federal Telecommunications Lab, prime target of the Sheehan inquest. Yet another was the seemingly laid-back attitude toward these matters in the higher reaches of the Army.[7]

A poster boy for all these troubles was one Aaron Coleman, who held an important job at Monmouth dealing with radar defenses. Coleman had been a schoolmate of Julius Rosenberg and Morton Sobell at the College of the City of New York, and in contact with Sobell up through the latter 1940s. He also admitted having attended a Young Communist League meeting with Rosenberg when they were students at City College. In this connection, ex-Communist Nathan Sussman, a CCNY alum, would testify that he, Coleman, Rosenberg, Sobell, Al Sarant, and Joel Barr had all been members of the YCL together. (Coleman would deny this, as he would deny Rosenberg's testimony at his espionage trial that Rosenberg and Coleman had been in contact at Fort Monmouth.)[8]

Coleman was also one of those at Monmouth who had a habit of taking documents from the office. In 1946, security agents at the post had become suspicious of his actions and searched his lodgings. There they found more than forty official papers, some of highly confidential nature. Suggestive of security standards then prevailing, he had received for this breach a ten-day suspension. When the McCarthy hearings opened, Coleman was still working at the post, and while this was on a security-restricted basis, he had full access to other workers with clearance and was hobnobbing with them freely.

Indicative of security attitudes at certain higher levels of the Army was the case of Coleman's roommate, one Jack Okun. Okun had been suspended from Monmouth on loyalty grounds in 1949, which meant someone spotted by the authorities as a loyalty risk had had access to the data Coleman kept in his apartment. Okun had, however, successfully appealed his case and been reinstated by the Loyalty Review Board in the Pentagon, then permitted to resign.[9] This was but one of many such security reversals that would draw the notice of McCarthy and his staffers.

Of similar implication was the case of Barry Bernstein, a top science official at Evans Signal, holding a sensitive job with secret clearance. The committee discovered that in 1951 Bernstein had been brought up on security charges, accused of pro-Red leanings and outside activities of kindred spirit that in the view of Monmouth officials made him a security risk. Granted a hearing by the First Army security board, Bernstein had been suspended from his duties. But when he appealed to the Pentagon board, the adverse ruling was overturned and he, too, was reinstated. However, unlike Jack Okun, Bernstein didn't resign. He was still holding down his job at Monmouth when the McCarthy hearings started.*[10]

---

*Bernstein's secret clearance was suspended a week before he appeared at the McCarthy hearings.

A third such in-and-out security case was Samuel Snyder, who had worked for the Signal Corps up through the latter months of 1952. Snyder, too, had gone through the strange revolving door of Pentagon security practice: suspended by the regional board of the First Army, reinstated by the Pentagon board, then permitted to resign. The favorable ruling at the Pentagon level was the more puzzling in view of information developed in the McCarthy hearings. Snyder, it turned out, had previously been in close and continuing contact with Eleanor Nelson, an identified Communist Party functionary (so named, e.g., by Whittaker Chambers). And when asked about his links to Nelson, Snyder refused to answer.

Some of the colloquy on this went as follows:

> QUESTION: Did you attend Communist meetings with Eleanor Nelson?
> ANSWER: I plead the Fifth Amendment on that . . .
> QUESTION: Did they [the Pentagon review Board] ask about your attendance at Communist meetings?
> ANSWER: I decline to answer that for the reasons I gave before. . . .

How this nonjuring witness had been given a clean bill of health by Pentagon reviewers was one of many security mysteries that swirled around Fort Monmouth.[11]

Similar questions arose regarding the Rosenberg-Sobell connection. As the hearings showed, there were numerous members of this group on the scene at Monmouth in the early 1950s, above and beyond the case of Aaron Coleman. One such was Joseph Levitsky, who had worked for the Signal Corps and thereafter at the Federal Telecommunications Lab handling classified Army projects, and had used Rosenberg as a reference in applying for this position. That background wasn't too reassuring as to his security status, but would get less so as Levitsky took the Fifth when asked if he and Rosenberg had been Communist Party members together. He would give a series of like responses about possible involvement in spying:

> MCCARTHY: Were you a member of the Communist conspiracy while you were handling classified material for the government?
> LEVITSKY: I decline to answer for the reasons previously given. . . .
> COHN: Did you ask persons who were employed at Fort Monmouth, in the Signal Corps, to commit espionage?
> LEVITSKY: I decline for the same reasons. . . .
> COHN: Since you left the Telecommunications Laboratory, have you asked any persons working at Fort Monmouth to commit espionage?
> LEVITSKY: I decline for the same reasons.[12]

The Federal Telecommunications Lab had been a particular focus of concern for the G-2 security squad, and the gravity of the situation there would be confirmed by the McCarthy inquest. A pivotal figure in the doings of the FTL was labor official Harry Hyman, employed at the lab until 1951, thereafter with the Federation of Architects, Engineers, Chemists and Technicians, a Communist-dominated union active among the Monmouth workers. Identified face-to-face as a Communist agent by ex-Reds Lester Ackerman and John Saunders, Hyman refused to answer. His exchanges with McCarthy suggested the "union activities" of this labor leader weren't confined to hours and wages:

> McCARTHY: Have you ever discussed the subject of espionage with any members of the Communist Party?
> HYMAN: I decline to answer for the reasons previously given. . . .
> McCARTHY: Have you ever turned government secrets over to anyone known to you to be an espionage agent? . . .
> HYMAN: I decline to answer on the same grounds.
> McCARTHY: Did you make 76 calls to the Federal Telecommunications Laboratory at Lodi, New Jersey between January 24, 1952, and October 21, 1953, for the purpose of getting classified information and for the purpose of then turning that over to an espionage agent or agents?
> HYMAN: I decline to answer on the same grounds.[13]

Still another conspicuous security suspect at FTL was Ruth Levine, who had worked at the lab for a decade, advancing to a high position with top-secret clearance, and was so employed when the McCarthy sessions started. Like Levitsky, she was one of those allegedly linked to Harry Hyman; Saunders and other witnesses in fact testified that she was a member of a Communist cell at this secret installation. Asked if she had been a CP member, attended party meetings, or engaged in spying, Levine too refused to answer:

> COHN: During that period of time [while employed at FTL] did you engage in conspiracy to commit espionage with a man named Harry Hyman?
> LEVINE: I decline to answer on the grounds of the fourth and fifth amendments.
> COHN: Did you participate in underground meetings of the Communist Party with Harry Hyman in his home?
> LEVINE: I decline to answer on the grounds of the fourth and fifth amendments.
> COHN: On the date that you were granted top-secret clearance, which was March 29, 1950, were you a member of the Communist Party?
> LEVINE: I decline to answer on the grounds of the fourth and fifth amendments.*[14]

---

* As a result of the McCarthy investigation, Ms. Levine would be removed from her job at the Telecommunications Lab. She would thus take her place as a minor victim in the pantheon of McCarthy martyrs. McCarthy would subsequently praise the management of the Lab for its cooperation with the committee, despite the adverse publicity that resulted.

To one of McCarthy's suspicious nature, so many refusals to answer questions on such topics suggested there had been espionage going on at the FTL and other parts of the Monmouth complex, and that problems of this sort were very much a present danger. In this, too, his conclusions would track with those of Captain Sheehan (though Sheehan never got a chance to tell his story in public). And there were other aspects of the McCarthy inquest that tended to confirm this verdict.

As the Monmouth probe unfolded, it found eerie similarities between the security picture at the post and previous wrangles on such issues. A main disclosure of the *Amerasia* case had been the vast hemorrhaging of confidential papers that wound up in the offices of this pro-Red publication. Revelations from other security probes suggested that looting of secret government data was a fairly common practice. There is no way of knowing how many U.S. secrets had been funneled to Moscow by Hiss at the State Department, White and the Silvermaster Treasury combine, or moles in the atom project, but the number was by most assessments in the several thousands.

Estimates of possible security damage at Monmouth were at this same stratospheric level. Literally thousands of official papers, it seems, had gone missing from the complex. Captain Sheehan would, for instance, tell McCarthy staffers of a case in which a Monmouth employee had signed out at one time or another for more than 2,700 documents (not a typo). Security officials tried to retrieve these, said Sheehan, but after thorough investigation, two-thirds of this enormous total was still missing. Sheehan added that, when the employee was brought up on security charges, this rather fantastic datum was omitted from the hearing record on orders from the higher regions.

Other estimates of secret data pilfered or copied and supplied to outside parties from the Monmouth complex were often in this same prodigious range. Such was, for instance, the post-McCarthy testimony of a defecting Soviet scientist named Andrivye (not his real name). Andrivye told congressional probers that in the 1940s secret U.S. materials involving radar had turned up in Russia in vast amounts, and that literally "thousands" of these had been identified on their face as having come from Monmouth. He remembered two sources especially, he said, "because I saw them quite often on the documents . . . One was from Fort Monmouth, and the other was RCA . . ."*[15]

That such problems stemming from the security stupor of World War II continued in the 1950s was indicated by other information uncovered in the Monmouth sessions. In pursuing the trail to Moscow, McCarthy came up with a further startling revelation: a report from Air Force intelligence concerning

---

*Like information would be provided by Aleksandr Feksilov, one of the Soviet bosses in charge of high-tech spying, concerning an "unknown radar source" in the United States who transmitted thousands of pages of secret data to Moscow.

an East German defector who said he had seen secret Monmouth data in 1950 while working with the Russians in Europe. His comments were recorded in a nineteen-page Air Force document that, as such items often did, wound up in the possession of McCarthy.

As recorded in this memo, the defector said he had been working at a Communist scientific lab in Poland when a Russian scientist shared some technical material with its staffers, prompting one to ask if it "had come from Evans Signal Laboratory in Fort Monmouth." The memo further quoted the defector as saying that, in previous confabs, "the name of Evans Signal Laboratory had been mentioned several times." He further said that, on another occasion, a Russian had shown a film about the atomic energy setup at Oak Ridge, Tennessee, and that the drill was "pretty much the same as with the microfilm I saw of Evans Signal Laboratory."[16]

When McCarthy shared the contents of this astounding memo with Army officials, they said they didn't know anything about it and seemed baffled by McCarthy's comments. As it turned out, however, the Army brass did know something of the matter but hadn't followed up because they were told the report was "fabricated," that the defector had recanted, and that he wasn't a credible witness.[17]

Nonplussed by this, McCarthy sent one of his aides to Europe to check the story out directly. In late October of 1953, committee investigator James Juliana tracked the defector down in a remote part of the (West) German Federal Republic. The object of this search turned out to be a youthful (twenty-four-year-old) technician named Harald Buettner, who talked with Juliana at length and gave him a notarized statement, the most obvious feature of which was that the witness had recanted nothing. The defector told Juliana he had been employed in September 1950 at a Soviet-run scientific installation in Poland, along with Red technicians from other countries. One evening, he said, he and his colleagues were told by a Russian scientist that he had some brand-new information to show them from the United States.

As the group followed the professor to his lab, said Buettner, he heard some coworkers talking in Russian. Asking for a translation, he was told, "I just wanted to know if it was from Evans Signal laboratory in 'Fort M' "—this accompanied by laughter. "Another person who interrupted our conversation said, 'From where else should it be?' " These comments, Buettner said, were borne out when the data were examined. "In his work room [the Russian] professor turned on a table sized microfilm projector apparatus, into which he inserted a Leica film," wherein "the term Evans Signal Laboratory was mentioned several times."[18]

These remarks, far from being a recantation, obviously confirmed the first report in its essentials. Who, then, had said that Buettner recanted? And what was there about this unpretentious story that was shown to be a fabrication?

As the authorities apparently never followed up, we don't have answers to such questions—or information about the missing papers described by Sheehan, or data on numerous other security problems surfaced in the McCarthy hearings. The proper response to all these matters would have been an in-depth investigation to sort things out in systematic fashion. The official response, so far as the available record shows, had been to drop the subject entirely.

With ample reason, McCarthy was appalled by the security muddle at Monmouth and its network of suppliers. However, the more he learned about the subject, the more he became convinced the problem wasn't with officials on the ground, either at Monmouth itself or at First Army. Captain Sheehan was an example of someone who had been on the scene and tried to get the problem corrected. Monmouth security chief Andrew Reid, who had first nabbed Aaron Coleman, was another.

Reid's perspective was of special value, as he had extensive knowledge of the Monmouth setup. He had been at the post since 1940 and thus had a good long-term view of the way things developed there, both in the generic security meltdown of the war and in the years that followed. Though under orders not to provide information on specific cases, Reid did tersely answer certain McCarthy questions. One brief exchange, in which McCarthy did most of the talking, went as follows:

> McCARTHY: Over that 13-year period of time [since 1940] have you repeatedly furnished information on individuals who you considered to be very dangerous to the security of this country, and discovered that they were kept on year after year even after you had supplied the complete facts on them?
> REID: Yes, sir.[19]

Of like implication were data the McCarthy probers gathered concerning the post commander, Major General Kirke B. Lawton (of whom more later), who had previously been a player in the muffled SCIA inquiry. According to an undated fall 1953 memo by McCarthy staffer Juliana, "General Lawton was commanding general at Fort Monmouth for one year and nine months prior to the [McCarthy] hearings and investigation . . . [During that period] even though he kept the Department advised of all the security risks at Monmouth, he was unable to suspend a single individual because of the Security Screening Board and the Secretary of the Army's letter of 1950 [forbidding security suspensions by the base commander]."[20]

In the light of such information, McCarthy became increasingly focused on the review board that had been overturning so many adverse security rulings. The situation had a striking resemblance to what had happened at the State Department, when suspects recommended for removal by security screeners were nonetheless approved at higher levels.* (McCarthy had raised the issue of Army security reversals as early as September 1953, when the probe was getting started, and would revert to it often in the hearings.)

McCarthy's concerns about these matters would soon link up with other, more famous Army cases, to be discussed hereafter. In all such instances, his main interest wasn't in the individual suspects, though he considered some of them quite important, but in the workings of a system that repeatedly granted clearance to people who, judged by the available record, were dubious security risks, to put the matter no more strongly. He accordingly planned to call before him members of the Pentagon Review Board, to find out who had been making such decisions and why they made them.

This would for some reason prove to be the most bitterly contested aspect of the whole Fort Monmouth battle, eventually provoking a constitutional showdown of epic nature between McCarthy and executive branch officials. The administration was determined that the Pentagon reviewers not appear before the McCarthy panel, and McCarthy was equally determined that they should. The conflict over this seemingly peripheral issue would become the most decisive single episode in the Red-hunting career of Joe McCarthy, and in many respects the most puzzling chapter of the entire McCarthy story.

Postscript

"Fort Monmouth" was the omnibus term for McCarthy's Army investigations, and the Monmouth complex the main focus, but the search for suspects funneling data to Moscow would lead to other venues also.

Among the more celebrated of these other cases was Prof. Wendell Furry, who taught physics at Harvard and MIT, had done extensive work on radar for the U.S. government, and knew many other scientists who did so. He was also, admittedly, a former member of the Communist Party and had scientific contacts who were, or had been, party members.

Called before the McCarthy panel, Professor Furry refused to name these CP-connected colleagues, though citing no constitutional basis for such refusal, would be cited for contempt and thereafter treated as an heroic figure for standing fast against McCarthy. As typically portrayed—by Furry himself and by numerous writers—McCarthy in this episode was trying to punish dissident

---

*On this point, as on others, later revelations would indicate McCarthy was right in his perception of the problem but underestimated its extent. In subsequent hearings Col. Ronald Thomas, former Chief of Counter-Intelligence for G-2, would testify that adverse security recommendations were routinely overturned by the Pentagon Review Board. "Under the previous [pre-1953] security regulations," said Thomas, "*out of say approximately 100 cases, 90 of these would be returned* by the Loyalty Board as reinstated cases rather than getting them out of the service." (Emphasis added.)

intellectuals for their political opinions, and Furry the defender of academic freedom had refused to be complicit in the witch hunt.

Omitted from this didactic treatment is that certain of the past or present CP members McCarthy wanted Furry to name had worked on radar-connected and similar projects involving the nation's defenses. It was this aspect of the case, not the political opinions of the academics, that concerned McCarthy. It was in his view quite possible that one or more of these onetime CP members might still be such, and—Professor Furry's assurances notwithstanding—might be providing secret radar or other military data to Moscow. Not quite, therefore, a simple morality play about academic freedom.[21]

CHAPTER 39

A Tale of Two Generals

T HERE is more to be said about the battle of Fort Monmouth, as it would prove to be a pivotal chapter not only in the saga of Joe McCarthy but in the political history of the nation. For the moment, a last installment must suffice.

The central figure in this phase of the story was the Army officer who knew more about the Monmouth probe than did any other, and was most directly affected by it: the commanding general of the post, Maj. Gen. Kirke B. Lawton, who testified before McCarthy at an executive session in mid-October 1953. In so doing, he would give an inside view of events at Monmouth, render judgment on the McCarthy inquest, then pay a price for his disclosures.

A thirty-seven-year veteran of the Army and former deputy director of the Signal Corps, Lawton had taken over at Monmouth in 1951. Shortly after his arrival, he became concerned about security problems at the post and set out to fix them. Unfortunately, as discussed, he hadn't been too successful in the effort. His testimony on this point went beyond the laconic answers of Andy Reid, though less discursive than the reports of Captain Sheehan. As post commander, however, he spoke with more authority than either of those officials.

Like Reid and Sheehan, Lawton would make it tolerably clear that efforts to get a tougher security stance at Monmouth had foundered on the rocks of resistance and/or indifference at higher levels. From the standpoint of his bosses, these comments would be considered less than helpful. Lawton, however, made things worse by adding some further incautious comment in praise of Joe McCarthy. The colloquy on this went as follows:

> McCARTHY: Would you say that since you have taken over, and especially in the last six months, you have been working to get rid of the accumulation of security risks in the Signal Corps and that you have suspended a sizable number? . . .
>
> LAWTON: That is a question I will answer "yes," but don't go back six months. . . . Effective results have been in the offing the last 2 weeks. I have been working for the past 21 months trying to accomplish what has been accomplished in the last two weeks.
>
> McCARTHY: . . . So that you would say that in the past several weeks you have been getting more effective results?
>
> LAWTON: Absolutely, than we have gotten for the past 4 years.
>
> McCARTHY: Could you tell us why it is only in the last 2 or 3 weeks that you have been getting effective results?
>
> LAWTON: Yes, but I had better not. I know this so well, but I am working for Mr. Stevens [Secretary of the Army].[1]

Lawton's views to this effect were given in executive session and wouldn't be published until somewhat later. However, Army counsel John Adams was in the room when the general testified and would have wasted little time in conveying the essence of the matter to Army Secretary Robert Stevens: That Lawton praised McCarthy for achieving results at Monmouth the Army itself had failed to get, and along the way made a not-so-flattering reference to Stevens. None of this would endear the general to the secretary, still less to others in high places.

Though contrary to the official line on Monmouth, the reason for the positive impact of the McCarthy probe as described by Lawton wasn't far to seek. By focusing publicity on security issues, McCarthy empowered officials at the Fort to move ahead with planned suspensions while staying the hand of whoever in the Army food chain had been reversing such decisions. In this respect, as in others, Monmouth developments tracked those at State; in both cases, the glare of the public spotlight had forced a tightening of standards.*

The general's judgment on the hearings would send another message also—rebutting the notion that McCarthy was conducting an unwarranted "attack against the Army." Lawton was very much of "the Army," as were

---

*In this respect, the figures on security suspensions would tell the story pretty clearly. Prior to the McCarthy probe, suspensions on such charges had been few and far between; but once the investigation started, the pace picked up briskly. In all, some forty-two employees were suspended—all but seven after the McCarthy hearings started. Conversely, once the hearings were over, most of the people suspended would be quietly reinstated. The before-and-after correlations jibe closely with the Lawton comment.

Colonel Allen at SCIA, Captain Sheehan, Andrew Reid, and others in the ranks who thought Signal Corps security deplorably weak. As McCarthy was fond of saying, his beef wasn't with "the Army" and its million-plus uniformed personnel, but rather with unknown civilians behind the scenes who were neutering security safeguards. Lawton was walking, talking proof that such decisions were far from being a consensus of "the Army."

At this stage of the proceedings, in fact, the positions of several Army players were in flux, changing on almost a daily basis. Initially, Stevens had voiced his desire to work with the committee, and McCarthy repeatedly praised him for cooperation. However, as the hearings wore on and drew heavy media coverage, they were seen as an embarrassment to Stevens and people in the echelons above him. The original revelations of lax security reflected on the preceding Democratic administration. But evidence of continued laxness reflected on the new one, or seemed to, spurring hostility to McCarthy in certain quarters where there was plenty of animus to start with.

In this unfolding conflict, Bob Stevens was caught squarely in the middle. A successful business executive in private life (J.P. Stevens and Co.), he was a conservative Republican and strongly anti-Red in his convictions. There is no doubt he wanted to clean out any subversives who might have been at Monmouth, or that he had been ready to work in tandem with McCarthy. However, he was in an awkward spot as revelations about Monmouth and its labs continued, and obviously under top-down pressure to contain the damage.

Accordingly, in late 1953, Stevens began to counter the negative press on Monmouth, saying there was no present espionage there that the Army knew of.* In time this stance would morph into an even more emphatic denial—that there was no serious security problem at the post and that McCarthy was raising an uproar over nothing. There had been problems in World War II and a while thereafter, but these had all been properly handled. Like many such denials from the era, this version has entered into the mainstream of historical writing and is commonly stated as the truth about the Monmouth inquest.

As in other cases, however, these assurances don't stack up too well—and didn't then—when gauged by the empirical record. There were the grave security issues described by Sheehan, stemming not from World War II but from the period 1951–52. There was the terse avowal of Andy Reid that he had been struggling with the security problem for years with small success to speak of. And now there was confirmation of the point by Lawton, the world's leading expert on the subject.

Ironically, Lawton hadn't at first been forthcoming with McCarthy staffers, unsure of how much to tell them, but on the instructions of Stevens had

---

*McCarthy's countervailing point, of course, was that there were plenty of indications of potential espionage that had been disparaged or ignored.

given them access to Monmouth workers (a further indication that Stevens was then trying to work in concert with McCarthy). Thereafter Lawton had been not only cooperative but active in the hearings, attending sessions, taking notes, and liaising closely with the panel. Now, after his October statement, he would be perceived by his superiors as being more cooperative—and talkative—than needed.

In fact, the general was now in serious trouble, and knew it. About a week after this session, McCarthy praised Lawton for the security stand he was taking. To this Lawton replied, per the account of Cohn, "Yes, but that stand will cost me my promotion. And I will be lucky if I survive much longer here at Fort Monmouth."[2] This was prophetic, as Lawton would indeed be passed over for promotion, and before another year had run would be gone from his command. He thus apparently knew what he was in for when he made his statements, but thought the situation was such that he went ahead and made them.

Second only to the general himself as a pivotal figure in these events was Army Counsel Adams. A self-professed moderate GOPer, former Capitol Hill employee, and holdover from the Defense Department under Gen. George C. Marshall, Adams had cast about for a job with the new regime after the Republican sweep of 1952. Somehow he got referred to Stevens and hired as the department's counsel. Despite the legal-sounding title, Adams would become in essence a full-time lobbyist with the McCarthy panel. Adams was by the same token the troubleshooter for Stevens with military figures such as Lawton and others called in the McCarthy hearings. The counsel thus became a busy go-between in discussions involving McCarthy, Cohn, Monmouth, Lawton, and a host of other topics.

The significance of Adams appears in retrospect the more so, as we have his own account of what he was privately doing and thinking when the hearings were in progress. As he later told it, he thought there was no serious security trouble at Monmouth, that the people seen as suspects were simply victims, and that his task as Army Counsel was to do all he could to make sure nobody got suspended. His views were thus at one with those of the Pentagon reviewers who kept reversing such suspensions, hence the opposite of McCarthy's.[3]

Also, Adams had other attitudes and contacts that put him on collision course with McCarthy, and also with Lawton. As a Pentagon official under Marshall, Adams had helped prep Mrs. Anna Rosenberg for confirmation hearings in 1950, when Marshall chose her as an assistant secretary of defense. Mrs. Rosenberg was at the time seen as a McCarthy "case," though McCarthy himself had little to say about her. However, McCarthy staffers had been in touch with ex-Communist witness Ralph de Sola, who said he saw Mrs. Rosenberg at a meeting of the Communist John Reed Club in the 1930s. She angrily denied this, saying there was some other Anna Rosenberg who was the John Reed member; the Senate accepted this denial and confirmed her.

John Adams was thus a partisan of Mrs. Rosenberg, while officers complaining of lax security in the Signal Corps in 1951 and '52 said she was a big part of the problem. Various memos in the McCarthy files pertaining to the SCIA dispute refer to suspect employees who were "Mrs. Rosenberg's people" or sent by Mrs. Rosenberg's office. These same documents show General Lawton, before his transfer to Monmouth, had sympathized with the complaining officials. Thus Adams was not only antagonistic toward McCarthy but de facto on the opposite side from Lawton before any of them ever got to Monmouth.[4]

Against that backdrop, it was perhaps unsurprising that when pressures were exerted on Lawton to ease up on security removals at Monmouth, those pressures came via Adams. Indicative of the process, and sharp clash of views, was an Adams-Lawton phone call in October concerning employees scheduled for suspension. Lawton himself would record this exchange as follows: "Adams asked Lawton on the phone, 'I hope you can see your way clear to withdraw certain cases which you have recommended for removal as bad security risks.' Lawton: 'I would not. Let the secretary take the responsibility.' "[5] That put the conflict in a nutshell.

In substance this was confirmed by Adams, who said there were nine Monmouth suspensions Lawton's bosses wanted him to reverse but that the general refused to do so. The critical nature of the episode was underscored as well by Stevens, who later discussed it with General Back, Chief Signal Officer of the Army. "I am a little concerned," said Stevens, "over General Lawton's continuing to suspend people at Monmouth . . . [He] is suspending people we haven't got anything on and we will have to take them back . . . When he suspends a fellow because he lives next door to a person who thought he was a Communist, that just isn't going to do us any good."*[6]

Things would turn still worse for Lawton a few weeks later, after he gave a series of security briefings to Monmouth workers. Though these talks were supposedly off the record, the contents of one—or what were said to be such— were leaked to New Jersey's *Asbury Park Press*. In this bootlegged account, Lawton once more allegedly sang the praises of McCarthy, commending him for helping get results at Monmouth and for the "fairness and courtesy" of the hearings. The general then added, according to the news report, that security

---

*This Stevens comment was suggestive as to his understanding of the cases—or, more accurately, lack thereof. As he would tell the Senate, he had no direct knowledge of the security files at Monmouth—which was only to be expected, given his many high-level duties. His description of the suspensions as unjustified, and one as absurdly trivial, would have been based on what someone told him. And the someone most likely to have told him something of this nature was John Adams (who thought, e.g., that Aaron Coleman was not a security risk but the victim of a witch hunt).

problems at the post stemmed from graduates of certain universities—CCNY foremost among them (which was of course quite true).[7]

By this time the Monmouth dispute was not only changing direction but undergoing a complete inversion. Somewhere in the higher reaches, the perceived problem at the research complex wasn't the presence of such as Aaron Coleman, Barry Bernstein, Samuel Snyder, Harry Hyman, or Ruth Levine, the hemorrhaging of secret papers, or the Rosenberg-Sobell contacts who had been hanging around the place for years. Instead the main problem to be dealt with was the budding McCarthyite, security hawk, and too-talkative witness—the commanding general of the installation.

Accordingly, in the manner of Colonel Allen and Captain Sheehan, Lawton would himself become a target of suspicion and a candidate for removal. In late November 1953, General Back obtained from Lawton and conveyed to Stevens a memo on the employee briefings—the predictable sense of which was that they had simply been attempts to make workers more security-conscious. Stevens was not impressed. A Senate memo capsuling Back's tête-à-tête with Stevens says, "Secretary Stevens questioned whether General Lawton was fit to continue in command at Monmouth, or should be relieved." Underscoring this all-but-explicit threat, the memo added that, on this same occasion, "General Lawton physically appeared outside Secretary Stevens' office. Stevens did not care to see him." For those who could read such obvious portents, Lawton's Monmouth days were numbered.*[8]

Actually getting rid of Lawton, however, would prove to be a tricky business. Though his views and actions were now seen as unbeneficial to "the Army," any move to oust him might trigger a reaction from McCarthy, and that wouldn't be too beneficial, either. Adams tried to test the waters, asking Cohn what McCarthy's reaction would be if Lawton were relieved at Monmouth. As might be guessed, the answer wasn't enthusiastic, so Lawton's job, for the time being, was officially safe. There would be no overt or immediate ouster.

Instead, something more circuitous was attempted: a subliminal effort to crack down on Lawton while he ostensibly remained in charge at Monmouth. He was told to stop attending hearings and otherwise pull back from collaboration with McCarthy. He would then be placed on "medical disability," complaint unspecified, and sent to Walter Reed Hospital, though people who visited him there said he seemed in good health. Meanwhile, Stevens in his public statements continued to tell the world Lawton was still in charge at

---

*The main reason alleged by Stevens for his pique with Lawton was the comment about the universities, this allegedly showing that the general had "bad judgment." This explanation seems lame, considering the things that had preceded—disagreement over the security drill, praise for McCarthy, refusal to restore suspended workers. All of this predated the briefing in which the universities were mentioned.

Monmouth. The evident purpose of all this was to keep McCarthy at bay and avoid a public blowup, while surreptitiously squelching Lawton.

A further remarkable chapter in the Lawton story would be written in the Army-McCarthy hearings in the spring of 1954. As these were intensely focused on Fort Monmouth, Lawton would have been an obvious person to hear from. Senators of both parties urged that he be called, and it was stated he would be. (As for Lawton's own outlook, according to one press account, he was "hopping mad" and anxious to have his say in public.)[9] But, in the fashion of Scott McLeod, Lawton would be strangely absent from the proceedings. Nor did Cohn and McCarthy, whose cause would have been helped by his testimony, insist that he be called. This was puzzling to John McClellan, who quizzed Cohn as to his seeming lack of interest in hearing Lawton.[10] Only later would an answer be provided. The McCarthy forces had been told that, if the general did appear, he would be punished further—losing benefits he was to receive as a long-serving member of the Army.

For this insight we are once more indebted to John Adams, who would relate that Sen. Karl Mundt (R-S.D.), Cohn, and others wanted to call Lawton but were warned off by Army spokesmen playing big-league hardball. The general, said Adams, "could not very well claim [publicly] that Stevens had driven him out of the Army, lest he lose his medical benefits. On the day Lawton was to testify, John Pernice, the Signal Corps chief counsel, met Cohn in Mundt's office and asked the two of them, 'are you prepared to do this to General Lawton?' Lawton was not called."*[11]

Mundt and the McCarthy forces weren't "prepared to do this" to Lawton, but his superiors were prepared to do things to him and would in short order prove it. Once the Army-McCarthy hearings were over and the public spotlight had gone elsewhere, the administration proceeded to finish breaking Lawton. Having already been passed over for promotion and sent to medical coventry at Walter Reed, Lawton would be removed from his command in the summer of 1954 and by the end of August retired from active duty. His premonition of the wrath to come had not been mistaken.

B Y COOPERATING with McCarthy, praising the work of the committee, and speaking his mind on security matters, Lawton not only blighted his career but ended it entirely. A second general pulled into the security whirlwind would learn to read the warning signs, take the opposite fork in the road, and

---

*Given the fact that Lawton's "medical disability" was of mysterious nature, and believed by many to be merely an excuse and not a reason for the handling he received, the short-term meaning of such denial is unclear. On the other hand, as everyone needs medical benefits sooner or later, the short-term meaning may not have mattered. At all events, the threat conveyed was clear and may have involved other benefits as well.

thus achieve official favor. This was Gen. Ralph W. Zwicker, a much-decorated veteran of World War II and now commander at Camp Kilmer, another Army post located in New Jersey, near New Brunswick.

In the course of the Monmouth probe, McCarthy and Co. received a tip about security goings-on at Kilmer that might be worth some digging. Following up on this, in late January 1954, committee staffer George Anastos placed a call to General Zwicker, saying he had heard of a security problem at the post involving someone in the medical corps but didn't know much else about it. Zwicker, not sure who was on the line, said he would call back, and an hour later did so.

The resulting conversation was momentous, as it led to not one but two historic McCarthy cases. With the relevant file before him, the general gave Anastos the name of the security suspect, said he was in the dental corps, and provided other data capsuled by Anastos in a memo for committee records. The next morning, Zwicker would call Anastos again, confirming what he had previously suggested, that the suspect was now scheduled for an honorable discharge. The general had gone an extra furlong to help McCarthy's staffer.

The suspect in question, as everyone would soon discover, was Dr. Irving Peress, a New York dentist drafted during the Korean War and given the entering rank of captain (as reflective of his professional civilian status).* He was also, according to sworn testimony and official records, a member of the Communist Party. This unlikely officer would soon become quite famous, subject of a pro-McCarthy rallying cry, "Who promoted Peress?" sounded often in the 1950s. And there were several other questions about the case that likewise needed answers.

At his induction, it developed, Peress had signed a statement—form 390—in effect foreswearing allegiance to the Communist Party or any other subversive group. But thereafter, in executing other, similar forms, he gave a different answer—equivalent to the Fifth Amendment—pleading "constitutional privilege." This not only meant he was unwilling to say whether he was a CP member, but by obvious implication suggested he swore falsely in his prior statement.

The matter of the loyalty forms (backed by other Army data) should have been enough to have Peress discharged forthwith, on a less-than-honorable basis. Instead, he had led a seemingly charmed existence—moving blithely from post to post, always a step ahead of his security records (once forwarded to the

---

*Discussions of this case invariably raise the question as to why anyone should have been concerned about a Communist dentist, in the Army or anywhere else. A parenthetical answer, slightly off the main point, is that oddly enough a dentist's office could be a very good cover for clandestine operations, as all sorts of people might come and go there without attracting much attention. It's noteworthy that a central figure in the Elizabeth Bentley spy ring in New York was a dentist, as was another such named by Whittaker Chambers. However, the main thing about Peress wasn't this, but rather what the case revealed about security procedures.

wrong command), so that nine months elapsed before the brass would focus clearly on the problem. Along the way, he received favored "compassionate" treatment in terms of posting, plus automatic promotion to the rank of major. Now there was to be an honorable discharge in the bargain.

Learning some of this, an incredulous Joe McCarthy called Peress before him at a hearing on January 30. At this session, Peress would be identified in sworn testimony by undercover police agent Ruth Eagle as a member of the Communist Party in New York and an alumnus of a Red leadership school in Queens. When Peress took the stand, rather than denying the identification, he proceeded to cite the Fifth Amendment across the board. Some of the exchanges went as follows:

> COHN: When you went down to Camp Kilmer . . . did you attempt to re-
> cruit any of the military personnel there into the Communist Party?
> PERESS: I again claim the [Fifth Amendment] privilege.
> COHN: When stationed at Camp Kilmer, did you have Communist Party
> meetings in your home, attended by one or more military personnel
> from Camp Kilmer?
> PERESS: I again claim the privilege.
> . . .
> McCARTHY: Is there a Communist cell at Camp Kilmer of which you are a
> member?
> PERESS: I again claim the privilege.
> McCARTHY: Did you not organize a Communist cell at Camp Kilmer?
> PERESS: I again claim the privilege.[12]

Amazed to have before him an Army officer named as a Communist, who took the Fifth Amendment about it, had recently been promoted, and was now scheduled for an honorable discharge, McCarthy immediately fired off a letter to the Army, hand-delivered to the Pentagon. This urged that Peress's honorable discharge be canceled, thus keeping him within the jurisdiction of the Army, and that he be held over for court-martial. Since Stevens was at this point on a trip to Asia, the letter was instead received, at a fateful moment, by Army counselor Adams.

Adams could at this point have held up the honorable discharge but, by his own account, in a sudden vindictive mood decided not to. (". . . I found myself deciding not to do what McCarthy demanded, and instead, to let the dentist go. In short, to hell with McCarthy.")[13] Thus, on February 2, the day after McCarthy's letter was received, Irving Peress ended his magical mystery tour in the Army with an honorable exit. The Pentagon, in the person of John Adams, had done the exact reverse of what McCarthy suggested.

Now thoroughly outraged, McCarthy redoubled his efforts to find out how such a thing could happen, a quest leading back to base commander Zwicker.

On February 13, McCarthy staffer James Juliana went up to Kilmer to interview the general and came back with further background on Peress and the impression, reinforcing the Anastos contacts, that Zwicker would be an informative and friendly witness. Specifically, as Juliana would testify, Zwicker said he was opposed to the honorable discharge of Peress. ("In fact," as Juliana later put it, "if Zwicker had testified on the stand to what he told me at Camp Kilmer, there is no question that it would have confirmed McCarthy's point about laxness in the Army's handling of security suspects.")[14]

Zwicker was thus scheduled to come before McCarthy, at an executive hearing, on the afternoon of February 18. It proved to be a stormy session. Zwicker would later say he was edgy and apprehensive, and that this affected his performance. McCarthy for his part had been sleepless the night before, as his wife had been injured in an auto accident, and he had been with her at the hospital until the small hours of the morning and again at noon the day of Zwicker's appearance. McCarthy rushed into the hearing room so frazzled his staffers wanted to postpone the session.

It would have been far better for all concerned if they had. What happened that afternoon shed no glory on McCarthy, but also none on Zwicker. Expected to be a knowledgeable and forthcoming witness, the general was neither. Instead, he bobbed and weaved, fenced verbally with McCarthy, and refused to answer many questions about the weird career and honorable discharge of Peress. As this cat-and-mouse game went on, McCarthy became increasingly angry and peremptory in his questions.

Particularly infuriating to McCarthy were pleas of ignorance with which Zwicker peppered his responses, ignorance McCarthy had reason to know was feigned. When asked why he hadn't himself held up the honorable discharge, Zwicker claimed he didn't know about Peress's Red connections. ("I was never officially informed by anyone that he was part of the Communist conspiracy.")[15] The general further implausibly said he was unaware of the well-publicized fact that Peress had taken the Fifth Amendment about his Red affiliations.

All this was dicey, but would get more so when McCarthy analogized the case to that of a GI accused of stealing $50. In that instance, he asked, would Zwicker have blocked an honorable discharge until the matter was settled? The general said he would. Then why, asked McCarthy, didn't you block an honorable discharge for someone accused of something a good deal worse? To this Zwicker didn't have much of an answer, except that he was following orders.*

McCarthy then posed a hypothetical case in which an officer okayed an honorable discharge for an identified Red who took the Fifth Amendment—all based on the facts about Peress. In this instance, McCarthy asked, should the

---

*Which he was. (See below.)

general who signed the order for the honorable discharge be kept on in the military? After several evasive comments, Zwicker finally answered, "I do not think he should be removed from the military." Whereupon McCarthy blew up and uttered the words that would thereafter plague him:

"Then, General, you should be removed from any command. Any general who has been given the honor of being promoted to general and who says 'I will protect another general who protected Communists' is not fit to wear that uniform, General. I think it is a tremendous disgrace to the Army to have this sort of thing given to the public."[16]

With this outburst McCarthy added another blotted page to the catalog of his famed abuses. It was indeed a grievous error thus to address a decorated combat hero, however evasive or false his statements—so much so it would eventually become one of the two counts officially voted by a Senate panel weighing McCarthy's projected censure. In the end, however, McCarthy's fellow senators refused to follow through on Zwicker. There was a widespread perception that the general had provoked the tirade, as in fact he did, and the votes couldn't be found to censure McCarthy for it. (See Chapter 44.)

And, as things turned out, that was not the half of it. Ultimately, the case would be reviewed by three committees of Congress—including an exhaustive inquiry chaired by John McClellan—whose findings would cast an entirely different light on Zwicker's conduct. Chief among these was that, far from being ignorant of the data on Peress, the general knew most of what was to be known about him. In fact, Zwicker himself had protested the lenient treatment of Peress in terms not too different from McCarthy's. On October 21, 1953, Zwicker had written the commanding general of the First Army: "This officer [Peress] refused to sign a loyalty certificate, and refused to answer an interrogatory concerning his affiliation with subversive organizations, claiming constitutional privilege . . ." The presence of Peress in the U.S. Army, said Zwicker, "is clearly not consistent with the interest of national security."[17]

Thereafter, on November 3, 1953, when Zwicker learned about the Peress promotion, he sent still another letter to First Army, repeating the point about the loyalty forms and adding: *"Investigation completed April 15, 1953, determined that this officer was a known and active Communist in Queens N. Y."*[18] (Emphasis added.) This was some three months before Zwicker swore on the witness stand that he hadn't been told about the Red activities and background of Peress.

On top of these disclosures, evidence would emerge from the Anastos phone logs that Zwicker had given the Peress info to the committee in the first place. Zwicker admitted that, in these talks, he named Peress, said the suspect was a dentist, and that he was scheduled for an honorable discharge. But, according to Anastos, the news from Zwicker went beyond this, including the fact that Peress had been identified as a CP member. Backing this testimony was committee staffer Mary Morrill, who had listened in on the Anastos-Zwicker conversation.[19]

Small wonder, then, that the McCarthy forces believed Zwicker would be a helpful witness, or that McCarthy was dumbfounded when he wasn't. It was this 180-degree U-turn that most inflamed McCarthy. Nor was the reversal lost on other members of the Senate. Georgia Democrat Richard Russell, in later questioning of Zwicker, would say: ". . . at this hearing, it appears that your earlier attitude of, I might say, friendly helpfulness, changed to one of hostility. What caused your attitude to change?"[20]

That was of course the $64,000 question, to which Zwicker addressed some sketchy answers, only one of which proved salient: that, on February 17, the day before his set-to with McCarthy, he received a flying visit from Army counsel Adams. And though Zwicker was vague about what happened at this meeting, it was apparent to members of the Senate that this changed everything, turning a potentially friendly witness into one hostile and evasive.* The point would be confirmed, again, by the forthright-in-hindsight Adams.

"We were anxious," said Adams of this visit, "*to make Zwicker understand that neither names nor security information would be revealed* [in testifying before McCarthy]. *We left the meeting with the impression that Zwicker had already made substantial revelations about Peress to McCarthy's staff,* starting off with the disclosure of his name. This would make McCarthy's interrogation of Zwicker awkward, *since Zwicker might now feel that he could not testify at the hearing concerning any information he had already informally told McCarthy's people.*"[21] (Emphasis added.)

That says it rather plainly—not only as to the once more decisive role of Adams and the peculiar change that came over Zwicker, but the "impression" that Zwicker had already shared data he would now be reluctant to confirm. That made for a very "awkward" scene indeed—for which read, angry confrontation. It was thus fairly obvious what had happened. Zwicker started out cooperating with the committee and in all probability did provide the Peress security data to Anastos. But after his visit from Adams, he got the message: Provide no further information. Hence the stonewalling before McCarthy; hence the blowup.

To all of which there are a couple of footnotes. As Zwicker's sworn denials were in direct conflict with the testimony of Anastos/Morrill, the McClellan committee in 1955 would refer the matter to the Attorney General for consideration of possible perjury charges. And since it would have been two witnesses against one, Zwicker was the obvious target. For some unknown reason, it took Eisenhower Justice nineteen months to respond to this referral, finally

---

*Sen. Styles Bridges (R-N.H.) put it this way to Zwicker: "It was very curious to me why you were so cooperative and so friendly in your relations one time, and all at once after Mr. Adams went to see you, your attitude changed, you bristled up. You certainly, as I read the testimony . . . were almost a new man in attitude. What did Mr. Adams tell you?"

answering in December 1956 that the matter didn't meet the "technical" requirements of a perjury indictment. The case was thus considered closed.

Then, a few weeks later, the final chapter of the story would be written. On January 17, 1957, Ralph Zwicker was nominated for promotion to full permanent rank as brigadier general and temporary major general. When he arrived for confirmation hearings, he was accompanied by Ike's new Army Secretary, Wilbur Brucker, and a full array of Pentagon brass, an impressive show of high-level support for someone who scant weeks before had been a candidate for a perjury indictment. After a ringing endorsement by Brucker, the promotion was approved, and Zwicker would go into the history books as a vindicated martyr. General Lawton, to judge by the silence of the record, still wasn't available for comment.

CHAPTER 40

The Legend of Annie Lee Moss

M cCARTHY martyrs weren't so thick on the ground in 1954 as they had been in 1950, when he inflicted his reign of terror on the State Department and reaped a bumper crop of victims. However, the later group of suspects would compensate for their relative lack of numbers with extra pathos. This was mainly owing to the newly risen influence of TV, which showcased several of these cases as pitiful targets of McCarthy's bluster.

There were several dramatic examples of this type, stemming from the VOA, Monmouth, and Army-McCarthy hearings—Reed Harris, Frederick Fisher, and some others. But the case that probably came closest to exhibiting the main features of McCarthy victimhood, and the lasting fame this conferred, was that of Annie Lee Moss, a black woman then working for the Army. Called before the subcommittee in early 1954, she was depicted at the time, and still is, as the quintessential McCarthy martyr. The most famous of all McCarthy cases, it's also a case that says a lot about McCarthy, his critics, and standard histories of the era.

A pivotal player in the Moss affair was FBI witness Mary Markward, an unsung foot soldier in the silent war conducted by the Bureau against the Kremlin's U.S. helpers. In 1942, Markward was recruited by the FBI as a deep-cover agent inside the Communist Party, a task she gamely carried out for seven years. In this guise she would become treasurer of the party in the District of Columbia, with responsibility for membership rolls and records of dues payments. This information she passed on to the FBI, keeping Hoover's men apprised of who was who inside the local party apparatus.*

In due course, Markward was considered so well informed about the doings of the comrades that the government would use her as an expert witness before the Subversive Activities Control Board (SACB), set up by Congress to monitor the party and its agents. This led the Communists to stage a vigorous counterattack against Markward, a dispute that dragged on before the board and in the courts for roughly a decade.

The immediate relevance of Mrs. Markward here is that she would identify Annie Lee Moss to the FBI as a Communist Party member in the District, information the Bureau passed on to the Civil Service Commission and the Army. This intel became the more important when Mrs. Moss, previously a cafeteria worker, somehow got appointed as a code clerk for the Signal Corps and was given security clearance for this duty. On the face of it, this seemed to be a security gaffe of huge proportions.

As such things had a way of doing, the case came to the notice of McCarthy, and, in a spin-off from the Monmouth probe, he would summon both Markward and Moss to appear before him to sort out the facts about the matter. This was in the immediate wake of the Peress-Zwicker confrontations, and in McCarthy's mind raised all the same disturbing issues. Given the Markward evidence, Civil Service data, and FBI reports, he wondered, how was it possible for Mrs. Moss to get clearance as an Army code clerk?

Markward testified before McCarthy in late February '54, a week after the Zwicker blowup. She said Annie Lee Moss had been known to her as a member of the D.C. party, based on its membership and dues-paying records, and a recipient of the *Daily Worker*. In 1945, Markward added, Mrs. Moss had been dropped from the formal CP rolls when she went to work for the General Accounting Office, as it was party policy to treat members holding official jobs on a separate, more confidential basis. (Mrs. Moss worked for the GAO from October 1945 until 1949, obtaining her code clerk post in 1950.)[1]

When Mrs. Moss appeared to answer Markward, she seemed a frail, distracted figure, not fitting the usual picture of a party apparatchik. Also, unlike many other suspects, she didn't plead the Fifth Amendment but proceeded to deny all: She wasn't a member of the Communist Party, never had been, didn't

---

*Mrs. Markward would identify many party functionaries to the Bureau, then to the House Committee on Un-American Activities, then later to McCarthy. Among those she named as CP members, to pick a few already mentioned, were Travis Hedrick, Andrew Older, and Ruth Rifkin. Hedrick, it may be recalled, was the OWI employee assailed by spokesmen for the AFL and CIO back in 1943. Older would be of special interest to McCarthy, as he preceded David Karr as reporter/legman for Drew Pearson. Ruth Rifkin—named by Elizabeth Bentley also—had twice worked for one of McCarthy's major targets, the State Department's William Stone. These were all significant security cases of more than local interest.

know anything about it. It was, she said, a mistaken-identity problem. There was some other Annie Lee Moss who must be the culprit they were after. This Moss explanation is featured in all the usual histories, which, with no known exceptions, have treated her testimony as conclusive on the subject.

A somewhat novel aspect of the case was that the mistaken-identity idea was first surfaced, and later pushed hard, by various subcommittee members. During the Markward testimony, before Moss came on the scene in person, the issue was raised by John McClellan. "Mr. Chairman," he said, ". . . may we determine whether the Annie Lee Moss that is now employed in the government is the same Annie Lee Moss about whom you speak, and whom you know to be a Communist?"[2] This wasn't an unreasonable thing to ask, as Markward had apparently never seen Moss in person, knowing of her through party records. It was, however, a bit unusual for the point to be made by a committee member before such a plea was entered by the suspect.

Then, when Mrs. Moss did appear, on March 11, Stuart Symington, aided by Scoop Jackson, went after the mistaken-identity theme in avid fashion, serving up leading questions the witness seemed well prepared to answer.

> SYMINGTON: Do you know anybody else in this town named Moss? *Have you ever looked up a telephone number**—are there any Mosses in Washington besides you?
> MOSS: Yes, sir, there are three Annie Lee Mosses.
> JACKSON: Will you state that again?
> MOSS: There are three Annie Lee Mosses.[3]

These responses were apparently all the proof required in certain circles to reach a verdict of not guilty. Symington announced himself persuaded by the mere statement of the Moss denial. "Mrs. Moss," he said, "I want to say something to you, and I may be sticking my neck out here, and I may be wrong . . . But I have been listening to you testify this afternoon and I think you are telling the truth . . . If you are not taken back into the Army (employment) you come around to see me, and I am going to see that you get a job."[†4]

This brought an outburst of audience applause, and for reasons that have never been quite clear was assumed to have settled the issue. Helping spread this notion was that the hearing including the Moss denial and Symington gesture was televised, most famously by Edward R. Murrow of CBS on his TV show, *See It Now*. Reinforcing the image of grievous wrong to Moss, when

---

*This false start by Symington was one of several indications that there was some prearrangement of these questions, but that he had gotten matters garbled. In the normal course of things, there would have been reason for somebody else to look up Mrs. Moss's telephone number, but no reason for Mrs. Moss herself to do so.

†Mrs. Moss had been suspended by the Army following the Markward testimony to McCarthy.

Roy Cohn brought up the previously noted point that still other witnesses could confirm the Markward statements, he was rebuked, and silenced, by McClellan.*

Such was the full extent of the story then broadcast to the nation, and such is the version appearing in all the standard write-ups, media retrospectives, and, most recently, entertainments. To cite the many books of alleged history in which this oft-told tale appears would be tedious for both the author and the reader. However, a few samples will suggest the prevalence of the treatment:

". . . Joe's old trouble of mistaken identity had cropped up again: as he had before indicted the wrong Anna Rosenberg, so now he indicted the wrong Annie Lee Moss, a Pentagon code clerk." (Jack Anderson) "He [McCarthy] claimed—erroneously—that the employee had access to decoded messages and belonged to the Communist Party. She had received Communist mailings, but hers seemed to be another case of mistaken identity—there were three Annie Lee Mosses in the Washington telephone directory." (Richard Fried) "To the dimmest intelligence it seemed clear that the case hinged on a bungle over identity—there were several Annie Lee Mosses listed in the Washington telephone directory—and it focused attention on the slipshod work of McCarthy's staff." (Lately Thomas)[5]

Unfortunately, what seemed clear to the "dimmest intelligence" wouldn't be clear at all to anyone who actually checked the records—as these authors obviously didn't. In fact, there was no mistaken identity in the case, no good reason to think there was, and plenty of reason to think there wasn't. Symington, the McCarthy critics of that day, and numerous facile commentators since would prove to be the bunglers.

Central to the Moss mistaken-identity plea was the contention that there were "three Annie Lee Mosses" in the D.C. phone book and that the McCarthy probers had simply collared the wrong suspect.† This led to considerable back-and-forth in the hearing record about the several addresses of Mrs. Moss, to verify that the same person was being talked of. On this point, Mrs. Moss herself would give the game away in an unguarded moment, volunteering one of the addresses where she lived in the 1940s. In an exchange with McCarthy about the *Daily Worker* being delivered to her home, she said: *". . . we didn't get this Communist paper anymore until after we had moved southwest to 72 R St."*[6] (Emphasis added.)

This comment would be of key significance later, when the SACB weighed arguments from the Communist party in its attack on Markward. Among the

---

*McCarthy, who might have protected Cohn from this onslaught, had by this time left the hearing room, relinquishing the gavel to Karl Mundt.

†As a matter of fact, there were *not* three Annie Lee Mosses in the D.C. phone book, but as this is a secondary issue, consideration of it is for the moment deferred. See below.

issues raised by the comrades were Markward's statements concerning a regional CP bigwig and whether she had received payment from the FBI for her undercover duties. To these counts, in response to the publicity given Moss, the party opportunistically added the charge that Markward had perjured herself in branding Moss a CP member.

This challenge caused the SACB to call for the FBI reports concerning Markward-Moss and examine the records of the Communist Party of the District. After this review, in a 1958 report, the SACB concluded: *"The situation that has resulted on the Moss question is that the party's own records, copies of which are now in evidence, and the authenticity of which it does not dispute, . . . show an Annie Lee Moss, 72 R St., S.W., as a party member in the mid-1940s."*[7] (Emphasis added.)

These findings about Mrs. Moss and her R Street address made the matter quite open-and-shut, rendering moot attempts to discredit Markward, conjure up three different Mosses, or other such rhetorical smoke screens. Whether Mrs. Moss was as befuddled as she appeared, or had been recruited into the party without knowing what she was doing, are debatable topics.* What isn't debatable is that this particular Annie Moss, and no other, had been listed in the Communist records as a party member. The Markward testimony to McCarthy was, per the SACB account, 100 percent on target.

That was the state of available information on the case in the fall of 1958, when the SACB released its findings. Decisive as these comments were, the record would get still more so when the underlying FBI reports about Mrs. Moss and the Communist records were later made available to researchers. These files show the accuracy of the SACB account, hence the veracity of Markward, but yield a number of other disclosures also, some of startling nature.

For one thing, as suggested by the SACB discussion, the FBI in its Moss reports wasn't simply relying on updates from Markward. It had also obtained, directly, copies of the membership, dues, and other records of the D.C. Communist Party via highly "confidential sources," which in Bureau lingo meant some variant of a bag job. As reflected in numerous Bureau summaries of these records, the Markward info about Moss—dues payments, shifts from one party unit to another, places of employment—was confirmed in systematic fashion. It was all the same information, all pertaining to the same person, all involving the same moves from one job or residence to another. (In which respect, the 72 R St. address was often featured.)[†8]

These were, however, among the least astonishing aspects of the Bureau

---

* That she had perhaps *unknowingly* signed up for membership in the Communist Party was hinted at by Moss both in her McCarthy appearance and in testimony to the House Committee on Un-American Activities.

† Having already nailed down all this, the Bureau later went through the drill of confirming that this Mrs. Moss wasn't some other Mrs. Moss, checking out the alibi about other people in the phone

records. A good deal more so was the revelation that, well before the McCarthy hearings, this same Annie Lee Moss had repeatedly been recommended for demotion or removal as a security risk by officials of the Army. Such recommendations had been made at least three different times in 1951 at different levels of the service, only to be overridden by the same review board that had been reversing security suspensions at Monmouth.* (Information that was in the possession of the McCarthy staffers.) Little wonder, then, that McCarthy considered the case to be part of a larger pattern.

Finally—the most jolting disclosure of them all—the FBI file reveals that the Democratic contingent on the McCarthy panel knew all about the Bureau data on the case well before the famous hearing in which Symington-Jackson-Moss floated the legend of multiple Annie Mosses. This is spelled out in a Bureau memo of February 24, 1954, the day after the Markward testimony, by FBI official Lou Nichols. In this update, Nichols said he had just discussed the case with Henry Jackson and minority subcommittee counsel Robert Kennedy, and had gone into minute detail about it with Jackson, as follows:

> I then told Senator Jackson that in addition to the Mary Markward testimony, we had secured through confidential sources access to an examination of membership records of the Communist Party of the District of Columbia in May of 1944, that these reflected the name of Annie Lee Moss of 72 R St. We had observed other records relating to members who had been dropped by the party and transferred to the party with the District; that the name of Annie Lee Moss appeared as transferring into the Party December 1, 1943.
>
> I further told the senator that a list of names had been observed believed to be . . . Group Captains in connection with the 1944 registration of Party members and this list contained the name Annie Lee Moss. In 1944, it had been ascertained that her name appeared on a list of CPA† members; that another list in the summer of 1944 reflected her name on a list of CPA

---

book with similar names and other alleged sources of confusion (e.g., variant spellings of the first name, including "Anna" and "Annie"). There was of course zero possibility that two people of identical name both lived at 72 R St. S.W., but the Bureau checked up anyway. The report on this says: "Based on information available in city directories and telephone directories, WFO [Washington Field Office] conducted investigation, results of which appear to indicate that none of the individuals with names similar to the employee's resided at the addresses for Annie Moss, reflected in the CP records."

* A Bureau report concerning this says "the Chief Signal Officer made the first indorsement of the file on June 30, 1951, recommending that she be removed from the government as a security risk. On July 5, 1951, the Military District of Washington placed a second indorsement on her file concurring with the Chief Signal Officer and recommending that she be removed as a security risk. On July 18, 1951, G-2, Department of the Army concurred on previous recommendation and recommended to the Loyalty Security Screening Board (LSSB), that subject be removed for security reasons." Despite all of which, "on October 23, 1951, after a hearing in the subject's case, the [Pentagon Review] Board recommended that she was cleared and that she be restored to her duties and be paid her back salary."

† CPA = Communist Political Association, the interim name given to the party by Earl Browder as part of the wartime effort to present the Communists as indigenous and patriotic.

NO MISTAKEN IDENTITY

As revealed in this FBI report of February 24, 1954, the Democratic contingent of the McCarthy panel had been informed of the Bureau's extensive data on Annie Lee Moss well before the March 11 hearings in which they pushed the mistaken-identity theory of the case.

I subsequently called Senator Jackson back and told him that I had checked and that the Director had wanted to be helpful to him if he could on a strictly personal and confidential basis. The Senator said he certainly would respect the confidence and expressed his deep appreciation for the Director's interest.

I then told Senator Jackson that in addition to the Mary Markward testimony, we had secured through confidential sources access to an examination of membership records of the Communist Party of the District of Columbia in May of 1944, that these reflected the name of Annie Lee Moss of 72 R Street. We had observed other records relating to members who had been dropped by the Party and transferred to the Party in the District; that the name Annie Lee Moss appeared as transferring into the Party December 1, 1943.

I further told the Senator that a list of names had been observed believed to be ~~supplied~~ to Group Captains in connection with the 1944 registration of Party members and this list contained the name Annie Lee Moss. In 1944, it had been ascertained that her name appeared on a list of CPA members; that another list in the summer of 1944 reflected her name on a list of CPA members under the heading "Unassigned."

Further, that a list had been observed dated January 2, 1945, wherein the name of Annie Lee Moss appeared under the heading of Cash Receipts for Daily Worker subscriptions.

Senator Jackson stated that this certainly was enough for him and that there could be no doubt about Annie Lee Moss's Communist Party affiliations, particularly in view of [ ] testimony this morning. However, he stated that this testimony reflected that [ ] was somewhat vague in her identification of Annie Lee Moss. Senator Jackson stated that he frankly could not see why the Army had not acted on this case. I told him we, of course, did not know what the results were of the loyalty hearing or what explanation she made. He stated that she should be called and be given an opportunity to explain, and then if she continues to deny, her case certainly should be referred to the Department for perjury prosecution.

121   2900   207

- 2 -

Source: FBI Annie Lee Moss file

members under the heading "Unassigned" . . . Further, that a list had been observed dated January 2, 1945, wherein the name of Annie Lee Moss appeared under the heading of Cash Receipts for *Daily Worker* subscriptions.[9]

This memo makes it crystal clear that Scoop Jackson was thoroughly briefed about the Moss affair on February 24, two weeks before the hearing in which the mistaken-identity plea was surfaced. The memo further shows Jackson was persuaded by what he heard, adding that "Senator Jackson stated that this certainly was enough for him and that there could be no doubt about Annie Lee Moss' Communist Party affiliations . . ."[10] Despite this, Jackson and his fellow Democrats on March 11 would act out the "three different Annie Lee Mosses" charade, thus obscuring before the nation the data that Jackson was given by the Bureau.

In fact, though Jackson kept quiet about what he was told and the SACB report wouldn't be published until four years later, there was ample reason in 1954 to know the Moss on the witness stand and the Moss in the party records were one and the same. Close study of the hearing records would have been enough to show this. For instance, the Moss named by Markward had been a cafeteria employee, lived for a time with a Hattie Griffin, and received the *Daily Worker*—all this testified to by Markward on February 23. The Moss appearing before McCarthy, by her own account, had been a cafeteria employee, lived for a time with Hattie Griffin, and received the *Daily Worker*. Anyone comparing the transcripts could see there was no identity mix-up.

Meanwhile, as the authorities knew but the public didn't, there was a long paper trail on Mrs. Moss and her security record with the federal government, first at the GAO and then with the Army. The trail would get even longer in August 1954—six months after Symington, Murrow, and others depicted Moss as a victim of McCarthy's slipshod methods—when the Army suspended her from her duties. This action was based on a series of charges addressed to Moss that tracked closely with the intel provided Jackson—but with one riveting addition: "You [Moss] are reported to have been given Communist Party membership book number 37269 for 1943."[11]

When these Army charges were made public, Stuart Symington, who had praised Mrs. Moss and generously offered to get her a job if she lost her post as code clerk, had a sudden change of heart. On August 5, 1954, he wrote McCarthy: "The press reports that the Army has suspended Mrs. Moss on the basis of information which was not previously available, pending further investigation . . . I think it is absolutely essential that we get to the bottom of Mrs. Moss' case . . . If Mrs. Moss is innocent that should be established. If she testified falsely before us, the matter should be referred to the Department of Justice for prosecution."[12]

The alternatives here were of course correctly stated. However, Symington curiously failed to note that he had already taken it on himself to clear Mrs. Moss, in a televised public hearing, based strictly on her own denials. That episode seems to have been forgotten, along with his chivalrous promise to get her a job if she were ousted from the Army.*

There was the further question of Mrs. Moss's duties with the Signal Corps, and whether she would have been capable in this job of doing any damage. In the March hearing, Symington, McClellan, *et al.,* treated her with utmost condescension, implying she was too ignorant to do any harm with the messages she was handling. (After Mrs. Moss had stumbled reading a notice sent to her by the Army, McClellan paternally asked, "Did you read that the very best you could?")[13] However, the official description of the Signal Corps post held by Mrs. Moss suggests this was by no means the job for an ignoramus. This reads in part:

> Examine messages received in tape form in code and clear text from Receiving Banks, to determine coherence thereof, whether numbers are in correct sequence, correctness of time and date group, precedence and whether complete. . . . Messages received in code must be more carefully scrutinized inasmuch as it is more difficult to detect omissions or errors in coded letter or number groups. . . . Process high precedence messages immediately by hand-carrying to overseas desk for quick routing . . . [Duties include] recognition, recording and disposition of encrypted messages destined for or received from the Crypto Center. . . . As workload requires, ascertain and record final disposition of messages addressed to this station and originating overseas or by State Department, Army Security Agency, Central Intelligence Agency, General Staff, etc. . . . If necessary perform research through the various files of Manual Teletype Unit to locate disposition actions, including commercial circuit files, misrouted files, staff Communication Branch files, etc.[14]

And so forth at some length. Looking at these requirements, it's hard to believe anyone as unsophisticated as Mrs. Moss seemed to be could have carried out the job in question. When we add the much-neglected fact that she was a licensed real estate agent in good standing in the District of Columbia, it would appear she wasn't quite the simpleton suggested by Symington-McClellan's patronizing questions. In which event, she would have been capable with her security clearance, working with clear text as well as coded data, of learning a lot more from the material she handled than her condescending champions suggested.

As instructive as the substance of the Moss case has been scholarly and journalistic treatment of it. Even after the dispositive ruling of the SACB and

---

* As to the business about info "not previously available," this reads like a lame alibi, given the data long since supplied to Henry Jackson by the Bureau (unless Jackson, for some perverse reason, had failed to share this information with his Democratic colleagues).

the matter of the R St. address, writers on the topic couldn't bring themselves to admit that McCarthy was right all along and that the mistaken-identity plea was bogus. In fact, the statements above quoted about the Moss affair from historians of the era were all written well after the SACB ruling was handed down in 1958. In most such cases, it appears, the writers didn't do their homework and just went with the legend, which is bad enough. But in other, still more troubling cases, it's evident the McCarthy critics do know about the findings of the SACB, but for motives we can only guess at have chosen to obscure them.

A prime example, earlier cited, is the handling of the case by associate Senate historian Donald Ritchie, who edited the executive hearings of the McCarthy panel released in 2003. The official status of this collection gives its discussion of the Moss affair, and others, a cachet exceeding that of any academic study and makes its errors less forgivable than if committed in some purely private writing. As Ritchie's version bears the imprimatur of the Senate, his comments will not unnaturally be thought by researchers to be established facts of record.

As already noted, Ritchie is remarkably free with dicta on the hearings, and nowhere more so than in his exegesis of the Moss case. In a fairly lengthy essay on the subject, he throws in a twenty-four-word reference to the findings of the SACB, but so phrased as to blur their meaning. He says the board confirmed Markward's identification of Moss, but then adds the cryptic comment that "the board conducted no further investigation of Moss" and had said "Markward's testimony should be assayed with caution." These asides can only suggest to readers that there is some lingering doubt about the matter— the more so as Ritchie follows up with an extended eulogy to Moss offered by a liberal writer, attesting to her blameless conduct.[15]

These Ritchie comments, however, are demonstrable obfuscations. For one thing, the point of the SACB inquiry, as the board itself observed, wasn't to investigate Moss but to gauge the credibility of Markward. Moss was not before the SACB, and as the board stressed in several places there was neither intent nor reason to pursue her case beyond acquisition of Communist Party records to check the Markward statements. Thus Ritchie's gratuitous comment about "no further investigation of Moss" is a red herring, suggesting some SACB action on Moss had been projected but never taken.[16]

Likewise, the board's comment about viewing Markward's evidence "with caution" pertained to other matters entirely, and specifically *didn't* pertain to Moss. In context, "assayed with caution" concerned the issue of payment from the FBI and the way Markward construed this. Reviewing the Markward testimony on Moss, the SACB repeatedly said the undercover agent was proved accurate in her statements on that aspect. As the board put it in yet another ruling (January 15, 1959), again citing the CP records, "we conclude that . . . the Communist Party's charge that Markward gave perjurious testimony is not substantiated. *Consequently Mrs. Markward's credibility is in no way impaired by the Annie Lee Moss matter. . . .*"[17] (Emphasis added.)

So despite the verbal fuzzballs of Donald Ritchie, the SACB unequivocally said Markward was vindicated in the Moss affair, and never made any findings that weakened this conclusion. In fact, reviewing half a dozen SACB references to the subject, it's evident the Moss case was the thing that most clearly bolstered Markward's credibility with the board.[18] All of which is the exact reverse of the impression conveyed to the American public by the associate historian of the Senate.

A second recent treatment of the Moss affair that deserves brief notice isn't a scholarly work, but undoubtedly has done more to spread disinformation about the case than a dozen history books together. This is the George Clooney film *Good Night and Good Luck,* released in 2005, based on the 1954 confrontation between McCarthy and Edward R. Murrow (the title of the film is taken from Murrow's habitual sign-off). This Clooney opus portrays McCarthy as a fearsome dragon and Murrow as the brave knight-errant who dared to slay him. In a mix of modern production methods and video clips taken from the archives, the movie affects to be a study in *cinema verité,* supposedly revealing the evil of McCarthy simply by showing him in action. The case of Annie Lee Moss is featured, as it was by Murrow himself back in the 1950s.

It's of interest that neither in the Clooney film nor in the original Murrow broadcast is there any *evidence* cited to indicate Moss was an innocent victim— the message being conveyed instead by video clips of Moss and of McClellan browbeating Cohn for allegedly treating her unfairly. In the case of the Murrow broadcast, when not all the relevant data were known, this was to some extent excusable (though had Murrow and Co. been the crack journalists they professed to be, they could have dug out the facts about Hattie Griffin and the like from the hearing transcripts). In the case of the Clooney film, there is no excuse whatever, as the truth about the case is fully available to anyone who bothers to review the voluminous SACB reports and archives of the Bureau.

Amazingly, in a press interview about all this, Clooney made it clear he had been informed that Mrs. Moss *was* a Communist and that he didn't deny it. Instead, he said, the real question stressed by Murrow and his colleagues, and therefore in the Clooney film, was that "they simply demand that she has a right to face her accuser."[19] We are thus informed, after fifty years of being told Mrs. Moss was not a Communist but a mistaken-identity victim, that wasn't the point at all! It was, instead, her right to face her accuser.

If Clooney was indeed aware of the copious evidence on the case, as he should have been in presuming to inform the world about it, he certainly disguised this knowledge in his movie. In the interests of historical truth, the data set forth above should at least have been alluded to, making it clear Mrs. Moss was in fact what Markward (and McCarthy) said, and not the victim of a mistaken-identity foul-up. But, of course, if Clooney had brought out these facts of record, he would have had no movie. Such information would have undercut the thesis of the film about the bullying and reckless lying of McCarthy.

As for "facing her accuser," Mrs. Moss was not denied such right by McCarthy. In keeping with its standard practice, the subcommittee notified Moss and her attorney that there would be testimony about her and summoned her to appear at that time to answer Markward's statements. Mrs. Moss herself, via a letter from her attorney received the day of the hearing, declined to do this, saying she was too ill to testify. She was then asked to appear the following day and came to the hearing room, but her attorney again said she wasn't in condition to take the stand. McCarthy, though skeptical of this, said if she were really too ill to testify he didn't want her to do so, but would reschedule her response to Markward. Mrs. Moss then appeared on March 11, the delay occasioned by her own requests, and not the doing of McCarthy.*

Finally, on the substance of the case, there are a couple of minor footnotes to be added. One is that, contra all the statements above quoted, there *weren't* three Annie Lee Mosses in the Washington phone book, at least not when the author, as a cub reporter, checked out the matter back in the 1950s. The occasion for this bit of niche reporting was a comment in December 1958 by William Shannon of the *New York Post,* who claimed there was no evidence the Mrs. Moss in the McCarthy hearings and the one in the Communist records were the same person, citing the inevitable "three Annie Lee Mosses" in the phone book. My response to Shannon read in part as follows:

> . . . there are not three different Annie Lee Mosses listed in the Washington phone directory, as you allege. There is one "Anna Lee Moss," one "Annie Moss," and one "Annie L. Moss." I have just this moment placed calls to all three of them. In the first-cited instance ("Anna Lee Moss"), I talked to the lady's husband, who said that his wife had never listed herself as "Annie Lee Moss," and had never been called by that name; in the second instance, I talked to the daughter of "Annie Moss," who said that her mother had never used the middle name "Lee," but called herself simply "Annie Moss." This leaves only one "Annie Lee Moss," who is listed in the Washington phone book as "Annie L. Moss," and she is the Mrs. Moss who was involved in the McCarthy hearings. (An interesting footnote is that when I talked to this Mrs. Moss, she would answer no questions whatever, other than to affirm that she was the woman who had testified; she insisted that I call the

---

*If the accuser-facing reference is to the film clip in which McClellan lambasted Cohn for mentioning other witnesses who would testify to the CP status of Mrs. Moss, that appears to have been still more humbug, and a bit of playacting by McClellan. The matter of such additional witnesses had been discussed in McClellan's presence by McCarthy, Scoop Jackson, and Cohn in the two previous hearings, the latter attended by Mrs. Moss and her attorney. On those occasions, McClellan hadn't said boo about the unfairness of alluding to these other unnamed parties. It was only *after* McCarthy left the hearing of March 11 that McClellan jumped Cohn for referring to this already mooted subject.

Department of the Army if I wanted any other information concerning her.)
Thus your statement on this point is in error.[20]

This missive to Shannon, a prominent writer for the then-liberal *Post,* also
noted the information on the 72 R St. house, and the unlikelihood "that there
should be two persons of that name living at the same address." These comments never received an answer, nor to my knowledge was the false assertion
about no evidence linking the Army Moss with the Markward data ever corrected by the *Post.* Writing Shannon was roughly equivalent to dropping a bottle in the ocean. That experience with media treatment of the case would be
uncannily replicated, almost half a century later, in further efforts to set the
record straight with journalists holding forth about Moss-as-victim.

One such episode involved Ken Ringle of the *Washington Post,* who in
2003 briefly capsuled the ersatz version of the case in a write-up of the McCarthy executive hearings and the views thereon of historian Ritchie.[21] Reporter
Ringle had zero interest in hearing any details about the matter or citations
from official records, saying the conventional version was plenty good for him
and that he didn't need to know any more about it. A similar episode concerned a misleading discussion of the case by Dorothy Rabinowitz of the *Wall
Street Journal.*[22] A letter to the editor correcting this mangled treatment and
setting forth some facts about the matter received no acknowledgment, was
never printed, and so far as I know resulted in no correction—another message
lost at sea in yet another drifting bottle. A lot can change in fifty years, but pur-
blind denial on the subject of Annie Lee Moss—and Joe McCarthy—is something you can always count on.

Postscript

As to why the Democrats on the McCarthy panel went through their charade
with Moss after Scoop Jackson had been so thoroughly briefed by the FBI, we
can only speculate. However, pending further revelations, a possible clue may
be found in the date of the hearing—March 11, 1954. This was the same day
an Army chronology regarding the situation at Fort Monmouth and asserted
misdeeds of Cohn-McCarthy appeared in the press, intimating among other
things that McCarthy's allegations of lax security in the Army Signal Corps
were phony.

In this context, the Moss case—wherein Pentagon security screeners at
high levels had overridden conclusive data from the FBI—would have been a
home run for McCarthy, especially coming on the heels of the all-too-similar
Peress fiasco. At a minimum, if the facts about the Moss affair had been clearly
understood, the case would have impeded the full-court effort that now commenced portraying McCarthy's quarrel with Pentagon security practice as

mudslinging without factual basis. Blanketing Moss with a smog of obfuscation could—and did—avert this danger.

That subcommittee Democrats and various of their colleagues at this time were in backstage contact with the Ike administration to drum up resistance to McCarthy is apparent from Bureau and other records—for instance, a rather improbable liaison between Assistant Attorney General William Rogers and ur-liberal Democrat J. William Fulbright. Further such contacts would be revealed in the Army-McCarthy hearings soon to follow and would become even more pronounced in the climactic struggle over censure. It thus does not strain credulity that the Democrats on the subcommittee, in successfully blurring over the facts concerning Moss, were helping out their allies-of-convenience in opposition to McCarthy. Why these same obfuscations have been repeated for fifty years by historians of the matter is a somewhat more difficult question.

CHAPTER 41

At War with the Army

PRECEDING chapters have noted certain parallels between the experience of the Dies committee and the later doings of McCarthy—like
effects and causes, similar issues, and sometimes the identical people.
There remains one further such connection to be considered, perhaps the most
suggestive of them all.

The *jihad* against the Dies committee was unceasing, but reached an
apogee of sorts in 1944. This was at the height of the wartime honeymoon with
Moscow and correlative efforts to abolish antisubversive records held in official
archives. On both counts the House Committee on Un-American Activities
was an obvious and inviting target. Its obdurate anti-Communism would of
course have been distasteful to our Soviet allies and their minions. As for antisubversive files, the committee was among the worst offenders, not only holding extensive records of this type but frequently sharing them with others in
Congress and executive agencies checking out security matters.

Given those factors and the longtime New Deal aversion to the panel and
all its works, it's not perhaps surprising that an attempt was made in 1944 to
close its doors and disperse its records.* In sync with this projected crack-

---

*Though ultimately averted, this effort reached the point that the committee files had been moved
out into the halls of the House Office Building, ready for transfer to the Library of Congress. It was
the threat of such dispersal that prompted publication of Appendix IX.

down, a campaign was launched to draft the committee's top professional staffer, chief investigator Robert Stripling, into military service. Stripling was then thirty-one years old, married and a father, held a key congressional job relating to security matters, and was specifically exempted from the draft by the Legislative Deferment Committee of Congress.

Notwithstanding all of which, as Stripling would relate, he was advised by his draft board that "there's been a lot of pressure on us to get you into the Army"—hence classified as 1-A and a candidate for conscription.[1] Columnist Drew Pearson and some of his journalistic brethren then mounted a vigorous press campaign to have Stripling called to active duty. This in fact occurred, and the ex–chief investigator would spend the next year and a half as an Army yardbird. Occasionally, efforts were made by Army officials to assign him to intelligence duties more suited to his background, but up until the tag end of his service these attempts were unavailing.

Stripling would later comment that, in all this, somebody at high levels "never lost sight of me—though I was indistinguishable from millions of other privates."[2] But of course he was quite distinguishable from other privates, precisely because he had been the top investigator of the House Committee. Neither Drew Pearson nor people at high official levels would have paid any attention to Bob Stripling had he been a plumber, carpenter, or insurance agent—or a State Department type like, say, Robert Miller or Alger Hiss, both in their thirties at the outset of the war but never drafted.*

The Stripling story would be repeated, *mutatis mutandis,* in 1953, with another staffer for yet another anti-Red committee, and with the ever-watchful Pearson once more hovering in the background. This staffer was G. David Schine, pal of Roy Cohn, part-time consultant to the PSI and soon to be the most famous private in the Army. He was also to be the proximate cause of yet another investigation of McCarthy, this one the most important in the series.

In terms of Hill prestige and clout, Schine was no Bob Stripling. Rather than being a top-line staffer, he was a somewhat marginal figure—an unpaid voluntary helper. However, he had done a fair amount of work on the VOA and USIS investigations and was involved in writing reports about those inquests. Also, as the executive hearings show, he assisted with the Monmouth probe, interviewing potential witnesses who would later come before the panel. Considering the committee's workload and small staff of about a dozen investigators, these contributions were of some value.

In context, probably the most distinctive thing about Schine was that he

---

*On December 7, 1941, Miller was thirty-one years old and Hiss had just turned thirty-seven. In 1940, Hiss had been classified 1-A but subsequently was the beneficiary of deferment requests by the State Department, filed in November 1940 and May 1941. Stripling would return to the House Committee from military service and play a substantial part in the investigation that brought both Miller and Hiss to public view.

was the McCarthy staffer most eligible for being drafted, though even this was a bit of a stretch. In 1947, he had been classified 4-F and draft-exempt because of a slipped disk in his back. He then obtained a position in the Army Transport Service, serving as the equivalent of a ship's purser before going on to Harvard. In the summer of 1953, Schine was approaching his twenty-sixth birthday (September 11), much older than the average conscript of that era, still classified 4-F, and helping lay the groundwork for the probe at Monmouth.

At this point, Drew Pearson would come back in the picture and, based on some combination of outside tips and inside sources, manage to obtain the Schine draft records. Pearson then began another press crusade to the effect that Schine was a shirker who ought to be conscripted. After a series of columns on this theme, the Schine case was reopened; he was classified 1-A and would enter the Army in November. When Drew Pearson spoke, it seems, local draft boards listened.

As Schine was at the outer age limit for the draft, this reopening of his file struck some observers as peculiar. One such naturally was Cohn, who believed the only reason Schine was drafted was that he worked for the McCarthy panel. McCarthy believed the same, though he was less vocal on the topic. These views were no doubt to be expected. It's noteworthy, however, that Army Secretary Robert Stevens was of the like opinion, voiced in January 1954 to Defense official Fred Seaton. "Of course," said Stevens, "the kid [Schine] was taken at the very last minute, before he was ineligible for age. My guess would be that if he hadn't been working for McCarthy, he probably never would have been drafted. . . ."[3]

However it was managed, and for whatever reason, the effect of Schine's induction was to give the Army a pressure point where influence over the McCarthy panel might at least in theory be wielded. It also created a two-way dynamic between McCarthy and the Ike administration. Schine was now under the thumb of the Army and subject to such treatment as it chose to give him. Meanwhile, the committee where Schine had worked was investigating his new bosses. Not quite two scorpions in a bottle, but the opportunities for mutual leverage were apparent.

At the fulcrum of these events was Cohn. Already believing Schine a victim of discrimination, Cohn soon became convinced of this more firmly. Citing Schine's educational level, age, and prior experience with the Army Transport Service, Cohn thought his pal and coworker should be eligible for a commission. This view was at first confirmed by Gen. Miles Reber, Army liaison with the Senate. However, Reber then got back to Cohn saying this was in error and that a commission wasn't going to happen. This persuaded Cohn that somebody in high places was watching over Schine, but not in a friendly manner. (Adding to these misgivings was the discovery that General Reber was the brother of Sam Reber, one of those with whom Cohn and Schine had clashed on their foray to Europe.)

While all this was going on, the Monmouth probe was grinding forward, and John Adams commenced his role as liaison between the committee and Bob Stevens. (Adams assumed his new position on October 1.) Thereafter, Adams and Cohn, and to a lesser extent subcommittee executive director Frank Carr, were in continuing contact on the basis of apparent friendship, with much hanging out together, attendance at prize fights, frequent dinners, and other forms of socializing. A similar if less intense bonhomie would develop between Stevens and McCarthy, and between Stevens and committee staffers—including a series of contacts with Schine himself and also with his family.

In these conditions, there were many informal off-the-record conversations among all the parties on a host of topics: Monmouth, Lawton, the review board, the status and activities of Schine, the linked cases of Peress and Zwicker, targets of other possible investigations. Who said what, who promised whom, who suggested a particular course of action, would in due course become sources of uncertainty and angry conflict.

Illustrative of both the original cordiality and later confusion were arrangements whereby Schine, while undergoing basic training at Fort Dix—yet another New Jersey Army post—would be given time off on nights and weekends to help wrap up committee business on which he was working. This was subject to the stipulation that such absences wouldn't interfere with Army training. Subsequently, the number of Schine's departures from the base, and whether he was really engaged in committee work rather than simply gadding about with Cohn, would be disputed fiercely.

The events that apparently turned good feelings into mortal combat occurred in January of 1954, when McCarthy made it plain he would press forward with the Monmouth probe and insist on calling members of the review board that had been reversing security suspensions at the complex. John Adams had done all he could to avert this but failed to get the job done. Accordingly, another and more powerful Adams, former New Hampshire governor Sherman Adams, top staffer in the Eisenhower White House, would enter the fray, moving it up to the highest levels. The result of this intervention would be the single most portentous episode in the entire McCarthy saga.

At a meeting in Herbert Brownell's office at the Department of Justice on January 21, John Adams, as he later testified, would give Brownell, Sherman Adams, Deputy Attorney General William Rogers, and other key officials (including U.N. Ambassador Lodge) a briefing on the Monmouth inquest, on what the counsel said were improper pressures from Cohn to get perks for Schine, and on Cohn's alleged threats against the Army. Having heard a fair amount of this, Sherman Adams told the counsel to put it all in writing so as to have a proper record. The next day, John Adams would begin compiling what would be known as the Army "chronology of events," concerning the activities of Cohn, the treatment of Schine, and related views and actions of McCarthy.[4]

While writing this account over the next few weeks, John Adams would share portions of it with members of the press corps—including columnist Joseph Alsop, Phillip Potter of the *Baltimore Sun,* Murray Marder of the *Washington Post,* and Homer Bigart of the *New York Herald Tribune.* Allusions to the chronology and its assertions soon began appearing in news columns. On March 10, the Army would make the indictment public, and thereafter proffer formal charges based on the John Adams version of what had happened. The gist of the complaint was that Cohn, with McCarthy's acquiescence, had used the bludgeon of committee power to get favors for Dave Schine. A further implication was that the Monmouth probe and calling of the loyalty board were efforts to exert such pressure, rather than a proper investigation.[5]

Alerted by press leaks to what was coming, McCarthy and Cohn had readied their defenses. The day after the Army document appeared, the duo held a press conference in which they made countercharges of their own, backed with a series of eleven internal office memos giving their version of the conflict. Their story was that the Monmouth inquest was legitimate and sorely needed, but unwelcome at the Pentagon, and that Schine was being used as a pawn to get the hearings canceled—the mirror image of the Army charges.

With dueling accusations now before the country, a Senate inquest was convened to sort out the muddle. Such was the genesis of the Army-McCarthy hearings that ran from April 1954 until the middle of June, filled 3,000 pages of printed transcript, and were viewed by an estimated daily TV audience of 20 million people. In the course of this inquiry, the public would hear much about Dave Schine, Fort Monmouth, General Lawton, and other topics, some far afield from the ostensible purpose of the hearings. TV viewers would get a close-up look at Joe McCarthy, Robert Stevens, Roy Cohn, John Adams, Stuart Symington, Everett Dirksen, Karl Mundt, and a then-unheralded lawyer from Boston named Joseph Welch, acting as special counsel to Stevens-Adams.

As the PSI was at the crossroads of the conflicting charges, it was decided the panel should conduct the hearings but that McCarthy as a party at interest would for the time being step aside as chairman. The new temporary chairman would be Mundt, second-ranking Republican on the subcommittee. To take McCarthy's place, the GOP named Henry Dworshak, a conservative backbencher from Idaho and member of the parent Government Ops committee. All other members of the subcommittee remained as in the previous lineup. Chosen after an extensive search to serve as chief counsel *pro tem* was Ray Jenkins, a flamboyant Tennessee lawyer of bulldog demeanor, recommended for the job by Dirksen.

As the hearings cranked up toward the end of April, the venerable Senate Caucus Room would again be packed with spectators, press, TV cameras, kibitzers from the Hill, and a glittering array of Army brass showing support for Stevens-Adams. The Army side went first, in an effort to document the alleged efforts of Cohn to get unwarranted perks for Schine. The opening witness was Gen. Reber, the Army liaison with the Senate, who testified that Cohn had been persistent, to the point of being a common nuisance, in repeatedly calling Reber's office about getting Schine a commission.

Reber was followed on the stand by Gen. Walter Bedell Smith, at this time with the State Department, who also happened to be an acquaintance of Cohn's. Smith testified that Cohn had come to see him about the possibility that Schine was a victim of discrimination, and that they also discussed the prospect of Schine's hooking up with the CIA, which Smith had previously headed. Both generals sketched a picture of Cohn as avidly bird-dogging the case of Schine, thus buttressing the Army charges.

However, the testimony of Reber and Smith also supported, in unexpected fashion, the contrasting views of Cohn-McCarthy. Asked if McCarthy had exerted any illicit pressure on behalf of Schine, for instance, Reber said he hadn't. Similarly asked if Cohn had made any "improper effort to induce or intimidate you to give Private Schine a commission," Reber answered, "None of Mr. Cohn's calls to me were of that nature." The problem, he said, wasn't "because of the language but because of the frequency." Smith would likewise testify about two Schine-related talks he had with Cohn:

> JENKINS: Did you regard those requests by Mr. Cohn on behalf of Schine as
> extraordinary or unusual or improper?
> SMITH: I did not.
> JENKINS: State whether or not on either of those occasions you felt that Mr.
> Cohn was being too persistent or was trying to high pressure anyone.
> SMITH: Not me, sir.
>
> . . .
>
> JENKINS: This final question: Do you regard anything said by Mr. Cohn to
> you on either of the two occasions you mentioned as being improper?
> SMITH: I do not.[6]

Thus on net balance, and to the surprise and probable dismay of many, these Army witnesses were actually helpful to Cohn-McCarthy. Their pro-McCarthy impact was, however, diluted when the senator abruptly raised with Reber his brother's status with HICOG, his encounter there with Cohn and Schine, and dismissal from his post for alleged security reasons. These questions were ruled relevant by counsel Jenkins as going to possible motives on the part of General Reber in handling the question of a Schine commission, but were otherwise widely viewed as an unfair personal onslaught. It would be the first of several McCarthy problems of this nature.

Following these warm-ups, the main Army witness to take the stand was Stevens, who would testify for fourteen days, spelling out the Army's case against McCarthy-Cohn and being subjected to withering cross-examination by Jenkins.* As all observers were agreed, the secretary's performance was not impressive. He seemed to have trouble getting his story straight and had great difficulty with specifics. His testimony featured many vague answers, memory lapses, and circumlocutions before the facts of any matter could be established. This was especially true of the Cohn-McCarthy contention that Stevens (and John Adams in his behalf) had wanted to get the Monmouth hearings canceled.

This Jenkins interrogation ran on for several pages, as Stevens at first denied any such intention, then by degrees admitted he was opposed to hearings of "this type" (meaning public), then at last conceded that, indeed, he wanted to get the probe suspended. The admission came, however, in circuitous, hesitant fashion:

"I said I didn't like this constant hammering in the headlines of the Army, because I thought it gave a picture to the public of considerable espionage or spying at Fort Monmouth, which was not in accordance with the facts. That is what I objected to. I therefore wanted to handle the job myself, but I specifically said, and I think you will find it in my testimony, that I wanted to make progress reports to Senator McCarthy, and that if we weren't doing the job right, I assumed that he would come right back into the picture."[7]

To be able to "come back into the picture," of course, McCarthy would first have had to step out of it, which is exactly what McCarthy and Cohn said Stevens-Adams were after. Thus, while taking the long way around the barn, Stevens was here confessing that, yes, he did want the hearings halted. This was a ten-strike for McCarthy.

As to the other side of the issue—the alleged threats by McCarthy-Cohn to do unspeakable things to the Army—the Jenkins questions were relentless. They brought out the point that during the period in which supposedly horrific pressures were being wielded against the Army, Stevens and John Adams had been on the friendliest possible terms with McCarthy, Cohn, and others from the panel. Stevens had, for example, visited with Schine's parents in their home, attended a party put on by Cohn, been driven in the Schine family Cadillac by Dave Schine, and had extended to McCarthy staffers the hospitality of a club he belonged to in Manhattan.

How, Jenkins wanted to know, did all this nonstop socializing stack up with the tale of bloodcurdling menace recited in the Army charges? If Stevens-Adams felt so terribly threatened, why were they on such cordial terms with McCarthy, Cohn, and Schine? Didn't it really add up to a concerted effort to ingratiate the Army with the committee? And wasn't the obvious purpose of

---

* It was in these opening sessions that McCarthy became known for his droning interjection "point of order," the device by which it was possible to get the floor. Others used it also, but none so frequently as McCarthy.

that to get the panel to call off its hearings? The Stevens response to all of which was that he always tried to have good relations with Congress (though no other cases of such unusual conduct were on record).

The Army did somewhat better when John Adams took the stand and spelled out his basis for saying McCarthy-Cohn, especially Cohn, had been abusive toward his clients. Adams recounted episodes in which he said Cohn had blown his stack, threatened to "wreck" the Army, and otherwise allegedly used the power of the committee to exert improper pressure. This would be followed by other Army officials who sought to document the special treatment given the notorious private. A graphic feature of this session was a display of charts purporting to show the absences of Schine from Fort Dix as compared to the number of leaves enjoyed by other privates—in which respect the discrepancy in Schine's favor seemed to be immense.

These charts, however, turned out to be of peculiar nature, and to observers following matters closely may have hurt the Stevens-Adams case more than they helped it. There was no question that Schine had many more passes than did the average private, as was implicit in the agreement reached with Stevens. However, Army graphic specialists weren't content to show this, but enhanced the contrast to make it seem even more enormous than it was. This was done by marking the absences of Schine with heavy black ink, explained in small white lettering, but showing the absences of a hypothetical average private in the opposite manner—white backdrop with small black letters.

As the rest of the chart in both instances was also white, the optical effect was a mass of black markings for Schine as against a chart that looked almost entirely white for others. This was further enhanced by the blacking out on Schine's chart of eight full days that elapsed between his induction and his arrival at Fort Dix. (See page 550.) Viewers seeing the two exhibits at the hearing or on TV would thus get an impression of Schine's absences far greater than the ample number he in fact was granted. When McCarthy and chairman Mundt made an issue of this, Army spokesmen said they had been in a hurry to get the graphics finished and perhaps had erred in showing the two cases in such contrasting formats.[8]

After all this was completed, Cohn and McCarthy would each take the stand and give a totally different version of the matter, from amiable start to dismal finish. The most knowledgeable testimony was that of Cohn, who had been at ground zero of events, the champion of Schine and, until near the end, in close contact with John Adams. Among other things, Cohn filled in certain blanks pertaining to the investigation of the Army and touched on several topics reviewed in previous chapters. He for instance alluded to the order of December 1944, discussed in Chapter 6, authorizing commissions in the Army for members of the Communist Party. Later he—and McCarthy—would refer to the question of possible pro-Soviet influence in G-2.[9]

BLACK AND WHITE

Army graphics showing Private David Schine's absences from Fort Dix, compared with those of the "average trainee." Note the contrasting formats used, and the emphasis given to Schine's absences by use of heavy black boxes—including eight full days in early November 1953 before he ever reported to Fort Dix.

RECORD OF ABSENCES AND TELEPHONE MESSAGES TO THE COMMANDING GENERAL, 9TH INFANTRY DIVISION, WHILE ASSIGNED TO FORT DIX, NEW JERSEY

FOR THE PERIOD 3 NOVEMBER 1953 TO 16 JANUARY 1954

NOVEMBER

SUNDAY	MONDAY	TUESDAY	WEDNESDAY	THURSDAY	FRIDAY	SATURDAY
1	2	3 SCHINE INDUCTED IN N Y	4 ON TEMPORARY DUTY IN N Y	5 ON TEMPORARY DUTY IN N Y	6 ON TEMPORARY DUTY IN N Y	7 ON TEMPORARY DUTY IN N Y
8 ON TEMPORARY DUTY IN N Y	9 ON TEMPORARY DUTY IN N Y	10 REPORTED IN NY FOR TRANSFER TO DIX, ASSIGNED TO RECEPTION CENTER	11 COHN & CARR CALLED ON GEN RYAN TO SEE SCHINE VISITED HIM AT RECEPTION CENTER (OFF KP AT 2 PM)	12 LAVENIA CALLED FOR WEEKEND PASS	13 ON PASS AFTER DUTY HOURS	14 ON PASS ALL DAY
15 ON PASS TO 10 PM	16	17 EVENING PASS FROM RECEPTION CENTER FOR DINNER WITH SENATOR MCCARTHY AT MC GUIRE OFFICERS MESS UNTIL 9:50 PM	18 LAVENIA CALLED GEN RYAN FOR PASS UNTIL 23 NOV	19 ASSIGNED TO 'K' CO, 47TH REGT FOR TRAINING ON PASS AT 4:15 PM	20 ON PASS ALL DAY	21 ON PASS ALL DAY
22 ON PASS TO 11:15 PM	23 BASIC TRAINING FOR 'K' CO STARTED	24 COHN CALLED LT BLOUNT FOR THANKSGIVING PASS	25 ON PASS AT 6:05 PM	26 ON PASS UNTIL 11:00 PM	27 COHN OR LAVENIA CALLED FOR WEEKEND PASS	28 ON PASS AT 12:00 PM
29 ON PASS UNTIL MIDNIGHT	30					

DECEMBER

SUNDAY	MONDAY	TUESDAY	WEDNESDAY	THURSDAY	FRIDAY	SATURDAY
		1 COHN OR LAVENIA CALLED FOR EVENING PASS TO TRENTON ON PASS FROM 5 PM TO 11:45 PM	2	3 COHN OR LAVENIA CALLED FOR EVENING PASS ON PASS FROM 6 TO 11:00 PM	4 COHN CALLED FOR OVERNIGHT PASS AND WEEKEND PASS ON PASS AT 6:30 PM	5 ON PASS TO 4:55 AM ON PASS AT 11 AM
6 ON PASS UNTIL MIDNIGHT	7 LAVENIA CALLED FOR EVENING PASS TO TRENTON ON PASS FROM 6 TO 10:45 PM	8 LAVENIA CALLED TO MEET SCHINE ON POST AT 5 PM GEN RYAN TOLD SCHINE NO MORE WEEK NIGHT PASSES. SCHINE LEFT KP DETAIL ON PASS TO 10 AM & GOT OUT OF 1 PM TRAINING FILM	9	10 COMMITTEE CALLED TO HAVE SCHINE MEET JULIANA ON POST AT 5 PM	11 COHN OR LAVENIA CALLED FOR WEEKEND PASS	12 ON PASS AT 12:10 PM
13 ON PASS UNTIL 12 MIDNIGHT	14 COMMITTEE CALLED TO HAVE SCHINE MEET LAVENIA ON POST AT 5 PM	15 COMMITTEE CALLED TO HAVE SCHINE MEET JULIANA ON POST AT 5 PM	16 COMMITTEE CALLED TO HAVE SCHINE MEET COHN ON POST AT 5 PM	17	18	19 ON PASS AT 4:30 PM, PER COMPANY POLICY
20 ON PASS UNTIL 11:05 PM	21	22	23	24 ON PASS AT 11:30 AM FOR CHRISTMAS WEEKEND PER COMPANY POLICY	25 ON PASS ALL DAY	26 ON PASS ALL DAY
27 ON PASS UNTIL 10:50 PM	28	29	30	31 ABSENT ABOUT 10:45 AM COHN CALLED RE TELEGRAM ON PASS PER GEN RYAN ABOUT 3 PM		

JANUARY

SUNDAY	MONDAY	TUESDAY	WEDNESDAY	THURSDAY	FRIDAY	SATURDAY
					1 ON PASS ALL DAY (VOCG)	2 ON PASS ALL DAY (VOCG)
3 ON PASS TO 10:50 PM (VOCG)	4 COHN CALLED TO ASK WHY AN INVESTIGATION OF SCHINE'S NEW YEAR ABSENCE COMMITTEE CALLED SCHINE TO CALL CARR	5 SUBCOMMITTEE STAFF MEMBER CALLED WITH MESSAGE FOR SCHINE TO CALL CARR OR COHN	6	7 SUBCOMMITTEE STAFF MEMBER CALLED WITH MESSAGE FOR SCHINE TO CALL LAVENIA	8 ON PASS AT 5:15 PM PER COMPANY POLICY	9 ON PASS TO 11:25 PM PER COMPANY POLICY COHN CALLED LT. BLOUNT. CARR CALLED ADAMS RE KP FOR SCHINE TOMORROW
10 ON PASS AT 11 AM PER REGIMENTAL COMMANDER KP DETAIL AVOIDED	11 ON PASS TO 6 AM PER REGIMENTAL COMMANDER	12	13 COHN CALLED TO REQUEST SCHINE AVOID END OF TRAINING CEREMONY REFUSED BY GEN RYAN	14	15	16 SCHINE CALLED LT BLOUNT FOR AUTHORITY TO LEAVE POST EARLY. GRANTED BY GEN RYAN *TRANSFERRED TO CAMP GORDON

Source: McCarthy Papers II

TYPICAL AUTHORIZED ABSENCES OF AN AVERAGE TRAINEE UNDERGOING
TRAINING CYCLE WHILE ASSIGNED TO COMPANY K, 47TH INFANTRY REGIMENT,
FORT DIX, NEW JERSEY.
FOR THE PERIOD 3 NOVEMBER 1953 TO 16 JANUARY 1954

NOVEMBER

SUNDAY	MONDAY	TUESDAY	WEDNESDAY	THURSDAY	FRIDAY	SATURDAY
1	2	3	4	5	6	7
8	9	10	11	12	13	14
15	16	17	18	19	20	21
22	23	24	25	26	27	28
29	30					

DECEMBER

SUNDAY	MONDAY	TUESDAY	WEDNESDAY	THURSDAY	FRIDAY	SATURDAY
		1	2	3	4	5
6	7	8	9	10	11	12
13	14	15	16	17	18	19 ON PASS AT 5:00 P.M. PER COMPANY POLICY
20 ON PASS UNTIL MIDNIGHT	21	22	23	24 ON PASS AT 11:30 A.M. PER COMPANY POLICY	25 ON PASS ALL DAY	26 ON PASS ALL DAY
27 ON PASS UNTIL MIDNIGHT	28	29	30	31 ON PASS AT 11:30 A.M. PER COMPANY POLICY		

ALL TRAINEES AUTHORIZED EITHER CHRISTMAS OR NEW YEARS PASS, BUT NOT BOTH.

JANUARY

SUNDAY	MONDAY	TUESDAY	WEDNESDAY	THURSDAY	FRIDAY	SATURDAY
					1 ON PASS ALL DAY	2 ON PASS ALL DAY
3 ON PASS UNTIL MIDNIGHT	4	5	6	7	8 ON PASS AT 5:00 P.M. PER COMPANY POLICY	9 ON PASS ALL DAY
10 ON PASS UNTIL MIDNIGHT	11	12	13	14	15	16

Though these references were brief, and indicated Cohn-McCarthy had not yet nailed down all the facts, they were correct in substance. They made the point that attempted Communist infiltration of the Army was not a fantasy dreamed up by McCarthy but an issue of long standing. (Likewise, Cohn-McCarthy would refer to the infiltration of OSS in World War II, which helped explain their collateral interest in the CIA, inheritor of the foreign intelligence mission, along with many staffers from the wartime unit.)

As to the conduct of Schine, Cohn stoutly if somewhat implausibly maintained that, during all his nighttime and weekend absences, the inductee had been working on committee business, not carousing in New York nightclubs (this even on New Year's Eve), all per the entente with Stevens. These comments were viewed with obvious skepticism by committee members. However, there were again countervailing statements by Army spokesmen that Schine, contrary to his playboy image, had completed his basic training in proper fashion and was considered a good soldier (and excellent marksman in the bargain).

Cohn's weakest moments on the stand concerned a blowup at Fort Monmouth when he had been barred from entry to the secret labs there and allegedly spouted curses against the Army. Though denying any "vituperative" language, he admitted he was angry and had expressed himself as such. Army witnesses were more explicit about his loss of temper and said he made threats about retaliation for the slight he suffered. All this was extremely negative for Cohn, but also had a downside for the Army: It had nothing to do with Schine, and thus had only marginal relevance to the subject of the hearings.

If Cohn was the most knowledgeable McCarthy witness, seemingly the most impressive to the panel was Frank Carr. The longtime FBI agent, taciturn and stolid, had merely casual interest in Schine—this mostly concerned with seeing that the draftee's committee work got finished—and there was no evidence from anyone, even John Adams, that Carr had done anything to get improper privileges for Schine.*

Carr was, however, most definite in backing Cohn on key elements of the conflict. One of these concerned a much-talked-of Manhattan lunch and car ride of mid-December 1953 in which, according to John Adams, Cohn had harangued him about Schine while McCarthy and Carr sat by in embarrassed silence. In fact, said Carr, the Cohn harangue was about an entirely different topic—the crackdown on General Lawton for having cooperated with the panel. (Cohn and McCarthy said the same.) As seen, General Lawton was a subject Adams and Stevens weren't eager to have brought before the nation.

Given the wide currency of the Adams version of this episode as a Cohn filibuster about Schine, the categorical statements to the contrary by Carr are

---

*Carr would eventually be dropped as a target of the Army charges, in exchange for the similar dropping of Cohn-McCarthy countercharges against Defense official H. Struve Hensel.

worth a bit of notice. ". . . it was," he said, "a monologue by Mr. Cohn . . . on the subject of Gen. Lawton and reprisals made against persons who helped the subcommittee in some way. *Mr. Adams kept trying to interject himself by making statements which I recall, in substance, as this: 'Let's talk about Schine.' Mr. Cohn replied, rather heatedly, 'I don't want to talk about Schine. Let's talk about Lawton.' . . . Mr. Adams tried on several occasions to swing the subject to Schine, but it never got there . . . Mr. Cohn wouldn't talk about Schine. He wanted to talk about Lawton."*[10] (Emphasis added.)

Who, in this maelstrom of conflicting statements, was telling the truth to a baffled nation? The whole thing boiled down to whose word was to be accepted. There was documentary evidence of a sort, but this was itself the subject of many questions. In particular, the eleven memos by McCarthy and his staffers, mostly chronicling contacts with John Adams, were viewed with sardonic skepticism by Army lawyer Welch and others. They seemed too pat and too convenient. In his cross-examination of McCarthy secretary Mary Driscoll, who had done the typing, and also of Frank Carr, Welch voiced serious doubts about the authenticity of these memos.

By his questions, Welch suggested the memos were written after the fact to substantiate the McCarthy version of the story. (There was later reason to believe this was true, at least with certain of the memos.) And, quite apart from when they were written, there was an obvious problem with the memos: They represented strictly the McCarthy version of events and could hardly be expected to include a record of any threats or other malfeasance by committee forces. They were thus no more credible on their face than the live testimony of McCarthy staffers.[11]

Over against the McCarthy memos was the chronology written by John Adams, which had similar evidential problems. This professed to be a phase-by-phase and sometimes day-to-day account of pressures and threats by McCarthy and Cohn to get privileges for Schine. But this was just as much *parti pris* as the McCarthy memos, well-shaded with subjective comment and plainly written after the fact—having been compiled in early 1954 about events that in most cases occurred months before then. (A point made by former Ike staffer William Ewald, who had access to the relevant papers on the Army side of the confrontation.)[12]

Obviously needed in these conditions was some impartial record of what really happened, drawn from a source whose validity wasn't subject to challenge. But in a he said/he said debate concerning private conversations, could such an account exist? Somewhat improbably, the answer was "Yes." A source of contemporaneous and accurate data, as opposed to self-serving memos, did exist and had been in the possession of the Army all along: a series of monitored phone calls involving most of the key players and discussing most of the relevant issues.

This store of data had been recorded by an Army stenographic expert who listened in on the office calls of Stevens and prepared transcripts of what was said on both ends of the phone line. The existence of these monitored calls would be initially brought out by Jenkins and confirmed by Stevens. Subsequently, Army lawyer Welch moved to introduce material from these transcripts—specifically, a talk with Stevens in which McCarthy downplayed the importance of Schine, said he didn't want any favors for him, and said Cohn was "completely unreasonable" on the topic.

This phone call, while showing McCarthy *not* seeking privileges for Schine, had the advantage for the Army of driving a wedge between McCarthy and Cohn—using McCarthy's words to help indict his counsel and deflating Cohn's contention that Schine was essential to the committee's labors. It's thus easy to see why Welch and Stevens would have wanted this conversation in the record. There were, however, serious dangers for the Army in this *démarche,* which Joe McCarthy was quick to notice.

While condemning the practice of monitored calls, McCarthy said he would consent to having this transcript read into the hearing record, provided it was indeed a verbatim transcript, and that *all other* monitored phone calls among the relevant parties were likewise entered. This was backed up by Democratic members of the panel. "We have the right," said Henry Jackson, "to subpoena all of these records that are relevant to this hearing." John McClellan put it as a motion, which was unanimously voted, that "all memoranda, all documents, all notes of monitored conversations as between the parties in this controversy, and all others that are relevant . . . be subpoenaed."[13]

This wasn't at all what Welch and Co. were after—was, indeed, the reverse. The monitored calls were extensive, including not only conversations between Stevens and McCarthy but further talks with other members of the Senate, various members of the Army, and officials of the Ike administration—conversations Stevens-Adams and those above them by no means wanted in the record. By opening up this Pandora's box, Army counsel Welch had blundered, and by so doing all but demolished the substantive case he had been building for his clients.

In the event, not all of the monitored phone calls would be obtained, but enough were placed in the record to torpedo the main contentions of the Army. Together with the testimony of Stevens, the calls showed the allegations of dire threats, intolerable pressure, and general hostility toward the Army by McCarthy-Cohn to be completely unsupported (nor, as brought out by Dirksen, did they reveal any vituperative or abusive language by Cohn). Instead, the calls reflected much congeniality and good feeling among the parties, with little or nothing by way of pressure from the McCarthy faction.

On this point, we can hardly do better than quote Army counsel Adams, who would write of the monitored conversations: "In fact, the transcribed calls favored McCarthy's side . . . Stevens' calls had been recorded all along, *and they showed more placation from the Army Secretary than pressure from McCarthy . . . There was certainly no smoking gun in the recorded calls that could be aimed at McCarthy or Cohn.*" (Adams would conclude this comment by quoting the *Washington Post*'s opinion that, "if anything they [the calls] were more damaging to the Army than to the subcommittee.")[14] (Emphasis added.)

While details to this effect were several, of particular interest was a March 8, 1954, conversation between Stevens and Stuart Symington, Democratic member of the panel. Rumors about the chronology had at that time abounded, and Symington was anxious to get a copy. The conversation, McCarthy argued, showed Symington's attempts to concert an alliance with Stevens against McCarthy-Cohn, which was certainly true enough.* But the transcript was still more suggestive in showing the views of Stevens on the main issues of the hearings. When Symington prodded him about problems with McCarthy and his staff, Stevens had answered:

> *I personally think that anything in that line would be very much exaggerated . . .* I am the Secretary, and I have had some talks with the committee and the chairman, and so on, and by and large as far as the treatment of me is concerned, *I have no personal complaint.* When he got after Zwicker, of course, then I hollered, but as far as I personally am concerned, *I don't have a lot of stuff so far as my contact with Joe, or the committee, is concerned.*[15] (Emphasis added.)

This previously off-the-record Stevens comment was made just two days before the administration, in his name, made its first public charges against McCarthy-Cohn, alleging a sinister plot to force special treatment for Dave Schine. The contrast between these charges of threat and pressure and the Stevens statement that he had "no personal complaint" could not have been more vivid.

It was of course possible that Stevens was being guarded in these comments and that they weren't his full and frank opinion. The fact remained that, in the record of conversations provided by the Army's own transcripts, Stevens was saying the exact reverse of what was in the Army charges. Likewise, there were no disclosures from the transcripts otherwise that sustained the Stevens-Adams accusations. Had those accusations been true, there should have been some evidence of it in the Army's records, but there wasn't.

Sen. Charles Potter (R.-Mich.) would later say the main contentions of

---

*In particular, as reflected in the monitored calls, and as McCarthy brought out in detail, Symington had recommended that Stevens seek counsel in the matter from leading Democrat Clark Clifford. As Clifford had been a high-level adviser to President Truman—and, as seen, a key participant then in security cases such as that of Robert Oppenheimer—he arguably was not the best counselor on such issues from a Republican standpoint.

McCarthy and the Army were both borne out by the hearings. A more considered judgment would seem to be that both sides were, in varying degree, *inaccurate* in their charges. What actually happened, stated early on by Jenkins and supported by the monitored phone calls, was the opposite of what the Army contended—but also different from the countercharges of McCarthy. Quite obviously, as Stevens admitted, he wanted to have the Monmouth hearings suspended. And having got Schine in their clutches, the Stevens-Adams team believed they had the leverage to do this.

That leverage, however, was wielded mainly in positive rather than negative terms—as an inducement rather than a threat: In handling Schine with velvet gloves, the Army faction hoped to get better cooperation from McCarthy. In this respect, Cohn's interest in the status of Schine was undoubtedly less offensive to Stevens-Adams than they let on, since it suggested that a strategy focused on Schine might be just the ticket for winding down the hearings. It was never likely this would work, and it didn't, but the message conveyed by Cohn's solicitude for Schine could only have encouraged Stevens and Adams in such notions.

There was in sum no evidence that Roy Cohn took or threatened any investigative action against the Army to get privileges for Schine, still less that McCarthy did so. But by combining these subjects in tangled fashion, Cohn, assisted by John Adams, had created the impression that some such attempts were made and that the kid-glove treatment of Schine resulted from these efforts. And in political Washington, then as now, reality often ran second to perception.

CHAPTER 42

On Not Having Any Decency

HAD THE Army-McCarthy fracas been decided on its merits, McCarthy, though suffering plenty of setbacks, would have been declared the winner, and by a substantial margin. Most relevant to the official outcome, the Army conspicuously failed to prove that the Monmouth hearings, subpoenas for the Loyalty Board, or any other investigative effort by McCarthy-Cohn had any linkage to Dave Schine—the essence of the original charges.

Conversely, the appointed judges of the matter were agreed that Stevens-Adams did try to use the famous private as a pawn to get the Monmouth hearings canceled. This didn't mean Cohn was off the hook for having pestered people about Schine, but that these efforts, instead of causing the Monmouth probe, most probably encouraged Stevens-Adams in attempts to stop it. On these key points, the opinions of Republican and Democratic members weren't far apart, though differing in the stringency of their comments. The GOP majority put it this way:

> We find Mr. Cohn was unduly aggressive and persistent in the contacts he made with various officials in the executive department in regard to his friend and associate, Mr. Schine . . . We find, however, that the investigation at Fort Monmouth was not designed or conducted as a leverage to secure preferential treatment for G. David Schine . . . The evidence reasonably inspires the belief that Secretary Stevens and Mr. Adams made efforts to

terminate or influence the investigation and hearings at Fort Monmouth . . . We find that Mr. Adams, at least, made vigorous and diligent efforts when the subpoenas were issued for the Army Loyalty and Screening Board to halt this action by means of personal appeals to certain members of this committee . . .[1]

The view of the Democratic minority was only slightly different:

The record fully warrants the conclusion that Secretary Stevens and Mr. Adams did undertake to influence or induce the subcommittee to discontinue at least some parts of its investigation of the Army . . . We are convinced that Secretary Stevens and Mr. Adams were most apprehensive and deeply concerned about the subcommittee's investigation of the Army and were anxious to and did undertake to appease and placate Senator McCarthy and Mr. Cohn. Unwarranted special privileges and preferential treatment were accorded Private Schine . . . Mr. Cohn, without justification, knowingly and persistently sought and secured special privileges and preferential treatment for Private Schine. To secure such favor, he knowingly misrepresented the record of Private Schine's service to the Investigations Subcommittee. In doing so, he misused and abused the power of his office and brought disrepute to the subcommittee.[2]

Thus, as might be expected, the Democrats came down much harder on Cohn than did the GOP contingent. Yet, even here, it's worth observing, there was no finding that the Monmouth investigation was connected to the fate of Schine. Cohn, on the Democratic reading, had badly overstepped his bounds, allegedly misrepresenting Schine's worth to the committee, but that wasn't the reason for the probe of Monmouth.

If that had been all there was, the hearings, though messy, harmful, and a huge distraction from other labors, would have been accounted a victory for McCarthy. However, the truth of the original charges wasn't to be a crucial factor in rendering a verdict on the inquest, either then or later. Instead, extraneous topics would become decisive, elevating issues of style and manner above the claims of substance. To some extent this was accidental, and some of it was the doing of McCarthy's gruff comments and demeanor, off-putting to many in TV-land, but most of it was owing to the tactics and improvisational skills of Army Counsel Welch.

Joe Welch, thanks to these hearings, would take his place as one of the more memorable characters of the era, a Dickensian figure transplanted to the 1950s. From a study of his forensic methods, strange way of phrasing things, and self-conscious quaintness, it's obvious he was a consummate actor and that he approached the hearings in this spirit. Welch treated the whole affair as a kind of melodrama in which fact and reason were distinctly secondary to image and impression. Much of what he said and did was geared to this soap opera conception of the process.*

As it happened, there was good reason for this approach, beyond the tastes and aptitudes of Welch. He may or may not have been a genius in the courtroom, but he was nobody's fool and could see his client's case was deplorably weak—particularly after the collapse of Stevens. It's thus no surprise that, as events permitted, Welch spent as much time as possible on topics that had only slight relation, or none, to the substance of the hearings. Or that, once he got hold of such a topic, he wrung it dry for dramatic impact.

In pursuing these tactics, Welch was eminently successful—so much so that side issues he developed would be virtually the only things many viewers remembered from the hearings. Even today, people who know little else about the conflict are likely to know something of these digressions—one in particular that's always mentioned. Nor, as usual with McCarthy cases, are most history books much better—generally treating these Welch asides, with varying degrees of accuracy, as the main highlights of the proceedings. Three episodes featured in the standard treatments are instructive.

• *The "Doctored" Photo.* In cross-examining Robert Stevens, Counsel Ray Jenkins had hammered away at the friendly contacts between the Army Secretary and the McCarthy staffers, especially his several gestures of good will toward Schine. Such behavior, said Jenkins, matched oddly with the contention that McCarthy, Cohn and Co. were abusing the Army in dreadful fashion.

In preparing for this line of questions, Jenkins learned that Schine had a photograph of himself with Stevens taken at McGuire Air Force base, adjacent to Fort Dix, where Schine was stationed. Jenkins asked Schine to obtain this picture, to be used in examining Stevens. The next day, the picture was delivered to the McCarthy staff, prints made from it, and a copy given to Jenkins. The counsel then proceeded to wave this in front of Stevens and question him about it.

Unknown to Jenkins, the picture from Schine's office had included a third person besides Schine and Stevens—Col. Jack T. Bradley, the commanding officer of McGuire, on hand to welcome the Secretary to the air base. This print showed Bradley and Stevens bracketing Schine, left and right, as they posed on the airport tarmac. In the version supplied to Jenkins, the base commander

---

*Welch liked it to be known that he worked at a stand-up desk in the Victorian manner. As to his methods of expression, the following is a fairly typical passage: "Hearings on Saturday are . . . repulsive because the chair knows my lovely habit of going back to my home . . . I am just as opposed as the dickens to night sessions. But I have said before, mine is a small voice. If I have to do it, I will hitch up my suspenders one more notch, etc." Welch later used his acting talents to more constructive purpose, playing a judge in the Jimmy Stewart movie *Anatomy of a Murder.*

was cropped out, leaving only Schine and Stevens. The next day, having discovered the omission, Army Counsel Welch opened the hearings by charging "trick," "doctored photograph," and other expressions of shock and outrage.[3]

Thus began a marathon procession in which Stevens, Schine, Cohn, Jenkins, photographers, committee staffers, and others filed before the panel to tell what they knew about the photo. In the end, the situation was matter-of-factly explained by McCarthy aide Jim Juliana when, after others had been heard from at length, he was at last permitted to take the stand. Told Jenkins wanted "the picture of Schine and Stevens," Juliana said, he had sent the original to the Senate photo shop with this instruction, the picture was cropped accordingly, and the resulting print was delivered to Jenkins. End of story.

That, as Juliana made clear, was the sum and substance of the whole affair. However, there were some footnotes that made the photo of further interest. As it turned out, the picture in question had *already* been cropped by the military, before it ever got to Schine, excluding from the shot a fourth individual in the original lineup. This fourth person was McCarthy staffer Frank Carr, standing sideways to the others, at the end of the queue to the left of Colonel Bradley. Carr obviously wasn't meant to be featured in the shot, though he was gazing pensively toward the camera; somebody thus decided he wasn't essential to the photo and cropped him out. So the picture allegedly "doctored" by Jim Juliana was already "doctored" before the McCarthy staffers ever got it.[4]

For some reason, *this* cropping of the photo elicited no cries of "trick" from Counsel Welch. Apparently, removing somebody from a picture was a dastardly deed only if this had some linkage to McCarthy. Done by a Pentagon photo lab, it was perfectly okay, not worthy of a moment's notice. Of course, as is well known, such "doctoring" of photos occurs on a daily basis at newspapers, magazines, and TV studios across the land deciding on key aspects of a wide-shot photo. Exactly the same thing had occurred with the Army version of the photo wielded by Joe Welch, and with Jim Juliana and the Senate technicians when told Jenkins wanted a picture of Schine and Stevens. The hassle stirred up by Welch was sound and fury over nothing.

Even this, however, wasn't the bottom line about the photo. Welch persisted in calling the Army version a "group picture," as if Schine and Stevens had bumped into each other in a milling subway crowd or some other gathering of the masses. But in the Army version of the shot, the only other person in the "group" was Colonel Bradley, *the commander of the air base*—not exactly a random stranger who happened to wander before the camera. His presence did nothing to change the point Jenkins was making—that Schine, a mere private, was being treated with utmost cordiality at the highest military levels. (Indeed, the fact that Schine was photographed standing *between* Bradley and Stevens, at the dead center of the Army version, emphasized the point more strongly.)

And, whether Bradley was in the shot or not, nothing could change the fact that Private Schine was indeed photographed cheek by jowl with Stevens.

• *The "Purloined Letter."* Fairly early in the hearings, McCarthy produced the two-and-a-quarter-page memo received from an Army intelligence officer the year before, relating to the security scene at Monmouth. As noted, this had been excerpted from a longer, fifteen-page memorandum sent to Army intelligence by the FBI, summarizing security data on Aaron Coleman and others at the Monmouth complex.

For obvious reasons, the contents of this memo would have been intensely relevant to the hearings. But these contents would never be entered in the record. Instead, at the insistence of Welch, abetted by some members of the committee and a disapproving letter from Eisenhower Justice, the document was explicitly barred as evidence on the points at issue. The data it contained about security risks at Monmouth, it seemed, were of zero interest. Instead, the main point stressed by Welch, hammered at from several angles, was how McCarthy came to have the document in his possession. "I have an absorbing curiosity," said the Army lawyer, "to know how in the dickens you got hold of it."[5] That was, per Welch, the all-important issue about the memo.

As with the "doctored photo," this Welch sally kicked off a prolonged discussion of what he called "the purloined letter." Logically considered, there was no reason his "absorbing curiosity" should have been quenched by McCarthy, and plenty of reasons that it shouldn't. McCarthy was the duly elected head of a Senate investigating committee charged with ferreting out official malfeasance, and in that capacity had many such data confided to him. As acting chairman Mundt pointed out, it was no business of temporary Army Counsel Welch to know who supplied the document to McCarthy, and very much the business of McCarthy not to tell him.

Though thus instructed by the chairman, Welch persisted in his efforts to find out who gave the document to McCarthy. In this endeavor he used one of his favored gambits, which was, after an elaborate and usually pious buildup, to implore the witness, please, please, sir, do the right thing here, as doing the right thing is so awfully important. His exchanges with McCarthy to this effect would go as follows:

> WELCH: Senator McCarthy, when you took the stand of course you understood that you were going to be asked about this letter, did you not?
> McCARTHY: I assumed that would be the subject.
> ...
> WELCH: Did you understand you would be asked the source?
> McCARTHY: ... I never try to read the minds of the senators to know what they will ask you.

• • •

WELCH: Could I have the oath that you took read back slowly by the reporter?

MUNDT: Mr. Welch, that does not seem to be an appropriate question. You were present. You took the oath yourself. He took the same oath you took.

WELCH: The oath included a promise, a solemn promise by you to tell the truth, comma, the whole truth, comma, and nothing but the truth. Is that correct, sir?

McCARTHY: Mr. Welch, you are not the first individual that tried to get me to betray the confidence and give out the names of my informants. You will be no more successful than those who have tried in the past, period.

WELCH: I'm only asking you, sir, did you realize when you took that oath that you were making a solemn promise to tell the whole truth to this committee?

McCARTHY: I understand the oath, Mr. Welch.

• • •

WELCH: . . . Then tell who delivered the document to you.

McCARTHY: The answer is no. You will not get that information.

And so on and so forth, until the whole line of questioning was ruled out of order by both Counsel Jenkins and Chairman Mundt. This ruling, as Mundt put it, was "sustained by an unbroken precedent so far as he knew [that] Senate investigating committees who come in contact with confidential information are not required to disclose the source of their information."*[6]

Linked to McCarthy's possession of the letter were two other Welchian sidebars. One was a suggestion that the two-and-a-quarter-page memo was—like the "doctored" photo—a "perfect phony" foisted on the committee by the devious McCarthy. Welch sought to develop this idea in interrogation of Robert Collier, a Jenkins aide who had discussed the memo with FBI Director Hoover. In this confab with Hoover, Collier had learned that the memo was in fact a condensation of a longer FBI report, not an identical copy. On this point the questioning went as follows:

WELCH: Mr. Collier, as I understand your testimony this document that I hold in my hand is a carbon copy of precisely nothing, is that right?

---

*This style of interrogation might be called, for want of a better term, "John Stewart Service syndrome." As has been seen, the fact that Service had absconded with confidential papers and handed these over to the Communist Philip Jaffe was of small concern to high officials, who dismissed the matter as an "indiscretion," kept Service on the payroll, and rigged the grand jury process to protect him. However, when somebody in the government leaked information *about* John Service to McCarthy, that called for instant firing. Communists running barefoot through official papers were no big deal, but informing McCarthy about such matters was a scandal. In the case of Monmouth, with obvious differences in detail, the identical drill would be repeated.

COLLIER: I will say that Mr. Hoover informed me that it is not a carbon copy of a memorandum prepared or sent by the FBI.

WELCH: Let us have it straight from the shoulder. So far as you know, it is a carbon copy of precisely nothing.

COLLIER: So far as I know, it is, yes, but that is only a conclusion.

WELCH: You just told us it is a carbon copy of precisely nothing, haven't you?

COLLIER: I have said it is not a copy of a document in the FBI file. I will not say it is a copy of nothing because if it was typed as a carbon there must have been an original.[7]

Having thus said thrice over the document was "a carbon copy of precisely nothing," Welch then reversed directions, describing the memo as too "hot" to be entered in the record and refusing even to read it. To do so, he said, would be a terrible breach of security regulations, and he would never, ever do that. His tribute to his own rectitude in such matters was emphatic.

"I have," said Welch, "higher standards in respect to my own conduct in respect to these documents than the senator and his staff does [*sic*]. I do not think it is proper for Mr. Collier to read it and he has declined to read it. I do not think it is proper for Mr. Welch to read it and he has declined to read it. I await with much interest the Senator's [McCarthy's] explanation of how it reached his hands and whether he read it."[8]

All of this, however, was fustian, as McCarthy—who had read the memo— quite lucidly explained it. In the condensed format, he noted, all information that might reveal FBI sources and methods, and specific data on the suspects, had been deleted. Thus, no security breach could occur from simply reading the bobtailed version. The sole but significant point established by the memo was that the FBI had duly warned the Army about the problem of Aaron Coleman and others in the Monmouth setup. This was of course a point Welch and Co. wanted to obscure—the sideshow about how McCarthy got the memo, and its allegedly phony nature, helping to achieve this.

In fact, the Collier testimony and other evidence in the record made it plain the two-and-a-quarter-page document was definitely not a "phony." Collier said the shorter memo covered the identical subject matter as did the original FBI report and, equally to the point, was verbatim as to phrasing—with the exception that the security information on the suspects was deleted.* Far from being a "perfect phony," as alleged by Welch, the document per Collier's

---

* As with the "doctored" photo, there were other Welchian solecisms that cried out for challenge. The most obvious of these is how he reconciled the very different positions he took within the span of a few minutes—that the memo was a "perfect phony" and "a carbon copy of precisely nothing," but that the mere act of possessing and reading it was a grave security dereliction. How reading a document that was a "perfect phony" and a "copy of precisely nothing" could violate security regulations Welch did not explain, nor was he asked to.

testimony was obviously the real McCoy.* As for the shortened format, such condensation of FBI reports—omitting certain sensitive data—was a common official practice. As earlier noted, there were hundreds of such condensed or paraphrased reports, based on Bureau information, in the security files at State, Commerce, the Civil Service Commission, and elsewhere.

Finally, McCarthy and Collier between them produced some other compelling facts about the bobtailed memo. An especially significant point was that the report bore the heading "Aaron Coleman—Espionage—R." As seen in the Owen Lattimore case, the "R" in such memoranda stood for "Russian." Beyond this, McCarthy reeled off a considerable list of other FBI reports on Monmouth, giving the dates on which they were provided, thus making it clear the Bureau's efforts to spotlight the problem had been persistent over a span of years since the latter 1940s.†

• *Fred Fisher.* Having thus exhibited his instinct for the capillary, Welch would outdo himself in a third notable episode of this nature—the matter of Frederick Fisher. Fisher was a young attorney from Welch's Boston law firm of Hale and Dorr, brought down to Washington to help prepare the case for Stevens-Adams. In getting ready for the hearings, Welch had asked Fisher if there were anything in his background that could prove embarrassing to the Army.

Well, yes, said Fisher, there was. He had been a member of the National Lawyers Guild, which was indeed a problem. As the Guild had the year before been branded by Attorney General Herbert Brownell as the "legal mouthpiece" of the Communist Party, and before that by the House Committee on Un-American Activities as the party's "legal bulwark," it was decided such past membership would be an incapacitating factor in hearings so heavily devoted to issues of subversion.‡ Fisher was sent home to Boston.

Nonetheless, his name would show up in the hearings, as Welch was cross-examining Roy Cohn in what would be a famous confrontation. This began with the standard Welch technique of exaggerated buildup, to the effect that Cohn had been remiss in not communicating whatever he knew about Communists in the Army directly to Robert Stevens. This colloquy is worth quoting *in extenso* as an example of Welch in action and the degree to which the lovable codger could change his mien as needed.

---

* A main substantive distinction between the documents, as earlier noted, was that the shorter version contained the designations "derogatory" and "no derogatory" [data], these evidently interpolated by someone in the Army. In terms of format, the main difference was that the shorter version had a typed signature, "J. Edgar Hoover," which the original did not.

† According to McCarthy, such reports had been provided at some time in 1949; on September 15, 1950; October 27, 1950; twice in December 1950; January 26, 1951; February 13, 1951; June 5, 1951; February 19, 1952; June 1952; September 1952; January 1953; April 1, 1953; and April 21, 1953.

‡ Brownell's designation to this effect was in a public speech, rather than via the Attorney General's list.

WELCH: If you had gone over to the Pentagon and got inside the door and yelled to the first receptionist you saw, "We got some hot dope on some Communists in the Army," don't you think you could have landed at the top?

COHN: Sir, that is not the way I do things.

· · ·

WELCH: And although you had this dope and a fresh and ambitious new Secretary of the Army, reachable by the expenditure of one taxicab fare, you never went during March, if you had it in March, did you, is that right?

COHN: Mr. Welch—

WELCH: Just answer. You never went near him in March?

COHN: No, I—

WELCH: Or April? Did you?

COHN: Mr. Welch—

WELCH: Tell me, please.

COHN: I am trying, sir.

WELCH: Or April?

COHN: No, sir.

WELCH: Or May?

COHN: I never went near him, sir.

WELCH: Or June?

COHN: The answer is never.

WELCH: Right. Or July?

COHN: I communicated—

WELCH: Or July?

COHN: No, sir—

SENATOR MUNDT: I think we have covered July.

WELCH: I think it is really dramatic to see how these Communist hunters will sit on this document when they could have brought it to the attention of Bob Stevens in 20 minutes, and they let month after month go by without going to the head and saying, "Sic 'em Stevens."

· · ·

COHN: May I answer the last statement?

WELCH: I only said you didn't say, "Sic 'em Stevens," and you didn't, did you? . . . You did not say "Sic 'em Stevens." Is that right?

COHN: Sir—

WELCH: Is that right?

COHN: Mr. Welch, if you want to know the way things work, I will tell you.

WELCH: I don't care how it works. I just want to know if it is right that you did not say, "Sic 'em Stevens."

COHN: No, sir, you are right.

WELCH: I am at long last right once, is that correct?

COHN: Mr. Welch, you can always get a laugh . . .

WELCH: Mr. Cohn, we are not talking about laughing matters. If there is a

> laugh, I suggest to you, sir, it is because it is so hard to get you to say that you didn't actually yell, "Sic 'em Stevens."[9]

When McCarthy finally objected to this burlesque, the discussion wandered off to other topics. However, Welch was soon back in "Sic 'em Stevens" mode, arguing that Cohn was at fault for not having personally rushed to inform Stevens the instant that data on security problems at Monmouth surfaced. This recapped what had gone before, but with additional Welchian furbelows:

> WELCH: . . . you didn't tug at his lapel and say, "Mr. Secretary, I know something about Monmouth that won't let me sleep nights?" You didn't do it, did you?
>
> COHN: I don't, as I testified, Mr. Welch, I don't know whether I talked to Mr. Stevens about it then [in September 1953] or not . . .
>
> WELCH: Don't you know that if you had really told him what your fears were, and substantiated them to any extent, he could have jumped in the next day with suspensions?
>
> COHN: No, sir.
>
> . . .
>
> WELCH: Mr. Cohn, tell me once more: Every time you learn of a Communist or a spy anywhere, is it your policy to get them out as fast as possible?
>
> COHN: Surely, we want them out as fast as possible, sir.
>
> WELCH: And whenever you learn of one from now on, Mr. Cohn, I beg of you, will you tell somebody about them quick?
>
> COHN: Mr. Welch, with great respect, I work for the committee here. They know how we go about handling situations of Communist infiltration and failure to act on FBI information about Communist infiltration . . .
>
> WELCH: May I add my small voice, sir, and say whenever you know about a subversive or a Communist or a spy, please hurry. Will you remember these words?[10]

This hectoring of Cohn, be it noted, came from the small voice whose clients had been pressuring General Lawton to *restore* asserted security risks at Monmouth. Even more ironic, if possible, it was premised on the selfsame "purloined letter" Welch had dismissively treated as a "carbon copy of precisely nothing." Now he was contending that Cohn was grievously to blame for not hand-delivering this copy of "precisely nothing" to Robert Stevens by the fastest possible method.

After sitting through these Welch sermonettes about exposing every subversive or Communist suspect Cohn had ever heard of, and being extra quick about it, McCarthy at last broke in by raising the issue of Fred Fisher. Having brought Fisher to D.C. to help out with the hearings, McCarthy opined, Welch had little standing to lecture others about proper methods of Red-hunting. In a tone heavy with disdain, McCarthy stated:

. . . in view of Mr. Welch's request that information be given once we know of anyone who might be performing work for the Communist Party, I think we should tell him that he has in his law firm a young man named Fisher, whom he recommended incidentally to do work on this committee, he has been for a number of years a member of an organization which was named, oh years and years ago, as the legal bulwark of the Communist Party . . . We are now letting you know that this young man did belong to this organization for either 3 or 4 years, belonged to it long after he was out of law school . . .

And subsequently:

Jim [Juliana], will you get the news story to the effect that this man belonged to this Communist front organization?[11]

This drew from Welch a much-celebrated answer, featured in all the usual write-ups and replayed innumerable times in video treatments of the hearings. It was the distilled essence of Joe Welch, worth studying in detail to get context and flavor. Along with certain other statements on Fred Fisher, Welch assailed McCarthy as follows:

Until this moment, Senator, I think I never fully grasped your cruelty or your recklessness. Fred Fisher is a young man who went to Harvard Law School and came with my firm and is starting what looks like a brilliant ca-reer with us . . . Little did I dream you could be so reckless and so cruel as to do an injury to that lad . . . *I fear that he shall always bear a scar needlessly inflicted by you.* If it were in my power to forgive you for your reckless cru-elty I would do so. I like to think I am a gentleman, but your forgiveness will have to come from someone other than me.[12] (Emphasis added.)

When McCarthy then attempted to give some background on the National Lawyers Guild, plus a strong *tu quoque* about the harm done to the reputations of Frank Carr and other young McCarthy staffers by the charges Welch had signed his name to, the Army counsel again lamented the injury to Fisher:

Let us not assassinate this lad further, Senator. You have done enough. Have you left no sense of decency, sir, at long last? Have you left no sense of decency?

And, finally:

Mr. McCarthy, I will not discuss this with you further. You have been within six feet of me, and could have asked me about Fred Fisher. *You have brought it out.* If there is a God in Heaven, it will do neither you nor your cause any good. I will not discuss it with you further.[13] (Emphasis added.)

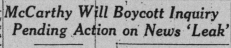

OUTED

Army Counsel Joseph Welch denounced McCarthy for outing Welch's assistant Frederick Fisher as a former member of a cited front group called the National Lawyers Guild. But *Welch himself* had publicly confirmed Fisher's former Guild membership weeks earlier in this *New York Times* story of April 16, 1954.

McCarthy Will Boycott Inquiry Pending Action on News 'Leak'

Continued From Page 1

ence indicated that their plans for continuing further investigation of the military installation at Fort Monmouth, N. J., were related to the importance attached by them to Private Schine's military assignment," said paragraph 13 of the charges.

Copies of the Army allegations were furnished to Senator McCarthy's associates, but the subcommittee withheld them from the public awaiting a formal reply of the McCarthy side of the case. Portions of the charges were made available last night to a few newspapers, including The New York Times, by a source who asked to remain anonymous.

Senator Stuart Symington, Missouri Democrat, broke through the secrecy barrier today and released the entire document, saying that he had done so because of "piecemeal leaks" and because he believed the public was entitled to all the facts of an investigation that should be conducted as if it were in a "gold-fish bowl."

Senator McCarthy, vacationing in Texas, acted through Mr. Cohn in protesting the part release of the Army charges last night. Mr. Cohn specifically said his complaint was not directed at Senator Symington's action today in releasing the full document.

[From Houston, Tex., The Associated Press said that Mr. McCarthy, however, had accused Senator Symington of violating the Senate subcommittee rule.]

Senator McCarthy demanded, in effect, that the investigation of the "news leak" should take priority over the public and televised hearings of the Army-McCarthy dispute scheduled to start Thursday.

Senator Mundt said Senator McCarthy's request would be placed before the subcommittee at its next meeting, probably Monday.

Other Senators said the diversionary attack by Senator McCarthy was not unexpected. By absenting himself from Washington all this week, first in Arizona and now in Texas, he has made it impossible for subcommittee members to confer with him personally about his counter-charges or about the ground rules of procedure that will apply to the investigation.

Senator Mundt reiterated today that Senator McCarthy had promised him by telephone last night to return over the week-end and be present for a meeting of the subcommittee at 10 A. M., Monday, unless his doctors advised against travel because of a persistent throat ailment.

Associated Press Telephoto

Frederick G. Fisher Jr., who said he had been dropped as one of the Army's lawyers for hearing on dispute with Senator Joseph R. McCarthy.

handling of resultant situations endangering our national security."

Part release of the Army charges, Mr. Cohn said, violated a subcommittee ruling that both sides would be made public together.

The Army allegations covered six typewritten pages, which both condensed and expanded the original charges made in the thirty-four-page report sent to Senators early in March.

One of the new charges is that Private Schine absented himself from Fort Dix, N. J., on special passes granted at the request of the investigating subcommittee "on occasions when in fact he did not work on behalf of this subcommittee."

The Army charges were signed by its new special counsel, Joseph N. Welch. Mr. Welch today confirmed news reports that he had relieved from duty his original second assistant, Frederick G. Fisher Jr. of his own Boston law office, because of admitted previous membership in the National Lawyers Guild, which has been listed by Herbert Brownell Jr., the Attorney General, as a Communist-front organization.

Mr. Welch said he had brought in another lawyer, John Kimball Jr. from his Boston office to take Mr. Fisher's place.

Subsequently, we're told, Welch broke into tears and the audience in the Senate chamber responded with sustained applause. Thus the incident most remembered from the hearings, and generally viewed as the moral Waterloo of Joe McCarthy. The reckless evildoer had exposed young Fred Fisher and his former membership in the National Lawyers Guild, thus scarring the innocent lad forever, and the good, decent Welch had protested this shameful outing of a youthful indiscretion.

All of which seems very moving, and is invariably so treated. It looks a little different, however, when we note that, well before this dramatic moment, Fred Fisher had *already* been outed, in conclusive fashion, as a former member of the National Lawyers Guild—by none other than Joe Welch. This had occurred in April, some six weeks before the McCarthy-Welch exchange, when Welch took it upon himself to confirm before the world that Fisher had indeed been a member of the Guild, and for this reason had been sent back to Boston. As the *New York Times* reported, in a story about the formal filing of Army allegations against Cohn-McCarthy:

> The Army charges were signed by its new special counsel, Joseph N. Welch. *Mr. Welch today [April 15] confirmed news reports that he had relieved from duty his original second assistant, Frederick G. Fisher, Jr., of his own Boston law office because of admitted previous membership in the National Lawyers Guild, which has been listed by Herbert Brownell, Jr. the Attorney General, as a Communist front organization.* Mr. Welch said he had brought in another lawyer, John Kimball, Jr., from his Boston office to take Mr. Fisher's place.[14] (Emphasis added.)

Giving this news item further impact, the *Times* ran a sizable photograph of Fred Fisher, plus a caption noting he had been relieved of duty with the Army's legal forces. (See inset, page 568.) Having caused this story to appear in the nation's most prestigious daily and reputed paper of record, Joe Welch would seem to have done a pretty good job of outing the innocent lad from Boston. (It was undoubtedly this news story, or an equivalent, that McCarthy was asking Jim Juliana to bring him.) It thus develops that Welch himself had already done the very thing for which he so fervently denounced McCarthy. So the suspicion once more dawns, as with the "doctored" photo, that something was unspeakably evil when, and only when, done by McCarthy, but perfectly proper when done by Welch and/or his clients.

What these several episodes tell us about the moral posturing of the Army's lawyer hardly needs much comment. There is, however, one further topic to be noted in taking the measure of Joe Welch. This was the effort of the Mundt committee to get from Welch's clients an Inspector General's report about the Peress case, including a list of Army officials involved in the mishandling of that matter. On this subject, as on others, the Army dragged its feet, so that four months elapsed between the date of the request and the time the report was finally delivered. Moreover, when the list was examined, it turned out to have some glaring omissions.

All this would be brought out the following year by the McClellan panel in its survey of the Peress debacle. In a scathing critique of the Army performance, the McClellan committee noted the obvious lack of candor in keeping back the IG report about the case. Even worse than the foot-dragging, however, was the deliberate *withholding* of the names of several officials involved in managing the Peress affair—including both John Adams and General Zwicker, among the most important players in the drama. As a result of such deletions, said the McClellan panel, "the list of 28 officials was deceptive and a gross imposition on the special Mundt subcommittee and this subcommittee." And why had the names of John Adams *et al.* been omitted? The information, said the McClellan report, "*was not furnished to the special Mundt subcommittee upon the advice received from the Army's special counsel, Joseph P. Welch* [sic] . . . *on or about May 11 (1954)* . . ." as "*not pertinent to the hearings.*"[15] (Emphasis added.)

Thus, what the McClellan committee described as "deceptive and a gross imposition" on two committees of the Senate was the doing of the virtuous Welch, this occurring "on or about May 11," 1954. That would have been roughly a week after the Army lawyer lectured McCarthy on the need for full disclosure of all relevant data, and the grave obligations in the solemn oath administered when the hearings started. It would appear that, in this brief span, Welch had forgotten this impressive moral sermon. Perhaps it would have helped if, as he requested, someone had read to him—slowly—the language of that oath, swearing "to tell the truth, comma, the whole truth, comma, and nothing but the truth." But then again, perhaps it wouldn't.

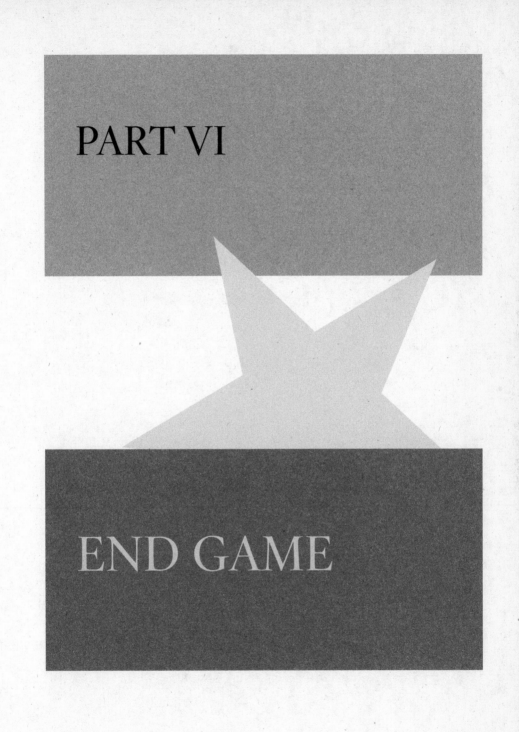

PART VI

END GAME

CHAPTER 43

The Sounds of Silence

W HEN Joe Welch advised his clients to withhold the names of John Adams *et al.* from the Mundt committee, he wasn't doing anything especially novel, but simply following standard practice on the Army side of the proceedings. In fact, suppression of critical data on controverted issues had been a favored administration tactic in its McCarthy battles for months before this.

Not, of course, that executive secrecy was invented by the new GOP regime and its bodyguard of Harvard lawyers. Official efforts to conceal important facts of record, especially on security matters, had been made often in the past, under Presidents Roosevelt and Truman. *Amerasia* was the most flagrant instance, Truman's secrecy order of 1948 the most far-reaching, and there were many related cases, several noted in this survey. It remained, however, for the Ike White House and Eisenhower Justice to wrap blanket gag decrees and secrecy measures in resounding phrases about the Constitution and noble objects of the framers.

In this respect, as in others, the policy being followed by the Ike administration was in jarring conflict with earlier Republican statements on the issues. In the 1952 campaign, the GOP had blasted the secrecy policies of the Truman White House and its agents. The gag order of 1948 had been denounced many times by party spokesmen as a cover-up and scandal, and there was copious evidence for such charges. However, as the various Ike-McCarthy disputes unfolded, the new administration would grow increasingly fond of Truman's order—invoking it, for instance, to silence General Zwicker in his set-to with McCarthy, stifle witnesses from Monmouth, and withhold security records from the panel.

Also, as has been seen, the administration along the way had improvised more specific and even tougher sanctions—the sequestering of Scott McLeod, the quarantine of General Lawton. These hardball tactics were in keeping with the spirit if not the letter of the Truman order, as they involved, in one fashion or another, access to security data. These *ad hoc* suppressions were, however, merely prelude to a more sweeping Ike dictate, extending the code of silence in ways that Truman, so far as we know, had not envisioned.

Given the pro-McCarthy trend of the Army-McCarthy hearings in terms of substance, the reasons for this further step would no doubt have seemed compelling. By May of 1954, two related bodies of data unknown to the public, neither favorable to the Army, were pushing to the surface. The more significant of these, or at least the one that later got all the notice, concerned the high-level January meeting mentioned by John Adams, when he was told by Sherman Adams to draft the "chronology" used in the arraignment of McCarthy. The other was the Army's stash of monitored phone calls, reflecting who said what to whom about Fort Monmouth, Lawton, the loyalty board, Dave Schine, and so on.

On both fronts, members of the Mundt committee were pressing hard for full disclosure. Only by getting information on these items, they said, would it be possible to extract the truth from the welter of conflicting charges. This view was reinforced by other developments in the hearings. Senators Dirksen, Mundt, and Potter would all reveal that they had been approached by administration spokesmen the day after the high-level January meeting, hinting at an indictment to be issued against Roy Cohn, this linked to McCarthy's plan to subpoena members of the Pentagon Review Board.

Dirksen testified that, on January 22, he was visited by John Adams and White House aide Gerald Morgan, both of whom had been at the meeting the day before, urging that the review board subpoenas be quashed and intimating that if they weren't, charges against Cohn might be forthcoming. Mundt said that, on the same day, he received a visit from John Adams, urging that subpoenas not be issued, this tied to the matter of Dave Schine, which seemed to Mundt a strange "juxtaposition of . . . topics."[1]

It thus appeared that the January meeting had been a crucial causative factor in the Army-McCarthy struggle, and that what was said and agreed to there was integral to the Mundt inquiry. However, it soon became apparent also that further information on the subject was not to be provided. On May 14, John Adams returned to tell the panel that he couldn't give any details about the mysterious meeting, "under instructions" from the Defense Department.[2] Committee members were perplexed, but would be even more so a few days later when a blanket secrecy edict was handed down, making it clear the information they sought was being withheld on orders from the highest levels.

On May 17, the White House released a letter from Eisenhower to the Department of Defense, forbidding provision of any data about internal conversations, meetings, or written communications among its staffers, with no exceptions as to topics or to people. This ukase cited the need for "candid" exchanges among executive employees in giving "advice" to one another, an elastic rationale that could be applied to any subject whatsoever. "It is not in the public interest," said the order, that any such conversations or documents be divulged to Congress. DOD employees were thus instructed "not to testify on *any* such conversations or produce *any* such documents or reproductions."[3] (Emphasis added.)

This was accompanied by a lengthy memo from Eisenhower Justice—a history of executive secrecy orders through the ages, dating from the nation's founding. Among the lofty precedents cited were the very Truman secrecy measures and denials the GOP had formerly protested—the 1948 gag order, the Condon case, the Remington case, concealment of the State Department security files, and others. These once-derided Truman actions were now invoked in reverent terms as instances of "the traditional executive view that the President's discretion must govern the surrender of executive files."[4] The legal basis for this stance, given in both the letter and the memo, was the "separation of powers," depicted as a most sacred and fundamental precept of the American system.

With this, the Mundt committee had run into a stone wall of denial, based on the broadest possible claim of privilege. The senators were less than pleased, Joe McCarthy less than others. "One of the subjects of this inquiry," he said, "is to find out who was responsible for calling off the hearings of the Communist infiltration of the government. At this point, I feel there is no way of ever getting at the truth, because we do find that the charges were conceived, instigated at the meeting which was testified to by [John] Adams. . . . [That meeting] didn't have to do with security matters. . . . It merely has to do with why these charges were filed."[5]

The Democrats on the panel took the same position. "I shall insist," said John McClellan, "upon making this record clear with respect to what was the result of the decisions made at that time, whether responsibility shifted from the Secretary of the Army to higher authorities. That we are entitled to know, because unless we can get that information, we will not have the evidence here upon which to make a decision that will place the responsibility."[6]

There were still other troublesome questions that begged for answers. What was known about the January meeting pointed to the White House, specifically to Sherman Adams. And considering that he was the topmost staffer to the

President, the further implications of that development were even more in-triguing. Was it possible Sherman Adams and other high officials were con-cocting an indictment of a member of the Senate but that the President knew nothing of it? And even without that information, as McClellan noted, what had been depicted as a midlevel action by Bob Stevens, allegedly launching charges at his own discretion, took on a very different aspect.

Some other puzzling questions were raised by Democratic members. Sym-ington wanted to know what U.N. Ambassador Lodge was doing at such a meet-ing, which apparently had nothing to do with the United Nations. Told by Army Counsel Welch this was off-limits because of the high-level nature of the confab, Symington asked: "Does that mean we are going to get the information about the low level discussions but not about the high level discussions?"[7] Now, with the Eisenhower order, the answer to that was clear: The committee would get neither.

McCarthy, as might be expected, had still other concerns and questions. All the legal/constitutional arguments and precedents to back up the secrecy edict were coming from Eisenhower Justice. But, McCarthy observed, both Attorney General Brownell and his deputy, William Rogers, had been present at the very meeting now ruled off-limits for discussion. In essence, therefore, Brownell and Rogers were propounding and defending an order that covered up their own behavior. Wasn't this, McCarthy rhetorically wondered, a self-evident conflict of interest?

These were significant issues that might have prompted similar questions from an inquisitive press corps. Traditionally, when faced with official efforts to withhold the facts on controverted topics, the instinct of the press has been in favor of disclosure—a well-known trait of the profession. Where Joe McCar-thy was concerned, however, the usual rules went out the window. As observed by journalist Clark Mollenhoff, who covered these hearings and later wrote a seminal book about the underlying issues, there was a prevailing view among his colleagues that "anything that is bad for Joe McCarthy is good for the country." If McCarthy was against it, they were for it.[8]

In keeping with that maxim, Ike's gag order, far from being assailed or questioned, was met with effusions of highest praise by leading members of the press. Especially voluble were those twin towers of elite opinion, the *New York Times* and *Washington Post*. According to the *Times,* a comprehensive secrecy order of the sort proclaimed by Ike was just the tonic needed by our body politic—a long-overdue rebuke to a pushy, interfering Congress. The real issue, said the *Times,* was "an attempt on the part of the legislative branch in the per-son of Mr. McCarthy to encroach upon the executive branch"—an affront to be resisted to the utmost.

The *Post* was equally supportive of the secrecy edict, using phrases that would read strangely down the road when the issue was something other than

McCarthy. "It is absurd," the *Post* opined, "to suppose that any congressional committee could compel this testimony if the President should decide to forbid it. . . . The President's authority under the Constitution to withhold from Congress confidences, presidential information, the disclosure of which would be incompatible with the public interest, is altogether beyond question."[9]

While the main subject of these exalted claims was the January meeting, the still mostly secret hoard of monitored phone calls was not forgotten—especially not forgotten at the White House. The Mundt committee had voted to subpoena these records on April 23, but as the weeks rolled by the subpoena had not been honored. And, as would later be revealed, some decisive steps were taken by executive fiat to make certain that it wasn't. On May 13, administration agents were ordered, on the double, to gather up the monitored phone transcripts and related data from the Pentagon and hustle them over to the White House. (This too in emulation of precedents from the Truman era, when the State Department security files were handled in like fashion.)

The purpose of this further secrecy measure would be described by William Ewald, an Ike aide who conducted an extensive study of the telephone transcripts and what had happened to them. "Neither the public nor most of the participants ever knew the contents of these documents," said Ewald, "because for reasons of strategy in the conflict, they were locked up in the White House by order of the President . . . Instantaneously, all relevant records in the Pentagon were gathered up and spirited across the Potomac to the White House against the possible threat of their being subpoenaed, on McCarthy's demand, by the investigating Senate committee."[10]

In this preemptive strike, the guiding hand of Sherman Adams was again apparent, as the removal was done on his specific order and the documents delivered to him personally at the White House. Nor were the reasons for this much in doubt. As seen, the small sampling of monitored calls made public wasn't supportive of Stevens-Adams, was indeed more helpful to McCarthy than to Stevens. The obvious inference had to be that any further calls the White House was concealing would be even less useful to the Army. Impounding the records, followed by Ike's all-concealing order, would prevent any new embarrassment of this nature. As Ewald summed it up:

> . . . by May 17, the transcripts had not been delivered to the committee. Then came the President's directive, slamming down the portcullis. The impounders had moved with dispatch and secrecy and effect. The long contemporaneous record—day by day, minute by minute—of the Army's fecklessness and compliance—a record that took the edge off the stridency of their charges and undercut many assertions in Stevens' testimony—that record would remain sealed. . . . The portcullis had indeed slammed down, and it slammed down just in time for the Army.[11]

Such were the facts, as conveyed by Ike's own assistant, behind the grandil-
oquent prose of the gag decree and Justice memo, facts that would not only
have weakened the Army's charges but "undercut" the testimony of Stevens
(and, one gathers, his agent John Adams), which sounds like a polite way of
describing perjury in the hearings. And such was the cover-up acclaimed by the
New York Times, Washington Post, and many others as a shining instance of
constitutional government at its finest.

Joe McCarthy didn't think it was such a shining hour for the Constitution,
thought it was indeed a cover-up, and said so. Beyond this, in what is generally
viewed as one of his more outrageous moments, he said there was no constitutional or legal warrant for suppressing evidence of wrongdoing by federal
officials, whatever secrecy orders might be issued. "As far as I am concerned," he
said, "I would like to notify those two million federal employees that I feel it is
their duty to give us any information which they have about graft, corruption,
communism, treason, and there is no loyalty to a superior officer that can tower
above their loyalty to the country."[12]

The shocked response to this McCarthy salvo was the flipside of the
worshipful view of executive secrecy that greeted Eisenhower's order. The Wisconsin brawler had now truly committed *lèse majesté*—pitting his view of the
constitutional/legal requirements against the dictate of the White House. So
grave was this offense considered that it would be one of the main points
alleged against McCarthy in the effort to have him censured. Senators Fulbright, Wayne Morse, and Ralph Flanders, for instance, all made this McCarthy
statement a major item in the accusations they proffered to the Senate.
As Morse would put it, "The supplying of such information would be illegal
and in violation of presidential orders and contrary to the right of the chief
executive under the separation of powers doctrine."[13]

Similar statements about McCarthy's incitement to lawbreaking have been
made often since. The essence of the charge was, and is, that a presidential
secrecy order by Ike or Truman was "the law," that executive employees were
bound by this, and that McCarthy by his audacious statements was urging that
the law be broken. Hence in the view of Richard Rovere, and others, he was
a rogue, "seditionist," demagogue, and outlaw. Had America been Imperial
Rome, or France under the Old Regime, such notions might have had some
standing—as "law" in those systems was held to be whatever the supreme executive said it was, and there was no legislature worthy of the name to counter-
mand him.

In the American governing setup, however, we were supposed to have
another kind of law (whether we actually did or not being a somewhat different question). This is called "statute law," meaning enactments passed by the
two houses of Congress, and assented to by the President, according to the

tenets of the Constitution. This kind of law, indeed, was once thought to be the essence of our system—the main object of Anglo-American constitutional struggles dating back to Magna Carta.

It so happened that, on the subject being addressed by McCarthy, there was some very definite statute law, which had been on the books for decades, most recently reenacted, at the time of the Army hearings, in 1948. This was the Civil Service Act, a law whose terms were quite familiar to McCarthy. In relevant part this statute said: "The right of persons employed in the Civil Service of the United States, either individually or collectively, to petition Congress, or any member thereof, or to *furnish information to either House of Congress, or to any committee or members thereof, shall not be denied or interfered with.*"[14] (Emphasis added.)

On the face of it, this language was both categorical and comprehensive, and would seem to indicate that it was the Ike gag order that was illegal rather than McCarthy's resistance to it. (This statutory language is conspicuously absent from denunciations of McCarthy appearing in many of our histories.) All of which raises a whole series of further questions that can't be settled in these pages—the most obvious of which, perhaps, is whether a presidential order can nullify a statute. In our system, the theoretical answer to this is "no," but the de facto answer at the time was "yes."

A T THE eye of this constitutional hurricane stood a most interested participant/observer, then–Vice President Richard Nixon. Beginning with his days in Congress and the security battles of that era, Nixon's brushes with executive secrecy issues were many. His repeated involvements with the topic, across a span of years, would have some instructive linkages to the anti-secrecy efforts of McCarthy.

As a member of the House in 1948, in an episode earlier noted, Nixon had attacked the Truman administration for its refusal to hand over the FBI's report on Dr. Edward Condon. Congress, Nixon then argued, had not only the right but the duty to canvass this material as essential to its oversight role in protecting the security of the nation. Now, however, he was part of an administration pursuing exactly the opposite course from that he had propounded, and inevitably had to tack with the changing winds of doctrine from the White House.

In his accustomed Janus-like role as mediator between Ike and the right wing in Congress, the Nixon of 1954 had ample opportunity to follow the executive privilege battle and was well acquainted with such active players in the drama as James St. Clair, the assistant to Joe Welch who helped shape the Army's legal tactics. Nixon would also have had many chances to savor and imbibe the tributes to executive privilege by the *Times* and *Post* and other powerful media voices. It would have been a memorable experience. Unfortunately for Nixon, the lessons he learned from it, or thought he did, turned out to be mistaken.

Some twenty years after these events, as is well known, Nixon was himself the nation's chief executive and the Watergate tide was rising all around him. The merits of that affair don't concern us here, except to note that key elements in the dispute were tapes of conversations recorded in the Oval Office among Nixon and his staffers. These conversations concerned methods of dealing with the scandal, strategies to be used in trying to contain it, and what exactly to say about it. The Senate Watergate Committee chaired by Sen. Sam Ervin (D-N.C.) and the office of a special prosecutor were seeking the tapes and transcripts of such meetings. Nixon's defense against these demands was a plea of executive privilege, based on the hallowed separation-of-powers doctrine.

Having lived through the heady days of 1954 when the wonders of executive privilege were being shouted from the rooftops, Nixon—with former Welch assistant James St. Clair as his lead attorney—would have had some reason to suppose the identical claim on his own behalf would be respected. Indeed, as the Oval Office tapes included his personal conversations with his closest aides, the tapes arguably would have been more entitled to protection than a talk between John Adams and Sherman Adams, not to mention the conversations or memos of staffers down in the ranks, all covered by the Eisenhower order.[15]

If Nixon had such expectations, however, he was in for a rude surprise. It turned out that what had been a sacred constitutional precept when invoked by Ike against Joe McCarthy wasn't so sacred when invoked by Nixon against Sam Ervin. Most especially, it wasn't sacred to the *New York Times* and *Washington Post,* both of which now turned on the proverbial dime and argued exactly the opposite view from that espoused against McCarthy.

According to the *Times,* commenting on Nixon's secrecy claim, the plea of executive privilege was now a cover-up and sham, worthy of no respect whatever. "A . . . refusal to produce the evidence as it pertains to Watergate," the *Times* averred, "would only create other problems for Nixon of a more consuming nature—problems of leadership and credibility which might be fatal to his presidency . . . There can be no practical justification for failure to make this evidence publicly available . . . ."

The *Post* turned on the same ten-cent piece, and in the same direction. Nixon's refusals to deliver up the tapes, it said, "have precipitated a crisis for no good constitutional or legal reason . . . What is at issue is only to what extent those issues we already know about have corrupted and compromised that high office."*[16] As with the earlier onslaught against McCarthy, these statements upbraiding Nixon were typical of opinion in many media outlets.

---

*In these musings by the *Washington Post,* there was no inkling that "the President's authority under the Constitution to withhold from Congress confidences," et cetera, "*is altogether beyond question.*" Apparently, questions that hadn't suggested themselves in 1954 had become visible two decades later.

Most to the present point, in the midst of all this furor, the distinguished Harvard law professor Raoul Berger brought out a scholarly tract on the subject of executive privilege, said by many to have demolished the doctrine altogether. This book was acclaimed by academic and media spokesmen as the definitive work about the topic, showing executive privilege was a farce and hoax, the opposite of constitutional, thus consigning Nixon's arguments, and Nixon himself, to the dustbin of discarded causes. That was basically it for Nixon.

This complete reversal of elite opinion on the matter did have, of course, the awkward side effect of seeming to justify *ex post facto* the position taken two decades before by Joe McCarthy, but this was a risk some opinion makers were willing to take. By 1974, after all, McCarthy was long since discredited, dead and buried; the evil that needed to be stamped out now was Nixon, and if turning backflips on executive privilege was required to do this, there were plenty of intellectual acrobats supple enough to try it, as would be proved in many forums.

For our purposes, the importance of this great reversal isn't the fate of the unhappy Nixon but the light shed on the original Ike-McCarthy fracas by these later insights. Of surpassing interest were the comments of Raoul Berger concerning the John Adams–Sherman Adams meeting in the office of Brownell. No fan of Joe McCarthy, Berger opined not only that this meeting wasn't legitimately subject to secrecy claims but that it may have been a legal offense of the most grievous nature. ". . . if the subject of this meeting is accurately stated," said Berger, "the discussion was of more serious import than McCarthy suspected. Executive scheming to interfere with the course of a parliamentary investigation would have in all likelihood been viewed as an impeachable encroachment on the prerogative of Parliament, and such offenses were dealt with harshly."[17]

It thus appears, on this legal-historical reading, that it wasn't McCarthy who was encroaching on the executive, but the executive that was encroaching on McCarthy. And, more than this, the high-level secret meeting that was the subject of the allegedly great and glorious plea of executive privilege may well have been an impeachable offense, according to the learned Berger. It was for denouncing this very meeting, and the gag order used to conceal it, that McCarthy was derided at the time, and still is in histories of the conflict.

CHARGES against McCarthy on the executive privilege issue connected up with others, most notably his possession of the two-and-a-quarter-page Monmouth memo that so terrified Joe Welch. The issues crisscrossed in that McCarthy's incitement to federal workers to supply him information on wrongdoing would presumably have resulted in other documents of this nature being smuggled to him. This, it was charged, would result in a violation, not merely of the Ike gag order, but of espionage and other laws concerning "classified" data, thus injuring the national security. McCarthy, said his critics, was not only violating such laws himself but encouraging others to do so.

McCarthy's retort to this was that he wasn't seeking or receiving military secrets or confidential Bureau records, but rather data showing whether laws and regulations pertaining to such matters had been ignored or broken. The Monmouth memo, as he described it, was a good example of the difference: It didn't contain any security information harmful to the national interest, as all pertinent info as to FBI sources and specifics about the cases had been deleted. What the memo did show, however, was that the FBI had duly warned the Army about Aaron Coleman *et al.,* though apparently little was done to rectify the problem.

Beyond this, there were anomalies in the stance of the administration condemning McCarthy for daring to have, read, and talk about the Monmouth memo. The argument of Joe Welch and others was that divulging information derivative from the FBI—for whatever purpose—was *ipso facto* a security violation, so much so that Welch, voicing the utmost trepidation, refused even to read an expurgated version. The essence of the position, argued at considerable length, was that any disclosure of such material for any purpose was damaging to security interests and legally verboten.

This appeared, however, to be another instance—like the "doctored" photo or the outing of Fred Fisher—in which something was evil when done by McCarthy but perfectly fine when done by others. In fact, as Joe Welch and all other parties to the conflict knew full well, the administration had itself made public copious security information from the FBI not long before this, in the case of Harry Dexter White. These disclosures were made by Attorney General Brownell in a Chicago speech of November 1953, and thereafter in testimony to the Senate. In addition, FBI Director Hoover had been authorized to follow Brownell to the stand to explain the facts of the case in more detail.

In testifying about the White case, Brownell had gone into many particulars of the FBI investigation of the Bentley suspects, extending well beyond the matter of White himself. In essence, Brownell gave the Senate, and the nation, a pretty good précis of the till-then super-secret data the Bureau had pulled together in the "Gregory" inquest. Quizzed about this in the 1953 Senate probe by a skeptical John McClellan, Brownell blandly said he had decided to declassify these confidential FBI records as a matter of public interest.[18]

Thus, the Ike administration had made far more extensive revelations of material from the vaults of the FBI than anything done or contemplated by McCarthy, certainly more than the meager helping of data in the brief memo that filled Joe Welch with fear and loathing. The purposes of this Brownell disclosure, moreover, were obviously to a great extent of partisan nature—to refute ex-President Truman's various denials about the case as well as to show

there had been a major security breakdown concerning it, which indeed there
had been.

An apparent distinction between the White case and the Monmouth
memo was that Brownell as Attorney General was the superior of the FBI, in
effect had the White security file in his possession, and could release it if he
chose to, the President assenting. McCarthy, on the other hand, had no such
authority and was prevented from doing what Brownell could do as a matter
of executive discretion. Of course, even if valid, this argument would contra-
vene the Welchian view that release of such material was a security violation
on its face, since it apparently wasn't such when Brownell decided to do it.
However, there were plentiful reasons to conclude that the argument wasn't
valid to begin with.

Foremost among these was that McCarthy was not only a member of the
U.S. Senate, this obviously bringing him within the ambit of the Civil Service
law about receipt of information from federal workers, but chairman of the
principal investigating committee of that body charged with sleuthing out malfeasance in executive departments. Receiving information of this nature was
integral to the performance of his sworn duties—arguably more so than the
public release of FBI data about the Gregory case to refute and embarrass
Harry Truman was integral to the duties of Brownell.

Add to this the significant fact that there were strong constitutional arguments countering the pro-secrecy position, and that these had been effectively
marshaled by Congress as recently as the Condon dispute in 1948. In that conflict, not only had Nixon and others argued that the Bureau's Condon report
be provided to the House, they had in their possession the Legislative Reference
Service survey of relevant data to support their version. As seen, the House
then demanded, by a huge bipartisan vote of 300–29, that the report be handed
over. In the new era of executive privilege as Holy Writ, this instance of Congress having stood up for its coequal powers was conveniently forgotten.

Finally, there was what might be called the real-world perspective on the
matter, known to any member of Congress seriously involved in investigations
of subversion. Time and again, the information on which Congress acted had
been brought to its attention by executive employees alarmed about some security matter allegedly being mishandled. A good deal of this information, in
turn, came either directly or indirectly from the FBI, another fact well known
to Hill investigators. A prime example was the series of hearings in the summer
of 1948, conducted by the House Committee on Un-American Activities, cul-
minating in the Hiss-Chambers case. All the numerous suspects dealt with in
that inquiry, and much of the initial evidence on them, matched point for point
with Bureau records on the cases.

In this connection, as McCarthy observed and Mundt confirmed, a major
breakthrough in the Hiss affair had occurred when an employee of the State

Department surreptitiously brought the department's security file on Hiss, containing considerable Bureau data, to Mundt's attention. This showed that the department had adverse information about Hiss, dating back at least to 1946, that confirmed and reinforced the Chambers allegations. (The employee who did this, as Mundt would one day disclose, was John Peurifoy.*) That was, as Mundt noted, the way things really worked in ferreting out evidence on subversion.

None of this, however, did the slightest good for Joe McCarthy in his battle with Stevens-Adams and the Eisenhower secrecy edict. Nor would McCarthy fare any better in the censure hearings that immediately followed, in which the same gag order would be used to stifle testimony—again—from General Lawton. Throughout, the administration invoked the allegedly sacred precept of executive privilege to conceal information adverse to its position, while readily divulging other data—most notably, pertaining to Dave Schine—seen as harmful to McCarthy. All in all, this tactic of selective secrecy and disclosure served administration interests nicely.

McCarthy would thus end his investigative career very much as he began it—up against a stone wall of denial. Truman had issued his secrecy edict of 1948, affecting all the early McCarthy cases, and Ike his even more stringent gag order of 1954 affecting the conflict with the Army. Truman had squirreled away State Department security records in the White House, and Eisenhower would follow suit with the Army phone transcripts. In both cases, McCarthy clamored for disclosure, but his protests availed him little. The wall of selective silence stood impervious against him.

To all this there was an Orwellian sequel that can't possibly be omitted. On May 31, 1954, two weeks to the day after issuing his secrecy order gagging federal workers and choking off information to the Congress, Eisenhower spoke to a Columbia University gathering in New York, a symposium on the weighty topic "Man's Right to Knowledge and the Free Use Thereof." On this occasion Ike asserted, to great applause, that "whenever man's right to knowledge and the use thereof is restricted, man's freedom in the same measure disappears." It was, the media sages agreed, a clear, long-needed rebuff to Joe McCarthy.

---

*This action, according to Mundt, brought great distress to Peurifoy, as he was thus going counter to the line on Hiss generally followed by Dean Acheson, Peurifoy's once and future boss. This and similar moves by Peurifoy garnered him kudos from anti-Communists on the Hill—including Joe McCarthy. On the other hand, Peurifoy would in other settings vouch for Hiss, suggesting the conflicted role he played in these mysterious matters. As seen, his part in the Hamilton Robinson business with Robert Miller and otherwise obscuring the State Department's security problems was more in line with the Hiss defense mode.

CHAPTER 44

Sentence First, Verdict Later

THERE is no getting around the fact that, in McCarthy's endless verbal battles, the invective was often scalding, including many sharp exchanges with other members of the Senate. It was for offenses of this type that he would eventually be censured by his colleagues, indicating that in their view the dignity of the upper chamber itself was the main victim of his conduct.

To gauge the ferocity of debate, we need only note that there were occasions on which members of the Senate were accused, in effect, of being agents of the Kremlin. Nor was it necessarily conceded that, in serving the nefarious ends of Moscow, the lawmaker thus assailed was mistakenly acting out of good intentions. Consider the following Senate broadside against one member of that body, accused of being a useful tool of Red subversion:

> We have marveled at the way in which the Soviet Government has won its military success in Asia without risking its own resources or its own men . . . What we are now seeing is another example of economy of effort and expansion of success in the conquest of this country for Communism. The preliminary campaign [in activity then occurring within the Senate] is successfully under way . . . Were . . . the senator [being attacked] in the pay of the Communists, he could not have done a better job for them.[1]

This was a pretty stiff indictment to be made by one member against another on the floor of the upper chamber, closely skirting, if not exceeding, the bounds of acceptable senatorial comment. It might thus understandably have brought down the wrath of the Senate on Joe McCarthy—if he in fact had said it. But, as it happened, this wasn't anything said by McCarthy but rather something said about him, on the road to his Golgotha. The person who made this accusation was Sen. Ralph Flanders (R-Vt.), laying the polemical groundwork for the motion of censure against McCarthy he would file a few days later.*

Flanders in this and further attacks made other charges against McCarthy of equally savage nature. One such was a passage in this same speech that implied, in innuendo so heavy no one could miss it, that McCarthy, Cohn, and Schine were a trio of homosexuals and that this perhaps accounted for their strange behavior.† In other statements—though this was common practice among McCarthy critics—Flanders analogized the Wisconsin senator to Hitler. So Ralph Flanders was perhaps not the ideal person to bring charges against a colleague on grounds of rhetorical violence or uncivil conduct.

This is, by the way, the same Ralph Flanders depicted in many standard histories as a supremely decent human being, second perhaps only to Joe Welch as a secular saint in the blessed crusade against McCarthy.‡ Based on the now-available record, however, it appears Flanders was neither saint nor demon, but an eccentric who, for whatever reasons, became the pliable front man for divergent interests bent on doing in McCarthy. His willingness to parrot charges devised by others was such that it may well be doubted whether any particular statement Flanders made was of his own devising or something simply handed to him on his way to the Senate cloakroom.

These comments are more than speculation. Some days after his blast against McCarthy, Flanders would follow up with a list of thirty-three specific charges that became the main bill of particulars in the censure battle. Some of these charges were extremely odd, as would be admitted even by McCarthy's critics. Questioned by majority leader William Knowland and Senator Herman

---

* Such rhetoric wasn't unusual on the anti-McCarthy side of the conflict. As earlier noted, Senator Tydings had made somewhat similar charges against GOP senator William Jenner of Indiana. President Truman had likewise described McCarthy as the Kremlin's "greatest asset" in America. Columnist Joseph Alsop would charge that McCarthy, plus Senators Kenneth Wherry and Robert Taft, among others, "have voted the straight Communist Party line in every major issue of foreign policy as laid down in the *Daily Worker* since the end of the war."

† These innuendos would later be supported by revelations concerning Cohn in books by Nicholas von Hoffman and Sidney Zion. There was never any credible evidence of such nature concerning either McCarthy or David Schine.

‡ One McCarthy biographer commends Flanders as a conservative but "with a broader concern for social values," another as "a deeply contemplative and spiritual man," qualities that presumably guided him in his combat with McCarthy. These tributes suggest that, as with Annie Lee Moss or Gustavo Duran, there was perhaps a second Ralph Flanders on the scene besides the one who addressed the Senate.

Welker of Idaho as to where this unusual list had come from, Flanders blandly acknowledged that the whole thing had been given to him by the National Committee for an Effective Congress. He had simply taken the NCEC material and read it out before the Senate.*

One consequence of such insouciant trashing of a colleague with second-hand data was that, when challenged on specifics, Flanders was hard-pressed to explain them. One item on his roster, Charge #8, said McCarthy had unleashed his investigative staff to spy on his committee colleague, Henry Jackson. When McCarthy categorically denied this, Sen. Homer Capehart (R-Ind.) asked Flanders what proof he had for his assertion. To this Flanders replied that the charge had appeared in a newspaper story but that he didn't know anything else about it.

Flanders would make the same response when asked about still other of his charges. He had dramatized his role by walking into the Army hearings, while McCarthy was on the stand, and handing McCarthy a note saying an attack would be forthcoming in the Senate. McCarthy interrupted his testimony and invited Flanders to make whatever allegations he cared to, under oath, then and there before the Mundt committee. Flanders not only didn't do this but, when asked about the matter later, said he might appear in such investigative format, "but I would have to begin by making a statement that I have nothing to testify, and that I read it all in the newspapers."[2]

The astonished reaction of Senator Capehart seems to have been apropos. Since when, Capehart asked, "does a senator of the United States, on the basis of reading something . . . in a newspaper, rise on the floor of the United States Senate and condemn a fellow senator?"[3] The answer to that, as events would show, was fairly simple: since Joe McCarthy had become a target for censure—an undertaking in which the usual rules of evidence and rational discourse were conspicuously not adhered to. The performance of Ralph Flanders and his inability to support his charges when quizzed about them were fitting prologue to the censure hearings.

Of course, questions about Flanders's newspaper reading were somewhat off the point, since he admitted he wasn't really the author of the charges. Such questions should have been addressed instead to Maurice Rosenblatt, George Agree, the aides of William Benton, and other officials and supporters of the NCEC, as they were the real instigators of the accusations. And even here, not too many questions were needed, as an examination of the list would have indicated rather plainly where the charges came from. Anyone familiar with the

---

*FLANDERS: "I accept every item on the list. It came from the Committee for a More Effective Congress [sic]."
   WELKER: "The senator received them from the Committee for a More Effective Congress?"
   FLANDERS: "That I have already said." (August 2, 1954)

Benton resolution, the activities of the Gillette committee, the battle of Fort Monmouth, or other disputes already noted would recognize most of these allegations at a glance.

Included in the rundown, for example, were the supposed mistaken-identity case of Annie Lee Moss, the blowup with General Zwicker, defiance of the Gillette inquiry, opposing the Bohlen nomination, possession of the Monmouth memo, resistance to the Ike secrecy order, and so forth. It was a kind of "greatest hits" collection, a potpourri of just about every kind of charge against McCarthy the NCEC could think of or that had been passed on to it by other critics of McCarthy. The whole thing had been hurriedly thrown together without much rhyme or reason by the Rosenblatt group and conveyed to Flanders, who then read it all verbatim to the Senate.[4]

While the charges were of disparate nature, there was one obvious common thread that tied them into a single package. If McCarthy did something with which the compilers disagreed—appointing J. B. Matthews, sending Cohn and Schine to Europe (both on the NCEC-Flanders list of charges)—then he should be censured for it. Censurable conduct could thus be anything and everything McCarthy said or did that his critics disapproved of, for whatever reason. Viewed from another angle, the hodgepodge nature of the list indicated the reverse-English method of proceeding: The notion that McCarthy should be censured was arrived at first, then divers items were pulled together, on whatever basis, to support the preconceived conclusion.*

The counts just mentioned, moreover, were those of relatively serious nature. Some others were so far-fetched as to suggest they were added simply by way of ballast. There was, for instance, Flanders's Charge #26—that *McCarthy* had caused the Army hearings, that this "necessitated the interruption of the subcommittee's work and its exclusive preoccupation" with that matter, and that for this hiatus McCarthy should be censured.[5] Thus, for having been targeted by the Army charges, then having to sit through two months of hearings on them, McCarthy was deserving of official condemnation. By this logic, he might have been censured also for having become the target of Flanders—since this would produce still another break in the work of the McCarthy panel.†

That a charge of this nature should have been submitted in all seriousness to the Senate, and on the basis revealed by Flanders, is suggestive of the polit-

---

*On this aspect, as on others, later disclosures by Maurice Rosenblatt and the records of the NCEC would confirm the curious—and helter-skelter—nature of the project. Flanders had made his original charges against McCarthy without citing any specifics. When other members of the Senate demanded a bill of particulars to support the accusations, Rosenblatt and Co. hastily patched together whatever charges they could think of and provided the resulting list to Flanders.

†At the end of this logic chain lay the unavoidable conclusion that McCarthy deserved to be censured *because he had been censured*—the censure process itself leading to still further interruptions in the work of his committee.

ical atmospherics then prevailing in the Capital City. And while most of the charges had more gravitas than this, a bland indifference to facts of record was notable throughout. Thus, while the full story on Annie Lee Moss had not yet developed, there was zero basis for such a charge, other than her own assertions, and ample reason to disbelieve it. Likewise, numerous data about the strange doings of the Gillette committee were available to the Senate, as were the facts about J. B. Matthews and other items in the Flanders lineup.

Notwithstanding all of this, it was decided that the Flanders charges—plus overlapping and reinforcing charges brought by Senators Fulbright and Wayne Morse of Oregon, making a grand total of forty-six—would be referred to a special committee of the Senate, to be given the most solemn consideration. Thus began the fifth and final investigation of Joe McCarthy—though, had it been needed, a sixth, or seventh, might have been laid on also. These anti-McCarthy inquests were conducted, indeed, like a relay race: As soon as one concluded, the next would instantly be started. Thus, the report of the Mundt committee on the Army-McCarthy battle would be filed on August 30, 1954. The very next day, brand-new hearings were convened, with McCarthy once more in the dock, to hear the charges that would produce his censure.

From the standpoint of his foes, this relay technique had several useful features. Most obviously, as long as McCarthy was defending himself in some investigation or other, his own subcommittee was virtually out of business. Equally important, while he was thus on the defensive, the spotlight would be on his alleged misdeeds rather than on the topics of subversion, lax security, or alleged cover-ups of such problems. And there was yet another helpful angle from the perspective of his critics: McCarthy was required to run the gauntlet again and again, each time facing a fresh set of inquisitors, albeit on overlapping charges, in the manner of interrogations designed to break the will of an imprisoned suspect.

The politics of all this were of interest, as both the Army-McCarthy probe and the censure hearings were conducted by a Senate nominally under GOP control, though closely divided as to numbers. Even more to the point, both inquests occurred with a Republican administration in the White House, and with its approval (to say no more), which was the crucial factor. As long as McCarthy had faced off against a Democratic president, he could with a few exceptions count on at least the tacit backing of his party in the Senate. Now, with a Republican White House aligned against him, there were GOP solons more concerned to work with a powerful Republican chief executive than to stand by a battered colleague obviously marked out for extinction.

One such Republican was Utah senator Arthur Watkins, at the time considered a conservative of moderate hue (though he would subsequently make many statements that belied this), who would head the special Senate committee weighing the charges against McCarthy. A former judge, Watkins was generally viewed as bland and unobtrusive, known for his attention to western water issues. His fellow Republicans on the panel, Francis Case of South Dakota and Frank Carlson of Kansas, were of like background and temper. All were Eisenhower loyalists and were chosen for the committee by Vice President Nixon in consultation with majority leader Knowland. None was likely to do anything remotely contrary to the wishes of the White House.

The Democrats on the panel—Edwin Johnson of Colorado, John Stennis of Mississippi, and Sam Ervin of North Carolina—were cut from the same bolt of homespun cloth: moderate conservative types not noted for flamboyance. (Ervin was the liveliest of the group, and his reputation to this effect would develop only later.) As condemnation of McCarthy would become a party-line issue for Democrats, it was certain none of these would take up the cudgels to defend him. All in all, a beige-and-gray committee, exactly what was wanted to handle a methodical, unswerving process after the wild and woolly shoot-out between McCarthy and the Army.

Linked to the committee's low-keyed personalities were its *sotto voce* methods. Though the hearings would be public, they weren't on TV, and Watkins ran them in eye-glazing fashion, featuring endless excerpts from the records of the Gillette and Mundt committees, legal memos, letters, assorted statutes, court decisions, and recitations of other printed matter. (One wag remarked that the panel might or might not decide to censure McCarthy but could conceivably bore him to death.) Integral to this approach were ground rules aimed at restricting McCarthy's role—stipulating that, when his attorney spoke in his behalf, McCarthy would be precluded from speaking also. All these measures were geared to reining in McCarthy—stifling his pugnacious debating tactics and penchant for appealing to the public.

McCarthy's counsel in these hearings was Edward Bennett Williams, one of the most renowned trial lawyers in the country, who would handle many high-profile cases in a long and colorful career before the bar. His preparation for the McCarthy defense lived up to his billing. He and his associates Agnes Weill and Brent Bozell had done their homework. They knew the Senate precedents, knew the law, knew a good deal about the charges, knew in particular about the peculiar antics of the Gillette committee. Williams was ready and more than able to conduct a legal defense of McCarthy and knock down the charges on their merits.

The famed attorney, however, made one huge miscalculation—though in the end it probably didn't matter. He was used to arguing cases in a courtroom where the process was open-ended, facts and law were salient, and outcomes decided on this basis. Such was the course he now gamely tried to follow, without much success to speak of. What he initially failed to realize, though he would grasp it fairly quickly, was that his legal tactics were nothing to the purpose in the assize run by Watkins. The hearings, while cast in legalistic form, were in fact a political process, the results of which would be, or already were, politically determined. Legalistic points could shape this in certain ways but couldn't fundamentally change it.

Williams would discover this early on, at the first session of the hearings, after learning that Colorado's Senator Johnson had been quoted in a Denver paper as saying all the Democratic leaders of the Senate "loathed" McCarthy. This raised some doubts as to Johnson's objectivity (though he pointed out that he didn't say he *personally* loathed McCarthy), as Johnson was now supposedly acting in a judicial role, impartially weighing McCarthy's conduct. Chairman Watkins, however, airily dismissed the matter as being of no concern whatever. Edwin Johnson had been chosen to be on the committee, and that was that; whether he made the statement in question and what exactly he meant by it were completely immaterial. After all, said Watkins, with faultless logic, "we are not trying Senator Johnson . . ."[6]

When McCarthy tried to argue against this, he was gaveled into silence; Williams had already spoken on the matter, so McCarthy couldn't. When McCarthy again protested, Watkins again banged the gavel, stopping McCarthy in midsentence. "We are not," said Watkins, "going to be interrupted by these diversions and sidelines. We are going straight down the line."[7] And so, in fact, they were. The episode was prophetic of what would happen in later sessions, indicating rather clearly where the line being followed would take the hearings.

Watkins gave a like response, outside the hearing room, to the oft-asked question as to why McCarthy was subject to charges for saying unflattering things about his colleagues, though they weren't subject to similar charges for saying unflattering things about McCarthy—the Flanders diatribe providing the premier, but no means the lone, example. The Watkins reply to this was once more revealing—"the Select Committee could function only within the limits of its assignment, that is to investigate McCarthy," period.[8] It wasn't investigating senators who said insulting things about McCarthy, but only what McCarthy said of others. The question thus contained its own irrefutable answer: We aren't doing what you suggest because that isn't what we're doing.

Similar logic would be applied to what would become the main issue of the hearings, McCarthy's supposedly contumacious behavior toward the Gillette committee. The centrality of this charge had been apparent from the beginning, and it was a charge attorney Williams was well prepared to answer. His main points were that the Gillette committee had been operating *ultra vires,* was prejudiced against McCarthy, and had transgressed the rules of right behavior in its relentless efforts to pursue him. McCarthy could hardly be blamed, said Williams, for failing to cooperate with a group so plainly out to get him and using illicit means to do it.

The Williams presentation on this was strong, and would have been still stronger had he known all the facts about it. Mostly he hammered the point that the Gillette committee had violated its mandate under the Benton resolution—to investigate alleged wrongdoing by McCarthy *since* his election to the Senate. As Williams knew, and McCarthy knew even better, the committee had blithely altered this proviso to rummage through every aspect of McCarthy's finances, and those of his friends and family, extending back for more than a decade before he ever ascended to the Senate. (And this, as seen, was prelude to still other efforts to stack the deck, including suppression of the Wheeling memo and refusal to print his testimony on Benton.)

However, Williams could have had ten times the documentation he did about the failings of the Gillette committee and it wouldn't have made the slightest difference. The responses Chairman Watkins had given on Edwin Johnson and rhetorical onslaughts against McCarthy presaged his answer on this one. What the Gillette committee might or might not have done to McCarthy in connection with its original mandate, said Watkins, "so far as I can see, is wholly immaterial. What is material is his conduct with respect to that committee and its activities."[9] Case closed, let's hear no more about it, and on to the next question.

Watkins reprised this performance yet again on the question of McCarthy's alleged incitement to federal workers to violate the law by providing him with information. When Williams and McCarthy tried to show that other members of Congress and committee chairmen had taken the identical stance vis-à-vis gag orders and attempts to cover up wrongdoing, this too was gaveled out of order. Various of the people Williams-McCarthy wanted to cite (including Vice President Nixon), said Watkins, were irrelevant to the hearings, "because they are not under charges here. We are not going to investigate the remarks of every fellow, every member of the Senate and the House, pro and con, on these various matters."[10]

In all such cases, the solipsism that we aren't doing that because that isn't what we're doing was hermetically locked and sealed, invulnerable to the legal skills of Williams. At this point, if not before, Williams knew the fix was in, that the outcome of the hearings was going to be decided by factors other than law and logic, and that this outcome had undoubtedly been arrived at before the hearings started. On the evidence of the Watkins rulings, McCarthy was going to be censured, no two ways about it; the only question remaining was exactly how the committee would structure and pronounce its verdict.

At this level, in the political realm where such matters would actually be decided, there were, however, a number of pending issues, and the way they were sorted out would be instructive. While the fact of McCarthy's censure seemed as certain as such a thing could be given the political vagaries of the process, the way it would be done intensely mattered—not so much to McCarthy himself, but to the people who condemned him. They didn't want any precedents that could be construed as limiting their own prerogatives as members of the Senate or committee chairmen.

Thus numerous charges that had any such connotation—treatment of witnesses, political speeches, the conduct of hearings, hiring of staff—would die a-borning. Many of the original forty-six counts were so flimsy as to fall immediately by the wayside, but even those of a presumptively serious nature would be discarded also if they contained any hint that they might be applicable to anyone other than McCarthy. All this would be hashed over by the committee, with the result that virtually all the original charges against McCarthy would be jettisoned for one reason or another.

When this winnowing was done, somewhat remarkably, forty-four of the original forty-six charges had been dismissed by the Watkins panel. The only counts remaining were McCarthy's alleged defiance of the Gillette inquest and his tirade against General Zwicker. The second of these, however, would soon be discarded also, as it came trailing too many problems to make it safely through the Senate. Even Senator Case, who had supported this count in committee, went wobbly after receiving information that Zwicker had behaved in such a way as to provoke McCarthy's outburst. The Zwicker charge was also unpopular with southern Democrats (many of whom had been committee chairmen and would soon be again as a result of Democratic victories in the 1954 election, and didn't want any precedents that would affect their powers).

So, in the end, the Zwicker charge was dropped, leaving only the count about the Gillette committee as the basis for McCarthy's censure. The rather amazing fact that a beginning mass of forty-six charges had now been reduced to exactly one might look like a sort of victory for McCarthy, but this was another angle from which the details were of little interest. The important thing was that McCarthy be censured for *something;* what it might be was pretty much a matter of indifference. And it was thought important also that this be voted by a substantial margin, providing cover all around for members of both parties, which meant political jockeying to get the lowest common denominator that everyone could agree on.

In the case of the Gillette committee charge, the denominator was low indeed—the weakest of the more serious counts against McCarthy, and the one on which he had reams of data to back his position. In this respect, the fact that the Gillette committee accusation was the last one standing was, to say the least, ironic. But it was in another way quite fitting, as the censure process itself, in both style and substance, was the lineal descendant of the Gillette inquest, as that probe in turn had been the son and heir of Tydings. (With a nice sense of what was proper, the Watkins panel would reprint, in its entirety, the final report of the Gillette committee, including its almost 300 pages dealing with McCarthy's finances.)

How all this was accomplished was an intriguing story in its own right. In particular, the already noted role of the National Committee for an Effective Congress is testimony to the leverage that can be exerted by a relatively small group that knows the ropes and is totally focused on its object. The NCEC and its "Clearing House" had well learned the lessons of the J. B. Matthews battle, and applied them on an even grander scale in the censure contest. Its role in preparing the thirty-three charges to back up the Flanders motion was but one example of its liaison with McCarthy's chief accuser.

The files of the NCEC are replete with such items as speech drafts prepared for Flanders, lists of specific accusations against McCarthy, whip counts of Senate votes, talking points on the censure charges, strategy memos advising Flanders on what to do and when to do it, and even a budget for supplying him with staffers whose salaries were to be paid from funds raised by the committee. (See page 595.) From these and other materials in the record there isn't much doubt that virtually the entire Flanders operation was orchestrated by the NCEC—and thus that an attack on McCarthy made under nominally Republican auspices was in fact directed behind the scenes by the far-left Democrats of the Rosenblatt committee.[11]

Given the innumerable praises heaped on Flanders for his "independence," all this puppetry by the NCEC was ironic also, but essential to the process. Had Democrats in the Senate taken the point in the effort to bring down McCarthy, it would have been viewed as a partisan move, undercutting the supposedly moralistic basis of the censure. It was thus critical that a Republican assume the lead, and the apparently limitless capacity of Flanders for accepting outside guidance made him the perfect candidate for the assignment. A further and especially important contact of the NCEC in this regard was liberal Republican businessman Paul Hoffman (sometime head of the Ford Foundation and a prominent Ike supporter).*[12]

Intriguing glimpses of the backstage maneuvers that led to McCarthy's censure are provided in the archives of the Rosenblatt committee. Among the major players at a series of meetings from April to June 1954, in addition to Rosenblatt himself, were former Senator Tydings, attorney Telford Taylor, Dean Clara Mayer of the New School for Social Research, Dean Francis Sayre of the Washington Cathedral, Benton attorney Gerhard Van Arkel, and former Truman staffer Philleo Nash. Pooling of left-liberal resources against McCarthy, agreement on the central role of the NCEC and fund-raising efforts for it, and the designation of former Senate staffer Laurence Henderson as the key liaison with Flanders were all on the group's agenda.

---

* As NCEC official George Agree put it in a memo to his colleagues Rosenblatt and Larry Henderson, "initial build-up has to be in establishing Republican character of the move." Agree said it was essential to keep arch-liberal Herbert Lehman quiet, and that Frank Carlson or some other GOPer "make statement favorable to the [censure] resolution." (This memo was titled "Ideas on Strategy and Timing re Operation Nut-Cutting.")

FUNDING FOR FLANDERS

This budget of the National Committee for an Effective Congress shows the organization's plans to provide staffers and other support to Senator Ralph Flanders in the campaign to censure McCarthy.

PROPOSED BUDGET

Six Week Period --- June 25 to August 10

Personnel

Key press relations expert	$1500
New York radio-press man	900
Researcher	750
Two secretaries	1000
One office manager	800
Reimbursement five executives for	5800

their salaries now paid in private employment. These men including Henderson, will cover the Senate, direct and conduct the phone campaign, travel. They will also provide the full-time assistance required by Flanders. (In event that project takes less than six weeks, total can be reduced. However, at least one month must be in hand before these men can obtain leaves of absence.) $10,750.00

Office Costs

Office rent (Capitol Hill hotel)	600.00
Office Supplies	300.00
Rental, office equipment	500.00
Postage	700.00
Total	2,100.00

Operating Costs *

Telephone -- Installation & Long D.	2,000.00
Telegrams and messenger	1,500.00
Printing and mimeographing	2,000.00
Travel	750.00
Miscellaneous expenses	1,000.00
Total	7,250.00

TOTAL BUDGET 20,150.00

* This does not include item for advertisments in three Washington papers which costs $3,500.00.

(It is expected that considerable volunteer service will be available for addressing, typing, and that other services will be contributed.)

Source: Maurice Rosenblatt papers, Library of Congress

Among the highlights of these records are scenes in which Dean Sayre, at a June meeting in Van Arkel's home, exhorted a group of twenty-five lobbyists, labor officials, and Hill functionaries to get behind the anti-McCarthy drive, this accompanied by a Rosenblatt pitch for funding of the NCEC as coordinator of the project. Revealing also are entries referring to Rosenblatt's "numerous conferences with [the] Democratic leadership," and the statement that on June 21, "Flanders received assurances of support from the highest administration leadership." We thus have a clear snapshot of leftward Democratic forces working in backchannel concert with the White House to push the censure effort forward.[13]

Given its liberal Democratic tilt, the NCEC not surprisingly had its best public entrée with members of the Democratic Party. Foremost among these was Arkansas senator Fulbright, an archliberal who despised McCarthy *a priori* and had directly tangled with him, most notably in the Jessup hearings. Fulbright was in essence the floor leader of the censure effort. He also provided guidance to the censure forces on how to bring around his conservative Arkansas colleague, John McClellan. Others with whom the NCEC had contact, either directly or at staff levels, were Sens. Mike Monroney, Thomas Hennings, and Herbert Lehman.

From this modest but solid foundation the campaign would be expanded outward to others in the Democratic ranks, including senators a good deal more conservative than Fulbright. Then–minority leader Lyndon Johnson would eventually put things together, as was his wont, on the basis of party-line requirements. In one way this would have been an easy sell, as the Democratic Party had suffered greatly from McCarthy. Once the southern Democrats were assured on matters that concerned them, an unbroken phalanx of Democratic votes would be arrayed against him.

It was, however, the lineup of Republican votes that was most crucial, as with the original leadership role of Flanders. In this respect, there is no doubt that the influence of the Eisenhower White House was decisive. Many White House connections to the censure effort were discreetly veiled, both then and later, but there are enough items in the record to tell the story rather plainly. The most obvious of these was the activity of Paul Hoffman, who not only aided the Rosenblatt group in numerous ways but had direct access to Ike himself and worked in tandem with White House adviser C. D. Jackson.

Behind the scenes, Hoffman had supported the Rosenblatt effort with financial contributions. In the midst of the censure battle, however, he would make the connection overt, underscoring the political links between the NCEC and the White House. Shortly after Flanders presented his resolution against McCarthy, the NCEC drafted, and Hoffman signed, a well-publicized telegram urging support of the censure motion. Like Hoffman himself, various of the twenty-plus other signers had been backers of Ike in the 1952 election. (The

NCEC authorship of this Hoffman missive is not in doubt, as Rosenblatt would later brag about it in an exultant letter to Benton aide John Howe.)[14]

In the background of the struggle, as he had been in the battles over J. B. Matthews and between McCarthy and the Army, was Sherman Adams. While he would later portray himself in almost clinical terms as a technician trying to moderate this and facilitate that, he made no secret of his aversion to McCarthy, and his known performance in the Matthews and Army conflicts belied his claim to purely procedural involvement with the censure.

Eisenhower himself, while professing a hands-off position, took pains to give special encouragement to Flanders when the accuser began his onslaught. Later, once the censure had been completed, Ike met with and congratulated Arthur Watkins on the fine service he had rendered. On leaving the President's office, Watkins was met by reporters who questioned him about the meeting. After filling in the press corps, Watkins also happily announced that the President had reconfirmed to him support for an important water project Watkins was pushing. Some cynics thought this looked suspiciously like a quid pro quo for McCarthy's censure.

In the end, these various overt and backstage efforts produced an even split among Republicans in the Senate: Twenty-two of the GOP contingent there— primarily from the northern and eastern sections of the country—voted in favor of the censure, while twenty-two others—mostly from the Midwest and West—opposed it. In addition, two GOP members, Homer Capehart of Indiana and John Bricker of Ohio, were paired in opposition, while McCarthy and his Wisconsin GOP colleague Alexander Wiley abstained from voting. Thus, while the recorded Republican votes were exactly equal, there were actually more GOP senators aligned with McCarthy than with the White House. The twenty-two Republican votes for censure nonetheless provided adequate basis for saying the condemnation was of bipartisan nature.*

While the censure battle was going down, McCarthy, William Jenner, Herman Welker, and a small band of others bitterly denounced what was occurring, and some McCarthy friends, including Everett Dirksen and Barry Goldwater, tried to broker a compromise that would avert an outright vote of condemnation. This would have involved some kind of apology by McCarthy, and a vote in the Senate that was something short of censure. According to Goldwater, McCarthy would have none of this and had thrown the pen he was asked to sign with across the room. He wouldn't crawl but would go down fighting.[15]

In this spirit, McCarthy presented a final defiant speech in which he criticized the methods of the Watkins inquest, calling it, among other things, the

---

*The one Democrat who almost unquestionably would have voted in favor of McCarthy, Pat McCarron, died in September 1954. The one Democrat who, rather famously, didn't vote at all was John F. Kennedy, who was in the hospital when the roll call was taken.

"unwitting handmaiden" of the Communists in derailing the work of his own committee. At the last moment, a completely new censure charge would be drafted for this further assault on the dignity of a Senate panel. This was duly added to the indictment—without any hearings or formal committee action— and adopted in the final tally of 67 to 22 in favor of McCarthy's condemnation. Of course, what McCarthy said about the Watkins panel was no worse, indeed was less severe, than what Flanders had said about McCarthy. But then, as Watkins had correctly noted, they weren't censuring Ralph Flanders.

Samson in the Heathen Temple

S O, FINALLY, they got him. How they did it is fairly plain, and instructive when the methods are considered. Why they did it is less apparent, as there were many "they"s involved, and a mélange of motives converging at the point of censure. Least clear of all is what the whole thing meant when it was over.

To all appearances, then and later, a crushing defeat was inflicted on McCarthy when his colleagues voted to condemn him. The defeat wasn't merely the three-to-one division in favor of the formal verdict but the informal penalties that followed. For many in the political world and press corps, he became a nonperson to be ignored and shunned, a ghost figure with no relation to the serious business of the Senate. Reporters who once hung on his every word now observed a tacit compact to treat him as if he were no longer there—which perhaps, in other than a purely physical sense, he wasn't.

Even worse for McCarthy was what happened to his name, record, and reputation in the ensuing decades. He died on May 2, 1957, just thirty months after the censure vote, and was taken back home to Appleton to be buried on a quiet hillside by the Fox River. He was only forty-eight when he died, an incredibly young age even then for one once physically so strong, albeit with his share of ailments.* Many observers thought he drank himself to death, others theorized foul play, still others that the censure and the ostracism had robbed him of the will to live.

Whatever the specific medical causes, it seems likely the terrific bouts of unremitting struggle and incessant pressure had taken their toll for some time before this. For most of the five years that his doings transfixed the nation, McCarthy was locked in mortal combat with the most powerful forces in the land, including two presidents of the United States, vast bureaucratic empires, formidable adversaries in Congress, relentless leftward lobby groups, and a horde of press, TV, and radio critics who made him their daily target.

Even more to the point, he had been put through the wringer of endless, back-to-back investigations and repetitive charges that drained time and energy, sapped his strength, and blocked him from pursuing the mission to which he was devoted. The psychological stress resulting from it all, while he was being portrayed to the American public as a monster, is hard to imagine. That it led him to drink, as many anecdotes allege, seems plausible indeed. So does the notion that the combined, unbearable burden finally broke his health and killed him.

However that may be, his early death, and the scattering of his staffers and records, put an end to whatever nucleus there was of pro-McCarthy information or expertise remaining after the censure was voted. Some, such as J. B. Matthews, still kept their files on cases, some like journalist Ralph de Toledano and committee staffer Jim Juliana squirreled away remnants of McCarthy's papers, some carried on the struggle in other venues. But there was no successor or political keeper of the flame, nobody in particular beyond his widow who would try to salvage his name or some kind of honorable place in history for him.†

Indeed, as time went on, the trend was all the other way around: McCarthy was dead and gone, his reputation in ruins after the Army hearings and the censure. Why bother trying to defend the indefensible? There were other things to do, other battles to be fought. No point in wasting time and resources on a cause so totally lost as that. And, perhaps more compelling, no desire to link other causes to the name of one thus reviled and battered, and now in death past caring.

For these reasons and some others, the field of McCarthy studies and related Cold War history was left mostly to his political foes, dominant in intellectual circles when he lived and virtually unchallenged in academic and media

---

* McCarthy's main physical complaint was a chronic sinus condition, painful and sometimes debilitating but not life-threatening.

†McCarthy's most likely successor in the internal security wars, his close friend Sen. William Jenner (R-Indiana), himself retired from the Senate the year after McCarthy's death.

precincts since. With a handful of exceptions, what purport to be histories of the era or biographies of McCarthy have been written by his severest critics. The views of his opponents are thus presented as the "facts," while significant data to the contrary have been denied, distorted, and in many cases suppressed entirely.

It was precisely here, of course, that the "total and eternal destruction" of McCarthy—or what appears to be such—was accomplished. Five decades of vilification, each new version heaped on and compounding those that went before it, scores of books and essays, countless media recaps driving home the message, spreading the villainous image to the widest possible public. And over this same span of fifty years, little or nothing of countervailing import.

As suggested in preceding pages, the costs of all this in terms of empirical truth and historical understanding have been great. We need only note that standard treatments of McCarthy, and histories of the age that delve into these matters, repeat in pertinent detail the spurious version of McCarthy's early cases invented by Tydings and his State Department allies: the Wheeling "205," the ersatz radio affidavits, the innocuous Lee list, the four committees, all recycled in pat formulations with no hint as to the bogus nature of these factoids.

As has been shown, this Tydings version of the matter is false in virtually every aspect, and where not conclusively so is sharply contrary to the available record. Its falsehood is the more egregious considering the deceptions used in putting it together: the backstage collusion with the State Department, vanishing documents and transcripts, the recording Tydings professed to have but didn't. Given all of which, we may well ask, why has the Tydings version been accepted, embellished, and purveyed to readers as a factual treatment of McCarthy's early cases?

Similar questions might be raised about other chapters in the story: naming the names, the Gillette committee's concealments and evasions, the multilayered cover-ups of *Amerasia* and felonious clearing of John Service, the Annie Lee Moss charade, and so on in grim procession. One has to search long and hard in conventional histories to find discussions of these matters that make the essential facts of record clear to the average reader.

That McCarthy made his share of errors, some contributing to his downfall, is true enough. A number of such have been noted in these pages: errors of detail in the presentation of his cases; the Marshall speech, a huge error of judgment and to some degree as well of fact; the unprovable "espionage" charge against Owen Lattimore; the emotional blowup with Zwicker; the use of harsh invective against various foes (though no harsher than the invective used against him). And errors, too, of omission: failure to tell the Senate he was mining data from the Lee list; not reining in Roy Cohn when he was badgering the Army about Schine.

These and other McCarthy miscues were important, not only because they were wrong or maladroit *per se* but because in the usual case they gave hostages to his opponents, who repeatedly used them to deflect attention from questions of lax security and loyalty risks on federal payrolls and make McCarthy him- self the issue. He thus strengthened the hands of powerful foes who had more than enough political/media muscle to begin with.

It would be possible simply by stringing such episodes together to build an indictment of McCarthy, which of course the usual histories do. However, these treatments invariably tilt the verdict by omitting or glossing over the cases in which he was proved right (*Amerasia,* the IPR, the debacle of State Depart- ment security practice, a long list of suspects from Gustavo Duran to Aaron Coleman, and countless others). A true balance sheet would have to include all this and a good deal more of similar nature to be even remotely accurate in its conclusions.

And, of course, the ledger can't be confined just to McCarthy, as if he were the only player in the drama. His record needs to be set over against that of his opponents, from Tydings and the State Department to Joe Welch and Stevens- Adams. On that kind of balance sheet, it's plain that McCarthy was far more sinned against than sinning, and that on the central issues he was chiefly right and his opponents chiefly in error. This was most obviously true in the early going against Tydings and the Gillette committee, but would remain so in later battles also.

Perhaps the easiest way of judging the matter is to note that McCarthy, throughout, was battling for public disclosure of the relevant data, while the typical stance of his adversaries was to suppress or obscure the facts, on what- ever pretext. Usually in such confrontations, it isn't difficult to figure out that the people trying to hold back information are the ones who will be embar- rassed by it, and thus the people who aren't being truthful. Concealment of data by his foes was so consistent a feature of the McCarthy saga it's hard to believe the writers who take the part of his opponents can't see it.

And of course it wasn't just concealment. It's impossible to study the gross deceptions of the Tydings report, the bizarre testimony of Tydings about the supposed recording from Wheeling, or the clanking contradictions of Bob Stevens and John Adams about the genesis of their charges against McCarthy, without seeing the pattern of flagrant falsehood.* The point is significant in itself but becomes the more so when we consider the things that were being concealed or palpably misstated. Despite all of which, our histories and biog-

---

* Stevens initially said he didn't know exactly where the charges had come from, while Adams clearly intimated that they proceeded from the high-level January meeting with top officials. After the May 17 secrecy order, and no doubt a good talking to by such officials, both got the message and changed their stories to read that the charges had been filed on the sole initiative of the Army.

raphies across a span of decades have depicted Tydings, Stevens-Adams, *et al.*, as the good guys, relatively speaking, and McCarthy as the villain.

In trying to understand all the slanted history, and why it continues, it's well to stress again that more is involved here than the doings of McCarthy. The real issue has always been the larger question of what actually happened to America—and the world—at the midpoint of the twentieth century, what it meant, and who was responsible for it. The point of the standard treatments, as seen, isn't merely that McCarthy was mistaken, but that the perspective he represented itself was evil and needs everywhere to be combated.

Nowhere is this more apparent than in discussion of the "China hands" in the State Department. There have been countless books and essays through the years not merely justifying but glorifying such as John Stewart Service, John Carter Vincent, John Paton Davies, and others at State for their alleged foresight on events in China. It is this view of the China issue and others like it that dictates the authors' attitudes on McCarthy. He was wrong because the China hands were right, or so these volumes tell us. From this angle, once more, McCarthy was almost an incidental figure. The motivations to write the history this way would be the same even if Joe McCarthy had not existed.

On the other hand, McCarthy in his heyday became a very consequential figure indeed, precisely because he threatened this reading of America's 'til-then feckless Asian policy and those complicit in it. His 1950 charges, and the explosion of public protest that followed, hit the Acheson State Department, its "China hands," and their various outside allies with stunning force—thus upsetting the plans and interests of many influential people. Numerous histories and biographies written in the intervening decades have been attempts to repair this damage, to win on the battlefield of history the war for public opinion that was lost so badly in the early 1950s.

And that, of course, is the other side of the story in deciding whether McCarthy was defeated or was in some sense the victor. It's true that, ultimately, they got him; but it's equally true that, before this happened, he got them—or at least a sizable number of them. In case after significant case—Service, Vincent, Lattimore, Jessup, Brunauer, O. Edmund Clubb, and scores of others—McCarthy's targets were driven from the field, and with them the *Amerasia*/IPR agenda for more Far East capitulations. It's doubtful that any other American figure, outside the confines of the White House, had more impact on the course of Cold War history. Whether that impact was for good or ill, of course, depends on one's perspective.

There were some other consequences also, in what might be viewed as collateral McCarthy damage. The Communist agent Mary Jane Keeney would finally lose her job at the United Nations, while the Soviet henchman Sol Adler decided in May 1950, at the fever pitch of the McCarthy furor, that the time had come to quit the Treasury and leave the country. Lauchlin Currie, though no longer holding a federal job, had been hanging around since 1945. He, too, departed in 1950. Perhaps it was mere coincidence that these two Soviet agents decided to skip precisely at this juncture; and perhaps it wasn't.

Still other direct and indirect examples of McCarthy's impact might be cited—most notably the firming up of security measures by the Truman administration in late 1951, switching from the unworkable "reasonable grounds" criterion to "reasonable doubt" (as recommended by Hiram Bingham), providing some realistic prospect of ousting egregious risks who lingered on the federal payroll. Such was the trend toward tougher McCarthy-driven security measures that developed in the early 1950s—aka the "reign of terror."

There are more instances of the McCarthy effect, but a couple relating to the Ike age and McCarthy's tenure as committee chairman are offered here by way of wrap-up. It's a remarkable but generally neglected fact that *every* major McCarthy investigation in the period 1953–54 resulted in some significant change in governmental practice: the State Department files, the business about Baker West, books in overseas reading centers, the loyalty drill at GPO, the Pentagon security daze suggested by Peress and Moss, and so on. In every instance, the officials in charge admitted there had been enormous foul-ups, and moved to take corrective action.

And there were also, as in the Truman era, some indirect consequences of McCarthy's hearings. As the executive sessions and backup committee records show, McCarthy beginning in mid-1953 was on the trail of Robert Oppenheimer, a fact well known to Ike and his lieutenants. There isn't much doubt this helped force the hand of the administration, impelling it to move on Oppenheimer before McCarthy did so. Thus Oppenheimer, too, could be added to the list of those who were in some fashion "victims" of McCarthy.

As to the why of the fierce opposition to McCarthy and reasons for the censure vote, there were as noted different motives that came together to produce that outcome. The situation is clearest with respect to the Senate's liberal Democrats and even with some of their conservative brethren. McCarthy was a thorn in the side of the Democratic party, as the issues of infiltration and security laxness all had their genesis under Roosevelt and Truman. The clamor McCarthy raised was extremely harmful to their party, which helps explain why under Truman every possible measure was taken to thwart McCarthy and obscure the truth about his cases.

Less understandable was the commitment of a Republican White House to cooperation in the censure—cooperation decisive to its success. Though there were obvious tensions all along, McCarthy until late in the day made it a point to say the problems he was addressing weren't the doing of the Ike administration. This became harder to maintain when it came to open warfare in the Army hearings, but even here, from the J. B. Matthews blowup forward, the moves that escalated the battle into fratricidal mayhem came more from the administration side than from McCarthy.

Add the fact that the Army hearings and the censure battle were disastrous for the Republican Party, heading into a tough election year that cost it control of Congress. Given all those factors, and even discounting for the detestation of McCarthy by many Ike advisers, the White House drive to annihilate him is something of a puzzle. One answer appears to be that the President and some of those around him thought McCarthy was trying to take over the party and planned to challenge Ike himself in the 1956 election.

These apprehensions weren't too realistic, and there is no evidence McCarthy seriously had such ambitions (beyond the why-not-me? syndrome familiar among politicians); he certainly had made no concrete plans to this effect that anyone was ever aware of. However, the Gallup poll in January of 1954 showed—rather incredibly, considering everything that had been said about him for four years running—that 50 percent of the American electorate had a favorable opinion of McCarthy, versus only 35 percent unfavorable. The Army hearings and censure battle would change those numbers in drastic fashion.

That McCarthy was a flawed champion of the cause he served is not in doubt (and who among us isn't?). It would have been better had he been less impulsive, more nuanced, more subtle in his judgments. On the other hand, somebody more nuanced and refined wouldn't have dreamed of grappling with the forces deployed against him. Those forces were powerful, smart, and tough, and they played for keeps. Taking them on was the task, not for a Supreme Court justice, but for a warrior. McCarthy, to his dying breath, was that.

Measured by the total record of his cases and political battles, McCarthy, whatever his faults, was a good man and true—better and truer by far than the tag teams of cover-up artists and backstage plotters who connived unceasingly to destroy him. The truth he served, moreover, was of the greatest import—the exposure of people who meant to do us grievous harm, and of long-standing indifference toward this menace by many at high official levels. In so doing, he summoned the nation to a firm-willed resistance to the Communist challenge, both abroad and on the home front. At the peak of his influence, the storm of protest he ignited shook a negligent ruling class to its foundations and scattered a host of furtive agents its lassitude had sheltered.

In the end he perished, politically and otherwise, in the rubble he pulled down around him. Yet when the final chapter in the conflict with Moscow was written, amid yet another pile of rubble, he was not without his triumph.

Notes

A Note on Citations

In the nature of the case, the names of certain individuals recur often in the titles of document collections, reports, and hearings cited in these notes. This is most obviously true of Joe McCarthy, the main character in the story. McCarthy maintained files, made speeches, conducted hearings, testified in other hearings and left certain materials now in the holdings of the National Archives and Records Administration (NARA). Also, he was himself the subject of various inquiries by the FBI, resulting in yet another file in which his name is featured.

A similar though slightly different situation obtains with McCarthy's first formidable antagonist in the Senate, Millard Tydings of Maryland. The Tydings name appears in the hearings he conducted on McCarthy's initial charges, the appendix to those hearings, and the report then issued by the investigating subcommittee. In addition, there are citations from the archive of the Tydings subcommittee, and from the file of Tydings's personal papers at the University of Maryland.

Still another source of multiple citations is the voluminous archive of the FBI, which conducted investigations on a host of subjects covered in this essay. Utilization of these records is further complicated by the highly technical "serial" numbering system with which the Bureau organized its reports and summaries—a system no doubt useful to the FBI but difficult for the layman to fathom. Also, while some of these files are paginated and indexed, a great many of them are not, making it hard to follow up citations.

In dealing with such issues, I have used certain procedures I hope will be helpful to the reader, sort out some complexities, and give a fairly clear idea of where the information came from.

As elsewhere suggested, there are three main tranches of McCarthy papers referred to in these pages: (1) A collection of McCarthy documents, case files, backup data, and other materials, pertaining mainly to his early cases; (2) some backup records of the McCarthy Permanent Subcommittee on Investigations, dating from 1953 and early 1954, held in the National Archives; and (3) a sizable group of later files, dealing with Fort Monmouth and potential investigations of other topics, extending both in subject matter and duration beyond the records in the archives. Rather than reciting all this each time one of these sources is mentioned, I have labeled these groups as McCarthy papers I, II, and III.

Otherwise, where McCarthy is referred to in the notes, the citations are from fairly standard public records—a collection of his speeches from the Government Printing Office, remarks in the *Congressional Record* or in public statements as reported by the press, hearings in which he testified or otherwise took part, and the hearings of the Senate Permanent Subcommittee on Investigations when he was its chairman.

In the case of Senator Tydings, the designations are as numerous but less complex. The citations used here, after the introduction of some formal titles, are: Tydings hearings, Tydings appendix, Tydings report, Tydings subcommittee archive, and Tydings papers.

As to the records of the FBI, rather than trying to follow the Bureau's system of "serials," the notes generally give the main title of the file—*e.g.,* FBI Silvermaster (Elizabeth Bentley) file, FBI Oppenheimer file, FBI Lattimore file, FBI *Amerasia* file, FBI McCarthy file, and so on. Throughout, the FBI volume number within the file is given (frequently called "section"), and where pagination is available the page number is likewise provided.

Prologue: The Search for Joe McCarthy

1. "Survey of Departmental Personnel Security Investigations," S. Klaus, August 3, 1946. For further comment on the Klaus report see Chapter 12, note 3.

2. Hearings of the Permanent Subcommittee on Investigations of the Senate Government Operations Committee (hereafter cited as McCarthy hearings), February 23, 1954.

3. "McCarthy Charges Reds Hold U.S. Jobs," *Wheeling Intelligencer,* February 10, 1950. Concerning which, see Chapter 14.

4. FBI Silvermaster file, Volume 71.

5. For discussion of this purported quote, see Thomas Reeves, *The Life and Times of Joe McCarthy* (Stein and Day, 1982), pp. 93–94 and accompanying note; and David Oshinsky, *A Conspiracy so Immense* (Free Press, 1983), p. 47 (especially footnote).

6. *New York Times,* May 24, 2000.

7. "Subversive Influence in the Educational Process," hearings of the Internal Security subcommittee of the Senate Committee on the Judiciary (hereafter cited as Senate Internal Security subcommittee), February 10, 1953, pp. 414–33; and February 24, 1953, p. 463.

8. Executive sessions of the Senate Permanent Subcommittee on Investigations of the Committee on Government Operations, 1953–54. (Hereafter cited as McCarthy executive hearings.) Five vols. Made public January 2003.

Chapter 1: An Enemy of the People

1. While by no means exhaustive, the list of books referred to includes the Reeves and Oshinsky volumes above cited; Robert Griffith, *The Politics of Fear* (University of Massachusetts Press, 1987); Richard Fried, *Men Against McCarthy* (Columbia University Press, 1976); Jack Anderson and Ronald May, *McCarthy: The Man, the Senator, the 'Ism'* (Beacon Press, 1952); Lately Thomas, *When Even Angels Wept* (Morrow, 1973); and Richard Rovere, *Senator Joe McCarthy* (Harcourt Brace, 1959). Briefer versions of the standard treatment are legion, usually provided as part of a more extensive survey of Cold War issues. Fairly representative are David Caute, *The Great Fear* (Simon & Schuster, 1978); Ellen Schrecker, *Many Are the Crimes* (Little, Brown, 1998); Richard Gid Powers, *Not Without Honor* (Free Press, 1995); Fried, *Nightmare in Red* (Oxford University Press, 1990); Anderson, *Confessions of a Muckraker* (Ballantine Books, 1979); and Fred J. Cook, *The Nightmare Decade* (Random House, 1971). A recent, more sympathetic treatment is Arthur Herman, *Joseph McCarthy* (Free Press, 2000).

2. The standard reference on the *Venona* decrypts is *Venona: Soviet Espionage and the American Response, 1939–1957,* Robert Louis Benson and Michael Warner, eds. (National Security Agency and Central Intelligence Agency, 1996). Two excellent studies of the subject, placed against a backdrop of other Cold War data, are Herbert Romerstein and Eric Breindel, *The Venona Secrets* (Regnery, 2000), and John Earl Haynes and Harvey Klehr, *Venona: Decoding Soviet Espionage in America* (Yale Press, 1999).

3. Valuable studies of data from the Soviet archives include Klehr and Haynes, *The Secret World of American Communism* (Yale Press, 1995); Klehr and Haynes, *The Soviet World of American Communism* (Yale Press, 1998); Allen Weinstein and Alexander Vassiliev, *The Haunted Wood* (Random House, 1999); and John Costello and Oleg Tsarev, *Deadly Illusions* (Crown, 1993).

4. The personal papers of Millard Tydings, as distinct from those of the Tydings subcommittee, are at the University of Maryland, College Park, Md. Various papers of William Benton are in the holdings of the State Historical Society of Wisconsin, Madison, Wis.

Chapter 2: The Caveman in the Sewer

1. Rovere, *Senator Joe McCarthy, op. cit.,* pp. 3, 19, 48, 73, 87.

2. On McCarthy's performance as a judge, see Ted Morgan, *Reds* (Random House, 2003), pp. 329 *et seq.*

3. Such denials were made to the author by two McCarthy associates who knew him in his final years, though others who were close to him then confirm the standard version. Most explicit on the subject was committee staffer James Juliana, who was with McCarthy almost daily until May 1957, and who categorically denied the chronic-drunkard image.

4. Morgan, *op. cit.,* p. 329; *New York Times,* April 20, 1955.

5. Such Russian-speaking occurred on at least two occasions—McCarthy's interrogation of Corliss Lamont, and thereafter of Igor Bogolepov, the defector referred to in the text. The exchange with Bogolepov was quoted in press accounts but dropped from the hearing record—apparently because the reporter misunderstood a dismissive comment by McCarthy. The exchange with Corliss Lamont is in the transcript. Both episodes occurred in McCarthy hearings, "State Department Information Program—Information Centers," September 28, 1953.

6. The North Dakota wheat farm stint is recounted in Anderson-May, p. 4, and Oshinsky, p. 57.

7. Among those protesting the Malmedy cases were *Christian Century* magazine, the Federal Council of Churches and the American Civil Liberties Union. See "Protests Increasing on Malmedy Trial," *New York Times,* March 2, 1949.

8. Quoted in Richard Gid Powers, *Secrecy and Power* (Free Press, 1987), p. 321.

Chapter 3: He Had in His Hand

1. Hearings of the subcommittee of the Senate Foreign Relations Committee, "State Department Employee Loyalty Investigation" (hereafter cited as Tydings hearings), June 23, 1950, p. 1376.

2. "William Henry Taylor, Treasury Department," McCarthy hearings, November 9, 1953, p. 20.

3. "State Department Information Program—Information Centers," McCarthy hearings, May 14, 1953. Among the *Venona* papers referring to "UCN9" and identifying him as Belfrage are cables of April 29,

May 19, May 29, June 21, June 22, and September 2, 1943.

4. The *Venona* message pertaining to Bisson and Bernstein is photographically reproduced in the NSA-CIA publication *Venona: Soviet Espionage and the American Response, 1939–1957,* p. 229.

5. "Transfer of Occupation Currency Plates, Espionage Phase," McCarthy hearings, October 20, 1953, pp. 25, 19.

6. *Major Speeches and Debates of Sen. Joe McCarthy* (hereafter cited as McCarthy speeches), Government Printing Office, June 14, 1951, p. 251.

7. Romerstein and Breindel, *op cit.,* pp. 138–39.

8. McCarthy speeches, February 20, 1950, pp. 45–46.

9. "Army Signal Corps—Subversion and Espionage," McCarthy hearings, December 14, 1953, pp. 159–64.

10. In the *Venona* decrypts, the cryptologists isolated the code name "Ruff" but were unable to establish the identity of the agent referred to. The identification of "Ruff" as Franz Neumann would be supplied by the so-called Gorsky memorandum of December 1948, which also confirmed many of the earlier identifications. See John Earl Haynes, "Comparative Analysis of Cover Names (Code Names) in the Gorsky Memo and Cover Names in Venona," October 2005. http://www.johnearlhaynes.org/page51.html

Chapter 4: "Stale, Warmed-Over Charges"

1. "Investigation of Communist Propaganda," report of the Special Committee to Investigate Communist Activities in the United States, U.S. House of Representatives, January 17, 1931.

2. Whittaker Chambers, *Witness* (Regnery, 1995), pp. 331 *et seq.* Chambers would rehearse these same details about the Washington apparatus in several appearances before Congress, most famously in the hearings of the House Committee on Un-American Activities in the summer of 1948.

3. Hearings of the Special House Committee on Un-American Activities, November 22, 1938, testimony of Ralph de Sola, pp. 2430–35.

4. For background on the founding, purpose, and proliferation of the fronts, see

Eugene Lyons, *The Red Decade* (Bobbs-Merrill, 1941), *passim.* On the specific role of Munzenberg, see Stephen Koch, *Double Lives* (Free Press, 1994).

5. Lyons, *op. cit.,* p. 47.

6. "Strictly Confidential," listing eleven organizations (Biddle's memorandum to department heads, prepared by the FBI). The organizations listed were, in order, the American League Against War and Fascism, the American League for Peace and Democracy, American Peace Mobilization, American Youth Congress, League of American Writers, National Committee for the Defense of Political Prisoners, National Committee for Peoples Rights, the National Federation for Constitutional Liberties, National Negro Congress, Washington Cooperative Bookshop, and the Washington Committee for Democratic Action. (Document in possession of the author.) These memos were placed in the *Congressional Record* at various times by Rep. Martin Dies and reproduced in Appendix IX of the House committee (see below). The number of groups on the list would later be expanded.

7. *Ibid.*

8. The full title of this volume is "Investigation of Un-American Propaganda Activities in the United States, Appendix IX, Communist Front Organizations, with special reference to the National Citizens Political Action Committee," U.S. House of Representatives, published 1944.

Chapter 5: Unthinking the Thinkable

1. *Parliamentary Debates (Hansard),* House of Commons, November 7, 1955. Kim Philby, *My Silent War* (Grove Press, 1968), p. 18.

2. There is a considerable literature on the Cambridge spy ring. Of note among more recent studies are Nigel West and Oleg Tsarev, *The Crown Jewels* (Yale Press, 1999) and, on the American aspect, Verne W. Newton, *The Cambridge Spies* (Madison Books, 1991). Earlier works include John Costello, *Mask of Treachery* (Morrow, 1988); Bruce Page, David Leitch, and Philip Knightley, *The Philby Conspiracy* (Doubleday, 1968); Barrie Penrose and Simon Freeman, *Conspiracy of Silence* (Farrar Strauss Giroux, 1987); and Chap-

man Pincher, *Their Trade Is Treachery* (Bantam, 1983).

3. Berle's notes are reproduced *in toto* in the proceedings of the Senate Internal Security subcommittee, May 16, 1953, pp. 329–30.

4. Because some of Berle's comments were construed as meaning he had given the Chambers data to the FBI, Hoover's agents confronted him on the matter, whereupon he conceded that he hadn't then given the information to the Bureau. Nichols to Tolson, FBI Silvermaster file, Vol. 142, Sept. 3, 1948.

5. When Duggan apparently committed suicide in December 1948, many eminent people sprang to his defense against allegations of subversion. Notable among his defenders was famed newscaster Edward R. Murrow. Murrow was a personal friend of Duggan and in his earlier career had worked for Duggan's father. See Joseph Persico, *Edward R. Murrow, an American Original* (DeCapa Press, 1997), p. 330. In the Duggan case, as in many others, the assertions of Whittaker Chambers (and fellow ex-Communist Hede Massing) would be borne out by *Venona* and data from the Soviet archives.

6. An extensive discussion of the Cambridge-American connection is provided by Newton, *supra.* In the specific case of Michael Straight, a recent study by Roland Perry, *Last of the Cold War Spies* (DaCapa Press, 2005), contends that Straight remained a Moscow agent for as long as the East-West struggle continued. Straight said he broke with the Soviets around the time of the Hitler-Stalin pact.

7. Michael Straight, *After Long Silence* (Norton, 1983), pp. 249–52.

8. The identifications of Norman and Greenberg as Communist Party member and Soviet agent, respectively, may be found in *Institute of Pacific Relations,* report of the Senate Internal Security subcommittee, 1952, p. 148. (Hereafter cited as IPR report.)

9. Costello, *Mask of Treachery, op. cit.,* p. 481. Of note is that Costello's reference here to Greenberg, and other comments on his case, were omitted from the paperback edition of this work later published by Warner Books.

10. Numerous details about this operation, Sorge himself, and such of his key contacts as Agnes Smedley and Guenther Stein are set forth in "A Partial Documentation of the Sorge Espionage Case," prepared by Army G-2 headquarters in the Far East under Maj. Gen. Charles Willoughby and supplied to Congress in May 1950. (Document in possession of the author.) Further data on the case, including the parts played by Ozaki and Saionji, as well as by Stein and Smedley, are given in "Hearings on American Aspects of the Richard Sorge Spy Case," House Committee on Un-American Activities, August 9 and August 23, 1951, featuring testimony by Willoughby and Japanese prosecutor Mitsusada Yoshikawa. Willoughby and Yoshikawa testified to similar effect in hearings of the Senate Internal Security subcommittee.

11. Maochun Yu, *OSS in China* (Yale Press, 1996), pp. 164, 280; and "Chen Hansheng's Memoirs and Chinese Communist Espionage," *Cold War International History Project Bulletin,* Issues 6–7, Winter 1995/1996, pp. 273 *et seq.*

12. Ralph de Toledano, *Spies, Dupes and Diplomats* (Duell Sloane and Pearce, 1952), p. 124.

13. IPR report, pp. 178–80.

14. Vitaliy Pavlov, *Operation Snow* (Geya Publishers, Moscow, 1996), Chapter I, "I Discover America"; see also Romerstein and Breindel, *op. cit.,* pp. 111 *et seq.,* and Toledano, *op. cit.,* pp. 72 *et seq.*

15. IPR report, pp. 156–57.

Chapter 6: The Witching Hour

1. The language of P.L. 135 appears in the files of the FBI pertaining to this investigation, designated as J. Edgar Hoover Official and Confidential file #59. These private Hoover files are usually cited as JEH O&C, and are so cited hereafter.

2. These standards were read into the record by Rep. Fred Busbey of Illinois in hearings of the House Committee on Un-American Activities, August 4, 1948, p. 626.

3. JEH O&C # 59. The memorandum containing this quote is followed by a lengthy entry setting forth the Dies list. As noted, the organizations used by Dies

to track federal workers—the American League for Peace and Democracy, Washington Book Shop, and Washington Committee for Democratic Action—were cited by Biddle himself in the roster of suspect groups he circulated to top officials.

4. Francis Biddle, *The Fear of Freedom* (Doubleday, 1951), p. 115.

5. Report of the Senate Internal Security subcommittee, January 3, 1955, p. 24.

6. *Ibid.,* p. 22.

7. This material was also read into the hearing record by Rep. Busbey, *loc. cit.,* pp. 633, 634.

8. "The Commissioning of Communists in the United States Army, 1941–1946," extension of remarks of Sen. Styles Bridges of New Hampshire, *Congressional Record,* January 2, 1951, p. 8002 *et seq.*

9. Hearings of Special Committee of the House Committee on Military Affairs, March 13, 1945.

10. Willard Edwards, "Bare Red Ties of 10 Officers in U.S. Army," *Chicago Tribune,* March 1, 1945; hearings of Special Committee of the House Committee on Military Affairs, March 13, 1945.

11. FBI Silvermaster file, Vol. 42.

12. Report of the Senate Internal Security subcommittee, January 3, 1955, pp. 25, 26.

13. "The Commissioning of Communists in the United States Army," *loc. cit.*

14. "Hearings of the Select Committee to Conduct an Investigation and Study of Facts, Evidence and Circumstances of the Katyn Forest Massacre," U.S. House of Representatives, November 1952, pp. 1852, 1883, 1932.

15. JEH O&C, #102.

16. *Ibid.*

17. These bizarre allegations were discussed by Lash himself in his book *Love Eleanor* (McGraw-Hill, 1982), pp. 445 *et seq.* Lash indicates that there was some kind of blowup by FDR that rebounded on G-2, but attributes this to the President's resentment that G-2 was spying on his wife.

18. Report of the Select Committee on the Katyn Massacre, December 22, 1952, p. 6.

19. *Ibid.,* p. 8.

20. *Ibid.*

21. George F. Kennan, *Memoirs* (Bantam Books, 1969), p. 88.

22. Summary FBI report (untitled) on Soviet espionage activity in the United States, November 27, 1945, p. 19. An unredacted copy of this somewhat celebrated report was in the files of Joe McCarthy (McCarthy papers III). It was frequently cited in congressional investigations of Communist infiltration of the U.S. government and other institutions. See Chapter 11.

23. *Ibid.,* p. 18.

24. "Communist Activities Among Aliens and National Groups," hearings before the Subcommittee on Immigration and Naturalization of the Committee on the Judiciary, U.S. Senate, September 15, 1949, p. 805. This Kerley testimony was in essence a paraphrase and digest of the FBI report of November 27, 1945, above cited.

25. Robert Lamphere and Tom Shachtman, *The FBI-KGB War* (Random House, 1986), p. 23.

26. Department of Justice statement, November 24, 1942.

27. JEH O&C, #102.

Chapter 7: The Way It Worked

1. Arthur Krock, "OWI's Critics Stirred by Broadcast on Italy," *New York Times,* August 1, 1943; and "President Rebukes OWI for Broadcast on Regime in Italy," *New York Times,* July 28, 1943.

2. Frederick Woltman, "AFL, CIO Hit OWI Radio as Communist," *New York World Telegram,* October 4, 1943.

3. November 27, 1945, FBI report, *loc. cit.,* pp. 30–32; FBI report, "The Comintern Apparatus," December 1944, p. 349.

4. Hearings of the Senate Internal Security subcommittee, April 24, 1956, p. 149.

5. Annual Report of the Senate Internal Security subcommittee for 1956, p. 163.

6. "State Department Information Program—Information Centers," McCarthy hearings, May 14, 1953; "Activities of United States Citizens Employed by the United Nations," second report, Senate Internal Security subcommittee, March 22, 1954, p. 22.

7. McCarthy hearings, "Army Signal Corps—Subversion and Espionage," February 23, 1954, p. 351.

8. Benjamin Mandel, "Memorandum on the Office of War Information for the Special Committee on Un-American Activi-

ties," May 1943, Sam Houston Regional Library and Research Center, Liberty, Tex.

9. "Study and Investigation of the Federal Communications Commission," hearings before the House Select Committee to Investigate the Federal Communications Commission, August 3, 1943, p. 324.

10. Remarks of Congressman John Lesinski of Michigan, *Congressional Record,* June 17, 1943, p. 6000; Jan Ciechanowski, *Defeat in Victory* (Doubleday, 1947), pp. 30–32.

11. Cranston's role was discussed in both the FCC hearings (August 5 and 20, 1943, pp. 378 *et seq.;* 1067 *et seq.*) and the Katyn investigation (November 11, 1952, pp. 1984 *et seq.*).

12. Remarks of Rep. Fred Busbey of Illinois, *Congressional Record,* November 4, 1943, p. 91455.

13. The Donovan testimony on Vucinich *et al.* is in the House Military Affairs subcommittee hearings above cited. Vucinich would plead the Fifth in hearings on "Interlocking Subversion in Government Departments," proceedings of the Senate Internal Security subcommittee, June 11, 1953.

14. Wolff and Fajans would both plead the Fifth before the Senate Internal Security subcommittee on June 16, 1953.

15. Duncan Lee makes frequent appearances in the *Venona* cables under the code name Koch. He would also be identified by Elizabeth Bentley as a member of the Washington spy ring that she managed for Moscow in the 1940s. (See Chapter 10.)

16. David Martin, *The Web of Disinformation* (Harcourt Brace Jovanovich, 1990), pp. 201, 150.

17. *Ibid.,* p. 150. Nora Beloff, *Tito's Flawed Legacy* (Westview Press, 1985), Chapter 3, "How Churchill Was Hoodwinked."

18. Martin, *op. cit.,* pp. 363–64.

19. Herbert Romerstein, "Aspects of World War II History Revealed through 'ISCOT' Radio Intercepts," *Journal of Intelligence History,* Summer 2005.

Chapter 8: Chungking, 1944

1. Louis Adamic, *My Native Land* (Harper, 1944), pp. 63 *et seq.;* McCarthy speeches, p. 227.

2. So noted, *e.g.,* by none other than John Service. Tydings appendix, p. 1974.

3. Service would discuss his rooming arrangements with Adler in materials reproduced in the Tydings appendix, *loc. cit.,* and in more detail during conversations recorded by the FBI. See FBI *Amerasia* file, note 13 below.

4. Don Lohbeck, *Patrick J. Hurley* (Regnery, 1956), p. 306.

5. An outline of Adler's career is provided in hearings of the Senate Internal Security subcommittee, December 3, 1953, pp. 1221 *et seq.*

6. Hearings on the Institute of Pacific Relations, Senate Internal Security subcommittee, August 14, 1951, p. 434. (Hereafter cited as IPR hearings.)

7. Philip Jaffe, *The Amerasia Case, from 1945 to the Present,* privately printed, 1979, pp. 1–2.

8. *The Amerasia Papers: A Clue to the Catastrophe of China,* prepared by the Senate Internal Security subcommittee, January 26, 1970, pp. 577, 592, 1015.

9. *Ibid.,* pp. 406, 410, 577, 579, 589, 1014.

10. *Ibid.,* pp. 943, 939, 1012–13, 724, 728.

11. *Morgenthau Diary: China,* prepared by the Senate Internal Security subcommittee, February 5, 1965, pp. 1463, 1948, 1134.

12. *Ibid.,* p. 1462.

13. *Amerasia Papers,* p. 592. FBI *Amerasia* file, Section 34.

14. *Amerasia Papers,* p. 94.

15. *Morgenthau Diary: China,* p. 1052.

16. *Amerasia Papers,* pp. 113, 112.

17. *Morgenthau Diary: China,* pp. 1996 *et seq.*

18. Albert C. Wedemeyer, *Wedemeyer Reports* (Holt, 1958), p. 285.

19. Maochun Yu, *OSS in China,* op cit., pp. 236, 221–22.

20. Jung Chang and Jan Halliday, *Mao* (Knopf, 2005), pp. 204–05.

21. *Amerasia Papers,* p. 583.

22. *Ibid.,* pp. 1014 *et seq.*

Chapter 9: Reds, Lies, and Audiotape

1. FBI report, November 27, 1945, p. 46 (also p. 33); see also "The Comintern Apparatus" (summary), March 5, 1946, p. 14.

2. The doings of Max and Grace Granich, their connections in the United States and China, and their linkage to John Service would be explored in hearings of the House Committee on Un-American Activ-

ities early in 1952. When asked if he knew Service, Max said he didn't, but Grace, when asked the identical question, took the Fifth Amendment. The House Committee was apparently in possession of information, obtained by the FBI, that Service had met with Grace, Tung Pi-Wu, and other Chinese Communists at a later date in Washington, D.C. Hearings of the House Committee on Un-American Activities, January 16 and 17, 1952, pp. 2265, 2299.

3. Tydings appendix, p. 2051.

4. FBI *Amerasia* file, Sections 34, 39.

5. *Ibid.,* Section 18.

6. *Ibid.,* Section 52.

7. *Ibid.,* Section 34.

8. *Ibid.,* Section 3.

9. *Ibid.,* Section 33.

10. The transcript of the Jaffe trial is reproduced in the Tydings appendix, pp. 1933–37.

11. *Congressional Record,* May 25, 1950, p. 7451.

12. *Ibid.,* p. 7452.

13. The wiretap logs appear in the Bureau *Amerasia* file at several places. These quotes are taken from a 1986 FBI release of this material, with cover memo summarizing key aspects, from D. M. Ladd to Director Hoover, June 30, 1952.

Chapter 10: When Parallels Converged

1. The FBI made extensive efforts to check out the bona fides of Bentley, which would be challenged when she went public with her testimony in 1948. FBI comments on her credibility include: "A studied attempt has been made to establish the basic truth or falsity of Gregory's [Bentley's] information . . . Gregory has mentioned over 150 names and in no instance has investigation indicated that a nonexistent person was mentioned . . . Gregory has reported with a high degree of accuracy situations within United States government policy which were known only within the government itself . . . In few instances has Gregory reported information which could not either directly or circumstantially be verified. A high degree of accuracy has prevailed throughout the revelations made by Gregory." FBI Silvermaster file, Vol. 82.

2. FBI Silvermaster file, Vol. 15; also appears in Vol. 54.

3. FBI Silvermaster file, Vol. 37.

4. Information about all these cases is strewn throughout the Bureau's Silvermaster file and, as indicated in Chapter 11, numerous reports that summarize the findings of the investigation. In these reports, the same names occur repeatedly, albeit with new cases and data added as the probe unfolded. The references here are chiefly taken from the report of October 21, 1946, "Underground Espionage Organization (NKVD) in Agencies of the United States Government," among the most thorough of the compilations, amplified in places by other data from Bureau records.

5. "Underground Espionage Organization (NKVD) in Agencies of the United States Government," October 21, 1946, FBI Silvermaster file, Vol. 82, pp. 131–32.

6. *Ibid.,* pp. 143 *et seq.* A further extensive discussion of Miller's contacts appears in the Silvermaster file, Vol. 56.

7. "Underground Espionage Organization," *loc. cit.,* pp. 160 *et seq.*

8. Hiss and Charles Kramer are discussed in this report as members of the Perlo group identified by Bentley. See discussion of Schwarzwalder in Vols. 18 and 58, Appleby in Vol. 42, Blaisdell in Vol. 64. Hiss himself is of course discussed much more extensively in the Bureau file devoted to the Hiss-Chambers case. Considerable information on Hiss would show up also in the internal records of the State Department. See Chapter 12.

9. "Underground Espionage Organization," *loc. cit.,* pp. 43, 52, 69, 163, 176.

10. *Ibid.,* pp. 259 *et seq.* Still more information on the Keeneys is provided in Silvermaster file, Vols. 55, 64, 65, and others.

11. FBI Silvermaster file, Vols. 25, 54.

12. "Underground Espionage Organization," *loc. cit.,* pp. 78 *et seq.*

Chapter 11: What Hoover Told Truman

1. William E. Odom, "Break Up the FBI," *Wall Street Journal,* June 12, 2002.

2. This report, though overlapping in many places with the Gregory-Silvermaster probe, obviously predated it and must be requested under the specific heading "the Comintern Apparatus" report, two volumes, December 1944.

3. FBI *Amerasia* file, Section 11.

4. Document in possession of the author. Copy found in McCarthy papers III, but report is also available in other files, including those of the House Committee on Un-American Activities.

5. FBI Silvermaster file, Vol. 25.

6. *Ibid.,* Vol. 23.

7. Must be specifically requested as "Comintern Apparatus/Communist Infiltration" summaries, March 5, 1946. (Documents bound together.)

8. FBI Silvermaster file, Vol. 16.

9. FBI Remington file, Section 1, July 29, 1948, and August 6, 1948. Contains a detailed summary of case, results of investigation, and lengthy recitation of dissemination of reports to high officials.

Chapter 12: Inside the State Department

1. Hearings of the House Committee on Un-American Activities, August 30, 1948, p. 1296. Though Berle would later make ambiguous comments about Hiss, it's noteworthy that he reemphasized his statement as to Acheson's position at this era. *E.g.,* ". . . I explained that Hiss was in favor of a much more complacent policy towards the Soviet Union than I was, therein following the lead of his immediate superior, Dean Acheson, but that honest men might differ on this subject and did . . ." And: "I testified before the House Committee that Acheson was one of the leaders of the 'appeasement' group at that time . . ." Adolf Berle, *Navigating the Rapids* (Harcourt Brace, 1973), pp. 584, 586.

2. Numerous Panuch-to-Russell memos on this subject, including several intensely critical of the OSS group and its designated leader at State (Col. Alfred McCormack, a transferee from Army G-2), may be found in the papers of J. Anthony Panuch, Boxes 7 and 8, Truman Library, Independence, Mo.

3. "Survey of Departmental Personnel Security Investigations," S. Klaus, August 3, 1946. This is the document that went missing from the Tydings subcommittee records and the State Department archive. A complete copy was found in the FBI McCarthy file. A further copy may be found in Tydings's personal papers, where

numerous other missing data from the subcommittee archives also came to rest. The portion quoted here is identical in relevant parts to that read by McCarthy into the *Congressional Record* for June 6, 1950, with the exception that Robert Bannerman's name was not given by McCarthy.

4. FBI McCarthy file, Section 5.

5. FBI Silvermaster file, Vol. 78.

6. Papers of Samuel Klaus, NARA, RG 59, Box 95.

7. FBI Silvermaster file, Vol. 149, p. 20.

8. There are several sources for this Bannerman memo on Miller, including the executive files of the House Committee on Un-American Activities. The copy quoted here is from McCarthy papers I.

9. The same is true of this memorandum on William Stone. The copy quoted here is from documentation presented by McCarthy to the Gillette subcommittee of the Senate Rules Committee, July 3, 1952. See Chapter 32.

Chapter 13: Acts of Congress

1. Extension of remarks of Rep. Paul Shafer of Michigan, *Congressional Record,* November 6, 1945, pp. A5091–93 and Rep. Carl Curtis of Nebraska, November 28, 1945, p. A5537.

2. "Soviet 'Situation' Halts House Bill," *New York Times,* March 15, 1946.

3. Memorandum to Donald Russell, July 19, 1946, J. Anthony Panuch Papers, Truman Library.

4. Panuch discussed his ouster in testimony to the Senate Internal Security subcommittee, June 28, 1953, pp. 907, 908. Acheson would give his version of the same episode in his memoir, *Present at the Creation* (Norton, 1969), p. 214.

5. Klaus memo, "Instructions for Mr. Wilson," February 3, 1947, papers of Samuel Klaus, NARA, RG 59, Box 95.

6. *Ibid.*

7. Klaus to Hamilton Robinson, February 24, 1947, *ibid.* (See also Box 103.)

8. Untitled Memorandum, February 11, 1947, *ibid.*

9. "Memorandum for the file," February 12, 1947, *ibid.*

10. "Memorandum for the file," April 11, 1947, *ibid.*

11. Klaus to John Peurifoy, "Inquiry from Congressman Stefan," March 21, 1947, *ibid.*

12. Remarks of Rep. Fred Busbey of Illinois, *Congressional Record,* May 14, 1947, p. 5398.

13. Peurifoy memo, "To Whom It May Concern," March 21, 1947, Papers of Samuel Klaus, *loc. cit.*

14. "Rees Bill Asks FBI to Aid in Loyalty Check," *Washington Times Herald,* April 11, 1947.

15. This meeting with Marshall would be described by Sen. Homer Ferguson of Michigan in remarks before the Senate, July 24, 1950, pp. 10805 *et seq.*

16. The details of this campaign and its results are set forth by Bert Andrews in *Washington Witch Hunt* (Random House, 1948). This book, written from the standpoint of the ousted employees and their attorneys, Arnold, Fortas and Porter, indicates that the dismissals were caused by congressional pressure.

17. The text of the Truman order, available in many places, is here cited from the Report of the House Interstate and Foreign Commerce Committee, "Directing the Secretary of Commerce to Transmit to the House of Representatives a Certain Letter with Respect to Dr. Edward U. Condon," April 15, 1948.

18. *Ibid.*

19. Interim Report of the House Committee on Un-American Activities, August 28, 1948, pp. 10–11.

20. Remarks of Sen. Homer Ferguson of Michigan, *Congressional Record,* August 7, 1948, pp. 10272–77.

Chapter 14: Wheeling, 1950

1. "McCarthy Charges Reds Hold U.S. Jobs," *Wheeling Intelligencer,* February 10, 1950.

2. See Tydings appendix, pp. 1756 *et seq.*

3. "Report of Preliminary Investigation of Senator William Benton's Charges Against Senator Joseph McCarthy, Relating to Senate Resolution 187," Subcommittee on Privileges and Elections, Senate Rules Committee (the Gillette subcommittee), January 1952. Papers of Sen. Robert Hendrickson, Syracuse University.

4. *Ibid.,* pp. 6–7.

5. *Ibid.,* pp. 30–32.

6. *Ibid.*, p. 28.

7. *Ibid.*, p. 32.

8. *Ibid.*, p. 28.

9. *Ibid.*, p. 31.

10. Interview with the author, March 2, 2000.

11. *Ibid.*

12. *Ibid.*

13. "Senator Joe McCarthy's Visit to Valley Area," *Wheeling Intelligencer,* February 11, 1950.

14. "Excerpts from Senator McCarthy's Address Before Ohio Valley Women's GOP Clubs," *Wheeling Intelligencer,* February 10, 1950.

15. *Denver Post,* February 11, 1950.

16. *Salt Lake Tribune,* February 11, 1950; *Salt Lake Telegram,* February 11, 1950; Gillette subcommittee memo, p. 9.

17. McCarthy speeches, p. 10.

18. "McCarthy Blasts State Department," *Nevada State Journal,* February 12, 1950.

19. "McCarthy's Attack on Reds Here Now Collector's Item," *Wheeling Intelligencer,* July 6, 1950.

20. Benton papers, Box 4.

Chapter 15: Discourse on Method

1. *Washington Times Herald,* February 19, 1950.

2. *Washington Sunday Star,* February 19, 1950.

3. McCarthy speeches, p. 6.

4. *Ibid.*, pp. 8–9.

5. *Ibid.*, p. 12.

6. *Ibid.*

7. *Ibid.*, p. 17.

8. *Ibid.*, p. 21–22.

9. *Ibid.*, p. 30.

10. *Ibid.*, p. 52.

11. *Ibid.*, pp. 34, 37, 39.

12. *Ibid.*, p. 51.

13. *Ibid.*, pp. 34, 36.

14. *Ibid.*, pp. 36, 38.

15. *Ibid.*, p. 54.

16. *Ibid.*, p. 48.

17. *Ibid.*, p. 11.

18. *Ibid.*, pp. 18–19, 24, 46.

19. *Ibid.*, p. 17.

20. *Ibid.*, p. 34.

21. *Ibid.*, pp. 35–36.

22. *Ibid.*, pp. 44–45.

23. *Ibid.*, p. 49.

24. *Ibid.*, p. 46.

25. *Congressional Record,* April 5, 1950, p. 4958.

26. Tydings hearings, pp. 17–18.

Chapter 16: The Tydings Version

1. Tydings hearings, p. 1.

2. Lately Thomas, *op. cit.* p. 124.

3. Tydings hearings, p. 6.

4. *Ibid.*, p. 11.

5. *Ibid.*, pp. 47, 40.

6. *Ibid.*, p. 47.

7. *Ibid.*, p. 70.

8. *Ibid.*, p. 25.

9. *Ibid.*, p. 780.

10. *Ibid.*, p. 28.

11. *Ibid.*, p. 257.

12. *Ibid.*

13. *Ibid.*, pp. 272–73.

14. Testimony of Owen Lattimore, IPR hearings, February 28, 1952, p. 3085.

15. Tydings hearings, p. 417.

16. *Ibid.*, p. 429.

17. *Ibid.*, pp. 490–95.

18. *Ibid.*, p. 491.

19. *Ibid.*, p. 628.

20. *Ibid.*, p. 685.

21. *Ibid.*, p. 698.

22. *Ibid.*, p. 702.

23. *Ibid.*

24. *Ibid.*, p. 706.

25. *Ibid.*, pp. 2519, 2521.

26. *Ibid.*, p. 2522.

27. Transcript of trial, *United States of America v. Earl Russell Browder,* March 8, 1951.

28. *Ibid.*

Chapter 17: Eve of Destruction

1. Tydings papers, Series V, Box 3.

2. Tydings papers, Series V, Box 2.

3. Benton papers, Box 4.

4. This letter and a similar one to Edward Connors appear in Tydings papers, Series V, Box 12.

5. Tydings appendix, p. 1754.

6. Correspondence of Edward Connors to John P. Moore, Chief Counsel, Gillette subcommittee, April 24, 1952. Document in possession of the author.

7. Tydings papers, Series V, Box 12.

8. Tydings papers, Series V, Box 9.

9. Tydings papers, Series V, Box 12.

10. Gillette subcommittee memo, *loc. cit.,* p. 24.

11. Tydings papers, Series V, Box 7.

12. Tydings papers, Series V, Box 6.

13. Eben A. Ayers, *Truman in the White House* (University of Missouri Press, 1990), p. 348.

14. "War on McCarthy," *Newsweek,* May 15, 1950.

15. *Congressional Record,* May 1, 1950, pp. 6108 *et seq.*

16. "Statement of Deputy Under Secretary John E. Peurifoy," State Department press release, May 2, 1950.

17. *Congressional Record,* May 3, 1950, p. 6247.

18. *Ibid.,* p. 6248.

19. *Ibid.,* pp. 6257, 6254.

20. "Memorandum for Mr. Dawson, Subject: Continuing the Counter-Offensive Against McCarthy," May 8, 1950, Truman papers, Official File, Truman Library.

Chapter 18: A Fraud and a Hoax

1. *Congressional Record,* July 24, 1950, pp. 10813–14.

2. *Ibid.,* p. 10813.

3. The omitted pages are printed in the *Congressional Record,* July 24, 1950, pp. 10815–19.

4. Tydings hearings, pp. 2523–25.

5. *Congressional Record,* July 17, 1950, p. 10397; and July 20, 1950, p. 10698.

6. *Congressional Record,* July 20, 1950, p. 10697.

7. *Ibid.,* p. 10686.

8. *Congressional Record,* July 21, 1950, pp. 10783, 10785.

9. Tydings report, pp. 149, 150, 151, 152, 167.

10. *Ibid.,* p. 150.

11. *Ibid.,* p. 167.

12. *Ibid.,* p. 153.

13. *Congressional Record,* July 24, 1950, pp. 10805–15.

14. *Ibid.,* p. 10701.

15. Tydings report, p. 124.

16. *Ibid.,* pp. 93, 148.

17. *Ibid.,* p. 73.

18. *Ibid.,* p. 149.

19. *Congressional Record,* July 20, 1950, pp. 10704–05.

20. *Congressional Record,* July 17, 1950, p. 10396.

21. *Congressional Record,* July 20, 1950, p. 10699.

22. *Congressional Record,* July 24, 1950, p. 10815.

23. *Congressional Record,* July 20, 1950, p. 10714.

24. *Ibid.,* pp. 10708–09, 10716.

25. Depositions of Millard E. Tydings and Edward P. Morgan, U.S. District Court for the District of Columbia, September 3, 1952, p. 80. Tydings's explanation was that he hadn't actually *said* he had a recording of the Wheeling speech—which he hadn't, merely implying it in every possible way.

Chapter 19: Of Names and Numbers

1. This version of the matter is set forth repeatedly in the Tydings report and in comments of the State Department. Conspicuous examples may be found in the Tydings subcommittee findings on "The Story of the '81 Cases' " and a lengthy State Department press release reprinted in its entirety by Tydings (Tydings report, pp. 6–9; 14–17).

2. McCarthy speeches, p. 29.

3. *Ibid.,* pp. 33, 31, 21, 82.

4. *Ibid.,* p. 30.

5. *Ibid.,* p. 57.

6. *Ibid.,* p. 21.

7. *Ibid.,* p. 53.

8. McCarthy letter to Tydings, March 18, 1950; supplementary names provided, March 14, 1950. Documents in possession of the author. (McCarthy papers I.)

9. This comparative table appears in the Tydings appendix, beginning at p. 1814.

10. Tydings hearings, p. 731.

11. Tydings appendix, p. 1817. (Fishburn-Washburn was McCarthy's case #80.)

12. The calculations concerning the State Department employees are based on the department's personnel listings for February 1950, Foreign Service listings for April 1950, and *Biographic Register* for 1951.

13. Tydings report, p. 15.

14. Alfred Friendly, "The Noble Crusade of Senator McCarthy," *Harper's,* August 1950.

Chapter 20: The Four Committees

1. Tydings report, p. 7.

2. *Ibid.,* p. 165.

3. Oshinsky, *op. cit.,* p. 110–14.

4. Reeves, *op. cit.,* pp. 227–28.

5. There are many copies of the Lee list

extant, mostly in mimeograph form as circulated in the halls of Congress (all identical as to text, but with different ancillary data). The version most accessible to researchers, though without name keys and somewhat buried in a voluminous record, is in the appendix to the Tydings hearings, pp. 1745 *et seq.*

6. Hearings on State Department appropriations, subcommittee of the House Appropriations Committee, January 28, 1948, p. 191.

7. *Ibid.*, p. 176.

8. Report of the House Committee on Appropriations, February 27, 1948.

9. *Congressional Record,* March 3, 1948, p. 2085; March 4, 1948, p. 2158.

10. *Ibid.,* March 3, 1948, pp. 2085–86.

11. Tydings report, p. 8.

12. Hearings of State Department subcommittee, House Committee on Expenditures, March 12, 1948.

13. *Ibid.*

14. FBI Silvermaster file, Vol. 109, pp. 51, 92.

15. Hearings of State Department subcommittee, House Committee on Expenditures, March 12, 1948.

16. FBI Silvermaster file, Vol. 94, p. 67.

17. *Congressional Record,* July 24, 1950, pp. 10805 *et seq.*

18. *Congressional Record,* August 2, 1948, pp. 9643–44.

Chapter 21: File and Forget It

1. McCarthy speeches, p. 35.

2. Tydings to Truman, April 12, 1950, Tydings papers, *loc. cit.*

3. Tydings hearings, p. 1.

4. "State Dept. to Open Files in Loyalty Probe," *Washington Post,* March 11, 1950.

5. Tydings hearings, pp. 249–55.

6. FBI McCarthy file, Section 1.

7. FBI McCarthy file, Section 1, Section 4b.

8. Alan Belmont to D. M. Ladd, March 30, 1950, FBI McCarthy file, Section 1.

9. Tydings subcommittee archive, Box 4; Tydings report, p. 173.

10. Tydings report, p. 12.

11. FBI McCarthy file, Section 4.

12. FBI McCarthy file, Section 5.

13. These statements are taken from a cover memorandum by House Committee investigators in connection with the so-called Lee list. See Chapter 19.

14. Associated Press report, June 21, 1950.

15. FBI McCarthy file, Section 5.

16. Hoover to McCarthy, July 10, 1950, McCarthy papers I.

17. Tydings report, p. 11.

18. FBI McCarthy file, Section 6.

19. McCarthy speeches, pp. 149–50.

20. Tydings report, p. 171.

21. McCarthy hearings, "State Department File Survey," February 4, 1953.

Chapter 22: All Clear in Foggy Bottom

1. Tydings report, p. 17.

2. Hearings of the subcommittee on State Department appropriations, Senate Appropriations Committee, supplemental appropriations for 1953, March 27, 1952, p. 502.

3. *Congressional Record,* February 20, 1950, p. 2071.

4. McCarthy speeches, p. 79.

5. This was the status of the matter as it stood in October 1951. It subsequently developed that three employees had been brought up on loyalty charges, but none had been dismissed at the time of Snow's orations.

6. McCarthy placed excerpts from these LRB minutes in the *Congressional Record* for January 15, 1952, beginning at p. 192. A more extensive, typewritten version of these proceedings was held in McCarthy's files (McCarthy papers I). The quotes given here are from this more detailed version.

7. LRB proceedings, McCarthy papers I.

8. *Ibid.*

9. *Ibid.*

10. Senate Appropriations subcommittee hearings, March 25–28, 1952, *loc. cit.*

11. *Ibid.*

12. *Ibid.,* p. 497.

13. *Ibid.,* pp. 499–500.

14. *Ibid.,* p. 542.

15. *Ibid.,* pp. 980–81.

16. *Ibid.,* p. 963.

17. *Ibid.,* p. 52.

18. *Ibid.,* pp. 387–89.

19. *Ibid.,* p. 419.

20. *Ibid.,* pp. 454–55.

21. *Ibid.,* p. 389.

22. *Ibid.,* p. 392.

Chapter 23: The Man Who Knew Too Much

1. McCarthy speeches, p. 11.
2. FBI McCarthy file, Section 1b.
3. Tydings hearings, p. 131.
4. FBI McCarthy file, Section 1.
5. *Congressional Record,* April 25, 1950, pp. 5897–98.
6. FBI McCarthy file, Section 1b.
7. FBI McCarthy file, Section 2.
8. Tydings hearings, p. 291.
9. McCarthy speeches, pp. 61–62, 125, *et seq.*
10. FBI Lattimore file, Vols. 20, 25.
11. FBI McCarthy file, Section 5.
12. *Ibid.*
13. Tydings report, p. 95.
14. Senate Appropriations subcommittee hearings, March 1952, *loc. cit.*
15. FBI McCarthy file, Section 1b.
16. Stanley to Rosen, November 23, 1954, FBI McCarthy file, Section 2.
17. J. B. Matthews papers, Duke University. Document provided by Ira Katz.
18. FBI McCarthy file, Section 1.
19. Statement of Miriam de Haas, *Washington Times-Herald,* November 2, 1952.

Chapter 24: The Trouble with Harry

1. FBI Oppenheimer file, Section 1.
2. *Ibid.* This same information, and much more like it, is repeated many times throughout the Bureau's voluminous file on Oppenheimer, and would be paraphrased in the charges later brought against him by the Atomic Energy Commission.
3. Hoover letter to Gen. Harry Vaughan, for the attention of President Truman, with accompanying memo summarizing key points in the Oppenheimer case, November 15, 1945. *Ibid.*
4. On Oppenheimer's multitude of new responsibilities under Truman, see James Shepley and Clay Blair Jr., *The Hydrogen Bomb* (David McKay, 1953), p. 29.
5. United States Atomic Energy Commission, Personnel Security Board, "In the Matter of J. Robert Oppenheimer," proceedings of the Gray Commission, April 1954, p. 48. The letters from Bush and Conant appear in FBI Oppenheimer file "Supplemental Release of Referred Documents" at end of series (no file number).

6. *Ibid.,* pp. 415, 420.
7. *Ibid.,* p. 425.
8. Testimony of Attorney General Herbert Brownell before the Senate Internal Security subcommittee, November 17, 1953, pp. 1109 *et seq.*
9. These issues are discussed at length in many Bureau memos, most notably in Section 3 of the FBI file on White, and in Vols. 155 and 158 of the Silvermaster file. As Bureau official A. H. Belmont summed up the matter to D. M. Ladd: "From the foregoing, it will be seen that, as of March 1946, the Treasury Department was in possession of all the essential allegations from Elizabeth Bentley and we had placed no restrictions on them from dismissing various persons in their employ named in the summaries." December 1, 1953. FBI Silvermaster file, Vol. 158.
10. Testimony of J. Edgar Hoover to Senate Internal Security subcommittee, November 17, 1953, p. 1146.
11. "Interlocking Subversion in Government Departments," proceedings of the Senate Internal Security subcommittee, Part 14, Appendix 1, p. 958.
12. This memorandum is photographically reproduced in *Venona: Soviet Espionage and the American Response, loc. cit.,* p. 117.
13. FBI Hiss-Chambers file, Vol. 6.
14. *Ibid.,* Vol. 12.
15. *Ibid,* Vols. 1 and 2.
16. Truman interview with Prof. Anthony Bouscaren, on television station WXIX, Milwaukee, Wis., September 3, 1956; transcript printed in *U.S. News & World Report,* September 14, 1956.
17. "A Synopsis of the Edward U. Condon Case," House Committee on Un-American Activities, November 11, 1958.
18. *Ibid.*
19. *Ibid.*
20. "Investigation of Edward U. Condon," testimony of Adrian Fisher, executive hearings of the House Committee on Un-American Activities, March 9, 1948.
21. "Interlocking Subversion in Government Departments," hearings of Senate Internal Security subcommittee, December 3, 1953, pp. 1221 *et seq.*
22. *Ibid.,* p. 1230.

23. "Export Policy and Loyalty," hearings of the Investigations subcommittee, Senate Committee on Expenditures in the Executive Departments, July 30, 1948, p. 57.

24. *Ibid.,* pp. 359–61.

25. *Ibid.,* pp. 336–37.

26. LRB Memorandum of Decision, January 27, 1949. The rationale for this decision by the Richardson Loyalty Review Board is discussed at sympathetic length by Gary May in *Un-American Activities* (Oxford University Press, 1994), pp. 111 *et seq.*

Chapter 25: A Book of Martyrs

1. FBI Silvermaster file, Vol. 114, p. 479.

2. FBI Silvermaster file, Vol. 155, p. 55.

3. Tydings appendix, p. 1794.

4. *Ibid.,* p. 1795.

5. McCarthy speeches, p. 71.

6. Hillenkoeter to McCarthy, March 2, 1950, Tydings papers, Series V, Box 7.

7. McCarthy speeches, p. 17.

8. Hearings of the Senate Internal Security subcommittee, October 8, 1957, pp. 1855–56.

9. "The Memoir of Gordon Griffiths," 1999, Library of Congress Manuscript Division, Shelf No. 23, 107.

10. Remarks of Sen. Joe McCarthy, *Congressional Record,* July 26, 1956.

11. Tydings appendix, p. 1815.

12. Jack Anderson, *Confessions of a Muckraker* (Ballantine Books, 1979), p. 221.

13. Tydings appendix, p. 1816.

14. FBI Lattimore file, Section 17, p. 13.

15. FBI McCarthy file, Section 3.

16. *Ibid.*

17. McCarthy speeches, p. 53.

18. The Chambers statements to Raymond Murphy concerning Post are included in Murphy memoranda of March 20, 1945, and August 28, 1946, both printed in proceedings of the Senate Internal Security subcommittee, December 2, 1953, pp. 1181–83.

19. FBI Silvermaster file, Vol. 42.

20. Remarks of Rep. Fred Busbey of Illinois, *Congressional Record,* March 25, 1948, p. A1912.

21. FBI Lattimore file, Vol. 10, p. 90.

22. Investigative memoranda and witness statements in proceedings concerning Charles W. Thayer. McCarthy papers I.

Chapter 26: Some Public Cases

1. Tydings hearings, pp. 189–99.

2. *Ibid.,* p. 208.

3. Haldore Hanson, *Humane Endeavour: The Story of the China War* (Farrar & Rinehart, 1939).

4. *Ibid.,* pp. 32, 101, 44–45, 267, 349.

5. *Ibid.,* pp. 305, 273, 311, 69.

6. *Ibid.,* p. 227.

7. *Ibid.,* p. 37.

8. Tydings hearings, pp. 590–91.

9. See Brunauer memoranda and related data in papers of Maurice Rosenblatt/National Committee for an Effective Congress, Boxes 12, 18, Library of Congress Manuscript Division; and Brunauer testimony to Tydings committee, pp. 295 *et seq.*

10. Tydings report, p. 29.

11. These data are provided in Appendix IX, pp. 550, 553; the same information is included in the Tydings appendix, p. 1518.

12. Tydings hearings, p. 91.

13. Tydings report, p. 29.

14. Report of the Special House Committee on Un-American Activities, March 29, 1944, p. 154.

15. Tydings hearings, p. 87.

16. Tydings report, p. 29.

17. Memoranda of loyalty board on Brunauer cases, #325 (Esther Brunauer) and #326 (Stephen Brunauer), executive files of House Committee on Un-American Activities, NARA. Document provided by Ted Morgan.

18. Tydings hearings, p. 119.

19. *Time,* October 21, 1951.

20. McCarthy speeches, pp. 334 *et seq.*

21. Statement of Henry Luce issued by Time, Inc., November 9, 1951.

22. Ronald Radosh, Mary R. Habek, and Grigory Sevostianov, eds., *Spain Betrayed* (Yale Press, 2001), pp. 306, 333.

23. "Review of the Scientific and Cultural Conference for World Peace," report of the House Committee on Un-American Activities, April 19, 1949, p. 11.

Chapter 27: Tempest in a Teacup

1. Tydings report, pp. 138–41.

2. An extended discussion of Walker Stone of the Scripps-Howard chain as the source for Hoover's "airtight" quote is contained in FBI *Amerasia* file, Section 59.

3. Tydings appendix, p. 2310; Tydings hearings, p. 999.

4. FBI *Amerasia* file, Section 54.

5. *Ibid.*

6. *Congressional Record,* May 25, 1950, p. 7543.

7. Tydings hearings, p. 974.

8. FBI *Amerasia* file, Section 53.

9. Alfred Friendly, "U.S. Denies Reports of 5 'Secrets,' " *Washington Post,* June 1, 1950.

10. FBI *Amerasia* file, Section 52.

11. Morgan memo to file, June 2, 1950, Tydings papers, series V, Box 3.

12. FBI *Amerasia* file, Section 29.

13. Tydings hearings, p. 974.

14. FBI *Amerasia* file, Section 53.

15. FBI *Amerasia* file, Section 51.

16. *Ibid.*

17. FBI *Amerasia* file, Section 52.

18. FBI *Amerasia* file, Section 53.

19. Hoover to James Hatcher, May 25, 1950, FBI *Amerasia* file, Section 51.

20. FBI *Amerasia* file, July 30, 1950, Section 53.

21. *Congressional Record,* May 25, 1950, p. 7453.

22. Tydings appendix, p. 2283.

Chapter 28: Little Red Schoolhouse

1. McCarthy speeches, p. 85; Tydings report, p. 41.

2. All these identifications, save Rose Yardumian, are given in the IPR report, p. 97 and pp. 147–59. The identification of Yardumian was made by former IPR official William Johnstone, McCarthy hearings (Voice of America), March 4, 1953, p. 432.

3. IPR report, p. 97.

4. IPR hearings, p. 437.

5. IPR report, p. 97.

6. McCarthy speeches, p. 83.

7. IPR Report, pp. 111–12.

8. *Ibid.,* pp. 208–09.

9. *Ibid.,* p. 79.

10. FBI IPR file, Section 47.

11. *Ibid.,* Section 14, part 2.

12. IPR report, pp. 223–25.

Chapter 29: "Owen Lattimore Espionage — R"

1. McCarthy speeches, p. 85.

2. Tydings report, pp. 52–53, 161.

3. *Ibid.,* p. 161.

4. Owen Lattimore, *Solution in Asia* (Little, Brown, 1945), p. 139.

5. Owen Lattimore, *The Situation in Asia* (Greenwood Press, 1949), pp. 79–80.

6. *Solution in Asia,* p. 141.

7. *Ibid.,* pp. 141–42.

8. *Situation in Asia,* p. 69.

9. IPR report, pp. 16–17.

10. Owen Lattimore, "New Road to Asia," *National Geographic,* December 1944.

11. IPR report, p. 119.

12. *Ibid.*

13. *Ibid.,* p. 46.

14. *Ibid.,* p. 225.

15. Tydings hearings, p. 484.

16. FBI Lattimore file, Section 10, p. 73.

17. FBI Lattimore file, Section 1, p. 1.

18. FBI IPR file, Section 3, p. 10.

19. FBI Lattimore file, Section 2, p. 81.

20. FBI Lattimore file, Section 1, p. 92.

21. FBI Lattimore file, Section 2, p. 67.

22. Memorandum to James M. McInerney, Assistant Attorney General, Criminal Division, and William E. Foley, Chief, Internal Security Division, June 17, 1952. McCarthy papers III.

23. *Ibid.*

24. FBI *Amerasia* file, Section 10.

25. IPR hearings, p. 3199.

Chapter 30: Dr. Jessup and Mr. Field

1. "Nomination of Philip C. Jessup," hearings of the subcommittee on nominations, Senate Committee on Foreign Relations (hereafter cited as Jessup hearings), September 21, 1951, pp. 24 *et seq.*

2. *Ibid.,* p. 4.

3. *Ibid.,* p. 170.

4. *Ibid.,* p. 172.

5. House Committee on Un-American Activities, *Guide to Subversive Organizations and Publications* (1957), p. 16.

6. "Un-American Activities in California," report of the California State Committee on Un-American Activities, 1948, pp. 169–72, and 1949, p. 412.

7. Appendix IX, p. 1067.

8. Jessup hearings, p. 43.

9. *Ibid.,* pp. 60 *et seq.*

10. *Ibid.*

11. "Un-American Activities in California," report of the California State Committee on Un-American Activities, 1949, p. 694.

12. Jessup hearings, pp. 231, 250, 182.

13. IPR hearings, p. 5228.

14. IPR report, p. 54.

15. Jessup hearings, p. 465.

16. *Ibid.,* pp. 480–81.

17. IPR hearings, p. 860.

18. *Ibid.,* p. 1049.

19. Jessup hearings, p. 619.

Chapter 31: A Conspiracy So Immense

1. McCarthy speeches, pp. 215 *et seq.; America's Retreat from Victory: The Story of George Catlett Marshall* (Devin-Adair, 1951).

2. A lightly fictionalized account of this episode may be found in William F. Buckley Jr., *The Red Hunter* (Little, Brown, 1999).

3. McCarthy speeches, pp. 305–07. The use here of "maledictions" is a dead giveaway as to the origins of the speech—a typical Davis word, atypical of McCarthy.

4. William F. Buckley Jr. and L. Brent Bozell, *McCarthy and his Enemies* (Regnery, 1995), pp. 388–92.

5. See the account in Forrest Pogue, *George C. Marshall, Ordeal and Hope, 1939–1942* (Penguin Books, 1993), Chapter IX, "So Little Time," pp. 193 *et seq.*

6. On Lend-Lease and Faymonville, see Leonard Mosley, *Marshall: Hero for Our Times* (Hearst Books, 1982), pp. 144–45; on Marshall's second-front ideas for Europe vs. the Churchill strategy, see Wedemeyer, *op. cit.,* pp. 228 *et seq.*

7. As to Marshall's role as team player—and political general—Mosley writes: "He was now a political soldier . . . He would have to become expert in a whole new set of skills." And: "By giving way to the President and going along with his stratagem [on Lend-Lease] he had taken a step into his [Roosevelt's] camp, and it would have both practical and psychological consequences." *Op. cit.,* pp. 123, *et seq.,* p. 143.

8. Among the more striking aspects of Vincent's record was that he opposed U.S. involvement in the war in 1940, at the height of the Hitler-Stalin pact, saying "it is not our war." Thereafter, when it did become our war with the Japanese attack in the Pacific, his most urgent concern was the fate of the Soviet armies—though he was then an official at our embassy in Chungking. Gary May, *China Scapegoat* (New Republic Books, 1979), pp. 58–59, 79.

9. For an extended discussion of the documents that made up the Marshall directive, and Vincent's role in their creation, plus the documents themselves, see Vincent's testimony before the Senate Internal Security subcommittee, February 1, 1952, pp. 2197 *et seq.*

10. Hearing of the Senate Internal Security subcommittee, December 3, 1953, p. 1230.

11. Maochun Yu, *OSS in China, op. cit.,* p. 276.

12. Jung Chang, *op. cit.,* p. 295.

13. Lucian B. Moody, "The Help Chiang Did Not Get," *The Freeman,* July 16, 1951.

14. IPR report, pp. 204 *et seq.*

15. Testimony to House Foreign Affairs Committee, March 20, 1947.

16. Chennault's testimony was given to the Senate Internal Security subcommittee on May 29, 1952, pp. 4673 *et seq.;* Badger testified before a joint session of the Senate Armed Services and Foreign Relations committees on the "Military Situation in the Far East" (the MacArthur hearings), June 19, 1951, pp. 2746 *et seq.*

17. David S. McLellan, *Dean Acheson: The State Department Years* (Dodd, Mead, 1976), p. 188.

18. The transcript of the Jessup-chaired policy conference is reprinted in an appendix to the IPR hearings, pp. 1581 *et seq.*

19. IPR hearings, pp. 1064–68; McLellan, *op. cit.,* p. 204.

20. The relevant portions of the Acheson Press Club speech are reproduced in "Military Situation in the Far East," *loc. cit.,* pp. 1811–12.

21. Frank Dorn, *Walkout: With Stilwell in Burma* (Thomas Y. Crowell, 1970), pp. 76–82; "Well-Kept War Secret Gets Its Due," *Chicago Tribune,* December 20, 1985.

22. W. W. Stuart, untitled memorandum, February 20, 1950, NARA RG 59, China, Box 18.

23. To the Secretary, from Dean Rusk, May 30, 1950, memorandum labeled "Top Secret," concerning U.S. policy toward Formosa, NARA RG 59, China, Box 18.

24. *Foreign Relations of the United States,* 1950, Vol. VI, p. 280.

25. A noteworthy exception to this comment is Ronald McGlothlen's *Controlling the Waves* (Norton, 1993), which discusses these events in some detail—albeit from a

different perspective—and led me to some of the data referred to.

Chapter 32: The Battle with Benton

1. "Maryland Senatorial Election of 1950," Report of the Committee on Rules and Administration, August 20, 1951, pp. 20 *et seq.*

2. "McCarthy and the Davis Incident," *Syracuse Post-Standard,* October 19, 1951; and "The McCarthy Record," *Syracuse Post-Standard,* March 15, 1953.

3. Howe to Benton, April 9, 1953, Benton papers, Box 5.

4. "Investigations of Senators Joseph R. McCarthy and William Benton," report of the Senate Subcommittee on Privileges and Elections, 1952, pp. 12–13.

5. Benton to Moore, Moore to Robert Shortley, Gillette subcommittee archive, NARA, RG 46, SR 187, Box 15.

6. Subject Index, Gillette subcommittee archive, NARA, RG 46, SR 187, Box 1.

7. "Investigations of Senators McCarthy and Benton," *loc. cit.,* p. 14.

8. McCarthy exhibits 37, 17, testimony to Gillette subcommittee, July 3, 1952, NARA RG 46, SR 304, Box 1.

9. Howe to Benton, Benton papers, Box 5.

10. Cf. the Murray Marder story in the *Washington Post* for July 4, 1952, "McCarthy in Hearing Says Benton Aided Reds." This portrays the hearing session as a shouting match between McCarthy and Benton and lists the people against whom McCarthy made allegations, but perforce provides no details about the cases or the documentation.

11. Griffith, *op. cit.,* p. 175; Oshinsky, *op. cit.,* p. 248.

12. Memorandum from Gerhard Van Arkel to William Benton, July 11, 1953; Benton draft letter to Sen. Guy Gillette (n.d.), Benton papers, Box 5.

13. Statement by Daniel Buckley, December 13, 1951, McCarthy papers I. Buckley would subsequently go to work as a McCarthy staffer and be subject to counterattack by pro-Benton forces.

Chapter 33: The Perils of Power

1. Quoted in Herman, *Joseph McCarthy, op. cit.,* p. 209.

2. Anderson, *Confessions of a Muckraker, op. cit.,* p. 303.

3. A deep-seated aversion to McCarthy is obvious in Eisenhower's memoirs and even more so in his diaries. These reveal wholesale acceptance of the standard version of McCarthy (claimed 205 Communists, then backed down, and so on) and contain many other hostile comments. Of note is a diary entry quoting an Ike acquaintance as saying McCarthy and certain others in the Senate were "disciples of hate"—with no Ike disagreement. This was recorded in June 1951, well before Eisenhower reached the White House. (Robert H. Ferrell, ed., *The Eisenhower Diaries* [Norton, 1981], p. 195.) For more comment on McCarthy, see Eisenhower, *Mandate for Change: The White House Years* (Doubleday, 1963), pp. 316 *et seq.*

4. See *America's Retreat from Victory, op. cit.,* pp. 24, 34, and others, all negative on Eisenhower, "who invariably sided with Marshall" (p. 34).

5. Among those Eisenhower didn't like, in addition to McCarthy, were Sens. James Kem of Missouri, Styles Bridges of New Hampshire, John Bricker of Ohio, George Malone of Nevada, William Jenner of Indiana, and William Langer of North Dakota. Ike did, however, like Acheson ally Charles E. Bohlen. (See Chapter 36.) Republican Senators who opposed Bohlen were, in Ike's view, "the most stubborn and small-minded examples of the extreme isolationist group in the party." (*Eisenhower Diaries, op. cit.,* p. 234.)

6. See *Retreat from Victory,* pp. 135 *et seq.,* wherein McCarthy stated: "I regard the assistance we voted to Greece and Turkey as the most statesmanlike approach made by the Truman administration to the whole post-war problem of the containment of Russia." McCarthy attributed the Truman Doctrine to the influence of James Forrestal, in contrast to the Marshall Plan, which he saw as the handiwork of the Acheson-Marshall combine. (McCarthy voted for the Marshall Plan, but later expressed regret for having done so.)

7. See Richard Nixon, *Memoirs* (Grosset & Dunlap), pp. 140 *et seq.*

8. For Taft's views on Yalta, the Marshall mission to China, and other Cold War

issues, see Robert A. Taft, *A Foreign Policy for Americans* (Doubleday, 1951).

9. For background on these matters see Eisenhower and Nixon memoirs, previously cited, Robert J. Donovan, *The Inside Story* (Harper, 1956), Emmet John Hughes, *The Ordeal of Power* (Atheneum, 1963), and Sherman Adams, *First Hand Report* (Harper, 1961).

10. Lodge had been a strong Ike supporter in the campaign for the 1952 nomination, entrusted with the task of assuring the party faithful that Eisenhower was, in fact, a Republican. Up until that point, no one had been quite certain. (See *Mandate for Change, op. cit.,* photo following p. 75.)

11. See Richard Whalen, *The Founding Father: The Story of Joseph P. Kennedy* (Signet Books, 1966), pp. 416 *et seq.*

12. In this speech, delivered on January 17, 1949, John Kennedy denounced "the Lattimores and the Fairbanks" who had created a disastrous policy toward China. Quoted in Evans, *The Politics of Surrender* (Devin Adair, 1966), p. 294.

13. The relationship between McCarthy and Robert Kennedy is discussed, from differing ideological perspectives, in Arthur Schlesinger Jr., *Robert Kennedy and His Times* (Ballantine Books, 1979), pp. 106 *et seq.;* and Ralph de Toledano, *RFK: The Man Who Would Be President* (Putnam, 1967), pp. 53 *et seq.*

14. Roy Cohn, *McCarthy* (New American Library, 1968), p. 28 *et seq.*

15. *Ibid.,* p. 47.

16. Cohn discussed his relationship with Robert Kennedy in many formats, including the book about McCarthy. Another was his brief memoir, *A Fool for a Client* (Hawthorn Books, 1971), devoted to his battles with the Kennedy Justice Department in the early 1960s. Kennedy would give his version in *The Enemy Within* (Harper & Row, 1960).

Chapter 34: Uncertain Voice

1. McCarthy papers III.

2. Fairly typical of such McCarthy statements is this: "I want to compliment the new Secretary of State for the attitude he has taken . . . I would like [also] to compliment the members of the committee . . . I have found that the Democrats on the com-

mittee have been just as eager and just as helpful in digging out anything that is improper, and just as careful of the rights of the witnesses, as members of the majority party. . . ." McCarthy hearings (Voice of America), February 28, 1953, p. 222.

3. The exchange on this subject showed, again, the collegiality then prevailing. When Stuart Symington urged that anyone adversely named in hearing sessions be called immediately to answer, McCarthy concurred and made this a rule of the subcommittee. Symington: "I want to thank the chairman for understanding the point, and I appreciate the position he has taken on it." McCarthy hearings (VOA), March 2, 1953, p. 251.

4. Memorandum by *Newsweek* correspondent Samuel Shaffer, "Re: Joe McCarthy," April 18, 1953. Document provided by Ralph de Toledano.

5. Willard Edwards, memorandum on McCarthy and the case of Gen. Ralph Zwicker, Papers of Willard Edwards. Document provided by Lee Edwards.

6. McCarthy executive hearings, January 27, 1953, p. 186.

7. McCarthy hearings (State Department file survey), February 20, 1953, pp. 126–28.

8. Annual Report, Senate Permanent Subcommittee on Investigations, January 22, 1954, pp. 54–55.

9. "Waste and Mismanagement in Voice of America Engineering Projects," report of the Senate Permanent subcommittee on Investigations, January 25, 1954.

10. McCarthy hearings (VOA), February 16, 1953, p. 7.

11. McCarthy hearings (VOA), *ibid.,* p. 27.

12. McCarthy executive hearings vol. I, pp. 769–70.

13. *Ibid.,* March 7, 1953, p. 792–93.

14. McCarthy hearings (VOA), March 5, 1953, p. 483.

15. *Ibid.,* March 2, 1953, p. 227 *et seq.*

16. *Ibid.,* February 20, 1953, p. 168.

17. Annual Report, Senate Permanent Subcommittee on Investigations, January 22, 1954, p. 4.

18. *Ibid.,* p. 10.

19. Reed Harris, *King Football: The Vulgarization of the American College* (Vanguard Press, 1932). Among the statements appearing in this volume: "Soviet Russia, a young nation which, whatever else may be said about her, is searching the world over for the best technical methods and the best ideas . . . has barred football from her new athletic program" (p. 24). "One of my friends on the Columbia faculty is, like my Princeton friend, a Communist . . . But there is tragedy in his eyes these days. He believes one thing and teaches another . . . He remembers the fate of others who disagreed—and remains silent" (pp. 148–49). And: "Among the students, the militant forward looking policies of the National Student League will bring new hope to the young people who must study in these fear centers [American universities]" (p. 158). The National Student League would later be described by FDR attorney General Francis Biddle as a "front organization for the Communist Party."

20. McCarthy hearings (VOA), March 3, 1953, pp. 331 *et seq.*

21. *Ibid.,* pp. 367, 368.

22. "Control of Trade with the Soviet Bloc," Interim Report of the Senate Permanent Subcommittee on Investigations, July 21, 1953.

Chapter 35: The Burning of the Books

1. McCarthy hearings (information centers), March 26, 1953, pp. 73 *et seq.*

2. *Ibid.,* pp. 79–80.

3. "State Department Information Program—Information Centers," report of the Senate Permanent Subcommittee on Investigations, January 25, 1954, pp. 3–4.

4. *Ibid.,* pp. 20–21.

5. McCarthy hearings (information centers), March 27, 1953, pp. 98, 111.

6. *Ibid.,* April 1, 1953, p. 135.

7. Other testimony was given as to some anti-Communist documents and periodicals in the system, but these evidently numbered in the hundreds rather than the thousands.

8. "State Department Information Program—Information Centers," report of the Senate Permanent Subcommittee on Investigations, January 25, 1954, pp. 3–4.

9. McCarthy hearings (VOA), January 25, 1954.

10. Document provided by Herbert Romerstein.

11. "Supplemental Appropriation Bill, 1954," hearings of the Senate Committee on Appropriations, June 15, 1953, p. 26.

12. Transcript of Eisenhower press conference, *New York Times,* July 2, 1953.

13. Report, "State Department Information Program—Information Centers," *loc. cit.,* p. 12.

14. *Ibid.*

15. McCarthy hearings (information centers), April 29, 1953, p. 197.

16. Nicholas von Hoffman, *Citizen Cohn, op. cit.,* p. 173.

17. Kai Bird, *The Chairman: John J. McCloy: the Making of the American Establishment* (Simon & Schuster, 1992), pp. 408–09.

18. McCarthy's view of Hammett was expressed at length in the Senate Appropriations Committee hearings above quoted, reproduced as an appendix to "State Department Information Program—Information Centers" report, pp. 18–19.

19. McCarthy's volleys back and forth with Wechsler are in McCarthy hearings (information centers), May 5, 1953, pp. 289 *et seq.*

Chapter 36: Scott McLeod, Where Are You?

1. Hughes, *op. cit.,* p. 11.

2. *Ibid.,* pp. 52, 84, 97.

3. A rationale for this approach would be offered by Arthur Larson, an official of the Eisenhower administration, in *A Republican Looks at His Party* (Harper, 1956), which received much favorable press notice at the time. Eisenhower himself was partial to such notions, as evidenced in his diaries, *op. cit.,* pp. 288 *et seq.*

4. Bird, *op cit.,* Chapter 22.

5. Such is the generally accepted story. However, according to Richard Nixon, he was the one who dissuaded McCarthy from a public attack on Conant. Richard Nixon, *Memoirs, op. cit.,* p. 139.

6. "Charles Eustis Bohlen," FBI reports and memoranda, JEH & OC, Sections 38, 104, 105.

7. *Congressional Record,* March 25, 1953, pp. 2278, 2281.

8. Dulles phone log summaries and related memoranda, Eisenhower Library. Documents provided by Ted Morgan.

9. Hughes, *op. cit.,* p. 85.

10. "Charles Eustis Bohlen," FBI reports and memos, *loc. cit.*

11. The government stance on homosexuals in the federal service is discussed in David K. Johnson, *The Lavender Scare: The Cold War Persecution of Gays and Lesbians in the Federal Government* (University of Chicago Press, 2004).

12. "Hearings Regarding the Administration of the Subversive Activities Control Act of 1950 and the Federal Civilian Employee Loyalty-Security Program," Part I, House Committee on Internal Security, September 28 and 30, 1970. Text of Executive Order 10450, April 27, 1953.

13. JEH O&C, Section 105.

14. *Ibid.*

15. JEH O&C, Section 105, p. 11.

16. *Ibid.,* pp. 14–15.

17. *Congressional Record,* March 26, 1953, p. 2385.

18. Hearings of Senate Foreign Relations Committee, "Nomination of Charles E. Bohlen," March 2, 1953.

19. *Congressional Record,* March 25, 1953, p. 2285; March 26, 1953, p. 2386; March 25, 1953, p. 2295.

20. Charles E. Bohlen, *Witness to History* (Norton, 1973), p. 309.

21. *Congressional Record,* March 25, 1953, p. 2296.

22. *Ibid.*

23. *Congressional Record,* March 26, 1953, p. 2379.

24. Dulles phone logs, *loc. cit.* However, according to the memo of another conversation, Eisenhower did suggest to Dulles that security checks henceforth be conducted *before* making nominations.

Chapter 37: The Getting of J. B. Matthews

1. "Investigation of Un-American Propaganda Activities in the United States," Special House Committee on Un-American Activities, August 19, 1938, p. 869.

2. *Ibid.,* pp. 918–19.

3. "Investigation of Un-American Propaganda Activities," report of the Special House Committee on Un-American Activities, January 3, 1939, p. 7.

4. "Reds and Our Churches," *American Mercury,* July 1953 (reprint), p. 3.

5. *Ibid.,* pp. 10–11.

6. *Ibid.,* p. 13.

7. Matthews, for instance, quoted Earl Browder as saying to a group of theological students: "You may be interested in knowing that we have preachers, preachers active in churches, who are members of the Communist Party." *Odyssey of a Fellow Traveler* (Mount Vernon Publishers, 1939), p. 9.

8. Remarks of Rep. Martin Dies, *Congressional Record,* February 1, 1943, p. 477.

9. *Ibid.*

10. "McCarthy Defeated and Matthews Ousted Because Opponents Attacked on Grounds of Their Own Choosing," *Congressional Report* of the National Committee for an Effective Congress, July 22, 1953.

11. Letter from George Agree of the National Committee for an Effective Congress to Sen. William Benton, October 7, 1953, Benton papers, Box 5; NCEC newsletter, *loc. cit.*

12. Joseph Alsop, "No Surrender Now," *New York Herald Tribune,* July 13, 1953.

13. Hughes, *op. cit.,* pp. 94–96.

14. "Eisenhower Scores Attack on Clergy; McCarthy Aide Out," *New York Times,* July 10, 1953.

15. Murray Marder, "Matthews Resigns as McCarthy Aide After Ike Condemns Attack on Clergy," *Washington Post,* July 10, 1953.

16. Drew Pearson, "Tragedy of the Matthews Case," *Washington Post,* July 11, 1953.

17. McCarthy hearings, "Security—Government Printing Office," August 18, 1953, pp. 62 *et seq.,* and August 19, 1953, pp. 72 *et seq.*

18. See, for instance, Kit Rachlis, "The Rise and Fall of Joe McCarthy," *Los Angeles Times,* November 7, 1999, portraying the GPO/Rothschild investigation as a hit-and-run witch hunt.

19. Senate Permanent Subcommittee on Investigations, Annual Report for 1953, January 22, 1954, pp. 53–54; McCarthy hearings (Security—Government Printing Office), August 18, 1953, p. 28. (This comment followed a series of questions directed to FBI witness Mary Markward by McCarthy at the request of Rothschild's attorney.)

Chapter 38: The Moles of Monmouth

1. Memoranda and correspondence concerning Signal Corps Intelligence Agency, McCarthy papers II and III.

2. Willard Edwards, "Secret Papers Miss-

ing, Army Sifts Red Plot—'Loyal' Group Asks Congress Probe," *Washington Times Herald,* January 20, 1952.

3. "Administrative Admonition," December 18, 1952, from Gen. George C. Back to Col. O. C. Allen, McCarthy Papers III.

4. Chronology and memoranda relating to G-2 investigation of Fort Monmouth, Captain Benjamin Sheehan, September 1954, together with memoranda discussing interviews with Sheehan by McCarthy staff. McCarthy papers III.

5. *Ibid.*

6. *Ibid.*

7. "Army Signal Corps—Subversion and Espionage," report of the Senate Permanent Subcommittee on Investigations, April 25, 1955, pp. 6, 20, 32, 33.

8. *Ibid.,* pp. 8–10; Coleman testified in public session before the McCarthy panel on December 8, 1953, pp. 51 *et seq.*

9. *Ibid.,* p. 9.

10. *Ibid.,* p. 23; Bernstein testified in executive session on October 22, 1953, in a hearing later printed with the public sessions.

11. McCarthy hearings (Signal Corps), December 16, 1953, pp. 252 *et seq.*; case summary in Signal Corps report, *loc. cit.,* pp. 23–24.

12. McCarthy hearings (Signal Corps), November 24, 1953, pp. 27–31.

13. McCarthy hearings (Signal Corps), November 25, 1953, pp. 35 *et seq.* McCarthy asked numerous other questions of Hyman concerning espionage and hundreds of alleged Hyman phone calls to military and scientific installations (*e.g.,* "Did you make a total of 242 calls between October of 1951 and September of 1953 to the Federal Telephone & Radio Corp., at Clifton, N.J.?," p. 40). On all such questions Hyman took the Fifth.

14. McCarthy hearings (Signal Corps), December 16, 1953, p. 278.

15. "Internal Security Annual Report for 1956," report of the Senate Internal Security subcommittee, March 4, 1957, p. 64.

16. Memorandum from James N. Juliana to Francis P. Carr, December 1, 1953, McCarthy papers III.

17. McCarthy executive hearings, testimony of Gens. George C. Back and Kirke B. Lawton, October 16, 1953, pp. 2563 *et seq.* The generals variously testified that the

Buettner report was said to be a "fabrication" and that Buettner had withdrawn it.

18. Juliana to Francis Carr, December 1, 1953, *loc. cit.*

19. Annual Report for 1953, Senate Permanent Subcommittee on Investigations, January 22, 1954, p. 7.

20. Memorandum for the files (n.d.), James N. Juliana, McCarthy papers III.

21. McCarthy hearings (Signal Corps), January 15, 1954, pp. 32 *et seq.*

Chapter 39: A Tale of Two Generals

1. McCarthy executive hearings, October 15, 1953; excerpt published in "Army Signal Corps—Subversion and Espionage," report of the Senate Permanent Subcommittee on Investigations, April 25, 1955, p. 7.

2. "Special Senate Investigation on Charges and Countercharges Involving: Secretary of the Army Robert T. Stevens, John G. Adams, H. Struve Hensel, and Senator Joe McCarthy, Roy M. Cohn, and Francis P. Carr" (hereafter cited as Army-McCarthy hearings), May 27, 1954, p. 1634.

3. John Adams, *Without Precedent* (Norton, 1983), pp. 50 *et seq.*

4. Numerous references to Mrs. Rosenberg are in memoranda submitted to the McCarthy panel by complainants in the matter of the Signal Corps Intelligence Agency. McCarthy papers II and III.

5. Army-McCarthy hearings, April 25, 1954, p. 425.

6. William Ewald, *Who Killed McCarthy?* (Simon & Schuster, 1984), p. 130.

7. "Say Lawton's Talks Had 'Political' Tone," *Asbury Park* (N.J.) *Press,* November 25, 1953, and "Lawton Will Be Called to Testify at Hearings," *Asbury Park* (N.J.) *Press,* April 29, 1954.

8. "Summary of Statement by Major General George I. Back [*sic*], Chief Signal Officer, United States Army, present, Mr. Jenkins, Mr. Prewitt, Mr. Carr, Mr. Cohn, Mr. Juliana," April 27, 1954, McCarthy papers III.

9. Martin S. Hayden, "Gen. Lawton Reported Ready to Help McCarthy in Army Row," *Washington Star,* April 30, 1954.

10. The case of Lawton and the question of why he wasn't called were discussed on several occasions in the hearings. Army Counsel Welch's stated reason for not calling

Lawton was that to do so would lead to more charges and countercharges and thus "would open up what seems to me a somewhat painfully wide field." Army-McCarthy hearings, June 10, 1954, p. 2522.

11. John Adams, *op. cit.,* p. 172.

12. McCarthy hearings (Communist Infiltration of the Army), January 30, 1954, pp. 112, 113.

13. John Adams, *op. cit.,* p. 118.

14. Hearings on S. Res. 301 (hereafter cited as Watkins hearings), September 13, 1954, p. 514 *et seq.*

15. McCarthy hearings (Communist Infiltration of the Army), February 17, 1954, p. 43.

16. *Ibid.,* p. 54.

17. "Army Personnel Actions Relating to Irving Peress" (McClellan hearings). March 23, 1955, p. 370.

18. *Ibid.,* p. 386.

19. *Ibid.,* p. 530.

20. Nomination of Brig. Gen. Ralph Zwicker, Hearings of the Senate Armed Services Committee, March 21, 1957.

21. John Adams, *op. cit.,* p. 124.

Chapter 40: The Legend of Annie Lee Moss

1. McCarthy hearings (Signal Corps), February 23, 1954, pp. 310 *et seq.*

2. *Ibid.,* p. 314.

3. McCarthy hearings (Signal Corps), March 11, 1954, p. 461.

4. *Ibid.,* p. 462.

5. The quotes are from Jack Anderson, *Confessions of a Muckraker, op. cit.,* p. 311; Richard Fried, *Men Against McCarthy, op. cit.,* p. 285; and Lately Thomas, *When Even Angels Wept, op. cit.,* p. 420.

6. McCarthy hearings (Signal Corps), March 11, 1954, p. 447.

7. Subversive Activities Control Board, Docket No. 51–101, William P. Rogers, Attorney General of the U.S. vs. The Communist Party of the U.S., recommended decision on second remand, September 19, 1958, p. 5.

8. FBI Annie Lee Moss file, Stanley to Rosen, February 26, 1954.

9. *Ibid.,* Nichols to Tolson, February 24, 1954.

10. *Ibid.*

11. "New Moss Charges Cite CP Membership Book Number & Date," *Washington Daily News,* August 5, 1954.

12. Symington to McCarthy, August 5, 1954, McCarthy papers II.

13. McCarthy hearings (Signal Corps), March 11, 1954, p. 458.

14. McCarthy hearings (Signal Corps), February 23 and 24, 1954 (appendix), p. 353.

15. McCarthy executive hearings, Vol. 5, p. xv. The sources cited for these assertions are McCarthy biographers Thomas Reeves, David Oshinsky, and Arthur Herman.

16. See, e.g., the SACB statements of December 3, 1956, that "the respondent [Communist Party] seeks to retry the Moss security hearing, and that is not a function of this board . . . " and December 13, 1956: "the Board will not permit a rehearing of the Moss case." (1 SACB reports, pp. 52, 57.)

17. William P. Rogers, Attorney General of the U.S. vs. Communist Party of the U.S., modified report of board on second remand, January 15, 1959 (1 SACB reports, p. 94).

18. See SACB reports and rulings of September 10, 1956; December 13, 1956; December 18, 1956; August 25, 1958; September 19, 1958; and January 15, 1959. All these board comments repeat or paraphrase the statements about Markward and the Moss case above cited.

19. Kerry Lauerman, "The Salon Interview: George Clooney," Salon.com, September 16, 2005.

20. Letter to William V. Shannon, December 10, 1958. Document in possession of the author.

21. Ken Ringle, "Tales from a Redbaiter's '50s Fishing Expedition," *Washington Post,* May 6, 2003.

22. Dorothy Rabinowitz, "A Conspiracy So Vast," *Wall Street Journal,* July 7, 2003.

Chapter 41: At War with the Army

1. Robert Stripling, *The Red Plot Against America* (Bell, 1949), p. 52.

2. *Ibid.*

3. Ewald, *op. cit.,* p. 165.

4. "Stevens-Adams Chronology," Army-McCarthy hearings (appendix), p. 135.

5. The formal Army charges, filed April 13,

1954, repeatedly stressed the notion that the Monmouth inquest was fueled by Cohn's effort to get privileges for Schine. See "Charges and Countercharges," etc., report of Mundt subcommittee, August 30, 1954, pp. 3–5. The McCarthy countercharges immediately follow.

6. Army-McCarthy hearings, April 22, 1954, pp. 47, 86–87.

7. Army-McCarthy hearings, April 26, 1954, p. 205.

8. Army-McCarthy hearings, May 25, 1954, pp. 1445 *et seq.*

9. Army-McCarthy hearings, May 27, 1954, pp. 1576.

10. Army-McCarthy hearings, June 14, 1954, pp. 2643–44.

11. According to Willard Edwards, a McCarthy backer, various of the McCarthy staff memos were indeed concocted *ex post facto*—allegedly in response to concocted memos by the Army. Untitled memorandum, Willard Edwards papers. Document provided by Lee Edwards.

12. Ewald, *op. cit.,* pp. 175 *et seq.*

13. Army-McCarthy hearings, April 23, 1954, p. 172.

14. John Adams, *op. cit.,* pp. 210–20.

15. "Charges and Countercharges," *loc. cit.,* p. 126.

Chapter 42: On Not Having Any Decency

1. "Charges and Countercharges," *loc. cit.,* pp. 79–80.

2. *Ibid.,* pp. 87–88.

3. Army-McCarthy hearings, April 27, 1954, pp. 256 *et seq.*

4. *Ibid.,* pp. 278 *et seq.;* April 30, 1954, pp. 534 *et seq.*

5. Army-McCarthy hearings, May 4, 1954, p. 703.

6. Army-McCarthy hearings, May 5, 1954, pp. 767–70.

7. *Ibid.,* p. 734.

8. *Ibid.,* p. 736.

9. Army-McCarthy hearings, June 9, 1954, pp. 2386–87.

10. *Ibid.,* p. 2426.

11. *Ibid.,* pp. 2426–27.

12. *Ibid.,* p. 2428.

13. *Ibid.,* p. 2430.

14. *New York Times,* April 16, 1954.

15. "Army Personnel Actions Relating to Irving Peress," report of the McClellan subcommittee, July 14, 1955, pp. 35, 32.

Chapter 43: The Sounds of Silence

1. Army-McCarthy hearings, May 14, 1954, p. 1187.

2. *Ibid.,* pp. 1169 *et seq.*

3. The text of the Eisenhower secrecy order, with appendix citing asserted precedents, is widely available. The text cited here is reprinted in full in the hearings on S. Res. 301 (McCarthy censure), conducted by Sen. Arthur Watkins, p. 122.

4. Clark Mollenhoff, *Washington Cover-Up* (Popular Library, 1963), p. 184.

5. Army-McCarthy hearings, May 17, 1954, p. 1263.

6. *Ibid.,* p. 1265.

7. *Ibid.,* May 14, 1954, p. 1169.

8. Mollenhoff, *op. cit.,* p. 41. Mollenhoff added that "seldom had there been more right on the side of McCarthy, but seldom had there been fewer people on his side."

9. Quoted in Evans, *Clear and Present Dangers* (Harcourt, Brace Jovanovich, 1975), pp. 64–65.

10. Ewald, *op. cit.,* pp. 8–9.

11. *Ibid.,* p. 374.

12. Army-McCarthy hearings, May 25, 1954, p. 1575.

13. *Congressional Record,* August 6, 1954.

14. The relevant portion of the statute is cited (and dismissed) in hearings on S. Res. 301 (McCarthy censure), conducted by the Watkins committee, p. 133.

15. Nixon ruminated on the executive privilege issue in his *Memoir* (pp. 772 *et seq.*), but didn't link it to McCarthy.

16. Quoted in Evans, *op. cit.,* pp. 62, 63.

17. Raoul Berger, *Executive Privilege* (Bantam, 1975), p. 264.

18. "Interlocking Subversion in Government Departments," hearings of the Senate Internal Security subcommittee, November 17, 1953, p. 1411.

Chapter 44: Sentence First, Verdict Later

1. *Congressional Record,* June 1, 1954, p. 7390.

2. "Meet the Press," NBC Television, June 13, 1954; p. 2.

3. *Congressional Record,* August 2, 1954, p. 12979.

4. The Flanders charges, and others, are set forth in the Watkins hearings, pp. 5–8.

5. *Ibid.,* p. 6.

6. *Ibid.,* p. 37.

7. *Ibid.,* p. 38.

8. Arthur Watkins, *Enough Rope* (Prentice Hall, 1969), p. 210.

9. Watkins hearings, September 1, 1954, p. 57.

10. *Ibid.,* September 8, 1954, p. 275.

11. The extensive contacts of Flanders and the NCEC are reflected in the papers of Maurice Rosenblatt/National Committee for an Effective Congress, Library of Congress Manuscript Division, *loc. cit.,* Boxes 18, 19, and 24.

12. *Ibid.,* Box 19.

13. *Ibid.*

14. Willard Edwards, "Well Heeled Group Works on Senators," *Chicago Tribune,* July 23, 1954; Maurice Rosenblatt to John Howe, February 24, 1961, Benton papers, Box 5.

15. Barry Goldwater, *With No Apologies* (Morrow, 1979), p. 261.

Appendix

THE McCARTHY LISTS

A frequent refrain of Joe McCarthy's critics was that the senator "had no names." But McCarthy supplied Senator Millard Tydings with the names of more than 100 suspects, as shown in the documents on the following eight pages. Source for all: McCarthy Papers I

March 18, 1950

Senator Millard Tydings
Chairman, Foreign Relations Sub-Committee
Washington, D. C.

Dear Senator Tydings:

Enclosed are the names which you, as Chairman of the sub-
Committee, demanded that I furnish in connection with the
eighty-one cases cited on the Senate floor.

They are being submitted herewith for insertion as part
of the record in Executive Session.

I believe you will find complete and detailed reports on
each in the various files which I indicated to the committee the other day, namely State Department, Civil Service, and F. B. I.

I would, however, like the right to present to the committee
additional documentation in cases of bad security risks from
time to time.

                          Very sincerely yours,

                          JOE McCARTHY

McC:d

1. **Herbert Fierst**

   I understand that this man was given loyalty clearance by the State
   Department's Loyalty Board, but that his case was referred back by
   the Civil Service Commission's Loyalty Board, expressing dissatis-
   faction in his loyalty clearance by the State Department's Loyalty
   Board.

2. **John Carter Vincent**

3. **Peveril Meigs**

4. **Gisella Illyefalvi-Vites**

5. **Jay Robinson**

6. **Frances M. Tachser**

7. **Marcia Ruth Harrison**

8. **Stanley Graze**

9. **David Demarest Lloyd**

10. **Marjorie S. Posner**

11. **Frances Perry**

    Letter from C.I.A. attached

12. **Helen Yuhas**

13. **Carleton Washburne**

14. **Ernst Theodore Arndt**

15. **Philip Jessup**

    There was no case #15 cited in the Record. Jessup's case should be
    inserted at this point. Jessup's file should be studied with the
    file of Owen Lattimore. Lattimore's files are, in my opinion, the
    most explosive and the most valuable which the committee can examine
    and will, in my opinion, be found extremely important in connection
    with the Jessup case.

16. **Robert T. Miller**

    Allowed to resign in 1946. Apparently still keeping close contacts
    with present State Department personnel.

17. Jeanne E. Taylor

I understand there is a decision in this case indicating that she was
a bad security risk and that she was allowed to resign in 1947. I
consider this case important in that the files would seem to indicate
that the security officials felt that if this woman had expressed a
change of heart and stated that she had reformed, she would not have
been forced to resign.

18. Blythe J. Lemmon

I understand that this woman is no longer with the Department. I consider this case important in the whole picture because it would seem
to be an example of continuing to retain an employee long after material
developed in the investigation would indicate absolute disirability of
her immediate discharge.

19. William Remington

20. S. Stevenson Smith

21. Nucie Belgado (Voice of America)

22. Alexander Rapoport

23. Mr. Chipchin

24. Mrs. Loss

25. Tegnel Conrad Grandal

26. Lowell M. Clucas, Jr.

27. Ivan Katusich

28. Hans Lansberg

29. Gerald Graze

This case is significant because it indicates how some of the bad
security risks got into government. I understand that in the early
war years when the Civil Service Commission was unable, because of
the vast number of applicants, to make final decisions in individual
cases, they appointed those who were known as liaison officers.
This case, I understand, was one of those Civil Service liaison officers.

29. Gerald Graze -- continued

I believe the files will give the committee a clear picture of this individual. I understand that this individual is now with the Department of Public Health, whose loyalty board refused to clear him and that the Civil Service Commission in January, 1949 reversed the findings of the Public Health regional loyalty board and ordered him restored to his job.

30. Joseph Josephson

31. Lewis Ross

I consider this case important as part of the picture because of the fact that the Congressional committee stated that a person with the same name signed a Communist petition, which information was handed over to the State Department in October, 1948, but over a year later, no effort had been made to check on this information.

32. Robert Ross

This case is practically identical with the last case in indicating laxity on the part of the security officials in the State Department to check information given to them by the House Un-American Activities Committee.

33. Herman Seigal

Roughly the same as cases number 31 and number 32.

34. Ella M. Montague

35. Melville Shell

36. Frederick W. Smith

37. Olga F. Ossnatch

38. Arthur Milton Kauffman

39. Max A. Volin

This case is considered important in that I understand he was hired without any security clearance whatsoever. His file should yield much valuable information to the committee.

COPY

40. Stella Gordon

41. Daniel F. Margolies

   I understand that this man was retained over the objections of
   Mr. Panuch who held the job which Mr. Peurifoy holds at the
   present time.

42. Gottfried Thomas Mann

43. Sam Fishback

44. William D. Carter

45. Norman T. Ness

→46. William T. Stone

→47. Esther Caukin Brunauer

(48. Mr. and Mrs. Robert Warren Barnett
(49.

50. Sylvia Shimmel

51. Rowena Rommel

   An important case who has a rather involved friendship with at
   least one high State Department official.

52. Philip Raine

53. Richard Post

   I understand that this man was allowed to remain in the Department
   over nine years after the Department received information that he
   was a member of a Communist underground cell in the Federal government with Alger Hiss.

→ 54. Val R. Lorwin   X   *Suspended*

55. Gertrude Cameron

Page 5

56. Paul A. Lifantieff-Lee

57. Fred Warner Neal

58. Lois Carlisle

59: Franz Leopold Neumann

This case was inadvertently skipped in the Record, but I understand that complete information on him will be found in his files.

60. Cora DuBois

61. Alice Demerjain

62. Isham W. Perkins

63. Stanley Wilcox

64. Hollis W. Peter

65. Victor Hunt

66. David Randolph (Rosenberg)

67. John Richard Lindsey

68. Aaron Jack Gross

69. Sylvia Magnite

70. Harold Berman

71. Stoian Stoanoff

72. The record of this individual is not in any way suspicious. He was cited to show that a loyal American who was well-qualified, found it impossible to get a job in the New York branch of the Voice of America, while at the same time security risks were being taken on so freely. For this reason, his name is not included but is available if the committee desires it for any reason.

73. Leonard Horwin

74. Joseph T. Jankowski

75. Mrs. Preston Keesling Lewis

76. James T. Ford

Page 6

77. The case of Davis Demarest Lloyd was read into the Congressional Record a second time by mistake. The case of Edward G. Posniak should have been read. I understand complete details will be found in his files.

78. Andrew W. Kamarck

May have been transferred to the Treasury Department.

79. T. Achilles Polyzoides

80. John T. Washburn

81. Ruby A. Parsons

(Zahodzietsky)

LIST OF 25 ADDITIONAL NAMES GIVEN TO SENATE FOREIGN RELATIONS SUBCOMMITTEE

COPY

Sent to Connors Mar 14, 1950

ASKWITH, Edna Jerry

BLAISDELL, Donald C.

DAVIES, Jr., John Paton

FISHBURN, John Tipton

HARRIS, Reed

HENKIN, Louis

HULTEN, Charles M.

HUNT, Victor M.

INGRAM, George Mason

LUDDEN, Raymond Paul

MEEKER, Leonard C.

NELSON, Clarence J.

NEWBEGIN, Robert

ROTHWELL, George J.

ROWE, James W.

SANDERS, William

TATE, Jack B.

THOMSON, Charles A.

TUCKERMAN, Gustavos

WOOD, James E.

ERDOS, Arpad

ZABLODOWSKI, David

RAMON, Josephina

RAPOPORT, Alexander

GRAJDANZEWE, Andrew (Also known as Andrew GRADE)

44

Acknowledgments

It's customary in book acknowledgments to say that the people being thanked bear no responsibility for the findings, errors, or opinions of the author.

In the case of a book that takes a favorable view of Joe McCarthy, such a disclaimer perhaps isn't needed. It can be assumed *a priori* that very few people, if any, would want to be connected to words in praise of so demonized a figure. On the other hand, the potential taint of "McCarthyism" is so great that maybe the usual disavowal is more requisite than ever. Either way, suffice it to note that the individuals mentioned here are in no way to blame for my effusions, unless somebody for some eccentric reason cares to step forth and endorse them.

That said, there are indeed many people to be thanked for their help in what has been a long and at times seemingly endless journey. Foremost among these is the late Ralph de Toledano, who shared with me his vast experience covering internal security issues of the late 1940s and early '50s, along with much documentary information concerning McCarthy's early cases. This material, including the data referred to in the notes as "McCarthy Papers I," is in a sense the foundation of the book, as it reveals the kind of information McCarthy had in his possession in 1950 and supplies the basis for tracking his cases in other long-neglected records.

Equally deserving of thanks, for similar reasons, is former McCarthy staffer James N. Juliana, who for five decades preserved vital remnants of McCarthy's papers from the period when McCarthy was a committee chairman. These files, referred to in the notes as "McCarthy Papers III," provide invaluable information on the investigation of Fort Monmouth and the ensuing conflict with the Army. They are to the later period what the Toledano information is to the era of the Tydings hearings. (As observed in the citations, "McCarthy Papers II" are records of the McCarthy committee held in the National Archives.) Jim also shared with me his personal recollections of McCarthy—these often in dramatic conflict with standard versions of the story.

In terms of detailed expertise on security matters, Communist infiltration of the government, and related topics, my principal thanks go to Herbert Romerstein, whose information on such questions is encyclopedic, and known to be so by everyone conversant with the subject. Herb has been an inexhaustible source of security data, insight on particular cases, and general background on the Soviet networks and pro-Red conniving through the ages. Any mistakes I may have made in dealing with such matters will have occurred despite his heroic efforts to inform me.

Likewise deserving of profoundest thanks is my office mate and long-time colleague, Allan Ryskind, himself a knowledgeable student of Cold War issues. On countless occasions he has provided me with documents, security hearings, and thoughtful counsel relating to my project, often at the expense of his own endeavors. Most of all, he is the person who more than any other helped crystallize the contents of this book, discussed in minute detail just about every day for more years than either of us cares to remember. I am grateful for his friendship.

Others who have assisted my researches make up a considerable roster. At the head of this lineup is Lee Edwards, another long-time valued friend and colleague and eminent historian of the American conservative movement. Lee kindly shared with me the files, memoranda, and voluminous newspaper stories of his father, Willard, the most knowledgeable journalist of the 1950s on the doings of McCarthy and the Communist infiltration problem in general.

A special word of thanks is owing as well to the late Anthony Kubek, who made available the results of his in-depth research on the *Amerasia* case, the Morgenthau diaries, and the ill-fated course of American policy in China. Tony served as editor of the *Amerasia* papers and the diaries for the Senate Internal Security subcommittee, and wrote the most comprehensive of all studies of the China meltdown—*How the Far East Was Lost.* (All these volumes may be read with profit today by scholars seeking insight on such matters.)

Contributing likewise to my researches —and here the disclaimer certainly needs stressing—are several Cold War experts and historians of intelligence issues from whom I derived significant data. One such is my former schoolmate, the distinguished biographer-historian Ted Morgan (no McCarthyite he), with whom I traded security dossiers of one sort or another. Others include Cold War/*Venona* scholars John Earl Haynes and Harvey Klehr, historian Maochun Yu, and McCarthy biographer Arthur Herman. While I doubt that any of them will agree with me about McCarthy (I'm pretty sure they won't), all have provided, by their writings and/or directly, information that shaped my understanding of the subject.

In the matter of disagreement, I have some rather awkward thanks to tender to Professor Thomas Reeves, generally regarded as the leading contemporary scholar of McCarthyana. Not only have I learned much from his comprehensive study of the McCarthy epoch, he was most generous in directing me to his research materials at the Wisconsin State Historical Society. His courtesy makes it painful for me to differ with him on key aspects of the record, which I have been constrained to do in sev-

eral places. Anyway, though it probably doesn't help much, I do thank him for his kindness.

In terms of institutional sources of information, the main ones are obvious from the text and notes. By far the most extensive and revealing of such sources, as mentioned frequently in the book, are the massive counterintelligence archives of the Federal Bureau of Investigation. As I have no doubt made sufficiently clear, the scope and nature of these files have given me new appreciation for the Bureau and for J. Edgar Hoover, who were faithfully standing watch, and keeping excellent records, while many of their official colleagues were at best indifferent to the infiltration problem and at worst complicit in it.

Next to the Bureau, the agencies that have contributed most to my pursuit of Cold War knowledge are what have to be two of the greatest research facilities on the planet—the National Archives and the Library of Congress. I can't begin to estimate the number of hours (and copy cards) expended at both places, the reams of data thus obtained, or the acts of expert assistance rendered by the archivists and library staffers. Particular thanks are owing to archivists Ed Schamel, Bill Davis, and John Taylor, who not only guided me to essential data but answered many research questions.

The databases I have relied on also include the Truman Library, where Dennis E. Bilger was an unfailing source of expertise and guidance, and the Wisconsin State Historical Society, where Dee Grimsrud was the same. Thanks as well to the librarians and archival staffers at the University of Maryland, West Virginia University, Hanover College, Syracuse University, and Duke University (where independent researcher Ira Katz, based in Durham, ably assisted my endeavors).

Others who have improved my understanding of McCarthy and his doings include the late Ruth Matthews (widow of J. B.); William Rusher, yet another long-time friend who among his many other achievements is an authority on security matters; Thomas Bolan (former law partner of Roy Cohn); Patricia Bozell (widow of L. Brent Bozell); Mrs. Patricia S. Gerlach (daughter of Don Surine); John Hoving of the *Mil-*

waukee Journal; and the witnesses from Wheeling: Mrs. Eva Lou Ingersoll, Douglas McKay, and Ben Honecker—all of whom shared with me their reminiscences of McCarthy. A special word of thanks is owing to the late Bob Ramsey, a great stalwart in the cause, and his wife Dorothy, who were my gracious hosts in Wheeling.

Among others who have supplied me with information, and/or encouragement in the task, are Ann Coulter, who has courageously (and truthfully) defended McCarthy in her writings and speeches; broadcaster/columnist Wes Vernon, a first-rate student of McCarthy and security issues; John Gizzi, whose extensive knowledge of political personalities has aided me in several places; the late Reed Irvine, who helped out on numerous McCarthy-related topics; former FBI agent John Walsh, who loaned me his detailed research on the *Venona* decrypts; Daniel Flynn, an astute collector of McCarthyana; and Jon Utley, who made available the considerable expertise about these matters of his mother, Freda. (Her excellent early volume, *The China Story,* is, like the works of Tony Kubek, required reading even now for students of these issues.)

Nor can I, in discussing all this, omit the Indiana contingent: William E. Jenner Jr., who directed me to his father's papers at Hanover College; Wilma Wood, who provided me with a priceless set of *Congressional Records* formerly belonging to Senator Jenner; Bob Galm and Dave Tudor, who arranged for the acquisition and delivery of these volumes. As to more contemporaneous developments in Congress, I am indebted to Representative Steve King of Iowa and his staffer Bentley Graves, who have taken an active interest in the security issues addressed herein and a leading role in seeking the release of relevant data. Thanks also to Phil Kiko on the staff of Representative Jim Sensenbrenner of Wisconsin for efforts to shake free long-secret records.

As for the production aspects of the book, special thanks are owing to Mark LaRochelle, researcher and computer maven par excellence, whose assistance in putting the manuscript on disk has been integral to the process, and who has otherwise aided me greatly in nailing down details on innumerable topics. He and the equally proficient Alex Adrianson, who did similar duty, have together put in almost as many hours on this volume as have I. Their expertise has been of utmost value in helping this incorrigible Luddite cope, if barely, with the realities of publishing in the computer era.

Production and research assistance were provided as well by my long-time assistant (and friend) Irma White; Malcolm Kline, who for many diligent years helped me research internal security and other matters; Don Todd and Brenda Carter, who assisted with the dubbing and transcription of tapes; Peter Spencer, who provided timely research aid on numerous subjects; Kathy Burns and Rick Henderson, who supplied background data on McCarthy's 1950 foray to Nevada; and Fred Mann, who tracked McCarthy's travels back to Washington via Wisconsin and other way stations on the journey. My thanks also to the estimable Mary Jo Buckland, who held things together at the office while I was struggling with this project.

Still others have assisted me in ways too numerous to mention. I am especially grateful to William F. Buckley Jr., whose long-ago McCarthy studies conducted with Brent Bozell have more than stood the test of time, and who through the Historical Research Foundation provided financial assistance for my own researches on the issue. Thanks also to Patrick Sullivan, Roger Milliken, Dan Hales, Joe and Augusta Petrone, Tom Pauken, Neal Freeman, Alfred Regnery, and Tom Winter, who have encouraged me in this and related efforts; my agent and wise counselor Alex Hoyt; and my perspicacious editor at Crown Forum, Jed Donahue. All have been valued companions on a lengthy expedition.

Index

About the Author

M. STANTON EVANS is the author of seven books, including *The Theme Is Freedom*. Now a contributing editor at *Human Events* and a contributor at *National Review*, he was previously the editor of the *Indianapolis News*, a columnist for the Los Angeles Times Syndicate, and a commentator for CBS and Voice of America. Evans founded the National Journalism Center, serving as director from 1977 until 2002, and is a visiting professor of journalism at Troy University. A graduate of Yale University, he has been awarded honorary doctorates from Syracuse University, John Marshall Law School, Grove City College, and Francisco Marroquin University. He lives near Washington, D.C.